CRITICAL SURVEY
OF
SHORT FICTION

CRITICAL SURVEY
OF
SHORT FICTION

Essays
1–406

1

Edited by
FRANK N. MAGILL

Academic Director
WALTON BEACHAM

SALEM PRESS
Englewood Cliffs, N. J.

LIBRARY OF CONGRESS CATALOG CARD NUMBER: 81-51697

Complete Set: ISBN 0-89356-210-7
Volume 1:   ISBN 0-89356-211-4

PRINTED IN THE UNITED STATES OF AMERICA

PUBLISHER'S NOTE

Critical Survey of Short Fiction is provided as an exhaustive examination of
the history, characteristics, structure, and prime examples of literature's most
popular form. There are three major divisions in this seven-volume work, as
outlined in the individual discussions below.

Essays

There is no aspect of the genre not covered extensively in this section. The
essays are long, detailed, analytic treatments which synthesize a wide range
of information, from the social and historical to the philosophic and religious
to the technical and semantic. Clusters of essays examine the genre's roots
in such ancient forms as the ballad, the Bible narrative, the medieval epic;
its development through modern chronological periods; its unique evolution
in particular countries (such as Ireland and Canada), regions (such as the
American West and South), and ethnic groups (such as black and Spanish-
American); its specialized branches such as detective short fiction and science
fiction; its linguistic underpinnings and literary devices such as narrative voice
and point of view; and its specific terminology and treatment in literary criticism. The result is an overview of the genre impressive for its
comprehensiveness.

Authors

Because of the nature of short stories, the set is arranged by authors rather
than by works. Each author article includes at the beginning a list of principal
short-fiction works and brief sections discussing other literary forms in which
the author wrote, influences on his work as well as the influence of his work
on the writing of others, characteristics of his short fiction as a whole, and
his biography. The major portion of the article is devoted to an analysis of
the author's short fiction in general, with in-depth critical examinations of
several particular works. The article closes with a recap of the author's publications other than short fiction followed by a representative listing of secondary research sources about the author.

The uniquely comprehensive index is an invaluable tool for retrieving all
information about a particular author to be found throughout the essays. For
example, after reading the article "Edgar Allan Poe," a reader consulting the
index could quickly locate specific treatments of Poe in several major essays,
from "Short Fiction: 1800-1840" to "Horror Short Fiction" to "Detective Short
Fiction." More than a bonus feature, the index is a key to the set, essential

in allowing users to move beyond the core article to locate a diversity of information about an author written from a variety of viewpoints by different writers. Thus, from the core article on Nathaniel Hawthorne, the index could guide a reader to examinations of Hawthorne's reception by his English contemporaries, his position as an innovator in the short-story form, his influence on modern writers of fantasy short fiction, and so on.

Current Authors

This section is the result of an invitation to several hundred current authors to contribute a one-page description of their work—their background, style, thematic concerns, and the like. More than ninety percent of the responses were written by the authors themselves, and these articles are unsigned; the signed entries are those written by someone other than the author whose work is described. Although some long-established authors are included in this section, most of the entries represent writers who have not yet received full critical recognition.

Reading a few dozen articles at random will reveal patterns about the present concerns and possible future directions of short fiction. The value of this section lies in the absolutely current nature of the material collected. Its value in future years will be to reveal which authors went on to establish lasting reputations in the field, as well as to indicate how the course of the genre's development shifted in response to influences and events that had not yet taken place at the time these articles were written.

PREFACE

CRITICAL SURVEY OF SHORT FICTION is an attempt to explore the development of the short-story form from its early loose beginnings to Hemingway's "zero endings"—and beyond. The first two volumes of the set provide some fifty essays that deal with the genre historically and critically from a broad base. Articles range from chronological overviews such as "Short Fiction: Beginnings to 1800," "The Romance Form in the Late Middle Ages," and "Short Fiction Since 1950" to specific areas of interest such as "The Fable Tradition," "The Saga and Tháttr," and "Themes of Women's Short Fiction"; also included are special subjects such as "The Adaptation of Biblical Story by Writers of Short Fiction," "The American Consciousness: 1880-1910," and "Fiction Writers on Writing Short Fiction," along with more than forty other major evaluations of the history and development of short fiction.

The remaining five volumes are devoted to a study of authors, their works, and their influence, the first four volumes comprising extended critical treatments of 261 important writers who contributed to the genre or who exerted an inescapable influence (Shakespeare, Chaucer, Marie de France, Homer, for example) and who vitally affected the form and content of the works of later writers. Volume 7 contains the general index for the entire work, although the volume is devoted primarily to 390 short articles on (mostly) contemporary writers of short fiction. Most of these short articles were written by the subject author, thus providing a self-analysis—the writer's own interpretation of his or her creative vision. No attempt has been made by the editors to evaluate the works of these authors or to place them within the history of short fiction, thereby leaving the reader free to appreciate, even savor, the intimacy of the writer's own appraisal of his artistic expression. To know to which of these younger writers, or to how many, will eventually be revealed the essence of the qualities essential for timeless literary expression is not within the province of critics or editors—now or ever.

The preparation of this work began with the selection of a staff to compile a concensus list of subjects and authors to be dealt with in depth. Once the tentative list of general essay subjects was established, scholars in the various areas were invited to contribute original critical essays concentrating on the general theme but free to examine pertinent influences and related literary figures. Selection of the 261 authors to be researched was almost a natural outflow from the historical articles established as essential to coverage of the growth and development of short fiction.

Once the names of authors to be studied were selected, known academic specialists and professional writers were asked to contribute scholarly articles within the following format: (1) Principal short fiction, (2) Other literary forms, (3) Influence, (4) Story characteristics, (5) Biography, (6) Analysis, (7) Major publications other than short fiction, and (8) Bibliography.

More than two hundred writers contributed original articles to this set. Quite a few contributors provided more than one article, and some wrote for both the author and the essay sections. From the beginning the purpose has been to present the long view of the growth of the short-story genre with emphasis on its historical development from tales, fables, and other early literary forms to the sophisticated short story of the 1980's. Through a series of general and special articles, the vast sweep of the concept has been brought under some measure of control, thanks to the provocative, instructive portrayals of growth and change delineated by scores of dedicated academicians.

Of the individual essays perhaps Professor Leonard R. N. Ashley's "Short Fiction: Beginnings to 1800" is the broadest in scope chronologically, for it reaches back to Homer, a writer "for kings," and Hesiod, who spoke to the peasants, and moves forward through *Beowulf*, *The Canterbury Tales*, and *Orlando Furioso* to such forerunners as certain of *The Spectator* and *The Tatler* entries.

Picking up at 1800 is an article by Walter Evans entitled "Short Fiction: 1800-1840" which offers a series of ten separate sections that review for the reader a wide range of short-story antecedents under these headings:

The Tale Tradition

The Essay-sketch Tradition

Washington Irving: The Creation of the Modern Short Story

Nathaniel Hawthorne

Edgar Allan Poe

Augustus Baldwin Longstreet and Frontier Humor

England and the Beginnings of the Modern Short Story

Germany and the Beginnings of the Modern Short Story

Russia and the Beginnings of the Modern Short Story

France and the Beginnings of the Modern Short Story

Readers will find in this article insights and interpretation that add much to an understanding of the various native influences that contributed to the development of the modern short story, examples such as, "It was a Briton [Darwin] who first proposed the biological theory of natural selection occurring over eons, an American [Michelson] who first measured the speed of light. In some way the British mind seems predisposed to the kind of gestalt a novel represents; the Americans seem more predisposed to that of the short story."

The article "Form and Language in Short Fiction" begins thus: "It may be assumed that a story has a point. A story, however, is much more than its point; it is an experience created by the formal control of language and literary convention. A point can be recapitulated, it can be paraphrased and remain intact. An experience is unchangeable; any change of the experience modifies, makes it other." The article then proceeds to deal at great length with the importance of form and how its change can disrupt, can alter the impact, of the story, Professor Richard Lyons has here provided a thoughtful, instructive essay.

Other essays that stress special aspects of the short-story genre include Charles E. May's "Short Fiction: 1840-1880" in which he deplores the critical and historical neglect of the short-story form, the novel often being treated as the only "prose fiction" worthy of serious consideration.

Attention should also be directed to William Peden's admirable study "Short Fiction in English: 1910-1950," and to Ferdinando D. Maurino's "Italian Short Fiction," which marks the enormous influence of the thirteenth century Italian *Novellino*, first on Italian writing that followed and finally on that of most of Europe. This erudite study enables the reader to follow easily the development of the short-fiction form in Italy down to writers of the twentieth century.

Emphasis thus far has centered on the objective material in the Essays, but the 261 author articles provide innumerable subjective insights, both delightful and instructive. One example is Bryant Mangum's article on Ernest Hemingway. The "Analysis" section begins: "After the publication of his last major work, *The Old Man and the Sea*, Ernest Hemingway explained his 'iceberg' theory of fiction writing in a *Paris Review* interview: 'If it is any use to know it, I always try to write on the principle of the iceberg. There is seven-eighths of it underwater for every part that shows. Anything you know you can eliminate and it only strengthens your iceberg. It is the part that doesn't show. If a writer omits something because he does not know it then there is a hole in the story.'" Having gained this intimate knowledge of Hemingway's own view of his art, the reader can thenceforth approach a Hemingway story with a special insight otherwise impossible. The author articles in this work endeavor to provide many such insights.

I wish to thank the individual writers for their contributions to this project, and to express my appreciation to the members of the Salem Press editorial staff for their dedication in helping to bring the disparate parts under control—often under severe time-pressure. All of us trust that we have provided a useful guide for those readers and teachers concerned with the appreciation and study of short fiction and the contemporary short story.

FRANK N. MAGILL

CONTRIBUTORS

Writing Staff for Essays

Leonard R. N. Ashley
Walton Beacham
Mark W. Booth
Laurence A. Breiner
Elizabeth Cook-Lynn
Joan DelFattore
Wilton Eckley
Walter Evans
Howard Faulkner
Ben Forkner
Howard M. Fraser
Ellen G. Friedman
George Garrett
May Frances Hopkins
Richard Lyons
Elizabeth MacAndrew
James MacDonald
Zita M. McShane

Marie-Antoinette Manz-Kunz
Patricia Marks
Ferdinando D. Maurino
Charles E. May
Helen Menke
Christina Murphy
Evelyn Newlyn
Bibhu Padhi
William Peden
Leon Perkins
Philip H. Pfatteicher
H. L. Prosser
Mary Rohrberger
Ruth Rosenberg
Amelia A. Rutledge
Brian Stableford
Christopher J. Thaiss
Gary F. Waller
Roger E. Wiehe

Writing Staff for Author Articles

Diane Ackerman
Thomas P. Adler
Carol Adorjan
Jeffrey Anderson
Joan Arias
Louisa Arndt
Marilyn Arnold
Robert W. Artinian
Leonard R. N. Ashley
Stanley S. Atherton
Jean Fawsett Atthowe
Michel Avallone
Lynne Baber
Peggy Bach
Peter Bailey
Tom Baker
Vincent D. Balitas
Jane L. Ball
Grady W. Ballenger
Mary Baron
Dennis Baumwoll
Walton Beacham
Peter S. Beagle

Bert Bender
John Bennett
Carol Berge
Sandra L. Bertman
Lydia Blanchard
Richard A. Blessing
Diana Bloom
Lynn Z. Bloom
Alec Bond
Laurence A. Breiner
J. R. Brink
Pierre E. Brodin
Rosellen Brown
Mitzi M. Brunsdale
Jerry H. Bryant
Louis J. Budd
R. L. C.
Jack Cady
Larry A. Carlson
Lorna Carlson
Ralph S. Carlson
Thomas M. Carlson
John Carr

Leonard Casper
Margaret Church
C. B. Clark
John C. Coleman
William Terrell Cornett
Maurice Custodio
Richard H. Dammers
Faye Dargenti
Nicholas Delbanco
Joan DelFattore
Walter DeMelle, Jr.
John F. Desmond
Kathryn Zabelle Derounian
Rochelle H. Dubois
Teresa Duran
Robert Dunkle
Grace Eckley
Wilton Eckley
Jeffrey M. Elliot
Steve Eng
Jean Ervin
Walter Evans
Grenfall Fields
Howard Faulkner
Jeanne A. Flood
James K. Folsom
Ben Forkner
David W. Foster
Kathy Ruth Frazier
Edith Freund
Miriam Fuchs
Kenneth Funsten
A. J. Furtwangler
Louis Gallo
Peggy C. Gardner
Frances A. Garvey
James W. Garvey
John Gerlach
Ray Giguette
Patricia Goedicke
James Gonzalez
Camille Gordon
Christopher Gould
Don Graham
Peter W. Graham
Julian Grajewski
James L. Green
William Frederick Greenfield
A. J. Griffith
David Mike Hamilton
Zia Hasan

Terry Heller
Cheryl Herr
Bruce Herzberg
William J. Higginson
Bill Hotchkiss
Sylvia Huete
Sandra Hutchins
Alex Jackinson
Hylah Jacques
Clarence O. Johnson
William P. Keen
John Keenan
Sue L. Kimball
Jerome Klinkowitz
John V. Knapp
Susan Koppelman
Daniel J. Kurland
Thomas D. Lane
Donald F. Larsson
Norman Lavers
Lane Lazarre
Marianne Lester
Milton Lomask
Larry McCaffery
Dermot McCarthy
Howard McCord
James MacDonald
Fred B. McEwen
James MacKillop
Robert J. McNutt
Clarence Major
Irving Malin
Bryant Mangum
Marie-Antoinette Manz-Kunz
Peter Marchant
Marion M. Markham
Patricia Marks
Ferdinando D. Maurino
Pablo Medina
Martha Meek
Helen Menke
Jennifer Michaels
Greg Michalson
Robert W. Millett
Robert A. Morace
Sara Morgan
Gilbert H. Muller
Christina Murphy
John M. Muste
George Myers, Jr.
Keith Neilson

Evelyn Newlyn
Martha Nochimson
Robert M. Otten
Cóilín Owens
David J. Parent
Elaine Parker
Richard Peabody, Jr.
William Peden
Natalie L. M. Petesch
Chapel Louise Petty
Robert Phillips
Constance Pierce
Joe Pires
L. H. Pratt
H. L. Prosser
Diana M. Rathbone
Donald H. Reiman
James Curry Robison
Mary Rohrberger
Ruth Rosenberg
Anthony Rudolf
Amelia A. Rutledge
Vanessa Ryder
Murray Sachs
David Sadkin
Joe Saltzman
David N. Samuelson
Charles R. Saunders
Lynda Schor
John Schultz
Daniel R. Schwarz

Shirley Clay Scott
Walter Shear
Allen Shepherd
Betty Shiflett
R. T. Smith
Ron Smith
Katherine Snipes
Sandra Whipple Spanier
Sharon Spencer
Brian Stableford
John Stark
Michael Stephens
William B. Stone
W. J. Stuckey
Eileen A. Sullivan
Henry Taylor
James D. Tedder
Christopher J. Thaiss
Jean L. Thompson
John H. Timmerman
J. J. M. Tobin
Rosemary Barton Tobin
Dennis Vannatta
Sandra Ventura
Larry Vonalt
Les Von Losberg
Lyn Walker
Gary F. Waller
Gordon Weaver
Roger E. Wiehe
Wirt Williams

LIST OF ESSAYS IN VOLUME 1

CRITICAL SURVEY
OF
SHORT FICTION

SHORT FICTION: TOWARD A DEFINITION

Any responsible study of literature must begin with the question, "why *study* it at all?" Or at least, "why articulate theories of what it means, or does, or how it functions on any level other than a personal one." Does it, in fact, make any difference that a piece of writing falls into some category which we label "poem" or "novel" or "short story"?

One answer, of course, is yes, it does make a difference, not because the label offers us a convenient way to group literature for anthologies, or even to establish a means for discussing a work of art which we admire, but because one primary function of art is to help us order things; and if we are to understand the ordering, we must know the form which orders it. That is to say, and to assume, that artists select their medium for a reason, whether or not it is selected rationally or intuitively, and that at least part of the message is conveyed by the medium itself. The medium may not be the message, but it greatly influences our response to it. Few people would argue that our response to a painting will be different from our response to a ballet, although the spirit of the message might be identical, and that we are moved not by the intellectual or thematic qualities nearly so much as we are moved by the dramatic force. Painting achieves some of its dramatic force through depth of vision; ballet through counterturn and stand. We experience the medium as well as the message and, as W. B. Yeats wrote, "Oh body swayed to music, oh brightening glance. How can we know the dancer from the dance?"

The short story is a gem, polished and honed so precisely that it is often compared to poetry. Anton Chekhov gave us perfect stories: not a word could be changed, we agree, and we can say the same of most short fiction which has survived and been admired—not like the clumsy, burdened novel that succeeds almost in spite of itself. As academic exercises, we would all prefer to clean up *The Scarlet Letter* (1850) and *The Adventures of Huckleberry Finn* (1884), and who would not cut hundreds of pages from Thomas Wolfe's fiction, and Leo Tolstoy's? The short story is another matter, however, and we often measure its success according to its perfection. Perhaps it cannot be any better although we can certainly add many more stories to the canon.

In terms of techniques, writers of short fiction have mastered the trade, and we can find many examples of difficult movements perfectly achieved. In terms of theme, we find short fiction dealing with complex emotions beautifully, exorcising powerful feelings from the reader. In terms of characters, settings, and symbols, we find outstanding pieces of short fiction, and we might be safe in saying that, given its traditional form, the short story cannot be improved. So why study it for the purpose of making it better? We certainly have not improved the quality of contemporary poetry through intensive academic attention.

Returning to the premise that one primary function of art is to help us order, we can argue that by studying short fiction, or almost anything for that matter, we come to know not only more about the form but also more about our need for order and our methods for achieving it. If that is true, and it seems reasonable that it is, and if the short story is a form which orders in a distinct way, then we can learn a great deal about ourselves, our values, and our needs by studying it. Landscape painting strikes different cords in us from portrait painting, or still lifes, and as we examine different schools of painting—classical, baroque, mannerism, impressionism, abstract—we understand clearly that the method of expression is an essential part of our response to it.

If we agree on this point—that art helps order and that different modes of art order in different ways—then the next logical step is to determine whether short fiction is a different mode or whether we should simply call it "fiction" and talk about it along with other fictional forms. Many writers have defined the short story in one manner or another, and the definition itself has generated continued argument among critics. To argue a definition seems almost to reject the value of definition at all. That is, if there is no definition, then studying the form does not help us order and evaluate our needs and values. Many critics who have argued a definition have looked at the story for its length or content, or in some historical context. Some critics have said that a short story is any piece of fiction shorter than fifty pages, or seventy-five to one hundred pages, depending on the critic. Others have defined the short story by the manner in which it covers content—the use of details, continuity of time, number of characters, completeness of theme. Still other critics have spoken of the history and evolution of short fiction from its roots in the poetic and dramatic arts. Certainly, these are valid and valuable ways of looking at various components of short fiction and, by definition, we can define the short story using any of those criteria.

Before embarking on yet another discussion of what short fiction is, there is some merit to observing that the short story is the most obvious and most likely verbal form for communicating whole ideas to other people. In fact, many of the subcategories within more standard definitions of short fiction account for the origins of the story, and when we speak of "tales" we acknowledge that short fiction originates out of ordinary language and the practical necessity of explaining an event to someone else. If cavemen, or early Egyptians, or medieval warriors did not tell short stories as we define them, they certainly accounted for events in full-bodied language which described not only the facts of the occurrence but also the emotion which surrounded it. The fact is that the fiery dragon, smelling of swamp mud and bellowing its lungs so that villagers far away could hear him, entered the camp, plucked four men from the campfire, hurled one into a nearby stand of trees, and fled back to the swamp with the other three. That is the journalism of the story;

yet there is something distinctly different between an *account* of a dragon and a *story* about the dragon.

The difference, we easily notice, is the process which imagination plays in determining the significance of the facts themselves. This process of imagination is indigenous to all art forms and to most human activities of all kinds, but it does establish a fundamental view, and perhaps a premise for studying art and language.

Consider the premise: an event occurs which is valuable information to impart to someone else. We may, in the school of pure journalism, convey only the facts, employing only the barest logical thought to create a context. A dragon abducted four men from their campsite last night. This dragon made noises loud enough to be heard a mile away, and he had a foul odor. He returned to the swamp with three of the four men he abducted and threw the fourth man into a tree.

By depriving this revision of textured language, we have reduced the potential for the listener to embellish the account with emotions which might be mistaken as fact. For example, in the original version, we were told that the dragon hurled one of the victims into a nearby stand of trees, which would lead us to believe that the beast was large, or at least strong; however, in making this logical deduction, we also face the potential of making the beast into more than he really is. The creature seems to have deductive powers, a sense of revenge and anger, and a clear intent for his action. Given this information, which we deduce from the textured language, we can then create an entire set of circumstances—or a myth—which accounts for the existence and actions of this creature, which is more difficult to do with *The New York Times*-style version of the event.

We can say without too much disagreement that one important element of the tale, story, or novel is the extent to which it allows fact to stand as fact. Consider this example: Mrs. Caveman gathered berries today is a fact, and we tend not to make very much of this ordinary act. People must eat, cavemen ate berries, women were berry pickers, and she was doing her job. A camera could observe her chore with no other information necessary to complete the scene. If we know that she is gathering the berries to celebrate the birth of a firstborn son, an entirely new dimension is added to the fact. We come to recognize that the berries are not being gathered for sustenance but in celebration of something—a ritual is being observed, and rituals come from a particular need, usually emotional or mystical. So there is more to the basic information than the simple fact that a woman gathers berries, and yet there is less to it than the account of the dragon's attack.

We say that the use of language to engender imagination is a characteristic of the tale. The reliability and nature of the facts to evoke response will greatly determine the depth and importance of the emotions we attach to the information. There is a certain element of *truth* which we consider crucial—

not necessarily that the data are *true*, but that they strike us somehow as containing truth. For modern readers, it may not seem very feasible that a dragon would behave in such a manner—probably there was not much factual validity for the medieval warrior either—but there is truth to those things that we fear in the night, and if they are represented by a terrible beast, then we all recognize how valid an emotion fear is.

How does that relate to short fiction, as distinct from long fiction? There are several postulations. First is that the writer must decide how long he can or wants to sustain the imagination. He can work the events surrounding the dragon for quite a while, but finally he must switch and go to some other event which, as correlated as it may be, is still another aspect of the tale. When this shift occurs, the context of the event changes, and the narrator's sense of his audience must account for this. If the bard narrating the story shifts from the action of the dragon to the warriors' pursuit of him, he must know that his audience's emotions have shifted, too. In this respect, the artist controls his story in order to shape his audience's response to it. The use of facts to relate events and the use of events to shape emotions are the basic building blocks for fiction writers, but the *way* in which the narrator/bard uses his building blocks will vary. In longer fiction the events (or incident and scenes) tend to stand as part of the larger unit, and while they often can stand by themselves, they contribute to a whole effect. In short fiction, however, incident serves as the unifying device, giving impetus to the story's emotional development. One significant difference between short and long fiction is that in short fiction the incident sets off a chain of related events which leads directly, without digression, to a culmination or resolution of the incident. An occurrence which serves as the impetus for a culmination is, at the very least, a story. An occurrence which sets off a series of events not culminating is a vignette.

Before we accept that distinction between vignettes and stories (or novels), we need to ask our initial question again: what difference does it make that we have made a distinction? To answer it, we have to go back to some basic ideas of relating incident as journalism, as tale, and as formulated fiction. Take this hypothetical news story as an example: on the sixth of May an armed man entered a branch of the Chase Manhattan Bank, forced all the bank's customers to lie on the floor, and gave the teller a note demanding the money in her cash drawer. Before the robbery was concluded, one of the customers on the floor, a woman sixty-four years old and later identified as Mrs. Harold Teague, began crawling toward the entrance, and she was shot and killed by the robber.

As a news event, we are given all the facts pertinent to the incident; and as a news event, we accept that information and ask for no more. Because people were involved, however, we will want to know much more about the event if it is to become personal. We will ask ourselves why this woman, who clearly had no real power to apprehend the gunman, would attempt to escape. Clearly the gunman was not interested in mass murdering the whole group of hostages; so what caused her to act? From her response, and from our own, we can see a principle of fiction, and especially of short fiction, emerging: *an event is important because of the effect it has on people.* We go through life as the recipient of occurrences, some of which we create and others which simply act upon us. When we are acted upon by some force, we must react to it, or decide not to react at all. Fiction shows us the process of that action/reaction. We identify a character and the force which is acting upon him. The force may be seemingly small, as with Mrs. Caveman who is required to gather berries for the ceremony, or it may be great, as with the dragon who abducts four warriors, but the force demands something of the character. For a while, these two elements may develop on their own, or they may begin influencing each other immediately, but eventually the character and force must converge.

character

force

If they do not, then we have the characteristics of the fiction we type as "vignette," meaning that we have been presented with a picture of some aspect of life without any attempt toward a resolution. The bank robber killed an old woman, and even if we know he was caught and tried, we have only an end to the event, not a resolution.

Consider this example: critics have questioned whether "Hills Like White Elephants" by Ernest Hemingway is really a short story or merely another one of Hemingway's vignettes. Two people, an unnamed American man and a woman of undetermined nationality called "Jig," are seated on the platform of a tiny train station located halfway between Barcelona and Madrid. While they are waiting for the train which will arrive in forty minutes, they talk about an operation which Jig is considering—probably an abortion. The American wants her to have it if she wants to, while Jig is not at all certain that an abortion is the right thing. She doubts if their lives will ever be the same again, or if they should be the same again. They argue, she looks out at the hills beyond, which she remarks look like white elephants, they argue some more, and he finally gets up, takes the bags around to the other side of the station, and on his way back to their table goes through the bar inside the station, observing that the people are "all waiting reasonably for the train."

There is no more to the story than that in terms of its "events," but there are many underlying forces which we see exerted on the couple. He considers her a romantic; she sees him as narrow-minded. She thinks that their previous life together, traveling around Europe trying new drinks, is superficial; for him it is their way of life. He thinks of himself as approaching the abortion logically: if she wants to have it, she should; if she does not, she should not. Jig, on the other hand, does not see the decision in such simplistic terms and probes him to think more deeply. The forces of their disunion build subtly yet steadily until she stands up, walks to the edge of the platform, and sees the fecund valley across the river standing in contrast to the barren area around the station. Many lines and many points of demarcation are established throughout the story. Parallel sets of train tracks are divided by the station. A bead curtain separates the outside from the inside. The River Ebro divides "there" from "here." The American and Jig are at a halfway point in both their journey and their decision about the abortion. As readers, we realize that somewhere the lines have to be crossed. If they are not, then the characters responding to their forces have not been resolved.

   If we accept the premise that a basic function of art—in this case story-telling—is to help us *order*, then we have no problem seeing Hemingway's story as artistic. Whatever form it is, it does delineate the feelings of each character so that we understand why they cannot agree. At the very least, vignettes, and perhaps certain journalism, perform this function. If, however, the function of storytelling is to help us *resolve* as well as order, the vignette falls short; and if the characters and forces seem important enough, we will demand a more complete rendering of the event. We will demand that the vignette become a "story." How does it do this?

   Let us take the dragon episode to its next logical step as an example: one of the witnesses to the dragon episode returns to the village and recounts the scene. He gives all of the details of the dragon: how he looked, what he did, what the men did in response. The elders of the tribe then take the matter under consideration to decide if this was merely an act of God, or whether appropriate actions can be taken to prevent a similar occurrence. How do the elders go about evaluating the events which our journalist/narrator has reported to them? How will they create a response which the rest of the tribe can understand and obey?

   The elders call our narrator/witness back and ask him what he thinks the event *meant*. He says that in his opinion the event meant that the warriors had not chosen their campsite wisely. It had been some time since the dragon struck their tribe because they had learned not to camp near swamps, and to make certain they always laid their camp on rocky ground. Apparently, the dragon has a foot disorder and will not step where there are helmet-sized rocks which trip him up. Because the plundering had been going so well these past years, however, the people had forgotten how terrible the dragon could be. In fact, when the dragon appeared in the camp, several of the men immediately headed into a rocky patch of ground, while others prayed fervently to Odin, and still others played dead. *Memory* is what this particular attack meant: how when you forget what is important, evil befalls you.

In his own mind, the witness has explained the event to his own satisfaction on two levels: that a carelessly laid camp invites trouble and that neglecting past experience may lead to death. So the next time he regales the event, he includes details which suggest that the warriors had forgotten what they once knew about the dragon, and as he develops the details his listeners anticipate the inevitable results. They may, in the process of the story, become fearful themselves, either of the dragon or of parts of their own lives which they have forgotten. The listeners begin identifying with the warriors in the story, not because they are warriors themselves, but because the warriors possess a human frailty which is like their own. Even the heroes are not able to conquer themselves, although they may be able to conquer most external enemies. The listener understands from the storyteller that the dragon is not the ultimate danger, for if the warriors had been prepared, the dragon would not have attacked. They failed themselves, however, by letting their guard down, and then disaster struck.

Two more principles of storytelling come from this example: *anticipation* and *identification*. A journalist usually begins with the event itself: at 2:00 P. M. the First National Bank was robbed; the storyteller usually begins with a character who will perpetrate some action before the story has ended. If the account of the bank robbery were a short story, we would probably see the robber beginning his day: drinking coffee, listening to police reports on the CB radio, polishing his handgun. We do not know he is going to rob a bank—perhaps even he does not know it that morning. The more we see his actions, however, the more we begin to realize that he is being driven to commit a crime, and it is important for us to see the forces which are compelling him. Unless we understand what forces act on him, his actions simply remain an event which, although startling, cannot move us to care very much about it. Stories may, of course, begin with an event. At 2:00 P. M. a robber walked into the First National Bank, stuck a gun through the change slot, and shot the teller through the left arm. Without demanding any money, he fled the lobby, disposed of his gun in a trash can, and disappeared into the streets of New York. This beginning event could allow the author to tell either the story of the wounded teller, a witness to the account, or the robber himself as he escapes into a bar on Second Avenue and talks with the guy on the bar stool next to him. The event of the robbery then becomes the same as watching the robber as he begins his morning drinking coffee.

Anticipation is important to effective storytelling because it makes the reader a participant rather than a witness. As readers, we will evaluate the forces acting on the character and think about what he will and should do under the circumstances. More importantly, we will think about what we would do if we were in his position. In "Hills Like White Elephants," we come to understand the man and woman's feelings about the abortion. They are incapable of resolving their differences, and as readers we are asked to consider how we would respond. In fact, through the tension, conflicts, and differences between these people, we may realize that it is not their story we are reading, but our own—perhaps not over an abortion but over one of the many differences we have with our mate.

Under the circumstances, we understand that both Jig and the American have limited choices. If she elects the abortion, she will lose the spontaneity and fecundity she desires. If she elects to have the child, she will alienate her lover. In either case, she may lose him. He, too, feels trapped, and even though we may not believe he is living up to his responsibility, we can understand why he does not feel the same need for fecundity as she does. A "white elephant" can be exotic, beautiful, and rare, or it can simply be a burden. She lives in an emotional world; he deals with his life rationally. Until the advent of her pregnancy, she had seemed content with their life together; now she wants something which he cannot understand. Other people in the bar were reasonable—"they were all waiting reasonably for the train" while the girl was ranting about the hills beyond. He has no idea what she wants of him.

As readers, we *do* know what she wants, and we are impatient with him for his absence of insight and caring for her. It is true that she does not know exactly what she wants, or at least not in "reasonable" terms which she can explain to him, and we strongly identify with her. By the end of the story, he has symbolically deserted her, aligning himself with the strangers in the bar rather than with the woman he has loved. Whether or not he actually abandons her at some future time or quite simply does not board the train when it arrives in a few minutes is only an afterthought and does not matter. This story has evolved from his effort to do what she wants, to his total alienation. It happens in only a few minutes—and with very few words passing between them. In this short story, Hemingway has shown us the power and the horror of a breaking relationship which most people who have ever tried to love will appreciate and care about. The resolution of "Hills Like White Elephants" may not be a cheerful one, but there is a resolution, and as readers, we identify with the outcome which the circumstances have produced.

Through the process of understanding characters in fiction, we come to know more about ourselves. Through imagination, we *project* ourselves into the world of the story, not necessarily in a direct manner but indirectly so that we begin to recognize pattern. That is to say, that with some types of short fiction, we might escape entirely into that world, riding with the cowboy as he drives cattle, believing that we are living in his time and place. For the duration of the story, we have left our world for his. Most serious fiction, however, does not provide escapism as its primary function. Rather, the storyteller attempts to bring the reader into the story's world only to impress upon him the forces at work. The author then hopes the reader will project the story into his own life, taking from it courage, hope, wisdom, or whatever virtues fiction can provide. The warrior, returning with his story of the dragon's attack, embellishes his tale not only with the facts of the event but also with elements of character so that the listener can entwine character with forces, extrapolate connections, and see how he, himself, fits into that pattern. Art does not exist as art, although it may exist as object, without someone to connect to it. The short story is a *process*: as characters in fiction begin to play upon the reader's sensibility, the reader will be stimulated to begin projecting himself upon the story, adding dimension to the character. Short fiction, as with many art forms, is the process of *suggestion*, and the real story lies within the reader's lower levels of consciousness.

With some art forms, such as lyrical poems, paintings, and certain dances, the art suggests rather than explains. With lyrical poetry, there is a "dramatic moment" in which something is being discovered, usually a moment of recognition in which we feel some truth about ourselves. The work of art forces us deep within ourselves in order to release a powerful feeling, but it is achieved through a highly refined and heightened ordering which may require a great deal of training to appreciate. Conversely, long fiction involves the reader by telling him much of the story and making the rest implicitly clear. In novels, time is an essential theme—we see a character develop through time, unlike in short fiction, in which we see him develop through epiphany. That is to say, the novel takes us through a period of time. Whether it is one day in James Joyce's *Ulysses* (1922), three days in *For Whom the Bell Tolls* (1940), or half a lifetime in *David Copperfield* (1849-1850), we see the force which time itself exerts on character. Given enough time, events will occur which will change people's lives, and the novel attempts to chronicle the relationship between passing time and event. The novel builds detail on detail, event on event, so that we can see that life is both a matter of coincidence and a product of will. We control and are controlled, establishing our lives and our values according to our perceptions of what life means. Of all art forms, the novel is best able to show connections. It establishes a sense that some kind of order does exist and that life is not simply a matter of cosmic coincidence. Our lives may not have been personally designed by a supreme being, but the events of our lives are linked together like a chain which either enslaves us or provides a lifeline to the source of things valuable.

Through the novel, we learn that time changes everything, or it changes nothing even though great change may have occurred. We are taken with the protagonist through a part of his life, examining at each step the forces at work. Not only do we see the forces, but we come to understand what they mean to him, leading eventually to some confrontation and reversal of circumstances. An American munitions expert goes to Spain to blow up a bridge, and, in the process of the novel, learns that the bridge itself is meaningless while the act of destroying it provides dignity and appreciation of life. The novel is a form which enables writers to age their characters, and the forces which cause them to age often constitute the theme. Frequently, the novel deals with the discernibly important elements of life: "marriage, birth, death, separation, and thoughts of these," as Philip Larkin has written. Many novels, and most American novels, take one of these important moments in life as their theme, or their driving force, and some critics have suggested that love and death are the only significant themes in American fiction.

Short fiction does not have to handle the big moments in our lives. The modern short story, particularly reflected by Nikolai Gogol, Ivan Turgenev, and Anton Chekhov in Russia and by other early practitioners, takes as its subject matter what are seemingly insignificant moments and teaches us why they may be the shaping forces of our lives. Ritual, custom, education, and rearing attempt to prepare us for the big moments of love and death which we will face, and while novels usually challenge the methods and effect of our training to face these moments, they do deal with them. The short story does not. Usually it cannot because the circumstances of the *big moment* must be carefully and intricately woven and there is simply not enough space in short fiction to do this. That is not to say that people do not love and die in short fiction—certainly they do, perhaps as often as they do in novels; but the great importance of short fiction is to illuminate the little moments in our lives. The modern short story, through its form, philosophy, and tradition, beginning with the nineteenth century writers in Russia, France, and America and continuing to the present, have adopted the illumination of seemingly insignificant events as the force and theme of short fiction.

The term "seemingly" is a crucial one, for the point of much short fiction is that the "little events" may be more important to us than the big ones. That is, marriages occur because we fall in love; we fall in love because we meet the right person; we meet the right person because, on a fall day when we saw a boy delivering his afternoon newspaper, we felt nostalgic enough to speak to the young woman standing at the bus stop. Or as in Chekhov's story "The Kiss," a soldier, alone and lonely, is mistakenly kissed by a stranger in a dark room, and from then on his life is changed. In William Faulkner's story "The Bear," which is both a story in several versions and a chapter of a novel, we understand that the major events are not as important as the seemingly less significant ones. Moments of *private* courage which Isaac endures build his character so that when, in Part IV, he discovers an entry about slavery in his grandfather's journal made long ago, that discovery is as important to him as the killing of the bear.

There are some reasons why short fiction is best able to deal with seemingly insignificant moments. First is the problem of focus. With any complex work of art, it is difficult for the artist to draw attention to the details of every area. In a wall-sized painting, there may be several different theaters of events so that the eye wanders in an attempt to locate the "focal point," both visually and thematically. A smaller painting may draw the eye immediately to a center and hold it there, pulling in peripheral data to complement the center. Although this analogy is dangerous in that it suggests that large paintings lack a central focus and small paintings achieve unity, the point is that given space, there are certain technical problems which face the artist. Scale of size is important to us, and psychologists tell us that people relate most directly to objects which are approximately their own size. So a wall-sized painting, which forces us to move far back in order to view it, sets a distance between us and it. With fiction, a portion (but not all) of this same principle operates. The novelist cannot expect that a reader will be able to keep the entire work in his head for the duration of the book. In fact, the reader usually cannot read the novel in one or two sittings, and may take days or weeks to finish it. To the novelist, this means that he cannot depend on the reader to remember specific details, and that if it is necessary to the development for a certain detail or element to be remembered, then the novelist must take special care to focus on it.

Obviously, the longer a work of fiction is, the more difficult it becomes to focus on an event, particularly a seemingly insignificant one. What seems insignificant in the novel is likely to remain that way; whereas in short fiction, the seemingly insignificant moment can remain the central event throughout, be developed, complicated, and finally resolved. So in this regard, one characteristic of short fiction is that it is short, but not by definition and not simply because it is less than fifty pages. "Short" would have to be defined as short enough so that the reader can sustain a single moment throughout the entire work for the purpose of seeing that single moment altered and refined in the protagonist's consciousness. In Faulkner's "The Bear," which is a relatively long story in its complete version, we understand from the beginning that Old Ben is a symbol for the difference between freedom and bondage, and that symbol is developed and changed at every turn of the story until the final closing passage in which Boone has freed a hoard of terrified squirrels who have no means of escaping. Most novels do not possess the potential of developing a single image, although some novels have achieved it very well. Thomas Mann worked ferociously to create "motifs" which may be viewed as a technical means of reinforcing otherwise forgettable images, symbols, or events. In *Ulysses*, Joyce establishes an image of Molly eating liver for breakfast, and that image shadows us through six hundred pages until the novel ends with Molly in bed late at night speaking of herself in carnal terms. We are not allowed to lose sight of *flesh* as a controlling element in *Ulysses*, and in that respect, Joyce has capitalized on a principal device of short fiction.

Combined with the problem of sustaining an insignificant moment over many pages is the problem of developing the details which will illustrate its complexity and importance. Return to the example of the man standing at a bus stop, watching a paperboy working his route, remembering his own route when he was a boy. He is filled with nostalgia and is compelled to speak in order to relieve his emotional tension. He speaks to the woman who is also waiting for the bus—not especially to her but because she happens to be there. He says:

> "The thing I remember most about my paper route was sitting on the corner with my friend Chris where the truck dropped the bundle of papers every afternoon. We'd sit there together folding the papers, maybe for an hour, talking about our day at school and waving at the mothers of our friends who would pass by on their way home from work. It was a corner like this one, and we felt very important knowing we would have the papers delivered before our fathers would be home and want their news."
>
> The woman waiting for the bus listened to him and moved one step closer to the stone obelisk which said "bus stop." "Oh," she muttered, not wanting to speak but responding from habit. Her blouse fluttered in the spring breeze, and for some reason she wished it would stop. April was too far gone for the cool wind to make your skin tingle. By now the air should be very still so that you felt yourself move within the spring, not that it moved around you.

Given such a beginning, the writer must make a choice. He can either catalogue a series of descriptions and conversation so that we receive an *impression* of the characters and forces, or he can take that opening moment and meticulously build on it, step by step, taking every word and couching it in such a way as to make it look forward and backward at the same time. That is to say, that with the second option the writer will take a step backward, then move forward two steps in order to connect each observation with the next. That is a laborious process for the reader and will establish an entirely different feeling to the fiction from that of the "impression" approach. If the writer opts for the step-by-step method, he will almost certainly develop a single moment directly to a single resolution, probably over a less than novel-length space. Almost certainly this type of development will result in a short story, and this is what short fiction achieves most effectively. The reader will follow every perception and resulting emotion which the man at the bus stop feels and will come to understand how an isolated moment in time can inextricably alter our lives. Longer fiction would necessarily have to move the place of action and follow the developing relationship between the man and woman. In doing so, it would diffuse the power of the moment when the man saw the paperboy and remembered his own childhood.

This distinction between the novel and short story is important for developing ideas of how we order and interpret life, and while the distinction holds true in almost all cases, it is not an entirely clear one some of the time. In short short fiction, say in a story under ten pages, the principle is easy to observe, but in longer fiction, especially as we approach the novella, that theory may appear to break down. Let us consider some examples. Faulkner's "The Bear" is a complicated story which takes place over a number of years. We follow Ike through several seasons of hunting Old Ben; we see him mature to a man and finally take charge of the family estate. Old Ben is killed, the dog named Lion is killed, Sam Fathers dies—many changes occur. There is not a simple, single moment which we follow step by step, as we might have in the bus stop example, and there are many techniques working here which the novelist would also use—certainly Faulkner used them in this particular story since it is also the last chapter of a novel. It is also true that some chapters in many novels form complete, autonomous units which function as short stories. In "The Bear," however, in spite of all the years and changes, there is a continued, unbroken sensibility which develops without digression to the culminating scene with Boone and the squirrels. With his highly refined internalization—a kind of stream of consciousness—Faulkner leads us to fuse our own consciousness with a more universal one steeped in the past and in archetypal contact with some collective force of which we are all a part. Rather than developing a single moment, as the man at the bus stop, Faulkner develops a single consciousness through a particular sensibility, asking the question, what is the meaning of symbol as it teaches us about freedom and bondage? We are never allowed to stray from that developing force.

Conversely, in Katherine Anne Porter's novella "Old Mortality," which is a fiction similar to "The Bear" in many ways, including length, we can see the novelist's techniques at work. There is, to be sure, a single image which begins the action: a portrait of Aunt Amy in a silver picture frame. Aunt Amy was "beautiful, much loved, and died young." Amy's two nieces are growing up under the spell of death in which everything is measured by Aunt Amy, or her time. This story, like "The Bear," takes us through the school years of the girls, ending with Miranda's train ride back home to another funeral in another time when she is eighteen years old. Both "The Bear" and "Old Mortality" cover about ten years in the protagonists' lives; both are steeped in the importance of family and tradition; both are lyrical and romantic; both deal with initiation and maturation. The potency of the image of Aunt Amy in the silver frame, however, is quickly diffused, twisted into different symbols, and is finally absolved altogether as Amy's fierce spirit is captured and altered in Miranda's visions of herself and her aunt.

What does unity, this single-mindedness of development, mean in our response to short fiction? In some ways, it sounds suspiciously like Aristotle speaking of the necessity of the "three unities" in tragedy, which William Shakespeare managed to do well enough without. Aristotle, recognizing the importance of "reversal" in drama, believed that the audience could best perceive the tragic downfall of man if the episodes were developed consistently so that there was a clear connection of cause and effect. Reversals occurred within an ordered structure. Sometimes man brought about reversals himself; sometimes they were perpetrated by the Fates or intervention of the gods. Understanding why the reversal occurred, however, would give man courage and help absolve him of his fears.

While Aristotle has been proven incorrect in his theory of unities, his theory of the importance of reversal still holds true in theater and in fiction, although the reversal might not necessarily occur on the modern stage or in the same way as it did in Greek or Elizabethan drama. In the "absurdist" drama *Waiting for Godot* (1952), the reversal occurs when we realize that Godot will never come, and usually most viewers do not feel the impact of the futility of waiting for Godot until long after the stage presentation ends.

Obviously, *where* the reversal occurs will have great impact on developing the remainder of the work, and on the reaction the reader has to it. In "The Bear," our expectations are that a reversal may occur at any time. There is suspense, and a feeling that once Old Ben appears, something extraordinary will happen; but it does not. Ben appears four times in the story, and each time only increases our expectation, but does not reverse it. Even when Ben is finally killed and Sam Fathers dies, we have no sense that the story is finished. There will be no more bear hunts, we know, but slowly, through Ike's consciousness, we have come to understand that this story is not about hunting bears any more than *Moby Dick* (1851) is about hunting whales. We must read on; must keep building the tension and expectation until reversal is inevitable. In "The Bear," it occurs at the end with Boone and the squirrels. In "Old Mortality," it occurs much sooner when the girls meet Uncle Gabriel, Aunt Amy's husband, at a horse race.

If the reversal occurs on stage, or early in the fiction (some critics have observed that in many novels the first reversal or climax occurs at three-fifths the length of the work), then there is some opportunity to explain or resolve the situation, and an obligation to do so. Having recognized the reversal, we then want to know how the protagonist will respond to it. Through projection, we ask ourselves how we would have responded and then we begin to measure ourselves against the protagonist. That is the normal course which a novel or novella will take.

With the short story, however, there is not so much a reversal as there is a moment in which the protagonist recognizes that life is or is not, or he is or is not the same as he once thought. In most short fiction, the narrator is the same person at the end as he was at the beginning with the essential difference that he has recognized something about himself (or that the reader has recognized something about him). Ike in "The Bear" is ten years older but still the same person, while Leopold Bloom is only one day older in *Ulysses*; yet the experience of his day, with all the reversals and expectations, has altered his character entirely—to the extent that Molly must reexamine her own life in the context of another Leopold whom she perceives to be a different man. With short fiction, we are not so much amazed by the shift in character as we are by the power which a moment or perception has to change us. The placement of the reversal causes this important difference between the forms of long and short fiction, and will result in different responses in readers.

To reiterate, let us review some differences between short and long fiction. To oversimplify, we may say that short fiction attempts to draw us into a moment and to show us how that moment changes our lives by changing an understanding of the significance of a seemingly small event. The novel attempts to draw us into a world where cause and effect establish some semblance of order. Therefore, the location of the climax or turning point will determine what a work of fiction can hope to accomplish and will finally determine whether we call it a vignette, short story, novella, or novel.

If a character is acted upon by some force, he must respond, and if the force, which may be an event (the dragon attacks), an image (a paperboy making his rounds), or a symbol (a bear representing freedom and bondage), is carried through a single course to a resolution, we then have a short story. That resolution will normally occur in the last paragraph of the story, and certainly within the final one-tenth.

character
force
moment of recognition

If, however, the emergence of character and force results not in a resolution but in a complication or reversal so that a new set of forces begin to act on the character, then we have a novella or novel.

reversal   recognition   recognition

character
force

In many novels, the first reversal is likely to have a substantial impact on the character's life so that everything he believed was true has been changed. That is, he responded to the force which initially acted on him in such a way as to expect one result, but he does, in fact, set into motion another set of forces which causes an unexpected result, and redefines what response he must make. We see the character as he works out the causes and effects on his life, which he will gradually understand and perhaps control, so that succeeding reversals will be seen in context of the chain of his life and not be quite as dramatic.

The difference between the endings of short fiction and the novel is important. Short fiction resolves. The resolution might not be what the character wanted, but at least he has come to some point of revelation. He understands what the force means to him, and in this respect short fiction is an optimistic literature. Given this new insight, he is faced with the potential to regroup and to alter the course of his life.

Novels, on the other hand, culminate. The end of the novel merely confirms that there is no beginning or end to life, but that in the greater science of living, this episode is but one account of the way things are. The series of reversals/responses/reversals have changed the character so that his life may have been broken, altered, or renewed, but the ending is almost insignificant. Or at least the very end is insignificant; it is the *process* of life that is important, not the outcome. For the novelist, we all come to one end or another, and once we arrive at the end, there is little we can do except to *understand* how we got there. Theoretically, any novel could continue through the character's death, even through generations of his descendants.

The short story, however, cannot follow whole histories, and so the treatment of subject matter must be different. In short fiction, the force is used to set the character in motion so that it is the character's *perception* of the force which is important, and not the force itself. The novel is able, and likely, to explore the nature of force—forces of evil, society, love, redemption, purgation—and having explored it, show how we deal with it. The short story does not explore what the force is, but how it leads to a character's realization about himself. In "Hills Like White Elephants" the force driving Jig and the American is her pregnancy, but Hemingway is not exploring the moral or even psychological issues of abortion. Rather, the driving force sets her in search of what life means to her and what "new life" really is.

Turning outside the story itself for a moment, it is necessary to recognize that social events do influence the practice of fiction. War, cheap printing, the film industry, and the economy will all affect how much short fiction is produced; and, as the world changes and society changes, the content of short fiction changes. Because short fiction is dealing with the *power* of the forces which act on us rather than the *nature* of the forces, however, short fiction remains surprisingly constant and has developed more consistently than the novel. That is to say, we equate certain ages of the novel with certain social themes. For example: many eighteenth century novels deal with class struggle and the plight of the middle class; nineteenth century novels deal with an industrialized world; twentieth century novels deal with psychological subservience which results from social repression. If we attempt to categorize short fiction, however, we are more likely to group it according to region (*Old Creole Days*, 1879; *In Ole Virginia*, 1887) or to type (detective, horror, romance) than we are likely to group it according to historical periods or social events. Only a few short-story writers are identified with their time. F. Scott Fitzgerald gave the name to his own period—"The Jazz Age," he called it—and he will always be associated with the 1920's, but most other story writers are less identifiably from a "time."

All this, of course, is of no consequence except as it illustrates differences between long and short fiction. Short fiction does not reflect the "human condition" as the novel does. It is not a sociological art form, and to approach it from a primarily sociological perspective is to distort and defy its inherent characteristics. As with the novel, however, short fiction does explore our methods and abilities to perceive correctly. The difference is that the novel bases perception on fact and circumstances, whereas the story depends on the relationship of one insight to the next. As readers of the novel, we are privileged to know much circumstantial information which helps us understand the characters. We may know about family background, history of the town, financial problems, and broken love affairs, all of which contribute to our feeling for the people. For a period of the novel's development, we look from the outside in, and even if we begin internally, as with *Ulysses* or *The Sound and the Fury* (1929), we must eventually pull outside. Although short fiction, too, may pull outside, it is much more capable of remaining focused and internal, and usually the story writer elects to look from the inside out. He allows characters to perceive slowly and to build one small perception on the next until some important, although "seemingly insignificant," revelation has occurred. Short fiction builds linearly, while long fiction builds laterally and allows many circumstances to come together at once, causing a turning point.

Because of this characteristic to build step by step, short fiction has offered experimental writers a technique of altering the sequence of steps and challenging the order of perception. With a technique analogous to cubist painting, these "experimental" writers have used the layers of short fiction as the cubists used planes, and in the stories of Donald Barthelme and Robert Coover, time becomes a structural device, not as in novels, but as a means of reordering. This fiction is not a departure from the form of short fiction, but a confirmation of the power of form. From the earliest recorded tales to modern stories, from children's ghost pieces to science fiction, listeners of short stories expect that the form itself is part of the message and entertainment. The fact that writers such as O. Henry, "The New Yorker School," or the Post-Modernists have frequently used the ending to alter our response demonstrates that essential difference between long and short fiction. Working from an oral tradition rather than from the novel's serialized, printed beginning, short stories engage audiences rather than assist their escape. Any good storyteller knows the importance of pacing the controlling event and of denying and fulfilling expectations. The essential formal qualities and lyrical nature make short fiction closer in some respects to drama and poetry than to the novel. Thus, in respect of those differences and achievements of short fiction, we offer a chronicle of its past and a forum to open its future, believing that of all modes of artistic expression, storytelling is most basic to the needs and means of man's heart and voice.

Walton Beacham

SHORT-FICTION CHRONOLOGY

B. C.

c. 4000	*Tales of the Magicians* (Egyptian)
c. 2000	*The Epic of Gilgamesh* (Sumerian)
c. 750	Homer flourished
c. 564	Aesop died
c. 5th century	*Jatakas* (Indian)
c. 300	Theophrastus, *Characters*
c. 270	Theocritus, idylls, mimes
c. 100	Aristides, Milesian tales
	Tale of Daniel and Susanna (from the Apocrypha)

A. D.

c. 8	Ovid, *Metamorphoses*
c. 1st century	Phaedrus, *Fabulae Aesopiae*
c. 400	*Vitae Patrum*
c. early 6th century	*Panchatantra* (Indian)
c. 6th century	Gregory the Great, *Dialogues*
c. 800	*The Thousand and One Nights* (in one form)
c. late 8th century	*Fates of the Apostles*
c. 9th century	*Romulus* (Latin)
c. 10th century	*Avian*
	Blickling Homilies (Anglo Saxon)
c. 990-997	Aelfric, *Sermones Catholici*, *Passiones Sanctorum*
c. 1000	*Beowulf*, manuscript written
c. 1100	*The Mabinogion* (Welsh), early tales written
	The Book of the Dun Cow (Irish)
	Chanson de Roland (*The Song of Roland*)
c. 1164-1180	Chrétien de Troyes, wrote earliest extant Arthurian romances *in the vernacular*
c. 13th century	*Ancren Riwle*
c. late 12th century	Marie de France, Breton *Lais*
c. 1200	*The Thousand and One Nights*, has substantially taken shape
	Odo of Cheriton, *Fabuale*
c. early 13th century	Snorri Sturluson, Prose Edda
	Aucassin and Nicolette
c. 1250	*Dame Siriz*
c. 1275	"The Fox and the Wolf"
c. 13th century	*Gesta Romanorum*
c. 1280-1350	South English Legendary
c. 1303	Robert Mannyng of Brunne, *The Handlyng of Synne*

c. early 1300's	*Northern Homilies*
	Northern Legendary
1313	Giovanni Boccaccio born
1353	Giovanni Boccaccio, *The Decameron*
1371-1372	*The Book of the Knight of La Tour Landry*
1375	Giovanni Boccaccio dies
c. 1383-1384	John Gower, *Confessio Amantis*
c. 1380-1390	Geoffrey Chaucer, *The Canterbury Tales*
1485	Sir Thomas Malory, *Le Morte d'Arthur*
16th century	*The Thousand and One Nights*, has taken final form
1526	Beatrice, *Hundred Mery Talys*
1550-1553	Giovan Francesco Straparola, *Le piacevoli notte* (*The Pleasureful Nights*)
c. 1553	*Lazarillo de Tormes*
1558	Marguerite de Navarre, *Heptameron*
1566	William Painter, *The Palace of Pleasure*
1567	Fenton, *Tragical Discourses*
1568	*Lazarillo de Tormes* (translated into English)
1576	George Pettie, *A Petite Pallace of Pettie His Pleasure*
1578-1579	John Lyly, *Euphues, The Anatomy of Wit*
1580	Michel Eyquem de Montaigne, *Essais*
1581	Barnaby Riche, *Riche His Farewell to Militarie Profession*
1591	Robert Greene, *Notable Discovery of Cozenage*
1593	Theophrastus' *Characters* translated into English
1597	Thomas Deloney, *The Gentle Craft*
1608	Joseph Hall, *Characters of Vices and Virtues*
1609	Thomas Dekker, *The Ravens Almanacke*
1613	Miguel de Cervantes, *Novelas Exemplares* (*Exemplary Novels*)
1614	Sir Thomas Overbury, *Characters*
1620	*Westward for Smelts*
1623	Charles Sorel, *Francion*
1628	John Earle, *Microcosmographie*
1664	Jean de La Fontaine, *Contes et nouvelles*
1688	Aphra Behn, *Oroonoko*
1691-1694	*The Gentleman's Journal*, edited by P. A. Motteux
1692	William Congreve, *Incognita*
1694	Voltaire born
1697	Charles Perrault, *Histoires et contes du temps passé, avec des moralités*
1700	John Dryden, *Fables*
1704-1712	*The Thousand and One Nights*, first European trans-

	lation (French) by Antoine Galland
1706	*The Thousand and One Nights*, partial translation of Galland's version into English
	Daniel Defoe, "The True Relation of the Apparition of One Mrs. Veal"
1709-1711	Sir Richard Steele and Joseph Addison, *The Tatler*
1711-1712, 1714	Joseph Addison and Sir Richard Steele, *The Spectator*
1720	Mrs. Manley, *The Power of Love: in Seven Novels*
1722	Benjamin Franklin, Dogood Essays
1725	Mrs. Haywood, *Secret Histories, Novels, and Poems* (2nd ed.)
1732	Benjamin Franklin, "Alice Addertongue," "Celia Single," "Anthony Afterwit"
1739	Voltaire, "Voyage de monsieur le baron de Gangan"
1747	Voltaire, *Zadig*
1750-1752	Samuel Johnson, *The Rambler*
1752	Voltaire, "Micromegas"
1759	Voltaire, *Candide*
1762	Oliver Goldsmith, *The Citizen of the World*
1773	Ludwig Johann Tieck born
1776	E. T. A. Hoffmann born
1795-1798	Hannah More, Tracts
1797	Ludwig Tieck, *Voksmärchen*
1778	Voltaire dies
1799	Sir Walter Scott, *An Apology for Tales of Terror*
	Honoré de Balzac born
	Alexander Pushkin born
1801	Maria Edgeworth, *Moral Tales for Young People*
1804	Maria Edgeworth, *Popular Tales*
	Nathaniel Hawthorne born
1805	Hans Christian Andersen born
1807	Washington Irving, *Salmagundi* ("Sketches from Nature" appeared in October, "The Little Man in Black" in November)
1809-1812	Maria Edgeworth, *Tales of Fashionable Life*
1809	Edgar Allan Poe born
	Nikolai Gogol born
1811	Théophile Gautier born
1812	Jacob and Wilhelm Grimm, *Grimm's Fairy Tales* (*Kinder- und Hausmärchen*)
	Charles Dickens born
1812-1817	Ludwig Tieck, *Phantasus*
1814-1815	E. T. A. Hoffmann, *Phantasiestücke in Callots' Man-*

	ier (*Weird Tales*)
1818	Ivan Turgenev born
1819	Leigh Hunt, "A Tale for a Chimney Corner"
1819-1820	Washington Irving, *The Sketch Book of Geoffrey Crayon, Gent.* ("Rip Van Winkle," May, 1819; "The Spectre Bridegroom," November, 1819; "The Headless Horseman," March, 1820)
1819-1821	E. T. A. Hoffmann, *The Brothers Serapion*
1819	Herman Melville born
1821	Fyodor Dostoevski born
1822	Charles Brockden Brown, *Carwin the Biloquist and Other American Tales and Pieces*
	Washington Irving, *Bracebridge Hall*
	Charles Lamb, "Dream Children"
	E. T. A. Hoffmann dies
1823	Charles Lamb, "Old China"
	Beginning of vogue in England of gift book annuals
1824	Washington Irving, *Tales of a Traveller* and letter to Henry Brevoort
	William Austin, "Peter Rugg, The Missing Man"
	Sir Walter Scott, "Wandering Willie's Tale" (in *Redgauntlet*)
1824-1832	Mary Russell Mitford, *Our Village*
1826	*The Atlantic Souvenir*, beginning of American gift book vogue
1827-1828	Sir Walter Scott, *Chronicles of the Canongate*, first series ("The Highland Widow," "The Two Drovers," "The Surgeon's Daughter")
1828	Leo Tolstoy born
1829	Sir Walter Scott, "My Aunt Margaret's Mirror," "The Tapestried Chamber"
	Prosper Mérimée, "Mateo Falcone"
1830	Nathaniel Hawthorne, "The Hollow of the Three Hills"
1831	Alexander Pushkin, *The Tales of the Late Ivan Petrovitch Belkin*
1831-1832	Nikolai Gogol, *Evenings on a Farm Near Dikanka*
1831-1861	*The Spirit of the Times*
1832	Washington Irving, *The Alhambra*
	James Hall, *Legends of the West*
	J. P. Kennedy, *Swallow Barn*
	A. B. Longstreet begins publishing his sketches
	Nathaniel Hawthorne, "My Kinsman, Major

	Molineux"
	Edgar Allan Poe, "Metzengerstein"
	Honoré de Balzac, "La Grande Breteche"
1834	Albert Pike, *Prose Sketches and Poems Written in the Western Country*
	Alexander Pushkin, "The Queen of Spades"
1835	A. B. Longstreet, *Georgia Scenes*
	Nikolai Gogol, "Diary of a Madman"
	Mark Twain born
1836	Charles Dickens, *Sketches by Boz*
	Nikolai Gogol, *The Nose*, "The Carriage"
	Théophile Gautier, "Fortunato"
	Bret Harte born
1837	Nathaniel Hawthorne, *Twice-Told Tales* (first series)
	Charles Nodier, "Inez de las Sierras" (part 1)
	Alexander Pushkin dies
1838	Thomas De Quincey, "The Avenger"
1839	Edgar Allan Poe, "The Fall of the House of Usher"
1840	Edgar Allan Poe, *Tales of the Grotesque and Arabesque*
	Thomas Hardy born
1841	T. B. Thorpe, "The Big Bear of Arkansas"
1842	Nathaniel Hawthorne, *Twice-Told Tales* (second series)
	Edgar Allen Poe's first review of *Twice-Told Tales*
	Nikolai Gogol, *The Overcoat*
1843	Harriet Beecher Stowe, *The May Flower*
	Charles Dickens, *A Christmas Carol*
	William Makepeace Thackeray, "Dennis Haggarty's Wife"
	Henry James born
1845	Edgar Allan Poe, *Tales*
1846	Nathaniel Hawthorne, *Mosses from an Old Manse*
	Ivan Turgenev begins *A Sportsman's Sketches*
1847	Edgar Allan Poe's second review of Hawthorne's tales
1848	Joel Chandler Harris born
1849	Edgar Allan Poe dies
	Sarah Orne Jewett born
1850	Honoré de Balzac dies
	Robert Louis Stevenson born
	Guy de Maupassant born
1851	Nathaniel Hawthorne, *The Snow Image and Other Twice-Told Tales*
1852	Ivan Turgenev, *A Sportsman's Sketches* (begun 1846)

	Nikolai Gogol dies
	Mary E. Wilkins Freeman born
1853	Ludwig Tieck dies
1855-1863	A. N. Afanasev, *Russian Folktales*
1856	Herman Melville, *Bartleby the Scrivener*
	Herman Melville, *The Piazza Tales*
	Wilkie Collins, *After Dark*
1857	Joseph Conrad born
1858	George Eliot, *Scenes of Clerical Life*
1859	Edward Bulwer-Lytton, "The House and the Brain"
1860	Anton Chekhov born
	Hamlin Garland born
1861	Rebecca Harding Davis, "Life in the Iron Mills"
1862	O. Henry (William Sidney Porter) born
1863-1864	Mrs. Gaskell, "Cousin Phillis"
1864	Nathaniel Hawthorne dies
1865	Mark Twain, "The Celebrated Jumping Frog of Calaveras County"
	Rudyard Kipling born
1867	Mark Twain, *The Celebrated Jumping Frog of Calaveras County, and Other Sketches*
1868	Bret Harte, "The Luck of Roaring Camp"
1869	Alphonse Daudet, *Lettres de Mon Moulin*
1870	Bret Harte, *The Luck of Roaring Camp and Other Sketches*
	Charles Dickens dies
	Ivan Bunin born
1871	Henry Kingsley, "Our Brown Passenger"
	Stephen Crane born
	William Dean Howells, *Suburban Sketches*
	Théophile Gautier dies
1873	Thomas Bailey Aldrich, *Marjorie Daw and Other People*
1875	Henry James, *A Passionate Pilgrim*
	Hans Christian Andersen dies
	Thomas Mann born
1876	Fyodor Dostoevski, "The Peasant Marey"
	Friedrich Spielhagen, *Novellen*
	Sherwood Anderson born
1877	Sarah Orne Jewett, *Deephaven*
	Gustave Flaubert, *Trois Contes* (*Three Tales*)
1879	Henry James, *Daisy Miller*
	Henry James, *The Madonna of the Future*

	George Washington Cable, *Old Creole Days*
1880	Joel Chandler Harris, *Uncle Remus: His Songs and Sayings* (8 more volumes to 1918)
	Guy de Maupassant, "Boule de Suif"
1881	George Washington Cable, *Madame Delphine*
	Guy de Maupassant, *La Maison Tellier*
	Fyodor Dostoevski dies
1882	Frank R. Stockton, "The Lady, or the Tiger?"
	Robert Louis Stevenson, *The New Arabian Nights*
	Charles Reade, *Readiana*
	Virginia Woolf born
	James Joyce born
	Guy de Maupassant, *Mademoiselle Fifi*
	Ivan Turgenev dies
	Franz Kafka born
1884	Charles Egbert Craddock (Mary Noailles Murfree), *In the Tennessee Mountains*
	Guy de Maupassant, "The Necklace"
	Anton Chekhov, *The Tales of Melpomene*
1885	Brander Matthews, "The Philosophy of the Short-Story"
	D. H. Lawrence born
1886	Sarah Orne Jewett, *A White Heron*
	Robert Louis Stevenson, *The Strange Case of Dr. Jekyll and Mr. Hyde*
	Leo Tolstoy, *The Death of Ivan Ilyich*
	Anton Chekhov, *Motley Stories*
1887	Mary E. Wilkins Freeman, *A Humble Romance and Other Stories*
	Arthur Conan Doyle, *A Study in Scarlet*
	Anton Chekhov, *In the Twilight* and *Innocent Wards*
1888	Rudyard Kipling, *Plain Tales from the Hills*
	Thomas Hardy, *Wessex Tales*
	Katherine Mansfield born
1890	Sarah Orne Jewett, *Tales of New England*
	Katherine Anne Porter born
1891	Hamlin Garland, *Main-Travelled Roads*
	Ambrose Bierce, *In the Midst of Life*
	William Dean Howells, *Criticism and Fiction*
	Herman Melville dies
1892	T. W. Higginson, "The Local Short-Story"
1893	Ambrose Bierce, *Can Such Things Be?*
	Guy de Maupassant dies

1894	Luigi Pirandello, *Amori senza amore* (*Love Without Love*)
	Kate Chopin, *Bayou Folk*
	Robert Louis Stevenson dies
	Isaac Babel born
1896	Sarah Orne Jewett, *The Country of the Pointed Firs*
	Stephen Crane, *The Little Regiment*
1897	William Faulkner born
1898	Henry James, *The Real Thing*
	Henry James, *The Turn of the Screw*
	Stephen Crane, "The Blue Hotel," *The Open Boat and Other Tales of Adventure*
	Anton Chekhov, "Gooseberries"
	Frederick Wedmore, "The Short Story"
	Charles R. Barrett, *Short Story Writing: A Practical Treatise on the Art of the Short Story*
	Anton Chekhov, "The Lady with the Dog"
1899	Stephen Crane, *The Monster and Other Stories*
	Edith Wharton, *The Greater Inclination*
	W. Somerset Maugham, *Orientations*
	Bret Harte, "The Rise of the Short Story"
	Ernest Hemingway born
	Vladimir Nabokov born
	Jorge Luis Borges born
1900	Stephen Crane, *Wounds in the Rain*, *Whilomville Stories*
	Jack London, *The Son of the Wolf*
	Stephen Crane dies
1902	Joseph Conrad, *Heart of Darkness*
	Bret Harte dies
1903	George Moore, *The Untilled Field*
	Thomas Mann, *Tonio Kröger*
1904	James Joyce, "The Sisters," "Eveline," "After the Race"
	Saki (H. H. Munro), *Reginald*
	Anton Chekhov dies
	Isaac Bashevis Singer born
	O. Henry, *Cabbages and Kings*
1905	Willa Cather, *The Troll Garden*
	Jean-Paul Sartre born
1906	O. Henry, *The Four Million*
1907	Alberto Moravia born
1908	O. Henry, *The Voice of the City*

Joel Chandler Harris dies
1909   Henry S. Canby, *The Short Story in English*
          Sarah Orne Jewett dies
          Eudora Welty born
1910   O. Henry, "A Municipal Report"
          Joseph Conrad, "The Secret Sharer"
          Lord Dunsany, *A Dreamer's Tales*
          Mark Twain dies
          O. Henry dies
          Leo Tolstoy dies
1911   Katherine Mansfield, *In a German Pension*
          Saki (H. H. Munro), *Clovis*
          E. M. Forster, *The Celestial Omnibus*
1912   Thomas Mann, *Death in Venice*
1913   Albert Camus born
1914   James Joyce, *Dubliners*
          D. H. Lawrence, *The Prussian Officer and Other Stories*
          Saki (H. H. Munro), *Beasts and Super-Beasts*
1915   Edward J. O'Brien, *The Best Short Stories of 1915* (annual volumes follow)
          Saul Bellow born
          Franz Kafka, *Metamorphosis*
1916   Ring Lardner, *You Know Me, Al*
          Lord Dunsany, *The Last Book of Wonder* (*Tales of Wonder*)
          Ivan Bunin, *The Gentleman from San Francisco*
          Anton Chekhov, *The Tales of Chekhov* (English translation by Constance Garnett completed in 1922)
          Henry James dies
1918   Theodore Dreiser, *Free and Other Stories*
          Maxim Gorky, *Stories of the Steppe*
1919   Sherwood Anderson, *Winesburg, Ohio*
          Franz Kafka, "Ein Landarzt" ("A Country Doctor"), "In der Strafkolonie" ("In the Penal Colony")
          First year of the annual O. Henry competition
1920   F. Scott Fitzgerald, *Flappers and Philosophers*
          Katherine Mansfield, *Bliss and Other Stories*
1921   Sherwood Anderson, *The Triumph of the Egg*
          Stephen Crane, *Men, Women, and Boats*
          W. Somerset Maugham, *The Trembling of a Leaf*
          A. E. Coppard, *Adam and Eve and Pinch Me*

1922	F. Scott Fitzgerald, *Tales of the Jazz Age*
	Katherine Mansfield, *The Garden Party and Other Stories*
1923	Ernest Hemingway, *Three Stories and Ten Poems*
	Sherwood Anderson, *Horses and Men*
	Katherine Mansfield, *The Dove's Nest and Other Stories*
	A. E. Coppard, *The Black Dog*
	Elizabeth Bowen, *Encounters*
	F. L. Pattee, *The Development of the American Short Story*
	Katherine Mansfield dies
1924	Ernest Hemingway, *In Our Time*
	Franz Kafka, "Ein Hungerkünstler" ("A Hunger Artist")
	Anton Chekhov, *Letters on the Short Story, the Drama and Other Literary Topics* (in English)
	Joseph Conrad dies
	Franz Kafka dies
1925	Ernest Hemingway, *In Our Time* (enlarged edition)
	Flannery O'Connor born
	Yukio Mishima born
1926	F. Scott Fitzgerald, *All the Sad Young Men*
	Isaac Babel, *Red Cavalry*
1927	Isaac Babel, *Odessa Tales*
	Ernest Hemingway, *Men Without Women*
1928	H. E. Bates, *Day's End and Other Stories*
	Thomas Hardy dies
	Gabriel García Márquez born
1930	Katherine Anne Porter, *Flowering Judas and Other Stories*
	Mary E. Wilkins Freeman dies
	D. H. Lawrence dies
1931	William Faulkner, *These Thirteen*
	Frank O'Connor, *Guests of the Nation*
1932	Conrad Aiken, "Mr. Arcularis," "Silent Snow, Secret Snow"
	Seán O'Faoláin, *Midsummer Night Madness and Other Stories*
	Marcel Aymé, *The Picture-Well*
1933	Sherwood Anderson, *Death in the Woods and Other Stories*
	Ernest Hemingway, *Winner Take Nothing*

1934	William Faulkner, *Doctor Martino and Other Stories*
	William Saroyan, *The Daring Young Man on the Flying Trapeze*
	D. H. Lawrence, *The Tales of D. H. Lawrence*
	Isak Dinesen, *Seven Gothic Tales*
	Marcel Aymé, *The Dwarf*
1935	F. Scott Fitzgerald, *Taps at Reveille*
	John O'Hara, *The Doctor's Son and Other Stories*
	Ignazio Silone, *Mr. Aristotle*
1936	Thomas Mann, *Stories of Three Decades*
	Rudyard Kipling dies
1938	Ernest Hemingway, *The Fifth Column and the First Forty-nine Stories*
	William Faulkner, *The Unvanquished*
	John Steinbeck, *The Long Valley*
	Richard Wright, *Uncle Tom's Children*
	Marcel Aymé, *Derriere Chez Martin*
1939	Katherine Anne Porter, *Pale Horse, Pale Rider*
	Jean-Paul Sartre, *Le Mur* (*The Wall*)
1940	William Saroyan, *My Name Is Aram*
	Dylan Thomas, *Portrait of the Artist as a Young Dog*
	Hamlin Garland dies
1941	Eudora Welty, *A Curtain of Green*
	Jorge Luis Borges, *The Garden of Forking Paths*
	Sherwood Anderson dies
	James Joyce dies
	Virginia Woolf dies
	Isaac Babel dies (?)
1942	William Faulkner, *Go Down, Moses*
	Mary McCarthy, *The Company She Keeps*
	Mary Lavin, *Tales from Bective Bridge*
	Isak Dinesen, *Winter's Tales*
1943	Eudora Welty, *The Wide Net*
	John Cheever, *The Way Some People Live*
	Virginia Woolf, *A Haunted House and Other Stories*
	Marcel Aymé, *The Walker Through Walls*
1944	Katherine Ann Porter, *The Leaning Tower and Other Stories*
	Frank O'Connor, *Crab Apple Jelly: Stories and Tales*
	Jorge Luis Borges, *Ficciones, 1935-1944*
1947	Vladimir Nabokov, *Nine Stories*
	J. F. Powers, *Prince of Darkness*
	Marcel Aymé, *Le Vin de Paris*

1948	Truman Capote, *Other Voices, Other Rooms*
1949	William Faulkner, *Knight's Gambit*
	Eudora Welty, *The Golden Apples*
	Shirley Jackson, *The Lottery*
	Truman Capote, *Tree of Night*
	Angus Wilson, *The Wrong Set*
1950	William Faulkner, *Collected Short Stories of William Faulkner*
	Mary McCarthy, *Cast a Cold Eye*
	Ray Bradbury, *The Martian Chronicles*
	Marcel Aymé, *En Arriere*
1951	Carson McCullers, *The Ballad of the Sad Café*
	W. Somerset Maugham, *The Complete Short Stories of W. Somerset Maugham*
1952	Frank O'Connor, *The Stories of Frank O'Connor*
1953	J. D. Salinger, *Nine Stories*
	Jean Stafford, *Children Are Bored on Sunday*
	Erskine Caldwell, *The Complete Stories*
	John Cheever, *The Enormous Radio and Other Stories*
	Ivan Bunin dies
1955	Flannery O'Connor, *A Good Man Is Hard to Find and Other Stories*
	Eudora Welty, *The Bride of the Innisfallen*
	Dylan Thomas, *Adventures in the Skin Trade and Other Stories*
	Thomas Mann dies
1956	J. F. Powers, *The Presence of Grace*
1957	Isaac Bashevis Singer, *Gimpel the Fool and Other Stories*
	James Purdy, *The Color of Darkness*
	Albert Camus, *Exile and the Kingdom*
	Isak Dinesen, *Last Tales*
1958	Vladimir Nabokov, *Nabokov's Dozen*
	Bernard Malamud, *The Magic Barrel*
	John Cheever, *The Housebreaker of Shady Hill*
	Isak Dinesen, *Anecdotes of Destiny*
	Samuel Beckett, *Nouvelles et textes pour rien* (*Stories and Texts for Nothing*)
1959	Philip Roth, *Goodbye, Columbus*
	John Updike, *The Same Door*
1960	Albert Camus dies
	Alan Sillitoe, *The Loneliness of the Long-Distance*

	Runner
1961	Isaac Bashevis Singer, *The Spinoza of Market Street*
	Tillie Olsen, *Tell Me a Riddle*
	Richard Wright, *Eight Men*
	John Cheever, *Some People, Places, & Things That Will Not Appear in My Next Novel*
	J. D. Salinger, *Franny and Zooey*
	Ernest Hemingway dies
1962	John Updike, *Pigeon Feathers and Other Stories*
	James Purdy, *Children Is All*
	Jorge Luis Borges, *Labyrinths* (in English)
	William Faulkner dies
1963	Bernard Malamud, *Idiots First*
	J. D. Salinger, *Raise High the Roof Beam, Carpenters* and *Seymour: An Introduction*
	Joyce Carol Oates, *By the North Gate*
	Doris Lessing, *A Man and Two Women*
1964	John Cheever, *The Brigadier and the Golf Widow*
	Jean Stafford, *Bad Characters*
	Donald Barthelme, *Come Back, Dr. Caligari*
	Flannery O'Connor dies
1965	Flannery O'Connor, *Everything That Rises Must Converge*
	James Baldwin, *Going to Meet the Man*
	Doris Lessing, *African Stories*
1966	John Updike, *The Music School*
	Joyce Carol Oates, *Upon the Sweeping Flood*
	Yukio Mishima, *Death in Midsummer and Other Stories*
1968	Saul Bellow, *Mosby's Memoirs and Other Stories*
	Donald Barthelme, *Unspeakable Practices, Unnatural Acts*
	William H. Gass, *In the Heart of the Heart of the Country*
	John Barth, *Lost in the Funhouse*
1969	Bernard Malamud, *Pictures of Fidelman*
	James Alan McPherson, *Hue and Cry*
	Robert Coover, *Pricksongs & Descants*
	Peter Taylor, *The Collected Stories of Peter Taylor*
	Jean Stafford, *Collected Stories*
	Frank O'Connor, *A Set of Variations*
1970	Isaac Bashevis Singer, *A Friend of Kafka and Other Stories*

	Donald Barthelme, *City Life*
	John Updike, *Bech: A Book*
	Joyce Carol Oates, *The Wheel of Love*
	Yukio Mishima dies
1972	Donald Barthelme, *Sadness*
	John Updike, *Museums and Women and Other Stories*
	John Barth, *Chimera*
	Joyce Carol Oates, *Marriages and Infidelities*
	Gabriel García Márquez, *La increíble y triste historia de la cándida Eréndira y su abuela desalmada* (*Innocent Eréndira and Other Stories*)
1973	Isaac Bashevis Singer, *A Crown of Feathers and Other Stories*
	Bernard Malamud, *Rembrandt's Hat*
1975	Isaac Bashevis Singer, *Passions and Other Stories*
1980	Eudora Welty, *Collected Stories*
	Italo Calvino, *Italian Folktales*
	Katherine Anne Porter dies
	Jean-Paul Sartre dies

Walter Evans

SHORT FICTION: TERMS AND TECHNIQUES

Because the short story is a form of fictional narrative that has never been adequately distinguished from other narrative forms, few of the terms and techniques that follow have been related specifically to the short story in the past. The approach of this article, therefore, is to include terms, approaches, genres, and concepts that have been, or could be, used to understand the form. The particular relevance of the term or technique to the study of short fiction has been indicated, and citations from other critics have been used whenever possible. By necessity, however, much of this effort to indicate the relevance of the terms to short fiction is a result of personal study of the form, and thus the use of many of the terms may not be widely accepted by the critical community.

Adaptation (film): Because of the compactness and elliptical nature of the short story, the genre does not adapt well to full-length feature films for the mass market—that is, unless the adapter invents new material or sentimentalizes existing material. For example, two film versions of Ernest Hemingway's "The Killers" must supply background motivation (including romantic interest) to account for the death of Ole Andreson. J. D. Salinger's story "Uncle Wiggly in Connecticut" was so sentimentalized in a Hollywood film entitled *My Foolish Heart* that Salinger has refused to sell film rights for any of his fiction since then. The short film (with a running time of fifteen to forty-five minutes) has been more appropriate to the short story. Excellent adaptations have been made of Herman Melville's *Bartleby the Scrivener* (1856), Ambrose Bierce's "An Occurrence at Owl Creek Bridge," and Katherine Mansfield's "The Garden Party." The best-known series of short films based on short fiction is "The American Short Story Series," shown on the Public Broadcasting System in 1978 and 1980.

Aestheticism: The literary movement predominant in England and France in the 1890's which focused on art for art's sake. As early as the mid-nineteenth century, however, Edgar Allan Poe described such an attitude in his "The Poetic Principle" and manifested such an approach in his short fiction. Poe would have agreed with Walter Pater's view that all art should aspire toward the condition of music and with Paul Verlaine's insistence that poetry is made with words, not ideas. The short story in England during the 1890's focused on bohemianism and the life of art and the artist; typical examples are Arthur Symons' "Spiritual Adventures" and Harry Harland's "Grey Roses."

Affective Fallacy: W. K. Wimsatt and Monroe Beardsley, in an essay in *The Verbal Icon* (1954), say that to approach a literary work from a consideration of its effect on the reader is to make the work itself disappear and to fall back on relativism and impressionism. Poe's definition of the short story in his famous 1842 Hawthorne review, in which he emphasized the short story's need to establish a single effect, has come under fire by formalist critics as an example of the affective fallacy. More recent literary theorists, however, such as Norman Holland, David Bleich, Wolfgang Iser, and Stanley Fish, have made more rigorous studies of the relationship of the reader to the work from psychological, phenomenological, and stylistic points of view. Such studies indicate that Poe's emphasis on effect perhaps deserves another look.

Allegory: A mode of literary expression in which a second meaning is encoded within the surface meaning of the story. The allegorical mode may dominate the entire work, in which case the encoded message is the work's primary excuse for being (as in the parable or the fable); or it may be an element within a work otherwise interesting and meaningful for its surface meaning alone. Nathaniel Hawthorne's stories constitute a range of the use of the allegorical mode, from stories that seem almost totally allegorical, such as "The Artist of the Beautiful," in which all the characters and events can be translated into abstract terms of the encoded story; to "Young Goodman Brown," which, regardless of the allegorical suggestiveness of such character names as "Faith," evades any easy equivalences to abstract terms; to "My Kinsman, Major Molineux," which combines social, psychological, mythic, and metaphysical issues so complexly that its characters and events defy simple conceptual equivalences.

Ambiguity: That state of communication in which an element of expression may be interpreted in more than one way. As opposed to its pejorative sense in discursive communication (in which a single meaning is usually intended), ambiguity has an honorific sense in literature. The formalist critics in America made ambiguity the central characteristic of literature. In the short story, ambiguity can be felt in the use of a single word, such as in the title of James Joyce's "The Dead," which refers both to the actual dead and the living dead. It may be felt in an event; for example, did Young Goodman Brown's experience in the forest really happen or was it a dream? It may be manifested in a character; for example, is Bartleby in Melville's story a mimetic figure or is he a symbolic figure? Because of the short story's highly compressed and poetic nature, ambiguity may play a more important role in the form than it usually does in the novel.

Annuals: A publishing fashion, which began in Europe and England in the early 1820's, for the publication of miscellaneous poems, extracts, and tales once a year in a single volume. The first annual in America was *The Atlantic Souvenir*, published in late 1825. In America the annuals were usually published for Christmas giving and constituted what are now called "coffee-table books." Until the middle 1840's, the annuals were the dominant publishing mode in America and thus gave an important impetus to the development of the short prose tale often published in them. Also called "gift books," the volumes were elegantly and elaborately printed. Because in America the annuals specialized in native writers and themes, they not only helped to create the distinctively American short story; they helped to create a distinctively American literature as well.

Antagonist: Usually a character in fiction that stands as a rival or opponent to the protagonist. In the short story, however, the antagonist is less often a character than a force, many times existing within the protagonist himself or herself. For example, the antagonist in Hawthorne's "Young Goodman Brown" is not the devil, but rather the antisocial desires within Goodman Brown himself. In William Faulkner's "Barn Burning," the antagonist is not Sarty's father, but rather the divided allegiances Sarty becomes aware of because of his father's actions. In Hemingway's "Hills Like White Elephants," the two central characters are not protagonist and antagonist; rather, as the two face the inexplicable loss of their relationship, that loss is the antagonist in the story.

Anthology: A collection of stories, usually by various writers. A group of stories by one author is most often called simply a "collection." Some important short-story anthologies which have influenced the way readers read stories and teachers teach them are *Understanding Fiction* (1943) by Cleanth Brooks and Robert Penn Warren, which has influenced several generations of readers in the so-called "New Critical" or "Formalist" method; and Philip Stevick's *Anti-Story* (1971), which introduced experimental writers to the current generation of readers. Most textbook anthologies of stories are organized according to stories which illustrate basic elements of fiction, such as plot, point of view, and character; or according to stories which illustrate various themes.

Antihero: Seán O'Faoláin characterizes this common figure in modern fiction as one who, deprived of social sanctions and definitions, is always trying to define himself or herself and establish his or her own codes. The antihero is often central in such "modern romance" fictions as *Wuthering Heights* (1847), *Moby Dick* (1851), and *The Scarlet Letter* (1850). The figure is also central to the short-story form generally. According to Frank O'Connor in *The Lonely Voice* (1963), the central figure in the short story is, by generic definition, an antihero, since the short-story character is always cut off from social definitions. Akaky Akakyevitch, the little clerk in Nikolai Gogol's *The Overcoat* (1842), is an early example. In the short story, says O'Connor, there is always a sense of outlawed figures wandering on the fringes of society.

Anti-Story: A term popularized by Philip Stevick in a 1971 anthology by the same name. Stevick defines the anti-story in terms of its contrariness to traditional conventions of fiction in the following ways: (1) The reality of the world out there is broken up to allow a reflexiveness about the fictional work itself. (2) Realism is violated to return to the earlier narrative world of the romance and the fairy tale. (3) Event is less important than subjective voice. (4) The story is apt not to have an identifiable subject—a core of abstraction that it is "about." (5) The extreme rather than the ordinary in human experience is emphasized. (6) The experiencing mind takes the place of the analytical author. (7) Given the writer's perception of an absurd universe, the story is apt to deny meaning. (8) There is more experiment with the minimal story. In general, the anti-story constitutes a reaction against traditional notions of "storyness." Other critics have termed such fiction "metafiction," "self-reflexive fiction," and "post-modernist fiction."

Archetype: Carl Jung defines archetype as a "primordial image," an "archaic remnant." Jung makes clear that by archetype he does not mean certain definite mythological images, for it would be absurd, he says, to suggest that such representations could be inherited. Rather, Jung says, the archetype is a "tendency to form such representations of a motif—representations that can vary a great deal in detail without losing their basic pattern." Northrop Frye, in his *Anatomy of Criticism* (1957), defines archetype as a typical or recurring image—"a symbol which connects one poem with another and thereby helps to unify and integrate our literary experience." Archetypal criticism, says Frye, is concerned with the study of conventions and genres in which it attempts to "fit poems into the body of poetry as a whole." That a great many short stories have been discussed in terms of archetypal criticism is not unusual, given the mythic nature of the short story and its origins in romantic and romance forms of poetry and prose. Short fiction is often a combination of the projective and the mimetic.

Architectonics: A term which refers to the qualities of unity and balance in a story. In its honorific sense the term refers to the achievement of organic unity; the work represents a synergistic whole in which the total impression or value of the work is greater than the sum of its parts. In its pejorative sense, architectonics refers to the so-called popular well-made story, in which the parts are so statically balanced that the whole seems an artificially constructed, inert object. The problem of unity and balance in the short story has been a critical issue for the form ever since Poe emphasized the importance of the writer's inventing and combining incidents for the purpose of bringing about a single effect. It may be that many critics have taken Poe's description of the methodical creation of his poem "The Raven" in "The Philosophy of Composition" too seriously and have thus associated this description of a carefully balanced technique with the construction of the short story. Brander Matthews, in his *Philosophy of the Short-Story* (1901), certainly made this mistake and influenced a great many critics and writers at the turn of the century to celebrate a formula-bound, architecturally constructed version of the short story. The reaction against this is sounded in *The Dance of the Machines* (1929) by Edward J. O'Brien, who decried the short story as being the most typical form of the industrial age in its machinelike standardization.

Atmosphere: The general mood of a story, which also sets up expectations in the reader. Atmosphere is often associated with the setting of a story, but it can be established by action or dialogue as well. For example, the atmosphere established at the beginning of Poe's "The Fall of the House of Usher" becomes a tangible element within the story itself and is materialized by the mist which rises up from "the decayed trees, and the gray wall, and the silent tarn—a pestilent and mystic vapor, dull, sluggish, faintly discernible, leaden-hued." Because it is an embodiment of Roderick Usher himself, as well as a supposed actual cause of Usher's madness, the atmosphere becomes an actual character in the story.

On the other hand, the opening of Katherine Mansfield's "The Garden Party" conveys a rapturous delight that the central character Laura cannot even articulate and then shifts to an atmosphere that so combines both squalor and beauty that she is left speechless once again. Shirley Jackson's "The Lottery" achieves its shock effect precisely because the dialogue in the early part of the story establishes a mood of eager expectation and then gradually shifts to an atmosphere of tense anxiety. Because the short story is primarily a lyric rather than a mimetic form, atmosphere may play a more important role in the form than in the novel. Eudora Welty has suggested that the first thing we notice about a story is that we really cannot see the solid outlines of it; "it seems bathed in something of its own. It is wrapped in an atmosphere." Atmosphere in a story, says Welty, "may be its chief glory."

Ballad: The basic definition of ballad is that it is a song which tells a story. The folk ballad is usually a highly conventionalized story of supernatural events which affect ordinary people. Characterization is slight and story itself is emphasized. The singer is usually objective, expressing no attitude toward the story itself. The ballad is the lyrical version of the folktale; in the former, song is foregrounded, whereas in the latter, story is foregrounded. In the early nineteenth century, William Wordsworth and Samuel Taylor Coleridge experimented with the ballad form in *The Lyrical Ballads* (1798) by presenting ballad stories from the point of view of a concrete speaker. Romantic poetry is a literary version of the folk ballad; the nineteenth century tale is a literary version of the folktale. The important difference in both is the introduction in the literary version of the tone and attitude of a particular persona.

Caricature: Caricature is a form of writing (or certain descriptive parts of a work) which focuses on unique qualities of a person and then exaggerates and distorts those qualities in order to ridicule the person or what he or she represents. Caricature is most often used in drawing; however, one of the earliest American short stories, "The Legend of Sleepy Hollow," makes extensive use of caricature in the figure of Ichabod Crane. Ichabod's gawky, long-legged figure, with his prominent Adam's apple and pointed nose, has become a grotesque icon in American literature. "His head was small, and flat at top, with huge ears, large green glass eyes, and a long snipe nose, so that it looked like a weather-cock, perched upon his spindle neck, to tell which way the wind blew." Contemporary writers, such as Flannery O'Connor, have used caricature for more serious, but no less satiric, purposes in such stories as "Good Country People" and *A Good Man Is Hard to Find* (1955).

Character: Character in fiction is the creation of a semblance of virtual people. One of the problems of character in short stories was noted very early by William Dean Howells, when he suggested that a defect in the form is that whereas we can remember certain stories, we can scarcely remember by name any of the people in them. Frank O'Connor (*The Lonely Voice*) points out that the characters in short fiction are not ones with which we can easily identify. The length of the form is one cause of this. In the novel, we live with characters for a longer period of time; in short stories, our encounter is brief, and the predicament rather than the person seems the focus. The short story, because it is more closely related to the romance form than to the novel, is more apt to present projective characters—that is, psychological archetypes rather than fully rounded characters with their own social personae and individual psychologys. The characters in short fiction are also apt to be in extreme situations; and characters in extreme situations are likely to act in terms of a deep level of subjectivity in which human differences are obliterated. In short fiction, we are often dealing with emotional states rather than with objective characters who seem to exist in the social world. W. H. Auden once referred to characters in Poe's stories as "unitary states."

Character Sketch: A seventeenth and eighteenth century literary form which presents types rather than individual characters; the form is predicated on the notion that human nature is everywhere the same. The short story usually focuses on situation rather than on character; however, when the short story does center on character, as does James Joyce's "Eveline," character is usually revealed by the character's reaction to a single crucial situation. When the short story focuses primarily on a character type, as does F. Scott Fitzgerald's "The Rich Boy," character is revealed primarily by the tone of the teller.

Coherence: That principle of writing which insists that the separate parts of the work be arranged in such a way that the meaning of the work is clear or the effect of the work is achieved. Coherence is a crucial element in short fiction because in its relatively short span it must organize materials in such a way as to strike singly at the reader. Lack of coherence in a short story is more apt to result in disaster than lack of coherence in a novel. Edith Wharton once noted that in the short story, "the least touch of irrelevance, the least chill of inattention, will instantly undo the spell." William Faulkner has said that whereas in the novel the author can be careless, in the short story "almost every word has got to be almost exactly right."

Comic Story: The comic story encompasses a wide variety of modes and inflections, such as parody, burlesque, satire, irony, and humor. Henri Bergson's famous definition of the comic as the "mechanical encrusted on the living, in which the comic character is usually comic in proportion to his or her ignorance of self," is illustrated in Eudora Welty's story "Why I Live at the P. O." Although both the comic and the tragic character are unaware of self, the reader usually does not identify with the comic character, but rather perceives the character from a detached point of view; the result is the impression that the character is not a person but a thing.

Complication: That point in the story in which the conflict is developed or when the already existing conflict is further intensified. It constitutes the rising action that must lead up to the climax and resolution.

Conflict: The struggle that develops as a result of the opposition between the protagonist in a fiction and the force that he or she encounters which necessitates a change in action. Traditionally in fiction, the opposing force is another person, the natural world, society, or some force within .the self. In short fiction, the conflict is most often between the protagonist and some ineffable force either within the protagonist or within the basic given state of the human condition. Resolution of conflict in a short story is usually not as clear and emphatic as in the novel. The protagonist's response is often in terms that suggest a helplessness in face of inexplicable forces, for example, Laura's "Isn't life. . . ." in Mansfield's "The Garden Party" or the narrator's "Ah, Bartleby! Ah, humanity!" in Melville's famous story.

Contextualist Theory: The contextualists pose that whereas the language of ordinary discourse refers to a preexisting reality, the language of art is constitutive. Rather than referring to preexistent values, the art work creates values only inchoately realized before. Primary advocates of this relatively new philosophic emphasis on formalist criticism are Eliseo Vivas (*The Artistic Transaction*, 1963) and Murray Krieger (*The Play and Place of Criticism*, 1967). Both critics owe a great deal to the theories of symbol, language, and myth developed by Ernst Cassirer (*An Essay on Man*, 1944).

Controlling Image (*Fundamental Image*): A central image around which the story turns. Usually if the image is a metaphor it is termed the "controlling image"; if the image is nonmetaphorical, it is termed the "fundamental image." The best-known discussion of this concept in short fiction is the theory of the "Falcon," set forth by the nineteenth century German critic, Paul Heyse. Based on a Giovanni Boccaccio *novelle* (the ninth tale of the fifth day), which turns on the gift of a falcon, the theory asserts that the *novelle* usually contains a central concrete image. For Heyse, the falcon is the specific concrete thing that distinguishes one story from thousands of others. Many short stories do contain a central controlling image, such as the house in "The Fall of the House of Usher," the wall in *Bartleby the Scrivener*, the gooseberries in Anton Chekhov's story of that name, the overcoat in Gogol's famous story, the flowering Judas in Katherine Anne Porter's story, and the beast in Henry James's "The Beast in the Jungle." Such images often appear in short fiction because of the need for a central device to unify the symbolic implications of the story.

Conventions: Although a short story may depict life, the depiction is always by means of devices of stylization and compression. Such conventions constitute the necessary difference between life and art. According to the Russian Formalists, these conventions constitute the "literariness" of literature and are the only proper concern of the literary critic. Because the short story has always been a less mimetic form than the novel, it is apt to be more convention-bound. As a result, making distinctions between stories which are highly "literary" and stories which are based on a simple "formula" has always been a difficult task for short-story critics. All short stories depend on conventions to communicate, but this does not mean that short stories are "conventional."

Crisis (*Climax*): Crisis denotes a turning point in fiction at which the opposing forces reach the point that a resolution must take place. A crisis and a climax do not necessarily have to occur at the same time, for while "climax" refers to the moment of the reader's highest emotional response, "crisis" refers to a structural element of plot only. Crisis marks a turning point in the plot and may indeed lead to climactic effects; there may be more than one crisis moment in fiction. In Melville's *Bartleby the Scrivener*, a crisis occurs when Bartleby decides to do no more copying at all; this necessitates that the narrator try to get rid of him. Another crisis occurs when the narrator decides to move from his present offices. These crisis moments bring on the climax of Bartleby's complete withdrawal from life. In Shirley Jackson's "The Lottery," the crisis occurs when the "winner" is narrowed down first to one family and then to one individual; the climax comes with the administration of the "prize." The climax of a short story is often presented in terms of an ironic reversal or an ironic understatement. The Russian Formalist critic, Boris Eichenbaum, says that a basic difference between the short story and the novel is that whereas the novel's ending usually involves a point of let-up, the short story amasses its whole weight toward the ending.

Defamiliarization: This basic principle of Russian Formalism, which distinguishes literature from nonliterature, was coined by Viktor Shklovsky in his 1917 essay, "Art as Technique." Shklovsky makes a distinction between practical language, which serves utilitarian purposes, and poetic language, which serves to renew perception itself. By the use of poetic devices, poetical language defamiliarizes or "makes strange" familiar experience. Shklovsky points out that as perception becomes habitual, it becomes automatic, and our thoughts become algebraic and abbreviated until we attend to the world of objects only as shapes. The result is an overautomatization in which habit devours everything. Shklovsky says that art exists so that one may recover the sensation of life.

> The technique of art is to make objects unfamiliar, to make forms difficult, to increase the difficulty and length of perception because the process of perception is an aesthetic end in itself and must be prolonged. Art is a way of experiencing the artfulness of an object; the object is not important.

The theory may be especially important to the study of the short story, for since its very beginning the form has been more "artful" and conventionalized and thus less mimetic than the novel.

Detective Story: A highly formalized and logically structured mode of short fiction, the origin of which is attributed to Poe in such stories as "The Murders in the Rue Morgue," "The Mystery of Marie Rogêt," and "The Gold Bug." Other well-known practitioners are G. K. Chesterton and Arthur Conan Doyle. More recently, Jorge Luis Borges, in such stories as "Death and the Compass," has made use of detective story conventions. Because the detective story is such a convention-bound form, it has come under more serious attention recently by critics who have been influenced by European structuralism. Previously, the form had been best known as a popular form, more akin to the crossword puzzle than to the short story. Poe termed his detective tales "ratiocinative."

Dialogue: The similitude of conversation in fiction. Dialogue serves functions of characterizing, furthering the plot, establishing conflict, expressing thematic ideas, and so on. Although often made to sound "natural," dialogue is highly stylized. Many of Hemingway's stories depend greatly on highly stylized dialogue; for example, "Hills Like White Elephants" and "Clean, Well-Lighted Place" depend almost solely on dialogue. The word "dialogue" also refers to a fictional form or genre in which two people converse on a given subject. The above-mentioned two Hemingway stories are complex psychological versions of this usually simple conceptual form.

Displacement: A term coined by Northrop Frye to indicate the author's attempt to make the story psychologically motivated and "realistic" even as the latent structure of the mythical motivation moves relentlessly forward. Tzvetan Todorov uses the term *vraisemblance* to refer to this attempt to make the reader believe that the work conforms to reality rather than to its own laws. The romance stories of Hawthorne are less "displaced," that is, closer to their mythic and conventional structure, than the more realistic stories of Henry James.

Dominant: A term coined by Roman Jakobson which forms part of the Russian Formalist and later Prague Structuralist notion that the study of literature is the study of the literary devices which defamiliarize familiar experience and thus constitute the "literariness" of works. Jakobson defines the "dominant" as that which "rules, determines, and transforms the remaining components" in the work of a single artist, in a poetic canon, or in the work of an epoch. According to Jakobson, the shifting of the dominant in a genre accounts for the creation of new generic forms. Within a set of poetic norms or system of devices, elements which were originally secondary become primary and thus the "dominant." For example, in a study of the historical development of the short story, the shift that takes place in the mid-nineteenth century with Melville's *Bartleby the Scrivener* indicates realistic conventions becoming dominant and romantic or fantasy elements becoming secondary. In the mid-twentieth century, fantasy elements are once again becoming dominant in the stories of such writers as John Barth and Donald Barthelme.

Doppelgänger: A common theme in short fiction in the nineteenth century, especially in the fiction of E. T. A. Hoffmann, in which a single character is split into two character objectifications of self. The *Doppelgänger* theme is a common one in short fiction because of the intensely subjective and romantic nature of the form, as well as because the short story often involves characters caught between the phenomenal and the psychic world of feelings and forces. The motif is usually a concern of psychoanalytic criticism. See Otto Rank's *The Double: A Psychoanalytic Study* (1971).

Dramatic Monologue: A poetic or narrative form, presented as the speech of one person, in which a dramatic situation is established and a dramatic listener is implied. Robert Langbaum (*The Poetry of Experience*, 1963) argues that such objective criteria for the form are less revealing than the characteristics of the dramatic monologue's "way of meaning." Langbaum defines the form as a modern genre which begins in the nineteenth century. Its particular tension is between the reader's initial sympathy for the speaker (which is primary) and the reader's moral judgment. A classic example of the form in short fiction is Part I of Fyodor Dostoevski's "Letters from the Underworld," in which the Underground Man addresses real or imaginary gentlemen and struggles with what Langbaum calls the essential philosophic position of the dramatic monologue—that immediate experience is primary and analytical reason secondary. Another basic characteristic of the form is that what the speaker of the dramatic monologue reveals is in disequilibrium with what he or she intends. We understand his or her point of view not only by what he or she says, but also by judging the speaker's limitations and distortions. Eudora Welty's "Why I Live at the P. O." and Ring Lardner's "Haircut" are typical examples of this disequilibrium.

Dream Vision: An allegorical form common in the Middle Ages, in which the narrator or a character falls asleep and dreams a dream which becomes the actual framed story. Major dream visions are Geoffrey Chaucer's *The House of Fame* (1380) and William Langland's *The Vision of William, Concerning Piers the Plowman* (c. 1362-1387). Although the dream vision convention is used in the short story, typically the line between dream and reality is blurred. For example, in Hawthorne's "Young Goodman Brown," the reader is not sure whether the events in the forest are meant to be actual, allegorical, or dream. In Poe's "The Pit and the Pendulum," the entire story seems to be a dream vision, although there is no actual dreamer dramatized in the story.

Effect: Probably the most misunderstood aspect of short fiction since Poe's use of the term in his 1842 review of Hawthorne's *Twice-Told Tales* (1842, 2nd edition). Poe says:

> A skilful literary artist has constructed a tale. If wise, he has not fashioned his thoughts to accommodate his incidents; but having conceived, with deliberate care, a certain unique or single effect to be wrought out, he then invents such incidents—he then combines such events as may best aid him in establishing his preconceived effect. If his very initial sentence tend not to the outbringing of this effect, then he has failed in his first step.

Because of Poe's definition of the short story, the form has often been stereotyped as a contrived trick. The emphasis of Poe's remarks, however, and indeed the emphasis of "effect" in the short story, is rather on what Poe calls "the deepest effects" which can only be achieved by the unity of impression and sense of totality the short story can create. The effect of the short story is to draw the reader into a mysterious dreamlike atmosphere in which events and phenomena transcend everyday reality and exceed the powers of the logical mind to comprehend or control them.

Epiphany: A religious term to suggest a showing forth of spirit. Its literary application was introduced into criticism by James Joyce in *Stephen Hero* (1944):

> By an epiphany he meant a sudden spiritual manifestation, whether in the vulgarity of speech or of gesture or in a memorable phase of the mind itself. He believed that it was for the man of letters to record these epiphanies with extreme care, seeing that they themselves are the most delicate and evanescent of moments.

Stephen draws his theory of epiphany from St. Thomas Aquinas and establishes the following stages for its achievement: apprehension of the object as one integral thing, recognition that it is a constituted entity (an organized, composite structure), and finally the manifestation of the "whatness" of the object when it achieves its epiphany. Joyce's stories in *Dubliners* (1914) have been analyzed many times as epiphanic stories in which either a character or the reader experiences a sudden revelation of meaning or significance.

Episode: An episode, which is composed of two or more scenes centering around a central event, is perhaps the most common type of action embodied in the short story.

Epistolary Story: A story told primarily or solely by means of letters. One of the most famous examples in nineteenth century American literature is Thomas Aldrich's "Marjorie Daw." The convention of letters is used in the story to conceal the fact that the young woman one of the writers describes does not exist. Prosper Mérimée uses the convention in his story "The Abbé Aubain" as an ironic device to allow the reader to see through the self-blindness of the female letter-writer and also to allow for a surprise ending in the final letter written by the priest.

Epithlamium: Usually a song written to celebrate a wedding. Because of its lyric quality, however, the short story can use such a form to create a lyric celebration or an ironic one. J. D. Salinger's story "For Esmé—with Love and Squalor" is a type of epithlamium written on the occasion of the narrator's receiving word of Esmé's marriage. Faulkner's "A Rose for Emily" is a kind of grotesque epithlamium commemorating the symbolic death/marriage of Emily to Homer Barron.

Essay (*Informal* or *Personal*): A brief prose work, usually on a single topic, which emphasizes the personal point of view of the author and reveals his or her own values and experiences. The periodical essay of the eighteenth century, as developed by Joseph Addison and Richard Steele in *The Tatler* and *The Spectator*, was an early influence on the development of the "sketch" form in American literature and therefore a progenitor of Washington Irving's sketches. The further development of the personal essay in the early nineteenth century by Charles Lamb, William Hazlitt, Thomas De Quincey, and others gave even further impetus to the development of the lyric-essay tone of Hawthorne's tales. The short story begins as a combination of the lyrical voice of the informal essay with the subject matter of the folktale.

Exemplum: A brief anecdote or tale often introduced into medieval sermons for edifying or illustrative purposes. Preachers of the period had collections of such *exempla* to draw from. In the fourteenth century, such *exempla* began to develop into exemplary narratives by the expansion of the anecdotes. Robert Mannyng of Brunne's "Handlynge Synne" contains sixty-seven *exempla* in short verses, many of which are expanded into exemplary narratives by the addition of concrete details. In *The Canterbury Tales* (c. 1380-1390), Chaucer also makes use of *exempla* in such tales as "The Nun's Priest Tale" and "The Pardoner's Tale." A typical example of the short story's use of the convention is Edward Everett Hale's *The Man Without a Country* (1863), which illustrates a social moral for the period.

Existentialism: Existentialism became recognized in France in the 1850's, but it more broadly began in the Romantic Period. Basic tenets are that *Logos* cannot account for the complexity of *Bios* and that the individual existent is concrete, singular, unique, free, and responsible. The short story is a particularly appropriate mode for existentialist writers in that they prefer the original, atypical, and emotionally charged complexity of situations and dislike the safe, secure, systematic life experience. Typical concerns of existential writers are man's estrangement from society, his awareness that the world is meaningless, and his recognition that one must turn from external props to the self.

Experience: John Dewey makes a distinction between "experience" and "an experience" in *Art as Experience* (1934), which may be helpful in understanding the nature of the short story. As opposed to continuous experience, which is inchoate, "an experience" has an individualizing quality and an aesthetic and emotional unity that gives it its name. "The existence of this unity is constituted by a single *quality* that pervades the entire experience in spite of the variation of the constituent parts." It seems quite clear that the short story deals with "an experience" rather than the more abstract and general sense of experience that the novel usually takes as its own.

Exposition: Exposition is usually the part or parts of a story which establish the antecedents of the central action. Exposition provides the reader with the necessary background information to understand the story—for example, the time and place of the action. Exposition also more generally provides an introduction to the nature of the fictive world of the story, such as the levels of probability the story employs. Exposition does not have to be located in the first part of a story, but can be scattered throughout and thus enable the reader to make a gradual discovery of the background. Exposition is usually elliptical and ambiguous in the short story. Even when it is extensive, its relevance is more apt to be related to the symbolic meaning of the story. For example, the narrator's description of his surroundings and his clerks in *Bartleby the Scrivener* is not made clearly relevant until the reader perceives the meaning of Bartleby's nonaction.

Fable: One of the oldest narrative forms, the fable has instruction as its primary function. The basic mode of the form is analogy in which animals or inanimate objects speak to illustrate a moral lesson. The form is usually highly abbreviated and epigrammatic with little or no effort to characterize. The most famous examples of the fable are those of Aesop, who used the form orally in Greece in 600 B. C. The modern fable, such as James Agee's "A Mother's Tale," may be more extended, may make more use of characterization, and may develop symbolic actions and characters rather than simple allegorical figures and events.

Fabliau: A short narrative poem, popular in medieval French literature and during the English Middle Ages. *Fabliaux* were usually realistic in subject matter and satiric in tone. Frequently, they involved bawdiness and shrewdness and satirized the weaknesses and foibles of human beings. They were popular with the common folk, appealing to a rustic sense of humor. Perhaps the most famous are Chaucer's "The Miller's Tale" and "The Reeve's Tale."

Fabulation: As Robert Scholes has defined it (*Structural Fabulation* 1975), fabulation presents a world which is radically discontinuous with the virtual world, but which makes us confront that world in some cognitive way. Fabulation is related to myth, fairy tale, folktale, and romance. A prominent modern example is John Barth's *Chimera* (1972), which uses myth to explore the conventions of story itself.

Fairy Tale: Various definitions have been posed for the fairy tale, a form of folktale in which supernatural events or characters are prominent. Fairy tales usually depict a realm of reality beyond that of the natural world in which the laws of the natural world are suspended. Bruno Bettelheim in his *The Uses of Enchantment* (1976) suggests that internal processes are externalized in fairy tales and represented there by the figures and events of the tales. The unrealistic nature of the stories is a clear indication that they are not concerned with information about the external world, but rather with the processes taking place in an individual. Fairy tales appeal to children and are valuable for the development of children because they conform to the way a child thinks and experiences the world, says Bettelheim. The projective nature of fairy tales helps the child reconcile and accept human dilemmas in a way that realistic stories cannot.

Fantastic: Tzvetan Todorov, in his study *The Fantastic* (1970), defines the fantastic as a genre that lies between the "uncanny" and the "marvelous." All three genres embody the familiar world, but present an event that cannot be explained by the laws of the familiar world. If the person who experiences the event is a victim of illusion, and thus the laws of the world remain what they are, we are in the realm of the uncanny. If the event has indeed taken place, then the work has created an alternate reality which is controlled by laws unknown to us, and we are in the realm of the marvelous. Todorov says that the fantastic occupies the "duration of this uncertainty. Once we choose one answer or the other, we leave the fantastic for a neighboring genre, the uncanny or the marvelous. The fantastic is that hesitation experienced by a person who knows only the laws of nature, confronting an apparently super-natural event." Because of the short story's basic folklore origins and romantic ancestry, the fantastic is a frequent theme in the form, as is also the uncanny and the marvelous.

Fiction: In the most general sense, fiction means a narrative that is made up or invented rather than an account of something that actually happened. Northrop Frye in *Anatomy of Criticism* (1957) uses the term to apply to any work of literary art "in a radically continuous form, which almost always means a work of art in prose." Frye distinguishes four forms of fiction: the novel, the prose romance, the confession, and the anatomy.

Flashback: A scene in a fiction which depicts an earlier event. The flashback can be presented as a reminiscence by a character in the story, or simply inserted into the narrative as exposition by the author. Contemporary fiction, at least since Joyce, has made use of flashbacks and flashforwards, not simply to provide details of previous events, but to break up the narrative's temporal flow itself. The result of such a time breakup is to create a spatial rather than a temporal form of narrative, which is closer to the conventions of poetry than to the usual linearity of prose. Typical examples are found in Conrad Aiken's "Silent Snow, Secret Snow" and Katherine Anne Porter's "The Grave." In both stories, the flashbacks and contemporary action are so in-termixed that time itself is broken up.

Folktale: A short prose narrative, usually orally handed down. The term is often used interchangeably with myth and fairy tale. A. E. Coppard has suggested that the folktale answered to an inborn need to hear tales, "and it is my feeling that the closer the modern short story conforms to that ancient tradition of being spoken to you rather than being read at you the more acceptable it becomes."

Form: One of the most recalcitrant terms to define in literary criticism, especially when it is used in juxtaposition to "content." As Rene Wellek and Austin Warren point out in *Theory of Literature* (1948), if we think of content as embodying the ideas and emotions in a work of art and form as all the linguistic elements by which content is expressed, we realize that such a distinction is not possible. If we take the most general definition that form is the organization of all the elements in a story in relation to its total effect, we can see that the short story is highly dependent on a perfection of form, that is, an integral relation between content and the structuring of content. R. S. Crane of the so-called Chicago Critics defines form as the "working" or emotional power that a fiction is to effect. Poe's discussion of the short story in his 1842 review of Hawthorne is the first discussion of the formal characteristics of short fiction.

Formalist Criticism: The term refers to two different schools of criticism—the Russian Formalists of the 1920's and the so-called "New Critics" in America in the 1940's. The major proponents of Russian Formalism were Boris Eichenbaum, Viktor Shklovsky, Roman Jakobson, Boris Tomashevsky, and Juri Tynyanov. The Russian Formalists were concerned with what constitutes the "literariness" of literature, that is, the conventional devices literature uses to "make strange" or defamiliarize that which habit has made familiar and thus "not seen." The American Formalists, John Crowe Ransom, Allen Tate, Robert Penn Warren, Cleanth Brooks, and R. P. Blackmur, were more concerned with the individual work as an object. The most succinct statement of the Formalist articles of faith is provided by Cleanth Brooks in a 1951 essay: the formalist believes that literary criticism is a description and an evaluation of its object, that the primary concern of criticism is with the problem of unity, that in a successful work form and content cannot be separated, that literature is basically metaphoric and symbolic, that the general and universal are seized upon only by the concrete and particular, and that specific moral problems are the subject matter of literature.

Frame Analysis: Developed by sociologist Erving Goffman (*Frame Analysis*, 1974), the concept springs from a phenomenological approach to reality that assumes, with William James, that reality is whatever is attended to for the time it is attended to; and with Alfred Schutz, that there are multiple realities governed by conventions. When an individual recognizes an event, he does so by applying a primary framework (in other words, prior interpretation) to make meaningful what would otherwise be meaningless. The perceiver does this even though he may be unable to describe the framework or even be aware of it. The task of frame analysis is to get at a set of conventions by which an event or activity, which is already meaningful in terms of a primary framework, is transformed into something which is indeed patterned on this prior interpretation, but which is seen by participants as something else. The issue may be important to short-story criticism in the sense that stories deal with events marked off from surrounding events and defined according to certain principles of organization and the reader's subjective involvement in them.

Framed Tales: The convention of including a story within a story. In such collections as *The Arabian Nights' Entertainments*, *The Decameron* (1353), and *The Canterbury Tales*, the frame serves simply as an excuse for relating a series of tales. In Henry James's *The Turn of the Screw* (1898) and Joseph Conrad's *Heart of Darkness* (1902), the interaction between the frame and the inner tale seems more complex. More recently, Samuel Beckett uses the frame convention in his trilogy (*Molloy*, 1950; *Malone Dies*, 1951; and *The Unnamable*, 1953) to develop a conflict between telling voices which constitutes the essential thematic thrust of the stories. John Barth makes use of the frame tale convention in his collections *Lost in the Funhouse* (1969) and *Chimera* both to parody the form and to push it to its inevitable self-reflexive implications.

Genre Study: The concept of studying literature by classification and definition of kinds is as old as the systematic study of literature itself. In fact, since Aristotle introduced the idea in the opening lines of *The Poetics* (fourth century B. C.), the genre principle has been an essential concomitant of the basic proposition that literature indeed can be studied systematically. In the field of poetics, as in any other science, classification and definition are synonymous with system and understanding. Such an assumption was not questioned until the nineteenth century when the Romantics rejected the species concept as part of neoclassical rigidity and rules. When later nineteenth century critics, influenced by Charles Darwin, tried to revive the concept by analogizing literary species with biological ones, the latter-day romantic Benedetto Croce laid the concept to rest for most of the twentieth century. It has been only since the mid-1950's, primarily due to the influence of Northrop Frye's *Anatomy of Criticism*, that the study of literature (poetics) has recognized the importance of the study of kinds (genre). The widespread influence of European literary theory in the 1960's has furthered the study of genre. Genre study is important for the short story precisely because it may allow for more serious discrimination between the short story and the novel and therefore better define the unique characteristics of the form. Recent genre study is usually of two types: theories which postulate some abstract principles for dividing all of literature into a few basic classes and theories based on an inductive analysis of examples of hypothetical kinds.

Gothic Romance: A form of fiction developed in the late eighteenth century, particularly in England, generally attributed to Horace Walpole. In the Preface to the second edition of *The Castle of Otranto* (1764), Walpole claimed that he was trying to combine the two kinds of fiction: events and story typical of the medieval romance and the delineation of character typical of the realistic novel. Clara Reeve in her Preface to *The Old English Baron* emphasized only enough of the marvelous to "excite attention," enough of the manners of real life to create probability, and enough of the pathetic to "engage the heart." Other examples of the form are Matthew Lewis' *The Monk* (1795) and Mary Shelley's *Frankenstein* (1818). Later in the century the typical Gothic thematic combination of romance and novel focuses on such Gothic hero figures as Heathcliff in Emily Brontë's *Wuthering Heights* and Ahab in Melville's *Moby Dick*. The focus in the Gothic romance is more on symbolic figures and events than on realistic ones. The Gothic genre had a strong influence on the development of short fiction because of Poe's familiarity with the Gothic from Germany and from the Gothic stories published in *Blackwoods Magazine* in England.

Grammar of Stories: On the assumption that stories are governed by rules, a grammar of stories is a set of statements describing these rules. A grammar of stories indicates how a story can be produced by using a set of rules and also provides a structural description of story. French Structuralists such as Roland Barthes, Claude Bremond, and Tzvetan Todorov have developed grammars of certain groups of stories. Gerald Prince (*A Grammar of Stories: An Introduction*, 1973) has attempted, by using the theory of generative grammar, to develop a grammar to identify what would be intuitively recognized as minimal story.

Grotesque: According to Wolfgang Kayser (*The Grotesque in Art and Literature*, 1963), the grotesque is a structure, an embodiment of the estranged world. In literature it is more common in the short story than in the novel and is most often embodied in a scene, although it can indeed dominate the entire short story, as it does, for example, in the stories of E. T. A. Hoffmann or Franz Kafka. The grotesque makes us aware that the familiar world is broken up by mysterious forces or that the everyday world is strange and evil. It is characterized by a disharmony in reader reaction, in which the reader is not sure whether to react with humor or with horror. It differs from fantasy in that the exaggeration which is manifested exists in the familiar world rather than in a purely imaginative world.

Hebraic and Homeric Styles: Terms coined by Erich Auerbach in *Mimesis: The Representation of Reality in Western Literature* (1953) to designate two basic fictional styles. The first is exemplified by the passage about Ulysses' scar in the *Odyssey* (c. 800 B. C.), in which everything is externalized and no contour is blurred. "Clearly outlined, brightly and uniformly illuminated, men and things stand out in a realm where everything is visible; and not less clear—wholly expressed, orderly even in their ardor—are the feelings and thoughts of the persons involved." The Hebraic style, characterized by the story of Abraham and Isaac in Genesis, externalizes the phenomenon only to the extent that it is necessary for the narrative, leaving all else in obscurity. In Auerbach's words:

> The decisive points of the narrative alone are emphasized, what lies between is nonexistent; time and place are undefined and call for interpretation . . . the whole, permeated with the most unrelieved suspense and directed toward a single goal (and to that extent far more of a unity), remains mysterious and "fraught with background."

These distinctions reflect the basic division in fictional forms between the romance fiction and the realistic fiction. Because of its origins in the romance form, the short story is more apt to be in the Hebraic style than in the Homeric.

Hermeneutics: Hermeneutics designates the theory of interpretation. The term originally referred to Hermes, the messenger of the gods, for the messages of the gods were mysterious and obscure and required interpretation to man. The difference between hermeneutics and exegesis is that the former is theory; the latter is practice. The theory of interpretation belongs originally to sacred texts and has only recently been used to apply to literary texts. The best-known discussion of the theory of interpretation in American criticism is E. D. Hirsch's *The Validity of Interpretation* (1967). Hirsch makes a sharp distinction between interpretation and criticism:

> Interpretation is the construction of textual meaning as such; it explicates those meanings, and only those meanings, which the text explicitly represents. Criticism, on the other hand, builds on the results of interpretation; it confronts textual meaning not as such, but as a component within a larger context.

Historical Criticism: A critical point of view that began with the French critic Hippolyte Taine in the mid-nineteenth century. Taine's focus was that literature resulted from three elements: the moment, the race, and the milieu.

Later in the century, Karl Marx and Friedrich Engels introduced the element of economics into historical criticism, and still later Leon Trotsky emphasized the political point of view in literature. The short story has never been a form that has lent itself to historical criticism. In the 1930's, James Farrell strongly criticized the form for its lack of political commitment; and as late as the 1960's, Maxwell Geismar has criticized the form for its lack of social concern. The short story, because it seldom deals with social reality, lends itself more to intrinsic and symbolic readings than to external readings.

Interior Monologue: Édouard Dujardin defines this form as the speech of a character designed to introduce us directly to the character's internal life. It differs from other monologues in that it attempts to reproduce thought before any logical organization is imposed. As Dujardin puts it:

> The internal monologue, in its nature of the order of poetry, is that unheard and unspoken speech by which a character expresses his inmost thoughts, those lying nearest the unconscious, without regard to logical organization—that is, in their original state—by means of direct sentences reduced to syntactic minimum, and in such a way as to give the impression of reproducing the thoughts just as they come into the mind.

Interpretation/Criticism: E. D. Hirsch (*The Validity of Interpretation*) says that interpretation occurs when we limit ourselves to the framework of the creation; criticism occurs when we measure a text's relevance by a framework we bring from outside. In interpretation we are dealing with meaning; in criticism we are dealing with significance.

Intrinsic Interpretation: Sigurd Burkhardt, in the Appendix to his book *Shakespearean Meanings* (1968), says that the method of intrinsic interpretation rests on the assumption of the work's infallibility. By "infallibility," Burkhardt does not mean that the work is infallible as an objective fact, but rather that it must be taken as it is. When one explains apparent inconsistencies through laws not derived from the work itself he has tacitly admitted that interpretation is no longer possible. Intrinsic interpretation means the attempt to know the poem solely from the poem itself. A complete interpretation means understanding the "law" that accounts for the necessary existence of every word in the poem; the work creates its own truth and establishes its own order.

Initiation Story: This mode of short fiction has been variously defined as the depiction of a fall through knowledge to maturity, a descent into the primitive sources of being, and a discovery of evil. Mordecai Marcus (*Short Story Theories*, 1976) divides initiation stories into three types: those that lead the initiate only to the threshold of maturity and understanding (for example,

Hemingway's "The Killers"), those that take the protagonist across the threshold but leave him or her uncertain (Mansfield's "The Garden Party"), and those that take the protagonist firmly into maturity (Conrad's "The Secret Sharer"). Because of their relation to primitive rituals, the initiation stories are apt to be highly informal, ritualistic, and symbolic.

Irrealism: Irrealism in contemporary short fiction is manifested as the story's loosening of its illusion of reality to expose the reality of its illusion. The story is presented self-consciously as a fiction rather than as-if-it-were-reality. Although this trend is a part of the so-called postmodernist movement in contemporary literature, the short story as a genre has always been more apt to lay bare its fictionality than the novel, which has traditionally tried to cover it up. The folk figures of Washington Irving, the allegorical figures of Hawthorne, the unitary figures of Poe, and the symbolic figures of Melville exist more as functions of the story than as problematical characters in an as-if-real world. The basic difference between these characters in the early short-story formmm and the completely function-bound characters in traditional folktale and parable is that such figures as Ichabod Crane, Young Goodman Brown, Roderick Usher, and Bartleby seem to exist both as if they were real people in an existentially real world and as representative figures manipulated for the purposes of the story. The basic difference between these early short stories and the stories of such contemporary writers as John Barth, William H. Gass, Robert Coover, and Donald Barthelme is that in contemporary fiction what is usually a background aesthetic tension is now foregrounded so that the conflict between "fiction" and "reality" becomes the self-conscious conflict of the characters in the story itself.

Irony: Generally speaking, irony is a speech device whereby the intent of an utterance is conveyed by a statement that has the opposite meaning from what is denoted on the surface. In the 1940's, the formalists made irony a central tenet of their view of literature. Cleanth Brooks (*The Well-Wrought Urn*, 1947) uses irony as a critical term to indicate a "recognition of incongruities which . . . pervades all poetry to a degree far beyond what our conventional criticism has heretofore been willing to allow." Irony in short fiction is most often a result of point of view, which is usually both distanced and involved at the same time. The detachment in the point of view in Chekhov's stories, for example, does not indicate indifference, but rather a recognition of incongruities that cannot, by their very nature, be resolved. Irony also often functions in the short story in the form of a concluding understatement which ironically enforces the impact of the story rather than deflating it.

Lay (*Lai*): A short narrative poem meant to be sung, popular in France in the twelfth century and later in England in the fourteenth century. One of the best-known twelfth century French examples of the form is *Lanval*, based on Arthurian legend, by Marie de France. One of the best-known fourteenth century English *lais* is *Sir Orfeo*. The *lai* form developed into the shorter romance form in the latter part of the fourteenth century in such tales as *Sir Launfal*, in which Thomas Chestre expands the earlier story by adding more details and new subordinate incidents.

Legend: A narrative that is handed down from generation to generation, usually associated with a particular place and a specific event. A classic early use of the legend convention in the short story is Washington Irving's "The Legend of Sleepy Hollow," which depicts the expulsion of Ichabod Crane from Sleepy Hollow and which signifies the triumph of the old Dutch atmosphere of New York over the attempted encroachment of Yankee exploitation.

Literary Short Story: A term which was current in American criticism in the 1940's to distinguish the short fiction of Ernest Hemingway, Eudora Welty, Sherwood Anderson, and others from the popular pulp and slick magazine fiction of the day. The most pervasive distinction between the two seems to be that the literary story rebelled against the sentimentalizing of reality in the popular short story. The literary story, according to critics of the period, marked a direction toward more intellectuality and subtler emotional treatment in the form.

Local Color: The term usually refers to a movement in literature, especially in America, in the latter part of the nineteenth century. The focus was on the environment, atmosphere, and milieu of a particular region. The movement forms a bridge between the romantic and the realistic movement and thus combines elements of both. The first phase of local color stories is romantic and tends to emphasize the strange and unfamiliar area, with the focus also on the somewhat regionally secluded area and folk. The shift to realism is inevitable since the local-color writer depends on particular detail of a region and maintaining verisimilitude in the dialogue of the characters. The realistic aspect is emphasized in the 1890's by Hamlin Garland. Local color for Garland means "that the writer spontaneously reflects the life which goes on around him. It is natural and unrestrained art." Local color for the realists means more than "a forced study of the picturesque scenery" of an area.

Lyric Short Story: Eileen Baldeshwiler (*Short Story Theories*, 1976) defines the lyric story as one that differs from the mimetic or epical story in that the lyrical focus is on internal changes, moods, and feelings. The lyric story is usually open-ended and depends on the figurative language usually associated with poetry. The most important writers in the history of this type of short fiction are Ivan Turgenev, Anton Chekhov, Katherine Mansfield, Sherwood Anderson, Conrad Aiken, and John Updike.

Metafiction (*Self-Reflexive Fiction*): These terms refer to certain contemporary stories which take the fictional process as their subject matter; however, the metafictional or self-reflexive tendency has always been a common element of the short story. Basically, this is due to the short story's hovering between conventions of fantasy and reality, in which characters from the everyday world confront projective embodiments of psychic states. Moreover, the short story has always been a more self-conscious "artistic" form than the novel. The illusion in such stories as "Young Goodman Brown" and *Bartleby the Scrivener* is that within a fiction itself, there is a mixing of fiction and reality. More obvious twentieth century examples of this mixing of fiction and reality within a fiction are Hemingway's "The Snows of Kilimanjaro," which mixes the writer's fictionalizing of his past with his actual present, and Sherwood Anderson's *Death in the Woods* (1933), which is about the storyteller's attempt to "make sense" of a mythically magic moment. Contemporary writers such as William H. Gass, Robert Coover, John Barth, and Donald Barthelme have pushed self-reflexiveness to such extremes that conservative critics such as Malcolm Cowley have cried for an end to stories about writing when authors do not have anything else to write about. Once we accept, however, the postmodernist assumption—that reality is not a given, but rather a constantly made process, a fictionalizing process—then we must agree with the meta-fictionalists that to write about fictional processes is to write about the only reality there is.

Metaphor: Perhaps the most basic trope in literature, for in metaphor one thing is described in terms of another; in fact, one thing is, in a quite purposeful "mistake," called something else in order to reveal something that cannot be revealed in any other way. I. A. Richards makes the distinction between the "tenor," or the subject of the comparison in metaphor, and the "vehicle," or the subject being communicated. Roman Jakobson (*Fundamentals of Language*, 1971) defines metaphor as one of the fundamentals of the two polar aspects of communication. Metaphor refers to the faculty for selection and substitution; metonymy refers to the faculty for combination and contexture. The metaphoric process predominates in the literary schools of romanticism and symbolism, whereas the metonymic process predominates in the so-called "realistic" schools. The short story, although primarily a metaphoric form, is influenced in the mid-nineteenth century by the metonymic thrust of realism. A study of the combination of the two processes in the short story is not only a study of a genre, but of the bipolar nature of language and thought itself.

Modernist Story: Modernism as a movement is usually said to have begun in the early twentieth century as an attempt to overturn nineteenth century bourgeois realism. In fiction, the effort was spearheaded by James Joyce and was manifested as an attempt to substitute a mythical for a realistic fictional method. The result in fiction has been the defeat of the usual expectations of linearity in narrative, of cause and effect, and of coherence of plot and character. Moreover, the inward consciousness is substituted for public or objective consciousness, and a subjective voice challenges the objectivity of the nineteenth century world view. This kind of shift can be seen in the American short story by comparing the "realistic" story of the late nineteenth century with the modernist short story of the 1920's. See Austin Wright's *The American Short Story in the Twenties* (1961) for a complete discussion of this shift.

Morphology of Fiction: To construct a morphology of a certain fictional genre is to see the episodes of individual stories in terms of a fixed form by converting the characters and actions into general categories. Vladimir Propp, in his *Morphology of the Folktale* (1928), terms the actions of stories "functions" which are constant elements regardless of who performs them. Propp ascertains that the number of functions known to the folktale is limited, that the sequence of functions is identical, and that all folktales are of one type in terms of their structure.

Motif: This term usually refers to a conventional incident or situation in a fiction which may serve as the basis for the structure of the narrative. In criticism, it is often used similarly to its use in music—to indicate a recurring idea or pattern. Russian Formalist Boris Tomashevsky uses the term to refer to the smallest particles of thematic material. "The theme of an irreducible part of a work is called the *motif*; each sentence, in fact, has its own motif." Mutually related motifs constitute the thematic bonds of the work, says Tomashevsky. He also distinguishes between "bound motifs," which cannot be omitted without disturbing the connections between events, and "free motifs," which can be omitted without disturbing the causal-chronological course of events.

Motivation: Although this term usually refers to the convention of justifying the action of a character from his or her own psychological makeup, the Russian Formalists use the term to refer to the network of devices justifying the introduction of individual motifs or groups of motifs in a work. Boris Tomashevsky classifies motivational devices as follows: (1) compositional motivation, which refers to the economy and usefulness of the motifs, the principle of every single property in the work contributing to the overall effect of the work; (2) realistic motivation, which refers to what Tzvetan Todorov has called *vraisemblance*, the realistic devices to convince the reader that the story is plausible and lifelike; (3) artistic motivation, which refers to the demands of the artistic structure.

Myth: Myth is story, story which tacitly symbolizes basic human experience. Philip Wheelwright suggests that primitive myths are early expressions of the "storytelling urge." The short story is a romantic revival of mythic story, in which the myth's original "semantic fluidity and plenitude" have been exchanged for "tidier narratives relying on firmer grammatical, logical, and causal relationships." Claude Lévi-Strauss says "Myth is the part of language where the formula *tradutore, tradittore* reaches its lowest truth value. . . . Its substance does not lie in its style, its original music, or its syntax, but in the story which it tells." Lévi-Strauss says that myth is made up of gross constituent units (that is, relations between motifs in the story), and that furthermore the true constituent units of a myth are not isolated relations, but "bundles of such relations." Lévi-Strauss illustrates his point about myth by analyzing the Oedipus myth.

Myth Criticism: A critical approach which assumes that literature develops both historically and psychologically out of myth. Northrop Frye asserts that in myth, "we see the structural principles of literature isolated." Richard Chase says that the artistic consciousness has much in common with the "primitive magico-mythical psychology." Myth criticism is not to be confused with "mythological criticism," which was primarily concerned with finding parallels to mythological stories in the surface action of narrative. Myth critics are concerned with deep mythic structures. Much of current myth criticism springs from the work of philosopher Ernst Cassirer in his *Philosophy of Symbolic Forms* (1955). Cassirer describes "mythic perception" and "mythical thinking" as an apprehension of reality which makes no distinction between the image and the thing itself.

Narrative: Narrative usually implies a contrast to "enacted" fiction. Wellek and Warren in *Theory of Literature* say that its chief pattern is its exclusiveness: "It intersperses scenes in dialogue with summary accounts of what is happening." Robert Scholes and Robert Kellogg in *The Nature of Narrative* (1966) say that by narrative they mean literary works which have the presence of both a story and a storyteller.

Narrative Essay: A form of the personal essay in which the essay either is told in narrative form or makes extensive use of anecdotal material. The popularity of the form in the eighteenth century helped give rise to the nineteenth century short story. Many critics have noted that Washington Irving's *The Sketch Book of Geoffrey Crayon, Gent.* (1819-1820) was strongly influenced by the tone established in the essays of Addison and Steele. Poe described many of the stories in Hawthorne's *Twice-Told Tales* as being narrative essay in tone and structure.

Narrator: In the most general sense, the one who tells the story or who recounts the narrative. Wayne Booth develops several different types of narrator in *The Rhetoric of Fiction* (1961). Even when an author is not dramatized in the story, the story creates an implicit picture of an author behind the scenes, which Booth calls an implied narrator. Various dramatized narrators which Booth describes are unacknowledged centers of consciousness, observers, narrator-agents, and self-conscious narrators. Booth suggests that the important element to consider in narration is the relationship between the narrator, the author, the characters, and the reader. The relationship of the narrator to the story has always been an important element in the highly subjective and lyrically relativist short story.

Naturalism: The term was brought to bear on literature in the late nineteenth century by Émile Zola, who insisted on the novel's telling of absolutely truthful instances. The term refers more to choice of subject matter than to technical conventions. Although the late nineteenth century stories of Guy de Maupassant and George Moore are often described as naturalistic, the focus on hard events and the rigid empiricism that dominate naturalism have not made the movement conducive to the short story. Jack London's famous story "To Build a Fire" is a classic example of naturalism in the American short story, but because of its adherence to physical facts, it is not typical of the short-story form. Many critics, trying to recover it from critical neglect, have attempted to suggest both metaphysical and symbolic significance for the story.

Novel: The novel is, of course, many things, perhaps even all things its author wants to put in it. It differs from the short story, however, not only in length, but also in its view of reality. The novel, says Lionel Trilling in *Liberal Imagination* (1953), pursues its quest for reality in the social world. What it analyzes as indicating the direction of the soul is manners of man in the social world. According to this definition, the novels of Henry James constitute the model for the form; for the real hero in a James novel, says T. S. Eliot, is a "social entity" of which the characters are constituents. Ian Watt (*The Rise of the Novel*, 1957) says that the novel is distinguished from other genres by the attention it pays to individual characterization and detailed presentation of the environment. Moreover, the novel is concerned with using past experiences as the causes of present action. "The novel in general," says Watt, "has interested itself much more than any other literary form in the development of its characters in the course of time."

Novella, novelle, nouvelle, novelette, novela: *Novella* is the Italian term for short story, from *nuovo*, meaning new, strange, extraordinary. The best-known example of the form in Italian is Giovanni Boccaccio's *The Decameron*. The Renaissance form focuses on plot rather than character, but differs from the fable in presenting the remarkable as being fact. Usually the story is built around a symbolic object, referred to as the "Falcon" (from one of Boccaccio's stories). The German form of short fiction is called *novelle* and indicates a form longer than a short story but shorter than a novel. The French term for this form is *nouvelle* and is distinguished from the short story or *conte* in both its length and its subject matter; whereas the *conte* arose as a French form that dealt with the fantastic, the *nouvelle* selects the strange and unusual from ordinary life. *Novela* is the Spanish term for the same form. "Novelette" is the term usually preferred by the British to refer to the form longer than the short story but shorter than the novel, whereas "short novel" is the term usually used to refer to American works of this genre. Henry James, using the French term *nouvelle*, found the form most conducive to his talents. Referring to it as the "ideal, the beautiful and blest *nouvelle*," he claimed that its main merit was the "effort to do the complicated thing with a strong brevity and lucidity—to arrive on behalf of the multiplicity, at a certain science of control." James also claimed that the *nouvelle* was about something that "oddly happened to someone."

Objective Correlative: This key critical concept in modern formalist criticism was coined by T. S. Eliot in an essay on Hamlet in *The Sacred Wood* (1920). An objective correlative is a situation, an event, or an object that, when presented or described in a work, evokes a particular emotion for which the object is the formula. Short stories, which must often focus on a single situation and depend on the evocativeness or emotional resonance of a situation or an event, expresses (like poetry) emotion by means of objective correlatives. Such objects or events need not be symbolic, although the garden in Mansfield's "The Garden Party," the flowering Judas in Katherine Anne Porter's story, and the card game in Stephen Crane's "The Blue Hotel" are symbolic because they objectify not only emotional complexes, but metaphysical ideas as well.

Oriental Tale: An eighteenth century form made popular by the translations of *The Arabian Nights' Entertainments* (*The Thousand and One Nights*) collection during the period. Benjamin Boyce, in a 1968 article on eighteenth century short fiction, characterizes these tales as vaguely biblical in manner and solemn in tone; there is little characterization, and the focus is on improbable events, supernatural places, and contrasts between simple peasants and luxurious royalty.

Parable: A brief allegory, often an analogue of an ethical situation, as in the parables of Jesus. The parable can be expanded to include characterization and complexity of incident, as it is in such stories as Hawthorne's "The Minister's Black Veil," Leo Tolstoy's "God Sees the Truth But Waits to Tell," and E. M. Forster's "The Other Side of the Hedge." In a 1960 essay, Richard Eastman defined a further form of parable, developed by such writers as Kafka and Beckett, which he terms the "Open Parable." In the open parable, the reader is not allowed to perceive a simple analogic structure and may feel he is reading a dream situation. By balancing sympathetic and antipathetic detail, the open parable does not allow the reader to endorse any one character or theme.

Phenomenological Criticism: The best-known example of phenomenological criticism is also called "Geneva criticism" or "criticism of consciousness." The most famous American practitioner is J. Hillis Miller, whose books, *The Disappearance of God* (1963), *Poets of Reality* (1965), and *Thomas Hardy: Distance and Desire* (1970), are strongly influenced by European critics Jean Starobinski, Jean-Pierre Richard, and especially Georges Poulet. The basic thrust of these critics is summed up in *Critics of Consciousness* (1968) by Sarah N. Lawall:

> They look upon literature as an act, not an object. They refuse to make distinctions between genres; they look for a single voice in a series of works by the same author; they will not consider each work as an autonomous whole. What is more, they seek latent patterns of themes and impulses inside literature, and do not discuss the symmetries and ambiguities of the formal text.

Plot and Story: The minimal distinction between plot and story is that story is a more general term referring to the narrative of character and action, whereas plot refers specifically to action with little reference to character. Russian Formalist critic Boris Tomashevsky, however, makes the distinction between plot (*fabula*) and story (*sujet*) by noting that in the plot the events are arranged according to the orderly sequence in which they are presented in the work, whereas story refers to the events arranged in causal-chrono-logical order. Plot is the sum of the same events as are in the story, but arranged so as to engage the emotions and develop the theme. Contemporary critics most concerned with plot are the Neo-Aristotelians or Chicago Critics. R. S. Crane, in *Critics and Criticism* (1952), defines plot as a temporal synthesis of action, character, and thought; it depends on our emotional involvement with characters—that is, whether we wish them well or ill. The form of a plot is its power to move our feelings in a definite way.

Plotless Story: In the late nineteenth and early twentieth century, when Chekhov seemingly eliminated the beginnings of endings of his stories, critics called his stories plotless. Gradually, critics recognized that this so-called plotlessness indicated a general shift in emphasis in fiction from external action to a concern with mood and motives—the drama of the mind.

Point of View: The means by which the story is presented to the reader, or as Percy Lubbock says in *The Craft of Fiction* (1921), "the relation in which the narrator stands to the story," a relation which Lubbock says governs the whole question of technique in fiction. Norman Friedman says that the basic questions to be asked about point of view are: who talks to the reader? From what position regarding the story does he tell it? What channels of information does he use? At what distance does he place the reader from the story? Wayne Booth, in his *The Rhetoric of Fiction* (1961), believes that additional questions need to be asked, such as what kind of person is the narrator? "How fully characterized? How much aware of himself as a narrator? How reliable? At what points shall he speak truth and at what points utter no judgments or even utter falsehood?"

Postmodernist Story: Postmodernism is an extension of the modernist movement which results from an increasing emphasis on self-consciousness and consequently self-reflexiveness in fiction. It moves beyond the modernist focus on the individual self to a fiction that is more and more about itself as fiction and about fictional processes. In the short story, the best-known practitioners are William H. Gass, Donald Barthelme, Robert Coover, John Barth, Jorge Luis Borges, and Vladimir Nabokov.

Protagonist: The central figure in a story, the character whose fortunes concern the reader most. According to Frank O'Connor, the protagonist of the short story is apt to be the "little man," or what O'Connor calls a "submerged population group." In such short stories as *Bartleby the Scrivener* and "The Fall of the House of Usher," it is not clear whether the unitary figures Bartleby and Usher concern us most or the narrators who confront these strange figures and try to understand them.

Psychological Criticism: The most influential form of psychological criticism is so-called "depth psychology," influenced by Sigmund Freud. Much psychoanalytic criticism, however, degenerated in the first half of the twentieth century into elaborate symbol-hunting of Freudian dream symbols or, as practiced by psychoanalysts, attempts to psychoanalyze either a fictional character or the author. More recently, psychoanalytic criticism has become more sophisticated and helpful in understanding the basic nature of literature and the reader's relationship to it. Perhaps the best-known is that form of criticism referred to as "transactive criticism," developed and practiced at the Center for the Psychological Study of the Arts at the State University of New York at Buffalo. Norman Holland, drawing on recent developments in ego psychology, especially the work done on "identity" by Heinz Lichtenstein, is concerned with the empirical study of how the themes of a reader's own identity match and shape the themes of the text. David Bleich has turned his attention to the more basic nature of subjective criticism and has tried to develop a theory for a new subjective paradigm in contemporary thought. Psychoanalytic criticism is now less concerned with the interpretation of the text, the character, or the author, and is more concerned with how the Freudian dream work of displacement, condensation, and symbolism are related to the conventions of literature itself.

Realism: A literary method or technique in which the primary convention is to create an illusion of faithfulness to external reality. As a reaction to romanticism in the mid- to late-nineteenth century, realism was not a hospitable technique for the short story, which has always been basically a romantic and symbolic fictional form. The only sort of "realism" suitable to the short story is the psychological realism of James, which, rather than maintaining a fidelity to external reality, instead creates a stylized representation of the mind itself.

Reception Aesthetics: Introduced in the late 1960's by German theorist Hans Robert Jauss, reception aesthetics derives from phenomenology and focuses on the study of a literary text through the reader's reaction to it. The best-known European practitioner is Wolfgang Iser (*The Implied Reader: Patterns of Communication in Prose Fiction from Bunyan to Beckett*, 1972); the best-known American practitioner is Stanley E. Fish (*Self-Consuming Artifacts: The Experience of Seventeenth-Century Literature*, 1972). For the reception critic, meaning is an event or process and is therefore temporal rather than spatial; form is also temporal rather than spatial. The form of a work, says Fish, is the form of the reader's experience. Meaning, rather than being embedded in the work, is created through particular acts of reading. Iser says there is no exact correlation between what is described in literary texts and objects in the real world. As a result, indeterminacy is characteristic of literary works. The reader must "normalize" the text either by projecting his or her standards into the text or by revising his or her standards. It is only in the act of reading that indeterminacy can be replaced with meaning.

Rhetorical Criticism: A mode of criticism which is concerned with the interactions between the work, the author, and the audience. The rhetorical critic is concerned with the work as a means of communication—the means by which the work affects or controls the reader. Such criticism thus works best with didactic works such as satire. Wayne Booth (*The Rhetoric of Fiction*, 1961), however, is concerned with nondidactic fiction and views rhetoric as the "art of communicating with readers"; he is therefore concerned with devices the author uses to "consciously or unconsciously impose his fictional world upon the reader."

Romance: The romance (whether it be the medieval romance or the modern romance form) usually differs from the novel in that the focus is less on realistic events and characters than on symbolic events and representational characters. Northrop Frye says the romancer does not try to create real people but rather stylized figures and psychological archetypes. Richard Chase has also defined the romance in terms of character, by noting that in the romance character becomes abstract and ideal, a function of plot, rather than a character complexly related to society. The romancer is more apt to be concerned with dream reality than with phenomenal reality, believing that reality itself is more complicated and complex than the novel will admit. Frye asserts that the romance form bears the same relation to the novel that the "tale" form bears to the "short story." These two fictional forms seem to correspond to two basic modes of artistic presentation defined by Carl Jung: the psychological and the visionary. The psychological deals with conscious human experience and belongs to the realm of the understandable. The visionary presents a primordial experience in which we are reminded not of the everyday world, but rather of the realm of dreams.

Romanticism: The Romantic Period in Europe and England had a strong influence on the development of the short story in America. The romantic fascination with the old romance form and with folktale and ballad, as well as their insistence that such forms be lyricized by a personal point of view, gave rise not only to Coleridge and Wordsworth's experiments in *The Lyrical Ballads* (in which the lyric element is foregrounded), but also to the short story of Hawthorne and Poe (in which the story element is foregrounded).

Satiric Story: A subgenre of the short story that works ironically by conveying to the reader a significance different from the literal or surface meaning and that usually attacks a character type, an institution, or a fictional form itself. The characters are usually types rather than individuals, and the theme is usually conceptual rather than psychological or emotional. Classic modern examples of the form are Flannery O'Connor's "Good Country People," J. F. Powers' "The Valiant Woman," Stephen Crane's "The Bride Comes to Yellow Sky," and Mary McCarthy's "Cruel and Barbarous Treatment."

Scene: A unit of fictional action or narration in which specific actions are narrated or depicted. The scene, as opposed to the summary of past events or events quickly passed over, gives the reader the sense of participation in the event at the same time that it occurs. Consequently, it is usually used for intense moments. Although a short story most often is an episode of several scenes, the entire story can be composed of one scene, such as in Hemingway's "Hills Like White Elephants."

Semiotics (*Semiology*): The science of signs and sign systems in communication. "Semiotics" is the favored term of Charles Sanders Pierce, which he defines as the formal doctrine of signs. "Semiology" is the term coined by Ferdinand de Saussure: "A science that studies the life of signs within society is conceivable; it would be a part of social psychology and consequently of general psychology; I shall call it *semiology* (from the Greek *sēmeîon* 'sign'). Semiology would show what constitutes signs, what laws govern them." Roman Jakobson says that every message is made of signs, and that the science of semiotics deals with the principles which underlie the structure of signs, their use in messages, and the specific nature of various sign systems.

Setting: Setting refers to all the circumstances and environment, both temporal and spatial, of a narrative. In the sense that setting is synonymous with atmosphere, setting has always played an important role in the short story. In 1902, critic Bliss Perry suggested that both character and action in the short story may be without significance, "provided the atmosphere—the place and time—the background—is artistically portrayed." Although Perry was focusing on the development of the short story in the late nineteenth century, it is nevertheless true that the short story generally, because it is usually not concerned with social situations, may depend more on atmosphere than more realistic fictional forms. Eudora Welty says: "Place in fiction is the named, identified, concrete, exact and exacting, and therefore credible, gathering-spot of all that has been felt, is about to be experienced" in the work of fiction. Setting in the short story is more apt to have a symbolic significance than in the novel; for example, the garden in Katherine Mansfield's "The Garden Party," Wall Street in *Bartleby the Scrivener*, or the hills like white elephants in Hemingway's famous story.

Sketch: The function of the sketch, a narrative form that originated in the eighteenth century, is to characterize. The focus is usually on a person or a place rather than on an event; whatever narrative or action is depicted exists less for its own sake than for the function of characterization. As a result of this lack of narrative, the focus on theme in a sketch is also minimal. The basic difference between the seventeenth century abstract characterization and the eighteenth century sketch is that the sketch makes use of concrete details and presents an individual person or place rather than a stereotype or concept. Washington Irving's pieces in *The Sketch Book of Geoffrey Crayon, Gent.* are early classic examples of the sketch form moving toward the short story.

Social Criticism: The social critic is concerned with the many relations of the literary work to society, such as the work within its social context (for example, Bartleby as representative of the alienated worker in nineteenth century society), the social implications of a work (for example, the decadent effect of wealth on the writer in Hemingway's "The Snows of Kilimanjaro"), the social effect of a work (for example, the questioning of social scapegoating in Shirley Jackson's "The Lottery"), or the broad relationship of literature to the class struggle. Many critics have taken the short-story form to task for not addressing social problems. David Daiches has rightly suggested that the sociological approach is best suited to the novel.

Spatial Form: Joseph Frank, in a now-famous essay, uses this term to describe an effort in modern fiction (beginning with James Joyce, Marcel Proust, Djuna Barnes) to make the reader apprehend the work spatially in a "moment of time" rather than sequentially. To do this, the artist breaks up the narrative into interspersed fragments. This is concomitant with the modern effort to supplant historical time in fiction with mythic time—the bodying forth of eternal prototypes apprehended totally. According to this point of view, a work of fiction cannot be read, but only reread. Frank says, "A knowledge of the whole is essential to an understanding of any part"; the work must be grasped as a unity. Creation and perception of spatial form is obviously more common and successful in the short story than in the novel because of length.

Stream-of-Consciousness Technique: A narrative technique by which an author tries to embody the total range of consciousness of a character, without any authorial comment or explanation. The usual distinction between stream-of-consciousness and the interior monologue is that the latter presents that aspect of consciousness in which the mind formulates thoughts and feelings in language, whereas the former is a broader term indicating the presentation of all ranges of consciousness: sensations, thoughts, memories, associations. In one of her essays, Virginia Woolf asserts the importance of this technique for capturing reality by noting that life itself is "a luminous halo, a semi-transparent envelope surrounding us from the beginning of consciousness to the end. Is it not the task of the novelists to convey this varying, this unknown and uncircumscribed spirit?"

Structuralism: The basic tenets of structuralism in all the varied fields of knowledge where it has made its mark in the last twenty years is stated by Jean Piaget. Structuralism is predicated on the ideal of intrinsic, self-sufficient structures which do not require making reference to extraneous elements. Furthermore, says Piaget, the structuralists hold that a structure is a system of transformations which involves the interplay of laws inherent in the system. "In short, the notion of structure is comprised of three key ideas: the idea of wholeness, the idea of transformation, and the idea of self-regulation." The structuralist approach to literary criticism is as varied as the many critics who practice it. Much of structuralist literary criticism as practiced by Roland Barthes, Claude Bremond, Tzvetan Todorov, and others owes much to the work of anthropologist Claude Lévi-Strauss's study of kinship systems in primitive societies. Lévi-Strauss in turn owes much to the Russian Formalist movement in the 1920's and to the linguistic school of structuralism developed by Ferdinand de Saussure in his *Course in General Linguistics* (1915).

The structuralist literary critic attempts to define structural principles that operate intertextually throughout the whole of literature as well as principles that operate in genres and in individual works. In one of the best primer introductions to structuralist literary theory, *Structuralism in Literature* (1974), Robert Scholes says that because narrative extends from myth to the modern novel, while preserving structural features, it offers a rich field for the structuralists: "Structuralism and formalism have given us virtually all the poetics of fiction that we have." Frederic Jameson (*The Prison House of Language*, 1972) suggests that formalism and structuralism find their most privileged objects in the smaller forms of narrative such as folktales, anecdotes, and short stories.

Subjective Criticism: Pioneered by Norman Holland in *The Dynamics of Literary Response* (1968) and David Bleich in *Readings and Feelings: Introduction to Subjective Criticism* (1975), this school of criticism proposes that literary texts are never the same for any two readers. Objectivity is only a paradigm, not an absolute. Consensually validated perception is a more viable way of understanding than the assumption of objective perception. Holland says a reader responds to a literary work by assimilating it to his own psychological processes, that is, to his search for successful solutions within his own identity theme to the multiple demands, both inner and outer, on his ego.

Symbol: Broadly speaking, a symbol is anything that means something else. In this sense, all words and all literary works are symbols. Usually a symbol refers to a word that both signifies a concrete referent and at the same time suggests another level of meaning. It differs from allegory in that the concrete referent in allegory has no meaning apart from the symbolized meaning, and from the image by actually suggesting something beyond the concrete referent. Coleridge says a symbol

is characterized by a translucence of the special in the individual, or of the general in the special, or of the universal in the general; above all by the translucence of the eternal through and in the temporal. It always partakes of the reality which it renders intelligible; and while it enunciates the whole, abides itself as a living part in that unity of which it is the representative.

Sympathy: According to Max Scheler in *The Nature of Sympathy* (1970), sympathy is the feeling which structures the experience we have when we reach a deep understanding of another's situation and his or her feelings by sharing it with him or her. Scheler says there can be no full knowledge of another unless based on the feeling of being with him or her as a unique spiritual-historical being in a common life. To have true insight into another, we must sympathetically share in his or her performance of a meaningful act. Sympathy, a key element in Romantic poetry, has also been a central element in the short story since its beginning.

Tall-Tale: A humorous tale very popular in the American West; the story usually makes use of realistic detail and common speech, but it tells a tale of impossible events which most often focus on a single legendary, super-human figure, such as Paul Bunyan or Davy Crockett.

Teaching Story: In traditional Hindu medicine, a story is given to a psychically disturbed patient for meditation. Such stories, often fairy tales, serve as parallels to states of mind. Internal processes are thus externalized in the characters and events of the story and embody the way the mind works. Meditation on the stories constitutes direct teaching and therapy.

Thematics: Northrop Frye says that when a work of fiction is written or interpreted thematically, it becomes an illustrative fable. The interest in thematic works, says Frye, is conceptual. A more specific definition is offered by Murray Krieger in his *The Tragic Vision* (1960). Krieger defines thematics as "the study of the experiential tensions which, dramatically entangled in the literary work, become an existential reflection of that work's aesthetic complexity."

Tone: Tone usually refers to the dominant mood of the work. Irving Howe has suggested that tone is more important in the short story than plot.

> If the short story writer is to create the illusion of reality, he must sing most aria and very little recitative. As a result, he uses a series of technical devices, often quite simple inflections of style, the end effect of which we call the story tone. A novel written in one dominant tone becomes intolerable; a story too often deviating from it risks chaos.

In a novel, says Howe, a second-rate writer may imitate a vision of life; in a short story, the second-rater tends to "echo a tone of voice."

Tragic Vision: The best definition of this central thematic concern in many short stories is given by Murray Krieger in his book, *The Tragic Vision*. Krieger says the tragic vision is an expression of man only in an extreme situation; it always represents extreme cases and rejects all palliatives. The central figure in such a thematic work is an extremist who, although he may be involved in actual experience, is transformed into parable. Bartleby, Kurtz, and the Swede in Crane's "The Blue Hotel" are examples.

Vraisemblance (*Verisimilitude*): Tzvetan Todorov defines *vraisemblance* as "the mask which conceals the text's own laws but which we are supposed to take for a relation to reality." Northrop Frye calls this concept "displacement"—a tendency to displace myth in a human direction. Frye says by displacement he means the techniques a writer uses to "make his story credible, logically motivated or morally acceptable—lifelike, in short." Similarly, Todorov says we speak of *vraisemblance* when we refer to the work's attempts to make us believe that it conforms to reality and not to its own laws.

Western Story: Usually a popular short-story form. The setting is the key element—Western America during the frontier period. The characters are usually stereotyped; the plot is usually melodrama. Bret Harte's stories of philosophic gamblers, whores with hearts of gold, and grizzled prospectors who turn sentimental are the forerunners of the form in the American short story. Stephen Crane satirizes the Western story in "The Bride Comes to Yellow Sky"; and in his "The Blue Hotel," the romanticized violence of the Western pulp story is the key plot element that leads to the tragic death of the Swede.

Yarn: The yarn is an oral tale or a written transcription of what purports to be an oral tale. The yarn is usually a broadly comic tale, the classic example of which is Mark Twain's "Baker's Bluejay Yarn." The tension in the yarn is usually between realistic detail and incredible events juxtaposed in such a way that the teller of the tale protests that he is telling the truth while the reader or listener knows that he is lying. In other words, the incredulity of the listener is crucial to the effect of the yarn. The basic difference between the yarn and the tall-tale is that the latter focuses primarily on the hero, whereas in the yarn the focus is on the teller.

Charles E. May

SHORT-FICTION CRITICISM

The most obvious fact about short-story criticism is that, compared to the novel, the form is seriously neglected. The following bibliography represents practically all the extended criticism which has been written on the short story since Edgar Allan Poe's famous 1842 review of Nathaniel Hawthorne's *Twice-Told Tales*. A similar bibliography on the novel would extend to several volumes. Although the short story has been called a unique American contribution to world literature, we do not even have a good critical history of the development of the form in this country.

There are many reasons for this neglect, not the least of which is a kind of literary snobbishness which equates bigness with importance and smallness with finger exercises. Moreover, there still exists a reaction against the formula-ridden criticism of the short story so popular in the first twenty years of the century. The problem began in 1901 when Brander Matthews, claiming himself to be the first to assert that the short story was a genre essentially different from the novel, published his *The Philosophy of the Short Story*. Attempting to create "set rules" out of Poe's cryptic suggestions, Matthews established formulas that gave rise to countless handbooks. The success of O. Henry's formulas for the short story at about the same time led to numerous imitators who so filled the magazines with rule-bound stories that critics cried for an end to it.

Reservations about the form persisted into the 1920's and 1930's with social-minded critics demanding that the short story address itself to social criticism, that it manifest an ideology, and that it have a serious thematic concern. In the 1940's, critics finally began to make distinctions between the popular commercial story and the quality or literary story. Moreover, they began to realize that the short story's characteristic mode of apprehending reality was closer to that of lyric poetry than to that of the novel. Consequently, they were more willing to accept its subjectivity, its lyric tone, its patterned structure, and its focus on moods and motives. This period marked the dominance of the so-called "New Criticism" in American English Departments; thus, the scholarly journals were filled with interpretations or "readings" of individual stories. The New Critics' approach so valued balanced tensions and imagistic patterns that the quality stories in the quarterlies and literary journals began to follow a new kind of formula—one that many claimed belonged only to the professors and the critics.

In the last thirty years, the short story has become even more "literary"—from the intricately crafted stories of Philip Roth, John Updike, and Bernard Malamud to the self-reflexive metafictions of John Barth, Donald Barthelme, and Robert Coover. This trend in the short story toward becoming more and more self-conscious, more and more aware of its own fictional processes, is simultaneous with the trend in literary criticism toward developing theories of literature which attempt to explain the modes of fictional communication itself. It has been only in the last two decades that American criticism has discovered the Russian Formalist school of the 1920's and has been highly influenced by European Structuralism which grew out of it.

This reaction against the New Critical focus on interpretation of individual works and the resulting shift toward considerations of the nature of literary conventions and generic modes has only recently stimulated a new interest in the short-story form. Indeed, the short story will perhaps benefit even more than the novel from structuralist approaches, for the short story has always been more highly patterned and conventionalized and thus "literary" than that "loose and baggy monster," the novel. Moreover, because the structuralists are interested in primitive structural patterns, in what might be called the "origins" of discourse or the minimal story, the short story, which is indeed a primary form of fiction, may come in for more attention than the novel, which is derived.

Admirers of the short story have been predicting a renaissance of critical interest in the form for the past century, only to be repeatedly disappointed; perhaps then, one should make predictions with hope rather than confidence. Obviously, the best way to begin such a new critical concern for the short story is to start with what has been done before. Therefore, the following annotated bibliography is offered as a stimulus and a starting point.

Bibliography of Short-Fiction Criticism

"The Art of the Short Story: Principles and Practices in the United States," in *Times Literary Supplement.* (September 17, 1954) pp. xl, xlii. Also included in *American Writing Today: Its Independence and Vigor.* Allan Angoff, ed. New York: New York University Press, 1957, pp. 176-191. A survey of the development of the American short story which suggests that the form thrived in prose-conscious nineteenth century America because it fulfilled a poetic need. American stories are usually better than British ones because the wide divergence of places in America makes the artist aware of the multifariousness of life; he is compelled to subdue, order, and yet preserve that experience in the short story.

Backus, Joseph M. "'He Came into her Line of Vision Walking Backward': Nonsequential Sequence-Signals in Short Story Openings," in *Language Learning.* XV (1965), pp. 67-83. A sequence signal is a word indicating that the sentence in which it appears follows another sentence on which it depends for its meaning. The short story makes frequent use of such signals out of sequence. For example, in the first sentence of Mary King's "The Honey House" ("He came into her line of vision walking backward . . ."), the personal pronouns are referentless and thus out of sequence.

The effect of the device is to pique the reader's curiosity, to plunge him *in media res*, and to reflect the slow process of identification by which he confronts the new experience.

Bader, A. L. "The Structure of the Modern Short Story," in *College English*. VII (1945), pp. 86-92. This article counters the charge that the short story lacks narrative structure by contrasting the traditional "plotted" story with the modern story, which is more suggestive, indirect, and technically patterned.

Baker, Falcon O. "Short Stories for the Millions," in *Saturday Review*. XIX (December, 1953), pp. 7-9, 48-49. As a result of Cleanth Brooks and Robert Penn Warren's *Understanding Fiction* (1943) and the New Criticism's focus on form, the short-story writer has begun to ignore entertainment value and the ordinary reader. Critics and editors have so disparaged the formula story that they have created another formula—"the literary formula of the unresolved impasse."

Baker, Howard. "The Contemporary Short Story," in *Southern Review*. III (Winter, 1938), pp. 576-596. A long review article of *Best American Stories of 1937* and fifteen other collections. Everything "worth saying about the short story bears in one way or another on the point that writing must be built up from a substructure of ideas." Urges that the short story be made deliberately much more intellectual than it usually is, or is recognized as being.

Baldeshwiler, Eileen. "The Lyric Short Story: The Sketch of a History," in *Studies in Short Fiction*. VI (1969), pp. 443-453. A brief survey of the lyrical (as opposed to the epical) story from Ivan Turgenev to John Updike. The lyric story focuses on "internal changes, moods, and feelings, utilizing a variety of structural patterns depending on the shape of the emotion itself."

Barth, John. "The Literature of Exhaustion," in *The American Novel Since World War II*. Marcus Klein, ed. New York: Fawcett World Library, 1969, pp. 267-279. This essay, which originally appeared in the *Atlantic Monthly* in 1967, is a celebration of the short fiction of Jorge Luis Borges, a justification for the kind of short fiction Barth has written, and a general discussion of so-called self-reflexive fiction common to both writers. The focus is on fiction self-consciously aware of its fictiveness rather than on fiction which accepts reality as an *a priori* to be rendered.

Bates, H. E. *The Modern Short Story: A Critical Survey*. Boston: The Writer, 1941, 1972. A history of major short-story writers and their work since Edgar Allan Poe and Nikolai Gogol. More focus on English and European short-story writers than most histories.

Beachcroft, T. O. *The Modest Art: A Survey of the Short Story in English*. London: Oxford University Press, 1968. A historical survey of the major figures of the English short story from Geoffrey Chaucer to Doris Lessing. The result of the basic difference between antique stories (listening) and modern stories (reading) is that the modern short-story writer attempts to portray rather than expound. He removes his own personality from the story and presents the flash of insight through poetic needs.

Beck, Warren. "Art and Formula in the Short Story," in *College English*. V (1943), pp. 55-62. A discussion of the difference between the popular short story and the literary short story. There is no sharp technical distinction; the literary story is the assertion of a different outlook—a protest against deceptive sentimentalizing of reality.

_____ . "Conception and Technique," in *College English*. XI (1950), pp. 308-317. Asserts the primacy of conception in fiction and the relative dependence of technique.

Beebe, Maurice. "A Survey of Short Story Textbooks," in *College English*. XVIII (1957), pp. 237-243. A review of forty short-story textbook anthologies in print at the time; the best one is Brooks and Warren's *Understanding Fiction*, the model for all critical readers since 1943.

Benjamin, Walter. "The Storyteller: Reflections on the Works of Nikolai Leskov," reprinted in *Modern Literary Criticism: 1900-1970*. Lawrence Lipking and A. Walton Litz, eds. New York: Atheneum Publishers, 1972, pp. 442-455. Benjamin claims that the art of storytelling is coming to an end because of the widespread dissemination of information and explanation. The compactness of story precludes analysis and appeals to readers by the rhythm of the work itself. In the storyteller (Leskov is simply used as an example) the old religious chronical is secularized into an ambiguous network in which the eschatological and the worldly are interwoven.

Bierce, Ambrose. "The Short Story," in *The Collected Works of Ambrose Bierce*. 1911; reprinted, New York: Gordian Press, 1966. X, pp. 234-248. Bierce criticizes Howells and the realistic school: "to them nothing is probable outside the narrow domain of the commonplace man's most commonplace experience . . . the truest eye is that which discerns the shadow and the portent, the dead hands reaching, the light that is the heart of darkness."

Bleifuss, William. "The Short Story in Text and Intact," in *College English*. XXIII (1962), pp. 402-408. A supplement to Beebe's review, covering twenty-seven short-story texts published from 1957 to 1961.

Borges, Jorge Luis. "Partial Magic in the *Quixote*," in *Labyrinths*. Donald A. Yates and James E. Irby, eds. New York: New Directions, 1964, pp. 193-196. A brief but important essay for the understanding of self-reflexive fiction, by the acknowledged master of contemporary short metafiction. Borges notes examples of characters in *Don Quixote de la Mancha* (1605, 1615) and *The Arabian Nights' Entertainments* (c. 1450) who are readers of their own fiction—an inversion that makes us as readers suspect that we might be fictitious.

Bowen, Elizabeth. "The Faber Book of Modern Short Stories," in *The Faber*

Book of Modern Short Stories. London: Faber and Faber, 1936. Bowen suggests that the short story, because it is exempt from the novel's often forced conclusiveness, more often approaches aesthetic and moral truth. She also suggests that the short story, more than the novel, is able to place man alone on that "stage which, inwardly, every man is conscious of occupying alone."

Boyce, Benjamin. "English Short Fiction in the Eighteenth Century: A Preliminary View," in *Studies in Short Fiction*. V (1968), pp. 95-112. A discussion of the types of short fiction found in the periodicals and inserted in novels: character sketch, oriental tale, stories of passion. Usually the purpose was didactic and the mode was either "hovering pathos" or "hovering irony." The most distinctive characteristic is the formal, even elegant language.

Boynton, Percy H. "American Authors of Today: The Short Story," in *English Journal*. XII (1923), pp. 325-333. The interest in technique has died down in short stories in the periodicals. The search is now for new subject matter, most of which is found in the realm of the supernatural or in faraway, exotic places.

Brickell, Herschel. "The Contemporary Short Story," in *The University of Kansas City Review*. XV (1949), pp. 267-270. Makes several generalizations about the decline of quality magazines willing to publish fiction, about the trend of the short story to be more subjective, psychological, and poetic, and about the lack of writers who find the short story a natural and inevitable form. Many writers of promise who began with the short story have now turned to the novel.

—————— . "What Happened to the Short Story?" in *Atlantic Monthly*. CLXXXVIII (1951), pp. 74-76. We have reached a very high plateau in the development of the American short story. Modern writers have succeeded in breaking the story away from its formal frame by drawing it nearer to poetry "in the precise and beautiful use of language" and by making it a "slice of the mind and the spirit rather than the body."

Canby, Henry S. "Free Fiction," in *Atlantic Monthly*. CXVI (1915), pp. 60-68. Criticizes the "well-made" or "formula" story of the day because it is based more on convention than on life, especially when contrasted with the "reality" of Anton Chekhov's stories. The multitudinous situations, impressions, and incidents in modern life are perhaps incapable of presentation in a novel because of their very impermanence, but they are admirably "adapted to the short story because of their vividness and their deep if narrow significance."

—————— . "On the Short Story," in *Dial*. XXXI (1901), pp. 271-273. The novel writer aims at a natural method of transcription; the short-story writer adopts the artificial method of selecting only what bears on his narrow purpose—the conveying of vivid impressions of one phase of a situation or character. The short story which "forsakes its natural field to delve deep into the mystery of things or the confusion of psychological character-subtleties is usually a flat failure."

_____ . *The Short Story in English.* New York: Holt, Rinehart and Winston, 1909, reprinted 1932. The Romantic movement gave birth to the modern short story; Poe is the first important figure in the changing fashions of storytelling since Chaucer. The rest of the nineteenth century and the first of the twentieth has applied Poe's theory of single effect to new subjects, primarily the contrasts of civilization in flux.

Canby, Henry S. and Alfred Dashiell. *A Study of the Short Story.* Revised edition. New York: Henry Holt and Company, 1935. A short-story anthology with a long introduction based on *The Short Story in English.* A survey of the development of short fiction from the varieties of medieval forms (all best represented in *The Canterbury Tales,* 1380-1390) through the American local-color story of the turn of the century. The comments on how the short story combines the elements of the exemplum, the essay, the novella, the Gothic romance, and the romantic sketch are still helpful.

Chatman, Seymour. "New Ways of Analyzing Narrative Structure, with an Example from Joyce's *Dubliners*," in *Language and Style.* II (1969), pp. 3-36. A "test" of the narrative theories of Roland Barthes and Tzvetan Todorov, with a detailed analysis of James Joyce's "Eveline." The story is considered both in terms of the internal relations of the narrative and the external relations between narrator and reader.

Chekhov, Anton. *Letters on the Short Story, the Drama, and Other Literary Topics.* Louis S. Friedland, ed. New York: Dover Publications, 1966. This translation by Constance Garnett, originally published in 1924, contains comments by Chekhov on his own stories as well as on the stories of others.

Clarke, John H. "Transition in the American Negro Short Story," in *Phylon.* XXI (1960), pp. 360-366. A shorter version of this article appears as the Introduction to *American Negro Short Stories.* John Henrik Clarke, ed. New York: Hill and Wang, 1966. A brief historical survey of the American short story from Paul Laurence Dunbar and Charles Waddell Chesnutt at the turn of the century, through the Harlem literary Renascence of the 1920's, to the emergence of Richard Wright, who marked the end of the double standard for black writers.

Column, Mary M. "The American Short Story," in *Dial.* LXII (April 19, 1917), pp. 345-347. A review of Edward Joseph Harrington O'Brien's *Best Short Stories of 1916* and Harry T. Baker's writing manual, *The Contemporary Short Story.* Criticism of the commercial standardization of the form. The short story is not so close to the novel, but rather somewhere between the drama and the essay form. The real writers of the day—Robert Frost, Edgar Lee Masters, Robert Lowell—present short stories in the guise of free verse or polyphonic prose.

Cory, Herbert Ellsworth. "The Senility of the Short Story," in *Dial*. LXII (1917), pp. 379-381. The short story has become obsessed with a unity which is abnormally artificial and intense. Seldom attaining high serious-ness, it is a literature of feverish excitement, "the blood kinsman of the quick-lunch, the vaudeville, and the joy-ride."

Cowley, Malcolm. "Storytelling's Tarnished Image," in *Saturday Review*. (September 25, 1971) pp. 25-27, 54. A diatribe against practitioners of the so-called "anti-story." Most of these, says Cowley, have no theme except the difficulty the writer finds "in writing fiction when he knows a hell of a lot about technique and has nothing but that knowledge to offer us."

Current-Garcia, Eugene and Walton R. Patrick. "Introduction," in *American Short Stories*. Revised edition (1964), pp. xi-liv. A historical survey of the American short story through four periods: Romanticism, realism, natu-ralism, and the modern period of both traditionalists (those who have carried on the Poe-Maupassant-James tradition) and experimentalists (those who have focused more on the fragmented inner world of the mind).

——————— , eds. *Short Stories of the Western World*. Glenview, Illinois: Scott, Foresman and Company, 1969. This anthology includes lengthy and detailed introductory comments on four different historical periods in the development of the short story.

——————— , eds. *What Is the Short Story?* Revised edition. New York: Scott, Foresman and Company, 1974. Although this is primarily a short-story anthology, it contains a generous selection of mostly American crit-icism on the short story arranged in chronological order. The book also contains a four-page general bibliography of the short story.

Dawson, W. J. "The Modern Short Story," in *North American Review*. CXC (1909), pp. 799-810. Applying the critical test that a short story must be complete in itself and consist of a single incident, Dawson can dismiss stories by Dickens and Hardy and praise those by Kipling, Stevenson, Poe, and Hawthorne. "The finest writing in a short story is that which takes up quickest to the very heart of the matter in hand."

Dollerup, Cay. "The Concepts of 'Tension,' 'Intensity,' and 'Suspense' in Short-Story Theory," in *Orbis Litterarum*. XXV (1970), pp. 314-337. Heav-ily documented survey of critical theory in German, Danish, and English on the concepts of intensity or tension in the short story and how these terms have been applied to linguistic rhythm, contrast, character, structure, and reader suspense in the form.

Duncan, Edgar Hill. "Short Fiction in Medieval English: A Survey," in *Studies in Short Fiction*. IX (1972), pp. 1-28. A survey of short pieces in the Old English period, primarily in verse, which have in common the characteristic of "artfully telling a story in a relatively brief compass" and which focus on "singleness of character, of action, and/or impression." The fall of the angels and the fall of man in the *Genesis B*, the flight of the Israelites and crossing of the Red Sea in the *Exodus*, the St. Guthlac poems, and *The Dream of the Rood* are analyzed.

_____ . "Short Fiction in Medieval English: II. The Middle English Period," in *Studies in Short Fiction*. XI (1974), pp. 227-241. A brief sampling of short-fiction elements in the "shorter romance" form, the exemplary narrative, the beast tale, and the *fabliau* introduced to Middle English by the French. Also noted are paraphrases of biblical stories, saints' lives, and the dream visions of *The Pearl* and Chaucer's *Book of the Duchess* (1369) and the "Prologue to the *Legend of Good Women*" (1380-1386).

Eastman, Richard M. "The Open Parable: Demonstration and Definition," in *College English*. XXII (1960), pp. 15-18. Using his own original story as an example, Eastman describes the parable form perfected by Franz Kafka and Samuel Beckett. It differs from the traditional parable because its "designed instability" leaves its ethical analogy open to the interpretation of the reader.

Eichenbaum, Boris. *O. Henry and the Theory of the Short Story*. Translated by I. R. Titunik. Michigan Slavic Contributions. Ann Arbor: University of Michigan Press, 1968. Originally published in 1925, this essay is a good example of the early Russian Formalist approach to fiction through a consideration of genre. Eichenbaum poses a generic distinction between the novel and the short story, suggesting that the former is a syncretic form while the latter is fundamental and elementary. Short stories are constructed on the basis of a contradiction, incongruity, error, or contrast; and, like the anecdote, they build their weight toward the ending.

_____ . "The Structure of Gogol's 'The Overcoat.'" Translated by Beth Paul and Muriel Nesbitt, in *The Russian Review*. XXII (1963), pp. 377-399. The classic example of Russian Formalist analysis of short fiction. The focus is on basic narrative devices and their interrelationships rather than on the mimetic or moral presentation of character and social interrelationships. Rather than a depiction of reality, the story presents a play with reality.

Elliott, George P. "A Defense of Fiction," in *Hudson Review*. XVI (1963), pp. 9-48. Reprinted as an Introduction to *Types of Prose Fiction*. George P. Elliott, ed. New York: Random House, 1964, pp. 3-30. Discussion of four basic impulses that mingle with the storytelling impulse: "to dream, to tell what happened, to explain the nature of things, and to make a likeness."

_____ . "Exploring the Province of the Short Story," in *Harpers*. CCXXX (1965), pp. 111-116. A review of seven collections including John Cheever's *Brigadier and the Golf Widow*, Isaac Bashevis Singer's *Short Friday*, and John O'Hara's *The Horse Knows the Way*. "The worst pitfall a writer dealing in extremes must watch out for is depersonalizing his characters. At the brink, people are apt to behave much alike, less according to their personal natures than according to human nature generally."

Engstrom, Alfred G. "The Formal Short Story in France and Its Development Before 1850," in *Studies in Philology*. XLII (1945), pp. 627-629. After making distinctions between the *nouvelle* and the *conte* (a complex line of action versus a compressed one), Engstrom points out the lack of any significant examples of *conte* until Prosper Mérimée's *Mateo Falcone* (1829), the first formal short story in French literature. The only other significant contributors to the form before 1850 are Honoré de Balzac and Théophile Gautier.

Esenwein, J. Berg. *Writing the Short-Story: A Practical Handbook on the Rise, Structure, Writing and Sale of the Modern Short-Story*. New York: Hinds, Noble and Eldredge, 1909. One of the best-known of the early "how-to" books. Discusses what a short story is not: not a condensed novel, an episode, a synopsis, a biography, a sketch, or a tale. Lists seven basic characteristics that add up to the following definition: "A Short-Story is a brief, imaginative narrative, unfolding a single predominating incident and a single chief character, it contains a plot, the details of which are so compressed, and the whole treatment so organized, as to produce a single impression."

Farrell, James T. "Nonsense and the Short Story," in *The League of Frightened Philistines and Other Papers*. New York: Vanguard Press, 1945 (written in 1937), pp. 72-81. Ridicules the crop of short-story writing handbooks that sprang from Brander Matthews' *Philosophy of the Short Story*. Their focus on form has made technical facility a value and has falsified the material of life. The typical American short story either affirms the ideological aims of capitalism or patronizes those of lower economic origin.

_____ . "The Short Story," in *The League of Frightened Philistines and Other Papers*. New York: Vanguard Press, 1945 (written in 1935), pp. 136-148. Decries the inadequacy of many revolutionary social critics practicing the short-story form. Too often the revolutionary point of view appears more glued on than integral to the story.

FitzGerald, Gregory. "The Satiric Short Story: A Definition," in *Studies in Short Fiction*. V (1968), pp. 355-361. Defines the satiric short story as a subgenre that sustains throughout a reductive attack upon its objects and conveys to its readers a significance different from its apparent surface meaning.

Friedman, Norman. "What Makes a Short Story Short?," in *Modern Fiction Studies*. IV (1958), pp. 103-117. Uses Neo-Aristotelian literary theory to determine the issue of the short story's shortness. To deal with the problem, Friedman says, we must ask the following questions: What is the size of the action? Is it composed of a speech, a scene, an episode, or a plot? Does the action involve a change? If so, is the change a major one or a minor one?

Frye, Northrop. "Myth, Fiction, and Displacement," in *Fables of Identity: Studies in Poetic Mythology*. New York: Harcourt, Brace and World, 1963. A central essay for the understanding of the relationship between spatial and temporal readings of a narrative; that is, between details of the plot in relation to a unity or theme and in relation to linear progression. Myth criticism is interested in the total design, those aspects of the fiction which are conventional and held in common with other examples of the same genre. "Displacement" is the sum of the techniques a writer uses to make his story credible and logically motivated.

Fuller, Henry B. "New Forms of Short Fiction," in *Dial*. LXII (1917), pp. 167-169. A survey of the types of magazine and newspaper fiction of the period and a discussion of how popular taste and the demands of weekly publication conditioned them.

Gardner, John Champlin and Lennis Dunlap, eds. *The Forms of Fiction*. New York: Random House, 1962. A text anthology which includes descriptions of the various forms of short fiction: sketch, fable, yarn, tale, short story, and short novel.

Gass, William H. *Fiction and the Figures of Life*. New York: Alfred A. Knopf, 1970. A collection of previously published essays and reviews by the most philosophical of the contemporary metafictionalists. The most pertinent essays for an understanding of the modern writers' attempts to create a language world rather than to render an external world are the title essay and "Philosophy and the Form of Fiction."

Geismar, Maxwell. "The American Short Story Today," in *Studies on the Left*. IV (1964), pp. 21-27. Criticizes the Salinger-Roth-Malamud-Updike coterie for their stress on craftsmanship in the well-made story and their ignoring of the social realities of the time. Even though there is much excitement in contemporary life, the "American artist has been shrinking further and further into the labyrinthian recesses of the tormented and isolated psyche, of the individual soul."

Gerould, Katherine Fullerton. "The American Short Story," in *Yale Review*. NS XIII (1924), pp. 642-663. Urges that the short story be read as critically as the novel. Poses the following requirements for the form: it must be well-made; it must offer situation, suspense, and climax; and it must focus on a significant event which is either truly momentous for the character or typical of the lives of many people.

Gold, Herbert. "The Novel and the Story—the Long and Short of It," in *Fiction of the Fifties*. Herbert Gold, ed. Garden City, New York: Doubleday & Company, 1959, pp. 12-15. The short story since Joyce has concerned itself with "scene and incident, striking hot, like the lyrical poem." The novel since Fyodor Dostoevski and Leo Tolstoy has made "the whole man face the whole world."

Gordimer, Nadine. "South Africa," in *Kenyon Review*. XXX (1968), pp. 457-461. One of the most suggestive articles in the International Short Story Symposium. The strongest convention of the novel, its prolonged coherence of tone, is false to the nature of what can be grasped as reality in the modern world. Short-story writers deal with the only thing one can be sure of: the present moment.

Grabo, Carl H. *The Art of the Short Story*. New York: Charles Scribner's Sons, 1913. A craft book for aspiring writers. Discusses the underlying principles of all narrative writing such as point of view, plot, character, dialogue, the unities, and description. The only difference between the short story and the novel is that the short story is more exacting in the selective process and more unified in action, place, and time. The short story aims at a single effect; writers of longer narratives aim at a variety of effects which "more nearly mirror the complexities of emotional life."

Gullason, Thomas A. "Revelation and Evolution: A Neglected Dimension of the Short Story," in *Studies in Short Fiction*. X (1973), pp. 347-356. Challenges Mark Schorer's distinction between the short story as an "art of moral revelation" and the novel as an "art of moral evolution." Analyzes D. H. Lawrence's "The Horse Dealer's Daughter" and John Steinbeck's "The Chrysanthemums" to show how the short story embodies both revelation and evolution.

——————— . "The Short Story: An Underrated Art," in *Studies in Short Fiction*. II (1964), pp. 13-31. Points out the lack of serious criticism on the short story, suggests some of the reasons for this neglect, and concludes with an analysis of Anton Chekhov's "Gooseberries" and Nadine Gordimer's "The Train from Rhodesia" to disprove the charges that the short story is formulaic and lacks life.

Harris, Wendell V. "Beginnings of and for the True Short Story in England," in *English Literature in Transition*. XV (1972), pp. 269-276. The true short story did not begin in England until Rudyard Kipling discovered the means to control the reader's angle of vision and establish a self-contained world within the story that keeps the reader at a distance. The externality of the reader to the story's participants is a basic characteristic of the short story.

——————— . "English Short Fiction in the Nineteeth Century," in *Studies in Short Fiction*. VI (1968), pp. 1-93. After distinguishing between "short fiction" appearing before 1880 and "short story" after 1880, Harris surveys examples from both periods. The turning point, as one might expect, is the definition posed by Brander Matthews which first appeared in the *Saturday Review* in 1884.

——————— . "Vision and Form: The English Novel and the Emergence of Short Story," in *Victorian Newsletter*. No. 47 (1975), pp. 8-12. The short story did not begin in England until 1880's because the presentation of isolated individuals, moments, or scenes was not considered a serious intellectual task for fiction to undertake. Only at the end of the century was reality perceived as congeries of fragments; the primary vehicle of this perception is the short story.

Harte, Bret. "The Rise of the Short Story," in *Cornhill Magazine.* VII (1899), pp. 1-8. More properly, Harte's subject is the "rise" of the local-color story in America, which he says is the true American story—as opposed to the earlier stories by Washington Irving which had English models.

Hartley, L. P. "In Defense of the Short Story," in *The Novelist's Responsibility.* London: Hamish Hamilton, 1967, pp. 157-159. A brief consideration of why short stories are not popular when collected in a single book; mainly it is reader laziness, for each story requires such close concentration.

Hendricks, William O. "Methodology of Narrative Structural Analysis," in *Essays in Semiolinguistics and Verbal Art.* The Hague: Mouton, 1973, pp. 175-205. Structuralists, in the tradition of Vladimir Propp and Claude Lévi-Strauss, usually bypass the actual sentences of a narrative and analyze a synopsis. This essay is a fairly detailed discussion of the methodology of synopsizing (using William Faulkner's "A Rose for Emily" as an example), followed by a brief discussion of the methodology of structural analysis of the resultant synopsis.

Hicks, Granville. "The Art of the Short Story," in *Saturday Review.* XLI (December 20, 1958), p. 16. A review of *Best American Short Stories of 1958* and *Stanford Short Stories—1958.* An emotional experience for the reader, rather than plot or character, is the focus for the modern short story.

Howe, Irving. "Tone in the Short Story," in *Sewanee Review.* LVII (1949), pp. 141-152. Review of *Best American Short Stories of 1948, Prize Stories of 1948,* and collections of stories by Delmore Schwartz, Isaac Babel, and others. Because the short story lacks prolonged characterization and the independent momentum of the novel, it depends more on those technical devices or inflections of style we call tone. "A novel written in one dominant tone becomes intolerable; a story too often deviating from it risks chaos."

Howells, William Dean. "Some Anomalies of the Short Story," in *North American Review.* CLXXIII (1901), pp. 422-432. The basic anomaly is that while readers seem to enjoy stories in the magazines, they do not read them when collected in a volume. Each story requires so much of the reader's energy that several together exhaust him. One of the basic defects of the short story in comparison to the novel is that it creates no memorable characters.

Hull, Helen R. "The Literary Drug Traffic," in *Dial.* LXVII (1919), pp. 190-192. The majority of short stories in the mass magazines are a mild literary dope, read by people who wish a substitute for their childhood daydreaming and fantasizing. "If there were a desire for stories with vitality or humor or beauty or vision or comment, there might be more such stories."

"Is the Short Story Necessary?," in *The Writer's World*. Elizabeth Janeway,
  ed. New York: McGraw-Hill, 1969. A panel discussion with Janeway, Shirley Hazzard, John Cheever, and Harry Mark Petrakis. Much of the discussion centers on Frank O'Connor's thesis in *The Lonely Voice* (1963).
Jameson, Frederic. *The Prison-House of Language: A Critical Account of
  Structuralism and Russian Formalism*. Princeton, New Jersey: Princeton
  University Press, 1972. A very helpful historical and critical survey of these
  two related literary theories; especially useful to the student of the short
  story for Jameson's explanation of why both Formalism and Structuralism
  are more applicable to the short story than to the novel.
Jarrell, Randall. "Stories," in *The Anchor Book of Stories*. Garden City, New
  York: Doubleday & Company, 1958. Jarrell's Introduction to this collection
  focuses on stories as being closer to dream reality than to the waking world
  of every day. There are two kinds of stories: stories-in-which-everything-
  is-a-happening (in which each event is so charged that the narrative threat-
  ens to disintegrate into energy) and stories-in-which-nothing-happens (in
  which even the climax may lose its charge and become one more portion
  of a lyric continuum).
Joselyn, Sister Mary, O. S. B. "Edward Joseph O'Brien and the American
  Short Story," in *Studies in Short Fiction*. III (1965), pp. 1-15. Attempts to
  synthesize O'Brien's philosophic and aesthetic attitudes which may have
  determined his choices of "best stories." Discusses O'Brien's contribution
  to the history, theory, and growth of the American short story.
Kempton, Kenneth Payson. *The Short Story*. Cambridge, Massachusetts:
  Harvard University Press, 1947. A book on the technique of the short story
  for aspiring writers. Kempton's basic principle is that a "good story entails
  an unwritten contract between its writer, the editor, and its reader, and that
  good story writing must reconcile these often conflicting points of view. . . ."
  Quite detailed and full of illustrations, but still just a craft book.
Kenyon Review International Symposium on the Short Story. Contributions
  from short-story writers from all over the world on the nature of the form,
  its current economic status, its history, and its significance. Plans were
  announced in 1970 for the publication of a single volume of the symposium,
  but the project was postponed indefinitely without explanation. Part I,
  XXX, Issue 4, pp. 443-490: Christina Stead (England), Herbert Gold
  (United States), Erin Kvos (Yugoslavia), Nadine Gordimer (South Africa),
  Benedict Kiely (Ireland), Hugh Hood (Canada), Henrietta Drake-Brock-
  man (Australia). Part II, XXXI, Issue I, pp. 58-94: William Saroyan
  (United States), Jun Eto (Japan), Maurice Shadbolt (New Zealand), Chan-
  akya Sen (India), John Wain (England), Hans Bender (West Germany),
  and "An Agent's View" by James Oliver Brown. Part III, XXXI, Issue 4,
  1969, pp. 450-502: Ana María Matute (Spain), Torborg Nedreaas (Norway), George Garrett (United States), Elizabeth Taylor (England), Ezekiel

Mphahlele (South Africa), Elizabeth Harrower (Australia), Mario Picchi (Italy), Junzo Shono (Japan), Khushwant Singh (India). Part IV, XXXII, Issue I, pp. 78-108: Jack Cope (South Africa), James T. Farrell (United States), Edward Hyams (England), Luigi Barzini (Italy), David Ballantyne (New Zealand), H. E. Bates (England).

Kostelanetz, Richard. "Notes on the American Short Story Today," in *Minnesota Review*. V (1966), pp. 214-221. Contemporary short-story writers focus on extreme rather than typical experiences and tend to emphasize the medium of language itself more than ever before. In a shift that pulls the genre farther away from narrative and pushes it closer to nonlinear forms of poetry, the contemporary short-story writer attempts to depict the workings of the mad mind, to simulate the feel of madness itself.

Langbaum, Robert. "Best Short Stories," in *Commentary*. XXIV (1957), pp. 171-173. Review of *Best American Short Stories of 1956*. Many of the stories deal with either minority groups ("For the minority culture offers definable mores which, in the more serious stories, can then be used to accentuate the lack of mores in the majority culture") or with the majority culture through odd points of view, most commonly that of childhood.

Lawrence, James Cooper. "A Theory of the Short Story," in *North American Review*. CCV (1917), pp. 274-286. Argues against Brander Matthews that the short story is a "new" genre. Develops a theory of the development of oral literature which establishes the short story as a primary unit, the basis of all literature except the lyric and the critical essay.

Lewis, C. S. "On Stories," in *Essays Presented to Charles Williams*. C. S. Lewis, ed. Grand Rapids, Michigan: Eerdmans, 1966, pp. 90-105. Although a story is a series of events, this series, or what we call plot, is only a necessary means to capture something that has no sequence, something more like a state or quality. Thus, the means of "story" is always at war with its "end." This very tension, however, constitutes story's chief resemblance to life. "We grasp at a state and find only a succession of events in which the state is never quite embodied."

Marcus, Mordecai. "What Is an Initiation Story?," in *The Journal of Aesthetics and Art Criticism*. XIX (1960), pp. 221-227. Distinguishes three types of initiation stories: those that lead the protagonists to the threshold of maturity only, those that take the protagonists across the threshold of maturity but leave them in a struggle for certainty, and decisive initiation stories that carry the protagonists firmly into maturity.

Marler, Robert F., Jr. "From Tale to Short Story: The Emergence of a New Genre in the 1850's," in *American Literature*. XLVI (1974), pp. 153-169. Using Northrop Frye's distinction between the tale (embodies "stylized figures which expand into psychological archetypes") and the short story (deals with characters who wear their "*personae* or social masks"), Marler surveys the critical condemnation of the tale form and the increasing em-

phasis on realism in the 1850's. The broad shift is from Poe's overt romance
to Herman Melville's mimetic portrayals, especially in *Bartleby the Scrivener*
(1856).

Matson, Esther. "The Short Story," in *Outlook*. CXXI (1919), pp. 406-409.
A consideration of why the short story had such an enormous appeal at the
time. Instead of playing on our intellectual or spiritual natures, the short
story plays on emotion, and at this time "our nerves are painfully close to
the surface." The danger of the short story is that the "writer must often
be tempted to harp upon the emotions that depress and devitalize instead
of invigorate."

Matthews, Brander. *The Philosophy of the Short Story*. New York: Longmans,
Green, 1901. An expansion of an 1882 article in which Matthews sets himself
forth as the first critic (since Poe) to discuss the short-story (Matthews
contributed the hyphen) as a genre. By asserting that the short-story must
have a vigorous compression, must be original, must be ingenious, must
have a touch of fantasy, and so on, Matthews set the stage for a host of
textbook writers on the short story that followed.

Maugham, W. Somerset. "The Short Story," in *Points of View: Five Essays*.
Garden City, New York: Doubleday & Company, 1959, pp. 163-212. This
long and "desultory essay," as Maugham himself calls it, combines his
earlier "Introduction" to *Tellers of Tales: 100 Short Stories from the United
States, England, France, Russia and Germany*. New York: Doubleday &
Company, 1939, pp. xiii-xxxix; and "The Short Story." *Essays by Divers
Hands: Being the Transactions of the Royal Society of Literature of the
United Kingdom*. NS XXV. Sir Edward Marsh, ed. London: Geoffrey
Cumberlege, Oxford University Press, 1950, pp. 120-134. As might be ex-
pected, Maugham's preference is for the "well-made story" exemplified by
Maupassant's "The Necklace." Most of the essay, however, deals with
Chekhov and Mansfield biographical material.

May, Charles E. "The Short Story in the College Classroom: A Survey of
Textbooks Published in the Sixties," in *College English*. XXXIII (1972),
pp. 488-512. An omnibus review of 110 short-story textbooks published in
America between 1961 and 1970. The texts are classified according to methods of organization (elements of fiction, thematic categories, modes of
fiction, major authors, and so forth) and evaluated according to the ap-
paratus (critical commentary, study questions, teacher manuals, bibliog-
raphies) featured in each.

_____ . *Short Story Theories*. Athens: Ohio University Press, 1976.
A collection of twenty previously published essays on the short story as a
genre in its own right.

_____ . "A Survey of Short Story Criticism in America," in *Minnesota
Review*. (Spring, 1973) pp. 163-169. An analytical survey of criticism from
Poe to the present, focusing on the short story's underlying vision and

characteristic mode of understanding and confronting reality.

_____ . "The Unique Effect of the Short Story: A Reconsideration and Example," in *Studies in Short Fiction*. XIII (1976), pp. 289-297. An attempt to redefine Poe's "unique effect" in the short story in terms of mythic perception. The short story demands intense compression and focusing because its essential subject is a manifestation of what philosopher Ernst Cassier calls the "momentary deity." A detailed discussion of Stephen Crane's story, "An Episode of War," illustrates the concept.

Millett, F. B. "The Short Story," in *Contemporary American Authors: A Critical Survey and 219 Bio-bibliographies*. New York: Harcourt, Brace and Company, 1940, pp. 85-97. An adequate survey of the American short story from the 1890's to the 1940's. The emphasis is on influences on the form: the rise of the large circulation slicks, Chekhov, O'Brien, and the aesthetic forces of both objective and subjective naturalism.

Mirrielees, Edith R. "The American Short Story," in *Atlantic Monthly*. CLXVII (1941), pp. 714-722. A complaint about the decline of consistently maintained talent in short-story writing since 1920. The promising writer who begins in the little magazines aims toward the wider popularity of the slicks; his quality declines accordingly.

_____ . "Short Stories, 1950," in *College English*. XII (May, 1951), pp. 425-432. A survey of the American short story during the first fifty years of the twentieth century, focusing especially on the typical subject matter of short stories in the late 1940's. Notes the increase of stories about childhood, stories of the supernatural, and stories sparked by racial and economic oppressions. Also notes a shift away from individual character interest to general significance of the situation or predicament.

Mish, Charles C. "English Short Fiction in the Seventeenth Century," in *Studies in Short Fiction*. VI (1969), pp. 223-330. Divides the period into two parts: 1600-1660, in which short fiction declined into sterile imitation and preciousness, and 1660-1700, in which it was revitalized by the influence of such French works as Mme. de Lafayette's *Princess de Clèves* (1678). The French direction toward interiorization, psychological analysis, and verisimilitude in action and setting, combined with the English style of the self-conscious narrator, moves fiction toward the novel of the eighteenth century.

Moffett, James. "Telling Stories: Methods of Abstraction in Fiction," in *ETC*. XXI (1964), pp. 425-450. Charts a sequence covering an "entire range" of ways in which stories can be told, from the most subjective and personal (interior monologue and dramatic monologue) to the most objective and impersonal (anonymous narration); includes examples of each type. The progression is the basis for *Points of View: An Anthology of Short Stories*. James Moffett and Kenneth R. McElheny, eds. New York: New American Library, 1966.

Moravia, Alberto. "The Short Story and the Novel," in *Man as an End: A Defense of Humanism*. Translated by Bernard Wall. New York: Farrar, Straus & Giroux, 1966. The basic difference between the novel and the short story is that the novel has a bone structure of ideological themes whereas the short story is made up of intuitions of feelings.

Munson, Gorham. "The Recapture of the Storyable," in *The University Review*. X (1943), pp. 37-44. A brief survey of the short story's escape from the O. Henry formula. The best short-story writers are concerned with only three questions: "have I discovered a storyable incident? how shall I cast my actors? who would best tell it?" To define "storyable" he turns to James's description of the writer's subject as a "tiny nugget" with a "hard latent value."

Newman, Frances. "The American Short Story in the First Twenty-Five Years of the Twentieth Century," in *Bookman*. LXIII (1926), pp. 186-193. There is little difference between a popular magazine story published in the first five years of the century and one published in the same type of magazine in the five years past. Those writers who are aware of Chekhov and Sigmund Freud and who try to see below the surfaces of their characters publish in the little magazines.

—————— . *The Short Story's Mutations from Petronius to Paul Morand*. New York: B. W. Huebsch, 1924. Although most of this book is story anthology, the interchapters chart the story's evolution from the "Matron of Ephesus" to Morand's "The Nordic Night"—an evolution of subtly changing techniques growing out of shifting philosophic attitudes. The broad movement is from the ironic mode to the impressionistic.

Oates, Joyce Carol. "The Short Story," in *Southern Humanities Review*. V (1971), pp. 213-214. The short story is a "dream verbalized," a manifestation of desire. Its most interesting aspect is its "mystery."

O'Brien, Edward J. *The Advance of the American Short Story*. Revised edition. New York: Dodd, Mead and Company, 1931. A survey of the development of the American short story from Irving to Sherwood Anderson. The focus is on contributions to the form by various authors: Irving's development of the story from the eighteenth century essay, Hawthorne's discovery of the subjective method for psychological fiction, Poe's formalizing, Harte's caricaturing, James's development of the "central intelligence," and Anderson's freeing the story from O. Henry formalism.

—————— . *The Dance of the Machines: The American Short Story and the Industrial Age*. New York: The Macaulay Company, 1929. Chapter Four of this rambling polemic against the machinelike standardization of the industrial age describes thirty characteristics which the short story ("the most typical American form") shares with the machine: for example, it is patterned, impersonal, standardized, speeded-up, and cheap.

O'Connor, Flannery. "Writing Short Stories," in *Mystery and Manners*. Sally and Robert Fitzgerald, eds. New York: Farrar, Straus & Giroux, 1969, pp. 87-106. In this lecture at a Southern Writers Conference, O'Connor discusses the two qualities necessary for the short story: "sense of manners," which one gets from the texture of one's immediate surroundings; and "sense of mystery," which is always the mystery of personality—"showing how some specific folks *will* do, in spite of everything."

O'Connor, Frank. *The Lonely Voice: A Study of the Short Story*. Cleveland, Ohio: The World Publishing Company, 1963. The introductory chapter is extremely valuable "intuitive" criticism by an accomplished master of the short story. The basic difference between the novel and the short story is that in the latter we always find an intense awareness of human loneliness. O'Connor feels that the protagonist of the short story is less an individual with whom the reader can identify than a "submerged population group"; that is, someone outside the social mainstream. The remaining chapters of the book treat this theme in Turgenev, Chekhov, Maupassant, Kipling, Joyce, Mansfield, Lawrence, Coppard, Babel, and Lavin.

——————— . "Prospectus for an Anthology," in *Nation*. CLXXXIII (1956), pp. 395-396. O'Connor's preference is for American, Russian, and Irish stories because they reveal a keen sense of human loneliness. "Sometimes I question myself and wonder whether I am attracted by certain great stories because they express an underlying mood of my own, or whether I am attracted to them because they are written close to the source of the story telling itself."

O'Faoláin, Seán. "The Secret of the Short Story," in *United Nations World*. III (1949), pp. 37-38. The secret lies in the French word *constater*, "meaning to establish the state or truth of a thing, to sum it up." Exploring why some countries are more accomplished in the short story form than others, O'Faoláin concludes that "the more firmly organized a country is the less room there is for the short-story, for the intimate close-up, the odd slant, or the unique comment."

——————— . *The Short Story*. New York: The Devin-Adair Company, 1951. A book on the technique of the short story which claims that technique is the "least part of the business." O'Faoláin illustrates his thesis that personality is the most important element by describing the personal struggles of Alphonse Daudet, Chekhov, and Maupassant; he also does his duty to the assigned subject of the book, however, by discussing the technical problems of convention, subject, construction, and language.

Overstreet, Bonaro. "Little Story, What Now?," in *Saturday Review of Literature*. XXIV (November 24, 1941), pp. 3-5, 25-26. A reply to protests that the current story is unpleasant and abnormal and that it has no plot. Having lost the faiths of the nineteenth century which underpinned a confident line of action (that one could tell the difference between right and wrong and that a reliable correspondence exists between inner character and outward behavior), the modern storyteller is concerned with psychological materials, not with events in the objective world.

Pain, Barry. *The Short Story*. London: Martin Secker, 1914. One of a series of pamphlets on various genres. The primary distinction between the short story and the novel is that the short story, because of its dependence on suggestive devices, demands more of the reader's participation. "The novelist gives more to the reader and asks less of him. The short-story writer gives less and asks more."

Patrick, Walton R. "Poetic Style in the Contemporary Short Story," in *College Composition and Communication*. XVIII (1967), pp. 77-84. The poetic style appears more consistently in the short story than in the novel because metaphorical dilations are essential to the writer who "strives to pack the utmost meaning into his restricted space."

Pattee, Fred Lewis. *The Development of the American Short Story: An Historical Survey*. New York: Harper & Row, Publishers, 1923. The most detailed and historically complete survey of the American short story from Irving to O. Henry. Charts the changes in taste of the short-story reading public and indicates the major contributions to the form of such classic practitioners as Irving, Hawthorne, Poe, and Harte. Surveys the effect of the "Annuals," the "Ladies' Books," local-color writing, Matthew's *Philosophy of the Short Story*, and the writing handbooks.

_____ . "The Present State of the Short Story," in *English Journal*. XII (1923), pp. 439-449. A reaction to the teaching of the short story in the schools as a new genre which made steady progress in America from the crude toward the perfect. All that Poe said had already been said by Aristotle: the form flourished because English novels were not protected by copyright. Short stories give us only fleeting sensations while novels give us a philosophy of life.

Peden, William. "The American Short Story During the Twenties," in *Studies in Short Fiction*. X (1973), pp. 367-371. A highly abbreviated account of the causes of the explosion of short stories during the 1920's, such as the new freedom from plotted stories, new emphasis on "now-ness," the boom of little magazines, and the influence of cinematic techniques.

_____ . *The American Short Story: Front Line in the National Defense of Literature*. Boston: Houghton Mifflin Company, 1964. Discussion of major trends in the American short story since 1940. The center of the book consists of a chapter on those writers who focus on everyday life in contemporary society (John Cheever, John O'Hara, Peter Taylor, John Updike, J. F. Powers, and J. D. Salinger) and a chapter on those who are preoccupied with the grotesque, abnormal, and bizarre (Carson McCullers, Flannery O'Connor, James Purdy, Truman Capote, and Tennessee Williams). An additional chapter surveys other short-story subjects such as the war, minorities, regions, and science fiction.

Perkins, Frederic B. "Preface," in *Devil-Puzzlers and Other Studies*. New York: G. P. Putnam's Sons, 1877. The short story compares with other prose types as the lyric does with the epic or narrative poem. A really fine story such as one by Poe, Hawthorne, Hoffmann, or Tieck is "the production of a faculty lofty, unique and rare."

Perry, Bliss. "The Short Story," in *A Study of Prose Fiction*. Boston and New York: Houghton Mifflin Company, 1902, pp. 300-334. The short story differs from the novel by presenting unique and original characters, by focusing on fragments of reality, and by making use of the poetic devices of impressionism and symbolism.

"The Persistent Mystery of the Modern Short Story," in *Current Opinion*. LXVII (1919), pp. 119-120. A very brief survey of some attempts to define and keep abreast of "a literary form which puzzles the critics and often perplexes the reader."

Pochman, Henry A. "Germanic Materials and Motifs in the Short Story," in *German Culture in America: Philosophic and Literary Influences: 1600-1900*. Madison: University of Wisconsin Press, 1957, pp. 367-408. Documents Irving's indebtedness to various German sources for much of his work, the influence of Tieck, Hoffmann, and Chamisso on Hawthorne and Poe, and Poe's debt to Schlegel for his theory of the short story.

Prince, Gerald. *A Grammar of Stories: An Introduction*. The Hague: Mouton, 1973. An attempt to establish rules to account for the structure of all the syntactical sets that we intuitively recognize as stories. The model used is Noam Chomsky's theory of generative grammar.

Prichett, V. S. "Short Stories," in *Harper's Bazaar*. LXXXVII (July, 1953), pp. 31, 113. The modern short story is a hybrid, owing much to the quickness and objectivity of the cinema, much to the poet and the newspaper reporter, and everything to the "restlessness, the alert nerve, the scientific eye and the short breath of contemporary life." Makes an interesting point about the collapse of standards, conventions, and values which has so bewildered the impersonal novelist but has been the making of the short-story writer—"who can catch any piece of life as it flies and makes his personal performance out of it."

Propp, Vladimir. *Morphology of the Folktale*. Svatava Pirkova-Jakovson, ed. Translated by Laurence Scott. Bloomington: Indiana University Research Center, 1958. All formalist and structuralist studies of narrative owe a debt to this pioneering early twentieth century study. Using one hundred fairy tales, Propp defines the genre itself by analyzing the stories according to characteristic actions or functions.

Poe, Edgar Allan. "Review of *Twice-Told Tales*," in *Graham's Magazine*. (April, 1842). The first critical discussion of the short story, or the tale as Poe terms it, to establish the genre as distinct from the novel. Because of its sense of totality, its single effect, and its patterned design, the short story is second only to the lyric in its demands on high genius and in its aesthetic beauty.

Pugh, Edwin. "The Decay of the Short Story," in *Living Age*. CCLIX (1908), pp. 387-395. The English short story has fallen into decay for the same reasons that the American short story has—the rise of the popular magazines which demand stories in the Poe mode, stories with "snap," "vim," "crispness," "breeziness."

Rhode, Robert D. *Setting in the American Short Story of Local Color: 1865-1900*. The Hague: Mouton, 1975. A study of the various functions that setting plays in the local-color story in the late nineteenth century, from setting as merely background to setting in relation to character and setting as personification.

Rohrberger, Mary. *Hawthorne and the Modern Short Story: A Study in Genre*. The Hague: Mouton, 1966. Attempts a generic definition of the short story as a form which derives from the romantic metaphysical view that there is more to the world than can be apprehended through the senses. Hawthorne is the touchstone for Rohrberger's definition, which she then applies to twentieth century stories by Eudora Welty, Ernest Hemingway, Sherwood Anderson, William Faulkner, and others.

Ross, Danforth. *The American Short Story*. Minneapolis: University of Minnesota Press, 1961. No. 14 of the Pamphlets on American Writers Series. A sketchy survey which measures American stories since Poe against Aristotelian criteria of action, unity, tension, and irony. Ends with the Beat Generation writers who rebel against the Poe-Aristotle tradition by using shock tactics.

Saroyan, William. "What Is a Story?," in *Saturday Review of Literature*. XI (1935), p. 409. The important distinction to be made is not between short story and novel, but between created things and imitated things. The created thing is "living substance, mutability, substance growing."

Schlauch, Margaret. "English Short Fiction in the 15th and 16th Centuries," in *Studies in Short Fiction*. III (1966), pp. 393-434. A survey of types of short fiction from the romantic *lai* to the *exemplum*, and from the bawdy *fabliau* to the *novella*. Schlauch's conclusions are that modern short-story writers are heirs both in subject matter (such as internal psychological conflict) and technique (such as importance of dialogue) to a long tradition that antedates the seventeenth century, a tradition that is still worth studying.

Scholes, Robert. "Metafiction," in *Iowa Review*. I (Fall, 1970), pp. 100-115. Using the short stories of John Barth, Donald Barthelme, Robert Coover, and William H. Gass as examples, Scholes develops a fourfold perspective on fictional forms and a corresponding fourfold perspective on fictional criticism. Metafiction assimilates the perspectives of criticism into the fictional process itself and attempts to transcend the laws of fiction from within fictional form, a process that makes metafiction tend toward the brevity of the short story.

_____ . *Structuralism in Literature*. New Haven, Connecticut: Yale University Press, 1974. A readable basic introduction to structuralist studies of literature by an American critic who believes that Structuralism and Formalism have given us virtually the only poetics of fiction we have. Indeed, the bulk of the book is taken up by summaries and discussions of the narrative theories of André Jolles, Gérard Genette, Roland Barthes, Tzevetan Todorov, and others.

Scholes, Robert and Robert Kellogg. *The Nature of Narrative*. New York: Oxford University Press, 1966. One of the best historical studies of narrative for the student of the short story because it examines all narrative forms rather than focusing on the novel as the end product of narrative development and therefore the narrative norm against which all other fictions must be judged.

Shaw, Harry. "Some Clinical Notes," in *Saturday Review of Literature*. XXIV (November 22, 1941), pp. 3, 23-25. The lack of worthwhile short stories at the time is the result of a shift in reader preference to the magazine article. While story technique has remained static, article writing has developed new appealing methods to interest the reader.

Shklovsky, Victor. "Art as Technique," in *Russian Formalist Criticism: Four Essays*. Edited and translated by Lee T. Lemon and Marion J. Reis. Lincoln: University of Nebraska Press, 1965, pp. 3-24. A seminal essay of Russian Formalism which proposes that the technique of art is to make objects unfamiliar and to increase the difficulty of perception. "Art is a way of experiencing the artfulness of an object; the object is not important."

"Short Stories: Their Past, Present and Future," in *Publisher's Weekly*. CXCVIII (December 14, 1970), pp. 12-15. Report of Doubleday's day-long symposium (November 20, 1970) to honor the publication of *Fifty Years of the American Short Story*, edited by William Abrahams. One of the panelists, Wallace Stegner, pointed out, "There has hardly been any systematic criticism in this country of the short story . . . we badly need a good critical history of it."

Smertenko, Johan J. "The American Short Story," in *Bookman*. LVI (1923), pp. 584-587. The rise of mass circulation magazines dependent on advertising has caused the deterioration of the short story. A number of magazines should be endowed to publish the best stories of both the masters and the promising unknown writers.

Smith, Frank R. "Periodical Articles on the American Short Story: A Selected, Annotated Bibliography," in *Bulletin of Bibliography*. XXIII (January-April, 1960), pp. 9-13; (May-August, 1960) pp. 46-48; (September-December, 1960) pp. 69-72; (January-April, 1961) pp. 95-96. This checklist of articles published between 1920 and 1950 is coded to indicate relative value of the items. Finding very few articles that give serious critical attention to the short story, Smith suggests his work might be considered a "negative" bibliography.

Smith, Horatio E. "The Development of Brief Narrative in Modern French Literature: A Statement of the Problem," in *PMLA*. XXXII (1917), pp. 583-597. Surveys the confusion between the *conte* and *nouvelle* and calls for a critical investigation of the practice and theory of the French forms similar to those published on the American short story and the German *Nouvelle*.

Stanford, Derek. "A Larger Latitude: Three Themes in the Nineties Short Story," in *Contemporary Review*. CCX (1967), pp. 96-104. The themes are the life of sex, illustrated by the work of Ella D'Arcy and George Egerton; the life of art, as seen in Arthur Symons' *Spiritual Adventures* (1905); and bohemian and *declassée* existence, reflected in stories by Henry Harland and George Gissing.

Stevenson, Lionel. "The Short Story in Embryo," in *English Literature in Transition*. XV (1972), pp. 261-268. Discussion of the "agglomerative urge" in eighteenth and nineteenth century English fiction that contributed to the undervaluing of the short story. Not until 1880, when the fragmentation of the well-integrated view of society began in England, did the short story come into its own in that country.

Stevick, Philip, ed. *Anti-Story: An Anthology of Experimental Fiction*. New York: The Free Press, 1971. An influential collection of contemporary short fiction with a helpful introduction that characterizes antistory as against mimesis, against reality, against event, against subject, against the middle range of experience, against analysis, and against meaning.

Strong, L. A. G. "The Art of the Short Story," in *Essays by Divers Hands: Being the Transactions of the Royal Society of Literature of the United Kingdom*. NS XXIII. Hon. Harold Nicolson, ed. London: Geoffrey Cumberlege, Oxford University Press, 1947, pp. 37-51. A survey of the rise of the English short story in the 1890's and how it split into two streams of serious and commercial short stories. The only rule for the short story is that it give the reader a sense of a completed experience.

───────────── . "Concerning Short Stories," in *Bookman*. LXXV (1932), pp. 709-712. Urges that critics and editors stop arguing about what a short story is and agree that the only thing that matters is that it be a piece of short prose fiction which has an aim worthy of an artist and which succeeds in that aim.

───────────── . "The Short Story: Notes at Random," in *Lovat Dickson's Magazine*. II (1934), pp. 281-291. Urges the return to narrative to invigorate the "somewhat anaemic body of the contemporary English short story." The new freedom in the short story, primarily due to the influence of Chekhov, has led too many writers snobbishly to scorn plot and situation.

Stroud, Theodore A. "A Critical Approach to the Short Story," in *The Journal of General Education*. IX (1956), pp. 90-100. Makes use of American "New Criticism" to determine the pattern of the work; that is, why apparently irrelevant episodes are included, why some events are expanded and some excluded.

Suckow, Ruth. "The Short Story," in *Saturday Review of Literature*. IV (1927), pp. 317-318. An extreme reaction to the formulizing of the genre. No one can define the short story; any such attempt is a "fundamental stupidity." An aesthetic method for dealing with diversity and multiplicity, the short story has always been a natural expression for American life, a life so multitudinous "that its meaning could be caught only in fragments, perceived only by will-o'-the-wisp gleams, preserved only in tiny pieces of perfection."

Sullivan, Walter. "Revelation in the Short Story: A Note on Methodology," in *Vanderbilt Studies in Humanities*. I, Richard C. Beatty, John Philip Hyatt, and Monroe K. Spears, eds. Nashville, Tennessee: Vanderbilt University Press, 1951, pp. 106-112. The fundamental methodological concept of the short story is a change of view from innocence to knowledge. The change can be either "logical" (coming at the end of the story) or "anticipated" (coming near the beginning); it can be either "intra-concatinate" (occurring within the main character) or "extra-concatinate (occurring within a peripheral character). Thus defined, the short story did not begin until the final years of the nineteenth century; *Dubliners* (1914) marks the completion of its development.

Summers, Hollis, ed. *Discussions of the Short Story*. Boston: D. C. Heath and Company, 1963. The nine general pieces on the short story are the Poe, Jarrell, and Bader essays listed above, Ray B. West's Chapter One, Seán O'Faoláin's chapter on "Convention," a chapter each from Percy Lubbock's *Craft of Fiction* (1957) and Kenneth Payson Kempton's *The Short Story*, Bret Harte's "The Rise of the Short Story," and excerpts from Brander Matthews' book. Also includes seven additional essays on specific short-story writers.

Tannen, Yoli. "Is a Puzzlement," in *Masses and Mainstream*. X (1957), pp. 14-18. A review of *Best American Stories of 1956*. The serious stories are in the little magazines which no one reads; the rest are the non-distinctive ones appearing in the big magazines. The problem of the "literary" writer seems to be his unwillingness to deal with the typical "white middle-class Protestant"; he prefers instead to focus on the comparatively simple delineation of the racial minority.

Targan, Barry. "The Short-Short Story: Etude," in *English Record*. XIX (1969), pp. 61-65. The major defining characteristic of this subgenre is that the situation and pace of the form create a terseness more extreme and immediate than in longer stories.

Thurston, Jarvis, O. B. Emerson, Carl Hartman, and Elizabeth Wright, eds. *Short Fiction Criticism: A Checklist of Interpretation Since 1925 of Stories and Novelettes (American, British, Continental), 1800-1958*. Denver: Alan Swallow, 1960. This checklist of interpretations of individual stories was brought up to date by Elizabeth Wright in the Summer, 1969 issue of *Studies in Short Fiction*, and has been supplemented by Wright, George Hendrick, and Warren Walker in each Summer issue since then.

Todorov, Tzvetan. *The Fantastic: A Structural Approach to a Literary Genre*. Translated by Richard Howard. Ithaca, New York: Cornell University Press, 1975. In this generic discussion of a form of fiction more often embodied in short stories than in novels, Todorov defines the concept of the fantastic in relation to neighboring thematic genres. When an event occurs that cannot be explained by the laws of the familiar world, two solutions are possible: either the event is the product of the participant's imagination, or the event has actually taken place. If we choose the first option, we are in the realm of the uncanny; if we choose the second we are in the genre of the marvelous. The fantastic exists during the period of uncertainty.

——————— . *The Poetics of Prose*. Translated by Richard Howard. Ithaca, New York: Cornell University Press, 1977. A collection of fifteen essays by the best-known structuralist theorist of narrative. The essays most indicative of the structuralist approach to short fiction are "The Grammar of Narrative" (with examples from *The Decameron*, 1353), "The Secret of Narrative" (with examples from the stories of Henry James), and "Narrative-Men" (with examples from *The Arabian Nights' Entertainments*).

——————— . "The Structural Analysis of Literature," in *Structuralism: An Introduction*. David Robey, ed. Oxford: Clarendon Press, 1973, pp. 73-103. The "figure in the carpet" in James's stories is the quest for an absolute and absent cause. The cause is either a character, an event, or an object; its effect is the story told. Everything in the story owes its existence to this cause, but because it is absent the reader sets off in quest of it.

——————— . "Structural Analysis of Narrative," reprinted in *Modern Literary Criticism: 1900-1970*. Lawrence Lipking and A. Walton Litz, eds. New York: Atheneum Publishers, 1972, pp. 436-441. The most basic summary introduction to Todorov's method of plot analysis, with illustrative schematic summaries from *The Decameron*.

Tomashevsky, Boris. "Thematics," in *Russian Formalist Criticism: Four Essays*. Edited and translated by Lee T. Lemon and Marion J. Reis. Lincoln: University of Nebraska Press, 1965, pp. 63-95. Seminal essay of Russian Formalism which explains the distinction between story (the action itself) and plot (how the reader learns of the action). The essay also makes distinctions between "bound motifs" and "free motifs" and lists various devices of "motivation"; that is, the network of devices which justify the introduction of individual thematic motifs.

Trask, Georgianne and Charles Burkhart, eds. *Storytellers and Their Art: An Anthology*. New York: Doubleday Anchor, 1963. A valuable collection of comments on the short-story form by practitioners from Chekhov to Capote. See especially Part I: "Definitions of the Short Story" and "Short Story vs. Novel," pp. 3-30.

Villa, José Garcia. "The Contemporary Short Story," in *Prairie Schooner*. (1936) pp. 231-233. The short story is taking on the characteristics of the sketch or the essay. The slice-of-life theory often neglects the integrative function of a short story and ignores its basically dramatic nature. "The mere episode—functionless, directionless, and pointless—is not a story."

Voss, Arthur. *The American Short Story: A Critical Survey*. Norman: University of Oklahoma Press, 1973. A comprehensive but routine survey of the major short-story writers in American Literature. Good for an overview of the stories and criticism, but contains nothing original.

Walker, Warren S., comp. *Twentieth-Century Short Story Explication: Interpretations, 1900-1966, of Short Fiction Since 1800*. 2nd edition. Hamden, Connecticut: The Shoe String Press, 1967. Checklist of interpretations of individual stories.

Ward, Alfred C. *Aspects of the Modern Short Story: English and American*. London: University of London Press, 1924. Brief discussions of representative stories of twenty-three different writers. In the Introduction, Ward lists five rather simplistic characteristics of the parable form by which to judge the short story. He does note, however, that the short story is ideally suited to the impressionistic effect and the territory of the unconscious.

Welty, Eudora. "The Reading and Writing of Short Stories," in *Atlantic Monthly*. (February, 1949) pp. 54-58; (March, 1949) pp. 46-49. An impressionistic but suggestive essay in two installments which focuses on the mystery of story, on the fact that we cannot always see the solid outlines of story because of the atmosphere it generates.

West, Ray B. "The American Short Story," in *The Writer in the Room*. East Lansing: Michigan State University Press, 1968, pp. 185-204. Originally appeared as his "Introduction" to *American Short Stories*. New York: Thomas Y. Crowell, 1959. Contrasts the short story's "microscopic" focus on inner motives with the novel's "telescopic" view of man from the outside. The novel is concerned with man's attempt to control nature through social institutions; the short story presents the individual's confrontation with nature as an indifferent force.

_____ . "The Modern Short Story and the Highest Forms of Art," in *English Journal*. XLVI (1957), pp. 531-539. The rise of the short story in the nineteenth century is a result of the shift in narrative view from the "telescopic" (viewing nature and society from the outside) to the "microscopic" (viewing the unseen world of inner motives and impulses).

_____ . *The Short Story in America: 1900-1950*. Chicago: Henry Reg-
nery, 1952. Probably the most familiar and often-recommended history of
the American short story. Takes up where Fred Lewis Pattee's book leaves
off, but it lacks the completeness or the continuity necessary for an adequate
history. Chapter I, "The American Short Story at Mid-Century," is a short
survey in itself of the development of the short story since Irving, Hawthorne, and Poe. Chapter IV is devoted completely to Hemingway and
Faulkner.

Williams, William Carlos. *A Beginning on the Short Story: Notes*. Yonkers,
New York: The Alicat Bookshop Press, 1950. In these "Notes" from a
writers' workshop session, Williams makes several interesting, if fragmentary and impressionistic, remarks about the form: the short story, as contrasted with the novel, is a brush stroke instead of a picture. Stressing
virtuosity instead of story structure, it is "one single flight of the imagination, complete: up and down." It is best suited to depicting the life of
"briefness, brokenness and heterogeneity."

Wharton, Edith. "Telling a Short Story," in *The Writing of Fiction*. New York:
Charles Scribner's Sons, 1925, pp. 33-58. The chief technical difference
between the novel and the short story is that the novel focuses on character
while the short story focuses on situation; "and it follows that the effect
produced by the short story depends almost entirely on its form, or
presentation."

Wright, Austin McGriffert. *The American Short Story in the Twenties*. Chicago: University of Chicago Press, 1961. Using a canon of 220 stories, one
set selected from the 1920's and the other from the immediately preceding
period, Wright examines differing themes and techniques to test the usual
judgments of what the "modern short story" is. The examination is bela-
bored for some four hundred pages and only ends in proving that the short
story of the 1920's is different from the short story of the naturalists.

Charles E. May

FORM AND LANGUAGE IN SHORT FICTION

It may be assumed that a story has a point. A story, however, is much more than its point; it is an experience created by the formal control of language and literary convention. A point can be recapitulated; it can be paraphrased and remain intact. An experience is unchangeable; any change of the experience modifies, makes it other. A point, an idea, is a static thing; it stands still for examination. An experience flies by, active, lost once past, but perhaps a compelling force in the memory. Ideas may excite the intellect; but until they are made dramatic, until they are incorporated into experience, they cannot be emotionally and humanly compelling.

The short story is narrative exposition. In order for exposition to be narrative, it must have a sense of expectancy, or drama. Whereas exposition employs conventions which are meant to culminate in clarity of idea, narrative employs additional conventions which are meant to culminate in a resonating effect on the heart and senses. An exposition may provide evidence which in accumulation leads to a conclusion. A narrative must do more: it must create the emotional environment of the accumulating points so that expectancy is controlled and intensified. Narrative not only concludes, it also expands.

The short story, like experience, is susceptible to various influences and can take many shapes. Basic to all the shapes of the short story, however, is one found repeated over and over, which can be called the traditional form. As human experience in the lives of individuals is repeated yet unique, so too is the traditional short story repeated formally, yet capable of evoking the unique in experience.

The center of the traditional short story is its climax: the highest point, the emotional apex. Climax is the heart of narrative, and it is reached by the development of expectancy and suspense, which is dependent on time. Events take place in time; they begin with time. Human consciousness is required to interpret events and therefore to produce dilemma, and language is required as a means of transmission to describe events to an audience. The traditional short story establishes a situation wherein a problem or conflict must be resolved. It takes time to work things out, and time becomes increasingly important as the pressures of the world (of the story) bear down. Emotion intensifies. Something must happen; a climax must be reached. From the climax a resolution derives. The problem is resolved; for better or worse, the conflict is over.

A classic of the traditional form, Jack London's "To Build a Fire" presents a man alone in the arctic wilderness. An obstacle, the terrible cold, must be overcome, thus generating the conflict: man in confrontation with nature at its most severe. It would not be unusual for another man, a different character, to turn back, but this man is limited by a peculiar incapacity:

> He was quick and alert in the things of life, but only in the things, and not in the significances. Fifty degrees below zero meant eighty-odd degrees of frost. Such a fact impressed him as being cold and uncomfortable, and that was all. . . . That there should be anything more to it than that was a thought that never entered his head.

Not only is he in conflict with the cold, but also with his incapacity to deal with the meaning of the cold. It is that incapacity which leads to his undoing. The theme, therefore, is evident, but it is still only an idea; it must next be brought to life. The tension in this man's quest is compounded by the contrast offered by his companion, a dog of the north, who knows nothing of degrees of cold but knows in his blood the significance of the cold; he knows it is time to burrow in the snow or to return to the camp and the warmth of fire.

> The animal was depressed by the tremendous cold. It knew that it was no time for traveling. Its instincts told it a truer tale than was told to the man by the man's judgment.

The terms of the conflict are clear, and so, too, is the implicit direction of the story. The man goes on across the windless waste of the vast arctic. He acknowledges the cold, but as far as he is concerned, there is no terrible danger. The dog warns him of the danger by stepping in a creek covered over by layers of snow. The icy waters turn to hard ice at once on the dog's paw. The dog chews off the ice, and although the man pays lip service to the danger, he pushes himself and the dog onward. Tension mounts as the time passes with each step he takes. Dangerous but quiet, nature is too mighty for this man, even though he has been warned through the dog's accident. And so,

> . . . at a place where there were no signs, where the soft, unbroken snow seemed to advertise solidity beneath, he wet himself halfway to the knees before he floundered out to the firm crust.

At this point the story achieves yet a greater increase in the tension. In order to remove the ice from his feet, the man must build a fire; but the nature he has not fully enough understood is relentless. To build a fire he must strike a match, which he cannot do with his mittens covering his fingers; so he must remove his mittens, prepare the wood, and strike the match. This all takes time, however, and expending valuable minutes in such a cold is a menacing proposition. The narrative insists on this point by making explicit all the details through which the man must proceed to make the fire. Because of the cold, time demands the severest acknowledgment; what would be ordinary in a warmer place is now extraordinary. The intensity of each moment is peculiar. Time contracts, and the atmosphere cracks with threat around him. He is granted only seconds to build his fire. Will he be successful? Until now he has not comprehended with his mind what the dog has known through his blood. Now, however, the horror of the cold dawns on him:

> Gradually as the flame grew stronger, he increased the size of the twigs with which he fed it. . . . He knew there must be no failure. When it is seventy-five below zero, a man must not fail in his first attempt to build a fire—that is, if his feet are wet.

Each act, each effort is desperate. The fire has started. There is relief, an easing of the tension, as the suspense relaxes temporarily; but then the greater issue, the man's incapacity to comprehend nature's significance, takes hold. At the moment when all seems most hopeful, he brings on his own doom.

> It was his own fault, or, rather, his mistake. He should not have built the fire under the spruce tree. . . . No wind had blown for weeks. . . . Each time he had pulled a twig he had communicated a slight agitation to the tree . . . sufficient to bring about the disaster. High up in the tree one bough capsized its load of snow. This fell on the boughs beneath. . . . It grew like an avalanche, and it descended without warning upon the man and the fire. . . . Where it had burned there was now spread a mantle of fresh and disordered snow.

His ensuing struggle to rekindle the fire constitutes the resolution (denouement). Failure is inevitable; the cold wins. The man sits back and dies, while the dog runs off to find warmth. The problem has been solved and the conflict obviated. The idea is brought to completion, and the drama resonates. The exposition has made clear the point that it is dangerous to misunderstand nature, presumptuous to feel in control of it; the conventions of premise and evidence align and conclude. The narrative conventions of the traditional form, dramatic situation, conflict, developing intensity, climax, and resolution compel the reader to the realization of experience.

"Once upon a time. . . ." The child hears those words and is attentive. Something happens in the child's imagination, as he prepares himself for the experience of a story, a drama. He is not seeking the inner refuge of his imagination to which he is driven by lectures, edicts, dogmas, rules, instructions, morals, and homilies. That little introduction, "once upon a time," a standard convention, suggests the strange yet identifiable, the mysterious yet tangible, the familiar yet desirable; it suggests the long ago, the exotic yet simple and comprehensible, and the activity and clarity of experience.

Although they are not examined here, some conventions in the great tradition of narrative form besides the formal, physical, structure of the story must be mentioned. The traditional story is told in the simple past tense: "Once upon a time there was a boy named Jack." There is a character—a convention to suggest human need in the representation, through language, of a person. Jack was a boy. He had a mother. He sold the cow because the family had no money for food. There is a mood and there is a tone, an atmosphere in which the events take place. There are descriptions to qualify the setting and there are images evoked by action and there are figures of speech. They were in rags. Her yellow hair was lifeless. His shoes had holes in them and were without laces. He led the cow along a winding road. There are symbols and there are themes. All these conventions, through history, have been employed in much the same fashion over and over again, as though they were aspects of a universal cycle, with a continued and undiminishing effect.

Like many things noble and enduring, the traditional form is open to corruption. When the basic structure of the short story is used to serve the shoddy and the shallow, it takes the shape of formula; for example: A Worthy Character Overcomes a Great Obstacle to Achieve a Valuable Goal. By implication, such a formula calls for the elements of traditional structure: the situation must place a character, Worthy, in conflict with Great Obstacle; it must develop the tension to the point of climax until the Obstacle is Overcome, and Worthy emerges victorious in the resolution—Achievement of Valuable Goal. Formulas, however, are limiting, since they cause the superficial to dominate, as in pulp romances, Westerns, and adventures. Such stories are prescriptive and automatic, and the result is predictability and dullness. Just as someone can follow the rules of verse and write doggerel, or can learn with precision how to mix paint and employ the rules of perspective and do no better than imitate, so does the formula writer achieve little. The short-story writer of any merit works to expand his formal limits at the same time he employs them. His work is more than the use of the form; it is the continued re-creation of it. The story he writes demands that it take a certain shape. It is for this reason that writers have continued to affect the form directly, modifying it and reshaping it, either to rediscover it as necessary or to innovate for their purpose.

Edgar Allan Poe redefined the concept of mood. He saw mood as the environment in which a reader immersed himself in order to experience fully the story. The mood, for Poe, was the external limit of the fictional world; all things were possible within that limit. The dead return to life; personal history becomes a tangible force; vengeance is sanctified. As Poe innovated with mood, others have done so with time and tense. The present tense has so often replaced the traditional past tense that it often seems as natural as the past tense. For example, here is the opening of John Updike's "A & P":

> In walks these three girls in nothing but bathing suits. I'm in the third checkout slot, with
> my back to the door, so I don't see them until they're over by the bread. . . .

It is a matter of necessity that this narrator speak in this tense, peculiar to his voice, his place, and his work, all of which are part of Updike's story. The story would be different, even impossible, if the tense were changed back to the simple past. The narrative quality would shift and feel awkward rather than natural. The slightest innovation, therefore—in this case the adjustment in tense—can be as essential as is the use of the past tense in so many thousands of other stories.

With each change in traditional convention, the sense of narrative expectancy is modified, thus modifying the total experience. Storytelling, however, does not evolve formally according to any predictable system; innovations come and go and perhaps return again. For example, the frame story (or the story within a story); the flashback (as well as other breakings of linear time); the monologue; and stories made up of dialogue only are not great intrusions on the fundamental form of the short story. The form is able to accommodate these innovations easily. The basic elements—situation, conflict, development of tension (suspense), climax, and resolution (denouement)—remain basically undisturbed.

There have been, then, innovations with mood and tense; there have been innovations with characterization, with symbols, and with the use of theme. Then there are the bolder innovators who have found it necessary to take up the form of the short story bodily, as a whole, and like wrestlers whirl it round, bend its backbone out of shape, tear something out of joint before subduing it, re-creating it, and making it artistically functional. It is as a result of these large-scale innovations that the most obvious and most troubling changes take place in short fiction. The limits of flexibility of the tradition are reached, strained, and broken. Innovation in fiction finally means change in the fundamental form, the re-creation of effect. Innovation startles, proclaims itself, and then, if proper, proves itself essential by obviating the question, "Was that really necessary?" Perhaps with time, as with the use of the present tense, innovation becomes familiar through judicious imitation.

If "To Build a Fire" is a clear representation of the traditional form of short fiction, then George Chambers' "The Trial" and Donald Barthelme's "Robert Kennedy Saved from Drowning" are clear representations of fictional innovation. Each is *apparently* an arbitrary series of selected and associated fragments In "Robert Kennedy Saved from Drowning," they are barely, if at all, dramatic; in "The Trial" the drama is established through the juxtaposition of dry presentation and the voice of the plaintiff. Barthelme's story places the figure Robert Kennedy in fragments as diverse as "Urban Transportation," "Karsh of Ottawa," "Dress," and "Sleeping on the Stones of Unknown Towns (Rimbaud)." In each fragment the unexpected is assumed. The total attitude is one of redefining expectation. The manner is so charged that when the reader comes to the end of the story, he realizes that he has encountered an extraordinary effect as well as a departure from traditional form.

Here is the final fragment of "Robert Kennedy Saved from Drowning":

K. Saved from Drowning
  K. in the water. His flat black hat, his black cape, his sword are on the shore. He retains

his mask. His hands beat the surface of the water which tears and rips about him. The white foam, the green depths. I throw a line, the coils leaping out over the surface of the water. He has missed it. No, it appears that he has it. His right hand (sword arm) grasps the line that I have thrown him. I am on the bank, the rope wound round my waist, braced against a rock. K. now has both hands on the line. I pull him out of the water. He stands now on the bank, breathing heavily.

"Thank you."

Innovation in Barthelme's story, fragments of the apparently unrelated, accumulate to a completion with that "Thank you," a resonance which, although arrived at differently from what is found in the traditional story, is nevertheless affecting. Humanity is confronted in all fiction, no matter what form the fiction takes, no matter what the attitude or extent of the ironic distance between the voice and the subject.

With Chambers' "The Trial," the experience is different in that the attitude toward the material is not bland and cold as it is in Barthelme's story. Although the presentation is similar—a series of deliberate and arbitrary fragments, as opposed to the derivative, continued narrative development found in traditional stories, such as "To Build a Fire"—the effect is closer to home and more poignant.

"The Trial" is the story of a young black woman, the victim of a rape, who has lived a life devoid of personal control. The story does not develop from situation to climax to resolution. The series of fragments—external voice and the young woman's statement—accumulate to a rising dramatic clarity. A declaration of her situation would tell readers the idea of the situation. The continued presentation of her situation and its aspects makes the problem more than obvious and clear; it becomes a definition of the horror of her life. The problem is developed in the manner of a lyric poem in which the final image, line, or word is essential before the total sense of the work can be clear. At the end of the story, the reader realizes that nothing has changed from beginning to end. The form is static; yet a dramatic tension is established by the technique of elaborating through fragments; the narrative shows a minimal dependence on time. Each of the fragments and their juxtapositioning serves the author's dramatic purpose. That is, when one has finished reading the story, it is clear that something has been experienced beyond a paraphrasable understanding.

If climax is the center and focus of the traditional short story, then ultimately there is only one innovation on the form: the excision of climax. Yet that is virtually impossible. If narrative is dependent on time and the sense of expectancy, then development to some point must take place. Nevertheless, as far as the form allows it—that is, as far as narrative can be taken and still remain narrative—it will continue to be challenged. The examples referred to above may hint at the changes possible in the form of short fiction as can be seen now, but they do not pretend to exemplify all the possibilities.

Innovation is the denial or reversal of expectation; it is the confrontation of time. Innovation is the refusal of tradition; or perhaps it is as Gustave Flaubert put it:

> What seems beautiful to me, what I should like to write, is a book about nothing, a book dependent on nothing external, which would be held together by the strength of its style, just as the earth, suspended in the void, depends on nothing external for its support: a book which would have no subject, or at least in which the subject would be almost invisible, if such a thing is possible. The finest works are those that contain the least matter.

When proper, innovation seems as conventional as tradition; it does not, like gimmickry, call constant attention to itself. It is not self-conscious and does not proclaim its novelty. It is required by style and intent and is as far from self-serving as genuine prayer. It is not required by an age but by a single artist who has arrived at innovation along a strait path.

One further technical concept tangential to the fundamental form of the traditional short story should be mentioned: point of view. The term "point of view" refers to the position from which the story is told—that of the persona, the mouth from which the story is heard, the singular intelligence which determines the manner of presentation. There is no narrative without point of view. Without a clear identification of point of view, reading a story is at best chancy. The reader must feel secure in his instinct for the point of view because it is the key to the attitude and therefore the language of the story.

Hence the language of the form, which is distinct in general from the language employed in other forms of composition and which is peculiar, every time, to each particular story. Or, as Paul Valéry puts it, "With every question, before making any deep examination of the content, I take a look at the language." To begin to comprehend the techniques of presenting human emotion and understanding, one must first examine the nature of language. Language is available to everyone; it is obvious and therefore a pitfall. Yet the control of language for the sake of fiction is not available to everyone. Most people can hear sounds; not many of them can make music. Everyone can touch clay and observe the forms of nature, but not many can make statues. Most people can see colors, yet how many are painters? Language is analogous to color, sound, or clay. In order for it to be used successfully in the art of fiction, it must be controlled, wrought. The analogy, however, can be taken only so far. Language is not solid like clay; it is not an aspect of direct perception as are music and color. Language is, rather, a tool of the imagination.

Language is, in and of itself, symbolic. Words represent things of the world and the mind. They are insubstantial, unlike clay and sound and color, although they represent them. It is only in the imagination that one can deal with words. Therefore, although it is true a person can speak his native tongue, it is equally true that not many people are fine storytellers. Sit down with friends and listen to them relate their experiences. Among them, is there one who is a joy to listen to? Who maintains the interest; who elicits the implied question from moment to moment: what happened then? Anyone can give information, like the dullest of friends, but only a few can recapture, activate, create, and transform through language and into the art of fiction the significance of human experience, dilemma, and emotion, as well as information.

Paint is used on walls. It would be clearly too limiting to say that paint therefore is simply paint, the same whether used on a wall or on a canvas. It is similarly limiting to assume that because language is used in conversation, language is therefore simply language, the same in fiction as it is in conversation. In conversation, in exposition, or in any nonartistic form, language rarely concerns itself with anything more than denotative accuracy. As Rainer Maria Rilke explained:

> No word . . . (I mean here every "and" or "the") is identical with the same-sounding word in common use and conversation; the purer conformity with the law, the great relationship, the constellation it occupies in verse or artistic prose, changes it to the core of its nature, renders it useless, unserviceable for mere everyday use, untouchable and permanent. . . .

Anything that is said in a piece of fiction, as in a poem, takes on a new meaning, a new and particular quality distinct from what it would be in a usage other than artistic. Meaning in exposition develops point by point until an idea is made complete. In narrative the idea is only a part of the meaning. The circumstance in which the idea is placed contributes to the deeper meaning. A suggestive, emotional quality begins to work its way out of the literal, denotative function of the language, and as the story accumulates—as incident and characterization, development and description, metaphor and symbol emerge and particularize—each word works distinctly in its service to the story. The accumulated use of the literal language is transcended by the artistic language at any given point in the narrative.

In James Joyce's "Araby," the young narrator concludes: "I saw myself as a creature driven and derided by vanity; and my eyes burned with anguish and anger." It is no doubt immediate and therefore easy for readers to say that the narrator has experienced the initiation of heartbreak and exposure to the false and shoddy in adult life. The reader would be correct in that he understood the denotative elements of the language, but he would clearly feel he was missing what he could not communicate, what only the story with its own special use of language has communicated: something of the emotional depth, singularity, and power of such an experience. The reader would be unable to communicate what the story made him feel, although he definitely felt it. The only way, finally, that he could make clear what was felt would be to give the story to the person with whom the reader was trying to communicate, and have him read it. The story's language is unparaphrasable and unique.

It is impossible to restate the fullness of what is effected in the prose of short fiction. It is as though the prose, the language of art, were separate from the form. Some—including André Gide as well as Flaubert—have gone so far as to say that artistic fiction is "free" and that there is no such thing, ultimately, as subject; that style, that is to say, language, is in itself absolute. The freest use of language would then amount to a usage which has no interest in what it refers to, which has no obligation to what is literal, which has a perfect sense of self and lives, "just as the earth, suspended in the void, depends on nothing external for its support."

Such a concept, of course, seems to preclude narrative entirely. Yet even in examples of certain short fiction, often called prose poems, in which language is employed for no purpose linked to time (that is, it is not concerned with event or climax) a sense of narrative expectancy arises, as though by itself, perhaps despite the abstracted, lyric intention of the language. Language in itself is narrative in that it establishes at once a sense of expectation. Begin with a word and certain requirements must be met in order for the word to have any life. Grammar and logic must be served. The need then for the word to achieve sense and meaning is dependent on time, a relationship with other words, and a system one can apprehend. That prose *can* tend away from narrative is undeniable; however, there is no reason to think it *must* do so. Storytelling is affected by a continued refinement of language. From time to time shifts in short fiction have taken place; the works of Henry James, James Joyce, Franz Kafka, Ernest Hemingway, and Katherine Anne Porter are examples. In each of their works, as in those of more recent writers such as George Chambers, Paul Friedman, William Gass, and Mark Costello, what emerges as the telling quality is the particularity and the deliberateness of their language. In each author's work, the use of language is distinct and stylistically singular; in any of their works the use of language indicates—as it has time and again—the special quality of language and its myriad possibilities for short fiction.

Although language is not form, without language there would be no form. What is taken to be form can be apprehended only through language. An experience which must be communicated is perhaps a formal thing, but it means nothing to anyone until it is put into language. It is the same for the imagined, or created, experience, the untold story. It is the choice of language that determines the quality of the story; language dictates the mood and the characterization, the tone and development, the pervasive atmosphere and attitude, and the continued qualifications of time and event. Although it has been said that there are no new stories, stories, one finds, are new, from age to age and from author to author. The individual, personal sense of experience and imagination is both joined by and is the outgrowth of a singular sense of language. The idea that there are no new stories is a mistaken idea: where language is new, the stories are new; where the language is unique to one author—whether Joseph Conrad or Paul Bowles, Eudora Welty or Flannery O'Connor—so too is the experience of the narrative.

Bibliography
Ellman, Richard and Charles Feidelson, Jr., eds. *The Modern Tradition.*
Friedman, Paul. "The Story of a Story" in *And If Defeated Allege Fraud.*
Poe, Edgar Allan. "The Philosophy of Composition."
Wellek, Rene and Austin Warren. *Theory of Literature.*

Richard Lyons

NARRATIVE VOICE

Any story requires a teller; the teller has a voice, and that voice provides his particular way of telling his story. It is the entire story. Readers are always aware that narrative voice is present though they may think of it as suppressed when characters are introduced, act, speak, and perhaps have their thoughts present. Narrative voice implies an author's second self. It is located always outside the plot events, dialogues, characterizing devices, summaries, and commentary which make up the story, although it is most often identified with the narrator's comments on his story. Even when so identified, it should not be confused with what the author himself believes or feels since the voice of the storyteller is a mask assumed for the occasion. It implies a consciousness working by means of the story and to whom assumed readers respond.

Narrative voice when associated with first-person viewpoint appears to come from "inside" the story framework since the voice is identified with that of an "I" who observes as a character or who interacts dramatically with other characters. Using the third-person viewpoint, the storyteller can make the narrative voice seem to come forth through the mind of a reflector character through the use of selective omniscience or even of objective viewpoint. The teller may assume a godlike, fully omniscient viewpoint in which narrative voice lays claim to know both subjective and objective facts about a variety of persons. This is often the voice of nineteenth century fiction writers; but since it has less psychological interest and can be abused, its employment in storytelling has rather abated in modern fiction. In any event, narrative voice works with viewpoint but it is *not* simply viewpoint since it forms the very basis of telling the story.

Distinction of Narrative Voice from Other Voices

Narrative voice can be distinguished from the voices found in poetry, drama, or expository prose. In drama, the speaking is performed through dialogue of the characters. The reader or viewer may be aware that the characters do not merely enter into certain situations or express certain problems; they have ways of delivering their speeches and of presenting ideas which are "in character." Readers, given a knowledge of the playwright's life or the influences upon it, may guess that the character speeches do, in varying degrees of directness, reflect the author's own thoughts. The presentation in drama, nevertheless, remains relatively objective, seeming to come forth from the consciousness of the characters themselves, with the exception of stage directions, in which expository prose explains dramatic effects.

In poetry, the voice may become entirely dramatic, using dialogue as in poetic drama; or, it may become relatively dramatic, as in dramatic monologue, which also has a narrative framework. In meditative, comic, or lyric poetry, the voice encountered by readers seemingly has no source. It is attached to no particular person unless readers associate it vaguely with the poet or with an assumed role the poet has adopted for the occasion. The voice becomes evident through direct speaking. Robert Frost's "Departmental" begins: "An ant on the tablecloth/Ran into a dormant moth" and, after humorously describing the lack of emotion and the bureaucratic mentality of ants called upon to deal with a dead companion, ends: "It couldn't be called ungentle/But how thoroughly departmental." The reader catches, through the comic understatement, slightly shifted word contexts, and imaginative incident, a speaker who is amused, affable, and tolerant of subhuman behavior. The speaker is not, however, necessarily Robert Frost; the voice is a free-floating consciousness.

In expository prose, a voice also exists. The reader assumes, by a convention, that the voice which speaks there is representing ideas, opinions, or information in a truthful manner and that the voice is the author's. It may use the first-person "I," becoming rather personal as does Robert Burton in *The Anatomy of Melancholy* (1621), speaking of his own writing style: "One or two things I was desirous to have amended if I could concerning the matter of handling this my subject, for which I must apologize . . . and upon better advice give the friendly reader notice." It can, on the other hand, be quite impersonal, as in Jonathan Culler's discussion of literary interpretation in *Structuralist Poetics*: "Both Jakobson and Greimas start from the assumption that linguistic analysis provides a method for discovering the patterns or meanings of literary texts. . . ." The reader recognizes in either case that he is being addressed by the voice from the printed text and, by implication, by the author himself.

Reliability and Location of Narrative Voice

The narrative voice can make readers doubt the truth of its own account as when a narrator asserts facts or ideas which elsewhere are contradicted by himself or by characters about whom he tells them. The narrator is then unreliable. As readers take the measure of this unreliability, they become aware that the arrangement of the narrative itself has caused the doubt and have the sense of "seeing behind" the narrator, often a first-person narrator. The narrative achieves a doubling of "upper" and "under" voices which deepen its meaning. This fact has made the use of the unreliable narrator of particular interest to modern fiction writers, as, for example, Sherwood Anderson in "I'm a Fool," in which a young horse handler at a race track, narrating in ungrammatical English, tries to persuade readers that he is happy with his style of life, despite an unfortunate blunder with a girl he admires, all the while dropping clues through his defensive remarks to a real ambivalence about his lowly social status.

The narrative consciousness is located, even in the omniscient viewpoint, at some definite time point, the "now" of the story from which events in the story take their pastness or futurity. It is located also at some definite spatial location from which movements in the story may be made in various incidents or from which those events assume nearness or distance. In its readiness always, as it appears on the page, to tell its story, narrative voice puts the reader into ever-enduring "now" even if the storyteller's tenses are past tenses as in the opening of Flannery O'Connor's "Greenleaf": "Mrs. May's bedroom window was low and faced on the east and the bull, silvered in the moonlight, stood under it, his head raised as if he listened. . . . " The reader becomes part of that scene regardless of when, in its own accounting, it is supposed to have occurred. The scene also forces a location somewhere outside Mrs. May's window. Fictional narrative voice has its own characteristic use of adverbs different from those of nonfictional narrative; for example: "Tallchief had often thought of his child, Redwing, who had gone into the big city. Where, he wondered, was that child *now*? *There* in Chicago or *far away* in San Francisco, perhaps, but he missed him *here* at home." Past or past perfect tenses are consistent here with a present-indicating adverb, and the placement of the narrator close to Tallchief makes Chicago and San Francisco assume location in relation to the narrative's own central point, probably somewhere in the Dakotas. Full omniscience has a greater looseness since it can move from mind to mind but even that viewpoint must assume a relatively coherent spatiotemporal integrity. The reader notices violations of the framework as in Tom Robbins' *Even Cowgirls Get the Blues* (1976), in which "Jelly is sitting in the outhouse. She has been sitting there longer than necessary. . . . On the other hand, Bonanza Jellybean, ranch boss, may be just looking things over. . . . Weather's hot but there's a breeze today and it feels sweet swimming up her bare thighs." The last sentence suddenly shifts from outside the character to inside her consciousness; the "here" becomes "there" and vice versa.

Stream of Consciousness and Narrative Voice

The stream of consciousness in which narrative voice seems to become plural, since it issues without mediation of the teller from the minds of the characters, still involves a centralizing narrative voice even if guide-directions such as "he said," "she thought," or "John entered" are absent. The interior monologue (which may, in fact, be dialogue of mind with itself) is organized on principles such as association of imagery, references to points in time or space, or a sequential plan of representing the monologue of each character. Otherwise, reader confusion can result. The interior voices are, after all, masks of a narrator.

Possibilities of Narrative Voice as Controlling or Commenting Agent

The possibilities are as follows: First, the narrator may see himself as a writer or, on the contrary, be rather oblivious of his relation to the story he tells. "If only Mr. Longman would allow me a fourth chapter for this love affair"; this is what Trollope's narrator says about his need to deepen his telling of his story. The narrator, on the other hand, may present characters, situations, ideas, or make other kinds of commentary without ever referring to how he tells his story or what he thinks of its recital. Second, the narrator may make commentary upon characters or their interactions with one another or with their environment. At least two generations of critics have objected to this use on grounds that commentary might break the illusion of reality in the story. It can be argued, however, that the narrator may appropriately speak about his own storytelling if his commentary furthers the objectives of the story.

Third, the narrator may also control the story by either presenting a scene in its varied details, making it relatively dramatic, perhaps with some summarizing, or by relying mainly on summary. In this way the narrative voice controls the speed of parts of the story, making its time flow unequal by the kind of concentration it gives to particular parts of the story. The particular events may be rather highly discriminated, or they may be rather abstractly summed up, as in Samuel Butler's *The Way of All Flesh* (1903): "Old Mr. Pontifex had married in the year 1750 but for 15 years his wife bore no children. At the end of that time Mrs. Pontifex astonished the whole village. . . ." Here readers find fifteen years summarized in one sentence before coming to a more specific event in the next sentence. A more concrete scene, from Ernest Hemingway's "The Three-Day Blow," offers the following: "The rain stopped as Nick turned into the road that went up through the orchard. The fruit had been picked and the fall wind blew through the bare trees." Summarizing may be put into the mind of a character, especially in modern fiction; but it may be subject to unreliability since the immediate authority in this case is not the narrator but the character.

Finally, narrative voice can control distance in fiction in terms of the reader's feeling of closeness or distance from the narrator or the characters, or of the characters' closeness or separation from the narrator, or of the narrator to the implied author, or of the reader to the implied author. For example, the first-person straightforwardness with which a barber of limited education and insight in Ring Lardner's "Haircut" presents the story of a vicious practical joker sets his lack of insight as the storyteller against what the reader sees through his story. Narrator here is distant from implied author. In Guy de Maupassant's stories, the characters, seen in third-person, often with limited omniscience, are given an objectivity setting the narrator distinctly apart from the characters. Franz Kafka's *Metamorphosis* (1915) has as its central character a traveling salesman who is transformed unexpectedly one morning into an insect, a millipede, and the narration proceeds largely through his consciousness. The narrator, in this instance, diverges markedly from the reader's own perceptions by offering unusual or uncustomary perspectives on reality or presenting deviant forms of behavior. Readers of Gustave Flaubert's stories are confronted with a highly specific knowledge of the social minutiae of provincial France in the nineteenth century which historians might have. If they take an interest, readers are awed by its inclusiveness. In this case, the narrative voice suggests an implied author distant from his reader.

Other Uses of Narrative Voice—Indirect Presentation of Story

Asking the reader to put his faith in a narrator whose storytelling forms a coherent and reliable account produces a straightforwardness and identification of reader with narrator; but it loses in vividness and immediacy of experience. Multifaceted engagement with events is diminished. Henry James, for example, used a "reflector" character through whose vision the story unfolds. It is a consciousness which presents and also interprets the story; but it can, as events unfold, be corrected or altered by what it knows. The story may, retroactively for the reader, take on a new aspect, and the reader can share in this new way of seeing the characters, their views of experience, or events themselves.

Unreliable Presentation of Story

The narrator may be honest as a first-person storyteller, but his unreliability asks the reader to make judgments. The narrative voice creates an ambiguity by setting events against characters' judgments about events or setting certain characters' perceptions against other later perceptions. Readers become implicitly aware of an implied author who does not share the same norms or view of experience as the narrator does. This carrying out of inferences by the reader from clues given by the narrative voice is part of the richness of modern storytelling, but it can, as in Henry James's famous ghost story, *The Turn of the Screw* (1898), also lead to endless puzzlement. A governess, isolated from any companionship but that of a few servants in an English country house and her two juvenile charges, finds herself in the presence of ghosts whose influence, as she discerns it, is malevolently directed against the children. Her efforts to ferret out the children's awareness of the evil, a fact they deny, increases their anxiety, a condition taken in her own view as further proof of malicious intention. In a moment of hysterical intensity, Miles, the boy, is overcome and dies, not before shouting, "Peter Quint, you devil!" Is the anguished cry directed at the male ghost suspected of haunting him? Or at the governess herself who may conceivably have imagined the ghosts and tormented the children by neurotic fears? The narrative voice has created its own instability since the reader cannot be sure which norms of judgment to apply.

Rhetorical Effects upon Story

The narrative voice may use its own rhetoric to persuade the reader to accept certain norms often by making generalizing statements such as "All men are of the opinion that a bad wife is better than none." It can heighten events: "After this happening at the inn, the talk of the whole village was about nothing but Mr. Henry's folly." The narrative voice may generalize about a whole pattern of experience in the story. In Anton Chekhov's "The Kiss," a diffident, unremarkable young officer indulges in romantic visions arising from a kiss accidentally bestowed upon him when he blunders into a darkened room where another man has been expected. His hopes of achieving for himself the love he has accidentally tasted are wrecked, however, and as he stands looking down at a stream the narrator says:

> And the whole world—life itself—seemed to Riabovitch an inscrutable aimless mystifi-
> cation. Raising his eyes from the stream and gazing at the sky, he recalled how Fate in
> the shape of an unknown woman had once caressed him; he recalled his summer fantasies
> and images—and his whole life seemed to him unnaturally thin and colorless and wretched.

Creation of Mood in the Story

The narrative voice can create mood as it does in Edgar Allan Poe's stories, in which the horror may become more intensified by being approached from within a character rather than by the less convincing mode of direct statement. The opening of "The Fall of the House of Usher" is noteworthy in this regard.

Attitudes Arising from Narrative Voice

Even with an objective or "effaced" narrator who seem oblivious to what is being spoken, some hint of narrator's attitude is revealed. Hemingway's "Hills Like White Elephants" very considerably relies upon dialogue and becomes close to dramatic narrative, telling the story of an irresponsible young American expatriate and his girl friend who quarrel over whether her expected child should be aborted or not. His claims to love the girl are accompanied by words indicative of his abandonment of responsibility. The technique seems to be totally objective; yet as the man waits for a Spanish train which will take them to a big city and the girl to the abortionist, the reader finds: "He drank an Anis at the bar and looked at the people. They were all waiting reasonably for the train." "Reasonably" hits the reader by its careful placement and offers, obliquely, a comment on the man himself: for him life is reasonable only in selfish terms which attempt to represent a real injury to the girl's love as if it were merely a reasonable compromise. The narrator has, quite deliberately, tipped his hand.

Narrative voice may also communicate an attitude to the reader through symbolism. The white elephants of Hemingway's title are distant hills to which the girl likens them. They imply an expensive, rare, but burdensome gift. Their location beyond the only fertile spot she sees in the landscape, a river, suggests an obtrusive sterility. The hills then represent the end of the love affair and its frustration of forthcoming life. The object here takes on extended meanings through repeated allusions by the narrator directly or by the characters presented through narrative voice.

Finally, narrative voice may utilize the opposite of significant details, the fact of absence or silence. Since all narrative, even that most dedicated to realism, must be selective, the voice may say nothing about certain events, feelings, motives, or ideas but imply them by suggesting gaps in what *is* said. Count Leo Tolstoy's *The Death of Ivan Ilyich* (1884) presents the reader with a Russian judge, now faced with death, whose life, despite his official position in society as the dispenser of justice, has been unconcerned with other people and given over to mere social conformity and money-grubbing careerism. In his death agony, he must confront having lived his life the wrong way, but, seeing a light, he can for the first time forgive others, "knowing that He whose understanding mattered would understand." Then comes the thought of the dying man, "It is finished." The narrative voice makes no comment on these Christian allusions; it permits the reader to supply appropriate inferences. In so doing, it deftly avoids forcing any kind of religious message upon the reader. Narrative voice, then, can create contexts in which silence is an effective speaking.

Bibliography
Booth, Wayne C. *The Rhetoric of Fiction.*
Hale, Nancy. *The Realities of Fiction.*
Warren, Austin. "The Nature and Modes of Narrative Fiction," in Robert Scholes's *Approaches to the Novel.*

Roger E. Wiehe

POINT OF VIEW

Point of view is a technical term of fiction referring to the position or vantage point from which a story is told. Custom dictates two broad categories: first person and third person. Within these categories several sub-groupings exist with many possibilities for intricacies.

In the first-person point of view, a narrator speaks in his or her own voice and manner to relate a series of events that is in some way significant to the storyteller. The first-person narrator could be simply an observer of the action or one who merely recounts events, as is found in Washington Irving's "The Legend of Sleepy Hollow"; could be a character involved only peripherally in the central conflict, as is Ratliff, the sewing machine agent involved in William Faulkner's "Spotted Horses"; or could be the protagonist of the story, as is the Captain in Joseph Conrad's "The Secret Sharer."

Since a short story is an orderly structure in which the component parts are integrally related to the whole, and since an author's choice of a narrator is dictated by the particular needs of a story, there are few narrators who are simply observers, who are, by definition, unnecessary to the action. In a story such as Nathaniel Hawthorne's "Wakefield," the first-person narrator seems at first glance to be nothing more than a storyteller: "In some old magazine or newspaper I recollect a story, told as truth, of a man—let us call him Wakefield—who absented himself for a long time from his wife." As the story proceeds, however, the skillful reader notices that the narrator is intimately involved in the conflict and, indeed, is trying to involve the reader as a kind of co-creator of a story about Wakefield: "What sort of man was Wakefield? We are free to shape out our own idea, and call it by his name." In William Faulkner's "A Rose for Emily," the first-person narrator is a spokesman for the town of Jefferson, using the plural pronoun "we" to indicate that position. If the first-person narrator is taken to be simply an observer of the action, then Miss Emily Grierson must be identified as the central character of the action, the protagonist whose story the narrator is relating. Yet an argument could be made that the narrator tells the story of Miss Emily not so much to elucidate Miss Emily's behavior as to explain the peculiar response of the townspeople who offer the rose to Emily.

The same kinds of observations could be made about a first-person narrator who is clearly a character in the story but one who appears to be peripheral to the central action. In "The Man Who Would Be King," Rudyard Kipling presents us with a first-person narrator, a newspaperman, who ostensibly is telling us a story about two men whose adventures are awesome and bloody and whose behavior is courageous. Still, a closer examination of the story suggests that the story may not be so much about the two adventurers who go out to make themselves kings, but rather about the newspaperman whose courage is not so great. In "The Egg," Sherwood Anderson makes it clear that the narrator is to be identified with his father about whom the story is ostensibly told, so that the story is seen to be as much the son's as it is the father's. In "I Stand Here Ironing," Tillie Olsen creates a first-person narrator involved in trying to understand her daughter, but the reader comes to understand that knowledge of the daughter is impossible without a concomitant knowledge of the mother. The point is that although it may be possible to find a first-person narrator who is simply an observer of the action or who is a character peripheral to the central action, more often such narrators are vehicles for further points made by the authors; they are the means by which authors create greater intricacies and more involved and consequently more interesting stories.

The first-person narrator who is clearly the protagonist of the action is commonly found in short fiction. In this kind of story intricacies derive from the character of the protagonist as well as from the sequence of events and conflict in which the protagonist is engaged. The first-person narrator is a human being like other human beings. He or she sees with a single pair of eyes, hears with a single pair of ears, cannot report what is not witnessed or heard about, and cannot enter into the minds of other people. In addition, the first-person narrator, like other human beings, is limited by particular prejudices, biases, ignorances brought on by lack of knowledge, age, and circumstance. In a sense, then, all first-person narrators are fallible, and a reader must take into account a narrator's particular fallibility.

One may, of course, wonder how a reader is to know about specific limitations of a narrator, since by definition of the point of view, all a reader has is the information a narrator tells, and a narrator may not be aware of his or her own limitations. In a situation like this it helps to remember that the narrator is not the author. The narrator is a character created by the author, and the author will let us know what we need to know. Let us consider, for example, a situation in a story in which we have a first-person narrator who tells us that she has always been shy and unable to get along with other people; has, indeed, been unable to make close friends. Later on in the story we see the narrator in interaction with other people, and we notice that although the narrator is quiet, her very manner makes it possible for other people to relate to her in significant ways. In addition, we notice that other people seem genuinely concerned about the narrator's well-being. Here it becomes obvious that, at the very least, the narrator knows little about herself and the situations in which she finds herself, and readers are, thus, alerted to the fact that they have to make such judgments for themselves and not rely on the narrator's judgment in every case.

In "Judas," Frank O'Connor makes skillful use of such a fallible narrator, a young man, who after the death of his father assumes the role of the father in his relationship with his mother and unknowingly acts out an Oedipal pattern. This pattern includes a completely unrealistic view of "good" girls.

In time the girl involved shows herself to be anything but the angel the young man thinks her to be; but, in still desiring her, the young man is overcome by guilt because he feels he has betrayed his mother as Judas betrayed Christ. James Joyce's "Araby" is told by an adult who recalls an experience that took place in his youth, but although the language is the adult's, the feelings are the youth's, as expressed in the famous last sentence of the story: "Gazing up into the darkness, I saw myself as a creature driven and derided by vanity; and my eyes burned with anguish and anger." It is, of course, the reader's job to discover why the boy feels as he does, because the boy is not yet old enough to know.

Other uses of the first-person narrator can involve different kinds of intricacies. In some of his stories, Imamu Amari Baraka makes use of a narrator acting in two different time periods so that the sense of disjunction is emphasized. In "That in Aleppo Once . . . ," Vladimir Nabokov makes use of three storytellers; and, when the various possibilities involving who, if anyone, is real, what, if anything, happened, and the references to *Othello* are added together, the result is many stories told by a lot of people. In "La Mère Sauvage," Guy de Maupassant uses a first-person narrator in an outer frame, inside which is a story told in the third person. Such a use of point of view both mutes the horror of the inner story and personalizes it.

The third-person point of view also involves several possibilities. An author may take complete omniscience and, like a god, enter into the minds of all the characters, moving at will from one locale or time to another. In "Roger Malvin's Burial," for example, Nathaniel Hawthorne enters the minds of Roger Malvin, Reuben Bourne, the protagonist of the story, Dorcas, Reuben's wife, and Cyrus, Reuben and Dorcas' son. In so doing Hawthorne explores the relationships among the members of the family as well as the interior dimensions of each character. In addition, the third-person narrator speaks in his own voice to record the incidents of the story: "Many circumstances combined to retard the wounded traveler in his way to the frontiers. . . . His scanty sustenance was supplied by the berries and other spontaneous products of the forest." In a story such as "The Man Without a Temperament," Katherine Mansfield also chooses to enter the minds of all the major characters, but her use of this point of view is somewhat different from Hawthorne's. In Mansfield's story no narrator's voice is discernible. Rather, the third-person narrator hovers barely outside each of the characters and, when entering their minds, uses the language and thought patterns appropriate to each character: "And she knoo it was there—she knoo it was looking at her just that way. She played up to it; she gave herself little airs."

Within the third-person point of view an author may choose to be selectively omniscient as Mansfield does in "The Daughters of the Late Colonel," in which she enters into the minds of some of the characters but not all. In this kind of situation, not entering the mind of a character is as important to characterization as entering the mind of a character. The point is clearly made in D. H. Lawrence's "The Rocking-Horse Winner," in which the father is the most elusive character in the story, but the fact that the father is isolated and withdrawn is important to the meaning of the story. It is, therefore, entirely appropriate that Lawrence should stay outside the father's mind, never recording a single one of his thoughts. Indeed, in the story the father says so little that one may wonder whether he has any thoughts.

Stream of consciousness functions within the third-person point of view as a kind of interior monologue set down in such a way that it gives the appearance of being an unending, disjointed flow of associations, thoughts, feelings, and memories reflecting the workings of a mind moving without apparent logic. People do not ordinarily think in sentence patterns or organize their thoughts into well-developed paragraphs. Thoughts often follow a process of association of which a person is not consciously aware. In attempting to reproduce this process, authors try to give the effect of chaos. Of course, in fiction, chaos is only apparent and not real. An author manipulates the thoughts of characters for a purpose which is ultimately significant. In fiction, stream of consciousness has been used more often in the novel than in the short story, although in a story such as Ronald Sukenick's "The Birds," stream of consciousness joins with a poetic collage of images and motifs arranged to suggest chance encounters.

Another possibility within the third-person point of view is that an author may enter the mind of a single character, focusing all or most perceptions through that character, as James Joyce does in "Clay," in which Maria's perceptions are of major interest to the reader and of great importance to the story. In "Clay," irony results from the contrasting of Maria's perceptions of herself with the reader's perceptions of Maria. Joyce's use of point of view in this story is very similar to the device used by Henry James which he called the "central intelligence," which is a character through whom all the story flows. In James's "The Tree of Knowledge," perceptions are restricted to the consciousness of the protagonist, Peter Brench, whose "awareness" is the subject of the story. This kind of limited omniscience is close to a first-person point of view but allows an author to move in and out of a character's perceptions as he desires, in accordance with the needs of a particular story.

Another possibility involved in the third-person point of view occurs when an author chooses to be completely objective, staying out of the minds of all the characters and simply reporting facts. This is the point of view used by Ernest Hemingway in his famous story "The Killers." In this story Hemingway records events as a camera would, and readers must speculate concerning the interior workings of the minds of the characters from the exterior facts of the story. The point of view that Hemingway uses in "The Killers" is entirely appropriate to the theme of the story, which concerns the absolute impersonality of a certain kind of evil.

Many people believe that authors did not become aware of the intricacies involved in a skillful use of point of view in prose fiction until after Henry James made his perceptive comments on the subject toward the end of the nineteenth century. Such an observation, however, is patent nonsense. One need only look to such earlier writers as Edgar Allan Poe and Herman Melville to see how an intricate point of view functions in their stories to provide complexity and help to direct meaning. In such stories as "The Tell-Tale Heart" and "Ligeia," Poe uses an insane narrator to intensify the horror of his tales, but his masterly use of point of view in these stories pales beside his use of point of view in what is probably his best story, "The Fall of the House of Usher." In that story, the first-person narrator is ostensibly sane; the madman is Roderick Usher. By the use of a "sane" narrator Poe is able to cause readers to make identification on a personal level with the narrator. Then, by means of various mirroring and doubling devices, Poe identifies the narrator with Roderick Usher. The ultimate horror and the final unmasking comes when readers must by a simple tautology identify themselves with Usher, because if the narrator equals the readers, and the narrator equals Usher, it follows that the reader must also equal Usher.

In *Benito Cereno* (1856), Melville focuses perceptions mainly through the consciousness of Captain Amaso Delano, but what is not focused through the mind of Delano is of equal importance. Indeed, it is necessary that readers separate themselves from Delano's perceptions fairly early in the story. Increasingly, then, as the story progresses, readers find themselves looking over Delano's shoulders rather than seeing through his eyes, becoming more and more aware that Delano's perceptions are in some way distorted or wrong but not knowing exactly how they are distorted or wrong until the end of the story. When the first revelation is made that Babo and not Benito Cereno is the masked "villain," Melville completely severs readers from Delano's consciousness. The reader follows Delano's men as they give battle to the mutineers, and then the reader withdraws even further from Delano as he goes through a long and involved legal deposition. Only then does Melville bring the reader back to the dramatic action and to the final revelation and climax of the story. Then one knows that just as Delano's perceptions were distorted by his patterns of thinking, so were one's own. A difference is that the reader comes to understand what Delano never does.

Point of view is a device used not only by writers of short fiction but also by writers of long fiction—that is, of novels. Novelists, however, often shift point of view within a novel. A novel can, for example, contain chapters that alternate between first- and third-person or between different narrators. This kind of shifting of point of view occurs very seldom in short fiction. Ordinarily, writers of short fiction choose the one point of view they consider best for the particular story they are writing and hold to that perspective through the whole narrative. In all other aspects, however, novelists use point of view with the same care and skill and in the same ways as short-story writers do.

Point of view is closely tied to a concept called "distance." Distance refers to how close to or far away from an action of a story readers must be placed if they are to apprehend total meaning. The concept can be better explained if looked at in reference to some of the other arts. Everyone knows what it means to get a good seat at the theater. One pays extra for the privilege of being able to sit in a select row of seats close enough to see the action on the stage in its entirety—not so close that the illusion is destroyed, and not so far or to either side that vision or hearing is impaired. Everyone knows that at a museum a piece of sculpture is set away from a wall so that a person can walk around it to see it whole. Museum directors pay attention to where a painting is hung, allowing enough wall space and sufficient light and often placing a bench at just the right distance from the painting so that the patron can sit down to peruse the whole painting. One may walk up close to view details, but one always walks back to see how the details function in the whole painting. For obvious reasons people do not choose to sit near the drums at a symphony or in the first row at a ballet. The perfect physical distance is sought so that one can apprehend the play, piece of sculpture, painting, symphony, or ballet in all aspects as those aspects relate one to another and function within the whole.

Closely related to the concept of physical distance is the concept of psychical distance. Psychical distance refers to attitudes which need, also, to be placed properly in relationship to the art object, so that nothing impedes a relationship with it. It is difficult, if not impossible, to listen to a symphony or watch a ballet if people feel intense pain or if their lives are in danger. One may react with aversion to a painting of a snake if one has an irrational fear of snakes. So, also, could prejudices and biases cause people to turn away from a work of art if its subject matter touches on an area close to something they dislike. If, for example, a person is embarrassed by nude bodies, he could never properly appreciate Michelangelo's statue of David; he probably would not be able to look at it in such a way that he could appreciate the whole form.

Writers, of course, from the early scops who engaged their listeners with a combination of heroics and strong rhythms to someone like Hawthorne who explored the subject of distance in some of his writings, have always known that people need to be in the proper relationship with a story so that they can gain its maximum effects. Although authors cannot do anything about any private irrational fears a reader may have, they can mute excessive horrors, avoid the intensely painful, sentimental, or maudlin, and do what they can to bring him close to or keep him far from the action of a story. On a graduated scale, a first-person point of view with the narrator as protagonist will place a reader closest to the action, and a third-person objective view will place a reader farthest from the action. Other point of view possibilities range in between. Of course other devices of fiction also effect distance—tone, mood, pacing—as other devices can effect or control point of view.

In the hands of a skillful writer, point of view not only helps to control distance and to delineate meaning, but also affects every aspect of the story-teller's craft. A proper point of view contributes to tone, mood, characterization, pacing, and plot. A story is a cohesive unit wherein all the parts contribute to the whole. It is, therefore, very difficult to separate a single device of fiction and speak of it as though it can be satisfactorily separated from the total range of techniques an author uses in the creation of a particular story. Point of view, thus, is a part of the total patterning of a piece of fiction.

Mary Rohrberger

SECOND-PERSON POINT OF VIEW

Although the current epidemic of narrative studies inexorably directs our attention to the hopeless generality of long-accepted terms such as "point of view" and "reader," these terms remain useful, even retain vestiges of their original sense, not only because they dominate our heritage of narrative theory, but also because, recognized as areas of concern rather than single items, they name what must still be our basic considerations. For example, although we recognize the distinctions between narratees internal to the story and the reader, who is always external, and even the distinctions between ourselves as flesh-and-blood readers and the "implied reader" or "ideal reader"—not to mention the even more subtle distinction between the "implied reader" of the rhetorical critic and the "implied reader" of the phenomenological critic—we still attend to "reader" in all its meanings, from noun-of-address to some kind of cocreator of text. We simply introduce additional terms and descriptions to clarify the distinctions.

Point of view, too, remains central, and despite full awareness of Wayne Booth's caveats in *Rhetoric of Fiction*, 1961 (and full agreement with their implications even in the face of rejoinders such as those of David Goldknopf, expressed in his article "The Confessional Increment: A New Look at the I-Narrator," in *Journal of Aesthetics and Art Criticism*), we still find the grammar of personal pronouns a convenient classification. We do note, of course, that the mere presence of the pronoun "I" does not assert a first-person narrator, and we offer significant subclasses in the two traditional categories of first-person and third-person point of view. Categories of person, however, pervade our discussions of point of view; therefore, "second-person point of view" can name a class of narratives or stretches within longer narratives distinct from first-person and third-person narratives. This class has been little noticed, in fact often summarily dismissed as composed of one or two experiments for the sake of experiment, but increasing numbers of whole works and increased awareness of the embedding of second-person narrative stretches within works invite analysis. Recent critical focus on the epic situation—the teller or narrator in the act of telling and the listener or narratee—offers further impetus to investigate the complexities of this category.

We are not the first to take critical interest in this kind of narrative. In 1965, Bruce Morrissette published an article, "Narrative 'You' in Contemporary Literature," in *Comparative Literature Studies*, the avowed purpose of which was to "trace a certain amount of historical background, through a survey of samples which cannot hope to be exhaustive; examine the evolution of narrative use of 'you' in the twentieth century; and analyse as closely as possible the structural, esthetic, and metaphysical significance of the second-person technique." The present paper is an extension of his third aim, attempting to describe more completely this category of narrative by extending

Morrissette's discussion of some of the examples he mentions and investigating several additional examples in order to describe more fully some of the various effects possible within the class. Our method is to analyze the narrative discourse as dramatic utterance (a full background discussion of dramatic analysis as a critical approach to literature and performance of literature being furnished in Don Geiger's *The Dramatic Impulse in Modern Poetics*, 1968) and to clarify relationships between narrator, protagonist, and narratee by substituting pronouns in order to compare their effects. Roland Barthes proposes this technique in "An Introduction to the Structural Analysis of Narrative" in *New Literary History*, and Katherine Passias discusses it in "Deep and Surface Structure of the Narrative Pronoun *Vous* in Butor's *La Modification* and Its Relationship to Free Indirect Style" in *Language and Style*.

A brief description of some characteristics of the other two modes will provide a necessary basis for our discussion. For example, we need to note possible variations of distance and opportunities for irony in the other two narrative modes before we examine the possibilities for second-person narratives. We accept Bertil Romberg's assertion, expressed in his *Studies in the Narrative Technique of the First-Person Novel* (1962), that first-person narrators are by definition within the fiction of the text. They may be major characters, minor characters, "runners beside the carriage," or even distant observers. Because they exist within the world of the text, they are subject to its limitations. The first-person narrator has human limitations of time and space. Irony, however, is possible because the I-narrator and the I-participant may be close or distant along many lines, most of those lines of distance (intellectual, moral, physical, psychological) made possible by distance in time between narrator and actant. Irony can result from a blend, such as in Frank O'Connor's "My Oedipus Complex," in which the vocabulary and observation are those of an adult but the viewpoint is limited to that of the child.

Third-person narrators, even observers, are external to the fiction. They may be fully omniscient, with privileged information about all characters, or partially omniscient, or omniscience may be limited to a single character. The latter of course most nearly resembles a first-person narrator; in both cases we get the story through the consciousness of one person. Each of these kinds of narration has different possibilities. Third-person observers may be the most nearly "neutral" narrators possible if, along with eschewing interior views, they also reject commentary. They may appear to be "absent" or at least totally uninvolved. The "absent narrator" may be the only effect not available to second-person narratives.

To appreciate fully the flexibilities of third-person narration, we look at some of Seymour Chatman's distinctions, outlined in *Story and Discourse: Narrative Structure in Fiction and Film* (1978), and discriminate between "camera angle," which we call "perspective," and "point of view" defined according to interior views. We must attend also to Chatman's other distinction, which he calls "voice." This "voice," recognized essentially through the vocabulary and world view of the utterance, accounts for distance between narrator and character when they share the same perspective and the consciousness of the character. Therefore, even though an author may achieve the ironic effects of a first-person narrator by limiting omniscience to a single character, even scrupulous adherence to this device allows variations in distance between narrator and character different from those of I-narrators.

It should be noted that perspective may establish point of view as well as do interior views. John Collier's "The Chaser," although it contains no privileged information of any kind, seems to be third-person limited because we always get only the young man's perspective, and we appreciate the irony of the old man's remarks no less than if the young man were his own narrator. The effects of perspective are especially important in Michel Butor's *A Change of Heart* (1957), probably the best known second-person narrative.

The traditional effect of third-person omniscience is, of course, that shift from the view of one character to that of another, called "bouncing" by E. M. Forster. By showing us the story first through one character, then through another, the author can heighten for the reader the irony of any single character's limited views. This bouncing can result from changes in interior views as well as from changes in perspective.

Narratees vary independently from the grammatical person of the narrator. From Albert Camus' *The Fall* (1956) to Eudora Welty's *The Ponder Heart* (1954), we find the narratees within first-person fiction and therefore at least somewhat distanced from the reader. We also have in first-person the external narratees of Camus' *The Stranger* (1942) and Charles Dickens' *David Copperfield* (1849-1850). Except under unusual circumstances, third-person narratives have external narratees, the entire epic situation outside the story. In second-person narratives the primary "you," because he or she is an actant by definition, is internal to the story, but the relationship of this "you" to the external reader may vary within the text, providing a source of complexity in the texture of the story.

It should be conceded here that the reader always has some sense of being the narratee regardless. Katherine Passias remarks that "The reader of any text, despite the narrative pronoun used, is always the receiver of the message. No matter how involved he may be in a narrative, there is an underlying awareness that the message is about 'the other.' " In other words, we always retain a sense of distance from the actants, however involved we get, and we never feel completely distanced as narratees no matter the circumstances within the text. We forget for long stretches of Erich Maria Remarque's *The Night in Lisbon* (1963) that the narratee is internal, like the speaker, a displaced person; and for most of Emily Brontë's *Wuthering Heights* (1847) we disregard the itinerant gentleman hearing this tale. Even when the narratee directly causes the narration, as Gerald Prince in his "Notes towards a categorization of Fictional 'Narratees' " in *Genre* reminds us about the caliph in *The Arabian Night's Entertainments*, we feel like the primary narratee, however unacknowledged.

Another effect allowed by third-person omniscience is indirect discourse, differing from both stream-of-consciousness and other interior views by being a blend of narrator and character, a blend that allows the reader to see from the character's view and at the same time to stand with the narrator outside the character, seeing both the character and what the character sees, a double vision that inevitably creates irony. (This effect is discussed in Judith C. Espinola's "The Nature, Function, and Performance of Indirect Discourse in Prose Fiction," in *Speech Monographs*.) This effect is also possible in first-person narrative, but usually functions in a different way. If the I-narrator is a major character and close to that character, then indirect discourse for that character is not possible, the enabling distance between the two thus being absent. Possibilities for indirect discourse in second-person narratives will be noted as specific examples are considered.

A careful study of second-person narrative mode will demonstrate its flexibility in allowing for all the various effects of the other two narrative modes; but first we must delineate this class. Obviously the "you" addressed must be an actant; otherwise, we are dealing only with the you-narratee present at least implicitly in every narrative even if it is the narrator herself or himself; but this distinction is not enough. Morrissette discusses the "guidebook you" ("You see the Cabildo on your left and the Presbytery on your right"), the "advertisement you" ("You will love your new car"), and the "cookbook you" ("You add four eggs, then the flour mixture"). Later, he alludes to the "courtroom you" ("You went to his house, found him alone, and shot him"). Perhaps the most common usage is "you" to mean the impersonal "one," as in "When you try too hard, you get tense," meaning "When one (anyone) tries too hard, one gets tense."

Morrissette denigrates the "journalistic you," becoming increasingly common in reviews, which is apparently an attempt to make the reported experience at the same time personal and generalized. "You walked from the subway exit at Sheridan Square down Christopher Street and entered the Theatre de Lys." Presumably the reader is invited to identify with the actant and simultaneously see the action as something anyone would do.

Narrative-you differs from most of the examples just mentioned in that this "you" has performed a specific action. The you-utterance is neither command nor accusation, nor yet generalization, but report. This reporting of action endows all narratives with a dual time, however close these two "tracts" may approach each other: the event or happening time and the time of the telling. Verbs in narrative are usually past tense, but the epic present is also possible, its essential "pastness" readily exposed by noting that past tense verbs are equally sensible in the context. This technique of substituting verbs unequiv-ocally distinguishes the present tense of Rumer Godden's "You Need to Go Upstairs" and Carlos Fuentes' *Aura* (1962) from the present tense of the guidebook/cookbook, in which past tense verbs create nonsense. We study the sense rather than the form to ascertain specific past action.

In narrative even future tense does not violate this dual time; that is, although future tense verbs appear in narratives, they are future to the nar-rated event rather than the narrative utterance. ("Jane will marry Ralph and they will have two boys" is understood to occur after that spot in the story but not after the utterance of the telling.) This distinction clearly eliminates, for example, Gerald Manley Hopkins' "Spring and Fall." "You will weep and know why" is prediction, not reported action, and not within any kind of fictional time; Margaret does not qualify as a protagonist. This dual time is a key to distinguishing second-person narratives from other kinds of "you-utterances" even when the you-addressee is an actant.

This same trait will help us eliminate that class of you-statements we call apostrophe, a class absent from Morrissette's discussion. The original meaning of "turning aside" is also a help. In a eulogy on Abraham Lincoln, for example, an extended address to him, even if it contained past-tense verbs, would hardly invite the classification of narrative. The context denies the label. What about the apostrophe that stands out of such a context, the entire utterance an address to a being or concept? Most examples contain the imperative "you"—"Death be not proud"—and the verbs of the indicative mode are in present or future tense, not reporting a past action but characterizing the object of address by generalized habitual or typical actions. Even apart from the verb distinctions, apostrophe is in a single time frame, what Jonathan Culler calls "the set of all possible nows," and therefore lacks the dual time necessary for narrative.

Past action alone, however, may make an event but not a narrative. "You made an error in yesterday's game" is not a narrative, although it qualifies as a segment of one. Contemporary experimental writers, rejecting scale and logical sequence as requisites of story, discourage criteria such as length and coherence as distinctive features of narrative, but we must at least nod toward length and some kind of development of events to explain why the sentence about errors is not a narrative whereas even the shortest story of Russel Edson is; see, for example, *The Very Thing That Happens: Fables and Draw-ings* (1964). We can agree that a narrative is at least a string of events as opposed to one, although they may occur within a short period of time and the telling of them may be brief.

A poem such as James Seay's "Let Not Your Hart be Truble" illustrates the need for the foregoing distinctions. With its thirty-one lines, it qualifies on the basis of length, in a way that Richard Brautigan's "Loading Mercury with a Pitchfork" does not. Further, the speaker reports an action performed by the you-addressee, and both speaker and you-addressee are within the same time, unlike the speaker and you-addressee of most apostrophe. Still, although both speaker and addressee are within the world of the text, no dual time is present; the action reported is single. To paraphrase unjustly, the speaker says, "You passed my car on a blind curve," and the rest of the utterance is merely address to the unseen, absent addressee.

Adrienne Rich's "Rape," on the other hand, although only thirty lines long, can qualify as a narrative. The third, fourth, and fifth stanzas, although the verbs are in the present tense, report a past action. In the first two stanzas the time is continuous present. We can change the "you" to "I" to illustrate that narrator and actant may be the same, like an I-narrator, but past tense verbs alter the passage significantly. The substitution of both verbs and pronouns works in the middle stanzas, that segment that qualifies the text as narrative. "And so, when the time came, I had to turn to him . . . I had to confess to him, I was guilty of the crime of having been forced. . . . And I saw his blue eyes, . . . his hand typed out the details. . . ." This "story" begins with "I had to turn to him" and ends with "he thought he knew what I secretly wanted." In the final stanza the shift in the "you" is exposed by the attempt to make the verbs past tense. The substitution does not work. We cannot allow "and if, in the sickening light of the precinct, my details sounded like a portrait of my confessor, did I swallow, did I deny them, did I lie my way home?" The past tense, no matter the pronouns, distorts the question.

Clearly one could make a case for this poem as not narrative but lyric, an utterance, hypothetical or fictionally real, from speaker to herself or to another woman, all of the utterance occurring in the "now" of the interrogation. In any case, the "you" of the final stanza functions differently from the earlier uses. Perhaps the narrative traits that exist at least as possibility contribute to the poem's resonance, but without doubt the final "you" invites the listener into the poem in a way different from the earlier ones.

This sort of shifting of referents for "you" is not unusual in second-person narratives and creates what we might call a "superficial ambiguity," superficial in that careful analysis of the terms will clarify differences and resolve the ambiguity, but otherwise we read allowing all the possibilities to hover around the "you." Mary McCarthy's "The Genial Host" is a good example of this kind of shifting. The first paragraph could be the utterance of an I-narrator using the indefinite "you" speaking to an undefined external narratee. We can illustrate by interpolating before the first words some inanity like, "I tell you, he was something else." Then the text begins, "When he telephoned to ask you to do something, . . . he let you know. . . . you never had to order blind." The end of the second paragraph, however, precludes the identity of "you" with an unidentified narratee or an impersonal "one": ". . . with your real friends you seemed to prefer those whose spheres of interest were larger rather than smaller than your own—or at any rate to see more of them, if you could—but in those cases you were able to be sure that you *liked them for themselves.*" This "you" is obviously not indefinite; the generality that remains is one of time—the habitual past, not the specific of the preterit or perfective past.

The next paragraph uses the same generalized verb but the "you" has changed again. No longer exclusively the specific "you" of the preceding paragraph, it includes a group of which that "you" is a member: "you poor ones," and "you half-hated him before your finger touched the doorbell." Both singular and plural meanings hover around the "you" of the following paragraph. For several more pages the narrator generalizes about experiences "you" have had with the host—sometimes the specific "you," sometimes the group.

Finally the event becomes specific—not "all those dinner parties" but "that night," and for two paragraphs "you" does not appear in the narration. In fact, at one point the narrator refers to all the guests as "them," the "you" apparently for the moment forgotten. "Pflaumen made a great bustle of seating the guests, and finally plumped himself down at the head of the table and beamed at them all as if to say, 'Isn't this cozy?' "

From that point the "you" is specifically the protagonist, though some generalized events mix with the specifics. "Across the table from you, someone refused," and "Sitting at his left hand, you looked down at your plate," but also "When you came to think about it, the Jewish paterfamilias was not the only figure that kept hovering behind your host's well-padded shoulder," and "In most of the men, . . . you saw only vestigial traces of the mother." This same mixture of generalized actions and specific actions with the specific "you" make up the rest of the story. The penultimate paragraph is mostly specific, but the final paragraph, a single sentence, manages to be both specific—a promise uttered in a particular time—and a generality about the future which matches the "every time" generality of the opening.

> You had forgotten about the Berolzheimers. Now you hesitated, weighing the invitation. Sooner or later you would break with him, you knew. But not yet, not while you were still so poor, so loverless, so lonely. "All right," you said, "you can pick me up at my place."
>
> The time after the next, you promised yourself, you would surely refuse.

Except for the ambiguity of the opening paragraph, the reader cannot be the narratee. The protagonist is the narratee throughout, except for those passages addressed to the group of which she is a member. Who is the narrator? This narrative seems equivalent to third-person limited in that we have only the protagonist's views, but like many third-person limited narrators, this narrator seems superior to the protagonist, wiser, even more articulate. We could label this narrative "second-person, limited omniscience."

Not all second-person narrators function in this way. Rumer Godden's "You

Need to Go Upstairs" seems like a first-person narrative. Godden wrote the story in response to a request from some nuns operating a home for blind children. The protagonist, Ally, is a blind child, and all the vocabulary and perceptions are suitable to her, the nature of the request for the story perhaps having influenced its vocabulary: "You sit with your legs straight in front of you; they have come out from their winter stockings and are very thin and knobbly, but the sun is beginning to warm them gently as if it were glad to see them again." This story contradicts, or at least offers an exception to, Butor's assertion, in "L'Usage des Pronoms Personnels dans le Roman," in *Les Temps Modernes*, that second-person narratives are always didactic in the sense that the narrator tells the other characters something they do not already know. Ally both knows and can articulate all that the narrator says; the narrative voice is neither didactic nor accusing. The only passages that become distorted with the substitution of "I" and past tense verbs are those in which the "cookbook you" occurs, making these passages seem to be interior speech and not the narrator's voice at all:

> From the chairs to the poplars is easy; you can hear them straining and moving their branches just enough to tell you where they are. There are two, and when you are up to them, you separate your hands the distance apart you think they will be and you do not hit them, you find them; their trunks are under your hands and you stay to feel those trunks; they are rough and smooth together; they are like people, they are alive.

The effect is that at that moment there is no distance between narrator and Ally; the voice is Ally's alone.

The only significant sense of "other" between Ally and the narrator occurs in passages of encouragement or caution: "You won't fall, the cinder smell has warned you," and "Are you facing the right way?" These passages could certainly be interior to Ally, but they at least signify a dichotomy of self— that voice we establish within ourselves to encourage, for example—a kind of intrapersonal discourse different from passages such as the following:

> With the smells come the house sounds, all so familiar: Doreen's footsteps in the kitchen: a whirring like insects from the refrigerator and the clocks: a curtain flapping in the wind and a tapping, a tiny rustle from the canary. You know all these things better than anyone else.

Still, the "other" voice addressing Ally is not more sophisticated or more knowledgeable than she.

If Ally is narrator, protagonist, and narratee, where is the reader? We are involved because the story is narrated as it happens, the telling time and event time simultaneous. Some phrases indicate that Ally is sharing the experience with an "other"—the reader, for example, "Now you let go of the door— like this. . . ." The phrase "like this" occurs several times. This expression and the "cookbook you" indicate some sense of audience for Ally. To note the relationship of this narrative to the "first-person-major-character" narrative, we might label it "second-person-personal." The narrator is entirely within the protagonist.

Butor's own novel more nearly corresponds to the you-narrative he describes in which the narrative voice is more knowing. So much has been written about *A Change of Heart*, some of it conflicting interpretations, that we need only nod toward it here. A few traits bear mentioning, however, as evidence of the diversity possible within second-person narratives, such as Butor's metaphysical positing, which reminds us of writers such as Jorge Luis Borges. This trait, although not typical of you-narratives, is at least permitted by the form. Another noteworthy device in *A Change of Heart* is the extensive use of perspective to establish that we experience this story from within (adulterous-husband) Léon's consciousness. Still, there is at times a distance between the narrator and Léon sufficient to allow irony. Does the narrator— or, better, the narrative voice, because we have not yet established a narrator—judge Léon to be justified?

This same kind of distance enables an irony in stretches of indirect discourse. About Léon's children we read the following words:

> Really they're at the worst possible age, they've lost the grace and charm of small children whom you can play with in the evenings like enchanting toys, and they're all too young still, even Madeleine, to be talked to like grown-ups, like friends; you can't take a real interest in their studies because of your job, your responsibilities and other preoccupations, yet you have to put up with their noise. . . .

Entirely absent here is the superior voice of earlier passages. These words are Léon's, uninterpreted by any other voice, but we as readers feel a kinship with the "consciousness" that chose to report them, and they are therefore evidence of distance. Other evidence of possible distance occurs in a description of Léon's response to Cécile: ". . . if at that time you had known Cavalcanti's poetry you'd have said that she made the air shimmer with light." Does Léon now, that is at the time of this utterance, know Cavalcanti? Or is it only the narrator who knows?

We can find an occasional utterance that betrays an awareness of audience other than narrator and protagonist. When Léon is reading the train schedule, we get information we could not expect the narrative voice to say to him or him to say to himself. "This train . . . will wait for twenty-three minutes at Chambery to allow for a connection, and again at the frontier from 4:28 to 5:18 for customs formalities (that tiny house next to the word Modane is the symbol for the Customs)." The information in parentheses seems to be an announcement to some kind of audience.

Clearly Butor's narrator eludes neat classification. Morrissette offers a tenable explanation: "The voice which says *vous* is less that of the character than of the author, or, better still, that of a persona, invisible, but powerfully present, who serves as the center of consciousness in the novel." We could label this narrative voice "second-person impersonal center of consciousness" because, although the voice seems to be inside Léon, it is strangely unemotional and uninvolved, compared with, say, the voice in "The Genial Host," which almost upbraids, and the voice in "You Need to Go Upstairs," which encourages.

Rex Stout's *How Like a God* (1929) was, according to Morrissette, "apparently, the first thoroughgoing second-person novel," but except for contemporary reviews, it caused little critical comment, perhaps because the innovative quality of the you-mode in the novel is difficult to isolate from the innovative handling of time. The novel contains sections in italics with third-person narration, which, juxtaposed, tell chronologically of the protagonist's suspense-filled trip up to the third floor of an apartment house to murder the woman whom he cannot resist despite his loathing for what she does to his life. Separating these third-person italicized sections are long stretches in the past-tense you-mode, enough longer than the italicized portions to put the novel in the class of you-narratives despite the mixture.

The second-person sections contain more "showing" than do those in *A Change of Heart* and less stream-of-consciousness, and we find none of that use of perspective. As in the other examples, however, we find a movement of the "narrative-voice" toward and from the protagonist. A paragraph will illustrate:

> You fairly and visibly trembled with timidity that first afternoon in the garden when Dick introduced you to this sister Erma. Yes, you were always timid with Erma Carr, damn her! Partly perhaps it was the house, the servants, the motor cars, the glistening fountains, the clothes-closets lined with fragrant cedar? Perhaps, but god knows Erma was enough. You see now that you resented her and felt her cold presumption that first day. Then you were charmed and submerged and inexpressibly timid.

The exterior voice of the first sentence blends easily into the interior expression of the expletives, surely the protagonist's. The narrator, although often judgmental, never seems more knowledgeable, more sophisticated, or more articulate than the protagonist, who is, after all, a writer himself, and a published one at that. Even more than the one in "You Need to Go Upstairs," this narrative seems to be a "second-person other self."

A full report of the analyses of other second-person narratives, although doubtless essential for the full study sure to be written some day, would not offer enough new insights here to justify the space. We note other examples only briefly, to call attention to their unique features that expand our description of the class. "Main Street Morning" by Natalie L. M. Petesch is perhaps the most "matter-of-fact" example we have in this group. Unwary readers may not even notice the second-person form. The "you" is unambiguous, the relationship stable between the narratee that is the you-protagonist and the unacknowledged narratee-reader. The style, however, unlike that of "You Need to Go Upstairs," changes even within one paragraph, suggesting that the voice is sometimes entirely Marie and sometimes an "other," much like that "invisible but present" persona Morrissette posits for *A Change of Heart*, although the presence here is less assertive and never distant from the you-protagonist. There is no irony here.

Another short story also demonstrates that you-narratives need not appear experimental. Robert Harvey's "Yes" appeared in the November, 1979, issue of *Blueboy*. The second-person protagonist is a young gay male fairly recently moved to California. The narrator, although not entirely unsupportive ("You are a lean and handsome and sensitive male," he begins), seems external, despite the fact that all of the perceptions seem to be those of the protagonist, perhaps because the language is unimaginative; the following paragraph is typical:

> It is 6:45 A.M. and your alarm clock snarls. You must wrench yourself out of the double bed in your new apartment. You must shower, shave, blow-dry your hair, guzzle a cup of instant coffee then catch the trolly to your new job. You are a teller at a bank. You are an artist, naturally, but at the moment no one will pay for your art.

Only the "naturally" betrays any spark of wryness or humor.

"The House of Ecstacy" by Ralph Milne Farley offers a unique relationship between you-protagonist and you-narratee. The narrator, although offering privileged information only about the protagonist, nevertheless seems external to both protagonist and story. The opening lines expose the device:

> This actually happened to you. And when I say "you," I mean *you*—now reading these very words. For I know something about you—something deeply personal—something which, however, I am afraid that you have forgotten.
> You're puzzled? You don't believe me? Read on, and I'll prove it to you—you'll see that I am right.

The narrator proceeds to tell "you" what "you" did under the spell of a madman, especially that "you" promised a despairing beauty that "you" would indeed remember the house number and return to rescue her. No other mention of the you-as-reader occurs until the final four paragraphs:

> You consider yourself to be a man of your word, don't you? And yet you have never returned to the house of ecstacy to rescue that girl, although you solemnly promised her that you would.
> I have now told you all that I myself know of the episode. But unfortunately I do not know the address of the house of ecstacy. You need that address. You have to have that address, if you are ever to rescue the girl who loved and trusted you.

Try hard, my friend, try hard.
Can't you remember? You *must* remember!

Two novels by Carlos Fuentes would offer conclusive proof that the second-person mode is flexible even if we had no other examples. *Aura* is in the realm of the marvelous as opposed to the fantastic, as the events are incredible even within the reality of the story. The present tense prevails except for the future use in Spanish that has the quality of present tense. The use of second-person familiar contrasts with Butor's use of *vous*, although apparently neither choice is significant. Morrissette reports that "even French critics, such as Delboville, have accepted the *vous* rather than *tu* as the character speaking to himself."

Aura could be told in the first-person except for those instances when the protagonist could not logically speak for himself, the action being in the present tense, such as when he is sleeping or dreaming: "Your sleep is heavy and unsatisfying." An italicized section identifies a dream: ". . . *in the depths of the dark abyss, in your silent dream with its mouths opening in silence, you see her coming toward you from the blackness of the abyss, you see her crawling toward you.* . . ." Otherwise, despite the present tense, an I-narrator could reasonably tell the story except for one other passage, the final paragraphs, in which substitution of "I" would undermine the authority of the prediction.

Fuentes' *A Change of Skin* (1968) is in a class alone, although most of it is you-narration. The novel is in so many ways experimental that to single out its second-person characteristics seems futile, even impossible; but its unique use of you-narrative must be noted. This intricate and elaborate novel, moving freely through time and space, both intertwining and merging several plot lines, uses verbs in both past and present tense and both "*tu*" and "*Ustedes*" for the second-person narration. The narrator is, paradoxically, "first-person omniscient," but the text nevertheless qualifies as a second-person narrative because most of it is addressed to various actants. The narrator refers to himself only occasionally, most of the novel being about other people, most of it addressed to them; yet the final words of the novel seem almost to seal the first-person quality. Although he places himself inside the novel, the narrator addresses several characters alternately as "you" and assumes all the powers of omniscience: internal monologues, privileged information, physical details available only to one who is present in the scene. We find the bouncing of third-person omniscience within this second-person mode uttered by an internal first-person narrator.

Beach Red (1945), a war novel by Peter Bowman, has much the same mixture in the narration that we have noted in other examples: the protagonist's thoughts, his observations, and some warning that could come from within himself, "Wind up all the little alarm clocks of your mind. Look around." Still, the narrator is distant from the you-protagonist by more than just wiser judgment and greater ability to articulate. He speaks after the hero's death:

> You do not see the unwashed face of Private Whitney poke itself through the grass and survey the ground in clinical analysis, then wave to the other members of your squad emerging from the brush. You do not see him approach you at a crouch and look down at the hole in your side and lift up your left wrist and press his finger against it to detect a pulse.

The form of the lines, according to the blurb on the jacket, was meant to represent not poetry but "the rigid timing by which each step of such an action is governed." This text is an obvious example of one advantage of second-person over first-person narrative. The I-narrator's voice stops with death.

One final example will illustrate that the you-narrative is distinct even from other kinds of you-allegories. The you-actant of W. S. Merwin's "Unchopping a Tree" does not make the text a true narrative. It is the "cookbook you," where past tense verbs would be nonsense. Joyce Carol Oates's "Journey," on the other hand, although no less allegorical, is a narrative. Past tense verbs could be substituted without distortion. Because the action is on a symbolic level, the reader could comfortably be the narratee. The narrator's utterance is "open," that is, directed toward any and all people outside the text. The story provides our only example of "second-person-open," since even "House of Ecstacy" could not be addressed to a collective "you."

In summary, the flexibilities within the second-person mode comparable to those within the other two modes have been noted. Second-person allows irony, indirect discourse, interior monologues, bouncing, various kinds of distance, and fluctuations of distance between narrator and protagonist. It admits flexible handling of time and space. Experimentation is possible but not inevitable. The only major narrative effect denied this mode is the "absent narrator." Narration sufficient to establish the "you" establishes a consciousness that generates the you-utterance.

What features does it offer different from those of the other modes? The most obvious distinction is the ambiguity, to an extent unavoidable, but often exploited within works. Especially in English any "you" offers a degree of ambiguity. It is the most ambiguous of the personal pronouns, having the same form and the same attendant verbs for singular and plural, masculine and feminine. Further, the only case change is for the possessive. Moreover, as has been mentioned earlier, everyday language offers a variety of you-usage: imperative, impersonal "one," and so forth. Because first and third person pronouns have less ambiguity of form and less flexibility of usage (even considering the possibilities for indefinite "we" and "they"), greater superficial ambiguity is inevitable in the second-person mode, and in some examples the ambiguity is pervasive.

The you-mode has yet another advantage. It offers the intimacy with the character enabled by the first-person mode without the presumptuous quality of the I-narrator. In *A Change of Heart*, for example, we might eventually resent Léon's assumption that we care enough for him to endure a report of his every perception. (See Goldknopf for a full discussion of this effect.) The "you," even in those cases in which it could be considered a "disguised I," is somehow less assertive. Consider "You are called Ishmael." Immediately the character is relieved of the responsibility for earning his right to our attention.

We do not presume to predict the growth and development of second-person point of view, but we insist that these examples already assert its flexibility and viability as a narrative mode. It will bear watching.

Mary Frances Hopkins and *Leon Perkins*

SHORT FICTION: BEGINNINGS TO 1800

Rudyard Kipling, one of the greatest tellers of tales in modern times, accepted the gold medal of The Royal Society of Literature with a speech in which he stressed the relationship between complex modern literature and simple primitive tales: he traced the first short story back to the cavemen. Some Urgk or Mneegleeg—human nature urges us to have a name for him, even if we have to make it up—returned (one supposes) from the hunt with an exaggerated tale of his own prowess; the art of fiction, artistic lying, was born.

Down the centuries we have invented names (Caspar, Melchior, and Balthasar for the Three Magi) for characters or tales to go along with names, to commemorate historic events, to raise a historic character (from Arthur the *dux bellorum* or war leader to "The Once and Future King," from John Chapman to Johnny Appleseed) to mythical importance, to enshrine the values of the society (Achilles, Aeneas), to make masterpieces, or to make jokes. People have told stories and read them to their children; sung them and written them down for posterity; used them to convey information and to preserve truths, as cautionary tales, as anecdotes, as jests, as parables; and preserved pieces of the past for us or cut them from whole cloth to satisfy man's desire for escape, for fantasy. Celebrating or mocking, instructing or merely entertaining, stories have been told and written for a thousand different purposes and even "without purpose" (for art's sake). The tales of the people have enshrined the history and the aspirations of the race, the myths of the past, the visions of the future. With sugar coatings of entertainment, facts and values were transmitted to generation after generation, handed down through stories told to the young and by the men around the campfires, long stories of heroic deeds and also traditional jokes and riddles—the whole great oral tradition of the people and, much later, the Great Tradition of literature.

When Elizabeth Bowen in the Preface to her *Faber Book of Short Stories* (1936) says that the short story is "a young art, is a child of this century," she is for her purposes very much limiting the definition of the short story. Brief narrative fiction is as old as mankind, and the literature of the short story is as old as writing.

Long before people could write, the tales generated by the various folk cultures were cast into verse (for both mnemonic and artistic reasons) and collected into huge narrative poems. Transmitted by word of mouth, these exciting and glorious legends of a heroic age were usually unified by the central figure of a hero; he united the various exploits much as the picaresque hero later found in the novel held together a string of exciting episodes. The hero was, in effect, involved in a series of short stories which were recited (sometimes with musical accompaniment, such as a harp) rather than sung (like lyrics) or acted (like plays).

All the elements of the modern short story (expert Laurence Perrine, for example, identifies them as escape and interpretation, plot, character, theme, point of view, symbol and irony, emotion and humor, fantasy, and values) were present in surprising sophistication in the early short-story collections and developments we call folk epics. Those, like Topsy, "just growed"; others were art epics, the product of a single author, but he often drew on ancient folktales for both content and technique. The anonymous and presumably Christian author of *Beowulf* (c. 1000), the oldest epic narrative in any modern European tongue (although a speaker of modern English, as harried students will testify, has a great difficulty with its Old English), may have given his monster a name (Grendel, suggesting *grund*, that is, bottom; Grendel's dam, who also appears strikingly in the epic, is a resident of the watery depths, a kind of sea monster, while the Dragon who guards the treasure trove at the end of *Beowulf* is a creature of earth and fire), but he drew on the unnamed monsters of folktales. In his character Wiglaf and in the relationships at the court of King Hrothgar, where much of the exciting action of *Beowulf* is set, the author presented the *comitatus* interdependence of the people of ancient times that is a feature of folktales, as are the characteristics of the bold hero who unifies the two separate stories of the poem which have clear analogues in Scandinavian folklore. Folktales certainly played a part in any other epics of *Beowulf*'s type and period that may have once fascinated the folk when *scops* or minstrels sang in the great halls. Of them we know nothing, for *Beowulf* is the only manuscript that has survived Henry VIII's dissolution of the monasteries. Its art and its appeal are such, however, that it cannot have been a unique creation.

The Anglo-Saxon writer, stitching together old pagan tales for the edification and entertainment of the Dark Ages in the late seventh or early eighth century, had his counterpart later in the authors of such art epics as the *The Song of Roland*, the earliest and best work of this sort from France (c. 1100). The author of *Beowulf* also used historical details from Icelandic sagas and other sources; and so did the author of the Roland epic (slightly more than four thousand ten-syllable lines to be sung, thus a *chanson*), the kernel of whose story is an ambush in the Pyrenees in the year 778, in which the Basques killed one Hruodlandus (as the Latin has it in the chronicles) of the army of Charlemagne. The interweaving of fiction and fact remains basic to storytelling today, and modern American novels and short stories, particularly, are noted for it.

Indeed, the movement toward making fiction sound like fact and fact like fiction is one of the major ones in the history of narrative. The ancient writers of epics were chiefly interested in larger-than-life heroes who could embody the life-preserving values of the society. *Beowulf* preaches love of glory and of freedom, respect for authority and for women, bravery in pursuit of truth and honor, strength, and the repression of sentiment, among other ideals. Similarly, in the *chansons de geste* (exploit songs) of which the *The Song of Roland* is the best of many, feudal virtues of loyalty, fortitude and the like are emphasized. Fact and fiction are enlisted in the cause of inculcating virtue.

The same is true of art epics such as Vergil's *Aeneid* (c. 29-19 B. C.) and John Milton's *Paradise Lost* (1667), which partake of both folklore and invention, myth and history, in the tradition of the writer (or writers) we call Homer, the author of the *Iliad* and the *Odyssey* (about the ninth century B. C.). Like the Bible and its Apocrypha, the Talmud with its Haggadah (illustrative stories, parables, and legends), and other ancient and immensely influential scriptures, epic poetry contains many short stories embedded in didactic and inspiring contexts.

There is, of course, more to be said about the nature and influence of epics of the Homeric tradition than can be hinted at in this brief survey, but we might in passing just note that some of the devices of the epic persist in narrative fiction. We may no longer write in quantitative hexameter with epic similes and stereotyped epithets, invoking the Muse, and so forth; but we often jump into the story *in medias res*, use monologues and descriptive passages, and even find equivalents (heredity, environment, psychology, economics, and the like) for the intervention of inexorable forces (the gods). Homer was the first genius of Western literature; his influence on narrative art is still strongly felt.

If Homer was (as Frank Byron Jevons in his classic *History of Greek Literature*, 1886, claims) "reading for kings," then the eighth century B. C. epic poet Hesiod, author of *Works and Days* and *The Theogony*, was "for peasants." He proposed to present truth, but he dealt in superstition and mythology as well and added something to storytelling, influencing the epics of Thebes, Troy, Hercules, and others that followed. Techniques of storytelling developed by Homer and Hesiod are still evident in fiction.

There were far more epics written by anonymous people, folk epics collecting old stories and legends and superstitions and myths. Sometimes they tell us more of how people lived and thought than such historical treatises as (for example) those of ancient China: the *Pan Piao, Pan Ku*, and *Pan Chao* histories of the Han Dynasty (covering the century before the birth of Christ), or the travels in India and beyond of Fa Hsien (c. 399-414) and other explorers and taletellers. In time, the impulses of epic and history created on the basis of many age-old tales collections such as *The Record of Travels in the West* (fourteenth century)—in which one Hsuan Tsang ventures to India to obtain Buddhist books and becomes involved in many escapades and wonderful adventures, the journey serving merely as an excuse—and even longer fictions of intrigue, love, lawlessness, and the miraculous. A still-popular Chinese novel of the middle fourteenth century is the *Romance of the Three Kingdoms* (attributed to one Lo Kuan-chung), a rousing series of episodes of derring-do a thousand years before.

Tales and legends were woven into other early masterpieces of Oriental literature, from the massive masterpiece (sixty thousand couplets) of *Shah Namah* (1010, *The Book of Kings*) of the court poet of Sultan Mahomet of Ghazna, Firdausi, the Persian genius (c. 935-1020), to little stories that served as source material for William Shakespeare and other geniuses of the West. *The Book of Kings* undertakes to cover about four thousand years of Persian history and to contain the histories of great reigns and minor adventures (such as that of *Sohrab and Rustum*, retold by Matthew Arnold in 1853). Short stories are interspersed also throughout the *Khamsa* (*Quintet*) of narrative poems by Persia's other great classical poet, Nizāmī Ganjāvī (c. 1141-1203). In the *Makhzanu 'l Asrar* (c. 1180, *Treasurehouse of Secrets*) he mixes anecdotes with religious matters. In *Iskandar Namah* (c. 1400, *Book of Alexander*, an epic on Alexander the Great) there is some relevance to brief narratives, and in *Haft Paykar* (*Seven Portraits*) he copies *The Arabian Nights' Entertainments* device to unify seven tales, a device well-known now in the West and originally brought from India by the Persians, reaching Arabic in time to center on the reign of Haroun al Raschid, Calif of Baghdad (763-809). In all Arabic literature, from the *Koran* (c. 622-632, *Reading*) revealed to Mohammed to the *Gulistan* (1285, *Rose Garden*) in prose and verse by Sa'di (c. 1184-1291), short stories in one form or another, as the essence of the work, as parables, as illustrations, or as decorations, play a significant part.

In fact, the art of history and of storytelling is essentially conceived in the early periods as the art of arranging. The Sanskrit epic (like the sacred scriptures of Zoroastrianism, *Zend-Avesta* or text and commentaries, equivalent to the Hebrew *Talmud*) arranges various sorts of material, including anecdotes and tales. The Sanskrit epic is called the *Mahabharata* (c. fifth century B. C.) and adds to the epic core (eighty thousand lines) so much that the whole eighteen books add up to a stunning 200,000 lines, or about eight times the *Iliad* and the *Odyssey* put together, or a whole shelf of epics such as *Beowulf* and Henry Wadsworth Longfellow's *The Song of Hiawatha* (1855). Its author appears in it as a character, Vyasa: but the name means simply "arranger"; and what this Vyasa has put together includes everything from the *Bhagavad-Gita* (divine song of Lord Krishna) and its philosophical speculations to the love story of Nala and Damayanti. It was obviously the product of many bards over a long period, from perhaps as early as four hundred years before the birth of Christ to two hundred years after that event. It tells in great detail the complex history of a dynastic struggle in Hastinapur as the Pandavas triumph over their cousins the Kauravas; in the process it teaches writers how to construct elaborate plots and the value of a clear-cut "good guys versus bad guys" approach. Subsequent fictions from fairy tales to detective stories can be measured in the light of the achievement of the *Mahabharata*. Moreover, the common attempt in fiction to impose a moral, to render entertainment didactic and improving, is well illustrated in the case of this Sanskrit library of fiction, for the barbarous tales of bloody battles and sly treacheries— the same materials as the Chinese novels were made of—chanted by early bards were in the *Mahabharata* extensively revised by philosophers and zealously modified for popular consumption.

The short story is, above all, short. It can never have the *Mahabharata*'s complexity, variety, and scope: it must be economical and make its points with a limited cast of characters and a directness, whether it is written in the style of Edgar Allan Poe (choose a single effect and concentrate on producing that and that alone) or W. Somerset Maugham ("stick to the point like grim death, and when you can—cut") or in one of the more recent and looser styles. When it tries to make a point, to point a moral, however, then it is very much in the tradition of the *Mahabharata*. Those who object to short stories that point a moral as old-fashioned seldom realize just how old-fashioned those stories are. Literature having a cortex of entertainment around a nucleus of truth was not a new idea even when St. Augustine entertained and lectured on it.

Part of the story of the *Mahabharata* occurs in another important Sanskrit epic, the story of Rama (an incarnation of Vishnu, like Krishna), called *Ramayana* (c. 350 B. C.); it is almost 100,000 lines long and is the product of perhaps seven centuries of accumulation ending in the second century of our era. Boy (Rama) meets girl (Sita); boy loses girl (to Ravana, an evil entity); boy gets girl (and the villain is foiled again). The story is attributed to one of its minor characters, Valmiki, itself a device often copied, and thus both story line and techniques are shown to be shared by the arrangers or creators of these long works. Semidivine brothers and obscure historical events are featured in *Ramayana*, and these are also to be found in the classical epics we have mentioned and in the Finnish epic called, after its paradisical setting, *The Kalevala* (1835). There is nothing new under the sun in ancient Greece, ancient India, or nineteenth century Finland, where Finnish folklore enthusiasts collected the miscellaneous rune stories of ancient days. By the second edition of his compilation (1849), Elias Lönnrot had arranged or knitted together fifty runes or episodes and created an epic almost a quarter as long as the sprawling *Ramayana*.

Early materials were handled in a similar fashion to construct the tales of the cursed hoard or treasure (shades of *Beowulf* and the Firedrake) we call *The Nibelungenleid* (*The Lay of the Nibelungs*), the most important German narrative of the Middle Ages (c. 1200). Ten thousand lines were arranged in quatrains by some South German or Austrian who put a thin veneer of Christianity over old bits of history, legend, and *Märchen* (fairy tales). Where the author of *Beowulf* used the history of the Geats and the Danes and the author of the *The Song of Roland* the paladins of Charlemagne, the author of *The Nibelungenleid* involved the hero and the dragon with ancient Goths,

Huns, and Burgundians, superimposing (as did the authors of those epics and of *The Mahabharata* and other such works) his own religious and social values, like Homer, Sa'di, and the Chinese. Once again there is love and intrigue, bravery and blood. The poetry is uneven, the story confused, but the message of chivalry and *Treue* (loyalty) is insistent and impressive—and influential. Witness *Der Ring des Nibelungen* operas by Richard Wagner: *Das Rheingold*, *Die Walküre*, *Siegfried*, and *Götterdämmerung*, with their echoes in modern literature and world politics.

Wagner also relied heavily upon the Icelandic prose *Völsunga Saga* (assembled about the same time as *The Nibelungenleid* and still very much alive in the literature of Wagner's period, as one can see in English in the work of William Morris). Other Old Norse sagas in prose and verse mix fact and fiction and have contributed narrative techniques as well as characters and situations to literature right up to the present time.

In other cultures, also, factual stories have been collected and aggrandized into epics. To cite but two examples, take the Spanish *El Cid* (c. 1140) and the Italian *Orlando Furioso* (1516-1532). El Cid Campeador (Ruy Diaz de Vivar) conquered Valencia and ruled it until his death in 1099, moving like Tristram and Iseult and Joseph of Arimathea (the Holy Grail legend, which was attached to a whole series of Arthurian romances) and the paladins of Charlemagne (Roland, Percival, Huon of Bordeaux) and other semihistorical characters from life to literature. El Cid became the hero of a twelfth century Spanish masterpiece. Orlando is the French Roland again; he was the subject of an unfinished epic by Matteo Boiardo in the fifteenth century (*Orlando Innamorato*, 1486-1495) and of one of the most important of Renaissance poems, *Orlando Furioso*, which Ludovico Ariosto completed supposedly as a continuation.

The short story or heroic episode as international currency is further exemplified by the work of Torquato Tasso: his epics *Rinaldo* (1562) and *Gerusalemme liberata* (1581), the story of Jerusalem delivered in the First Crusade, made use of stories and designs to some extent familiar in older forms. Farther afield, the reader notices that Odysseus returning in disguise in Homer's epic is much like the story of the returning husband in one tale of the *Samhita* ("collections" of tales) of the very ancient Vedic scriptures of India. Other stories of India and Persia and many other old narratives were also pieced together (supposedly related night after night by Scheherazade, wife of Schariar, legendary king of Samarkand) to make *The Thousand and One Nights* (c. 1450). These tales include Aladdin and his wonderful lamp, Sindbad the sailor, and Ali Baba and the Forty Thieves—stories known now from nursery books, Christmas pantomimes, comic books and television cartoons, the cinema, and even in very primitive places where the peasantry has neither books nor films nor television but only itinerant storytellers in the marketplaces. After 1001 nights, *The Arabian Nights' Entertainments* tells us, the king relented and withdrew his threat to put Scheherazade to death. The tales did not perish, either. They reached the West in various ways but principally through the French of Antoine Galland, who published French translations in 1704-1717. They then went through various hands before being translated unexpurgated by Sir Richard Burton in sixteen volumes (1885-1888). They are as deathless as the stories of ancient vintage which Charles Perrault gave us in the seventeenth century as *Histoires ou contes du temps passé* (1697)—Cinderella, the vicious Bluebeard, the Sleeping Beauty.

Fairy tales, told to children one at a time at bedtime, perhaps, tend to remain separate from one another. The frame device of Scheherazade to link stories, however, was as useful in narrative fiction as it had been in epic; it became the basis of organization of those anthologies of the short story that one knows as *The Decameron* (1353) and *The Canterbury Tales* (1380-1390). Before coming to Giovanni Boccaccio and Geoffrey Chaucer, however, let us look briefly at the short stories they so ingeniously welded into masterworks.

The Decameron takes its title from the Greek for "ten days"; the plot concerns the plague of 1348, and Giovanni Boccaccio (1313-1375) has his refugees from it flee to a country villa and tell stories to pass the time. The ten days of storytelling range over the conversion of a Jew to Christianity, the evils of the very Church to which he is converted, "the attainment or recovery of a much-desired thing," "happy conclusions of unlucky love affairs," and other set categories involving love, lust, and life in general. The tales include a story that winds up in Shakespeare's *Cymbeline* (1609); a famous tale of Tancred and Ghismonnda which Robert Wilmot made into an Elizabethan play; something like Chaucer's "Pardoner's Tale" or his "Reeve's Tale"; an Enoch Arden situation; a fairy tale of the Patient Griselda; a joke played on the simpleton Calandrino; a joke or two which has turned up in *Reader's Digest* or *Playboy* lately; and maybe even a story you have heard told by a friend as something that happened to himself or someone he knows. *The Decameron* was later regretted by its author, but it has never been regretted by anyone else: it is a magnificent portrait of an age and good entertainment for any age. Ambitious writers of the short story—which has tended to appear as an individual piece ever since the great boost given to short fiction by the emergence of the popular magazine at the beginning of the nineteenth century—can read these linked tales, really groups of tales on certain subjects, with profit as well as pleasure. Boccaccio was a master of yarn-spinning, of dialogue and description, and of all the arts of this genre.

So was an Englishman, Geoffrey Chaucer (c. 1343-1400), who copied and adapted Boccaccio in many ways, retelling the Italian stories in his *Troilus and Criseyde* (1385). If one excludes the author of *Beowulf* and Caedmon, and whoever wrote the heroic poems such as *Widsið* and *Deor* and elegies such as "The Wanderer" and "The Seafarer," Chaucer was the first great English poet. He was also a great master of narrative. He translated some part of the *Roman de la rose* (1360-1372) and under French influences constructed his beautiful *Book of the Duchess* (1369), but it was when his love-vision approach yielded *The House of Fame* (1374-1386) and he came under Italian influences (which produced in addition to *Troilus and Criseyde* such works as *The Parliament of Fowls*, 1375-1385; *The Legend of Good Women*, 1380-1386; and parts of *The Canterbury Tales*) that he moved securely toward his great unfinished symphony of stories, *The Canterbury Tales*.

To present his portrait gallery of English life, Chaucer contemplated a frame which would involve 120 tales (or 124, if one is to count the Canon's Yeoman, who overtakes the party of pilgrims on the road to the shrine of St. Thomas à Becket at Canterbury after they have set their plan of storytelling). The plan was that, at the suggestion of the Host (Harry Bailey) who is to lead the party, each of the thirty pilgrims should while away the time of the traveling by telling two stories on the way to Canterbury and two on the way back to London. The prize was to be a celebration dinner given to the best storyteller when the company got back to The Tabard Inn in Southwark, just across London Bridge from The City. The plan appealed, of course, to the travelers; it also appeals to Chaucer and to the reader, for it enables the author to present and the reader to savor a cross section of English people (or at least those who would go on such a religious pilgrimage—the lowest classes are pretty much ignored) and to avoid monotony involved in a Boccaccio-like set topic for the day or in a too limited social group.

A General Prologue introduces the personages, and then we are treated to a lively collection of stories more or less suited to the teller's personality (unlike Boccaccio's work, in which the emphasis is on the theme of the day). The stories are a veritable summary of Chaucer's narrative inheritance: chivalric romance, *fabliaux*, jests, virtue stories, folktales, miracles of The Blessed Virgin, moral tales, exempla, *de cassibus* warnings about the fall of great men, fables, beast fables, German *Märchen* and Hindu tales and French *lais*, prose sermons and saints' lives, and everything else from classical stories to a modern attack on alchemical impostures. The Manciple recalls Ovid's *Metamorphoses* (a favorite source of Chaucer), and the Canon's Yeoman in heroic couplets recounts what may be a fictionalized bit of Chaucer's own experience. If it is true, as T. H. Ward wrote, that Chaucer was "the first great painter of character, because he is the first great observer among European writers," Chaucer was also a great observer of many European, and non-European, earlier writers.

Other writers of the Middle Age "moralized" Ovid and drew extensively on older narratives. The Middle High German period remodeled old tales of Alexander the Great (*Alexanderleid*, 1150) and Roland (*Rolandsleid*, c. 1170) and in the work of Konrad von Ratisbon fictionalized the history of emperors. The minstrels also sang of historical figures (*Herzog Ernst*), and by the close of the twelfth century Heinrich der Glîchezaere had already created the beast epic of Reynard the Fox (*Reinhart Fuchs*, c. 1240). Court poets wrote new epics based on Vergil (Heinrich von Veldeke's *Eneit*, 1189), the "Arthurian matter" of writers such as Crétien de Troyes (Hartmann von Aue's *Erec*, c.1180-1185; and Wolfram von Eschenbach's *Parzifal*, c. 1210), and similar material such as Gottfried von Strassburg's incomplete *Tristan und Isolde* (c. 1210), based on the Tristram and Iseult story as treated by Thomas of Brittany in c. 1160; and anonymous poets of the people were responsible for *The Nibelungenleid*. Middle High German writers avoided the boredom of versified encyclopedias in medieval Latin, unlike the Italians, and to some extent the religious romance of the French (such as *Le Tombeur de Notre-Dame*, a sweet story of an acrobat whose devotion gains him a visitation from Our Lady); and (for example) forged more northern myths of the Frisians and others into the tale of *Gudrun* (1210), which ranges widely (Ireland, Friesland, Zeeland, Normandy) and traces maidens in distress generation after generation. Sebastian Brant's *Das Narrenschiff* (*The Ship of Fools*) was, in 1494, really the first German book to achieve international and lasting fame, but before and after this the Germans with their own folklore and their redaction of foreign tales were adding continually to the rich treasury of European story.

Teutonic peoples were also responsible for invading France, mixing cultures, and driving the Celts further West. As the Celts moved they took with them their old stories of battles and great heroes (Cuchulain, Finn) and heroines (Deidre, Maeve). These stories subsequently entered English literature; so did the *chansons de geste* and romances of Brittany. From the distant past came Benoît de Sainte-Maure's *Roman de Troie* (c. 1160), influencing Boccaccio and Chaucer among later writers, and many other romances of far-off places and high deeds. From Geoffrey of Monmouth's *Historia Regnum Britanniae* (1135-1138) and Robert Wace's *Roman de Brut* (1155) came Breton romances, and tales of Arthurian legend, stories of Launcelot and Merlin, from Crétien de Troyes (c. 1130-1180) and such successors as Robert de Boron (c. 1170-1212). From the *chansons de geste* developed the *romans d'adventure*—the French word for novel is still *roman*—and the earliest extant metrical romance in English, *King Horn* (c. 1250). Related to *King Horn* is *Guy of Warwick* (c. 1300), with its combination of chivalry and religion, and *Bevis of Hampton* (1622), with its quick changes of scene and plethora of characters and effects. As time went on, these swashbuckling tales which sometimes lost track of the point or of a major character (such as Brunhilde in *The Nibelungenleid*) perfected the art of popular fiction, gaining strength from beast fables, Welsh tales for the instruction of an apprentice bard (*The Mabinogion*), assorted "matters" of Rome, France, and Britain, stories incorporated into histories or pious tracts, and so on. The tradition of "farcing" out sermons with anecdotes, of making moral points with illustrative tales, of praising The Blessed Virgin or the saints with more or less fictional material in devotional books and hagiographies, of cramming didactic and humorous material into defenses of religion or attacks on corruption in the Church (say, John Gower's *Confessio Amantis*, 1386-1390)—this entire tradition of storytelling was available to Boccaccio and Chaucer.

It took a genius such as Chaucer to come along at the right time, as Bach did in music, and pull it all together. The economy of the short story does not permit one to stray very often from the main road to pick a few flowers glimpsed in a nearby field. The desire for variety must be kept in check, for the short story must begin at the beginning (or later), go on to the end, and then stop. It need not even present the end (as writers of what came to be called *The New Yorker* story, with the "walk-away ending" that sometimes suggests that the writer has lost or discarded the last few pages of typescript discovered); it can suggest it. Nor does it have to be written backwards in the Poe manner. The end must be kept in constant view, however, and a singleness of effect does enable a story, like concentrated acid, to etch deep. Chaucer found a way to be quintessentially English and varied and at the same time effective in short pieces. He made each piece of his narrative afghan different but designed to fit together with the other pieces; then he stitched the whole thing together.

The short narratives, which became the components, he drew from sources as different as Guillaume de Lorris' dream allegory and the Buddhist collection of tales called *Vedabbha Jataka* (which later served Kipling well). In those days Cecilia was a saint—she has now been demoted, a mere storybook character—and he gave her pious tale to a nun to relate in rhyme royal; in stark contrast he placed the Wife of Bath (although her tale is without the coarseness her Prologue would suggest) and the bawdy story of the Miller. There is a story of men "yfallen out of high degree" and another of women fallen. Chaucer mocks long-winded storytellers with the rime of Sir Thopas (a satire on knight-errantry which is mercifully and humorously left unfinished) and with a compendium of all the worst faults of medieval storytelling called "The Tale of Melibee" (typically from the French and going back to Albertano de Brescia's *Liber Consolationis et Concilii*, heavy with moralizing). The latter plods along in a clumsy prose which suggests that the lively author has, once again, his tongue in cheek.

The Canterbury Tales has been examined at this length because it is truly a summary of all the narrative techniques developed to that time, important to the history of the novel because of its framework and to the short story because of its components, a mosaic of magnificence. Especially in its organizing principle and didactic purpose, it extracted from French *contes populaires* and, of course, from religious works already mentioned; it added to the traditions of romance, folklore, and fairy tale. Chaucer's "hie sentence" and boisterous satire are still strenuously sought in modern fiction. Chaucer would approve of the allegory of George Orwell's *Animal Farm* (1945) and the humor of John Barth's *Floating Opera* (1956), and he has something in common with modern writers as different as Jorge Luis Borges and Donald Barthelme. To note but one more concern of the modern writer of the short story that was articulated and magisterially manipulated by Chaucer, the ways in which Chaucer fits presentation of the story to content and in which the teller colors the tale are still copied in modern fiction. Chaucer's work represented a skillful summation and advance in the art of fiction.

The period immediately following Chaucer, however, did not see much improvement in the art. John Lydgate (c. 1370-1450) tended to be wordy, although his *London Lickpenny*, 1515, (if it was he who wrote it) exhibits a lively if episodic structure and presages the pictures of the London underworld that enliven the catchpenny journalism of Shakespeare's contemporaries. The Scottish followers of Chaucer, such as Robert Henryson (c. 1425-1506), also tended to be verbose, although Henryson's *Morall Fables of Esope* (1621) are to the point. They are in a great tradition that stretches back past Chaucer and Marie de France (twelfth century) to the ancients and forward to Jean de La Fontaine (1621-1695, author of both *Fables*, 1668 and *Contes*, 1692), John Dryden (1631-1700), John Gay (1685-1732), and lesser-known but important authors such as Gotthold Lessing in Germany and Ivan Krylov in Russia; the same tradition influenced such American authors as, for example, Nathaniel Hawthorne and Joel Chandler Harris (creator of Uncle Remus), George Ade (*Fables in Slang*, 1899), and popular authors of this century.

In the fifteenth century the pioneer printer William Caxton (c. 1422-1491) did much to widen the audience of *The Canterbury Tales* and of authors such as Sir Thomas Malory (c. 1395-1471), whose collection of Arthurian tales in *Le Morte d'Arthur* (1485) later influenced Edmund Spenser's romantic epic *The Faerie Queene* (1590-1596), almost persuaded Milton to write on an Arthurian subject, and was reworked in Alfred Tennyson's *Idylls of the King* (1859-1885), Edwin Arlington Robinson's *Tristram* (1927), Mark Twain's *A Connecticut Yankee in King Arthur's Court* (1889), and T. H. White's trilogy *The Once and Future King* (1958).

The imitators of *The Canterbury Tales* are weak; Stephen Hawes's *The Passetyme of Pleasure* (1506) is typical, a bloodless allegory featuring cardboard characters which make the abstractions of the Morality Play *Everyman* (c. 1500) look positively three-dimensional. The technique of embodying abstractions to lend stories profundity if not credibility, however, is still in the short-story writer's armamentarium.

At the same time, the popular ballad, with its concision, shorthand characterizations, swift changes of scene, and all the other devices of economic narration (not to mention the extremely popular elements of the supernatural, the sensational, and the sentimental), was achieving effects in verse that were soon to become universal in the short prose narrative. They have had a very long run in popular fiction, including the journalistic sensational or true-crime story, the ghost story and the horror story, the Gothic tale, the detective story and the spy story, and so on. Ballads, whether the work of the folk or a single author (art ballads), taught short-story writers many tricks of their trade.

With the Renaissance, the Italian *novella*, dealing as it might with romance or satire or practical jokes and buffoonery, exerted considerable influence. Some writers, such as Franco Sacchetti (who wrote three hundred *novelle* in Florence in less than a decade after 1388), ground out these short fictions at an alarming rate. In the next century the quality improved (as in Masuccio Salernitano's *Novellino*, 1476) and the quantity increased. In the sixteenth century, collections of *novelle* of great distinction were published in Italy by inheritors of the great Marguerite de Navarre (1492-1549), whose seventy-two tales in the *Heptaméron des Nouvelles*, 1558, are excellent—her inspiration, Boccaccio. Among those works which greatly influenced English writers were *Ecatommiti* (1565, *Hundred Tales*) by Giambattista Giraldi Cinthio, the *novelle* (especially his retelling of Romeo and Juliet's story, which reached Shakespeare eventually) of Matteo Bandello—a Dominican monk who became a bishop and a great writer—Antonio Francesco (or Antonfrancesco) Grazzini's *Le Cene* (c. 1550, *Banquets*), and Gianfrancesco Straparola's *Tredici Notte Piacevoli* (1550, *Thirteen Nights' Entertainment*). Also, many minor writers were read abroad with major interest by both the public and competitors.

Fiction also owes something to the style or content of Renaissance Italian leaders of thought such as Niccolò Machiavelli (1469-1527), who was blamed for the "true Machiavelli" villain; Baldassare Castiglione (1478-1529), whose dialogues on *The Courtier* (1528) were internationally important; Benvenuto Cellini (1500-1571), whose free-flowing *Autobiography* (1730) was replete with dash and daring; and many others, even playwrights (such as Ludovico Ariosto of *I Suppositi*, 1509; and Giambattista Guarini of *Il Pastor Fido*, 1580) and poets (Teofilo Folengo of *Baldus*, 1517, 1521, 1534-1535; and Giambattista Marino of *Adnoe*, 1623, the former vulgar and vigorous and the latter a sort of precious Italian lily, or Lyly). High-flown speeches, pastoral settings, plots of intrigue, the slapdash spontaneity of a Cellini, and the constipated classicism of some of the more precious (but less valuable) poets—all these things entered into Italian fiction and, because Italy was the nurse of the whole European Renaissance, into the literature of the Continent.

Renaissance fiction in Spain began about the time that García Rodriguez de Montalvo launched the great popularity of *Amadís de Gaula*. This was originally a Welsh tale but was elaborated in Spain and Portugal, and when the version of 1508 appeared, it started a whole fashion of romances. It was translated into French (1540) and English (1619), and it influenced Sir Philip Sidney's *Arcadia* (1590) and many other works, from popular novels to operas. Then came Miguel de Cervantes Saavedra (1547-1616), whose satire of *Amadís de Gaula* and its ilk grew into *Don Quixote de la Mancha* (1605-1615), a novel which contains many short stories within its wonderful variety and which in its themes of the dreamer and the vagabond (*picaro*) sums up all Spanish literature, some think. Other great novels of the period are *La Celestina* (1499), with its emphasis on common life, and *Lazarillo de Tormes* (1553), a masterpiece of the picaresque (superior even to Francisco Gomez de Quevedo Villegas' *La Vida del Buscón*, 1626), not as magnificent, perhaps, as *Don Quixote de la Mancha* but equally significant, because of its episodic structure, in the development of short fiction.

In Portugal, Jorge de Montemayor (1520-1561) adapted the pastoral novel in *Diana* (1559), complicating plotting, which was not lost on yarn-spinners elsewhere, especially those who had to string out a jest or an anecdote to short-story length or (unfortunately) longer.

In many other countries of Europe, fiction was developing—in simple jests and folktales of the people its essence was always there—even though in some (Russia, for example) it was the eighteenth century before the short story in recognizable form was developed. In Russia, Vassili Trediakovski, 1703-1769, helped by translating Aesop.

France had already flowered in the genius of François Rabelais (c. 1495-1553), who turned the seed of an Arthurian romance of *Gargantua* into the vast and marvelous *Gargantua and Pantagruel* (1534), which is something of a textbook on how to handle short scenes; France learned more of economy in the *Essais* (1580) of Michel de Montaigne (1533-1592). These examples, however, did not seem to influence Honoré d'Urfé's *L'Astrée* (1607-1627), a mishmash of the Italian pastoral and the Amadis of Gaul romance; and for quite some time France, which had produced the Queen of Navarre and other seminal writers of short fiction, contributed comparatively little to the development of the genre. This is surprising, considering that in the eighteenth century Bernadin de Saint-Pierre's *Paul et Virginie* (1788) was to sketch in new backdrops for fiction, and in the nineteenth century such short-story masters as Prosper Mérimée (1803-1870), Gustave Flaubert (1821-1880), and Guy de Maupassant (1850-1893), flourished. Introducing an anthology of *French Short Stories of the 19th and 20th Century* (1933), Professor Frederick Charles Green argues persuasively that the genre is, in fact, especially attractive and suited to the French character, demanding as it does "a profound respect for form, an instinct for clarity and conciseness, and an unerring *flair* for the truly dramatic situation." Given this, France really ought to have produced her giants of the short story much earlier.

Germany also had a somewhat infertile period between the Middle Ages with its *Kalendergeschichten* (1949) collections and its superb attainments in the short story and especially the novella in the nineteenth and twentieth centuries. "The most distinguished writers of German novellas in the nineteenth and twentieth centuries," says Professor Harry Steinhauer in his Introduction to a dual-language book *Die Deutsche Novellen* (1936), "are

Goethe, Kleist, Tieck, Hoffmann, Stifter, Storm, Keller Meyer, Raabe, Hauptmann, Schnitzler, Hermann Hesse, Thomas Mann, Paul Ernst, Wilhelm Schäfer, Ricarda Huch, Hans Franck, Kafka, Werner Bergengruen; and this catalogue is anything but exhaustive." It is not exhaustive at all: it does not include Ilse Aichinger, Heinrich Böll, Paul Heyse's *Novellen* (1855), and the many exciting masters of the short story since the beginning of World War I (the year of Heyse's death). Not to be neglected in the history of the short story are many names not in these very literary lists: candidates for the most neglected are the Brothers Jacob Ludwig Karl and Wilhelm Karl Grimm, essentially philologists but forever to be thanked for *Kinder- und Haus-Märchen* (1812-1815), the famous fairy-tale collections. All short-story writers begin as children: they learn much of their art at their mother's knee.

To return now to English literature, we can go back to the *aeglogai* (goatherd's tales) or eclogues of Edmund Spenser's *The Shepheardes Calendar* (1579). That work is not merely a milestone in Elizabethan lyricism; it also has a certain relevance to his masterpiece, *The Faerie Queene*, in terms of storytelling as well as in its use of deliberate archaic language. The romantic approach to storytelling is also seen elsewhere in Elizabethan literature, as in the works of The University Wits (such as Thomas Lodge, c. 1577-1625). Others of that group (such as George Peele, c. 1558-1596) are connected with the yarn-spinning traditions of the jestbooks or (as in the case of Thomas Nash, 1567-1601) the early English picaresque novel. Nash's *The Unfortunate Traveller: Or, The Life of Jack Wilton* (1594) is one of the earliest if not the very first English historical novel, probably influenced by *Lazarillo de Tormes* and similar tales of adventure, journalism, and imagination; it did much to establish comic realism in place of fuzzy pastoral and chivalric romances. The episodes are linked with rather too much moralizing, quite at odds with the vitality and even raciness of the story, but when later ages weeded out this sort of material they were well on the way to new frontiers in fiction. Throughout the Elizabethan period the basic movement in the direction of the modern short story involved works tending in this direction rather than those which looked backward in the style of William Painter's collection, *The Palace of Pleasure* (completed in 1567, published in a new edition of both volumes in 1575, which had considerable influence on Shakespeare). Whereas the Elizabethan drama leaned toward the exotic (with notable exceptions: one was the tragedy of *Arden of Feversham*, 1592), the important short fiction was moving closer to a striking, if often sensational, realism.

Shakespeare was a considerable picker-up of fictional trifles for the plots of his plays, although he preferred the old-fashioned to the new. A few of the sources he mined for the "fable" that Aristotle said was "the soul of drama" should be mentioned. He seems to have derived his *Two Gentlemen of Verona* (1594-1595) from Montemayor's *Diana* before Bartholomew Young translated it (1598), which may indicate the extent to which popular stories circulated in conversation. *Romeo and Juliet* (1594-1596) came from Arthur Brooke's poem (1562), derived from François de Belleforest's *Histoires tragiques* (1559), which in turn came from Bandello's *Giuletta e Romeo* (1554), which had even earlier Italian analogues. This example indicates how a good story passed from country to country and from genre to genre in that period, much as today a short story can become a movie and a movie a television series (filmed short stories again). The Romeo and Juliet story was also included in Painter's *The Palace of Pleasure*, a work that yielded suggestions likewise for the play *All's Well That Ends Well* (1602-1604) and the poem *The Rape of Lucrece* (1594).

A *Midsummer Night's Dream* (1595-1596) draws ideas from several tales Chaucer in turn had borrowed, from Montemayor again, and from others. Some features of *The Merchant of Venice* (1596-1597) go back to the *Mahabharata*, and some to more recent (thirteenth century) sermonizing tales from the *Gesta Romanorum* (1473, "Deeds of the Romans"), plus Boccaccio, "the moral" Gower, and others. The temperament of Elizabethan audiences, along with the fact that the stage had many acting areas and was capable of swift changes of location, joined with other factors to produce a drama that could combine short-story material from various sources. Shakespeare was "the only Shake-Scene in the country" for the masterly combination of diverse elements, but he had many competitors and imitators. The practice was common, although the Bard's results were extraordinary.

Another Elizabethan dramatic habit was the rewriting of old scripts. *The Taming of the Shrew* (1593-1594) looks like a revision of an anonymous *Taming of a Shrew*, but *that* play owes much to Ariosto's *I Suppositi* (*The Substitutes*) for its subplot. That type of subplot was an Elizabethan convention after Henry Medwall's play of *Fulgens and Lucres* (c. 1497) of nearly a century before, which appealed mightily to the Elizabethan penchant for comedy mixed with tragedy (Sidney derided it as "hornpipes and funerals") and the theater's demand of something for everyone in the very mixed audience. The old "Arabian Nights" ploy was adapted for the frame story.

Then there was the exciting and risible play of *The Merry Wives of Windsor* (1597-1601). The Italian writer Giovanni Fiorentino was among several authors borrowed from when Shakespeare somewhat uncharacteristically wrote about English contemporary characters and apparently tried something new for him: inventing a rather original plot. Straparola and Painter were used as well. Bandello, *Orlando Furioso*, *The Faerie Queene*, and other sources went into the making of the delightful *Much Ado About Nothing* (1598-1599). *As You Like It* (1599-1600)—like Lodge's *Rosalynde* (1590) and the pseudo-Chaucerian Cook's "Tale of Gamelyn"—went back to *The Tale of Gamelyn* (c. 1350) with an admixture of typical English material such as Robin Hood and the Greenwood. Playwright Robert Greene (who also dabbled successfully in romances and novels and other popular fiction) accused Shakespeare of decking himself with others' feathers, but everyone was doing it. Today the writer tries to be as original as possible; then he did not have plagiarism to bother about, and he borrowed boldly from contemporary and ancient sources with as much public acclaim as now greets writers of "fiction" which looks very much like autobiography or novelization of fact.

For *Twelfth Night* (1599-1600), Shakespeare was free to do as he willed with a story by Barnaby Rich, probably "The History of Apolonius and Sila" in *Riche . . . His Farewell to Militarie Profession* (1581). After all, Rich had taken it from Bandello's *Novelle* (1554), or Belleforest (1570), or maybe Cinthio's *Ecatommiti*. (From the latter Shakespeare also got *Othello*, 1604.) A collection of prose tales told onboard a ship from Rome to Marsailles also gave George Whetstone his basis for *Promos and Cassandra* (1578); Shakespeare took that for his *Measure for Measure* (1604-1605). For *Troilus and Cressida* (1601-1602), Shakespeare looked up Caxton's *Recuyell of the Historyes of Troy* (1475), Lydgate, Chaucer, and other works, all of which harked back to Guido delle Colonne's tales of 1287, *Historia Troiana*.

Hamlet (1600-1601) was a rewrite of what the Germans call the *Ur-Hamlet* (1589), a play by Thomas Kyd (author of *The Spanish Tragedy*, c. 1585, which is similar in many important, actually Senecan, features). In the background of Kyd's (lost) play are Belleforest (1582) and a history of the Danes in Latin by Saxo Grammaticus (c. 1200) as well as Snorri Sturluson's *Prose* or *Younger Edda* (also about 1200), a guide to the scaldic poetry in which the age-old stories and myths of Iceland are preserved. Likewise partly from mythology (in this case Celtic) is *King Lear* (1605), owing its inspiration to poets (such as Spenser) and historians (such as Geoffrey of Monmouth, who claimed to be translating very ancient records). *Macbeth* (1606) is fully from old chronicles, albeit adapted.

A decade before he wrote *Timon of Athens* (1605-1608), Shakespeare alluded to a story in a passage in *Love's Labour's Lost* (1595; IV, iii, 170) which he later expanded with a digression in Plutarch (a favorite source for his Roman plays), a bit of Lucian, and so on. Or *Timon of Athens* may be just a rewriting of an old play. For a fable of Menenius in *Coriolanus* (1607-1608) he borrowed from William Camden's *Remaines . . . Concerning Britain* (1605), supplementing the Plutarch he had on his desk to write *Antony and Cleopatra* (1606-1607) and *Coriolanus*. The story of *Pericles, Prince of Tyre* (1608) he could have found in any number of places; Gower or the *Gesta Romanorum* seem likely. *Cymbeline* found him consulting a number of typically Elizabethan sources: Raphael Holinshed's *Chronicles* (reprinted and enlarged in 1587, it was one of his standbys; like his useful translation of Plutarch's *Lives* by Sir Thomas North, 1579, it was basically a history book but not free from fictional and legendary material), the Belarius story (probably from a play first printed in 1589, somehow related to Francis Beaumont and John Fletcher's *Philaster: Or, Love Lies Ableeding*, c. 1609), and a wager plot from Boccaccio (either directly from the ninth novel of the second day of *The Decameron* or from an English translation of the Dutch *Frederyke of Jennen*, 1509, version of the Boccaccio story of Frederick of Genoa). *The Winter's Tale* (1610-1611) is altered from *Pandosto: Or, Dorastus and Fawnia* (1588), an English pastoral prose romance derived from a Polish folktale.

Small wonder Greene accused Shakespeare of borrowing. Why all these details of that borrowing here in an article not on Shakespeare but on the short story? It is simply to show the rich heritage of short fiction accumulated as early as Elizabethan times, its international currency, and its contribution to an artist who never even ventured into writing prose fiction himself but contented himself with becoming the world's best playwright and a supreme poet. In later times the short story was to contribute much to other arts: to the opera and the ballet, to the cinema and television, and so on. Today it is often said that the markets for the short story are few, that the novel has replaced collections of stories in the favor of publishers and readers, that the genre has diminished in importance; but the value of the short story to Shakespearean drama stresses the inescapable fact that the short story is the basis of all narrative art.

Now to continue with this high-spot summary of its development. We had arrived at *Pandosto*. It was somewhat uncharacteristic of its time in the nature of its moralizing and in its freedom from the over-elaborate style (which we now call euphuism) widely copied from two novels by Elizabethan poet and playwright John Lyly (c. 1553-1606): *Euphues, the Anatomy of Wit* (1579) and *Euphues and His England* (1580), fictions that changed the verbal mannerisms of the period in a way perhaps unequaled until Dashiell Hammett, Ernest Hemingway, and Raymond Chandler in twentieth century America introduced the "tough-guy" pose. More in the mainstream were the conneycatching pamphlets and scenes of gulling and lowlife depicted elsewhere by *Pandosto*'s author, Greene. It was the streets and not pallid, played-out pastoral scenery that were to hold the short story's future.

Of course there were other streams that fed the great river. *The Tempest* (1611) is one; its only really noteworthy source is an essay on cannibals by Montaigne, but it also had connections with another narrative art, the *commedia dell'arte*, whose sketchy *scenario* tradition is obscurely connected to Renaissance storytelling. The other is Shakespeare's collaborative play *The Two Noble Kinsmen* (1634), going back to "The Knight's Tale" in Chaucer, itself a long (but shortened) version of Boccaccio's *La Teseida* (c. 1341), an epic in *terza rima* exactly the length of the *Aeneid*, with a triangle plot from Statius' *Thebais* (the latter "Englished" by King Alfred, Queen Elizabeth, and lesser English people and long influential) and Boethius. The play more nearly captures what must once have been the short-story essence of the tale. *The Canterbury Tales*, of which it is the longest and perhaps the best piece, suffers from typically medieval overelaboration of details and anachronisms which bother the modern reader. (Chaucer's original readers welcomed both, but fashions changed.) Shakespeare had to be more to the point, handling the story of Palamon and Arcite in a way foreign to both Chaucer and Boccaccio, let alone Ancius Manlius Severinus Boethius (c. 475-525) and Publius Papinius Statius (c. 40-96). The twelve books of Statius' *Thebais* have been denounced as having "no national interest, no moral conception, no religious or philosophical doctrine," nothing in fact but this useful story, which also appealed to Dante Alighieri (1265-1321, the stunning accomplishment of whose *La Divina Commedia*, c. 1320, and also his important stress on the vernacular as a literary language, could not avoid greatly affecting the course of narrative art) and to writers of the eighteenth century. A good story has an extremely long life. Consider that Aesop, a slave on the island of Samos six centuries before the time of Christ, still has influence. Although the ornate style of George Pettie's *A Petite Palace of Pettie His Pleasure* (1576) has given way to new perversities in presentation (so that some of the most skillful writers of the 1970's go almost unread, except by critics), some of his stories could still be used, fixed up perhaps with a modern version of the thieves' slang that decked John Awdley's *Fraternitye of Vacabones* (1565) or the direct approach to the lives of ordinary people seen in the work of Thomas Deloney (c. 1543-1600).

Deloney was a bridge to the seventeenth century along with Thomas Dekker (c. 1572-1632), a writer of enormous talent in creating a London teeming with gulls and gallants. The century also rejoiced in miscellaneous books of jests (often fathered on famous men who had had nothing to do with them, and told with clumsiness), characters, translations such as James Mabbe's *Exemplary Novels* of Cervantes (1640), and other kinds of popular literature. A new reading public was emerging which kept yarns and jokes alive despite puritanical suspicion of all arts and made a market for picaresque fiction about the lower class and sentimental fiction about the middle class.

Later in the seventeenth century there were triumphs of the "novel" as later defined by Dr. Johnson ("a small tale generally of love") from women authors such as Mrs. Aphra Behn (1640-1689). There were works of allegory (John Bunyan's *Pilgrim's Progress*, 1678, 1684, with what might be called short stories imbedded in it). There were sermons with scenes of common life for illustration, and there were stories stolen from French sources (of the forty-six stories published in twelve volumes as *Modern Novels* in 1692, most are thefts from the better-established French tradition of the period, for it was a time for fiction in England, as the nineteenth century largely was for drama, when it looked as if French products might sweep the local English manufacturers right out of business). At the time the French had no outstanding novelists of the calibre that was to come with Stendhal, Honoré de Balzac, Émile Zola, and others, but they outclassed the English in both short and longer pieces.

Typically English at the time and germane to the history of the development of the short story because of subject matter or approach were: rogue fiction such as Richard Head's *Meriton Latroon* (1665-1671, added to by Francis Kirkman); the *"voyage imaginaire"* (with classical origins but note the French term—an example was Henry Neville's *The Isle of Pines*, 1668, which was in time to lead to trips to the moon, to Lilliput with Gulliver, and far into space with modern science fiction); the sentimental novel such as William Congreve's *Incognita* of 1692; and the sensational "true stories" of horrible murders which as broadsides were years and years before an extremely popular kind of the cheapest literature.

Each of these types of fiction was to have its counterpart in the increasingly popular short story once periodicals began to call for brief fiction in quantity. The rogue fiction of Dan Foe, the butcher's boy who became Daniel Defoe (c. 1660-1731) and at sixty a sudden master of fiction, was to reach impressive heights artistically. The modern short story was taking form in the pages of Peter Anthony Motteux's *Gentleman's Magazine* (founded 1692) when along came Defoe to unite journalism and popular fiction. He had the energy to write his review (called *The Review*, 1704-1713) almost single-handed and at the same time to turn out embryonic modern short stories and episodes in best-selling novels which much affected writers for years to come. The novels hit the public in dazzling succession: *Robinson Crusoe* (1719, with two sequels later), *Captain Singleton* (1720), in 1772 two books about the Plague Year plus *Colonel Jack* and *Moll Flanders*, and so on.

With one of his ghost stories, the one in which Mrs. Veal appears to Mrs. Bargrave although Mrs. Veal is dead, Defoe almost incidentally created what one might call the modern short story, the sort of thing that Joseph Addison and Richard Steele kept skirting around in their near-stories and chats in *The Spectator* (1711-1712) and *The Tatler* (1709-1710). People say that the closest they ever got to a short story as we would recognize one today is the essay numbered 116 in which Sir Roger de Coverley goes out on a hunt in *The Spectator*. Actually, they did not write that one. T. O. Beachcraft in his concise pamphlet for The British Council on *The English Short Story, I* notes that "this number of the Spectator was written by neither Addison nor Steele, but by [Eustace] Budgell," Addison's cousin, a hack writer who drowned himself in The Thames in 1737 in despair. Therefore, one might argue that it was Defoe—or Eustace Budgell—and not Addison and Steele who invented the modern short story.

The modern short story had to wait for a more popular press and the magazine format more clearly established before it triumphed. Meanwhile the essay and the sermon and sentimental novels of considerable length gained sway. Yet nothing like the short story, as ancient as *Tales of the Magicians* (a collection of Egyptian stories of about 4000 B. C.), as well-known and revered as the stories and parables of the Bible or the hallowed bedtime stories of childhood, could ever perish. The Italian *novella*'s realism and the French *roman*'s romance were already at work producing the modern novel, but the smaller and not lesser genre of the modern short story had also been born.

The magazine markets of the late eighteenth and early nineteenth centuries brought forth a modern story with a history that stretches, back to the beginnings of man. In fact, in *every* age there has been a "modern short story" of some kind to answer the persistent demand of people for a gripping tale, a tale which (as Sir Philip Sidney said nearly four hundred years ago) "holdeth children from play, and old men from the chimney corner."

Leonard R. N. Ashley

SHORT FICTION: 1800-1840

By the year 1800 various Western literatures could boast isolated examples of works which, if they were published today, would almost certainly be called short stories in the modern sense of the term. These works are in one sense rather like those hypothetical Phoenicians or Greeks or Vikings who stumbled onto America before Columbus. In the final analysis we celebrate Columbus not so much for being the first as for being the first to make much historical difference. By the same token, the father of the modern short story is the writer whose first short story made the most dramatic difference to the genre and to subsequent literary history. By 1800, although well on the way, he had not yet arrived. What was found then in short fiction throughout the Western world was a dizzying variety of forms, traditions, genres, and subgenres which sometimes approached quite closely the modern short story, which in fact seemed to have produced splendid isolated examples, as in Sir Richard Steele's *Spectator* 113, but which—although generating fine literature according to other criteria—finally fell short of a consistent vision, a full conception of the short story as it is thought of today.

This short narrative current in the year 1800 can be arbitrarily divided in as many different ways as might a custard pie, but the most meaningful division would seem to be into the broad categories of work in the tale tradition on the one hand and in the essay-sketch tradition on the other.

The Tale Tradition

The tale tradition had by far a longer and more complex history than the essay-sketch tradition. Virtually every anthropologist, linguist, and literary historian would agree that tales in one form or another are approximately as old as language, and if language is the distinguishing feature of Homo sapiens, then tales must have originated at almost exactly the same time as human beings. Judging from what is known of human nature, one can assume that the first tales took the form of either lies or gossip, which remain among the most seductive categories of narrative today. Mankind, or womankind more likely, must have soon varied the literary fare with the sorts of oral tales which seem to have flourished then and which still flourish today among preliterate peoples in just about every culture on the face of the earth: myths, legends, folktales, jokes, anecdotes, and so on—and subsequently with the sorts of refinements and variations of these forms which develop in diverse guises in various cultures at various times. Among the terms (often overlapping) for specifically oral tales with which Stith Thompson deals in his classic study, *The Folktale*, (1851), are *Märchen*, fairy tale, household tale, *conte populaire*, novella, hero tale, *Sage*, local tradition, local legend, migratory legend, *tradition populaire*, explanatory tale, etiological tale, *Natursage*, *pourquoi* story, animal tale, fable, jest, humorous anecdote, merry tale, *Schwank*, and so on.

Of course, such genres invariably alter, sometimes quite subtly, sometimes fundamentally, when the means of transmission becomes not the more or less dramatic human voice (with accompanying facial expressions and physical gestures and so on) of a person immediately present, but impersonal pen and ink. Earlier sections of *The Folktale* describe some of the forms of written tale that have spanned the centuries since the paleolithic oral tale: Geoffrey Chaucer's *fabliaux*, saints' legends, beast fables, and Chivalric romances, for example.

About the year 1800, as for many decades before and after, there were basically three avenues by which these works in the tale tradition reached the public. The first is the oldest, the most widespread, and in many ways the most important—oral storytelling. It is safe to say that until television metastasized so dramatically in the 1950's almost everyone on the planet was introduced to literature by way of tales such as "Snow White" and "Jack and the Beanstalk" or stories of Spider or of Rabbit and Coyote or of Fox or Bear. Even the Saturday morning television programs so many children now watch are fundamentally in the same tale tradition. The second means of transmission was books. European children had long enjoyed chapbooks like *Jack the Giant Killer*, and adults titillated their own imaginations with fare as varied as jest books and saints' legends. Countless European fairy tales had appeared in print, among them Charles Perrault's *Histoires et contes du temps passé, avec des moralités* (1697), but a powerful new influence entered in 1704-1717 with Antoine Galland's first European translation (into French) of *The Thousand and One Nights* (or *The Arabian Nights' Entertainments*). Something of the international character of these stories may be inferred from the fact that Englishmen translated the French translation which was itself an Arabic (largely Persian) translation of stories primarily derived from India and China. Where the stories ultimately originated and how old they really are no one will ever know. The magnificent example of *The Thousand and One Nights* and the growing interest in the past and in primitives which helped stimulate the rise of Romanticism led to Jacob and Wilhelm Grimm's *Grimm's Fairy Tales* (*Kinder- und Hausmärchen* or *Childhood and Household Tales*, 1812-1823) and to a host of similar folkloric collections in the early 1800's.

The tales in books tended to be one step from the traditional oral tales, but by 1800 a third medium, periodical publications—chiefly newspapers and magazines—offered a bewildering variety of forms of tale. Many were quite traditional; magazines published forms such as fables, anecdotes, fairy tales, and legends. Many, however, were quite different forms; many were much closer to what would be recognized as the modern short story. James Louis Gray lists among the many subgenres of short fiction in late eighteenth and early nineteenth century periodicals forms he calls tales of character, moral tales, histories, dialogues, sentimental tales, adventure tales, and allegories of the heart.

By the year 1800 all these antecedent forms continued to exist—orally or in print—and inevitably had a tremendous impact on the mind of anyone concerned with short fiction.

The Essay-sketch Tradition

The second grand tradition dominating short prose works in the year 1800 was that of the essay, especially the periodical essay or sketch. One can trace full-fledged tales back to the evolution of language, but the essay or sketch can hardly have existed before the creation of a fairly sophisticated system of writing. In one form or another essays must have existed from the time the first writer attempted (the word *essay* comes from the French word meaning to try or to attempt) to capture in prose his thoughts or feelings about some subject; alternately the sketch must have begun when the writer attempted to characterize or to describe some subject in prose.

Most historians of Western literature recognize as the first great writer of sketches the Greek philosopher Theophrastus, who around 300 B. C. composed a book called *Characters*; the work was composed of several short prose pieces, each representing some basic character or personality type. Theophrastus' sketches had a tremendous influence on later writers of sketches, especially those in the seventeenth century: Joseph Hall, John Earle, Sir Thomas Overbury, and Jean de La Bruyère. These writers in turn influenced Joseph Addison and Sir Richard Steele, who in *The Tatler* and *The Spectator* developed a number of more or less typical characters; the most important was Sir Roger de Coverley, a good-natured provincial squire with whom the sketch approached the sort of sophistication with which subsequent novelists were to treat character. In the decades preceding 1800 various writers such as Benjamin Franklin and Oliver Goldsmith, inspired by the example of Sir Roger, carried the character sketch further and further from idealized abstraction, closer and closer to the sort of uniqueness and individuality associated with character in fiction. With the gradual waxing of Romanticism and the slow shift of emphasis from thought to feeling, the character sketch had evolved into a form only slightly removed from the modern short story.

The essay has a similar lengthy history. From the beginnings of the form, the subject discussed seems to have held precedence over the individual mind acting on that subject, but in 1580 a minor literary revolution occurred when the Frenchman Michel de Montaigne published his *Essais*. Wishing to explore the nature of humanity and convinced that each man was a microcosm of the whole, he determined to plumb his own mind in detail ("I myself am the matter of my book. . . . It is myself that I depict"). Few subsequent essayists ever achieved a style or tone approaching Montaigne's charming intimacy, but his intensive compelling introspection helped others, even writers such as the relatively formal Sir Francis Bacon, shift their own focus more in the direction of personality. Again Addison and Steele played a crucial role; in

The Tatler and especially in *The Spectator*, they popularized what had been a relatively esoteric form and established a most successful model for a periodical series; these periodical series offered a variety of brief compositions on a dizzying miscellany of topics, unified by little but the persona of the essayist, the anonymous Tatler or Spectator. Benjamin Franklin and other followers cultivated a richer personality in the essayist; and by the year 1800, with the rise of sentimentality and Romanticism, the personality of the essayist became dramatically more important, to reach a plateau shortly in the familiar or personal essay as practiced by Charles Lamb and his contemporaries and followers.

Absolutely pure prose forms are approximately as rare as unicorns. Although the essay takes the natural form of exposition and the sketch inherently, irresistibly gravitates toward description, some narrative did invade both forms. We are familiar with narrative essays and with sketches which are almost stories; these were popular phenomena long before the birth of the modern short story.

Washington Irving: The Creation of the Modern Short Story

Precisely when did the modern short story begin? The question is like asking precisely where it is that the blue shades into violet in a rainbow. The more specific and dogmatic the answer the less reliable it is likely to be. It is known, however, that by the early 1800's in America, and in various degrees throughout the Western world, two distinct traditions existed side by side: one, the tale tradition full of narrative bursting with drama and incident, extraordinary situations and settings, and rather flat characters depicted for the most part externally; the other, the essay-sketch tradition, more subtly developed, largely ignoring striking incidents to focus on the vagaries of character, preferring the more normal and usual (in one sense more realistic) characters, situations, events, and settings, depending more on sharply observed detail, introspection, and thoughtfulness than on drama. The union of these two traditions was to mark the creation of the modern short story— but precisely when did that happen?

Literary historians, although less than unanimous, show a surprising degree of agreement that the modern short story began in America and that the American it began with was Washington Irving. The finest scholar of the American short story, Frederick Lewis Pattee, wrote that the form began in October, 1807, with Irving's publication in the periodical series *Salmagundi* of "The Little Man in Black." The piece is short and a story but has decidedly too little sophistication, too little psychological depth, and too little successful imagery really to succeed as a modern short story. At least as good, if not better, a case could be made for "Sketches from Nature" (perhaps by Irving or by his collaborator James Kirke Paulding, although in fact more likely by both), which appeared a month earlier in the same periodical series. Here we have a focus on mood and psychological subtleties, on sharply observed imagery, and on interior states. The problem is that finally the psychic change on which the piece ends does not add up to very much. The solution seems simple enough now: merely blend the virtues of "The Little Man in Black" (those of the tale tradition generally) and the virtues of "Sketches from Nature" (those of the essay-sketch tradition); but the evolution which had waited several thousand years after the introduction of writing to the Western world, tens and perhaps hundreds of thousands of years after the invention of story-telling, was in no hurry to occur.

No one with any degree of certainty can point to any given work as indisputably the world's first modern short story. We can with confidence, however, point out the first truly great modern short story produced in the Western world: "Rip Van Winkle," which appeared in the May, 1819, debut of Washington Irving's periodically published book, *The Sketch Book of Geoffrey Crayon, Gent.* Earlier writers had managed various blends of the tale and essay-sketch traditions before Irving, but none managed so brilliantly to blend the best of both traditions as to create from these two an irresistibly successful example of a wholly new form. How did Irving do it?

The most memorable parts of the story, the striking incident pattern involving Rip's experience with the dwarfish sailors of the *Half-Moon* and his two-decade-long nap, Irving based on a tale about a goatherd taken from Germanic folklore. In another bow toward the tale tradition, within the text itself, Irving's narrative persona, Diedrich Knickerbocker, relates that he heard the tale told orally by Rip himself and by other old Dutch settlers in the Catskills. The supernatural motifs of encountering the crew of Henrick Hudson's *Half-Moon*, who return every twenty years to tipple and to play ninepins in the mountains, and of course Rip's long sleep, also derive from the traditions of oral narrative.

In one form or another, however, all these elements existed long before Irving. His genius consisted in the brilliance with which he transmuted the elements which the tale tradition offered to him and to every other writer of his time. Irving transformed those basic elements by treating them as he might have treated the essential matter of a periodical essay or sketch. He developed Rip not as the flat character so common in tales, not as a kind of cardboard marker to be pushed from square to square in a board game, but as a rich, full, complete human being. Rather than merely assert certain abstract qualities in his character, Irving shows us through rich details a Rip who is good-natured, lovable, feckless, irresponsible, and (inevitably, given the above qualities and a wife too) terribly henpecked. The details with which Irving develops Rip are realistic, credible, and concrete—precisely the kinds of details with which the contemporary sketch-developed characters descended from Sir Roger de Coverley. Few if any previous prose tales could boast a character so effectively developed in terms of a credible human personality.

For many, the most characteristic aspect of the modern short story is its quality of psychological analysis, and of course the short prose form most inclined to intimate personal revelation came from the essay-sketch tradition, the familiar or personal essay. It is no accident that *The Sketch Book of Geoffrey Crayon, Gent.*, generally credited with containing the first great American successes in the personal essay, also contained a minutely detailed analysis of Rip Van Winkle's slowly dawning recognition of the immense changes twenty years made in himself and in his environment. Rarely if ever in a prose tale before Irving's masterpiece has the reader spent so much time minutely analyzing a character's mind.

Yet in "Rip Van Winkle," Irving pays quite as much attention to setting as to personality and psychology. With the rise of Romanticism, verbal sketches of nature achieved the same sort of popularity as those in the visual arts. Unlike almost any previous tale, "Rip Van Winkle" opens not by introducing a character or by outlining an incident or a situation, but with a subtle, sensitive, and thematically quite relevant description of a setting: the Catskills and a sleepy Dutch village within them. The careful arrangement and coloring, the sharp detail, and the attention to atmosphere in "Rip Van Winkle" help set it apart from earlier prose tales, which tended either to ignore setting or to dismiss it in brief idealized summary.

Some define the modern short story in terms of its realism, another quality much more characteristic of the essay-sketch tradition than of works in the tale tradition. For many readers the supernatural tipplers and Rip's incredible twenty-year sleep absolutely destroy any of the story's claims to realism—as they should if these elements reflect the mood of the story as a whole; but they do not, for three reasons. First, the great mass of the story (all but about six paragraphs) takes place in a densely realistic environment, in a setting developed with detail rich and credible enough to be all but photographic; few stories, for example, picture a scene more powerfully realistic than the long account of Rip's homecoming. Second, Irving gives us every reason to disbelieve that anything supernatural ever occurred. For one thing, most of the townspeople themselves refuse to believe Rip's story; for another, we learn that Rip himself told several versions of his story before finally fixing on one. A third point (one that cannot be appreciated if readers consult only various anthologies' butchered reprintings of the story) is that Irving chooses to tell the story *not* through an omniscient narrator, *not* through the reliable Geoffrey Crayon who supposedly authors *The Sketch Book of Geoffrey Crayon, Gent.* as a whole, but through the credulous dunderhead Diedrich Knickerbocker, purported author of Irving's ridiculous *A History of New York* (1809). In a note at the end we learn that even Knickerbocker realizes how unbelievable Rip's story is and feels obliged to offer corroborating evidence. The evidence: he has heard of equally incredible stories supposed to have occurred in the Catskills, and, for the clinching argument, he heard the story from Rip Van Winkle himself who even (and before a rural justice of the peace) signed, with an *x*, a document testifying to the tale's accuracy. In a technical strategy as old as time, Irving allows us our choice between alternative explanations: the story is literally true or, if we prefer, Rip ran away from his henpecking shrew of a wife and, hearing that after twenty years she died in a fit of anger at a peddler, he promptly returned with an outrageous lie to explain his long absence, a lie which only the most naïve will believe in the least. For those inclined to look closely, behind the façade of fantasy Irving displays an architecture grounded in solid reality.

It was particularly the confluence of these elements from the tale (plot and striking incident) and from the essay-sketch (character, psychological depth, setting, realism) which created the modern short story. Certain other, rather more unique, factors of "Rip Van Winkle" pioneered various subsequent trends in the short story. The intense focus on a unique place—the physical surroundings, the habits and customs and peculiar modes of thought of a subculture—showed the way for the local color movement which dominated Western literature in the second half of the century. In the bookish outsider Diedrich Knickerbocker bamboozled by a backwoods native's outrageous tall tale (and in "The Legend of Sleepy Hollow" the outsider Ichabod Crane's unhappy experiences with the native frontiersman Brom Bones), there is found an early example of frontier humor, a mode that burst on the scene in the 1830's and eventually gave rise to Mark Twain and *Huckleberry Finn* (1884) and in the present time to much of William Faulkner's work. Other important aspects of "Rip Van Winkle" are the story's toying with conventions of literary realism through its claim to truth based on a statement taken before a notary public; and its layering of narrators—from Irving to Crayon to Knickerbocker who bases his version on Rip's oral tale; its recycling of Knickerbocker from *A History of New York* and *Salmagundi* and reference to one of Rip's cronies, Peter Vanderdonk, and to his ancestor, Adriaen Van der Donck, who actually lived and who wrote an actual description of New Netherland (New York), to which Irving also refers in the story. This "deconstructive" technique of calling into question the essential "reality" of the narrative itself looks forward to O. Henry and beyond to the Postmodernists among our contemporaries.

Irving's literary earthquake, "Rip Van Winkle," was followed by a series of aftershocks that began the new decade of the 1820's for the short story. "The Spectre Bridegroom" and "The Legend of Sleepy Hollow" and "The Adventure of the German Student," all read with pleasure today, show an increasing tendency toward the Gothic mode which Nathaniel Hawthorne, Edgar Allan Poe, and Herman Melville were to employ to create some of the finest short stories in world literature. There were some other American stories of the 1820's read with genuine pleasure today—William Austin's "Peter Rugg, the Missing Man" (1824), for example—but most of the decade was given over to melodrama, to sentimental romance, or to didacticism. The popular reputations of the literary lions of the day have biodegraded quite as thoroughly as most of the paper on which they imposed their writings. Even the best among them—James Kirke Paulding (1778-1860), Catharine Sedgwick (1789-1867), Nathaniel Parker Willis (1806-1867), John Neal (1793-1876), Timothy Flint (1780-1840), James Hall (1793-1868)—are now little more than historical footnotes.

Point of view may be as important in literary history as in literature. In America the decade of the 1820's represented a tremendous falling off if the standard of comparison is the best of Irving's *The Sketch Book of Geoffrey Crayon, Gent.* On the other hand, if the standard is all other short narrative of the immediately preceding decades, then the 1820's represented a period of regular, if unhurried, advances in the skill and sophistication with which writers approached short fiction in general and this new form, the modern short story, in particular.

The true decade of advance for the genre—in America and, as shall be seen, in Europe—was the 1830's, which saw three different kinds of revolutions, one authored by Nathaniel Hawthorne, one by Edgar Allan Poe, and one by Augustus Baldwin Longstreet.

Nathaniel Hawthorne

Hawthorne's career began in a kind of imitation of the development of the modern short story. His earliest works were rather old-fashioned tales—"The Hollow of the Three Hills" (1830) and "Sir William Phipps" (1830)—and he also produced an early sketch, "Sights from a Steeple" (1831), which was much vaunted in his day; but these early works are finally insignificant. Hawthorne created the kind of artistic success destined to stand time's most stringent tests only when he combined the best of these two antecedent traditions in "My Kinsman, Major Molineux" (1832). Here, on the one hand, is a form close to the local New England legends he so loved to read and to compose— he opens with a paragraph of history referring to a real historian, sets the scene in historical Boston, gives a rough time for the event, builds his climax around the kind of episode (tarring and feathering a minor Tory official) which might have earned a brief footnote or inspired some oral tale. To this frame, however, Hawthorne adds the sort of rich imagery, the close psychological analysis, and the compelling specific detail which characterized his many experiments in the essay-sketch tradition. The result is neither essay, sketch, nor tale, but one of the finest modern short stories anyone ever wrote.

Similar patterns dominate "Young Goodman Brown" (1835). Many mistakenly try to read the story as a kind of simplistic parable, but Henry James, among others, emphatically disagreed: "this, it seems to me, is just what it is not. It is not a parable, but a picture, which is a very different thing." As in "My Kinsman, Major Molineux," Hawthorne here relies on intensive imagery and detailed psychological analysis to move well beyond the traditional tale and to create a truly modern short story. Here, as in many other short pieces, he borrows a great deal from the tale tradition—striking incident, dramatic situation, Gothic motifs, and so on. In his best work he does not, however, borrow plot in the strict sense of the term: that is, plot in the sense of a causal sequence of events leading to a climax. J. Donald Crowley and many other critics have described a "processional mode" which Hawthorne tends to substitute for plot. In these two stories, as in many others, Hawthorne develops the central experience through a series of tableaux or vivid scenes which occur in front of the character's eyes. The mode, which tends to be much more passive than active, seems to have been instinctive with Hawthorne, but a case could be made that he borrowed the technique from the contemporary descriptive sketch. Certainly the pattern dominated his own sketches; and, oddly enough, until he published *The Scarlet Letter* in 1850, it was these works firmly in the essay-sketch tradition rather than the short stories (or "tales" as his contemporaries would have called them) for which Hawthorne was principally recognized. In various personal comments, such as the 1851 Preface to *Twice-Told Tales* (1837), Hawthorne alluded to the public conception of himself as "a mild, shy, gentle, melancholic, exceedingly sensitive, and not very forcible man," generally, that is, as the author of such popular pieces as "Little Annie's Ramble," "A Rill from the Town Pump," and "The Toll-Gatherer's Day." What R. H. Fogle called "a general nineteenth-century mistrust of plot" helped cause many of those works least read in our own day to be among the most popular in his own. A contemporary, Henry T. Tuckerman, noted a "melodramatic" and a "meditative" strain in Hawthorne's fiction, and, like a great many contemporary readers and critics, revealed a decided preference for the latter, those more akin to the essay-sketch tradition.

Edgar Allan Poe

One tends to think of the early nineteenth century as the heyday of the "traditional" short story, that is the short story dominated by plot, but in fact experimental or innovative or unplotted short fiction was at least as popular in the time of Hawthorne and Poe as it is in our own. Perhaps the most important reason for our myopia is that in May, 1842, Edgar Allan Poe's highly laudatory and immensely influential review of Hawthorne's *Twice-Told Tales* was published; Poe's essay is almost universally recognized as the very first attempt to develop a cogent formal theory of the modern short story. Most critics today recognize that Poe's theory applies much more closely to his own work than to that of Hawthorne, who himself wrote Poe in June, 1846, that he admired Poe more "as a writer of tales than as a critic upon them. I might often—and often do—dissent from your opinions in the latter capacity, but would never fail to recognize your force and originality in the former." In an 1847 review for *Godey's Magazine*, five years after his first attempt, Poe was still refining his theory, but in essence he still held that a story must be judged wholly on the basis of the effect it creates; he further insisted that only the most finely adapted and consciously applied technical skill could ensure the desired effect. The technical skill itself should focus tightly on incident and arrangement of incident (in 1847 he added "tone" to his blueprint).

Many scholars credit Poe's theory with an immense influence on the subsequent development of the short story. Certainly Poe's disciple Fitz-Jam ›s O'Brien (c. 1828-1862) and many others would seem to have constructed their houses of fiction brick by brick according to Poe's blueprint; but how well does the blueprint describe antecedent fiction, such as Hawthorne's? According to Hawthorne and according to the best critics among his contemporaries and among our own, not very well. How well does the blueprint fit Poe's own fiction? Again, not very well. Poe does often have a climactic scene at the conclusion of his stories, but he most often and most successfully prepares for that conclusion not by developing a strong plot, a strong series of tightly integrated actions, but by intensely, powerfully, mercilessly overwhelming his readers with a dizzying atmosphere of sensually overwhelming imagery. As countless critics have commented, even in his most dramatic stories, in "The Fall of the House of Usher" (1839), in "Ligeia" (1838), and in "The Masque of the Red Death" (1842), Poe relies on a minimum of incident and on a maximum of imagery to prepare for his final effect.

Poe seems to have intuitively realized the fact and to have acknowledged its truth in the text of his most popular, and perhaps his finest, short story, "The Fall of the House of Usher." The story's epigraph keys us to the significance of an intensely sensitive awareness, and the story's first paragraph depicts a narrator powerfully affected not by any incident or arrangement of incident, but by imagery—the aspect of the house he describes so powerfully. Poe as book reviewer focuses on effect created by consciously manipulated patterns of incident; Poe's narrative protagonist focuses on effects created by the subconscious powers of imagery: "there *are* combinations of very simple natural objects which have the power of thus affecting us, still the analysis of this power lies among considerations beyond our depth." The reader who falls under Poe's spell in the story can only agree. Poe does have some stories more dependent on incident—"The Black Cat" (1843), for example, and "The Pit and the Pendulum" (1843)—but strangely enough he has other works which he called "tales" that have practically no incident whatever and which even today most readers would be much more inclined to consider sketches than true stories—"The Elk" (1844) is an example.

What conclusions should one draw? Poe's description of the intensively plotted story of effect described Hawthorne's best fiction and Poe's own best relatively poorly. Much more was going on than reasoned analysis could master. On the other hand, Poe might be said to have outlined his analysis as more an ideal to be sought (various desirable but unattainable ideals form the constant focus of his poems and stories) than as a reality already achieved. In this sense—that is, as a call to greater artistry in a genre too often considered a subcategory of journalism rather than as a nascent art form—Poe's theory seems to have been much more successful. Earlier writers treated structure, form, and technique with a rather cavalier disregard; N. P. Willis, for example, had a habit of writing a loose introductory descriptive sketch and following it with an only marginally related incident. Poe's insistence on applying the kind of unremitting attention to technique which conventional wisdom associated only with lyric poetry demanded for the short story a respect as literature which it had never before achieved.

Augustus Baldwin Longstreet and Frontier Humor

Irving created the modern short story by combining the inherent narrative interest of incident and plot (which already existed in the tale) with a tendency toward fully developed character, realism, specific detail and vivid imagery, and close psychological analysis (which characterized work in the essay-sketch tradition). Hawthorne brought to the form an intellectual commitment and a profound moral depth which raised the short story above mere entertainment and endowed it with the high worth associated with the finest poems, novels, and plays. In his criticism, Poe demanded on the one hand that readers acknowledge the new form's right to be considered as true literature, and, on the other, insisted that writers must bring the sorts of technical, artistic resources that alone could justify such a claim. In his own fiction, Poe demonstrated the power and subtlety possible when a writer marshaled the vast array of resources at hand.

Had these pioneering giants left anything out? Evidently many of their contemporaries felt so, for, quite independently of the short-story tradition which these men conspired to create, a quite different mode of short fiction was inventing itself.

Irving, Poe, Hawthorne, and their associates considered themselves among the cultured elite. Each took many of his most fundamental literary values from the Eastern establishment which borrowed its own from Europe, particularly from England. Meanwhile, below and beyond the Appalachians, in the barbarous regions of the "Southwestern frontier," in Tennessee, Georgia, Alabama, Mississippi, Arkansas, and other relatively unsettled areas of what then constituted the United States, relatively primitive living conditions had reduced the cultural level of the pioneering settlers below that of the established section of the Eastern seaboard. Down here, literature consisted not of delicate sensibilities written in Latinate phrasings, but in a vigorous telling of exaggerated oral tales. Scholars such as Constance Rourke and Bernard De Voto consider this oral tradition of outrageous storytelling to be the true original American art form and feel that it is as old as America. Scholars usually identify as the first appearance of this mode in written literature Augustus Baldwin Longstreet's *Georgia Scenes, Characters, Incidents, Etc. in the First Half Century of the Republic* (1835), but three years earlier Longstreet had begun publishing these treatments of the barbarous Georgians native to the Augusta area. A year before that, in 1831, William T. Porter had begun publishing the *Spirit of the Times*, a national magazine that soon began publishing narrative letters and other contributions from its widely distributed readership. The popularity which Longstreet and Porter achieved inspired a number of later frontier humorists, among them George Washington Harris (1814-1869), Joseph Glover Baldwin (1815-1864), Johnson J. Hooper (1815-1862), and Harden Taliaferro (1818-1875). In the opinion of many, the two great individual masterpieces of the genre are "The Big Bear of Arkansas" (1842) by Thomas Bangs Thorpe (1815-1878) and "The Celebrated Jumping Frog of Calaveras County" (1865) by Mark Twain.

Longstreet and his peers tended to isolate the more literary and sophisticated elements of the essay-sketch tradition in a gentleman (or a dude) who dominated frame material bracketed at the beginning and at the end. Within this frame, as Walter Blair long ago explained, we have a "mock-oral tale," a story designed as nearly as possible to capitalize on the virtues of the orally rendered stories any traveler could hear on the frontiers of the polite establishment.

One important element was humor, a feature with which Irving succeeded but with which Poe, Hawthorne, and most of their polite contemporaries seem to have failed miserably. These writers from the frontier based much of their humor on violence, physical grotesqueness, and cruelty, however, and a good deal of their material is offensive to modern sensibility. Another element important to the genre was an almost exaggerated realism. Except for his two great stories, Irving's fiction tended to drift toward the same Romantic environments that so often seduced Hawthorne and Poe. The frontier humorists wrote of immediate life, full of spavined horses, ripped trousers, spilled liquor, and hostile husbands; they wrote of their farms, shops, quiltings, revivals, militia meetings: of all that was most vivid, vital, and real to them.

In many ways the most significant element of Southwestern humor, and perhaps its greatest gift to Mark Twain and his finest gift to subsequent American literature, was the sense of a genuine speaking voice. The writing style of the established writers to the Northeast was emphatically artificial and valued highly for that very quality. No one ever really spoke as Poe and Hawthorne wrote, and their artificiality was central to their art. The frontier humorists delighted in introducing a gifted folk storyteller and, so far as possible, allowing him to exploit on the page the priceless virtues of a concrete, unaffected, vital, and vivid oral narrative. Nothing quite like it had ever been seen before. In its finest form, *Huckleberry Finn*, it would never be bettered by anything in American literature.

England and the Beginnings of the Modern Short Story

By 1840, then, in the modern short story, American literature could boast the triumphs of Southwestern literature as well as masterpieces by Irving, Hawthorne, and Poe, even though as an independent country America could measure its existence only in decades. What was being produced in the great European literatures, especially in English literature? Curiously enough, the country with the greatest literary heritage on earth, although it could boast much excellent short fiction, had not yet produced creditable modern short stories. Many of England's finest writers experimented, often unsuccessfully, with shorter forms: Sir Walter Scott (1771-1832), who had helped give Irving's career a great boost, produced some fine ghost stories and an interesting tale, "The Two Drovers" (1827), which develops from an essay framework. Beginning in 1820, Charles Lamb (1775-1834) published his *Essays of Elia* in the *London Magazine*; these were a series of brilliant familiar essays with everything required of a short story—psychologically rich character, sharply imaged setting, at least a minimal narrative flow—everything but a focus on a unique, particular experience meaningful for its own sake (the only likely exception might be "Dream Children," published in 1822, which is sometimes anthologized as a short story). Hannah More (1745-1833) published an enormously popular series of moral tales much too didactic to be considered true fiction. Maria Edgeworth (1767-1849) and Mary Russell Mitford (1787-1855) produced work marred by sentimentality and superficiality, but some pieces verge close to the modern short story.

Again and again, however, as T. O. Beachcroft points out, the best English writers seemed inclined to treat the kind of material most appropriate to a short story only as an episode in a novel or as a brief narrative poem. Countless examples of short stories *manqué* from the early nineteenth century might be drawn from Jane Austen's novels or from certain narrative poems of such poets as William Wordsworth or Lord Byron. William Makepeace Thackeray (1811-1863) published a series of condensed novels, summary parodies of popular contemporary genres, and a handful of other short fictions, mostly old-fashioned series of incidents unified chiefly by the life of a central character.

England's great popular and artistic success in short fiction during this period was unquestionably *Sketches by Boz*, which Charles Dickens (1812-1870) published in 1836; yet the fact that the greatest book of British short fiction from 1800 to 1840 hardly stands comparison with the least of that writer's novels gives us some sense of the way the British imagination scaled its proprieties. The *Sketches by Boz*, Dickens' first great success, owes much more to the essay-sketch tradition than to the tale. The young journalist who authored these sketches devoted his time, considerable energies, amazing powers of observation, and incomparable imagination to representing in brief prose pieces some of the multifarious scenes, characters, and activities he encountered in his endless jaunts through the London streets. In these pieces his sentimentality and melodrama are at (for him) a minimum, and his comic appreciation of color, contrast, and human oddity under no perceptible restraint. The book is absolutely delightful, but contains no real short stories. Some of these narratives have something of a plot, but in none does the author focus on creating a tightly focused, genuinely meaningful human experience of the sort we expect in the modern short story. It is senseless to try to fault Dickens for failing to achieve something he never attempted, but many writers much inferior to Dickens in all but a sense of form have produced much finer short fiction.

Why is it that, working from essentially the same literary traditions, the Americans produced so many very fine modern short stories by 1840 when the English had produced none? There have been many half-baked theories to explain British predominance in the novel and American precedence in the short story during the period in question (and in fact it was well into the 1880's before a writer born and bred in England produced a respectable—not outstanding—volume of short stories, Thomas Hardy's *Wessex Tales* in 1888). Some suggest that the rushed pace of American economic life and its business morality equating time and money forced American writers to generate works which might be read in short snatches of time, the physically slower pace of British life promoting longer narratives. This is nonsense. For one thing, during the period in question the rush-quotient did not differ appreciably from one side of the ocean to the other. For another, a great many British magazines flourished because of serialized novels, each monthly segment approximating a short story in length. Thus the consideration of physical length or of reading time seems finally an irrelevant consideration.

Much more important, and more commonly accepted as a reason for the national tendencies toward novels or toward stories, were the contemporary copyright laws, or the lack of them. In essence a writer's works were protected by copyright only in his own country. As a result American publishers could reprint any British novels they chose without paying a penny in royalties. The relatively higher status of British writers, and the fact that their works were freely available, made American publishers reluctant to publish novels by Americans. Economic conditions thus forced, or at least strongly encouraged, American writers to focus on publishing short fiction in magazines and gift-books (books usually of prose, poetry, and artwork which were published annually and intended largely as Christmas gifts), where payments to authors were minimal. Even the copyright theory should be taken with a grain of salt. For one thing, it does not explain the fact that the English, novelists of brilliance, failed to produce higher quality short fiction for their own magazines (which published discrete fictions as well as serialized novels). For another, it ignores the triumphs of James Fenimore Cooper (1789-1851) and others who, long before the copyright laws were altered at the turn of the century, demonstrated that American novels could reward American publishers (and readers) quite handsomely. The contemporary copyright laws were a factor, but should not be overrated.

Another factor, as Hawthorne, James, and other American writers have lamented, is that the novel as a form seems best adapted to a complex social environment, one in which manners, classes, and traditions carry enormous weight. The short story as a form has traditionally had a focus more psychological than sociological, more individual than social. Those cultures, or those individual minds, which pay relatively more imaginative attention to society than to the individual would seem naturally to have more affinity for the novel than for the short story.

Of more importance seems to have been a quite distinct factor, one which helps explain not only why the British turned to novels during the period and the Americans to stories, but also why so many individual writers who have attempted both forms are able to achieve real success only in one or in the other. Although many individual exceptions exist, in general the novel as a form tends to emphasize evolutionary changes which take place over a long period of time; the short story as a form tends to focus on a sharp change which occurs in a brief period of time, sometimes no more than a moment. Americans as a people are notorious for a mentality which demands immediate results and which focuses on the short term; Britons as a people are famous for their historical sense which emphasizes the part each smaller unit plays in some much longer evolutionary change. It was a Briton who first proposed the biological theory of natural selection occurring over eons, an American who first measured the speed of light. In some way the British mind seems predisposed to the kind of gestalt a novel represents; the Americans seem more predisposed to that of the short story. For whatever reason, the best short stories in English in the nineteenth century were not written by the English.

Germany and the Beginnings of the Modern Short Story

Previous discussion has shown how the early nineteenth century American short story developed essentially from a synthesis of the best which two divergent traditions offered. The Americans' model for the essay-sketch tradition came primarily from England; for contemporary Americans and Englishmen, however, the dominant written model for the other strain, that of the tale tradition, consisted chiefly of the literary *Märchen* (folktales) and *Novellen* (longer and relatively more realistic stories) of then fashionable German writers. As was earlier noted, for example, the vast and immediate popularity the brothers Grimm, Jacob (1785-1863) and Wilhelm (1786-1859), achieved by publishing short narratives based on their researches into Germanic folklore. Irving based "Rip Van Winkle" on a tale in a similar collection by Otmar. Such stories we call "fairy tales" in English, although often they contain no fairies at all, but witches, trolls, giants, or ogres. What they all *do* contain is emphasis on a striking incident or series of incidents which take precedence over character, setting, and all other elements. In addition, if true folktales, they share a common origin in folk traditions; each, in this sense, is (despite the inevitable variations incorporated by each individual narrator) a very old story.

In contrast to these traditional folktales there developed in Germany a tradition of *Novellen*. The term *Novellen* derives from the Italian term *novella*, which signifies "a small new thing." The sense of the word "new" in "*Novellen*" and "novella" (and in the French term "*nouvelle*") might be taken to mean "unusual or surprising," but in fact it seems most probably to have developed to distinguish a basically or at least largely original story from an essentially traditional story. The *Novellen* do tend to have a relatively more complex and realistic social background, but otherwise any artificial distinction between *Märchen* and *Novellen* becomes quite problematic when there is in both genres of German tale a fondness for particular settings (often isolated and grotesque), a frequent use of type characters (young lovers, bellicose aristocrats, sinister intellectuals), a focus on dramatic incident (some define the *Novellen* in terms of a requisite surprising "turning-point" or *Wendepunkt*), and so on.

Historically, the German form itself, like its name, owes an imposing debt to the largely Latin tradition of short tales involving—to mention only a few of the very best among many other works—Giovanni Boccaccio's *The Decameron* (1348-1353), Marguerite de Navarre's *Heptameron* (1558), and Miguel de Cervantes' *Exemplary Novels* (1613, *Novelas ejemplares*). Apparently the first German author to use the term *Novelle* was Christopher Martin Wieland (1733-1813), a particular favorite of Poe, who in 1772 offered the following brief description:

> The term "Novelle" is applied especially to a kind of narrative [tale] that differs from long novels by the simplicity of [its] plot [plan] and the small bulk of [its] fable, or, the relationship between them [the *Novellen* and novels] is like that of a small play to a great tragedy or comedy.

A. G. Meissner, who published a German translation of Boccaccio's *The Decameron* in 1782, published a volume of original stories, *Novellen des Rittmeisters Schuster*, four years later. The first genuine artistic climax in the German form, however, came in 1813 with Johann Wolfgang von Goethe's *Unterhaltungen deutscher Ausgewanderten*, a series of frame tales told within a contemporary setting which reflects the troubled political situation of the times. The relatively more rational social and moral emphases in Goethe's

Unterhaltungen in the later history of the *Novelle* altered in the direction of irrationality and exploration of personal and more specifically imaginative concerns.

Among the more important and more widely influential early nineteenth century writers of the *Novelle* were E. T. A. Hoffmann (1776-1822), Ludwig Tieck (1773-1853), Heinrich von Kleist (1777-1811), and Friedrich La Motte-Fouqué (1777-1843), and among the form's prominent critics (whose influences on Poe's theories are problematic) were Friedrich von Schlegel (1772-1829) and his brother August Wilhelm von Schlegel (1767-1845). The Schlegels' intensive emphasis on the artistic importance of unity of effect seems to have captured Poe's critical imagination much as the German fiction writers' dramatic, surprising, emotional, mysterious, often fantastic, and at times quite grotesque stories popularized the mode Anglo-American writers called Gothic, a mode which dominated much of the best short fiction in English until the 1850's, and some even beyond that. Yet various theorists of their time and of today would remind us that despite a heavy emphasis on fantasy, on the irrational, and on the supernatural, there was also a contrary impulse toward realism, one which entered the form in embryo when the *Novelle* initially divorced itself from the *Märchen* and which gradually grew throughout the nineteenth century until in the later decades, up to about 1890, the form's dominant mode was "Poetic Realism." This impulse to acknowledge the actualities of coherent environment and at the same time to emphasize irrationality and chaos; the antithetical impulses toward amoral narcissistic self-analysis on the one hand and toward moral imperative on the other; the vacillation between the asocial individual and the socially dominated individual; and the loyalties divided between the comic and the tragic—these and other tendencies of the early nineteenth century *Novelle* have been variously exploited in myriad patterns into the present century.

Russia and the Beginnings of the Modern Short Story

The origins of the Russian short story, like those of Russian literature itself, most scholars trace to Alexander Pushkin (1799-1837). Before Pushkin, in prose as in verse, there were two predominant "literary" strains in Russia: on the one hand, a vigorous tradition of oral folklore and, on the other, a written tradition dominated by foreign models, especially by the French. In fact, during Pushkin's time, French was the language affected by the elite; Pushkin's education was essentially French, his early reading emphasized French literature, and, startling though the fact may be, the father of Russian literature began his career as a writer in the French language.

As with the great American and European short-story writers, however, although his formal education emphasized polite written literature, Pushkin was informally introduced to a rich folkloric tradition of oral tales bursting with sharply defined characters, improbable incidents, and marvelous settings—the Russian *narodnye skazki* (folktales) and *volsebnye skazki* (fairy tales).

Pushkin began as a poet, and a long-verse narrative, *Ruslan and Lyudmila* (1821), was his first great success. He went on, however, to produce master-pieces in all the major genres—the play *Boris Godunov* (1826), the brilliant verse novel *Eugene Onegin* (1823-1831), and, most important for our pur-poses, in 1831 *The Tales of the Late Ivan Petrovitch Belkin*, a framed group of five dramatic and romantic short stories—but his masterpiece of short fiction is "The Queen of Spades" (1834). By Poe's standards the piece is long (about ten thousand words, it is divided into chapters) and rambling, with a need for tighter focus, but it may be considered the first great short story in Russian literature.

Normally considered the second great Russian writer, although actually much more of a contemporary, Nikolai Gogol (1809-1852) brought to the form emphases which magnificently complemented those which dominated Pushkin's work. Pushkin was drawn relatively more to the Byronic mode of Romanticism, to European models, and to aristocratic characters and back-grounds. The much earthier Gogol began his career with a group of stories strongly based on Ukranian folklore, *Evenings on a Farm Near Dikanka* (1831-1832). Here the folk models and backgrounds are as important to Gogol as the aristocratic and European are to Pushkin. The following years saw Gogol's great innovative fantasies "Diary of a Madman" (1835), *The Nose* (1836), and finally the masterpiece on which he worked for a number of years, *The Overcoat* (1842). The latter work brilliantly combines three distinctive elements of Gogol's work—first, a humor quite alien to the short story as Pushkin imagined it; second, a marvelous strain of fantasy akin to but finally quite distinct from that of the folklore he so loved; and third, a marvelous sense of realism. Fyodor Mikhailovich Dostoevski and Ivan Turgenev, and various other Russian Realists, have had attributed to them the quip, "We all came out from under Gogol's overcoat." Paradoxical as it may seem, this humorous tale of an insignificant clerk who wreaks revenge as a ghost did contain the seeds of precisely observed detail, of a specific social group's mores and behavior, and of a fidelity to life as the mass of his readers would recognize it, that led directly to the fictions, short and long, of the giants of Russian literature, Turgenev, Dostoevski, Count Leo Tolstoy, and even be-yond to Anton Chekhov and to various others, to the social criticism in Yevgeni Ivanovich Zamyatin's fantasies, in Mikhail Mikhailovich Zosh-chenko's mild satires, and to much of the very best of modern Russian fiction.

France and the Beginnings of the Modern Short Story

Anomalies and paradoxes abound in the short story. One is that the French, celebrated for their emphasis on logic and rationality (or alternately reviled for their penchant for contentious rationalization), have spent much less energy defining their basic critical terms for short fiction, *conte* and *nouvelle*, than people such as the Germans and the Americans have expended analyzing their own. Yet the French have among the world's very richest traditions in short fiction generally and in the short story in particular.

Conte, apparently the older French term, seems quite close to the world "tale"—on the one hand connoting emphasis on a dramatic (often supernatural or fantastic) central incident or incidents, and on the other hand forming part of numerous compound terms: *conte de fées* (fairy tale), *conte moral* (moral tale), *conte oriental* (oriental tale), and so on. *Nouvelle*, which in one sense means "news," would seem a literary term derived from the Italian term *novella* and the Spanish *novela* to indicate works such as the short fictions of Boccaccio and Cervantes which tend to be more realistic than *contes*, more integrated with a social milieu, and which often have more narrative complications.

The French critic Ferdinand Brunetière distinguished between the forms by setting the *conte* and the *roman* (the novel) as two poles with the *nouvelle* in between. The *roman* he considered the most realistic, the *conte* the least realistic. The *nouvelle* he felt dealt with subjects which might be extraordinary, unusual, or quite rare, but between the poles represented by the other two. Alfred Engstrom recognizes the same polar arrangement, but distinguishes among the three primarily on the basis of length and of narrative complexity, with the *conte* limited to a single and tightly integrated focus, the *nouvelle* limited to a single line of development (which may involve several linked incidents, no one of which is the story's primary focus), and the *roman* with plural lines of development. The *nouvelle* Engstrom equates with the English term novelette; the *conte* he considers the true short story, and he exiles from the genre any work with unrationalized supernatural elements, that is, works which contain incidents which cannot be considered "realistic" in the common sense of the term.

One may assume, in fact should assume, that neither scheme is really definitive, for both *conte* and *nouvelle* are quite elastic and even overlapping terms. One may assert, however, that a quite new and distinct sort of *conte* or *nouvelle* developed in France in the early decades of the nineteenth century and that this new form may be identified with the modern short story. In many ways the finest candidate for the first true French short story is *Mateo Falcone*, which Prosper Mérimée (1803-1870) published in the *Revue de Paris* in May, 1829. In this brilliant, powerful story and in three others published later that year, "La Vision de Charles XI," "Tamango," and "L'enlèvement de la redoute," Mérimée showed the ability to compress his action and to focus on a single incident, to create through closely observed detail a sense of a real environment, and to develop characters with genuine psychological depth.

The following year, 1830, saw the first short stories of France's great colossus of the nineteenth century novel, Honoré de Balzac (1799-1850): "El Ver-dugo," "Une Passion dans le désert," "Un Episode sous la Terreur," and in the following years several more, many of the later ones figuring as integral elements of his vast complex of novels, *La Comédie humaine* (1842-1848). Balzac constantly favored the more dramatic, more romantic materials, com-pulsively highlighting violence and strong emotions and at the same time constantly exploiting the novelist's predilection for questions of social forces and of social identity.

Théophile Gautier (1811-1872), the third important French writer to figure prominently in the short story's early history, published "La Cafetière" in 1831 and a handful of others at irregular intervals in the following years. Of the three, Gautier is indubitably the most Poesque (although in fact Poe did not publish his first short story, "Metzengerstein," until 1832), favoring ideal-ized type characters, fantastic incidents, and exotic settings; in fact, as with Poe, Gautier's powerfully suggestive imagery often carries the burden of emphasis, meaning, and power in his short stories.

Other French writers produced significant short fiction before 1840—Charles Nodier (1780-1844), Gérard de Nerval (1808-1855), and others—but it was these three early masters who provided French literature with a new kind of short fiction, a story which tended to concentrate its interest tightly on a single, focused narrative event rather than dissipating its energies in a long train of incidents, a story which valued the psychological dimension of its characters quite as much as it valued their predilection for fantastic situ-ations, and a story which replaced summary background with a sharply ob-served imagery designed to create a powerful and often suggestive environment in which the characters and incidents could credibly exist.

The grounds had been laid for one of the world's greatest short-story tra-ditions, although the form's greatest writers, among them none greater than Guy de Maupassant, were yet to arrive on the scene.

Walter Evans

SHORT FICTION: 1840-1880

Notes Toward a Theory of the Short Story

During the past thirty years American literary critics have become increasingly concerned with what Aristotle termed the art of literature in general as well as its various species. As a result of René Wellek and Austin Warren's *Theory of Literature* in 1948, the revival of the Aristotelian tradition encouraged by R. S. Crane's *Critics and Criticism* in 1952, and Northrop Frye's *Anatomy of Criticism* in 1957, as well as the more recent American discovery of early Russian Formalism and modern European Structuralism, books on poetics and literary theory roll off commercial and university presses in growing numbers. Particularly energetic have been efforts to establish a poetics for that species of literature which seems most resistant to theory—that is, prose fiction or narrative. Studies on the nature of narrative, the rhetoric of fiction, the theory of fiction, and the poetics of prose dominate the field both in number and importance.

On making even the most casual survey of these studies, however, one soon discovers an assumption so pervasive that it is seldom announced, much less questioned. When critics use the terms "prose fiction" and "narrative," they mean that relative latecomer to the hallowed realms of art and adademic concern—the novel. They seldom mention, except as an afterthought, the form of prose fiction which has developed with sophistication and vigor alongside the novel—at least since the beginnings of the nineteenth century—the short story. This attitude toward the short story, an attitude which hardly makes the form worth mentioning in the rarefied atmosphere of current criticism about "serious" literature, is not new in Anglo-American literary studies; it is, in fact, as old as criticism of the short story itself. In 1884, when Brander Matthews published the first discussion of the short-story genre since Edgar Allan Poe's famous 1842 review of Nathaniel Hawthorne's *Twice-Told Tales* (1837), he noted the "strange neglect" of the short story in histories of prose fiction.

The reasons for this neglect, which has persisted up to the present, are too complex to recount here. One of the most basic reasons, however, is the general devaluation of genre theory in Anglo-American criticism until recently; and a truly critical history of a literary form is simply not possible without a generic theory of that form. Fifty years separate Fred Lewis Pattee's *The Development of the American Short Story* (1923) and Arthur Voss's *The American Short Story: A Critical Survey* (1973), but their similarities sum up histories of the American short story. Both are surveys, filled with names, titles, dates, and sketchy considerations of influence, but neither is critical or theoretical and neither is informed by a generic theory of the form. R. S. Crane, in his *Critical and Historical Principles of Literary History* (1971), insists that the inductive development of distinctions of species is an essential task before one can write a narrative history. Wellek and Warren suggest that one of the most obvious values of genre study is that it calls attention to the internal development of literature; Wellek even goes so far as to say that the "history of genres is indubitably one of the most promising areas for the study of literary history."

Most comments about the short story focus on the form's midway position between the novel and the lyric poem. Poe himself placed the short story next to the lyric as offering the opportunity for the highest practice of literary art. Most critics since have not really disagreed and have, in fact, compared the short story to the lyric in various ways. Except for the fact that the short story shares with the novel the medium of prose, there is a fundamental difference between the two forms: although the short story is committed to prose fictional representations of events, it makes use of the plurasignification of poetry—using metaphoric overdetermined language because of the basically subjective nature of the form or its *multum in parvo* necessity to use the most suggestive but economical means possible.

The Russian Formalist critic, B. M. Ejxenbaum, says that the novel and the short story are not only different in kind, but also "inherently at odds." Genetically, the novel is a syncretic form, either developed from collections of stories or complicated by the incorporation of "manners and morals" material. The short story, on the other hand, is a "fundamental, elementary (which does not mean primitive) form." The difference between the two, says Ejxenbaum, is one of essence, "a difference in principle conditioned by the fundamental distinction between big and small forms." According to Ejxenbaum, the important implication arising from difference in size has to do with the difference between the endings of short stories and novels. Because the novel is structured on the linking of disparate materials and the paralleling of intrigues, the ending usually involves a "point of let-up." The short story, however, constructed on the basis of a contradiction or incongruity, "amasses its whole weight toward the ending." This built-in necessity of the form has, of course, been the source of much of the popular appeal of the short story and also the cause of the resultant scorn by the critics. Not all short stories depend on the kind of snap ending that O. Henry mastered, yet shortness of the form does seem inevitably to necessitate some sense of intensity of structure that is lacking in the novel.

Another suggestion about the implications of the shortness of the form has been made by Georg Lukács in his pre-Marxist *The Theory of the Novel* (1916). Although Lukács has since repudiated this early attempt to formulate a general dialectic of literary genres, his comments on the short story here offer some fruitful bases for further consideration. Perceiving that the short story is a fictional form which deals with a "fragment of life," lifted out of life's totality, Lukács says that the form is thus stamped with its origin in the author's "will and knowledge." The short story is inevitably lyrical because of the author's "form-giving, structuring, delimiting act." Its lyricism lies in pure selection. Yet, regardless of this lyricism, the short story must deal with event; and the kind of event it focuses on, says Lukács, is one that "pin-points the strangeness and ambiguity of life," the event that suggests the arbitrary nature of experience whose workings are always without cause or reason. The result of the form's focus on "absurdity in all its undisguised and un-adorned nakedness" is that the lyricism is concealed behind the "hard outlines of the event" and thus the view of absurdity is given the "consecration of form: meaninglessness *as* meaninglessness becomes form; it becomes eternal because it is affirmed, transcended and redeemed by form." Consequently, says Lukács, the short story is the most purely artistic literary genre.

When Lukács says that the short story is the most purely artistic form, he means, of course, that it is the least conceptual form—that it deals with experiences which refuse to be reduced to a concept or to be integrated into a larger conceptual system. Such experiences can only be selected. This is what Frank O'Connor means in *The Lonely Voice* (1963) when he says that whereas the novel makes use of the essential form of the development of character or incident as we see it in life, for the short-story writer there is no such thing as essential form. "Because his frame of reference can never be the totality of a human life, he must forever be selecting the point at which he can approach it, and each selection he makes contains the possibility of a new form as well as the possibility of a complete fiasco." Thus the basic difference between the two forms is the difference between pure and applied storytelling, and the pure storytelling that is found in the short story is more artistic than the applied storytelling that is found in the novel. Lukács says that the short story expresses the "very sense and content of the creative process." The result is that the short story is a highly self-conscious, even a self-reflexive, form that often tends to be about the nature of story itself.

The fact that the short story pinpoints the strangeness of life is due precisely to the fact that the short story focuses on fragments that are not only detached from the conceptual framework we call the totality of life, but fragments that also reveal the absurdity of that conceptual framework, even, as Albert Camus would put it, the absurdity of hoping for a meaningful conceptual framework. Because the individual experience thus detached is always meaningless, it can have nothing but form; the only possible integration for it is the integration within itself. He who focuses on the fragment of experience must necessarily sense absurdity or meaninglessness, or else its polar extreme, meaningfulness that transcends the "normal," the conceptual, the everyday. It is a clear indication of the modern temperament that a contemporary short-story writer such as Donald Barthelme can say, "Fragments are the only forms I trust."

The revelation in the short story is, as Robert Langbaum describes the revelation of nineteenth century poetry in his *The Poetry of Experience* (1957), not a formulated idea that dispels mystery, but a perception that advances in intensity to a deeper and wider, a more inclusive mystery. When Mark Schorer said that the short story is an art of "moral revelation" and the novel an art of "moral evolution," he was assuming the nonconceptual character of the experience depicted in short stories and the conceptual nature of experience in the novel. Evolution is a linear process manifested as cause and effect—the essence of the conceptual experience. Revelation is, by its very nature and definition, without cause. Something shows forth that was not there before. Evolution implies a teleology, an evolving toward some end; revelation has no such end.

The short story's method, however, is to present a glimpse through external meaninglessness to essential and immanent meaning. At least since James Joyce, it has been recognized that the short story's way of meaning is by means of the epiphany. Moreover, the "whatness" of the object that Joyce describes in aesthetic terms is equivalent to the "thouness" Martin Buber describes in moral terms. As Langbaum suggests, the epiphany is a way of knowing or apprehending value when value is no longer objective. This simply means that the epiphany mode is a radical return to the primitive mythic mode when there was no such thing as objective value, when all value by its very nature was subjective. The modern return to this mode begins with the early nineteenth century when external values are discredited and the short fictional form and the short lyric form become the most appropriate genres for the new milieu. The short story has always been an antisocial form, either in its adherence to mythic relationships or in its adherence to secularized psychological replacements of the lost mythic relationship. The short story as a modern artistic form seeks to replace the lost mythic perception with intense subjectivity and a revival of archetypes.

Short stories thus present synchronic invariants of human action, not the diachronic variants of social interaction. Since the short story does deal with such universals regardless of social surroundings, there was a need to hear stories long before there was a need to read the mimetic depictions of everyday reality. It is the liminal nature of human existence, even the religious nature of human existence as Philip Wheelwright and William James have described it, that gives rise to the short story. The English short-story writer Christina Stead says: "The belief that life is a dream and we the dreamers only dreams, which comes to us at strange, romantic, and tragic moments, what is it but a desire for the great legend, the powerful story rooted in all things which will explain life to us and, understanding which, the meaning of things can be threaded through all that happens." Human beings need to hear stories for the same reason they need to experience religion, says Canadian writer Hugh Hood. "Story is very close to liturgy, which is why one's children like to have the story repeated exactly as they heard it the night before. The scribe ought not to deviate from the prescribed form. That is because the myths at the core of story are always going on."

This notion of the story as liturgy is also suggested by Indries Shah in his discussion of the Sufi teaching story. Such stories do not teach by concept but rather by some more intuitive method of communication, by rhythm, or, as the structuralists would say, by a deep structure that lies beneath the conscious level of concept. We must go back to an early stage to prepare ourselves for story, says Shah, a stage in which we regard story as the "consistent and productive parallel or allegory of certain states of mind. Its symbols are the characters in the story. The way in which they move conveys to the mind the way in which the human mind can work.

The fact that the short story does not deal with social reality means that it tends to thrive best in societies where there is a diversity or fragmentation of values and people. This diversity has often been cited as one reason why the short story became quickly popular in the nineteenth century in America. In 1924, Katherine Fullerton Gerould said that American short-story writers have dealt with peculiar atmospheres and special moods, for America has no centralized society. "The short story does not need a complex and traditional background so badly as the novel does." Ruth Suckow also suggested in 1927 that the chaos and unevenness of American life made the short story a natural expression. The life in America was so multitudinous that "its meaning could be caught only in fragments, perceived only by will-of-the-wisp gleams, preserved only in tiny pieces of perfection." The more firmly organized a country is, says Seán O'Faoláin, "the less room there is for the short story—for the intimate close-up, the odd slant, or the unique comment." Frank O'Connor also notes that in those countries in which society does not seem adequate or sufficient for the repository of acceptable values we find the short story to be the most pertinent form. "The novel," says O'Connor, "can still adhere to the classical concept of civilized society, of man as an animal who lives in a community . . . ; but the short story remains by its very nature remote from the community—romantic, individualistic, and intransigent."

These considerations lead O'Connor to formulate his famous theory that the short story always presents a sense of

> outlawed figures wandering about the fringes of society. . . . As a result there is in the short story at its most characteristic something we do not often find in the novel—an intense awareness of human loneliness. Indeed, it might be truer to say that while we often read the novel again for companionship, we approach the short story in a very different mood. It is more akin to the mood of Pascal's saying: *Le silence éternal de ces espaces infinis m'effraie.*

The antisocial nature of the short story is one of its most predominant features. To understand this aspect of the short story, we might use, *mutatis mutandis,* a description T. S. Eliot once made of Henry James's fiction:

> The general scheme of James's fiction is not one character, nor a group of characters in

a plot or merely in a crowd. The focus is a situation, a relation, an atmosphere to which the characters pay tribute. The real hero in any of James's stories is a social entity of which the men and women are constituents.

The focus of short fiction is also an atmosphere or situation to which the characters pay tribute and of which they are constituents. Because the short-story situation, however, is like that of dream or myth, indeed, because the short story is always more atmosphere than event, its meaning is difficult to apprehend. As Joseph Conrad's Marlow understands when he attempts to tell the story of Mr. Kurtz and the journey into the heart of darkness, the meaning of an episode is not within like a kernel, "but outside, enveloping the tale which brought it out only as a glow brings out a haze." Marlow impatiently asks, "Do you see the story? Do you see anything? It seems to me I am trying to tell you a dream—making a vain attempt. No relation of a dream can convey that notion of being captured by the incredible which is the very essence of dreams."

The atmosphere that plays about the short story is not the social atmosphere or social entity of James's fiction, or by extension, of the novel generally; rather, it is an antisocial entity. If it is religious or numinous, we must remember that Herbert Otto in his study of the Holy has pointed out that the numinous can have a violent and frightening Dionysian aspect as well as a Christ-like one. Regardless of which aspect it takes, the short story, like the mythic aura of Christ and Dionysus, represents both the human and the divine; for both Christ and Dionysus are gods of showing-forth, of revelation, of epiphany. Both demand of their followers strange and paradoxical requirements: that we lose ourselves to find ourselves, that we plunge into the irrational, the incredible, into all that is against social law and human order in the everyday world.

Historical and Formal Background to the Short Story Before Poe

There is no such phenomenon as a totally new genre. Genres that appear to be new, such as the American short story in the 1840's, are the results of reactions against and integration of preexisting literary forms. The short story drew primarily from five such forms: the folktale, the medieval romance, the eighteenth century essay or sketch, the eighteenth century novel, and the romantic lyric. From the folktale, the short story takes its focus on a single event, usually an event that cannot be explained in terms of everyday reality. From the eighteenth century essay or sketch, it takes its focus on a personalized point of view—a definite teller whose attitude toward the story he is telling is as important as the story itself. Washington Irving's famous tales are perfect examples of this combination of folktale and point of view. Although Irving borrowed his plots from German folklore, he borrowed his teller's tone from Joseph Addison and Richard Steele. Irving himself drew attention to his concern with tone and point of view in a letter:

> For my part, I consider a story merely as a frame on which to stretch my materials. It is the play of thought, and sentiment, and language; the weaving in of characters, lightly, yet expressively delineated; the familiar and faithful exhibition of scenes in common life; and the half-concealed vein of humor that is often playing through the whole—these are among what I am at, and upon which I felicitate myself in proportion as I think I succeed.

From the medieval romance and the eighteenth century novel, the short story gets its focus on a symbolic or projective fiction, but one in which real people are involved. This experiment in fiction began in the late eighteenth century, of course, with Horace Walpole's *The Castle of Otranto* (1764). Walpole said that *The Castle of Otranto* was an attempt to "blend the two kinds of romance, the ancient and the modern." That is, he wished to retain the imagination and improbability of the medieval romance, but make use of the convention of character verisimilitude of the novel. As Walpole says in his Preface,

> Desirous of leaving the powers of fancy at liberty to expatiate through the boundless realms of invention, and thence of creating more interesting situations, he wished to conduct the mortal agents in his drama according to the rules of probability; in short, to make them think, speak, and act as it might be supposed mere men and women would do in extraordinary positions.

The result in the Gothic story is essentially a projective fiction embodying emotional states, yet a fiction in which characters with their own thoughts, fears, and anxieties—in short, psychologies—are enmeshed. The effect, to use Mary Shelley's *raison d'être* of another famous Gothic fiction, *Frankenstein* (1818), is a fiction that, however impossible as a physical fact, "affords a point of view to the imagination for the delineating of human passions more comprehensive and commanding than any which the ordinary relations of existing events can yield."

This is a basic romantic view, of course, which also infused the epoch-making *The Lyrical Ballads* (1798) and which underlies an important distinction between the romantic lyric and the eighteenth century poetry that went before it. The basic romantic fascination with medievalism and folk material springs from their realization of the basic religious or spiritual source of both the old romance and the folk ballad. The romantics' fascination with the old ballads and tales was part of their effort to recapture the primal religious experience, to demythologize it of the dogma that had reified the religious experience and to remythologize it by internalization and projection. In order to preserve the old religious values without the old mythological trappings, they secularized the religious encounter by perceiving it as a basic psychic process, by taking it back from the priests who had solidified it and experiencing it in stark uniqueness and singleness. This is indeed the focus in the "Preface to *The Lyrical Ballads*" and in Samuel Taylor Coleridge's discussion of his and William Wordsworth's dual tasks in *Biographia Literaria* (1817). The uniting of the old ballad material with the lyric voice of a single individual perceiver in a concrete situation gave rise to the romantic lyric. Robert Langbaum has discussed this creation of a subjective point of view in a concrete dramatic situation in his *The Poetry of Experience*. The positioning of a real speaker in a concrete situation encountering a particular phenomenon which his own subjectivity transforms from the profane into the sacred is the key to the romantic breakthrough.

The ballad story previous to Wordsworth and Coleridge existed detached from a teller, a projective fiction independent of an individual teller and tone. In the nineteenth century it became infused with the subjectivity of the poet and projected on the world as the basis for a new mythos. The thrust was dual. As Coleridge says, his own task was to focus on the supernatural, "yet so as to transfer from our inward nature a human interest and a semblance of truth sufficient to produce for these shadows of imagination that willing suspension of disbelief for the moment, which constitutes poetic faith." Wordsworth was to choose subjects from ordinary life and "excite a feeling analogous to the supernatural by awakening the mind's attention from the lethargy of custom and directing it to the loveliness and the wonders of the world before us." Clear examples of this dual project are Coleridge's lyrical story "The Rime of the Ancient Mariner" and Wordsworth's lyrical story "Resolution and Independence." The poems are representative of two primary modes of fiction—what Carl Jung calls the "visionary" and the "psychological" respectively. In Northrop Frye's terminology, they correspond to the basic difference between the romance mode and the novel mode, and therefore the basic difference between the tale and the short story. In the first, the characters are psychic archetypes; in the second they are primarily social personae.

The moral values in these poems are those of sympathy, identification, and love—the primary values of romantic axiolgy, most explicitly delineated in Percy Bysshe Shelley's *A Defence of Poetry* (1840). They later become the primary values of Nathaniel Hawthorne's stories in America. In *The Lyrical Ballads*, the ballad or "story" element, the hard outlines of the event, are subsumed by the lyrical element, which is foregrounded. For Hawthorne and Poe, however, in America it is the story element that is foregrounded. The lyrical element exists as the personal voice of the teller, a teller who responds personally to the event, but whose tone is somewhat delyricized by the influence of the "talk-of-the-town" tone of the eighteenth century essay and sketch.

Both Fred Lewis Pattee and Edward J. O'Brien in their 1923 histories of the American short story place the birth of the form with Washington Irving's combination of the style of Addison and Steele with the subject matter of German Romanticism. Pattee says about Irving's *The Sketch Book of Geoffrey Crayon, Gent.* (1819-1820): "It is at this point where in him the Addisonian Arctic current was cut across by the Gulf Stream of romanticism that there was born the American short story, a new genre, something distinctly our own in the world of letters." O'Brien, focusing more on the classical Arctic than the Gulf Stream romanticism, says that the short story began when Irving detached the story from the essay, especially the personal essay of the "talk-of-the-town." It is obvious that Irving's Diedrich Knickerbocker is more like the eighteenth century Roger de Coverley than he is the anonymous folk storyteller of the ancient ballad.

H. S. Canby has also noted Addison's influence on Irving which resulted in a classical restraint and a gentle humor in his stories, but it is with Hawthorne's and Poe's mutations and development of the romantic impulse that the short story more properly begins. Poe's contribution, says Canby, was to do for the short story what Coleridge and John Keats were doing for poetry: to excite the emotions and to apply an impressionistic technique to his materials to hold his stories together. Hawthorne, however, uses a moral situation as the nucleus to hold his stories together. Hawthorne was, in fact, the first American story writer to build a story on a situation, an "active relationship between characters and circumstances." Pattee agrees that Hawthorne was the first to touch "the new romanticism with morals" and that both Hawthorne and Poe differ from E. T. A. Hoffmann's and Ludwig Tieck's "lawless creative genius" and "wild abandon" by exercising deliberate control and art. Pattee also suggests that Poe's important contribution was his realization that the tale is akin to the ballad form, but that like the lyric, it was dependent on an emotional, rather than a conceptual unity. For Poe, says Pattee, the story was a "lyrical unit, a single stroke of impressionism, the record of a moment of tension." Alfred C. Ward, in his 1924 study of the modern American and English short story, is quite right in noting that what links Hawthorne's stories with those of writers of the twentieth century is that they both "meet in the region of half-lights, where there is commerce between this world and 'the other-world.' " The difference between short-story writers before Hawthorne and those after him, however, is that while this region of half-lights for the preromantic existed in the external world of myth and the religious externals of allegory, for writers after the romantic shift the realm exists within what James has termed Hawthorne's "deeper psychology." Many critics since Ward have agreed with him that the brief prose form "affords a more suitable medium than the novel for excursions into the dim territory of the subconscious." In the first "theory" of the short story after Poe, Brander Matthews makes a brief suggestion that the short story has always been popular in America because the Americans take more thought of things unseen than the

English. Matthews was also the first to notice, although he does not develop the point, that although Poe depicts things realistically or objectively, a shadow of mystery always broods over them. The subtle movement from Hoffmann's and Tieck's fairy tale-like unrealities and supernatural events to Poe's psychological stories which push psychic responses to such extremes that they *seem* supernatural marks the beginnings of the short story.

Bliss Perry, in an unusual departure from usual histories of prose fiction at the turn of the century, devotes a chapter to the short story in his 1902 study entitled *A Study of Prose Fiction*. He notes that because of the shortness of the form, if the story is concerned with character, the character must be "unique, original enough to catch the eye at once." The result of this necessity for choosing the exceptional rather than the normal character is that the short story is thrown upon the side of romanticism rather than realism. Perry also notes another point about the short story that has remained constant since its inception:

> Sanity, balance, naturalness; the novel stands or falls, in the long run, by these tests. But your short story writer may be fit for a madhouse and yet compose tales that shall be immortal. . . . The novelist has his theory of the general scheme of things which enfolds us all, and he cannot write his novel without betraying his theory. . . . But the short story writer, with all respects to him, need be nothing of the sort.

Both Alberto Moravia and Richard Kostelanetz have recently noted this characteristic of the short story in opposition to the novel.

This insistence on the basic romantic nature of the short story, both in its focus on unusual events and on the subjectivity of the form, was strongly voiced in the late nineteenth century when Ambrose Bierce entered the argument then raging between William Dean Howells and Henry James over the romance versus the novel form. In his attack on the Howells school of fiction, Bierce says, "To them nothing is probable outside the narrow domain of the commonplace man's commonplace experience." The true artist, says Bierce, is one who sees that life is "crowded with figures of heroic stature, with spirits of dream, with demons of the pit. . . . The truest eye is that which discerns the shadow and the portent, the dead hands reaching, the light that is the heart of darkness." Even James says that he rejoices in the anecdote which he defines as something that "oddly happened" to someone. More recently, Flannery O'Connor has placed the short story within the modern romance tradition, a form in which the writer makes alive "some experience which we are not accustomed to observe everyday, or which ordinary man may never experience in his ordinary life."

The only extended critical discussion of this romantic element in the short story is Mary Rohrberger's *Hawthorne and the Modern Short Story: A Study in Genre* (1966). Comparing Hawthorne's comments in his prefaces with comments by modern short-story writers, Rohrberger notes that both share the romantic notion that reality lies beyond the extensional, everyday world with which the novel has always been traditionally concerned. "The short story derives from the romantic tradition," says Rohrberger:

> The metaphysical view that there is more to the world than that which can be apprehended through the senses provides the rationale for the short story which is a vehicle for the author's probing for the nature of the real. As in the metaphysical view, reality lies beyond the ordinary world of appearances, so in the short story, meaning lies beneath the surface of the narrative.

Poe, Hawthorne, and Gogol:
The Beginnings of the Short Story

Poe's romantic allegiance to poetry and his debt to Wordsworth and especially Coleridge for his theories about the nature of poetry and the imagination is made clear in his many reviews and critical essays. For Poe, the highest genius can be best employed in the creation of the short rhymed poem; it is poetry that elicits the poetic sentiment—"the sense of the beautiful, of the sublime, and of the mystical." If one wishes to write in prose, however, Poe says, "the fairest field for the exercise of the loftiest talent" is the tale; for the tale is the closest one can get to poetry when writing mere prose. The basic difference between poetry and the tale form for Poe is that while the tale is concerned with truth, the poem is concerned with beauty and pleasure; and truth, Poe makes quite clear in his discussion of Hawthorne's *Twice-Told Tales*, means the presentation of a theme by means of the author's ability to use a "vast variety of modes or inflections of thought and expression." Furthermore, what Poe admires in Hawthorne in addition to the central attribute of the short story—"Every word *tells* and there is not a word that does *not* tell"—is that Hawthorne not only displays a novelty of theme but a novelty of tone as well.

The most troublesome element of Poe's theory of the short story, however, lies in his remarks on the tale's "single effect," for these comments led in the early twentieth century to a misplaced concern with the tricks a writer may use to construct a story for effect rather than with how a story complexly affects the reader. For a further consequence of misreading Poe has been that many critics have taken the phrase "single effect" to mean "simple effect." Part of the problem is the critical bias against the very "shortness" of prose narrative that Poe most insisted on. The usual assumption is that narrative by its very nature is concerned with movement and therefore character development and change. Since change is a complex phenomenon influenced by a multitude of forces, it follows that the novel can more plausibly present change than the short story. As Thomas Gullason has recently pointed out (*Studies in Short Fiction*, 1973), Mark Schorer's famous distinction between the short story as the "art of moral revelation" and the novel as the "art of moral evolution" does seem to contribute to various stereotypes which have deadened the response of readers to short fiction. The distinction is damaging to the short story, however, only if we accept the prevailing bias that the nature of narrative is to present change plausibly and that the novel is thus the narrative norm. Unfortunately, Gullason does accept this, asserting that "it is mainly in terms of 'moral evolution' or growth that a fiction becomes organic—lifelike, plausible, multidimensional, and long-lived. Moral revelation alone usually leaves a fiction artificial, unrealistic, one-dimensional, and short-lived." In short, Gullason attempts to defend the short story by suggesting that it is really more like the novel than previous stereotypes have led us to believe—that it is realistic and has an "everyday quality" applicable to general reality. The best way to redeem the short story from previous critical neglect is not to ignore its unique characteristics, but rather to focus on how the very shortness of the story compels it to deal with a different mode of reality and knowledge from that of the novel and therefore how it has a different effect on the reader. One way to achieve this and better understand what Poe meant by "single effect" is to make use of approaches developed by philosophy and anthropology to the nature of myth. The most helpful are those of Ernst Cassirer. What is being suggested is that the short story, although separate stories may indeed structure myths as different constitutive units, is primarily a literary mode that embodies and recapitulates mythic perception itself.

Once we hypothesize this as a central characteristic of the short story, we can better defend Poe's insistence on the unique or single effect of the form; we can better combat the bias against it which, confusing novel with story and history with myth, insists that the short story have a plausible, everyday quality; and we can better justify the comments already made that the short story is centered around emotion, intuition, and fleeting perceptions that consequently give it its mysterious, dreamlike quality. In short, we can begin to see that the bias for the novel as narrative norm and the consequent neglect of the short story is the same bias that Cassirer describes as modern man's preference for theoretical thinking over mythical thinking.

Not only is mythic perception impregnated with emotional qualities and surrounded by a specific atmosphere, but it is also characterized by a focus on the immediate present. Cassirer says, thought is "captivated and enthralled by the intuition which suddenly confronts it. It comes to rest in the immediate experience, the sensible present is so great that everything else dwindles before it." From this point of view, Poe's stress on the "immense force" of the short story "derivable from *totality*" and the great importance of "unity of impression" to make possible the "deepest effects" becomes more significant. The short story, more than other modes of narrative, requires complete absorption. Moreover, it is the only form of narrative with which the reader can be completely absorbed for the *totality* of the narrative experience. As Poe says, "During the hour of perusal the soul of the reader is at the writer's control. There are no external or extrinsic influences—resulting from weariness or interruption." Similarly, Cassirer says, when one is under the spell of mythic thinking, "it is as though the whole world were simply annihilated; the immediate content so fills his consciousness that nothing else can exist beside and apart from it." Cassirer says the characteristic of such an experience is not expansion, but an impulse toward concentration; "instead of extensive distribution, intensive compression. This focussing of all forces on a single point is the prerequisite for all mythical thinking and mythical formulation."

The short-story form manifests this impulse toward compression and demands this intense focusing for the totality of the narrative experience primarily because it takes for its essential subject the mysterious and dreamlike manifestations of what Cassirer calls the "momentary deity." The production of these deities, the first phase of the development of theological concepts, does not involve investing them with mythico-religious images. Rather, Cassirer says:

> it is something purely instantaneous, a fleeting, emerging and vanishing mental content. . . . Just let spontaneous feeling invest the object before him, or his own personal condition, or some display of power that surprises him, with an air of holiness, and the momentary god has been experienced and created. In stark uniqueness and singleness it confronts us . . . as something that exists only here and now, in one indivisible moment of experience, and for only one subject whom it overwhelms and holds in thrall.

Many, perhaps most, short stories present characters thus overwhelmed and enthralled by something within or without them which they invest with mythic rather than logical significance. Roderick Usher's obsession with the horror of the house that he can neither name nor understand, Goodman Brown's compulsion toward the witches' sabbath, Bartleby's absorption with the wall that makes him prefer to do nothing—none of these experiences can be accounted for logically; neither can they be presented in terms of everyday reality. In fact, they are characterized by their removal from everyday reality. Thus, the short story is the form best able to embody this mythic experience. As Cassirer says:

> It is as though the isolated occurrence of an impression, its separation from the totality of ordinary, commonplace experience produced not only a tremendous intensification, but also the highest degree of condensation, and as though by virtue of this condensation the objective form of the god were created so that it veritably burst forth from the experience.

Hawthorne's critical comments about art are less developed than Poe's and confine themselves primarily to prefaces in which he discusses the nature of the romance form. Hawthorne, however, no less than Poe, is concerned with the mythic and the mysterious. Hawthorne's comments about the romance can be applied equally to the short tale, for as Northrop Frye has pointed out, the romance bears the same relation to the tale form as the novel does to the more developed short story. In the former, the characters are archetypes which serve the function of the mythic plot; in the latter, the characters are wearing their social masks. The romance and the tale are visionary forms, while the novel and the short story tend more toward psychologizing and verisimilitude. Hawthorne, although he may have expressed a longing to master the techniques of realism, found such techniques impossible to reconcile with his own vision of the superiority of moral truth over physical truth. In fact, Hawthorne's technique is to spiritualize the material and thus, in true romantic fashion, discover true or "sacred" reality always immanent in the "profane" physical world. As he notes in his Preface to *The House of the Seven Gables* (1851), Hawthorne finds that the romance, while governed by its own laws, is not bound by the laws of fact and is therefore freer than the novel. Hawthorne's stories, like Poe's, follow the laws of their own conventions rather than the laws of external reality. Thus, to use Northrop Frye's term, they are less "displaced" than the novel; they do not try to conceal their conventions under the cover of verisimilitude.

Another central element of fiction for Hawthorne, one that accompanies Poe's emphasis on tone, is the importance of atmosphere. In the Preface to *The Blithedale Romance* (1852), Hawthorne laments the loss of the "old world" conventional privileges the romance had. Among American writers there is no "Faery Land" which has its own rules that govern it so that it can be placed equally alongside nature, no realm of reality that is so much like the real world in its truth and laws that in its "atmosphere of strange enchantment," the "inhabitants have a propriety of their own." Without such an atmosphere, Hawthorne says, the characters of the imagination "must show themselves in the same category as actually living mortals." It is precisely this atmosphere of fantasy in which real people dwell, however, that begins to make itself felt as central to the genius of the short story. It is that "neutral territory somewhere between the real world and fairy-land, where the Actual and the Imaginary may meet and each imbue itself with the nature of the other."

One final element in Hawthorne's fiction which further contributes to the development of the short story as a genre is a thematic view also shared by Poe—the importance of sympathy. For Hawthorne, as it was for Shelley in *A Defence of Poetry*, sympathy was the great secret of morals. Shelley says, "A man, to be greatly good, must imagine intensely and comprehensively; he must put himself in the place of another and of many others; the pains and pleasures of his species must become his own." It is obvious that in Hawthorne's fiction, isolation and alienation exist for those who, like Ethan Brand and Giovanni, lack "the key of holy sympathy." Although Poe's fiction, because it seems less obviously concerned with moral themes than that of Hawthorne, appears to lack the element of sympathy; this is not, however, the case. Poe's first-person narratives, such as "The Tell-Tale Heart," "The Black Cat," and others, demand of the reader a sympathy and participation in much the same way that Robert Langbaum says is required for the narrators of Robert Browning's monologues. Moreover, the nature of sympathy becomes a metaphysical principle for Poe in his prose poem *Eureka* (1848), in which he points to a universal brotherhood of atoms themselves. It is a cosmology which for Poe has a moral implication: "No one soul is inferior to another."

Lest one might think these combinations of elements—the fantastic and dreamlike with the real, a focus on sympathy, an emphasis on unity, and a concern with the story following its own laws—are an isolated American occurrence, it is best that we now turn to a development in Russian literature in 1842—the same year as Poe's famous review—the publication of Nikolai V. Gogol's *The Overcoat*. Frank O'Connor in his study of the short story has suggested that Ivan Turgenev's famous remark, "We all came out from under Gogol's 'Overcoat,' " is applicable not only to Russian writers, but is a general truth as well. O'Connor points to this story as marking the origin of the short-story form. For O'Connor, *The Overcoat* is like nothing in the world of literature before it.

> It uses the old rhetorical device of the mock-heroic, but it uses it to create a new form that is neither satiric nor heroic, but something that perhaps finally transcends both. So far as I know, it is the first appearance in fiction of the Little Man, which may define what I mean by the short story better than any other terms I may later use about it.

O'Connor goes even further and suggests that if one wanted an accurate key description of what is central to the short story, he could do no better than quote Akaky Akakyevitch's plaintive tacit cry to those who harass him: "I am your brother." The phrase indicates both the isolation of Akaky and his need for sympathy. In Akaky, O'Connor finds a central type of figure in the short story, because always in the short story, O'Connor says, there is a "sense of outlawed figures wandering about the fringes of society. . . . As a result there is . . . an intense awareness of human loneliness."

This cry for human sympathy, this sense of isolation and loneliness, however, is not the only thing that characterizes *The Overcoat* and makes it stand out as a unique new fictional creation. The passage from which O'Connor quotes is referred to in Russian criticism as the "humane passage." Indeed, the classical Russian view of the story in the nineteenth century is that the story is one of the first Russian works about the "little man" oppressed by the crushing regime of the Tsars, that the story is a realistic one with social significance; its only blot is the introduction of the fantastic at the end. In the 1920's, however, in what has now become a significant contribution to the Russian Formalist movement, the critic Boris Ejxenbaum discovered the technical and formal genius of Gogol's story. Ejxenbaum says that *The Overcoat* is a masterpiece of grotesque stylization in which Gogol takes the basic narrative technique known in Russian criticism as *skaz* (the oral narrative of a lowbrow speaker) and juxtaposes it against the sentimental rhetoric of the tone to make the reader uneasy about whether to sympathize with Akaky or laugh at him. The "humane passage" exists not simply to make us feel the oppression of the "little man," but rather to create a contrapuntal tension between comic *skaz* and sentimental rhetoric. "This pattern," says Ejxembaum, "in which the purely anecdotal narrative is interwoven with a melodramatic and solemn declaration, determines indeed the entire composition of 'The Overcoat' as a grotesque." The effect of the story is a "playing with reality"—a breaking up of the ordinary so that the unusual logical and psychological connections of reality turn out, in this constructed world of the story, to be unreal.

This is precisely the kind of play with reality, although admittedly with a different tone, in which Hawthorne was engaged; it is also similar to the tone of combined mock seriousness and sarcasm in which Poe delighted. Ejxenbaum says that the structure of a short story always depends in large part on the kind of "role which the author's personal tone plays in it."

Hawthorne's stories are obviously very close to their folklore and Gothic origins. The genius of Hawthorne that sets him apart from the anonymity of folklore and the plot focus of the Gothic, however, is not only his own personal tone, but also his awareness that the conventions of folklore and the Gothic are really the embodiments of unconscious, even mythic, reality. Moreover, although many of his stories seem allegorical, they are less allegorical in the traditional sense than they are early attempts to perform in prose fiction the function that romantic poetry had served: to find the spiritual and moral meaning beneath the external physical and social reality of human life and events. The result, says Haytt H. Waggoner, is that we have no name for Hawthorne's type of story—not quite allegories, not quite symbolic, but somewhere in between. In fact, Hawthorne's type of story is the result of a merging of the representative fiction of allegory and the mimetic fiction of the novel. Thus, the stories seem both to be determined by the characters within them, and at the same time determined by the story of which the characters are only functions. This focus tends to make the short story more aware of its own artifice and illusion than the novel, therefore more aware of its own process of ordering. The result is often a dreamlike story that is aware of itself as dream.

The problem of the dream nature of "Young Goodman Brown" is related to its modal situation halfway between realism and romance. If we ask whether the story is a dream told as if it were reality, or whether it is a reality told as if it were a dream, we realize that we cannot make that determination. The story begins with a concern with the oneiric as Faith tells Brown that she has been troubled with dreams; he wonders if a dream has warned her of his journey on this one night of the year. Of course at the end of the story, Hawthorne teases the reader with the question: "Had Goodman Brown fallen asleep in the forest and only dreamed a wild dream of a witch meeting?" The problem of the story is: if it is a dream, when did the dream begin and who is dreaming it? There is certainly no point in the story when Brown falls asleep, as is typical of the traditional dream-vision story. Moreover, if the forest meeting is a dream, then the whole story must be dream, for Brown knows where he is going from the beginning; and indeed from the point of view of the story as a projective fiction, both Faith and Brown are merely functions of a dreamlike folklore allegory—that is, Hawthorne's "dream."

Because Brown seems to have his own consciousness and seems at times to be uncertain about what lies before him in the forest, the story has its mimetic aspect as well. The crucial moment in the forest when Brown calls out to Faith to resist the evil one is clearly a breakthrough moment when he manifests his own will and becomes a psychological character rather than a parabolic function. This uncertainty as to the nature of reality in the story is intrinsically related to the moral-thematic impact of the story. "Young Goodman Brown" is not a simple initiation story of a youth becoming aware of evil, but rather a mimetic-symbolic story of the movement from *faith* that reality is simply its surface appearance to *knowledge* that reality is complex and hidden; it is a movement from an unquestioned sense of community to a realization that community must be constantly developed. In this sense it is a romantic story of the fall in perception from a unified sense of reality to the awareness of separation and the realization of the necessity of healing that separation. Instead of making the effort of sympathy and love to unite himself with others, however, Brown turns from them forever; having lost the absolute, he cannot live with ambiguity.

Another Hawthorne story that seems part parable and part mimetic representation is "The Minister's Black Veil." Although the minister has his own psychology and thus much of the story depicts his personal suffering, Hawthorne transforms the veil (rather the minister himself makes this transformation) into a symbolic object and the story into a parable—not a parable in the usual sense of a simple story to illustrate a moral, but rather a parable in the basic root sense of the word; that is, a story that probes basic mystery. The minister does not hide his face to conceal some secret personal sin (as he might in a realistic story), but rather to objectify his metaphysical awareness that the meaning of sin is separation. The thematic thrust of the story is similar to that in "Young Goodman Brown"; the minister, made aware of basic human separation, now tries to perform his ministerial function by teaching others that same awareness through the emblem of the veil. The moral implication of this awareness, as it often is for Hawthorne, is that life must be lived with the realization of separation so that the individual will see the need to have sympathy for the other—the need to project the self into the other, penetrate behind the social veil that we all wear. The story is also similar to Herman Melville's *Bartleby the Scrivener* (1853) in that the minister's black veil is like Bartleby's wall: an emblem of all that stands in the way of human communication. What makes Hawthorne's story more than a simple allegory is not only the complex meaning of the veil, but also the fact that the minister is consciously aware of the meaning of the veil. His "madness" in the mimetic world of the story, which makes him treat a simple object as if it were its metaphysical meaning, is a function of his symbolic role in the parabolic world of the story.

The loss of the absolute and the entrance into ambiguity is also depicted in "My Kinsman, Major Molineux," a story which combines actuality (this time a historical transition that takes place in America) with myth and dream-like reality. Young Robin, the rustic youth on his first visit to town just after his eighteenth birthday, has all the characteristics of the conventional folktale initiate setting out to seek his fortune in the world. His evening of ambiguity as he searches for his kinsman from whom he seeks preferment is a symbolic journey in which he encounters figures of human ambiguity: sexuality in the form of the young girl with the scarlet petticoat, death in the elder man with his "sepulchral hems" which evoke the "thought of the cold grave," authority in the nightwatchman who warns Robin he will be in the stocks by daylight, and ultimate duality in the Janus-faced man who suggests both a fiend of fire and a fiend of darkness.

Each time Robin is rebuffed in his quest for his kinsman, he tries to rationalize an explanation; finally reason is rebuffed so often that he begins to doubt not only reason, but also the state of his present reality. He recalls his father and home and asks: "Am I here or there" and his mind vibrates between fancy and reality. When a stranger comes by, he cries, "I've been searching half the night, for one Major Molineux; now, sir, is there really such a person in these parts, or am I dreaming?" Indeed, at this point in the story the reader may well feel that Robin's encounters have been so grotesque and mysterious that the story *is* the embodiment of a dream or a myth. Also at this point, however, the mystery is explained by reality itself as Robin sees the crowd coming down the street with the tarred-and-feathered kinsman; the historical framework—of the colonists rejecting governors appointed by the king— supplies the realistic motivation to account for all the seemingly mythical events of the night. Hawthorne, however, never completely "naturalizes" his fictions; the realistic explanation does not dislodge the mythic aura of the events. Furthermore, the stranger with Robin at the end is not realistically explained; he is solely a function of the parabolic story—a mythic elder companion to Robin's new awareness, a denizen of the fable element of the story.

The same kind of fantasy and reality integration constitutes the nature of

Hawthorne's most difficult story, "Rappaccini's Daughter," probably Hawthorne's most complex treatment of reality, fantasy, fairy tale, myth, legend, and symbol. In the Preface to the story (which Hawthorne attributes to M. de l'Aubépine), Hawthorne recognizes his own ambiguous situation between the transcendentalists, who are concerned with the spiritual and the metaphysical, and the great body of writers who address the "intellect and sympathies of the multitude," that is, the realists. Aubépine, says Hawthorne, "generally contents himself with a very slight embroidery of outward manners—the faintest possible counterfeit of real life—and endeavors to create an interest by some less obvious peculiarity of the subject."

Giovanni, like Goodman Brown and Robin, is primarily an inhabitant of the real world (that is, the mimetic aspect of the fiction) who is confronted with a dreamlike or fablelike fantasy. This encounter is complicated by the fact that the story is a maze of inversions of our usual expectations of good and evil, spirit and body, innocence and experience. Beatrice, like Dante's guide, is a spiritual figure of allegory; but she is also, like Mary Shelley's Frankenstein monster, a creation of nineteenth century science. When Giovanni first sees Rappaccini in the garden walking through the flowers as if they are malignant influences, his imagination connects the garden with the mythic story of the Garden of Eden. "Was this garden, then, the Eden of the present world?" Giovanni thus both creates and walks innocently into the stuff of myth itself; however, it is the Eden story turned upside down. Rappaccini is both God figure who created the garden and serpent figure who sets up the downfall of Giovanni, who is indeed the new Adam. Beatrice is Eve, brought up without contact with the fallen world. Giovanni is fallen man who must be seduced back into paradise again. The result of the story is that Giovanni, like Goodman Brown, cannot live with the mysterious mixture of spirit and body that Beatrice seems to represent: "Am I awake?" he cries. "Have I my senses? What is this being? Beautiful shall I call her, or inexpressibly terrible?"

Thus, instead of a story of the fall from grace into reality, we have instead a story of how fallen Adam tempts Eve into reality, even as she tries to tempt him into the fall back into grace again through faith and love. Giovanni's efforts to bring Beatrice into the "limits of ordinary experience" is evidence of his lack of acceptance and love; it means the death of the denizen of the romance world of fiction and thus the end of the story. "Rappaccini's Daughter" is about the conflict between reality and fantasy, materiality and spirit, empiricism and faith; and thus it is about the very conflict between characters like Giovanni, with psychological verisimilitude, and characters like Beatrice, who exist for the sake of the story as parable. The conflict is an inevitable one for the short story, taking as it does elements both from the old parable and romance form and from the conventions of the realistic eighteenth century novel. The classic example of a Poe story which involves this same kind of interaction is "The Fall of the House of Usher," in which the realistic narrator confronts Roderick, who by his very obsession has been turned into a purely symbolic figure. Melville exploits the mixture of the two fictional conventions even further in *Bartleby the Scrivener* as the short story moves more within the realistic tradition of the late nineteenth century.

The European mind has always been more hospitable to Poe than the American mind. Charles Baudelaire led the French in a discovery of Poe while he was still being scorned as a hack and a misfit in America. Recently, the French Structuralists have resurrected Poe from many years of critical condescension by considering his stories from a point of view of both new theories in psychoanalysis and new theories of narrative. American empiricism has simply been unconcerned with the basically phenomenological point of view of Poe's works. One of the most basic criticisms of Poe's stories, and an influential one because it is by W. H. Auden, is that Poe's stories have one damaging negative characteristic: "There is no place in any of them for the human individual as he actually exists in space and time." Poe's characters, says Auden, are "unitary states" who cannot exist except operatically. Yvor Winters' famous criticism of Poe as a classic case of obscurantism is based on a similar assumption—that Poe is not concerned with human experience, only emotion, and that he exhibits a "willful dislocation of feeling from under-standing." In fact, says Winters, Poe is interested in the creation of an emotion for its own sake, not in the understanding of experience." These views of Poe are common in American and English criticism. They result from a common genre error when a critic approaches a short story and scorns it because it does not follow the mimetic conventions of the novel. One can certainly admit that many of Poe's characters are unitary states without at the same time admitting that Poe is unconcerned with human understanding. As has already been shown, the short story from its beginnings is more closely aligned to projectionist fiction and a lyrical point of view than to the realistic fiction and rational point of view of the novel.

The best place to begin a consideration of the nature of Poe's stories is with a relatively unassuming story depicted in a basically realistic technique: the simple revenge story of "The Cask of Amontillado." The key to understanding the story is to perceive it as a monologue with a listener within the story. The narrator at the beginning addresses a definite "you" who he says "well know the nature of my soul." At the end of the story we discover that the present telling-time of the story takes place fifty years after the told event. The final line of the story—"*In pace requiescat*"—thus refers both to Fortunato, whose bones have never been discovered, and to Montresor, who is making the present confession, we assume, to a priest. The entire story is a complex tissue of irony; just as Montresor has made sure that none of his servants will be home by ordering them not to leave, so does he lure Fortunato into the catacombs by urging him to go home. Moreover, the irony takes on a structure of mocking and grotesque echo-action. As Fortunato begs Montresor to release him and screams in despair, Montresor echoes his words and screams. The central irony of the mock action in the story, however, turns on a reversal of Montresor's dual requirements for the perfect revenge and an ironic inversion of the symbolic meaning of Montresor's family coat of arms. Montresor says: "A wrong is unredressed when retribution overtakes its redresser. It is equally unredressed when the avenger fails to make himself known as such to him who has done the wrong." When we realize, however, that the mocking screams of Montresor border on hysteria, when we realize that he is now making confession of his crime, when we note that his heart grew sick after walling up Fortunato, and when we remember that Montresor does not let Fortunato know that his murderous act is indeed an act of revenge—then it becomes clear that Fortunato has more closely fulfilled the revenge criteria than has Montresor. The coat of arms—a human foot which crushes a serpent, but whose fangs remain embedded in the heel—is equally ironic. If the Montresor family is represented by the foot which crushes the serpent Fortunato, then we note that the serpent still clings to the heel. The family motto—No one harms me with impunity—thus applies to Fortunato as well as it does to Montresor. Every element in the story contributes to this single, but certainly not simple, ironic effect. Tone is the key to the story's meaning. There is, however, one more ironic turn of the screw in the story; although Montresor is now confessing, and thus, presumably, repentant for his crime, the very fact that the reader enjoys the clever ironic ways he tricked Fortunato indicates that by his very tone of telling, Montresor is enjoying it again also and is thus not repentant. Even though he is on his deathbed, he relives with glee the experience; and although he confesses, his tone damns him completely.

Although Poe disliked allegory, calling it the lowest form of art, his "The Pit and the Pendulum" and "The Masque of the Red Death" are both forms of allegory; however, they are more complex than the traditional conceptual allegorical fiction because of their dreamlike nature and because their elements symbolize complex metaphysical and psychological reality. "The Pit and the Pendulum" is very close to a self-contained dream story, but, like Franz Kafka's stories, it has enough of verisimilitude to give it the feeling of reality experienced as if it were nightmare. The entire story is dream and Poe is the dreamer; it is pure projective fiction from the beginning when the narrator says "I was sick—sick unto death" until the end when the loud blast of the trumpets marks his rescue from the dream by awakening him. The story is marked by many considerations of dream phenomenon in the beginning, as if the dreamer could consciously consider the curious epistemological and ontological status of dream itself. "Arousing from the most profound slumber," he says, "we break the gossamer web of *some* dream. Yet in a second afterward (so frail may that web have been) we remember not that we have dreamed." Moreover, the story is marked by a struggle to control the actions of the dream instead of being controlled by them; throughout the story the narrator undergoes a constant struggle to escape the machinations of the dream mechanism that controls him, but each time a danger is thwarted, a new danger is thrown in his way; for there is no way to escape the dangers that threaten one in dream except to awaken from the dream itself. The events that threaten the narrator—the pit, the pendulum, the walls that close in on him, the rats—are thus all of his own making; yet they are outside his control at the same time, for they are products of his own unconscious. The dilemma of the narrator is an objectification of the dilemma of all characters in this kind of self-conscious fiction—the dilemma of making one's story and being trapped by the story at the same time. The thematic content of the dream, however, is universal rather than personal; for it is a dream of being trapped by time (the pendulum), being prey to the nausea of body itself (the rats), and being threatened by the unknown and unnamable (the pit). As Harry Levin says of this story, it is an existential allegory that transcends the conceptual nature of allegory and becomes oneiric symbolism.

"The Masque of the Red Death" is allegorical fiction also, but again it is more complex than we usually assume allegory to be, both because it is tempered by Poe's characteristic irony and because it is infused with his concern to symbolize the nature of art itself. Prince Prospero is, like William Shakespeare's master magician in *The Tempest* (1611), a representation of the desire not simply to escape from death, but to escape from life into a re- placement world of fantasy and art. The story is an objectification of the attempt to escape from dynamic life (which inevitably results in death) into the static life of the art work (which means eternity). The first key to this understanding of the story lies in the title. The avatar of the pestilence death in the story is red, the color of blood, and blood is the symbol of life; however, it is Poe's view that life itself is the curse because it leads inevitably to death. Thus, Prospero shuts himself up within the castle and surrounds himself with clowns, improvisatori, dancers, musicians, actors; in short, figures who mimic life rather than participate in it. What Prospero in effect does is to enclose himself within the hermetically sealed art work itself, which says, as all ro- mantic art works do: "the external world could take care of itself." The masked figure dabbled with blood is Poe's image of death masquerading as life, for it suggests that the sign of blood is always as masque for the death that lies beneath life or is inherent within it. When the revelers try to seize the figure, they find that it has no tangible form; for death that is inherent in life is a nothingness that can be neither grasped nor escaped.

Poe deals with the problem of trying to escape death in another story that is not so much allegory as it is surrealistic and symbolic psychological fiction. "The Tell-Tale Heart" presents a narrator who is mysteriously obsessed with the eye of the old man with whom he lives. The key to this unexplained obsession lies in the double meaning of the title of the story and in the pun

Poe plays on the word "eye" itself. Although the title seems to refer to the end of the story, when the narrator thinks that the old man's beating heart has "told on him," that is, exposed his crime to the police, more generally the title refers to the only tale the heart can tell: the tale of time, as each heartbeat echoes the tick of the clock bringing one closer and closer to death. This is the tale that the narrator wishes to escape, and his obsessive concern to slow down and stop time altogether in his spying on the old man indicates this. The narrator's obsession with the eye is related to his identification with the old man. As he spies on him, the narrator delights that the old man is "listening just as I have done." He comments on the old man's groan of fear, "I knew the sound well." He then chuckles, "I knew what he felt and pitied him." The madness of the narrator is a metaphysical madness, for he hates the eye because it has come to mean "I" to him. The irony of the story is that the narrator wishes to escape death by destroying the "I"; that is, his own ego. He wishes to escape the tale the heart tells by destroying the self he has projected on the old man. The narrator's attempts to destroy the "I" by destroying the "eye" are ironically fulfilled at the end when he hears the beating of his own heart and thinks it is the old man's. The story consistently mixes up external and psychological reality to reveal a metaphysical meaning. Its refusal to separate the inner reality from the outer one is a typical device of Poe, and it is an influential one that characterizes the short story as a genre.

Poe's "The Fall of the House of Usher" presents a character configuration and a plot development that is typical of the short story from its beginnings up to the present day. It is the story of an actual or mimetic character, the narrator, who encounters a character who has been transformed into a parabolic figure by his own obsession with metaphysical mysteries. The story begins with the narrator's entrance into a world of ambiguity and myth; it is an entrance into the realm of story itself. It looks backward to Rip Van Winkle's entrance into the world of legend even as it looks forward to the encounter the narrator has with the ambiguous Bartleby in Melville's famous story. That the narrator enters the world of the art work itself is emphasized by his unsuccessful attempts to account for the feeling of gloom the house creates in him. He notes that while "there *are* combinations of very simple natural objects which have the power of thus affecting us, still the analysis of this power lies among considerations beyond our depth." What he is considering here is the romantic notion of the mystery of the imaginatively constructed art work—that it is not the elements but their combination that constitutes the mysterious unexplainable effect the art work has on us.

Usher himself is best known as one who is fascinated by art, especially the intricacies of music—that art form which Poe thinks to be the highest, because the most mysterious, source of the poetic sentiment. The effect of "The Fall of the House of Usher," however, is that of the poetic sentiment carried to its disastrous logical extreme—the poetic sentiment that has distanced itself so completely from material reality that it no longer has contact with the actual. Roderick Usher lives completely within the house of art, so detached from physicality that his senses cannot tolerate anything but the most insipid food, can stand only certain kinds of clothing, cannot bear odors, can bear only the faintest light. His music is wild and abstract; his paintings are not of things but ideas. When the narrator tries to determine what Usher fears, Usher can only suggest that it is fear itself. Indeed, Usher is afraid of nothing, but it is a nothing similar to that experienced by the old waiter in Ernest Hemingway's "Clean, Well-Lighted Place"—a felt nothing that he knows too well. It is the *nada* that waits for the artist who so pursues his quest of pure art that he cuts himself off from any external reality and thus can only feed on his own subjectivity. Roderick's twin sister Madeline functions to embody (as the old man's eye does in "The Tell-Tale Heart") a projection of Roderick's gradual withdrawal. His attempt to bury his own obsession returns to destroy him. Roderick's dilemma of being caught between the world of the art work and the real world—in which the art work gradually displaces the real world— is objectified in the scene in which the narrator reads to Usher from a Gothic romance; the actions of the fiction are echoed by the actions of Madeline as she breaks out of her entombment. At the end of the story when Madeline enters the room and collapses onto Roderick, she symbolically collapses back into him. Then in a compressed symbolic climax, Roderick collapses back into the house and the house collapses back into the nothingness that is the tarn. The ultimate end of the artist who cuts himself off from actuality to live in the realm of the art work is the nothingness that results from devouring the self.

This is the Poe in whom Baudelaire saw the genius, and this is the Poe who contributes so much to the genius of the short story as a form—a form that combines mimesis and romance, myth and actuality, and that is supremely conscious of its own processes of doing so. The narrator of "The Fall of the House of Usher" is left with the memory of the encounter and thus with an obsessive tale to tell. The end of the events of the story is the beginning of the endless telling of it. As Randall Jarrell says about stories, "we take pleasure . . . in repeating over and over, until we can bear it, all that we found unbearable."

Before moving on to Melville's *Piazza Tales* (1856), which mark a transition, especially in *Bartleby the Scrivener*, toward a more realistic emphasis in the short story, the romantic stories of the 1840's and 1850's in France and England, as well as the beginnings of poetic realism in Russia, will be briefly examined.

Romantic Short Fiction in Europe and England

Albert George, in his book *Short Fiction in France: 1800-1850* (1964), notes that the history of short fiction has been mostly ignored in France because of its oral origins and plebian associations. In the 1820's and 1830's, however, the short story began to be popular in France in the magazines even though the romantics continued the long tradition of the short tale in the folktale and the oral anecdote. Almost all critics agree that the formal short story, as Poe defines it, came into being in France in 1829 with the publication of Prosper Mérimée's *Mateo Falcone*. Honoré de Balzac's "Passion in the Desert" and "La Grande Bretèche" appeared in 1830 and 1832 respectively. Yet regardless of this introduction of a new formal control in short fiction, the short story, or *conte*, during the romantic period of the 1840's and 1850's in France is a combination of romantic fantasy, the supernatural, and a whimsical or satiric tone.

Typical of romantic whimsy and the supernatural is Théophile Gautier's "The Mummy's Foot," published in 1840. It is a story which derives from the earlier Gothic fiction of E. T. A. Hoffmann, but is presented in a new lightness of tone by a first-person narrator whom the reader cannot take seriously. The narrator buys the foot of an Egyptian princess in a bric-a-brac shop and then later dreams of returning the foot and traveling with the princess to a mummy afterlife; he awakes to find the foot gone. The plot is, as the narrator says of the foot itself, "charming, bizarre, and romantic," but it is ultimately silly; however, the plot is the least of the story. Tone, in fact, is everything here, as the romantic dilettantish narrator confronts in mock seriousness the absurdity of a one-footed princess and later is introduced to "the mummies of her acquaintance." What the story represents in the development of short fiction is a movement toward the sophistication of the supernatural and a satire of the dream-vision convention itself; it both develops the romantic dream vision and ironically undercuts that vision at the same time; it signals a trivializing of a convention and a self-parody which is the first step toward the establishing of a new convention, in this case the convention of realistic verisimilitude.

Gérard de Nerval's story "Pandora," although presented in more brittle satiric tones, is similarly a sign of the naturalizing of romanticism. Published in 1854, it integrates mythical and dream reality into the sophisticated social setting of the realistic convention of Balzac. If Gautier's inspiration is Hoffmann, Nerval's is Johann Wolfgang von Goethe; and his story, embodying the tension between the sensuous and the supernatural, has a more significant metaphysical thematic base than does Gautier's. The central character, in his adoration of Pandora, elevates her to a symbolic status even as he transforms himself into the tormented Prometheus. The dream of hallucinatory vision embodied here is more believable than in "The Mummy's Foot," because it is inextricably intertwined in the story rather than set apart from it. In this way, Nerval anticipates the style of Kafka by confusing reality and dream so purposefully that dream takes on an ontological status equal to that of phenomenal reality. Moreover, the narrator in "Pandora," a writer self-consciously aware of his own work, notes in the story that "Pandora" is a continuation of an earlier work and also inserts a confidential letter into the narrative addressed to Gautier himself in which the narrator and the writer of the letter are the same man. This self-reflexive technique confuses the point of view quite purposely to entangle elements of fiction and reality within the fiction itself. Again, when a work of fiction becomes self-consciously aware of itself as fiction and thus parodies the very conventions upon which it depends, we know we are on the brink of a shift to another generic convention.

It has often been noted that Prosper Mérimée's later stories do not match in impact and artistic control his earlier ones such as *Mateo Falcone*. One of his best-known stories, however, published in the 1840's, "The Abbé Aubain," marks a complete break from the romantic supernaturalism and self-parody of Gautier and Nerval and establishes the short story as a realistic and radically ironic form. On the one hand, the story is reminiscent of the early Italian novella of Giovanni Boccaccio in its satire on human vanity; on the other hand, because of its ironic reversal at the end, it points toward the kind of trick story that Guy de Maupassant made so popular in the latter part of the century in France. The story is told almost entirely in the form of letters from a wealthy sophisticated society woman (who has moved to the country) to a friend in the city. As is typical of such a radically first-person form (which is actually transcribed monologue), much of the pleasure of the story lies in the reader's opportunity to mock the lady for her superficiality, which she reveals unawares. Her condescension toward the parish priest throughout the story allows the reader to laugh at her foolishness at the end. For although she fancies that the priest is in love with her (an infatuation that she finds amusing and which she uses to entertain herself), we discover in the last letter (which the priest writes to his old professor) that he has instead been using her to gain preferment and thus escape the country to a higher position in the Church. The concealment of this information, which is the only thing that makes this a story at all, is possible, of course, by the use of the letter convention. At the end of the piece, we are left with two unappealing characters who have not only underestimated each other, but who also remain self-deceived. The story contributes nothing to the short story except to move it toward the kind of ironic plot reversal that Maupassant perfected in "The Necklace."

The fact that the short story did not fare well in England in the nineteenth century seems partial support for Frank O'Connor's thesis that the short story deals with the individual detached from society. Lionel Stevenson has drawn attention to the Victorian assumption that any serious work of literature should offer a well-integrated view of society—an assumption which made English authors ignore the short-story form as trivial. Not until the 1880's, when the "fragmentation of sensibility" set in in England, did the short story begin to be seen as the most appropriate form for representing such a sensibility. As has already been noted, the romantic impulse in England found its form primarily in poetry, especially the romantic lyric moving toward the dramatic monologue. The short story is a fictional parallel to such forms because they, like the short story, depend on a particular point of view, usually of a single event. In certain ways, Coleridge's "The Rime of the Ancient Mariner" is a model short story, as is Browning's "Andrea del Sarto" and "Fra Lippo Lippi." The fictional embodiment of romanticism in nineteenth century England was only an undercurrent to the development of the Victorian novel, taking its direction from the Gothic fiction of Horace Walpole, Ann Radcliffe, William Beckford, and Matthew Gregory Lewis. That short fiction in England during this period often dealt with strange and unexplainable (or at least seemingly unexplainable) events springs partially from the old folktale tradition of dealing with such events and partially from the influence of the darker side of German Romanticism. The English way to deal with the supernatural, however, is to explain it away naturalistically or play it for its simple shock effect, rather than, as in America, to exploit its metaphysical and psychological implications.

A typical example is Wilkie Collins' "The Traveler's Story of a Terribly Strange Bed." The story is about a single narrator who begins winning at gambling prodigiously and is encouraged on and seemingly protected by a dirty and wrinkled old man with vulture eyes. After breaking the bank at the gambling house, the narrator is almost killed in a four-poster bed when the top is lowered down to crush him. The story has the kind of plot and character potential of which Dostoevski could have made metaphysical capital, or that Poe could have developed into a psychological nightmare. For Collins, however, the story is a simple one of a thwarted murder attempt, in which the mysterious old man turns out to be the owner of the gambling house and the perpetrator of the plot to kill the narrator. The story is not without its suspense and not without its elements of mysterious hallucination. The bed, however, turns out to be not very "terribly strange" at all—only a smooth-running mechanism for murder. The story is indeed short and self-contained, but it is told more in a novelistic manner that focuses on realistic motivation and verisimilitude than in the true short-story manner which focuses on psychological and metaphysical mysteries.

Edward Bulwer-Lytton's story "The Haunted and the Haunters: Or, The House and the Brain" (1859) is a ghost story with a ratiocinative twist. The narrator of the story is a dilettantish ghost hunter who spends a night in a mysterious house in order to disprove, or at least to explain, the strange phenomena that have been reported there. Indeed, mysterious manifestations do take place during his night in the house: a child's footprints are seen, ghastly exhalations are felt, and ghostly voices are heard. The narrator discovers clues that the previous residents of the house had been involved in mysterious events of love and death—events that somehow had given rise to the phenomena. The narrator, however, is little interested in the lives that seem perpetuated in the house; his only concern is to explain the events and to prove his theory that the supernatural is only a natural law of which we have been previously ignorant. The final solution involves not the elaborate ratiocinative devices of Poe's detective figures, nor does the haunting of the house suggest the sort of psychological hallucination and dream reality of Poe's horror stories. In fact, the discovery of a powerful lodestone, some amber and rock crystal lumps, and a magic symbol in a secret chamber do little to explain anything. The final discovery is that a famous charlatan who once lived in the house has left behind a mechanism which preserves his own powerful will and affects the occupants of the house. The motivation for his action, however, is left vague and unexplored. A more typical short story would have involved the narrator in the story in some crucial way; but here, he only exists to explain, in pseudoscientific ways, the mystery of the phenomenon. How the events take place is all that is important, not why they happen or what they mean.

A more pertinent example of the failure to exploit the particular characteristics of the short-story genre in England can be seen in a tale by Charles Dickens. One would think that Dickens, with his focus on the outcast figure on the fringe of society and his mastery of the grotesque and extreme situation, would have found the short story a most viable vehicle. In "The Signalman" (1866), however, Dickens has all the plot and character elements of a successful short story, but fails to use them in an intense and revealing way. The narrator of the story, who identifies himself as a "man who had been shut up within narrow limits all his life, and who being at last set free, had a newly awakened interest" in the world around him, encounters a railway signalman. The narrator descends through an extremely deep cutting of clammy stone, that becomes oozier and wetter as he goes down, to the signalman's post; it is solitary and dismal and has an earthy, deadly smell and so much cold wind rushing through it that the narrator feels as if he had "left the natural world." The signalman himself has the potentially symbolic task of watchfulness and exactness; in fact, he seems to exist only for this purpose and has learned a language of telegraphic communication that sets him apart from the phenomenal world.

The story, however, is a structure of potential elements that are never realized. The signalman's function and his cavernous location down the ravine, which the narrator finds "easier to mount than to descend," seem the materials of symbolic fiction; the narrator himself, who has been confined within narrow limits, seems the stuff of psychological drama; the central event of the story—the signalman's perception of a specter with the left arm across the face and the right one waving violently as if to say, "For God's sake, clear the way"—has all the elements of the doppelgänger motif; and the final event in the story, when the signalman has been killed and the narrator sees an actual embodiment of the specter make the waving gesture, has the potential of involving the narrator in the story. All these elements could have come together in a story about the nature of isolation, concretely realized and vividly symbolized. Instead, what we have is a simple demonstration of the psychic phenomenon of precognition. The potential of the story, either psychologically or morally, that a Poe or a Hawthorne could have developed is never fulfilled or even suggested in a unified way. For Dickens, these elements are interesting in themselves, but they do not come together in the single and unified complex effect that marks the mastery of the short-story genre.

For whatever reason, because of individual poetic genius or because of the difference in social milieu, Turgenev could have transformed the Dickens material into a unified, lyric, and symbolic story. There is no question that *A Sportsman's Sketches* (1852) is one of the great collections of short fiction in the nineteenth century. Frank O'Connor says it may well be the greatest book of short stories ever written. Turgenev is a distinctly romantic writer, but a romantic writer moving toward realism. Strongly influenced by the German Romantics—Hoffmann, Tieck, Novalis—Turgenev had a strong sense of the irrational and an adherence to the mysterious saving power of love. Marina Ledovsky, in her 1973 study entitled *The Other Turgenev*, describes the characteristics of Turgenev's tales in a way that could be a description of the short-story form itself: "The peculiarity of the structure of the mysterious tales consists in the alternating and at times fusing of extremely realistic, prosaic events with fantastic episodes. . . . Thus the irrational and alogical are woven into banal reality to create a grotesque setting on two planes." As is true for the short story generally, Turgenev's realism is not an indication of a philosophic acceptance of the primary reality of the physical and phenomenal world; rather, it is simply a technique for involving everyday reality with the immanently mysterious world of the irrational. This is why the short story often involves the grotesque, and why the form, as exemplified in Turgenev, suggests the entanglement of the physical world with the dreamlike world of story itself. Turgenev's two best-known stories—"The Country Doctor" and "Bezhin Meadow"—are exemplars of the short story as a form; so completely do they represent the short story that their subject matter is the world of story itself.

"The Country Doctor" is a framed story in which the sportsman narrator, taken by a fever, calls in a district doctor who tells him a "remarkable story" which the sportsman then relates to the reader in the doctor's own words. The story is one about the doctor's trip to tend a beautiful sick young girl in the home of her poor but cultivated mother. The girl's slow death over a period of days is ironically the doctor's one moment of life—life elevated from his everyday routine. The tale the doctor tells of his falling in love with the girl and her falling in love with him reaches its climax and crux when the doctor realizes that she loves him only because she is going to die. The doctor says he understands that "if she had not believed herself on the point of death, she would never have given me a thought; but say what you like, there must be something appalling about dying at twenty-five without ever having loved; that was the thought that tormented her, and that was why, in despair, she seized on me." What adds another excruciating turn of the screw is that the girl, having proclaimed her love for the doctor, is desperate to die. When she begs the doctor that she must die, that he promised her that she would die, he says, "It was a bitter moment for me, bitter for many reasons."

The conception of the story is a stroke of genius, for it combines for the doctor a moment of the highest fulfillment, yet at the same time a moment of the deepest despair precisely because of the fulfillment itself. Yet the real genius of the story lies in the telling itself, as the doctor in his hurried yet halting way tries both to justify the experience and to understand it. It is a typical Turgenev device, as it was later to be for Anton Chekhov, to have the story end in understatement. After the story is told and the narrator takes the doctor's hand in unspoken sympathy, the doctor suggests a game of Preference and offhandedly says he has since married a woman as common as he is, "a spiteful hag, I must say, but luckily she sleeps all day." The last paragraph of the story is: "We got down to Preference for copeck stakes. Trifon Ivanich won two and a half roubles from me—and went home late, very pleased with his victory." Such an ending is not to suggest that we have been tricked into a sympathy for the doctor which he does not deserve. On the contrary, it is an indication of the depth of his significant loss that he is content with the trivial win. For the central irony of the story that is if he had won, that is, if the girl had lived, he would have lost. His only win is the memory, the story itself, and that is a constant source of both joy and torture for him. There is no sentimentality in the story, nor is there cynicism. It is simply the recounting of a moment in time when the evanescent possibility to be elevated from the everyday occurred—a recounting which indeed suggests that the only possibilities for such transcendence are, by their very nature, evanescent. Transcendence is a strange and lyrical moment surrounded by the mundane and the ordinary; it is one of the functions of the short-story form to depict such moments in all their bittersweetness.

"Bezhin Meadow" is an even more complex story about the transition from the ordinary phenomenal world into the extraordinary world of dream, wish, and thus story itself. The tale begins with the sportsman getting lost; as he experiences a sense of disorientation, he cries "where on earth am I?" and we realize as we do with Rip Van Winkle's strange trek up the mountain, with Young Goodman Brown's journey into the forest, and with the narrator in "The Fall of the House of Usher" as he approaches the ominous house that the sportsman is nowhere on earth, that he has moved from the terrestrial into a realm of folktale and dream. The landscape he travels through is a familiar one in romantic poetry and the short-story genre:

> The hollow was like an almost symmetrical cauldron with sloping sides. At the bottom of it rose, bolt upright, several large white stones, which seemed to have crept down there for a secret conclave, and the whole place had such a deaf-and-dumb feeling the sky hung so flatly and gloomily above it, that my heart shrank. Some little creature was squeaking faintly and plaintively among the stones.

Floundering through this mythic landscape, the sportsman comes upon a group of peasant boys tending horses. As he pretends to sleep, he hears the five boys tell the following stories. Fedya tells the first story of a ghost in a papermill which frightened him and some of his friends and then made a sound of choking and coughing like a sheep. Kostya tells the story of a carpenter who confronts a water sprite in the forest and crosses himself in fear that it is the devil; at this act she begins to cry and tells him that if he had not crossed himself he could have lived with her merrily forever; since that time the carpenter goes about grieving. Ilyusha tells a story of the kennelman Ermil, who, seeing a lamb on the grave of a drowned man, strokes it and says "Baa-lamb, baa-lamb," to which the lamb bares its teeth and answers him back. Pavel tells a story of the coming of Trishka, the antichrist, who turns out to be only the barrelmaker who had bought himself a new jug and had put the empty jug over his head. Finally, Kostya tells of a little boy who drowned in the river near where the boys are and whose mother has not been right in the head since. At the end of this story, Pavel, who has told the only "supernatural" story with a naturalistic explanation, comes back from the river and says that he has heard the drowned boy call to him from under the water.

The story has no plot, is not *about* a single event except for the narrator's encounter with the realm of story itself. "Bezhin Meadow" projects a basic romantic image of man; like Shelley's poet who is a nightingale singing in the darkness, the boys tell their stories and light up a small place. The stories themselves are kernels of short stories—folk legends of mysterious encounters with hope, wish, pathos, madness. Pavel is central in the narrator's consciousness because of his attempts to find some rational explanation for the supernatural events; but he too is drawn into the dream world of story until the virtual world itself is transformed and he hears the voice of the drowned child. The irony of the story is the irony of all the stories we tell of those things that frighten us, for we tell them as a way of dealing with our fears. It is a story of the storytelling impulse as an example of Freud's repetition compulsion, a basic urge to control the uncontrollable by managing it in the form of story itself. For Turgenev, as for all great storytellers, the nature of reality lies not in hard events, but rather in human emotions that construct those events and make them meaningful. Story is a primal form of expressing the emotion-made nature of reality—a primal form of expressing the reality of wish, of dream, of feeling, of the ultimately unexplainable, that yet must be integrated and coped with.

Although Dostoevski is often praised as a prophetic voice of the twentieth century existential sensibility, and his novels are often cited as exemplars of the philosophical novel, little has been said of his use of, and contribution to, the short-story form. Indeed, in his short fictions, the focus is less on the formal perfection of a lyrical form to penetrate psychological and metaphysical mysteries than it is on the presentation of a conceptual philosophic position. Among his stories, "The Crocodile" is a satire of civil service bureaucracy and "The Dream of a Ridiculous Man" is a parable which sets forth his own Christian existentialism. Even the two stories singled out for discussion— *Notes from the Underground* (1864) and "The Peasant Marey"—have been analyzed mainly for their conceptual or parabolic content. What is to be suggested is that, both formally and thematically, the stories fall within the tradition of short fiction in the nineteenth century.

First of all, the Underground Man is a clear example of that isolated individual which Frank O'Connor suggests is central to the short-story form. He is a "characterless creature" who has cut himself off from the social world and feeds instead on his own subjectivity. Like Melville's Bartleby, he has confronted a wall before which he is impotent. In his story "Apropos of the Wet Snow," he recounts the experiences which have led him to the underground and thus to his philosophic monologue. Basically, "Apropos of the Wet Snow" recounts his attempts to involve himself in real life, attempts to love and be loved; but they are attempts which fail because of his morbid self-consciousness and his bookish posturing and artificiality. The Underground Man's relationship with the characters in the story are basically the same as his relationship with the readers in the monologue: he tries to win them over even as he mocks them. The Russian critic Konstantin Mochulsky sums up this dilemma and the theme of the story in a way that marks its similarity to the theme of many of the stories of Hawthorne: "A strongly developed person recoils from the world, desperately defends his own autonomy, and, at the same time, is attracted to others and understands his dependence on them." The tragedy of "Apropos of the Wet Snow" is, Mochulsky says, the tragedy of human communication. Mochulsky notes that this tension also dominates the monologue section of the story, for it is a monologue which is in the nature of a dialogue. Although the Underground Man insists that he needs no reader, each statement is intended to make an impression on the reader.

Although the monologue has received the most critical attention, it is the story "Apropos of the Wet Snow" which constitutes the center of the work. The monologue is, as Ralph Matlaw has suggested, a false start, leading the reader away from the real subject of the work. Before he can recall and reveal, the narrator evades and attempts to build up an image of the self through philosophic speculation. It is the story that depicts his encounters with "the real thing" and his failures both because of his confusion between real life and art life and his own self-consciousness. His situation in the two parts of the stories are echoed in the monologue of J. Alfred Prufrock and in James's story of John Marcher in "The Beast in the Jungle" a generation later.

"The Peasant Marey" is a story within a story which depicts the relationship of a memoried or storied past event to an intolerable present situation. The present time of the story is Easter week and the narrator is in prison. Disgusted by the violence and disorder of his surroundings, and affected by a hissed whisper to him by a political prisoner—"I hate these scum"—the narrator loses himself in memories of when he was nine years old and heard a shout of "wolf," but was comforted by one of his father's peasants, Marey, who told him that the shout was in his fancy only. After the narrator resurrects this incident (which he says must have lain hidden in his soul for twenty years), he looks on his fellow prisoners with more sympathetic eyes; for now he feels that the very criminal he had found so disgusting may be the very Marey who had comforted him as a child.

The parabolic nature of the story is simple enough: that one must recognize the basic humanity of all men regardless of their external appearances. The mode of the story—in which a memory is revived and relived as a key to a present situation—is more complex. For the story of Marey and the boy who heard "wolf" is a play with the folktale of the boy who cried "wolf." Whereas the folktale is about a boy who so often presents a fantasy as if it were a reality that when he confronts the reality no one believes him and he is devoured by it, Dostoevski's story is about a fantasy (or memory or story) which reminds the narrator that the external reality he perceives around him is appearance only—that the significant reality resides in the story—the very story that he remembers and constructs. Thus, as often in the short-story form, the fiction becomes more real than the external reality.

The Well-Made Story and the Movement Toward Realism

After the era of Hawthorne and Poe in America, the short story ceased to be a distinctive form until Henry James revived it as a serious art form in the 1880's. This does not mean, however, that important changes in the form did not take place in the 1850's, 1860's, and 1870's—changes that have affected the development of the form up to the present day. The primary movement in this period was, of course, the shift toward realism; and realism is neither a philosophic assumption nor a literary convention that is conducive to the basically romantic and psychological/metaphysical nature of the short-story form. Herman Melville's *Bartleby the Scrivener* is an exception, because even as it points forward to the highly polished psychological tales of Henry James, it points backward to Poe's psychological hallucinations and Hawthorne's moral parables. Beyond Melville's distinctive contribution to the short story in the 1850's, the other two movements in the development of the form that dominate the period up to the 1880's are the stories of local color and the so-called "well-made" stories. Of the many examples of local-color stories that dominate the period, the short stories of Bret Harte and Mark Twain have been chosen to comment on. Of the well-made story, the best-known stories of Fitz-James O'Brien, Thomas Aldrich, and Edward Everett Hale have been selected for commentary.

Frederick Lewis Pattee, in his 1923 study of the short story, has noted the avalanche of female authors that followed Hawthorne and Poe in the 1850's and filled the magazines with sentimental stories. Hawthorne himself said in 1855, "America is now wholly given over to a d----d mob of scribbling women. I should have no chance of success while the public taste is occupied with their trash—and should be ashamed of myself if I did succeed." Besides Melville, the only other figure in the 1850's to contribute (for better or worse) to the future of the short story was Fitz-James O'Brien. His 1859 story, "What Was It?," makes use of the fantasy and supernatural elements that Poe perfected, but it also points ahead to the journalistic style of O. Henry. "What Was It?" is a well-made, formally constructed story far superior to similar stories by Wilkie Collins and Edward Bulwer-Lytton, but very much inferior to the intricate blendings of fantasy and reality that Poe achieved.

Character development in the story is slight; Harry, the narrator, serves primarily to tell the story of his capture of an invisible ghoulish figure. He is a writer and a smoker of opium and somewhat of an amateur expert on supernaturalism. The central event takes place in a boarding house, reputed to be haunted, on a night after he and a friend, Dr. Hammond, have been smoking opium and talking. On this particular night, instead of talking about the light or Ariel side of life, as was their custom, they discuss the darker or Caliban side. Hammond brings up the philosophic question to Harry: "What do you consider to be the greatest element of terror?" Dr. Hammond thinks of various effects in the works of Brockden Brown and Bulwer-Lytton and thinks that if only he were master of a literary style he could write a story like Hoffmann on this particular night.

After retiring, the narrator of "What Was It?" tries to get the horrible thoughts of the discussion out of his mind; he feels something drop from the ceiling onto his chest and try to strangle him with bony hands. After a struggle, he subdues the thing and turns on the light, only to find nothing. In contrast to the usual such dream-vision awakenings, however, the thing is still there; it is invisible, but it is still a concrete "thereness." Later when they call in a doctor to chloroform the thing and make a cast of it, what is revealed is a four-footed, manlike creature with muscular limbs; the narrator describes it only as something that surpasses figures from Doré or Callot. Now the creature becomes a burden—something they can neither release, nor keep, nor kill. Finally the creature dies, seemingly having starved to death, and is buried. What the story is, given O'Brien's fascination with *The Tempest*, is an objectification of fantasy—the intrusion into virtual reality of an abstract, yet emotionally created, object of terror that the narrator and doctor have been discussing. In fact, the entire house of boarders has been infected psychologically with dark fantasies, for they have been reading a book entitled *The Night Side of Nature* before the creature appears. Thus within the fantasy entitled "What Was It?" we have an actual objectification of the fantasies of the fictional characters. Such a self-reflexive motif, while not as expert as similar motifs in Poe, is more polished than stories of other supernatural writers in the 1850's and 1860's.

Herman Melville's short fiction has been little appreciated until recently. Pattee only briefly mentions him in his 1923 study of the short story. Of the mass of criticism that has been published on Melville's short stories in the last twenty years, the story that has received the most attention (and rightfully so) is *Bartleby the Scrivener*. In nothing else that Melville wrote, says Newton Arvin, "did he achieve by the accumulation of details themselves commonplace, prosaic, and humdrum, a total effect of such strangeness and even madness as this." The story has been discussed by numerous critics as an autobiographical parable of Melville's feeling of artistic failure, as a case study in schizophrenia, and as a social allegory of how the system crushes the little man. The one discussion that approaches the story as a short story is an article by Robert Marler (*American Literature*, May, 1974), which argues that *Bartleby the Scrivener* marks a transition from the "tale" form, in which characters are unitary figures or archetypes, to the true "short story," in which characters have their own psychologies and are wearing their social personae. Marler says that *Bartleby the Scrivener* is a fully developed short story because it is embedded in a social context and is a reflection of the narrator's mind. It is not Bartleby's story, says Marler, but a story of the narrator's movement from a state of ignorance to a state of knowledge.

There is not sufficient space here to argue with all of Marler's points which indicate that the story is the first true short story and therefore radically different from the "tale" form that preceded it; it is not a point worth belaboring. The difference between *Bartleby the Scrivener* and the stories of Hawthorne and Poe is indeed a result of a step toward realism. Even though Melville focuses on the prosaic and the commonplace in the story, however, the effect is as psychologically mysterious as a story by Poe and as morally complex as a story by Hawthorne; for the prosaic and the commonplace are transformed here into symbol. Although the story takes place in an actual setting—an office in New York's Wall Street—as the story develops, we gradually discover that Wall Street serves less as a social situation than as a symbolic backdrop to Bartleby's story. Indeed, it is a story filled with walls—both blank walls which Bartleby faces and dividing walls that separate him from others. The story is symbolic in the sense that Bartleby himself, for no discernible reasons, has transformed the physical walls around him into metaphors for all the psychological and metaphysical walls that stand between man and understanding of the world. If Bartleby is mad, his madness is that of one who, like Dostoevski's Underground Man or Hawthorne's minister with the black veil, has understood too clearly that nothing can be understood at all. By his transformation of a real object—the wall—into a symbolic object and his consequent reaction to the object as if it were the significance he has projected on it, Bartleby himself is transformed into a symbolic figure. Bartleby then becomes a "wall" for the narrator, something opaque and mysterious, something that cannot be explained rationally. Indeed, the story *is* the narrator's story; it is his effort to "replay" the experience with Bartleby both as a means of justifying his actions and of understanding what the experience meant.

The basic conflict between Bartleby and the narrator is, as pointed out by Norman Springer (*PMLA*, 1965), that while the narrator is a man of assumptions, Bartleby is an embodiment of preferences. Thus, Bartleby exists to demonstrate the inadequacy of all assumptions. The narrator perceives, as does the narrator of "The Fall of the House of Usher," that the mysterious figure before him has "nothing ordinarily human about him." When the narrator asks Bartleby during one of his "dead-wall reveries" why he will do no more copying, Bartleby replies, "Do you not see the reason for youself?" His reference is to the wall he stares at. Even if the narrator could see in the metaphysical, yet mad, way that Bartleby sees and were to ask him why the wall makes him withdraw from life, Bartleby could answer only that the wall means "nothing." It would be a nothing that is a tangible, felt reality in the way Hemingway's old waiter understands it in "Clean, Well-Lighted Place," a *nada* that butts all heads at last. The frustration that the narrator feels at not being able either to understand Bartleby or to help him is a result not only of the narrator's safe and secure position, which Bartleby comes to challenge, but also of the impossibility of what Bartleby tacitly demands. For what Bartleby presents is the radical challenge to charity and love that Christ requires. Bartleby tacitly asks to be understood although he refuses to aid in that understanding; he asks to be loved although he infuriatingly rebuffs all efforts the narrator makes to help him. Bartleby is indeed a particularly painful case of the inability of one to penetrate to the core of the other and say "I-Thou," for he is the "other *par excellence*" who comes solely to challenge the narrator's easy assumptions.

The relationship between Bartleby and the narrator is different from the relationship between Roderick Usher and his narrator only in that the focus shifts. In "The Fall of the House of Usher," the symbolic figure Usher is foregrounded, and we know little of the narrator's mind except his puzzlement and inability to understand. In *Bartleby the Scrivener*, it is indeed the narrator's inability to understand, and by extension the basic human inability to understand, which is foregrounded into the subject matter of the story. Although there are no immediate heirs to this shift of emphasis in the short story in America, it does dominate the form from Henry James and Joseph Conrad on up through the twentieth century. We now see in Flannery O'Connor, Eudora Welty, Bernard Malamud, and other contemporary writers short-story situations in which an ordinary person in the phenomenal world confronts some mysterious character or figure who throws him or her out of an often uneasy placidity into the mystery of human communication and love (or the impossibility of either), and we see the loneliness that inevitably results.

Fred Lewis Pattee points out that the gradual rise of realism and the magazine *Atlantic Monthly* dominated the short-story form in America in the 1860's. Of the many stories published in *Atlantic Monthly* during this period, commentary will be kept to the most famous, Edward Everett Hale's "The Man Without a Country," a tremendously popular story at the time, which remains worthy of note because of its so-called realism. The story is told by a first-person narrator, and the tone is that of a cautionary tale for young military men. Philip Nolan, the man without a country, is presented as a "real" man involved in an actual event (Aaron Burr's attempted overthrow of the country), but the historical framework serves only the purpose of establishing the event as having really happened and of motivating Nolan's unique sentence—the carrying out of which is the main material of the story. Nolan's character is not explored, and his personal motivation is not developed. The traitorous act itself is described rather in terms of some sort of a satanic temptation. Burr is described simply as a "gay deceiver" who "seduces" Nolan "body and soul."

When Nolan damns the United States at his trial and vows, "I wish I may never hear of the United States again," the court sentences him to fulfill his wish. He is transferred back and forth on Navy vessels for fifty years, never closer than one hundred miles to United States soil. All officers and crewmen on the ships are forbidden to make any reference to the United States; his reading material is carefully censored, even to the deletion of references to the United States in foreign books and newspapers. The story is primarily narrative, with only a few scenes that indicate Nolan's growing loneliness and awareness of the extremity of his situation. The actual thematic thrust of the story, for all its realistic plot detail, is of a man tempted into a traitorous act by a figure who has become legendary in American history. The result of Nolan's act is that he is not only forced to have his wish fulfilled—a wish he discovers to be a curse—but he himself is also turned into a legendary figure in a cautionary tale. Just as the early short story concerns a mythic figure presented as a man, Hale's story presents a man being transformed into a mythic figure—the stuff of continuing story. Regardless of whatever surface verisimilitude a short story may manifest, its so-called "realism" is always mixed with the mythic and the storylike.

Bret Harte is not a realist in any sense except for the fact that he situates his stories in a specific locality for which he establishes a Western atmosphere and a set of social customs. His characters are types who serve the ironic function of his stories. Moreover, Harte's "local color" is primarily romantic, for he creates his own self-contained little world in which he stylizes the customs, caricatures the characters, and romanticizes the surroundings. Although his effect was strongly felt at the time his first stories appeared in *Overland Monthly* in 1868, his reputation has not fared well since. In his best story, "Tennessee's Partner," his humorous and ironic point of view and his carefully controlled technique make a definite contribution to the short-story genre; for here he creates a story that, as all good stories do, seduces the reader into a response quite contrary to what the actual events of the story suggest on the surface.

Arthur Hobson Quinn has said that Harte taught nearly every American writer of short stories some of the essentials of his art. Quinn suggests that Harte's sense of humor "preserved in him that sense of proportion which was one of his great gifts to the development of the short story." Harte would have been happy to accept this as his major contribution, for in his *Cornhill* article of 1899, he singles out humor as the factor which finally diminished the influence of English models on the short story in America and helped create a distinctly American form:

> It was *Humour*—of a quality as distinct and original as the country and civilization in which it was developed. It was first noticeable in the anecdote or "story," and after the fashion of such beginnings, was orally transmitted. It was common in the barrooms, the gatherings in the "country store," and finally at public meetings in the mouths of "stump orators."

According to Harte, it is the storyteller's tone and point of view that determine the meaning of a short story, for it is his moral perspective which should direct the reader's response to the story. "Tennessee's Partner" has a dramatically defined narrator with a voice and purpose of his own. After relating how Tennessee's partner went to San Francisco for a wife and was stopped in Stockton by a young waitress who broke at least two plates of toast over his head, the narrator says that he is well aware that "something more might be made of this episode, but I prefer to tell it as it was current at Sandy Bar— in the gulches and barrooms—where all sentiment was modified by a strong sense of humor." It is this barroom point of view, in fact, which dominates the whole story; and once we are willing to accept this tone, the story takes on a new and not so pathetic dimension. The narrator fully intends for this story to be, not the occasion for tears, but for sardonic laughter.

When Tennessee's partner invites the men to Tennessee's funeral, the narrator says, "Perhaps it was from a sense of humor, which I have already intimated was a feature of Sandy Bar—perhaps it was from something even better than that, but two thirds of the loungers accepted the invitation at once." That "something better," which sentimental readers have always been willing to accept as an indication of sympathy and perhaps regret on the part of the men for their condemnation of Tennessee, might be seen instead as the final necessary act in the ritual of complicity between the partner and the town in their vigilante justice on Tennessee. The "popular feeling" which had grown up against Tennessee in Sandy Bar could end no other way. At the trial, the narrator makes it abundantly clear that Tennessee's fate was sealed, that the trial is only to justify "the previous irregularities of arrest and indictment." The men have no doubt about his fate; they are "secure in the hypothesis that he ought to be hanged on general principles." It is this very knowledge that they are going to hang Tennessee not so much for a concrete wrong as on general principles that makes them begin to waver, until the partner, who *has* suffered a concrete wrong by Tennessee, enters the game with his attempted bribe of the judge. As a result of his taking a hand, the town helps Tennessee's partner avenge himself on Tennessee for stealing his wife, and the partner helps the town get rid of a bothersome blight on the body politic. The economical use of detail in the story, as well as its combination of sardonic humor and moral complexity, is similar to Poe's masterpiece, "The Cask of Amontillado." In its use of a narrator who quietly and cleverly controls his satiric intent, it is surely as well done as Ring Lardner's "Haircut" or Mark Twain's "The Celebrated Jumping Frog of Calaveras County."

In contrast to Harte's humorous story, about which little has been said, Mark Twain's jumping frog story has come in for a great deal of critical commentary. The story has been called a multilevel satire pitting the simplicity of the West against the cunning of the East in which, although the Westerner Jim Smily is bested in the contest by the Easterner, the West gets its revenge on the East by imposing Simon Wheeler's long-winded story on the Easterner, Mark Twain. The story itself is a clear example of Twain's own definition of the humorous in his 1895 piece, "How to Tell a Story." The humorous is told gravely, says Twain; "the teller does his best to conceal the fact that he even dimly suspects that there is anything funny about it." The humorous story always depends on the manner of the telling rather than on the matter, says Twain; and Simon Wheeler tells his story with such earnestness that "so far from imagining that there was anything ridiculous or funny about his story, he regarded it as a really important matter, and admired its two heroes as men of transcendent genius in finesse." The irony of the story is that although an Easterner beats the inveterate gambler Jim Smily, the Western story itself is the champion. The genius in finesse is Simon Wheeler (or rather his creator Mark Twain—not his auditor Mark Twain), and the framed story triumphs over the frame itself. Truly, as Bret Harte has said, the genius of the American Western story is the tone of the telling; the tone in Twain's tale is one that hovers uneasily between seriousness and triviality and between reality and parable.

The beginnings of the well-made story in America have already been noted in the stories of Edward Everett Hale and Fitz-James O'Brien. The form did not become overwhelmingly popular and influential, however, until Thomas Bailey Aldrich's "Marjorie Daw" appeared in 1873 in *Atlantic Monthly*. Its impact was similar to that created by Harte's "The Luck of Roaring Camp," Frank R. Stockton's "The Lady or the Tiger?," or more recently Shirley Jackson's "The Lottery." Like these stories, "Marjorie Daw" has come to stand as an exemplar of the short-story form in the popular imagination. As Fred Lewis Pattee has noted, "Marjorie Daw" became a type "standing for controlled artistry, a whimsical wit, and a totally unexpected denouement that sends the reader back over the story again." Although it is often suggested that Aldrich's surprise ending is the key to the story's success, the basic thematic impulse of the story is as characteristic of the short-story form as is the characteristic turn at the end. As we have been discussing it, the short story often presents a realm in which fantasy and reality are blurred or one in which fantasy becomes more real than the phenomenal world. "Marjorie Daw" is a story that takes this central characteristic as its primary theme. The epistolary form of the story, in which Edward Delaney writes letters to the laid-up John Fleming describing a beautiful young girl who lives across from him and Fleming writes back describing his growing love for the girl, is the point-of-view device that makes possible keeping the secret that there is no such girl.

The story is about the power of the writer's ability to create an "as if" reality that is more real than a real person. Delaney wishes he were a novelist with the skill of Turgenev as he begins to weave his tale of the young girl in the hammock across the way. As the letters progress, Fleming seems to feel he has known her in some previous state of existence or has dreamed her. Indeed, she is an embodiment of dream, a shadow or chimera; and Delaney marvels that Fleming could fall in love with her, even as he writes Fleming that the chimera is falling in love with him. Thus both Marjorie Daw and Fleming are transformed into fictional figures by Delaney, "a couple of ethereal beings moving in finer air than I can breathe with my commonplace lungs"; and Delaney, caught up in his own fictional creation, begins to "accept things as persons do in dreams." The end of the story is told in Delaney's last letter to Fleming, which Fleming reads when he has finally come to see Marjorie for himself, and it catches the reader with what Mark Twain would call a "snapper": "For oh, dear Jack, there isn't any colonial mansion on the other side of the road, there isn't any piazza, there isn't any hammock—there isn't any Marjorie Daw!" The reader's surprise at this ending and his subsequent going back over the story for clues to the trick is an objectification of what every reader feels when he or she has taken a fictional character to be real. "Marjorie Daw" is a story of the storytelling function itself—a discovery that characters are made of letters only.

The final figures in the development of the short story in the period from 1840 to 1880 are the self-conscious masters of fictional technique in the nineteenth century: Gustave Flaubert and Henry James. Poe's discussion of the importance of form and the artistic nature of the short story in 1842 is echoed by James in his discussion of the art of the novel in 1884. Poe's insistence that "In the whole composition there should be no word written, of which the tendency, direct or indirect, is not to the one preestablished design" is repeated by James's insistence that the novel is a "living thing, all one and continuous, like any other organism, and in proportion as it lives will it be found, I think, that in each of the parts there is something of each of the other parts." This is indeed a new criterion for the novel, one that redeems it from the realm of the popular and includes it within the realm of the artist. Furthermore, Poe's insistence on the importance of the point of view of the teller and its predominance over a simple mimetic presentation of events is also echoed by James's assertion that experience in fiction is an "immense sensibility, a kind of spider-web of the finest silken threads suspended in the chamber of consciousness . . . the very atmosphere of the mind." It is a curiosity of literary criticism that while James's essay is hailed as marking a new direction for the novel at the end of the century, Poe's similar insistence for the short story forty years earlier has been scorned as simplistic. In spite of the similarity of the two essays, many critics seem to believe that James's discussion is the first effort to justify fiction itself as an art form.

What James and Flaubert contribute to the novel form at the end of the nineteenth century is possible because of the development of the short story from the beginnings of the century. The importance of both point of view and form and their intrinsic relation to content, which seems a new departure for fiction at the end of the century, seems so only because the short story has always taken a back seat to the novel. The so-called modern novel may begin with the twentieth century, but for fiction generally "modernism" begins with the nineteenth century short story. Albert George in his study *Short Fiction in France: 1800-1850* says that Flaubert's *Three Stories* (1877) are an indication that Flaubert was the first to profit from romantic attempts to understand short fiction; they are "the superb refinement of the accumulated knowledge of a half-century." The same might be said of Henry James's *Daisy Miller*, published in 1878. Flaubert's "A Simple Heart" and James's *Daisy Miller* constitute a new beginning for the short story, a definite movement away from the romantic tale form that had dominated the century toward a new focus on realism, but a realism controlled by an ironic tone and a continuing focus on sympathy and an undercurrent of symbolism that has been unique to the short story since Gogol and Hawthorne. Flaubert's Félicité and James's Daisy are similar to Gogol's Akaky and Melville's Bartleby. They differ in that instead of being primarily functions of the story, they move to the forefront of the story and are presented as characters that can be identified with, even as they are symbolic. The kind of case that Robert Marler makes for *Bartleby the Scrivener* as marking the beginning of the true short story can be made also for "A Simple Heart" and *Daisy Miller*. In fact, Ray B. West, Jr., in his *The Short Story in America* (1952), notes that James's collection *Daisy Miller: A Study; And Other Stories* (1883) may be the first use of the term "story" in the title of a work in English. "Story" rather than "tale" has been used almost exclusively ever since.

The key to the power of "A Simple Heart," a story that Flaubert himself thought so much of that he sent it to a friend as an illustration of what he thought a story should be, lies in the complex mixture of irony and sympathy in the point of view of the teller, as well as in the use of realistic details that even in their ordinariness seem resonant with suggestive symbolism. It is the kind of technique that James Joyce brings to perfection in *Dubliners* (1914) and the kind of tone that Chekhov masters in his short stories. The interesting aspect of characterization in the story is that the only character of importance is Félicité, and she herself is characterless; she is the servant *par excellence* in that she gives herself completely to others. For all the particular detail of Félicité's life, she is finally not so much an individual character as she is representative of simplicity itself. In reading the story, one takes it incident by incident as a character study of the concrete universal, Félicité/Simplicity. It is not until the final pages of the story when she gets Loulou the parrot that we begin to suspect the symbolic nature of the story. For the parrot is a grotesque image of the kind of iconic figure that Félicité herself becomes. Flaubert says that by the age of fifty she was like a "woman made of wood," although she herself is hurt when people compare Loulou to a log of wood. Just as Félicité becomes deaf and her circle of ideas grows narrower, transforming her into a static iconic figure, so does the parrot become an iconic figure to Félicité after it is stuffed. While alive, the parrot is like a son and a lover to her; when dead he becomes an image of the Holy Ghost.

> They were linked in her thoughts; and the parrot was consecrated by his association with the Holy Ghost, which became more vivid to her eye and more intelligible. The Father could not have chosen to express himself through a dove, for such creatures cannot speak; it must have been one of Loulou's ancestors, surely.

Félicité begins to kneel to the parrot to say her prayers, and as she deteriorates, so does the bird. On her deathbed, he is brought to her with a broken wing, the tow coming out of his stomach, and the worms having devoured him; but Félicité is blind now as well as deaf and she kisses him. Although Félicité's devotion to the parrot throughout the last part of the story has something of the absurd about it, her simplicity and deteriorating condition prevent the reader from laughing at her. Although the tone of the story never drops from a kind of sympathetic distance, the conclusion runs the risk of dropping into bathos. In the moment of most poignancy, we are also confronted with the moment of most absurdity: "The beats of her heart lessened one by one, vaguer each time and softer, as a fountain sinks, an echo disappears; and when she sighed her last breath she thought she saw an opening in the heavens, and a gigantic parrot hovering above her head." The story of Félicité's treatment of the parrot is a symbolic echo of Flaubert's treatment of Félicité herself. Little more than a shadow throughout her life, Félicité can do little more than parrot others. She acts by instinct rather than rationality; she is, in the early part of the story, a representative of simplicity itself, but by her very simplicity she is transformed. In the later part of the story as the parrot becomes an iconic figure to her, so does she become an iconic figure to the reader; and that the Holy Ghost is perceived as a parrot by a peasant girl is no more absurd than that a peasant girl is perceived by the reader as a Christ figure. What Flaubert has done is what Frank O'Connor says that Gogol did so boldly and brilliantly. He has taken a mock-heroic character and imposed her image over that of the crucified Jesus, "so that even while we laugh we are filled with horror at the resemblance."

Henry James also creates a figure of simplicity in *Daisy Miller*. In a work that James himself called "the purest poetry," he creates a character that becomes a type. "Poor little Daisy Miller was, as I understand her," says James, "above all things innocent. . . . She was too ignorant, too irreflective, too little versed in the proportions of things." The whole idea of the story, James concludes, "is the little tragedy of a light, thin, natural, unsuspecting creature being sacrificed as it were to a social rumpus that went on quite above her head and to which she stood in no measurable relation." When considering why he called the story a "study," James said the reasons had escaped him, unless "they may have taken account simply of a certain flatness in my poor little heroine's literal denomination. Flatness indeed, one must have felt, was the very sum of her story." The sum of Daisy's story, however, is no more flat than that of Félicité, and for the same reasons—point of view and a symbolic undercurrent. James makes use of a *ficelle* in the story, a foil and a figure on which Daisy makes her impression. Giles Winterbourne, as his cold name implies, has an attachment to Geneva, the little metropolis of Calvinism, and has thus lost his instinct in the matter of innocence; his reason cannot help him in regard to Daisy. He can only apply a formula to her, that she is unsophisticated, even as he knows that is not the answer. The story deals with the inextricable nature of innocence and guilt. Moreover, it is a story of form versus formlessness.

Daisy Miller is very similar to Hawthorne's "Rappaccini's Daughter" in its placing a creature from another world into contact with the real world. The difference, of course, is in the mode of the telling. Instead of creating symbolic settings and using supernatural events to convey such a conflict, as Hawthorne did, James uses the realistic conflict between American innocence and European social order and sophistication. The terms of innocence and guilt, vulgarity and sophistication, formlessness and form seem natural elements of this realistic situation. Winterbourne becomes more and more angry at himself for being "reduced to chopping logic about this young lady; he was vexed at his want of instinctive certitude as to how far her eccentricities were generic, national, personal." Finally, with horror and relief, the ambiguity and the riddle of Daisy's behavior flash upon him in an ironic illumination of his own simplicity; that she was "a lady whom a gentleman need no longer be at pains to respect." Like Hawthorne's Giovanni, Winterbourne has made the mistake of judging when he should have loved; and Daisy, like Félicité, has been transformed from realistic character into icon, "a living embodiment," says Leslie Fiedler, "of the American faith that evil is appearance only." Like Bartleby, Daisy is the victim of the tragedy of being misunderstood; and like many short stories, Daisy's story is the drama of the need for the irrationality of love to transcend reason.

Conclusion

In the modern world since the beginning of the nineteenth century, when religious sanctions no longer apply; not only morality but also reality itself has become problematical, even arbitrary. Anyone who is secure in his or her own absolutist view of reality is likely to be challenged in fiction by the romantic perception of the irrational. The encounter with this mysterious deeper reality immanent in external categorical perceptions of reality can so challenge one and unsettle one's comfortable and familiar framework that he or she is unable to readjust, or at least must see that readjustment requires a radical reorientation or perspective. This is surely the significance of Goodman Brown's journey into the forest, Giovanni's encounter with Rappaccini's daughter, the narrator's encounter with Bartleby, or the guest's sojourn in the house of Usher; and in the twentieth century the irrational is confronted by Eudora Welty's traveling salesman, Flannery O'Connor's unfortunate family who meets the inevitable misfit, and Bernard Malamud's reluctant rabbi in "The Magic Barrel."

Often in the short story we are presented with characters who are *too* comfortable, too settled in their illusion that their lives are controlled and regular; they must be made aware of the problematic and arbitrary nature of their perceptions and the limitations of their awareness. Their unauthentic lives must be challenged. The short story does not reassure the reader that the world is as he or she usually sees it, nor does it assure him or her that leaps of faith can be made with anything but fear and trembling. It only presents one with the realization that "I-Thou" encounters are ambiguous, mysterious, and problematical. The reality the short story presents us with is the reality of those subuniverses of the supernatural and the fable. It presents us with the reality of the *mysterium tremendum* that suddenly erupts in the midst of the profane everyday. It presents us with those magical episodes in which we are torn away to what Martin Buber calls "dangerous extremes," in which security is shattered. It presents us with moments that make us aware that life is a becoming, a possibility of not-yet existence. As Flannery O'Connor says, it appeals to the kind of person who is willing to have his or her "sense of mystery deepened by contact with reality and sense of reality deepened by contact with mystery." It is both "canny and uncanny" at once.

The short story represents both desire and the frustration of desire, our deepest wishes censored and distorted by the external reality we must affirm to ourselves every day in order to survive. It says to us, however, that surviving is not enough, that we must make superhuman efforts in a superhuman world that always lies immanent in the world of the everyday. The short story is the most paradoxical of all fictional forms, for it gives us reality and unreality at once—gives us both the familiar and the unfamiliar, the universal and the particular. It reminds us of our separation and our possibility for unity—a unity that is not given to us, but that we must constantly make.

Charles E. May

THE AMERICAN CONSCIOUSNESS: 1880-1910

Ralph Waldo Emerson died on April 27, 1882; Mark Twain, on April 21, 1910. The nearly three decades between the deaths of these two literary figures mark a significant time not only for American literature, but also for American society generally. Spawned by revolution and saved by civil war, America was a young and robust nation, stretching and flexing itself as it faced the coming of the twentieth century. While the calendar may mark the end of one century and the beginning of another with the stroke of a clock, history, literary or otherwise, does not. America actually began moving into the twentieth century quite some time before midnight of December 31, 1899. Before beginning an examination of American short fiction between 1880 and 1910, therefore, it will be helpful to take a brief look at what was happening to American society in the years between the end of the Civil War and 1880.

If the American Revolution marks the birth of the American nation, the Civil War represents its trial by fire. More than that, the Civil War might well be termed a kind of rebirth for America. Certainly it was a pivotal point in American history, unleashing forces that were to move the country away from the Jeffersonian ideal of an agrarian society toward an urbanized industrial society—that is, toward the twentieth century.

By the mid-nineteenth century, America had developed a clearly defined ideology that consisted of a cosmic optimism, a belief in progress and perfectability, a concept of egalitarianism, and a middle-class, agrarian way of life—all undergirded by the Protestant ethic. Such an ideology would, of course, have been gradually redefined even without the war, but the war brought the redefinition with a dramatic abruptness. Secession destroyed the agrarian control of Congress and opened the way for government to please the industrial and commercial interests of the Northeast. More than that, however, it brought into clear focus the conflict between idealism and materialism—a conflict that had not gone entirely unnoticed even before the war. With all his idealism, Thomas Jefferson, for example, knew that America was destined to become an industrialized nation.

America, however, was being affected by more than industrialization. Rapid territorial expansion between 1870 and 1890 brought settlers to the vast area between Kansas and California. The call of the West was strong, and there were many with dreams of land or gold who heard and answered that call. At the same time, paradoxically enough, there were others who answered the very different call of the towns and cities—so many that by the 1880's the states of the Northeast were already feeling the pressures of urbanization. The closing of the frontier in 1890 merely exacerbated these pressures, as did the great influx of immigrants from Europe between the end of the war and the end of the century. So sweeping were the changes in American society that anyone who might have gone to sleep at the end of the eighteenth century to wake in 1880 would have felt the same trauma as Julian West, the hero of Edward Bellamy's Utopian novel *Looking Backward* (1888), who awakens in the year 2000 to exclaim, "The past was dead, crushed beneath a century's weight, and from the present I was shut out."

One of the best studies of the changes occurring in America during this period is Henry Adams' brilliant autobiography, *The Education of Henry Adams* (1907). In it Adams, using his own life as a kind of microcosm, traces the forces that brought about these changes. Born in the nineteenth century, Adams was given an eighteenth century education to face the twentieth century. The reality of the eighteenth century was being redefined throughout the nineteenth: Aristotelian logic was replaced; Euclidian geometry with regard to space was overthrown; Newtonian physics lost its primacy; and new theories of the origin of man were being advanced. What once appeared to be a world of unity now seemed a world of multiplicity—indeed, one of chaos. Returning from abroad in July of 1868, Adams was aware of the changes taking place in America, and he described the new Americans, of whom he was to be one, as having to "create a world of their own, a science, a society, a philosophy, a universe, where they had not yet created a road or even learned to dig their own iron. They had no time for thought; they saw, and could see, nothing beyond their day's work; their attitude to the universe outside them was that of the deep-sea fish." America, in short, was a nation of power with no idea of how to direct it.

Even though Emerson and the other Transcendentalists had misgivings regarding the rise of materialism in America, their views, based on the absolute of intuition, were optimistic. When Emerson in "The American Scholar" made a plea for an American declaration of independence from other lands, because the "millions that around us are rushing into life, cannot always be fed on the sere remains of foreign harvests," he was expressing the same faith in America that Walt Whitman was later to echo in "Democratic Vistas." Such optimism and faith in the destiny of America were in no small way predicated upon the concept of America as a new Eden and manifested in the Westward movement of the first half of the nineteenth century. Thomas Jefferson in his first Inaugural Address spoke of America as having "room enough for our descendants to the hundredth and thousandth generation." America, however, was being transformed much more rapidly than Jefferson could have imagined.

Prior to the Civil War, the open land of the West served as a safety valve for discontent in the large cities of the East; following the war, however, as the century drew to a close, such was not the case. Industrialism had brought with it many economic inequities that were to result in conflicts between a proletariat of ignorant and often unskilled workers and the industries that exploited them. Even the farmers of the Midwest found themselves dependent upon the industrial East. While the farmers were eventually to organize through the Grange, it was the laborers who made the first steps toward the betterment of their economic situation by seeking strength in unions. Unionism, points out Jay Martin, "sponsored its own martyrology in books like C. Osborne Ward's *The Ancient Lowly* (1888), and its own myth of success in the novels of social awakening that flourished in the '90's and on into the new century." A good example of the latter, of course, is Upton Sinclair's *The Jungle* (1905)—a book that Jack London called the *Uncle Tom's Cabin* of wage slavery.

Just as the times demanded a redefining of philosophical, social, political, and economic concepts, so too did they call for a new kind of literature. England might still bask somewhat in the setting sun of Romanticism, but America needed a literature that was a more natural reflection of the changing conditions and the shifting perceptions of life. The new theories of the history and laws of the physical world stimulated broad interest in the hard actualities of science—those things that can be seen as real. Henry James perhaps phrased it best when he said that "the real represents to my perceptions the things we cannot possibly *not* know," whereas the romantic represents "the things that . . . we never *can* directly know."

The years from 1880 to 1910, then, may be seen as the period during which realism became the dominant literary mode in America, a mode that has been characteristic of American literature up to the present day. While realism was a revolt against an outworn romantic tradition, the irritation out of which it developed in America was, according to Warner Berthoff, "as much with prevailing conditions of social and economic life, with the latest forms of disorder and inequity (however they might masquerade as progress), as with the insipidness of other, feebler literary methods." The optimism of Western expansion may have served well enough as a metaphor for such men as James Fenimore Cooper or even Walt Whitman, but the serious writers of the latter decades of the nineteenth century needed a different metaphor. They could not, even had they wanted to, ignore the changes mentioned earlier that were affecting America in so many ways. Optimism gave way, if not to pessimism, at least to an attitude of questioning concern regarding the complexities of American development.

A major tenet of the realists was the concern for man in society. A Captain Ahab might view the world from his philosophical vantage point on the quarterdeck of a whaling ship, but the average man views it from behind a plow, in the dark depths of a coal mine, amid the inferno of a steel mill, in a small New England village, or in the slums of a large city. In such places was the stuff of fiction to be found. Although the opponents of realism, in both Europe and America, might decry the penchant of the realist for drawing his characters from the lower levels of society and focusing on the more common human relationships, the latter declined to accept the view that art, literary or otherwise, could not address itself successfully to the commonplace.

While not as somber perhaps as its European counterpart, American realism was nevertheless in the 1890's moving toward naturalism, as the attitude
of questioning culminated in a feeling of disillusionment. Seeing man as living
in an indifferent universe where human reason can discover no rational principle, fiction writers wrote with an objectivity and frankness infused with a
philosophy of determinism—a great shift, indeed, from the philosophy of
optimism of Emerson. By the first decade of the twentieth century, naturalism
was in full sway—with such writers as Stephen Crane, Frank Norris, Jack
London, and Theodore Dreiser—and the perception of man and his world
had changed drastically from that of earlier periods. Instead of being in control
of his destiny and moving like a comic hero through his cosmos, man was
now a wisp in the winds of determinism, and the pattern for American literary
development in the twentieth century was set. To understand the progression
of short fiction from 1880 to 1910, it is with the realists that one must start.

One of the leading proponents of literary realism in America was William
Dean Howells, for many years considered the dean of American letters. From
his "Editor's Study," a column written for *Harper's Monthly*, he carried on
the battle against Romanticism, and in so doing faced some vocal defenders
of that tradition—among them Thomas Bailey Aldrich, who wrote in "Funeral
of a Minor Poet,"

> The mighty Zolaistic Movement now
> Engrosses us—a miasmatic breath
> Blown from the slums. We paint life as it is,
> The hideous side of it, with careful pains,
> Making a god of the dull commonplace.

A critic of the *Literary World* expressed the view that many of Howells' dicta
regarding realism were "as entertaining and instructive as that of a Pawnee
brave in the Louvre." Howells nevertheless persevered, viewing such attacks
as the latter as coming from those whose intellectual mission was "to represent
the petrifaction of taste, and to preserve an image of a smaller and cruder
and emptier world than we now live in." He continued with his plea that
fiction should cease to lie about life and begin to portray men and women as
they really are, and that it sould "speak the dialect, the language, that most
Americans know—the language of unaffected people everywhere." He also
continued to defend the writers who were attempting to make their fiction
do just that.

Among the writers that Howells referred to were those of the local-color
school of the short story, who produced the first significant examples of
American realism. Focusing on specific regions of the country, the writers of
this school portrayed the commonplace scenes and surface characteristics of
their chosen locales, paying close attention to such things as geographic setting, character types, speech patterns, social mores, and codes of conduct.

Because they were concerned with an exact portrayal of character and setting, they represented a clear turn toward realism. "Nothing could testify with more force," wrote H. H. Boyesen in *Literary and Social Silhouettes* in 1894, "to the fact that we have outgrown romanticism than this almost unanimous desire on the part of our authors to chronicle the widely divergent phases of our American civilization." Gone was the predilection of American writers to treat the strange and the remote. They were to find not only an appropriate subject matter in the several regions of America, but also an extremely receptive audience for their stories. The result was that in the last decades of the nineteenth century the short story in America reached its maturity as a form of fiction and was generally thought to be America's unique contribution to the literary genres of the world.

Accepting the dictum that the short story as a literary form demands a unity of effect, the local colorists worked to make their settings vivid and real. Aware, too, that locality can serve as a significant source of motivation for a character, these writers knew that they could not write about what they did not know and understood that honest, accurate observation will discover the stuff of fiction anywhere. Of all the regions of America, probably none stirred the interest of the reading public, both at home and abroad, more than did the West. The last of the American frontiers, the West epitomized the freedom of opportunity that has always been so significant an aspect of the American dream. Rich in materials for fiction, the West has received considerable attention from writers over the years; but it was Bret Harte, whose "The Luck of Roaring Camp" is often seen as the first local-color story, who pioneered in Western writing. While some may debate whether Harte can justifiably be called the founder of the local-color school of writing, no one would deny that he made a significant contribution not only to that genre, but also to the American short story in general. Combining a clear talent for developing narrative and creating scene and incident with a formula that was based on the contrast between appearance and reality, that utilized stock characters, and that redeemed sentimental plots with humor and irony, Harte caught not only the flavor of the region, but also the favor of the reading public.

"The Luck of Roaring Camp" offers a clear illustration of Harte's writing technique. Essentially a story of the regeneration of a rude mining camp, it is set in an area of stark isolation and striking natural beauty. At the opening of the story, a group of hard miners stand nonplussed outside a cabin in which the camp prostitute is giving birth. Although they are not aware of it at the time, the "sharp, querulous cry,—a cry unlike anything heard before in the camp" sets in motion a change in Roaring Camp that in some way will affect them all. Cherokee Sal dies giving birth, but her baby survives—becoming, as it were, a son to the whole camp. Nourished by milk from a jackass and protected by the watchful attention of the men, the Luck, as he is called, works a near miracle on the camp. Hard and crude as they seem, the men are all touched by the subtle influence of the Luck as his presence awakens their finer sentiments. Less than a year later, however, Roaring Camp is inundated by flood waters and literally swept away. After a frantic search, the survivors find the Luck dead in the arms of Kentuck, who is also dying. As he clings to the Luck, his last words are "he's taking me with him,—tell the boys I've got the Luck with me now."

By focusing clearly on the specific setting and on the general characteristics of the miners, Harte leaves the reader with the impression that only at this given place, at this given time, and with these given people could the story occur. Moreover, by blending humor and sentiment so that each either undercuts or highlights the other at just the right moment, he avoids cheap sentimentality or low comedy. Thus "The Luck of Roaring Camp" succeeds as a short story and serves as an exemplary effort in local-color fiction.

In addition to Harte, of course, there were many minor writers who, following his lead, used the West as settings for their stories—including E. H. Clough, who wrote about mining and ranching; Yda Addis Storke, who treated the semi-Spanish civilization; Edward Waterman Townsend, who pictured life in San Francisco; William S. O'Neil, who depicted life on the frontier army posts; and R. L. Ketchum, who portrayed the "real cowboy" on the great cattle ranches of Wyoming and Utah. One writer who, interestingly enough, wrote approximately eighty stories with Western settings was O. Henry. His own experience in the West gave him firsthand knowledge of cattle ranches, cowboys, and badmen. Mostly, however, he used and reused the same plots with a few different twists. He was often criticized by Eastern critics for injecting too much fantasy into his stories and for gross exaggeration, but there was considerable real-life basis for many of the characters and episodes that he depicted.

In contrast to the rawness of life lived close to the surface in the West, the South represented a funded past, a sense of gentility and tradition that, while not as violently dramatic as the various aspects of Western life, nevertheless provided writers of local color with rich sources of materials. Three of the most important of these sources were the plantations, New Orleans, and the remote areas of the Southern Appalachians.

Just as in much of the rest of the country, there was, prior to 1865, little concern with literature in the South. Following the Civil War, however, the nation's readers exhibited a growing and sympathetic interest in Southern life, as well as in the scenes and episodes of the war itself. Southern writers rose to the occasion; there were a significant number of local colorists who tried to present the South and its inhabitants to the reading world, among them Joel Chandler Harris, George Washington Cable, and Mary Noailles Murfree.

Harris was born in Georgia and spent his childhood there, learning to set type on the plantation of Joseph Addison Turner. More than that, Harris learned much about plantation life and, in the process, developed a deep sympathy and understanding for the plantation black. In his stories of the Southern plantation, he effected the felicitous combination of black character and dialect as he tried to achieve the goals he set for himself: to embody the quaint and homely humor of the black, to suggest his picturesque sensitiveness, and to portray his curious exaltation of mind and temperament. His vehicle for achieving these goals was not only his own imagination, but also the beast fables and legends of the plantation, which he sought to present without embellishment and without exaggeration. For a narrator he created the delightfully unlettered storyteller Uncle Remus, a slave who spins his tales with an artful simplicity.

Holding a privileged place on his master's plantation, he has general supervision over all things and free rein to do as he pleases. In "How the Birds Talk" his duties are enumerated: "He did no great amount of work, but he was never idle. He tanned leather, he made shoes, he manufactured horse collars, fish baskets, footmats, scouring mops, and ax handles for sale; he had his own watermelon and cotton patches; he fed the hogs, looked after the cows and sheep, and, in short was the busiest man on the plantation." Most importantly, however, Uncle Remus tells stories to a spellbound little boy (probably the master's son)—stories of the adventures of such animal characters as Brer Rabbit, Brer Fox, Brer Wolf, and Brer Snake—all of whom are thinly disguised, strongly individualized human beings. Brer Rabbit, for example, is very quick-witted and clever, while Brer Fox is thievish and sly, although not generally successful; indeed, he is never able to catch Brer Rabbit. Most critics agree that these animal characters are reflections of various black types with whom Harris came into contact during hiw own plantation experiences.

Discussing his use of a rabbit for a hero in his stories, Harris said,

> The story of the Rabbit and the Fox . . . is artistically dramatic in this: it progresses in an orderly way from a beginning to a well-defined conclusion, and is full of striking episodes that suggest the culmination. It seems to me to be to a certain extent allegorical, albeit such an interpretation may be unreasonable. At least it is a fable thoroughly characteristic of the Negro; and it needs no scientific investigation to show why he selects as his hero the weakest and most harmless of all animals, and brings him out victorious in contests with the bear, the wolf, and the fox. It is not virtue that triumphs, but helplessness; it is not malice, but mischievousness.

Typical of the incidents in which Brer Rabbit triumphs is the tale in which Brer Fox spends a whole day hunting, bagging considerable game. Brer Rabbit waits till Brer Fox is returning home, then lies down in the road playing dead. When Brer Fox sees him, he thinks that the rabbit, although mighty fat, has been dead too long to take home, so he goes on. Brer Rabbit then springs up and gets ahead of Brer Fox and once more lies in the road playing dead.

This time the temptation is too great for Brer Fox. He decides not only to take this rabbit home, but also to go back and get the first one. Leaving his bag of game, he retraces his steps back to the first rabbit. At this point Brer Rabbit jumps up, takes the bag of game, and runs home. When he sees Brer Fox later, he asks him what he caught on his hunting trip. Brer Fox says, "I kotch a han'ful er hard sense, Brer Rabbit." Brer Rabbit replies, "Ef I'd a know'd you wuz atter dat, Brer Fox, I'd a loant you some er mine."

If Americans felt that the Southern plantation was a strange and exotic setting, they felt the same about New Orleans and its rich blend of races and cultures. George Washington Cable in his stories and novels focusing on the Creoles of Louisiana attempted to picture their romantic culture before it passed away in the coming homogenization of American society. His treatment was unapologetically romantic. The very title of his best work, the collection of stories called *Old Creole Days* (1879), implies an idealization of the past. In the short pieces making up the book, Cable was accurate and thorough in his use of materials, although he was not beyond blending in what he called the "harmoniously supposable."

Among the stories in *Old Creole Days*, "Posson Jone' " (Parson Jones) was one of Cable's favorites. Found too coarse for *Scribner's Monthly* and some other magazines, the story first appeared in *Appleton's Journal*. Like all of Cable's stories, "Posson Jone' " is a series of dramatic episodes interspersed with descriptive passages that combine to produce an interesting climax and a unique ending. Parson Jones is a huge preacher from West Florida who is visiting New Orleans and carrying a large roll of bank notes that belong to his church. He meets Jules St.-Ange, a young Creole of questionable character, who hopes to trick him out of his money. Prior to a scheduled fight between a tiger and a buffalo, St.-Ange succeeds in getting Jones drunk. In this condition the latter gives a sermon to the crowd and hurls the tiger onto the back of the buffalo, shouting, "The tiger and the buffler *shell* lay down together! You dah to say they shayn't and I'll comb you with this varmint from head to foot!" Whereupon he is jailed. St.-Ange is so admiring of Jones's strength that he effects his release. The money, however, is missing, and Jones is remorseful that he has let his church down. St.-Ange offers to make up the loss with money that he has won from gambling, but Jones refuses the offer. All ends well, however, when the next day Jones boards a schooner for home and finds that his slave has safeguarded the money all along. St.-Ange himself is moved to the point that he resolves to become an honest man. "Posson Jone' " is a comical study of the differences between the moral codes of the Creole and the Anglo-Saxon. While Jones may come off as morally superior to St.-Ange, the latter nevertheless does have his moments of generosity and compassion.

Cable's picture of Creole culture and Creole lingo may have been challenged later by Grace King, but he certainly succeeded in laying out for his readers a view that from his vantage point was one of honesty and truth. "The sharp originality of Mr. Cable's descriptions," wrote Lafcadio Hearn in 1883, "should have convinced the reader of 'Old Creole Days' that the scenes of his stories are by no means fanciful; and the strict perfection of his Creole architecture is readily recognized by all who have resided in New Orleans." And J. K. Wetherill, five years later, wrote, "What Bret Harte has done for the stern angularity of Western life, Mr. Cable has wrought, in infinitely finer and subtler tones, for his soft-featured and passionate native land. Those who come after him in delineation of Creole character can only be followers in his footsteps, for to him alone belongs the credit of striking this new vein, so rich in promise and fulfillment."

If Cable found his literary inspiration among the Creoles of New Orleans, Mary Noailles Murfree found hers among the people of the Tennessee mountains. Writing under the pen name of Charles Egbert Craddock, Murfree produced stories of the rude mountaineers living routine lives in a spectacularly impressive and isolated setting. Born into the Southern aristocracy herself, she depicts in her stories a world where civilization has yet to make many inroads. Circumscribed though it may have been, however, mountain life had its elements of drama; focusing on them, Murfree opened up the Southern mountains both for her readers and for later writers.

Her first, and perhaps best, collection of stories is titled *In the Tennessee Mountains* (1884), published at the urging of Thomas Bailey Aldrich by Houghton Mifflin. Aldrich was proved right in his recommendation, for the book went through more than a dozen editions in two years; indeed, it has been held by some to be as significant a contribution to local-color writing as Harte's "The Luck of Roaring Camp." Dominant in all these stories are the mountains—so dominant that Murfree has been accused of lugging in description by the ears. Yet it is the mountains that strongly establish in the reader a sense of place. It would, moreover, be hard to deny that to the mountaineer the mountains were the central fact in his existence. The opening scene of "A-Playin' of Old Sledge at the Settlemint" serves as an example of Murfree's description:

> No broad landscape was to be seen from this great projecting ledge of the mountain; the valley was merely a little basin, walled in on every side by the meeting ranges that rose so high as to intercept all distant prospect, and narrow the world to the contracted area bounded by the sharp lines of their wooded summits, cut hard and clear against the blue sky.

Murfree's mountain characters are generally depicted as fatalistic and accepting. The men are shiftless and prone to disregard domestic responsibility in favor of hunting, fishing, drinking, and generally loafing. The women, when young, are naturally beautiful, but when they grow older, they lose their beauty and become like Mrs. Ware in "Drifting Down Lost Creek," who looks at her daughter "with a gay grin, which, distorted by her toothless gums and the wreathing steam from the kettle enhanced her witch-like aspect and was spuriously malevolent." Like so many primary societies, that of the Tennessee mountains is male-oriented and male-dominated; it is the woman's lot to accept without complaint.

The basic theme of Murfree's stories is that of common humanity. Reginald Chevis, an outlander in "The Star in the Valley," for example, realizes that the humble mountain girl Celia Shaw is a person of stature and feeling—that "despite all his culture, his sensibility, his yearnings toward humanity, he was not so high a thing in the scale of being; that he had placed a false estimate upon himself." In her use of this theme of common humanity, however, Murfree often falls into a didacticism that militates against her stories. Perhaps too much the outsider in relation to mountain life, she tends on occasion to adopt a moral stance out of keeping with mountain mores or to manipulate her characters to the point that they are more like chess pieces than they are human beings. Even so, her work stands as an important contribution to regional literature; through it she brought to view the colorful inhabitants of one of America's most remote and romantic areas.

Harris, Cable, and Murfree are but a few of the Southern writers of short fiction between 1880 and 1910. Some others were Thomas Nelson Page, whose stories of antebellum plantation life reflect a sense of regret at the passing of the days before the war; Constance Fenimore Woolson, whose settings range from Virginia and the Carolinas to Ohio and Michigan; Grace Elizabeth King, who, as did Cable, treated the Creoles of New Orleans; and James Lane Allen, who utilized Kentucky as a setting for his stories.

Like the South, New England had a strong sense of tradition, and preachers, statesmen, and writers came forth regularly to prove it. Following the Civil War, however, New England lost its signal position as the cultural and religious center of America. The Puritanism that had provided Nathaniel Hawthorne his inspiration was dead, and the Federalists were long gone. The brash city of New York was becoming America's cultural, as well as commercial, center. The character of a people does not so readily change, however, and the two major writers of New England local color between 1880 and 1910—Sarah Orne Jewett and Mary E. Wilkins Freeman—found their métier in the descendents of the Puritans and in the starkness of the New England landscape.

Born in South Berwick, Maine, and living most of her life in the stately pre-Revolutionary home of her birth, Jewett wrote of what she knew—the fishing villages and upland farms that dotted the area around her birthplace. Chronicling a disappearing social order and decaying seaports, her stories are primarily sketches, told with restraint and grace. Her characters are taken from people she knew well. As one reviewer wrote in 1910,

The people of her books are familiar to us all. Her stories are constructed from material

of the most elemental kind: of the pathos incident to old age and loneliness, of the joy
of friendship, the peace of quiet paths, of the struggle of trying to make both ends meet,
of the humorous development of character where isolation lays its emphasis on heart and
mind, or perhaps the odd cranks and whimsies induced by like cause.

Because she chose such materials, Jewett was one of the few writers of
local color able to portray the universal through a focus on the local. The
story "Miss Tempy's Watchers" is a good example.

Basically, the theme of this story is the posthumous effect on two women
of the character of Miss Tempy Dent. Mrs. Crowe and Miss Binson, longtime
friends of Tempy, sit in her kitchen carrying out her last request that they
perform the traditional watching over the body of their friend the night before
the funeral. There is a marked contrast between the two women. Mrs. Crowe,
a stingy woman of some wealth and social status, has a kindly look, but "when
she gave away anything, or lifted a finger to help anybody, it was though a
great piece of beneficence, and compliment, indeed, which the recipient accepted with twice as much gratitude as double the gift that came from a poorer
and more generous acquaintance." Miss Binson, on the other hand, has had
to toil on her little farm in order to support an "inefficient widowed sister
and six unpromising nieces and nephews." Still, pleasureless though her life
seems to others, "it was brimful of pleasure to herself." Tempy's hope was
that through their watching, these two women would forget the differences
that had grown between them and come closer together.

As the night progresses, the conversation between them rises to "an unusual
level of expressiveness and confidence"—moreso than either has intended.
Moreover, they get the feeling that they are being watched over, as in one
sense they are, by the spirit of Tempy. What Tempy had in mind comes to
pass. As Mrs. Crowe and Miss Binson recall their deceased friend's many
virtues, all the barriers that have stood between them fall; and as Miss Binson
dozes, Mrs. Crowe glances at her "compassionately, with a new sympathy for
the hard-worked little woman." Through death, then, the "loving-hearted
soul" of Tempy Dent has brought about a new degree of human awareness.
Perhaps Willa Cather phrased it best when she said that Jewett did not write
about Othellos or Iagos or Don Juans or people at war with their environments, but of "everyday people who grew out of the soil."

In 1887, Mary E. Wilkins Freeman published her first book of short stories,
A Humble Romance and Other Stories; these tales are about the village people
of New England. Four years later she published another volume of stories,
A New England Nun and Other Stories, most of which are about provincial
New England women caught in a rigid tradition of village repression. The
title story of this latter volume portrays the archetypal old maid who shuns
marriage because it would change the routine of single life to which she has
become accustomed. Engaged fifteen years to Joe Dagget, who has spent
most of that time earning money in Australia, Louisa Ellis occupies herself

with domestic tasks; she is an almost perfect picture of spinsterhood.

When Joe returns, the couple realize that they are no longer in love. For her part, Louisa is hesitant to change her life-style, and Joe has become enamored of Lily Dyer, a girl who works for his mother. All three characters, however, in the name of decorum, play self-sacrificing roles, and marriage plans go on. When Louisa accidentally overhears Joe and Lily expressing their love for each other, she releases Joe from the engagement—thus resigning herself to her nun's existence for the rest of her life—but with no real regret: "Louisa, all alone by herself that night, wept a little, she hardly knew why; but the next morning, on waking, she felt like a queen who, after fearing lest her domain be wrested away from her, sees it finally insured in her possession. . . . Serenity and placid narrowness had become to her as the birthright itself." In commenting on this decision by Louisa, Perry Westbrook in his book on Freeman sees Louisa as redeeming herself to a degree. She has, in his view, learned to live with her inadequacies, and her decision not only interrupts the "unrippled flow of years of passivity, but it marks her as the possessor of a sense of moral realism which Howells . . . repeatedly declared goes hand in hand with literary realism." Like Jewett, Freeman, in her compact and poignant tales of New England, created a gallery of individualized characters who are very much products of their environment. In so doing, she gave to local-color characterization a heightened sense of seriousness.

To shift from the provincially restrictive villages of Jewett and Freeman to the throbbing metropolis of O. Henry's New York City involves considerably more than a geographical displacement. It is like leaving one world for another, in the sense that the boiling surface of New York life at the turn of the century stood in stark contrast not only to New England but also to the South and the West.

Born William Sydney Porter in North Carolina, O. Henry began his career working at various kinds of jobs in Texas. Involved later in a bank embezzlement scheme, he spent three years in prison, where he began writing short stories. In addition to his tales of the West, mentioned earlier, he wrote of the Latin American banana republics; but his greatest contributions to short fiction are his stories of city life. A good-natured writer, he often relied on humor, plots with surprise endings, or overt sentimentality to carry his stories. He made these elements, which in lesser writers would have been detrimental, work to his advantage, primarily because his characters were genuinely human and his settings strikingly real. The result was that at the turn of the century he was one of America's most widely read authors.

When he arrived in New York, O. Henry, in his own words, "spent a great deal of time knocking around the streets." Because of this immersion into the life of the city, he was able in his stories to record the essence of New York and its inhabitants. There was, in short, no corner of the city that he could not find a story in. The stories he found ranged from "The Gift of the Magi," a Christmas story in which a young wife sells her long hair to buy her husband a chain for his watch, while he in turn sells his watch to buy her a set of combs for her hair; to "The Cop and the Anthem," in which a hobo tries unsuccessfully to get arrested so that he can get food and shelter and then *is* arrested after he decides that he will give up his vagabond ways; to "The Last Leaf," in which a young woman is given the will to live by a poor painter who braves the cold to paint a leaf on a wall outside her window and then dies from his efforts; to "Brickdust Row," in which a wealthy man gains a broader and more idealistic perspective of humanity as he watches the jostling masses at Coney Island.

The last region to be mentioned here as distinct in terms of local color is the Middle West. Although a number of writers treated this area around the turn of the century, Hamlin Garland stands out, not only for his literary talent, but also for his position in American realism. Born in a log cabin in Wisconsin, Garland wrote movingly of the hardships and deprivations of pioneer life. He saw himself as a realist, or veritist, attempting to "hasten the age of beauty and peace, by delineating the ugliness and warfare of the present." In that sense he believed that fiction must be a vehicle for social and moral improvement, and his indignation at the social system under which the Midwestern farmer labored caused him to ask, "Why have these stern facts never been put into our literature as they have been in Russia and England? Why has this land no storytellers like those who have made Massachusetts and New Hampshire illustrious?" To remedy such a situation, Garland set about writing stories in which his characters, as Carl Van Doren has so aptly described them, "wrestle fearfully with sand and mud and drought and blizzard, goaded with mortgages which may at almost any moment snatch away all that labor and parsimony have stored up."

"Among the Corn Rows" is a good example of Garland's descriptive ability and his emphasis on the harsher aspects of Midwestern farm life. In this story, Rob Rodemaker, a bachelor homesteader in the Dakotas, decides to return to Wisconsin to get a wife. He meets Julia Peterson, a supple, handsome girl of Norwegian stock who is plowing a field under the hot July sun. She is an example of the overworked farmer's daughter who longs to be free of the hardship and constriction of farm life. She willingly accepts Rob's offer of marriage and a shanty home on a "rattlin' good claim," where all she will have to do is cook for him. A simple story, "Among the Corn Rows" is powerful in its unyielding portrayal of the boredom and hopelessness of such people as Julia Peterson as they participate in the struggle for mere existence in the stifling corn fields or wheat fields of the Middle West. While Julia is rescued from her father's fields, she is bound for a not much different life in a shanty house on a "rattlin' good claim"—where the sun still shines hotly and where existence is still a struggle.

While Garland may have considered himself an opponent of naturalism—pointing out that he was simply trying to present life as he saw it and was not interested in exploiting such "naturalistic themes as murder, seduction, and adultery," and that he was "against the idea of viewing men and women as returning to the morality of monkeys"—his stories, in their choice of subject and character and in their emphasis on social determinism, exhibit tendencies toward naturalism. Indeed, critics in the Middle West were enraged by the ugly pictures of life that they saw in *Main-Travelled Roads* (1891), Garland's first collection of stories; William Dean Howells, however, rose to its defense. While it is true that writers of local color were more concerned with presenting and interpreting segments of the American scene than in delving into the universal, and while modern critics might decry their penchant for photographic realism and their tendency toward one-dimensional characters and specifically labeled settings, these writers certainly contributed to the realistic movement in America.

One writer of short fiction who refused to be swept up in the currents of realism and local color running so strongly in the latter nineteenth century was the enigmatic Ambrose Bierce. Exhibiting in his fiction the same penchant for the macabre and the supernatural as Edgar Allan Poe, Bierce rejected the dictum of probability espoused by Howells and the other realists. Close to Hawthorne in this sense, he believed that the capable writer ignores probability "except to make what is related *seem* probable." That Bierce passed over into the realm of romance and beyond would not be questioned by anyone reading many of his stories. His most famous, "An Occurrence at Owl Creek Bridge," published in *Tales of Soldiers and Civilians* (1891), is a good example. In a staccato style similar to Ernest Hemingway's, the story opens with Peyton Farquhar, a plantation owner, standing on a bridge in Alabama waiting to be hanged by Union troops during the Civil War for having sabotaged a bridge. As he falls downward through the wooded supports of the bridge, he loses consciousness. After what seems ages later, he awakens with "the pain of a sharp pressure upon his throat, followed by a sense of suffocation." The rope has broken. Freeing himself in the water below the bridge, Farquhar begins a suspenseful flight home. As he finally drags himself to his doorstep where his wife awaits, "a blinding white light blazes all about him with a sound like cannon—then all is darkness and silence. Peyton Farquhar was dead; his body, with a broken neck, swung from side to side beneath the timbers of Owl Creek Bridge." In the detailed account of Farquhar's attempt to reach freedom, Bierce succeeds in getting the reader to cheer the fugitive on. When he finally reaches his home, the reader sighs with relief. Then it is all abruptly pulled away. Though the reader may feel cheated that death has prevailed after all, Bierce shows that in the end there is no escape from death.

In 1893 Bierce published *Can Such Things Be?*, a collection of stories replete with such psychic phenomena as time displacement, visions of previous lives, and the death experience. "The Death of Halpin Frayser" from this collection not only presents an interesting pre-Freudian study of the Oedipal theme, but also illustrates Bierce's use of coincidence in his plots. In the story, Halpin Frayser, who has been unnaturally close to his mother, is lost on a hunting trip and decides to lie down on the ground to sleep. He awakens to speak the unfamiliar name Catherine Larue. Going back to sleep, he has hideous dreams that culminate in a vision of his mother dressed for her grave. Not knowing that she had remarried, he also does not know that her second husband (named Larue) brutally murdered her. Moreover, he has unknowingly gone to sleep on her grave. The next day two detectives, while searching for an escaped madman, find Halpin murdered—either by the madman or by the ghost of his mother, whichever the reader prefers.

Another American writer very active during this period was Henry James, although in many respects he seems more European than American. Recognized more widely for his efforts in the novel, James nevertheless wrote many pieces of short fiction—although often these come closer to being short novels than short stories. He himself preferred to call them tales rather than short stories, or to use the French word *nouvelle*, because it gave more flexibility with regard to length of a story. He believed in the concept of "masterly brevity," of a piece being "beautifully shaped." His average tale runs from ten to twenty thousand words, with the result that he found it difficult to place his stories in the magazines of the day. James's subject matter is also quite distinct from that of the other American writers of the time. Educated abroad, James had a familiarity with international society that carried him beyond any concern with economic or social conditions in his writing. Unlike Howells and the other realists, he was an interpreter of the upper classes, more concerned with how money was spent than with how it was acquired.

A reflection of his interest in the upper classes, James's style is involved and circumlocutious almost to the point of ostentation. H. G. Wells once compared it to a hippopotamus trying to pick up a pea; but Pelham Edgar defends the style, which is more concerned with the landscape of the mind than with physical action or geographical setting, by pointing out that James "neglects these excrescent attachments of fiction, and concentrates all the powers of his intellect on the artistic presentation of human behavior under conditions designed to reveal character at the maximum of intensity that situations on the hither side of tragedy may bear." James's approach, then, is basically psychological, and his novels and stories are filled with psychological subtleties.

Among the tales that may be more justifiably labeled short stories, "The Beast in the Jungle" is a good illustration of James's psychological orientation. It begins with a chance meeting between a somewhat impoverished May

Bartram, at age thirty, and John Marcher, a shy and financially independent man of thirty-five. She recalls for him an earlier meeting in which he had confided a "sense of being kept for something rare and strange, possibly prodigious and terrible" that was sooner or later to happen to him. His feeling becomes the chief topic of their conversation as the acquaintance stretches through years. He never legalizes their relationship nor concerns himself much with May's affairs; his principal concern is with discovering the identity of the unknown force which he senses. The pair grow old discussing his mysterious fate. Then, on Marcher's next-to-last visit, May is moribund and resembles an "imperishable sphinx," but he fails to perceive a connection and only fears "she might die without giving him light" about his fate's identity. Because of the delicacy of their communication—containing much Jamesian indirection, such as "what I allude to was what you said to me"—and because of her unselfish love for him, May refuses to confide her understanding of the beast's identity, but without words she makes a supreme effort to stand: the beast has sprung. Marcher, however, fails to comprehend. On the last visit, she explains that he was to suffer his fate, not to know it.

A visit to her grave still tells him nothing about himself; on her stone her two names become "a pair of eyes that didn't know him." After a year of empty travel, he returns to the grave once more and observes a deeply stricken mourner at another grave. He now realizes that such a passion as this stranger's has always been beyond him, that his fate was to be the person to whom nothing happened—except that *she* had offered him "the chance to baffle his doom." In the "Jungle of his life" he now sees "the lurking Beast," ready to spring "for the leap that was to settle him."

James presented a different kind of reality from that advocated by Howells or Émile Zola. Focusing on the conventions and manners of society, he plumbed the psychological depths of his characters to seek out the substance of their moral values. Rejecting such forces as history and religion, he isolated the contemporary, and in so doing, he surely achieved what he called the "obstinate finality" of the artist.

As the nineteenth century came to a close, the final phase of American realism was evidenced in the trend toward naturalism. While much has been written regarding the differences and likenesses between realism and naturalism, the only sure point is that definitively labeling literary movements is difficult, if not impossible. The shadings among them are broad and often subtle. Realism, for example, has always been a part of literature in one way or another. To be sure, the new conception of the universe being framed in the nineteenth century demanded a new literary response, one governed by truth, sincerity, honesty, and objectivity, and these characteristics marked the new directions for literature that Howells and other realists were charting during the 1880's and 1890's. There were those, however, who wished to go beyond the rather quiet and simple realism of Howells and the local colorists toward that of Zola and the French realists. While Howells advocated the common and usual for literary subjects, Zola went after the uncommon and the abnormal for his subject matter. Howells was unable to view America as a country with the same experiences as Europe; thus, Zola's realism, or what is more appropriately called naturalism, might have been acceptable for France, but it certainly did not fit the prosperous, well-ordered society of America. American writers, Howells thought, should "concern themselves with the more smiling aspects of life, which are the more American, and seek the universal in the individual rather than the social interests."

As previously mentioned, Hamlin Garland declined to see himself in the naturalist camp, writing in *Crumbling Idols* (1894) that "No nation can endure and transact business whose citizens are as depraved as those set forth by Zola or his feeble imitators here in America." Still, anyone giving Garland a careful reading cannot help noticing the strong deterministic tone in his stories of the Middle West; and perhaps the one thing that differentiates naturalism from realism most clearly is this addition of determinism as a significant factor in human existence. Three writers who, in one sense, picked up where Garland left off are Frank Norris, Stephen Crane, and Jack London.

It is generally agreed that Frank Norris provided a link between the Zolaistic and the American schools of naturalism. Interestingly enough, he did so because he equated naturalism with Romanticism. Romance, he said, was serious business, not simply "an affair of cloaks and daggers, or moonlight and golden hair." Consequently, Norris saw Zola not as a naturalist, but as a true romanticist. His point was that realism, by dealing only with the surface of things, stultifies itself, whereas Romanticism (naturalism) delves beneath the surface to the depths of the human heart and the "unsearched penetralia of the soul of man."

Producing all of his work in a single decade, the 1890's, Norris is most remembered as a novelist. He did, however, write a considerable number of short stories which, although they hardly add to his literary reputation, are of some interest to the scholar of short fiction because they illustrate some of the same characteristics as his novels. These stories were written in two groups: the first between 1895 and 1897 and the second a few years later. Warren French characterizes the first group as "designed to provide sadistic pleasure" and astonishing because they seem "so entirely out of keeping with the character of a man with any pretensions as a serious artist." Of these early stories, only "Boom," which treats the real-estate booms of the 1890's, has any redeeming qualities. According to French, these early stories show that, far "from being an objective naturalist, Norris was an extremely unrealistic idealist who could not stomach the constant compromise of ideals demanded by life in an urban society."

The second group of stories, however, are structurally better and more accurately reflect Norris' literary talent. Of these, "A Deal in Wheat" presents a tight circle of economic determinism which sees the farmers and workingmen fall victim to the buying and selling machinations of the great operators of the Chicago grain market. In the first scene, Sam Lewiston, a small wheat farmer in Kansas, has to sell wheat that costs a dollar a bushel to produce at the artificially low figure of sixty-two cents a bushel. Ruined, he moves to Chicago to work for his wife's brother. In the ensuing scenes Norris describes the clever market manipulations of two men, Truslow and Hornung, in Chicago that have caused the ruin of farmers such as Lewiston. In the last scene, Lewiston stands in a bakery bread line only to learn that, because further manipulations have raised the price of wheat to two dollars a bushel, the bakery can no longer give free bread to the poor. Lewiston is left with the bitter knowledge that at the two ends of a great wheat operation is ruination— first for the farmer who grew the wheat and second for the workingman who consumed it—while in between, the great operators grow richer through greed and chicanery.

Like his character Presley in the novel *The Octopus* (1901), Norris searched for the "true Romance." While Presley never quite succeeds in his search, Norris, at least in his own mind, did succeed in his. He found the romance he was looking for in "the people." While such a view would seem to ally him to the Populist movement of the time, Richard Chase points out that the "main difference between the folklore of Populism and the imagination of Frank Norris is that naturalist doctrine has given him an underlying pessimism about nature itself and man's place in it." The real voice of Norris, of course, is to be found in his novels. Still, "A Deal in Wheat" serves as a clear hint of that voice.

Considered one of the more brilliant turn-of-the-century writers in America, Stephen Crane represents as well as anyone the turn toward naturalism. Joining the revolt against the genteel tradition of letters and the social conditions of the times, he produced, in his short life of twenty-nine years, two highly significant novels—*Maggie: A Girl of the Streets* (1893) and *The Red Badge of Courage* (1895)—and a number of quality short stories that have combined to assure him a secure place in American literature. Like his compatriots in the battle for realism, he felt "that the nearer a writer gets to life, the greater he becomes as an artist." A minister's son who received his training as a journalist, his ambition was to maintain a strong dimension of personal and artistic honesty, even if such lofty ambition might never be fully realized. He wanted "to write plainly and unmistakably, so that all . . . might read and understand." Although he felt that fiction should have an intention, he was always "very careful not to let any theories or pet ideas of my own creep into my work." If there was to be any moral, the reader would have to find it out for himself.

Crane, like the other naturalists, saw man as quite small in the universe, destined to struggle not only against the merciless forces of nature, but also against the impersonal forces of society, with only his persistent intelligence as a weapon. Crane's "The Open Boat" is a powerful portrayal of the human struggle for existence in the face of an indifferent universe. The story is based on Crane's own experience in a shipwreck in 1896. In the story, four men—the cook, the oiler, the correspondent, and the captain—are the survivors of a shipwreck and are struggling to get their lifeboat to the shore. The sea, with its huge, sweeping waves, is their enemy; it cuts them off not only from the shore, but also from everything else. Against the raw power of nature the men throw up a subtle human brotherhood: "No one said it was so. No one mentioned it. But it dwelt in the boat, and each man felt it warm him." At last they can see land and people moving about; but no one on land seems to be aware of their plight, and the four must spend a night at sea with sharks lurking nearby. The next day they decide to run through the surf to the shore. The boat is swamped, and, with Billy the oiler leading the way, they begin swimming. Billy is drowned, and the welcome of the land is shadowed by a "still and dripping shape" being "carried slowly up the beach." In his death, Billy represents the sacrifice of love—the one human element that nature cannot crush.

Such Crane stories as "The Open Boat," "The Blue Hotel," and "The Bride Comes to Yellow Sky" are among the best American efforts in short fiction and have greatly influenced such writers as Sherwood Anderson, William Faulkner, and Ernest Hemingway. Although perhaps an exaggeration of sorts, Carl Van Doren's comment in 1924 that modern American literature began with Stephen Crane has at least an element of truth to it.

Jack London, another very popular writer of his time, also viewed man as living in an indifferent and even hostile universe. Called a dreamer as well as a social reformer, he was aware of the profound tragedy of life, yet fascinated by the evolutionary history of man. A follower of Friedrich Nietzsche, Herbert Spencer, Karl Marx, and Charles Darwin, he believed that evolution is the fundamental law of the social as well as the physical process and that a close relationship exists between civilized man and brute man. Individual struggle and primitive violence characterize the grim world of London. He was not a writer of American society; on the contrary, he rejected it. He wrote of the elemental struggle to survive, which he believed constituted the truth of life.

No better illustration of this truth appears in London's stories than in "White Silence." Two men, Mason and Malamute Kid, and Mason's Indian wife face two hundred miles of unbroken trail with only six days' supply of food and none for their dog-sled teams. The temperature is sixty below zero, and a "white silence" permeates all. As they are camped, as if in a conscious effort to prove man's frailty, a pine tree falls on Mason, mortally injuring him. Mason tells Malamute Kid that he must shoot him and continue on the journey. Reluctantly, Malamute sends the woman on and then shoots Mason—"and Malamute Kid, sole speck of life, lashed the dogs into a wild gallop as he fled across the snow." Thus the ruthless game of natural selection is played out once again.

Accused of manufacturing sensationalism in his writing, London once told an interviewer that he had no unfinished stories. "Invariably I complete every one I start. If it's good, I sign it and send it out. If it isn't good, I sign it and send it out." As flippant as such a comment may sound, London was serious about his work. His aim was to present life in its rawness and man in his strength as well as in his weakness, and certainly his short stories contribute in no small way to that presentation.

The foregoing examination of the short fiction being written in America between 1880 and 1910, and of the social, scientific, and philosophical forces that combined to produce it, is of necessity cursory. The three decades in question represent a dynamic period in American development, a period of change to which American writers of all kinds reacted—and none more than short-story writers. The true significance of short fiction between 1880 and 1910 was that it recorded the life and thought of America in dramatic fragments which, taken collectively, present a composite view that is both artistically and historically rewarding. From the realism of the local-color writers, to the psychological realism of Bierce and James, to the naturalism of Norris, Crane, and London, American short fiction, answering the great demand of its readers, undertook an unyielding examination of man and his surroundings, with the result that the short story as a genre was given new impetus. The writers who followed in the ensuing decades of the twentieth century owe no small debt to those practitioners of that genre between 1880 and 1910, who not only fought the battle for realism, but also provided informative and entertaining reading.

Wilton Eckley

SHORT FICTION IN ENGLISH: 1910-1950

Although short fiction—tales, fables, *fabliaux*, narrative sketches, and so on—is apparently the oldest of literary forms, the "short story" is distinctly a product of the nineteenth century. Edgar Allan Poe and Nikolai Gogol are its most clearly demonstrable parents, followed a generation later by Anton Chekhov and Guy de Maupassant; and by the 1890's, as H. G. Wells has commented, "short stories broke out everywhere." What is immediately apparent about this *new* short fiction—one hesitates to use the term "modern," remembering Henry James's statement that "it is as difficult to suppose a person intending to write a modern . . . novel as to suppose him writing an ancient [one]"—is its *cosmopolitanism*, the international quality of its origins and antecedents. Poe, Gogol, Chekhov, and Maupassant were followed by Stephen Crane, James Joyce, D. H. Lawrence, and Katherine Mansfield; subsequent masters and seminal influences included Ernest Hemingway, William Faulkner, and Franz Kafka. (Also, it is surely more than coincidental that so many of these major figures were expatriates.)

This "new" short story in English—in the United States, England, Ireland, and Wales—attained its greatest heights during the decades framed by the prelude to World War I and the aftermath of World War II, approximately from 1910 to 1950. The period began auspiciously. Three collections of enormously popular stories by O. Henry (William Sidney Porter) were published in 1910, the year of his death. *Reginald in Russia* by Saki (H. H. Munro) came out in the same year, to be followed by *The Chronicles of Clovis* (1911) and *Beasts and Super Beasts* (1914), only two years before Saki was killed in action on the French front. Katherine Mansfield's first volume, *In a German Pension*, and E. M. Forster's *The Celestial Omnibus* were in print by 1911 and Kafka's first stories two years later, although they would not be available in English translations until the middle 1940's. Major books such as D. H. Lawrence's *The Prussian Officer and Other Stories* and Joyce's *Dubliners* were published in 1914 and Ring Lardner's *You Know Me, Al* in 1916; the decade closed with Sherwood Anderson's *Winesburg, Ohio* in 1919.

Before the great early achievements of Joyce, Mansfield, Lawrence, and Anderson, the battle against what E. M. Forster called the "tyranny of plot" had been joined by various rebels and innovators, particularly the *Yellow Book* coterie including H. M. Crackanthorpe's *Wreckage* (1893) and *A Set of Village Tales* (1895), at approximately the same time that Stephen Crane was producing his memorable sketches of contemporary American life in frontier towns and big-city slums, along with his better-known stories collected in *The Little Regiment* (1896), *The Open Boat and Other Tales of Adventure* (1898), and *The Monster and Other Stories* (1899).

Social, literary, moral, and economic change was everywhere. Social protest and social consciousness had their roots in English and American literature almost from the beginnings, but its modern origins were in the mid-nineteenth century with the novels of Charles Dickens and Harriet Beecher Stowe's *Uncle Tom's Cabin* (1852), books which are said to have altered the course of history more than the governments of England and the United States combined. In short fiction, the turn of the century had seen the fictionalized protests of H. G. Wells and Jack London, but the major early Communist/Marxist/Socialist thrust was the period from 1910 to 1920, highlighted by the writings of Emma Goldman, Mabel Dodge, Floyd Dell, John Reed, Max Eastman, and Big Bill Haywood.

By the early 1920's, however, with the exception of the highly vocal Mike Gold, most American writers had lost interest in proletarian literature *per se*. It was only after the international furor accompanying the execution of Nicola Sacco and Bartolomeo Vanzetti in 1927, followed by the stock market crash and the beginnings of the American Depression, that many writers and editors on both sides of the Atlantic became increasingly social-minded. Distinguished small-circulation magazines such as *Story*, founded in Vienna in 1931 by Americans Whit Burnett and Martha Foley, had a completely open-door policy, welcoming good stories by authors of any nationality, any political persuasion; John Lehmann's *New Writing* (1936) was particularly receptive to left-wing, anti-Fascist authors, although he claims that simple propaganda was not the primary purpose of their efforts. On the other hand, four years later Cyril Connolly would announce in the first issue of *Horizon* that "Our standards are esthetic and our politics are in abeyance."

The major influence on the "new" short story, however, was World War I. That the "War to end all Wars" furnished both subject and theme for the new generation hardly needs restating; more important was the climate of life *after* the war. Postwar explosions in the arts and letters are not uncommon, and change is a common factor in the wake of all wars; but literary and social change was more dramatic, more conscious, in the 1920's than during any other period of recent history. Rebels or strangers in a world whose values they could not or would not accept, the Lost Generation writers tended to reject or defy rather than accept tradition, to ask questions rather than provide answers. Theirs was a literary rebellion that manifested itself both in subject matter and narrative method; it involved a consideration of the relationships between form and content in which conventional manners and mores, like conventional fictional techniques, were challenged, mocked, or rejected.

To such a generation of writers the conventional popular magazine story with its formularized structure, one-dimensional characters, and surprise or trick ending—the sort of story labeled by Sherwood Anderson as those "bastard children of de Maupassant, Poe and O. Henry"—seemed as old-fashioned as a Gibson Girl bathing suit, as odious as the values of a Babbitt, and as archaic as the claims of earlier authorities that a short story must have a plot with a beginning, middle, and end. The new writers similarly questioned or rejected traditional concepts of time, replacing them with a sense of the *nowness* of fiction in a manner supportive of Ezra Pound's concept of the *image*, that "which presents an intellectual concept in an *instant of time.*" More and more the short story depicted action at the moment of its taking place rather than retelling an already twice-told tale. Cinematic techniques were similarly altering the basic concepts of narration: characteristic was A. E. Coppard's insistence, "I want to *see* it. . . . I must *see* it."

At the same time, Freudian and Jungian explorations of the inner tensions and realities beneath the surface of human experiences opened up hitherto unexplored concepts of individual and collective consciousness that had been anticipated in fiction by Marcel Proust, Joseph Conrad, and Dorothy Richardson: novels such as Joyce's *Ulysses* (1922), Virginia Woolf's *Orlando* (1928), and John Dos Passos' trilogy *U.S.A.* (1938) were just around the corner, and the art and technique of prose fiction, long and short, would never be quite the same again.

In such a climate, and further influenced by the postwar acceleration of technology, the brief, allusive, elliptical mode of the short story seemed increasingly compatible. It could adhere to Poe's concept of a unified whole from which nothing could be taken or to which nothing could be added without disturbing or destroying the effect of the whole, thus creating a work of art admirable and worthy in itself and at the same time something to entertain, delight, or add to the reader's awareness of the human situation. At the other extreme, it could be a "trip" in the contemporary sense of the word, a hallucinogenic happening in which a character's process of vision is altered or changed, knowingly or unknowingly, temporarily or permanently. It could be an allusive form that suggests more than it states and in which the whole is greater than the sum of the individual parts and what is left out is often more significant than what is included. It could be a form that often does not *really* begin until it is finished, arousing echoes in the reader's consciousness which remain long after specific incidents and details have faded from his memory; increasingly it was in the process of becoming more poetic and lyrical. In short, in the large and spacious house of short fiction there was and would continue to be rooms to accommodate guests as different as the early unplotted Nick Adams pieces of Hemingway; the relaxed fictions, as much essay as conventional short story, of Anderson's *Winesburg, Ohio*; the complex stories of Faulkner with their wrenching of chronology and floating points of view; Mansfield's probings into the warfare between men and women and their hidden inner lives; Lawrence's obsessive concern with sexual, sociological, and psychological hangups; and the traditionally structured stories of a W. Somerset Maugham or a Wilbur Daniel Steele. It was a "lonely, personal art," as Frank O'Connor was to observe, challenging and difficult enough to engage the talents of the most dedicated artisan yet still potentially popular enough to entice the most money-conscious craftsman (F. Scott Fitzgerald comes to mind). At the same time, it was so increasingly concerned with ideas as to attract the most avant-garde intellectual or the most militant advocate of social reform. The short-story writer, as H. E. Bates was to comment later, was becoming the "freest of all artists in words . . . the short story [could] be anything the writer decides it shall be."

Thus, merely to list the names of representative authors whose careers began, matured, or in one or two cases ended during the period between the world wars suggests the richness and diversity of the epoch: Conrad Aiken, Sherwood Anderson, H. E. Bates, Stephen Vincent Benét, Elizabeth Bowen, Kay Boyle, James Branch Cabell, John Collier, Erskine Caldwell, Willa Cather, John Cheever, A. E. Coppard, Water de la Mare, Theodore Dreiser, William Faulkner, James T. Farrell, F. Scott Fitzgerald, Graham Greene, Ernest Hemingway, Langston Hughes, Aldous Huxley, Mary Lavin, D. H. Lawrence, Ring Lardner, Katherine Mansfield, William March, W. Somerset Maugham, Frank O'Connor, John O'Hara, Seán O'Faoláin, Liam O'Flaherty, Dorothy Parker, Katherine Anne Porter, V. S. Pritchett, William Sansom, William Saroyan, Irwin Shaw, Wilbur Daniel Steele, John Steinbeck, Jesse Stuart, James Thurber, Sylvia Townsend Warner, Eudora Welty, William Carlos Williams, Angus Wilson, P. G. Wodehouse, Richard Wright. . . .

It is one of the paradoxes of literary history that the short story has with relatively few exceptions been a financial failure in book form. (Notable exceptions include some of O. Henry's collections and the Flying Officer "X" stories of H. E. Bates.) Perhaps even more significant, until relatively recently, the short story has been considered a minor literary genre—indeed, almost relegated to the role of subliterature—particularly among academic critics and "specialists." In this context, there is relevance to Walt Whitman's comment that to have great writers a nation must also have great readers; the statement should be extended to include—indeed, to emphasize—the need for equally great publishers.

Short stories had been the staple of the American mass-circulation magazine from *Godey's Lady's Book* or *Graham's Magazine* during Poe's editorship until the decades between the wars when such magazines as the *Saturday Evening Post*, *Collier's*, and *Cosmopolitan* were paying writers such as Lardner and Fitzgerald three thousand dollars and occasionally more for a single story (even Faulkner, early in his career, had aspired to writing "commercial short stories" but fortunately abandoned the idea). The 1920's and 1930's were the golden age of "little magazines"; equally influential (and continuing to be) were the annual collections of "prize" or "best" short fiction: Edward J. O'Brien's *Best English Short Stories* and *Best American Short Stories*, both founded in 1916, and the corresponding *Prize Stories* (The O. Henry Memorial Awards for American short stories) founded in 1921.

If there is any real validity in the often-quoted statement—ascribed, in slightly differing versions, to both Ivan Turgenev and Fyodor Dostoevski—

that "we all sprang out of Gogol's 'Overcoat,' " it can similarly be said that many of the writers in English between the wars descended from, or out of, James Joyce's "dear, dirty Dublin." As we have seen, the "new" short fiction was a kind of hybridization, a cross-pollination occurring in various places by various writers at approximately the same time, and it is both unwise and critically unjustifiable to be dogmatic about its ancestry. If any writer in English can be said to have fathered the new twentieth century fiction, however, Joyce's claim is the most legitimate.

Like the naturalists, Joyce was concerned with the influence of heredity, environment, and "things as they are" on the lives and actions of his characters. Also, like Chekhov and Crane, he rejected what he considered the romantic nonsense of his predecessors. He sought his subject matter in what he termed "places most hostile to romance," the streets and homes and public houses of contemporary Dublin; his stories, he claimed, constituted a series of chapters in the moral history of his country. Rejecting the cumbersome, artfully plotted stories of the past, he achieved simplicity of form and language in his portrayal of what he considered his "city of the dead," emphasizing the "special odour of corruption" which he hoped hovered over his emotional and spiritual misfits in an environment reeking of the "odour of ashpits and old weeds and offal."

Yet Joyce was never enslaved by the limitations of naturalism. His major concern is more with his characters' responses to ordinary situations than with the situations themselves. His people are revealed in moments of sudden awareness, in times of crisis, indecision, bewilderment, entrapment; through these revelations—the Joycean *epiphanies*—the reader is made aware of the very essence of his people and their harassed, usually futile attempts at self-realization and fulfillment in an environment in which paralysis is more attainable than salvation. It must be remembered, too, that even the earliest *Dubliners* stories, written almost a decade before their publication in book form in 1914, are illuminated by passages of lyric beauty culminating in the unforgettable final passage of "The Dead." This, together with Joyce's use of symbols, irony, paradox, compression, and *omission*—the uncompleted action, the words never spoken, the relationships never consummated, the gestures never made—make many of the *Dubliners* pieces more akin to poetry than to the late-nineteenth century English novels-in-miniature classified as short stories, despite Joyce's conscious style of "scrupulous meanness." *Dubliners* altered the direction of the stream of the "new" short fiction less dramatically, less obviously, than *Ulysses* influenced the novel, but no less certainly.

It is perhaps more than coincidence that D. H. Lawrence (1885-1930) and Katherine Mansfield (1888-1923) were finishing their careers at approximately the same time that their major English and American successors were beginning theirs: Sherwood Anderson with *Winesburg, Ohio* in 1919; Ernest Hemingway with *Three Stories and Ten Poems* in 1923; H. E. Bates with *Day's End and Other Stories* in 1928; William Faulkner with *Doctor Martino and Other Stories* in 1929; and Katherine Anne Porter and V. S. Pritchett with *Flowering Judas and Other Stories* and *The Spanish Virgin and Other Stories*, respectively, both published in 1930, the year of Lawrence's death.

Different as they are, both as writers and individuals—Mansfield was the daughter of the allegedly wealthiest man in New Zealand, Lawrence the son of a semiliterate Nottinghamshire coal miner—the two share much in common. Both were enormously talented, but plagued by ill health, and both died young—she at thirty-five and he at forty-five. Both were driven and tormented by forces which hastened their destruction; each was sexually ambivalent and voracious, Mansfield torn between an unfulfilling marriage and various lesbian relationships, Lawrence striving to attain the unattainable human relationship.

Their publishing careers similarly coincided. *In a German Pension*, Mansfield's first book, based on her experiences while temporarily recovering from consumption, was published in 1911, three years before Lawrence's first collection, *The Prussian Officer and Other Stories*. Her last, *The Dove's Nest*, came out in the year of her death, 1923; Lawrence's *The Lovely Lady* (1933) and *Love Among the Haystacks* (1930) were published shortly after his death. They share, too, the seriousness with which they approached their work. Of the two, Mansfield was the greater artist, striving constantly to create the truth and the peace she was unable to find in her personal life; for her, nothing short of the truth was the goal of art. Her ironic, perceptive, and often malicious commentaries on contemporary society—some seventy stories during her brief lifetime—are admirable in form and sophisticated in technique. Often classified as a disciple of Chekhov, the one writer she adored, she speaks with her own voice, sees with her own interior vision. Rather than Chekhovian, her stories are essentially *Mansfieldian*, and her influence both on her contemporaries and on those who came later is difficult to overestimate.

Lawrence, similarly hounded by burning ambition and ill health (his comment that "one sheds one's sickness in books" was not mere rhetoric), was even more driven, more compulsive, and much more prolific (some fifty books). Although he wrote in many forms—novels, plays, poems, journals, and essays, to say nothing of his translations and his paintings—his best work is in his short stories, which have the power of his novels without the verbiage and repetition that so often flaws them. His stories, often brutal in their naked exposure of human relationships, their preoccupation with sexuality, and the superiority of the individual to society, were as controversial as the man himself. Lawrence's career was one of continuous controversy, evoked as much perhaps by what apparently was one of the most obnoxious personalities in English literary history as by his revolutionary beliefs, his contempt for the Bloomsbury Establishment, and the frankness and brutality of his fiction.

The short stories of Mansfield and Lawrence have in common their authors' intensity, their sense of the drama in the human spirit, and their almost obsessive preoccupation with tormented human relationships. Although relative traditionalists in form and structure, between them they opened doors and banished old taboos and reticences. Their work is a landmark: the culmination, in England, of the fiction writers' battle for freedom from taboos of any sort.

An enormously popular writer of quite different kinds of stories, W. Somerset Maugham (1874-1965), had his first collection, *The Trembling of a Leaf: Little Stories of the South Sea Islands*, published in 1921, two years before Mansfield's death; it was followed by ten other collections before Maugham abandoned the form in 1945. Although he was one of the first English writers to praise Chekhov, in whom he had "found a spirit greatly to . . . [his] liking," Maugham was admittedly and deliberately an "old-fashioned" storyteller who eventually rejected Chekhov: "if you try to tell one of his stories you will find there is nothing to tell."

A kind of latter-day and more cynical Rudyard Kipling, Maugham had few illusions about life, art, or his own stature as a writer; he belonged, he claimed, "in the very front row of the second raters." A storyteller par excellence with a concern for what an earlier generation would have termed "forbidden" subjects, Maugham's stories were enormously popular, bringing him what one critic called "almost unrivalled success and fame." He had a keen eye for the dramatic event, a psychoanalyst's interest for the reality beneath the surface of his characters, and a naturalist's preoccupation with credibility and verisimilitude. Maugham's continuing depiction of pretense, hypocrisy, and human absurdity elevates even his less successful stories above the level of competent literary journalism. Although most of his short fiction has not weathered changes in contemporary taste and the test of time, few readers would disagree with his comment that "One thing you will notice about it [a Maugham story] is that you can tell it over the dinner table or in a ship's smoking room and hold the attention of listeners."

The life story of Jean Rhys (1894-1979) is as romantic and bizarre as any of Maugham's tales. Born in the West Indies of Welsh-Creole parents, she was sent to England in her teens for a proper schooling which she soon abandoned to study dance. She eventually made her way to Paris, where she knew Hemingway, Fitzgerald, Ford Madox Ford, and other Left Bank expatriates, and where her first story was published in Ford's *Transatlantic Review*. Her first book, *The Left Bank and Other Stories*, was published in 1927; it was followed by four novels in the next decade. Rhys suffered a quarter of a century of oblivion until the middle 1960's, when she was "discovered" in Devon where she had been living in isolation after the death of her third husband. A decade of literary activity followed (*Tigers Are Better Looking*, with a selection from *The Left Bank and Other Stories*, was published in 1968; two new stories in *Penguin Modern Stories* in 1969; and *Sleep It Off, Lady*, sixteen new stories, in 1976), and even before the posthumous publication of her unfinished autobiography, *Smile, Please* (1980), Rhys had become a cult figure almost unparalleled in recent literary history.

Rhy's stories, with only occasional exceptions, depict a contemporary purgatory peopled with what a recent critic has aptly termed the most empty, the most tired, souls in the world: her Montparnasse is "full of tragedy—all sorts—blatant, hidden, silent, voluble, quick, slow . . . even lucrative. . . . 'Eat or be eaten' is the inexorable law of life." Yet even the darkest of these brief (with only one exception, the twenty-two pieces average three or four pages in length) and expertly crafted narrative sketches and episodes are illuminated, if only momentarily: "lovely words," reflects the ubiquitous narrator of "Hunger," "or the sound of a concertina from the street: even a badly played piano can make me cry. Not with hunger or sadness. No. But with the extraordinary beauty of life." More characteristic, however, are the concluding lines of "A Night":

> Mater Dolorosa: Mother most sorrowful. Pray for us, Star of the Sea. Mother most pitiful, pray for us.
> Ripping words.
> I wonder if I dare shut my eyes now.
> Ridiculous, all this. Lord, I am tired. . . .
> A devil of a business.

The Left Bank and Other Stories is a remarkable book, and it is good to have it, like its remarkable author, rescued after the years of oblivion.

During a remarkably productive period in the 1920's Aldous Huxley (1894-1963) published four collections of short stories considered by some critics to be superior to his early novels: *Limbo* (1920); *Mortal Coils* (1922); *Little Mexican and Other Stories* (American title, *Young Archimedes and Other Stories*, 1924); and *Two or Three Graces* (1926). Like the early novels, the best of Huxley's shorter pieces are entertaining, witty, sophisticated commentaries on contemporary English manners and mores, ranging in setting from London to English country life to the Continent.

A characteristic Huxley story moves with a deliberately snail-like pace and is frequently narrated in retrospect; the story-within-the-story is one of his favorite modes. The "I" of "Eupompus Gave Splendour to Art by Numbers," like many of Huxley's narrators, is a "consummately good talker" with the power of "stimulating others to talk well." It is wonderful conversation, on art, literature, politics, manners; it is a leisurely, overflowing cup of conversation seemingly unmatched since the heyday of Samuel Johnson.

Huxley's often-acerbic comedies of manners—"Living is hard enough without complicating the process by thinking about it" is one of the more genial comments of one of his narrators; the "hideous triumph of things" is more characteristic—are usually conventional in form, leisurely, consciously literary in diction, and as far removed from the "new" stories of an Anderson, Hemingway, or a Jean Rhys as can be imagined.

Some of Huxley's best-known and most-frequently anthologized stories— "The Giaconda Smile," for example—seem over-contrived and melodramatic to the point of approximating vaudeville, and lack the pace and bite of his early novels. Others, "Young Archimedes," for example, seem as moving and powerful as ever, and destined to become a part of the permanent repertory of the short fiction of the 1920's. Huxley tends to be at his best, it seems, in some of his briefer pieces, such as "Fairy Godmother," a delicious single-episode depiction of a pompous fraud of a grandmother and a boisterous baby which is pure delight, with a sting; or "The Bookshop," a brilliant five-page contrast between two very different kinds of collectors.

Meanwhile, equally important developments were taking place in the United States. Among the earliest of the post-Joycean realists, Ring Lardner (1885-1933) and Sherwood Anderson (1876-1941) are the most important. The first of Lardner's many collections, *You Know Me, Al*, written while Lardner was sports columnist for the Chicago *Tribune*, was published in 1916, three years before Anderson's *Winesburg, Ohio*. Others include *Treat 'Em Rough* (1918); *The Big Town* (1921); *The Love Nest* (1926); and the posthumous *First and Last* (1934). Lardner's swiftly moving narratives are characterized by an effective use of the vernacular seldom seen in American short fiction prior to his gallery of professional athletes, traveling salesmen, Rotarians, drugstore cowboys, and pool hall hangers-on; his contemporary America is coarse, vibrant, strong, comical, pathetic, and odious. Traditionally considered a humorist, he is closer in spirit to some of the black-humorists of the 1960's than to an S. J. Perelman or a James Thurber; beneath the clowning and the breezy action runs a strong undercurrent of sadness, frustration, isolation, even disgust. A story such as "Some Like Them Cold" is much more than brisk slapstick; there is more pathos than comedy in poor Mabel Gillespie's attempts to snare a husband. "Golden Honeymoon," perhaps his most frequently anthologized story, is a similarly bleak picture of marriage characterized by utter boredom in a world of individual and collective emptiness.

Like O. Henry, Lardner was a gifted and indefatigable writer who never achieved his potential, and few today are likely to agree with a recent English critic's comment that he is "on the whole a better short-story writer than even Hemingway." His influence on Hemingway and others, however, was both pervasive and profound. Like O. Henry he was an alcoholic, plagued by real and imagined illnesses, working frantically against time and fate, never achieving or approximating greatness, but always readable, entertaining, and at his best, beneath the clowning, a serious commentator on the contemporary scene.

Quite the opposite of Lardner's breezy, tongue-in-cheek, slangy fictions, often dark beneath their engrossing surfaces, are the quiet and fastidious stories of Willa Cather (1875-1947). Her first collection, *The Troll Garden*, was published in 1905, about the time that Joyce was writing most of the *Dubliners* pieces; but her major work in the short story was done in the 1920's and 1930's: *Youth and the Bright Medusa* (1920), *Obscure Destinies* (1932), and *December Night* (1933). A final posthumous collection of three long stories, *The Old Beauty and Others*, was published in 1948, the year after her death. A realist in the tradition of her acknowledged masters, Gustave Flaubert, Henry James, and Edith Wharton, Cather produced works in both the longer and shorter forms that are distinguished by high seriousness that never lapses into solemnity, artistic integrity, and poetic sensitivity. Somewhat akin to the naturalists in her concern with the effect of heredity and environment on her people, she broke from them completely in her sympathetic but unsentimentalized attitude toward her characters and their problems. The youthful protagonist of perhaps her best-known story, "Paul's Case," is characteristic; Paul, a pitiful adolescent caught in the trap of spiritual and artistic poverty "destined always to shiver in the black night," is memorable both as a believable individual and a symbolic victim of unfortunate heredity and relentless environment.

If much of Lardner's work today seems less important than some of his contemporaries found it to be, Sherwood Anderson's *Winesburg, Ohio: A Group of Tales of Ohio Small-Town Life* is a major landmark. Anderson's subsequent collections—*The Triumph of the Egg* (1921), *Horses and Men* (1923), and *Death in the Woods and Other Stories* (1933)—although less impressive than *Winesburg, Ohio*, underscore the fact that for years he was perhaps the most undervalued major short fiction writer of his generation. The Winesburg stories, like the stories in Joyce's *Dubliners*, are narrated with simplicity, economy, and directness. Like Joyce, Anderson probed beneath the surface of the lives of his characters, average individuals in a spiritually stifling environment confronted with the universal problem of the loneliness of modern life and the inability to communicate meaningfully with their fellows. What in the hands of a less compassionate writer might have become a series of clinical studies of the so-called average man and woman are made meaningful by Anderson's sympathetic understanding of his characters and by his almost compulsive need "to see beneath the surface of things."

"Man, I don't know who is right and who wrong," he wrote to Upton Sinclair in 1917; "I want to try to sympathize and to understand a little of the twisted maimed life that industrialization has brought on us." Typical, for example, is his characterization of George Willard, a projection of Anderson himself, who appears and reappears throughout the *Winesburg, Ohio* stories and sketches, a troubled youth who sees himself as "a leaf blown by the wind [who] must live and die with uncertainty . . . [surrounded] on all sides [by] ghosts, not of the dead but of the living." Tormented by "the meaninglessness of life," Willard has a brief encounter with the daughter of the local banker; in spite of the brevity of the coming-together, George knows that "man or boy, woman or girl, they had for a moment taken hold of the thing that makes the mature life of man and woman in the modern world possible."

Anderson's shortcomings—his lack of a sense of humor and his flatness of style, for example—were parodied or ridiculed by some of his younger contemporaries, including Hemingway and Faulkner. His rebellion against plot, his rejection of the romantic nonsense about the inherent virtues of small-town life, and his sincerity, however, far outweigh his limitations. His preoccupation with "grotesques" who were not strong enough to triumph over the rigors of contemporary American life and his concept of a group of stories unified by a common setting and a recurring character or groups of characters were to constitute a common chord among writers as different as Ernest Hemingway, William Faulkner, Eudora Welty, Carson McCullers, and William Saroyan, to name only a few. If Faulkner overstated as well as redressed an old wrong in the draft of his Nobel Award acceptance speech when he declared that "we all failed but Anderson," he was closer to the truth when he called Anderson the "father of my generation of American writers and the tradition of American writing which our successors will carry on. He has never received his proper evaluation."

Of the major post-World War I United States writers of short fiction, F. Scott Fitzgerald (1896-1940), William Faulkner (1897-1962), and Ernest Hemingway (1898-1961), Fitzgerald was the most immediately popular, Hemingway had the most immediately pervasive influence on the genre, and Faulkner was the slowest to achieve recognition. Fitzgerald's debut was auspicious. After working with a New York advertising agency for ninety dollars a week (and receiving some hundred and twenty rejection slips for his stories), he became a celebrity almost overnight with his first novel, *This Side of Paradise*, and in its wake his first collection of short stories, *Flappers and Philosophers*, both published in 1920. These were followed by *Tales of the Jazz Age* (1922), *All the Sad Young Men* (1926), and *Taps at Reveille* (1935).

Fitzgerald's fame as the chronicler of the Jazz Age (as well as his life, which encapsulates both the glamor and the shallowness of the period, with its excitement, zest, and crack-up) is perhaps more permanent than the recognition gained by all but a handful of his some hundred and sixty stories, most of which are routine and undistinguished mass-circulation magazine fiction. His disillusioned debutantes, pleasure-seeking millionaires, and sad, bored, no longer young protagonists fight a losing battle against alcohol, boredom, and their expanding waistlines. Along with their world of exclusive clubs, Long Island and Westchester estates, New York City brownstone houses, and speakeasies, they are perhaps destined to survive as social history rather than as fiction. With the exception of stories such as "The Diamond as Big as the

Ritz," "May Day," "The Baby Party," "The Rich Boy," "Winter Dreams," and "Babylon Revisited," Fitzgerald's best work was done in the novel rather than the short story. Even his better stories tend to be conventional in the least praiseworthy sense of the word: they are often novels-in-miniature, rather heavy-handed, predictable, and lacking tension, allusiveness, and perceptiveness.

Fitzgerald's stories *read* well. As has so frequently been observed, his narrative gift is, at his best, superb. His stories, despite their repetitiveness, move swiftly, and his characters are types with which even the least perceptive reader can identify. Only a small percentage of Fitzgerald's stories, however, survive the test of rereadings. His people, like their creator, have so strenuously dedicated themselves to the pursuit of the "goddess of waste" that the inevitable attainment of their quest tends to be too predictable to move, astonish, sadden, or satisfy the reader.

With the exception of *Winner Take Nothing*, 1933, Ernest Hemingway's best short stories were published during the 1920's: *In Our Time* (1924), *Today Is Friday* (1926), and *Men Without Women* (1927). His stories were later collected in *The Fifth Column and the First Forty-Nine Stories*, 1938; unfortunately, Hemingway never wrote the "twenty-five more stories" he anticipated in his brief Preface to this collection. The most influential and widely imitated short-story writer since Chekhov, Hemingway himself had many masters, as diverse as Joyce (to whom he inscribed and sent copies of his early work); Gertrude Stein, Ring Lardner, and Sherwood Anderson (whom he parodied and ridiculed in *The Torrents of Spring*, 1926); and from them back to Guy de Maupassant, Gustave Flaubert, Arthur Rimbaud, and Charles Baudelaire. Whatever his early sources and influences, however, Hemingway almost from the beginning spoke with his own voice and saw things through his own process of vision. Studied simplicity of language, economy of narrative method, the use of dialogue both as narrative device and a mode of characterization, and understatement are Hemingway's unmistakable hallmarks, whether he is depicting a few minutes of conversation and confrontation between a Jewish wine-seller and three Roman soldiers who shortly before had witnessed the crucifixion of Jesus of Nazareth ("Today Is Friday"); or a more conventionally narrated story of a man who fails in the initiation-through-courage ritual on the African veldt ("The Short Happy Life of Francis Macomber"). His stories range from a young boy's introduction to courage and cowardice, life and death in the Michigan lakes ("Indian Camp"); to the impending "execution" of a second-rate professional pugilist ("The Killers"); to a returned soldier's inability to adjust to stultifying small-town and family mores ("Soldier's Home"). Similarly, his subject matter and themes follow a predictable pattern: war, love, the conflict between men and women; the strenuous life, ordeal by combat, and the virtues of courage and loyalty; initiation-through-experience of sex, violence, and death; the quest for self-understanding; loyalty to oneself and to one's friends; stoicism, endurance, grace under stress, and "looking good in there."

Hemingway's work changed the direction of short fiction for a generation, influencing a whole school of American, English, and Irish authors including H. E. Bates, who acknowledged his indebtedness to Hemingway's simplicity, rejection of "false romance," and depiction of life not in "wooly, grand, or 'literary' prose, but in pictures." Similarly, V. S. Pritchett began his career as much under the influence of the Joycean epiphany as of Hemingway's style and manner. Even a romanticist such as William Sansom was as much influenced by Hemingway as by the surrealist painters, while to Seán O'Faoláin, Hemingway was "the real man."

Like Fitzgerald and Hemingway, William Faulkner began writing early, but unlike them his apprenticeship as a writer of short stories was painful and slow. One of his early efforts ("Landing in Luck") had been printed in the student daily newspaper during Faulkner's brief postwar enrollment at the University of Mississippi, but it was not until 1930, by which time he had published five novels, that "A Rose for Emily" was finally accepted by a national magazine. His first collection, *These 13*, was published the following year, by which time Fitzgerald, a year older than Faulkner, and Hemingway, a year younger, had virtually finished their careers in short fiction. Subsequent collections include *Doctor Martino and Other Stories* (1934), *The Unvanquished* (1938), *Go Down, Moses, and Other Stories* (1942), *Knight's Gambit* (1949), and *The Collected Short Stories of William Faulkner* (1950).

Like Hemingway and many of his contemporaries, Faulkner was influenced by Joyce ("the greatest of the century"), Sherwood Anderson ("the father of modern American literature"), a variety of writers from the Old Testament to Dostoevski, and, rather surprisingly, by Thomas Beer, creator of the immensely popular *Saturday Evening Post* stories of Mrs. Egg of Ohio.

Faulkner's Yoknapatawpha and its people are among the major achievements of twentieth century short fiction; few authors have evoked more successfully the essence of time and place and ways of life. With very few exceptions, the best of Faulkner's stories are those concerned with the saga of his mythical Mississippi county. They involve a wide range of characters— landed gentry, poor whites, blacks, and Indians—and take place during a time span of more than a century, the most important event of which was the defeat of the Confederacy. Yoknapatawpha and its leading citizens (the Sartorises and Compsons who fought gallantly in the war and whose descendants were seldom able to forget the lost cause, and the poor whites such as Ab Snopes of "Barn Burning" and *his* descendants who profited by it) furnish subject and theme for the best of Faulkner's stories; individually brilliant, collectively Faulkner's stories of the decay of the Sartoris world and the rise of the Snopes have about them the unmistakable ring of permanence.

Much has been written concerning Faulkner's preoccupation with violence, decay, and abnormality. It is true that many of his best and most renowned stories—"A Rose for Emily," "That Evening Sun," "Dry September," "Barn Burning"—are somber, tragic, or grotesque. On the other hand, such pieces as "Shingles for the Lord," "A Bear Hunt," and "Mule in the Yard" are characterized by robust good humor and sheer horsing around which removes them far from the world labeled by one of his critics a place of "mania and doom." Comic or somber, straight or grotesque, Faulkner's Yoknapatawpha, like Joyce's Dublin, is as integral to his fiction as character or incident, as much his hallmark as his narrative method and style. That style—what has been called the "chartered chaos" of his storytelling—uses stream-of-consciousness and multiple or floating points of view; counterpointing of past and present and a wrenching, indeed dismembering, of time; a Joycean concern for language; and an at times almost obsessive indirection, obliquity of approach, and revelation of reality in fragments, piece by piece, a little at a time.

For years, Faulkner's work, in both the shorter and longer forms, was underestimated, patronized, misunderstood, or ridiculed by the contemporary critical and literary establishment; not until he won the Nobel Award in 1950 (the same year that his collected stories were published) was he grudgingly admitted into the hierarchy of contemporary American literary saints. Since then, his reputation and influence both at home and abroad have steadily grown. With the exception of Hemingway and Kafka, whose works were beginning to circulate via English translations in the 1930's, and of Jorge Luis Borges, whose writings became prominent in the 1960's, no twentieth century short-story writer's influence has been more pervasive or more profound.

Not to be overlooked is Thomas Beer (1888-1940), a popular writer partially if only temporarily resurrected because of Faulkner's remarks concerning Beer's influence upon his own early stories. During the crowded decade from 1920 to 1930, Beer led one of the most active literary lives in our history: he wrote three literary studies (*Stephen Crane*, 1923; *Hanna*, 1929; and *The Mauve Decade*, 1926); three novels; and more than a million words of widely read *Saturday Evening Post* stories about Mrs. Egg of Ohio and her son Danny. Beer professed only contempt for these stories, which a reputable critic years later was to call "an indispensable chapter of the true saga of America." He was nevertheless a good storyteller with a flair for drama, and his concept of a group of stories related in setting—again the influence of Anderson is apparent—was probably what appealed most to Faulkner. Beer's stories read well but reread less well, and in the final analysis they are more important as reflections of popular reading tastes of the period than as permanent fiction.

Jean Toomer (1894-1967), on the other hand, wrote only one book of short fiction, *Cane*, published in 1923, but it has the distinction of being the first really important collection by a black writer of the century. The book was praised by many of his contemporaries, but like Beer, Toomer was virtually forgotten until the revival of interest in black literature during the 1960's and 1970's. The revival is both fortunate and eminently just. *Cane* is a small classic. It is small in length, large in achievement, one of the remarkable books of the 1920's, and a precursor of the so-called "Innovationist" short fiction of the 1960's. Its structure is threefold. The first section is a series of interrelated and interlocking poems and brief narrative sketches of Georgia life, mostly about women; the second is set in Washington, where Toomer had been born of educated black Creole stock, and focuses on the black settlement in the District of Columbia; the third, a short novel, returns to a Southern setting. From beginning to end, *Cane* is a remarkable achievement, individualistic without being freakish, brilliant in its contrasts of lyric beauty and ugliness, and highlighted by a searing scene as powerful as the climax of James Baldwin's "Going to Meet the Man."

Among the most controversial writers of the 1920's was Kansas-born Robert McAlmon (1896-1956). Ford Madox Ford called him one of the "two worst writers" he had known in Paris; Katherine Anne Porter considered his stories "vastly superior" to Hemingway's; Katherine Mansfield thought *A Hasty Bunch* (1922) "extraordinarily good"; Fitzgerald labeled him a "bitter rat" and Joyce called *Being Geniuses Together* (1938) "the office boy's revenge"; even William Carlos Williams, with whom McAlmon had helped launch the avant-garde *Contact* in 1920, described him as a "dedicated dropout." Today, McAlmon is remembered primarily as the author of perhaps the major book about the postwar expatriates, *Being Geniuses Together*, and as the publisher (at his own expense) of writers such as Ernest Hemingway, Ezra Pound, Ford Madox Ford, and Gertrude Stein, most of whom he was later to castigate in his memoirs. As a creative writer, he was a not-unimportant rebel and minor innovationist, driven by the same energy and frenzy that characterized him as a human being; between 1921 and 1925 he produced three collections of short stories, two novels, and a volume of poetry. The best of these, *A Hasty Bunch*, is a small but memorable milestone in the new realism; it contains twenty-three stories and a handful of what McAlmon termed "Momentary Essays," along with an unclassifiable piece called "Creation."

Like his literary forefathers, Mark Twain and Sherwood Anderson, McAlmon is concerned with the effects of bigotry, provincialism, and societal stupidity. The best of his brief narrative sketches and fictionalized essays are set in Merivale, South Dakota, his version of *Winesburg, Ohio*. Particularly notable is "Abrupt Decision," about the "most charming woman" in town who rebels against the "ravaging mediocrity of her existence" by committing suicide. McAlmon is also good, in spite of occasionally sloppy writing, in his portrayal of young people in stories such as "The Baby of the Family," "Three Girls," and "A Boy's Discovery." He is equally effective in "The Psychoanalyzed Girl," a savage lambasting of artistic pretentiousness and sham.

Meanwhile, in Ireland during the 1920's, a post-*Dubliners* generation was creating a new kind of Irish short story. Of the new authors, Liam O'Flaherty, born in 1896, is best known for his many novels, including *The Informer* (1925), which was made into one of the most powerful films of the period. *Spring Sowing*, the first of several collections of O'Flaherty's stories, was published in 1924; *Two Lovely Beasts* (1948) is perhaps his best single collection. O'Flaherty's is essentially a harsh world of man's continuing struggle for survival against the barren land and the implacable Irish sea; his affinities are closer to John Millington Synge and D. H. Lawrence than to Joyce. Many of his stories of the Irish peasantry are concerned with a similar continuing combat between man and his fellow men and between men and beasts, yet the harshness and violence of his world is often depicted with lyrical beauty. Nature can be friend or enemy; as such a story as "The Mirror" suggests, man's happiness is more likely to result from yielding than from battling. Only occasionally, as in "The Sow," does nature "assert herself with tenderness."

Born in 1900, Seán O'Faoláin's *Midsummer Night Madness*, his first collection of short stories, was published in 1932; his most recent novel was published in 1980. Of his short-story collections published prior to 1950, *The Man Who Invented Sin* (1948) is his most representative and one of his best. In addition to his fiction, both long and short, O'Faoláin is the author of travel books, biographies, translations, miscellanea, and two excellent books of criticism, *The Short Story* (1951) and *The Vanishing Hero* (1957).

In his book on the short story, O'Faoláin has said that the genre eludes definition, but should possess "punch and poetry"; in a brief foreword to a subsequent collection he likens it to a "child's kite, a small wonder, a brief, bright moment." The tale is something else again, freer, "carries a bit more cargo, roves farther, has time for . . . more complex characterization, more changes of mood, more incidents and scenes. . . ." In either form, he is, as a critic commented years ago, "one of the wonderful 'O's' of contemporary Irish literature." Like O'Flaherty's stories, O'Faoláin's best and most characteristic pieces are deeply and firmly set in Ireland, and central to his effectiveness is his unsentimentalized love for the Irish people which constitutes what Frank O'Connor has termed a "common chord" in his fiction both short and long. Few writers have more effectively captured the ambivalences and contradictions of Irish life; stories such as "I Remember! I Remember!," "A Shadow, Silent as a Cloud," "Passion," and "The Heat of the Sun" are part of the permanent literature of the Irish short story.

Frank O'Connor (1903-1966) was a witty, urbane, and unwinking recorder of what he labeled the "Irish middleclass Catholic way of life with its virtues and its faults without any of the picturesqueness of earlier Irish writers." Like O'Flaherty and O'Faoláin, he was as versatile as he was talented; his works include several collections of short stories, several novels, plays (at one time he was director of Dublin's famous Abbey Theater), verse, essays, biographies, and the best recent book about the short story, *The Lonely Voice* (1963).

The Common Chord: Stories and Tales of Ireland (1948) is characteristic: priests and penitents, squeamish maidens and reluctant matrons, barroom dudes, shopkeepers, breeders of greyhounds, or aging Don Juans—O'Connor knew these people as he knew the palm of his hand. Sex is the "common chord" among these carefully crafted stories, as it is in his earlier and most frequently anthologized piece, "My Oedipus Complex." Here are men who suddenly become aware that their wives "hate the living sight of them" or women whose maidenhood is terrified by the "ghosts of love and marriage." The tyranny of sex and sexual repression, along with the domination of the clergy, is the force which shapes the lives of his people. Although many of his stories are either essentially humorous or at least leavened with a sense of the comic, in the final analysis the characters are more somber than contented, more likely to meet frustration and disappointment than their opposites.

Elizabeth Bowen (1899-1973), quite a different kind of Irish writer, belongs with the Henry James-Katherine Mansfield school of short fiction rather than with that of Joyce, O'Flaherty, O'Faoláin, and O'Connor. Born in Dublin, she was educated in England and traveled widely on the Continent and in the United States. Not uncharacteristically, her best-known collection, *Ivy Gripped the Steps* (1946), was written in wartime London. She began writing early: *Encounters*, her first collection, was published in 1923; *At Ann Lee's*, in 1926.

From the beginning, Bowen's stories are characterized by a carefully disciplined but flexible prose style, intelligence, and a Jamesian concern for probing beneath the façade of human relationships, particularly family relationships involving youth and childhood, children and parents, and the young and the old. At the same time there is often an element of fantasy in her work, dramatically evident in stories such as "The Demon Lover" (1945), that underscores the relevance of her comment that "the short story, as *I* see it to be, allows for what is crazy about humanity: obstinacies, inordinate heroisms, 'immortal longings.'"

Her best and most characteristic work grows out of relatively nonexceptional situations involving relatively complex individuals. "Coming Home," from her first collection, is typical, turning as it does on the relationship between a young girl and her mother. Bowen is fascinated by the problem of human unknowableness and by the rites of passage from innocence to experience. In the title story of *At Ann Lee's*, for example, a pair of matrons in a hat shop are interrupted by the sudden entrance of an uncouth man, arrogant and at the same time curiously servile; later, on a half-deserted street, the same man rushes by them, seemingly overcome by sheer terror, and "stabs his way on into the fog." The reader, like the matrons, does not know the cause of this strange action; we see and feel it, and are left to draw our own conclusions.

"Places more often than faces have sparked off [my] stories," Bowen comments in the Preface to her collected stories. The remark is applicable to much of her work, particularly the stories set in wartime London, a place teeming, she felt, with "untold but tellable stories," and glittering "with scenes that cry aloud for the pen." Characteristic of this mode, "Ivy Gripped the Steps" is as complex as James's "The Jolly Corner" (which it resembles in a curious kind of way, although two stories could hardly be less similar) yet at the same time simple and universal in its implications. The story bears witness to Bowen's marvelous evocation of atmosphere and place which in her stories is as important as characters and situation.

Mary Lavin, born in 1912 in Massachusetts but a resident of Ireland since her childhood, rounds out this distinguished group of Irish writers. As talented as she is prolific, she has produced stories with a classic quality of permanence, whether she is writing about the harsh islands of Western Ireland or Dublin or about the green farmlands where for years she and her lawyer-husband and their children have lived on a farm she has called "one of the loveliest places in Ireland." Lavin is an orthodox, conservative writer. She employs no tricks and offers no great subtleties. The strength of her stories lies in her understanding of her people and in her effective evocation of time and place. The struggles of the human heart are her subject; her stories are built around nonspectacular incidents embodying universal themes, and this universality reminds us, as one of her characters states, that "life is just the same in the town, in the city, and in the twisty countryside. Life was the same in the darkness and the light." Little-known and seldom written-about in the United States, Lavin's stories have earned the praise of such writers as Frank O'Connor ("She fascinates me more than any of the Irish writers of my generation because, more than any of them, her work reveals the fact that she has not said all she has to say") and V. S. Pritchett, who has called her "one of the finest living short-story writers," ranking her with Hemingway and Joyce. Thomas Beachcroft says of one of her stories, "The Great Wave": "No finer story has appeared in fifty years."

It has been observed that, as the century has progressed, the short story "written in English has become increasingly the British story." Of the Welsh writers whose first work was published during the 1920's, Rhys Davies, born in 1903, is the most important. Like the best Irish and American so-called regional writers, Davies' many collections, some twenty in all, are deeply rooted in his country, small Welsh villages or mining communities. Also, in the best regional fiction tradition, his work transcends the purely local and suggests the universal, always exhibiting a sympathetic understanding of his people and capturing the beauty of their language. Davies employs an admirable variety of form and method in his stories, which range from highly concentrated sketches to longish episodic stories. The former are frequently humorous: typical is "Alice's Pint," a light-hearted episode about a green-grocer's beer-drinking donkey. The longer pieces, including such stories as "The Dilemma of Catherine Fuchsias," tend to be essentially somber or tragic. Characteristic are the words of one of the characters of "Resurrection," per-haps the most powerful single story in the collection: "Not worth living is life, Meg. . . . A dirty business it is. Black is the future. Go you now, please, and follow soon we will, true enough. Better comfort in the other world than this."

It is in his blending of the tragic and the comic that Davies' great strength lies. Underlying the sorrow, misfortune, and tragedy of so many of his stories, there exists a vital life force which animates his vision and gives a glowing warmth to his stories and their people. Like the strapping collier of "Night-gown," who wonders what woman will replace the worn-out wife lying before him in her coffin, even Davies' bleakest stories throb with the "warm dark energy of life."

It is a truism that the first half of the twentieth century saw the rise, flowering, and decline of naturalism in the short story in English; the dominant mode of the writers already discussed was the essentially realistic depiction of nonexceptional characters confronting universal problems in realistically observed places (obvious exceptions include some of the stories of William Faulkner and Elizabeth Bowen). At the same time, however, a varied group of major writers were finding their subject matter in very different domains, which from the beginnings of English literature had attracted, fascinated, or repelled the imagination of the greatest writers. These domains were the world of the bizarre, the romantic, the hallucinated, and the abnormal, as seen in the world of Puck, for example, or the witches of Macbeth. The world of ghosts and goblins by the end of the nineteenth century had produced "Monk" Lewis' *The Monk* (1795), Mary Shelley's *Frankenstein* (1818), and the tales of Poe; Hawthorne's "blasted allegories"; the ghost stories of Joseph Sheridan Le Fanu; Henry James's *The Turn of the Screw* (1898); and the science-fiction stories of H. G. Wells.

Among the English, the most important and the most representative were Walter de la Mare (1873-1956) and A. E. Coppard (1878-1957). As prolific as they were versatile (de la Mare published a score of collections of poetry, five novels including the masterly *Memoirs of a Midget*, 1921, a play, four collections of essays, and fifteen or sixteen collections of short stories), they were at their best as tellers of tales, as explorers of a world of dreams, the unusual, and the bizarre. Many of de la Mare's stories begin in what appears to be a specific segment of the "real" or "ordinary" world; but to him, realism was little more than a "kind of scientific reporting," a recording of "life at low pitch in the sunless light of day." His goal was to pierce the veil of the *usual* and to discover ultimate reality through dreams, the power of the imagination, or the uncontaminated eye of childhood. He was fascinated by the "twilight side of life"; like William Blake he created his own heaven and hell; and his best indirect and implicational stories elude conventional analysis.

Within his own self-imposed boundaries, de la Mare's skill in juxtaposing the commonplace and the ordinary with the fantastic and the bizarre is extraordinary. Few writers have written more memorable tales of terror and the supernatural, yet he is seldom interested in terror for its own sake. He is concerned with the enigmas of the human soul and spirit, glimpsed through fantasy and the oneiric rather than through the senses. "The Riddle" is characteristic. De la Mare lulls his reader into a momentary sense of false security by relating small and seemingly insignificant details concerning seven young children who come to visit their grandmother who lives alone in a substantial Georgian house. Then, devastatingly, the children one by one disappear within a curiously carved oaken chest in a corner of the grandmother's bedroom and the story ends with the grandmother's mind a

> tangled skein of memories—laughter and tears and little children now old-fashioned, and the advent of friends, and long farewells. And gossiping fitfully, inarticulately, with herself, the old lady went down again to her window-seat.

Like many of his best stories ("Seaton's Aunt," "Old Hallows," "The Creatures"), "The Riddle" is as much prose poem as conventional narrative. Characterized by a memorable lyric quality and the effective use of symbols, the story evokes a curious, indefinable terror which defies analysis. Yet de la Mare's evocation of mood and his extraordinary technical skill and virtuosity were never ends in themselves. In the final analysis, he is concerned with some of the profoundest issues that confront the human soul.

Perhaps the most undervalued short-story writer of the first half of the twentieth century, A. E. Coppard is important for his incomparable tales of fantasy and the supernatural and his equally effective realistic stories and sketches, some two hundred in all published between the early 1920's and late 1930's. He is important, too, for his firmly held beliefs on the nature of the short story and his influence on the younger generation of English writers such as H. E. Bates.

Perhaps Coppard's most important historical contribution to what he called that "unconscionable lying which is styled the Art of Fiction" is his concern for the relationship between film and fiction: "I want to *see* it," he insisted to the young H. E. Bates; "I must *see* it." This insistence on the visual is one of the dominant elements in his work, which, in effect, is a series of scenes so like paintings that the images linger in the reader's consciousness long after some of the incidents themselves have faded from memory: the golden field illuminating the gray afternoon that mirrors the gray lives of the "sere, disvirgined" women of "The Field of Mustard," the amputated mouse of "Arabesque: The Mouse," and the Monet type of loveliness of "The Fair Young Willow Tree." Equally important, perhaps, is his repudiation of the nineteenth century concept that the short story was simply a novel-in-miniature:

> I want to crush the assumption that the short story and the novel are manifestations of one principle of fiction, differentiated merely by size. . . . In fact the relationship of the short story to the novel amounts to nothing at all.

Coppard is an expert craftsman and teller of tales. His effective use of symbols as specific details or structural elements is as much his hallmark as his visual imagery; together they transport the reader into a Kafkaesque world more real than reality itself.

Other English writers who chose not to concern themselves with traditional verisimilitude range from E. M. Forster (1879-1970) to T. F. Powys (1875-1953) to John Collier (1900-1980). Forster, best-remembered for *A Passage to India* (1924) and his connections with the Bloomsbury Group, published two early collections of what he described simply as "fantasies": *The Celestial Omnibus* (1911) and *The Eternal Moment* (1928). Place plays an important-to-dominant role in these fictions. "The Story of a Panic," for example, Forster's earliest story, in effect sprang into his consciousness, demanding to be written, while he was resting after a walk in Italy; in "Other Kingdom," in which a bride is turned into a dryad in the wood given her by her husband, place *is* the story. Forster's tales, fantasies, and allegories are permeated with a delicious sense of irreality. The best of them have the quality of fading, long-hidden water colors, landscapes with figures (not fully fleshed human beings) that tend to become diminished when subjected to the full, hard light of day.

T. F. Powys, a member of a distinguished literary family, a "heretical Christian" and recluse, did his best work between 1921 and the early 1930's. His grotesque fables and allegorical sketches range from "fables of sticks and stones and animals in converse with human beings" to brief narratives depicting the horrors of life, and they influenced such different authors as Sylvia Townsend Warner and Dylan Thomas.

John Collier was as popular as Powys was obscure. British-born but a longtime resident of the United States, Collier was a novelist and scriptwriter best known for his nine collections of stories and tales of the unusual, the supernatural, and the macabre published between 1931 (*No Traveler Returns*) and 1958 (*Pictures in the Fire*). *Fancies and Goodnights* (1951) is his best-known and perhaps his best collection.

Among the Americans primarily concerned with depicting the shadows or the realities beyond the curtain of conventional naturalism, the most important is Conrad Aiken (1889-1973). Like de la Mare and Coppard, Aiken was an indefatigable and versatile writer (some forty books of fiction, poetry, criticism, and autobiography), and his major work, like theirs, was his short stories.

Most of Aiken's best and most memorable stories, such as "Silent Snow, Secret Snow," "Gehenna," "No, No, Go Not to Lethe," and "Life Isn't a Short Story," begin in a conventionally realistic manner. The real and the recognizable are illusory, however; Aiken's stories are forays into the dark night of the soul, into dreams, nightmares, and hallucination, into a world seemingly stable but always threatened by unseen forces. The lament of the protagonist of "Gehenna" is the key to his creator's universe: "How easily . . . our little world can go to pieces." Like de la Mare and Coppard, Aiken demands a good deal of the reader and has suffered accordingly, being little-read, seldom anthologized, and mostly ignored by recent critics in his own country. It is an English critic, Martin Seymour-Smith, rather than an American, who has stated that it "is arguable that as a short story writer . . . Aiken is in the first half-a-dozen English language practitioners of the century."

Other representative United States writers who in one way or other turned their backs on traditional realism range from Wilbur Daniel Steele and James Branch Cabell to Stephen Vincent Benét and H. P. Lovecraft. Of these, Wilbur Daniel Steele (1886-1970) gained national recognition during the 1920's, being hailed by one major critic as the "dean of living American short short writers." (Another important critic called Steele "at present [1924] our American best"; yet another more specifically said he was superior to Hemingway and Faulkner.) By the end of the decade, however, the inevitable reaction against his eminently readable but often contrived and melodramatic stories had set in, and the new generation began criticizing him as old-fashioned and unrealistic, or worse, ignored him. Steele, a perceptive critic as well as master of his particular kind of story, abandoned the form he had once tended to dominate. Similarly, James Branch Cabell (1879-1958), who in numerous novels and short stories created his imaginary medieval kingdom of Poictesme (which became notorious when his best-known novel, *Jurgen*, was banned in 1919), suffered a decline in popularity. Likewise, Stephen Vincent Benét, best-known for his Pulitzer Prize-winning poem *John Brown's Body* (1928), gradually lost his popularity in the genre of short fiction, although like Cabell and Steele he had been a prolific fiction writer. H. P. Lovecraft (1890-1937), although tremendously popular for his tales of horror and fantasy, is best remembered today for his book on the genre, *Supernatural Horror in Literature* (1930).

As the 1920's came to an end, the short story in English had become a deepening, widening river with many tributaries and many eddies, a genre sufficiently flexible to challenge the most dedicated artist, avant-garde intellectual, or militant advocate of social reform. Despite the American Depression and the European rumblings presaging the beginnings of World War II, the 1930's were to produce some of the most important short stories in the history of the genre. Although Hemingway and Fitzgerald had already done their major work, Faulkner's first collection of short stories was not published until 1931. Members of the older generation such as Willa Cather had either departed or abandoned the short story. (*The Old Beauty and Others* was published in 1948, two years after Cather's death; except for the title story it is relatively unimportant), and a new generation was coming into being. In England. H. E. Bates published *Day's End and Other Stories* (1928), V. S. Pritchett *The Spanish Virgin and Other Stories* (1930), and Graham Greene *The Basement Room and Other Stories* (1935). Major first collections in the United States included Katherine Anne Porter's *Flowering Judas and Other Stories* (1930), Erskine Caldwell's *American Earth* (1931), John Steinbeck's *The Pastures of Heaven* (1932), William Saroyan's *The Daring Young Man on the Flying Trapeze* (1934), and John O'Hara's *The Doctor's Son and Other Stories* (1935).

Among the major directions and achievements during the years after World War I were the vigor, variety, and quality of stories about the American South by Southerners. These stories were far removed from the romantic glorification of the pre-Reconstruction Virginia of a Thomas Nelson Page or a John Esten Cooke, or the essentially decorative techniques of the local colorists and the so-called regionalists. Place and a preoccupation with the Southern past—its history, its culture, its realities, and its myths—were vital to this new sectional fiction. Heirs to a legacy of defeat and what in effect had amounted to four decades of occupation, these writers examined what was good and enduring in the past—and what was not—in order to help understand the present. As many of Faulkner's best stories suggest, for example, the pre-1860 South had been weakened as much by the rapacity of its Snopeses and the failure of its Sartorises as by Yankee bullets or carpetbag occupation; if the Sartorises were to a degree symbols of the good life, they were instruments, too, of failure and defeat.

Ellen Glasgow's only collection of short stories, *The Shadowy Third* (1923), had sounded this new note, one which would be heard again and again, in Faulkner in particular and in the writers of what has been called the Southern Renascence in general. Among Faulkner's contemporaries, Katherine Anne Porter (1894-1980) was almost universally acclaimed as the most significant. Few writers have received from the beginnings of their careers such unqualified praise for what in the final analysis is a relatively small body of work: *Flowering Judas and Other Stories* (1930; an enlarged edition, 1935); *Pale Horse, Pale Rider* (1939), three long stories including *Noon Wine* (1937), which some of her admirers consider her masterpiece; and *The Leaning Tower and Other Stories* (1944), generally considered her least important collection. Her *Collected Stories* (1965) received the National Book Award.

If her canon is relatively small, Porter's artistry and insight are consistently high. A craftsman in the James-Mansfield tradition, she shares with them an almost obsessive concern for the inner lives and conflicts of her characters and the forces that determine their behavior. Like a surgeon seeking cause and cure for an undiagnosed malady, she probes beneath the surfaces of her people, individuals struggling against what she tends to depict as the crippling forces of tradition and the stubborn realities of changing manners and mores in an unsettled society. She is particularly effective in her delineation of family relations; among her best stories are those centering around or narrated by Miranda, Porter's alter ego. Miranda appears as the child in "Circus," a masterly story, deceptively simple and disarmingly brief, in which what was supposed to be a happy afternoon at the circus turns into a nightmare with Miranda feeling rejected by everyone except Dicey, a black mother-figure closely akin to Faulkner's unforgettable Dilsey.

At the other extreme is "Flowering Judas," perhaps Porter's most frequently anthologized work, a stunning, highly complicated story illuminated by complex and open-ended characters, incidents, and events climaxed in a powerful betrayal and nightmare-eucharist scene that is one of the high points in the literature of the short story in English. Equally memorable and similarly characteristic of Porter's best work in the long short story or novella is "Old Mortality," a rite-of-passage fiction delineated with unerring specificity centered around the Miranda of "Circus" whom we see successively as child, girl, and finally young adult, her own woman, freed of past and family.

Quite a different vision of life and art characterizes the short stories of Erskine Caldwell, born in Georgia in 1903. During a remarkable decade and a half, in addition to *Tobacco Road* (1932), the novel that made him famous, Caldwell wrote some one hundred and fifty stories which appeared in a wide range of magazines from small avant-garde, or socially militant magazines to the *Atlantic Monthly*, *Esquire*, *Scribner's*, *The New Yorker*, and the *Saturday Evening Post*. His best black-white stories are so powerful as to evoke in the reader an overwhelming visceral sense of horror, disgust, and pity. At the same time, he writes with equal intensity of a world in which whites are victimized by whites; the individual is humbled, debased, and often destroyed; white families live in dry-goods boxes or sleep in ditches; a young widow sells her two-year-old daughter for twenty-five cents; and old men and women die and their bodies are dumped into the Savannah River. If such stories are at times overmanipulated and overcontrived, they will endure as sociological documents of a dark period in American history, dreadful testimony to the devastating effects of man's inhumanity to man, and somber examples of the effect of poverty on the human spirit.

Caldwell is equally facile in his humorous stories, pieces such as "Country Full of Swedes," "Meddlesome Jack," and "August Afternoon," which have a permanent place in the humorous literature of the United States. Underestimated because of his astounding productivity and sometimes overfacility,

Caldwell is a better craftsman than most critics have admitted. At their best, more than a handful of his stories are part of the permanent literature of the genre.

Less known but highly deserving of adult readership and critical attention are the stories of William March (1893-1954), a native of Alabama. March is not even mentioned in most recent or relatively recent studies of the American short story, nor do his stories turn up in the many college and university anthologies of short stories. He is remembered, if at all, for his novel, *The Bad Seed* (1954), and the enormously popular and influential motion picture based upon it. *Company K* (1933), one of the classics to come out of World War I, is a series of more than a hundred brief narrative sketches, reflections, and incidents involving a varied group of enlisted men, conscripts, non-coms, and officers in and out of combat. His collected stories, in *Trial Balance* (1945), constitute a major and similarly neglected contribution to the short fiction of the twentieth century. The world of *Trial Balance* is one more of gloom than of sunshine, stories involving a memorable series of spiritual or physical misfits in a world generally indifferent or hostile to its inhabitants. There is a clown, for example, who wanted to be a hero but became instead a deserter ("The American Diseur"); a happy halfwit whose madness is exorcized only to be replaced by fear ("Mist on the Meadow"); a salesman who dreams of love and terror in the arms of a series of tawdry women ("The Shoe Drummer"); and a mother of eight who on her deathbed laments on the emptiness of her wasted life and wishes she had "run off to a circus" ("The Arrogant Shoat"). At the other extreme is an occasional lighthearted story "The Borax Bottle," a not-so-tall tale of a boy's peculiar sexual mishap—unique, delightful, unforgettable.

Jesse Stuart, born in 1905 in Kentucky, became one of the most prolific short-story writers of his time. He published his first collection, *Head o' W. Hollow*, in 1936; since then he has written approximately five hundred stories, collected in some fifteen individual volumes. Despite this prodigal productivity, Stuart maintains a thoroughly professional balance; his work combines the simplicity of the oral tale with the accomplished technician's skill and artistry. Notable, too, during the spate of drearily pessimistic Marxist-oriented stories of the Depression, Stuart's work is permeated with a genuine love for the Kentucky hill country and its people.

Meanwhile, the first stories of a young Mississippi writer were appearing in relatively small-circulation literary quarterlies such as the *Southern Review*, where six of her first seven pieces were published. With the publication in 1941 of *A Curtain of Green*, Eudora Welty, born in 1909, was recognized and acclaimed as the highly individualistic and disciplined writer she has remained. Without in any way underestimating the value of her later work, *A Curtain of Green* and *The Wide Net* (1943) are perhaps her two most enduring books; with her subsequent collections of short fiction, novellas, novels, and superb essays, she is the most distinguished living American woman fiction writer. With the exception of *The Bride of the Innisfallen* (1955), Mississippi has furnished both subject and theme for Welty's best work. The range, variety, and universality of her stories, however, are as much her hallmarks as her brilliant evocation of place and peoples.

Paradox and contrast are central elements in Welty's stories, as Katherine Anne Porter commented in her perceptive and warm-hearted Introduction to *A Curtain of Green* (an essay, incidentally, that remains after almost four decades one of the most important commentaries on the stories which have become perhaps the most written-about short fiction of any twentieth century author). Welty's range is remarkable; she writes with equal perceptiveness and is equally at home with gentle comedy and mordant satire; her characters range from the commonplace to the bizarre to the grotesque and back again to the ordinary; as an artist, a master of her craft, she is equally effective when employing conventional narrative structure or working with indirection, implication, and allusion; she dramatizes external events and interior emotions, thoughts, suppressed desires, or unrealized frustrations with extraordinary facility and insight. She is, in short, in complete control of her materials at all times, regardless of subject matter, place, mood, or method.

Central to all of Welty's work is the enigma of human personality and individual identity. "Human relationships," she has said, are "a pervading and changing mystery"; the interior world is "endlessly new, mysterious, and alluring." Her stories are "explorations into the nature of this mystery," and it is this sense of undiminished interest and wonderment that is the common denominator of Welty's varied stories with their wise, compassionate, but never sentimentalized concern with the realities of love and loneliness, happiness and sorrow, life and death.

Similar craftsmanship characterizes the work of Caroline Gordon (1895-1981), such as *Forest of the South* (1945). This is not to imply that Gordon's carefully wrought stories are imitative or derivative; although she was primarily a novelist, the title piece and "Hear the Nightingales Sing" challenge comparison with Faulkner's best stories of the War Between the States, and "The Last Day in the Field," "Old Red," "Her Quaint Honor," "The Captive," and "The Ice House" are permanent additions to the genre.

The renascence of stories from the American South continued. Other outstanding collections by authors better-known for their work in the novel or poetry include Robert Penn Warren's *The Circus in the Attic and Other Stories* (1948); Marjorie Kinnan Rawling's *When the Whippoorwill* (1940); Paul Green's *Salvation on a String* (1946) and *Dog on the Sun* (1949); James Still's *On Troublesome Creek* (1941); and Peter Taylor's *A Long Fourth and Other Stories* (1948).

Meanwhile, two young Californians had published their first collections of short stories, work as deeply rooted in place as that of the Southern writers just discussed: John Steinbeck with *The Pastures of Heaven* in 1932 (it had been preceded by his first novel, *Cup of Gold*, in 1929) and William Saroyan with *The Daring Young Man on the Flying Trapeze* (1934). At approximately the same time, two very different kinds of writers who shared with Saroyan and Steinbeck a high awareness of social consciousness had made their debuts: Kay Boyle with *Wedding Day and Other Stories* (1930) and William Carlos Williams with *The Knife of the Times* (1932).

Steinbeck (1902-1968) was to become internationally famous for his novels, particularly *Of Mice and Men* (1937) and *The Grapes of Wrath* (1939), rather than for his short stories; although it could be argued that, except for *Tortilla Flat* (1935) and *The Grapes of Wrath*, *The Long Valley* (1938) is his best book. Steinbeck's anti-Horatio Alger concept of life; his sympathy for misfits, racial minorities, the oppressed and the underprivileged; and his dramatic contrasts between the "good" elemental life of rural and country people as opposed to the growing sickness of contemporary city life constitute an important chapter in the history of the revolt from the cities during the Depression. Although never a dedicated Marxist, his works are an integral part of the anticapitalist, pro-Marxist proletarian literature of the years between the Depression and the beginnings of World War II. If his politics today may seem oversimplified, Steinbeck is an engrossing storyteller and a painter of vivid scenes and memorable episodes. His best and most frequently anthologized stories, including "Johnny Bear," "The Leader of the People," "Chrysanthemums," "Flight," and "The Red Pony" (which has deservedly become a contemporary classic) have about them a narrative excitement that redeems their creator's fondness for melodrama and sentimentality.

"The Daring Young Man on the Flying Trapeze," the first published story of William Saroyan, born in 1908, came out, after numerous rejections, in *Story*, perhaps the most influential American "little magazine" of the 1930's. As the title piece of his first collection (1934), it brought Saroyan, the son of an Armenian minister-turned-California grape rancher, fame and notoriety. As a boy, Saroyan stated, he had discovered that all the "rules" about writing stories were wrong, and as a result he had decided a writer should "forget everybody who ever wrote anything." The results were fortunate: Saroyan's brisk, eminently readable stories and his unabashed love for life brought freshness and simplicity to a literary scene becoming mired in militant social protest on the one hand and the artifice and shallowness imposed by the mass-circulation family magazines on the other. Like Anderson before him, Saroyan "opened the windows and aired the room" at a time when fresh air was badly needed.

If his many subsequent collections at times seem to lack the freshness and impact of his first, Saroyan's spontaneous good nature and narrative simplicity continue to be impressive, even when his characters dissolve into self-pity or simultaneously utter both profound truths and nonsense. The best of Saroyan remains as wonderful and new as the works of his first collection of pieces. They have about them the warmth of a summer afternoon, with the scent of ripening fruit in the air, when Saroyan and his characters were ambitious, truculent, warm-hearted, expectant, voluble, indefatigable—and young.

Kay Boyle, born in 1903, is a different kind of socially conscious realist, a sophisticated recorder of the human and ideological complexities of her era and a meticulous craftsman. Hers is a cosmopolitan outlook; she lived on the Continent much of her adult life, first in Paris, where she was on intimate terms with the Hemingway-Fitzgerald coterie including Robert McAlmon; later in various parts of Europe; where she spent several years as a foreign correspondent for *The New Yorker*.

From the beginning, Boyle was highly socially conscious, both as a writer and as an individual; "we considered ourselves," she wrote later concerning her early years in Paris, "a portion of the contemporary conscience, and we had no pity on the compromiser . . . of our time." She practiced what she advocated, writing and distributing pamphlets and reading aloud her own manifestos on the streets of Paris. Fiction too, she insisted, should deal with contemporary issues ("an . . . important responsibility of the short story is that it attempt to speak with honesty of the conditions and conflicts of its time"), but it should be taken seriously as an art form and as entertainment as well.

In addition to her novels and poetry, Boyle's subsequent short-story collections include *The First Lover and Other Stories* (1933); *The White Horses of Vienna and Other Stories* (1936); *Thirty Stories* (1946); and *The Smoking Mountain: Stories of Post-War Germany* (1951). Boyle practiced what she preached: individual stories such as "Defeat," "The White Horses of Vienna," and many of *The Smoking Mountain* pieces succeed as art, entertainment, and social-political-ideological commentary. She is consistently good and deserves to be better-known and more widely read.

For James T. Farrell (1934-1980), as different from Kay Boyle as two socially conscious contemporaries could possibly be, his native Chicago furnished subject and theme for most of his many novels and fourteen collections of short stories, the first of which, *Calico Shoes and Other Stories*, was published in 1934. A confirmed Socialist but never a card-carrying Communist, Farrell's political ideas were molded by John Dewey, his fiction by Sherwood Anderson. His fictional world, that of deteriorating Southside Chicago, is one of spiritual poverty and social injustice. The lives of all men, one of his people comments, are "miserable things"; nobody, says another, "likes their work"; life is merely a slow "journey to senility," reflects a third. In Farrell's contemporary urban jungle, slatterns drag their aching bones along dimly lit streets, and sensitive youths dream in boyhood only to be disillusioned or destroyed in manhood. Farrell is at his best in his depiction of isolated incidents in the gray lives of these victims of the disease of contemporary big-city life.

Despite his most conspicuous limitation, the absence of a sense of humor and the perspective that usually accompanies it, Farrell has created a segment of the American past as authentic as Mark Twain's Hannibal or Faulkner's Yoknapatawpha. Too often taken for granted, perhaps for being so prolific and repetitive, Farrell's sincerity was as unrelenting and admirable as his intelligence. Almost to the time of his death he had something important to say and said it more than tolerably well, and his genuine concern for the tragedy of human waste illuminates and informs his best short fiction.

Although remembered today primarily and justifiably as one of the major poets of the twentieth century, William Carlos Williams (1883-1963) was also a distinguished critic and essayist; a novelist and autobiographer; an influential avant-garde editor; and a very good short-story writer who shared with such varied authors as Steinbeck, Saroyan, and Farrell a passionate concern for the small, voiceless human beings lost or overwhelmed in contemporary society. Unlike Steinbeck with his flair for the melodramatic, or Saroyan with his ebullient optimism, Williams' stories were written with the cool but far-from-disinterested detachment of the doctor he was. (Williams practiced medicine for many years in Rutherford, New Jersey, where he was born. "The Use of Force," perhaps his best-known and most frequently anthologized story, is a classic among "doctor-patient" fiction, short or long.)

Williams' first book of short fiction, *The Knife of the Times*, was published in 1932; it is one of the most undervalued collections of the 1930's, a small but genuine classic. It was followed by *Life Along the Passaic River* (1938) and *Make Light of It: Collected Stories* (1950). Williams rejected conventionally plotted structure (one critic has complained that his stories are "almost wilfully incomplete"), but beneath their consciously understated surfaces, his stories are alive with power, insight, and unsentimentalized compassion and understanding.

The militantly Marxist school of proletariat short fiction had almost run its course by the late 1930's; the Soviet-Nazi nonaggression pact sounded its obituary. Meanwhile, socially conscious stories continued to contribute to the short fiction of the decade; they were as varied as those of Langston Hughes, John O'Hara, Irwin Shaw, Richard Wright, Chester Himes, and Albert Maltz.

Missouri-born Langston Hughes (1902-1967) published his first collection, *The Ways of White Folks*, in 1934, the same year as Saroyan's *The Daring Young Man on the Flying Trapeze*; the coincidence is interesting in view of some of the similarities between these two very different kinds of writers. As a black born in southwestern Missouri, Hughes, like Saroyan's first- and second-generation Armenians, knew something about prejudice; the two writers share a kind of ebullient good nature in the face of adversity and a relaxed, semiformal, and leisurely narrative method. Hughes's approach to the realities of racial intolerance is gentle rather than violent, more compassionate than bitter; yet beneath the humor and the relaxed surface of his stories, he can sting. Stories such as "Who's Passing for Who?," "Trouble with Angels," or "Something in Common" suggest as much about the evils of intolerance and the stubborn *wrongness* of black-white relations and responses in the 1930's as the later savage work of Richard Wright.

John O'Hara (1905-1970), a kind of latter-day Ring Lardner, possessed an uncanny ear for the nuances of contemporary speech; at the same time he was a hard-boiled, skeptical observer of the human situation. Central to O'Hara's effectiveness was his thorough, if frequently jaundiced, understanding of characters, whether he was writing of small-town life in Pennsylvania where he was born and reared (the "Gibbsville" of his early fiction); "show biz" in New York or Hollywood; or the upper-middle-class suburbanites of his later work.

There are few, if any, heroes in O'Hara's short fiction. His impressively large canon is characterized as much by his dislike and impatience with pretention, sham, arrogance, and social stupidity as it is by his admirable professionalism. Always competent, never dull, and an expert journalist-sociologist, O'Hara in the final analysis is likely to be valued as much by sociologists as by students of *belles-lettres*. In addition to his many novels, O'Hara's pre-1950 collections include *The Doctor's Son and Other Stories* (1935), *Files on Parade* (1939), *Pal Joey* (1940), *Pipe Night* (1945), and *Hellbox* (1947). Following *Hellbox*, O'Hara abandoned the short story for more than a decade. After writing several novels, he returned to the short story: *Assembly* (1961) was the first of several collections which, with the exception of *The Doctor's Son*, contain much of his best work.

Born in 1913, Irwin Shaw achieved sudden notoriety with his savage antiwar play, *Bury the Dead*, in 1936. With the subsequent publication of *Sailor off the Bremen and Other Stories* (1939), *Welcome to the City and Other Stories* (1942), and *Act of Faith and Other Stories* (1946), Shaw became perhaps the most widely read exponent of the socially conscious, topical story of his generation. His best and probably best-known stories are directly or indirectly concerned with war or its effects ("Gunner's Passage," "Sailor off the Bremen," "Act of Faith," "Medal from Jerusalem," "Walking Wounded"). At the same time Shaw is equally effective with his stories of American civilians during the 1930's and 1940's ("80-Yard Run," "The Climate of Insomnia," "Welcome to the City").

Even at his less-than-best, Shaw is a first-rate storyteller with a flair for the dramatic and a Dickensian facility for creating memorable characters. If, at times, he stacks his cards too neatly and tends to oversimplify important moral, sociological, and geopolitical problems (as he does in "Act of Faith" and "Medal from Jerusalem"), his people seem wonderfully alive, and his sense of pace is remarkable. Like the trained journalist and dramatist he is, Shaw handles scene and setting superbly: from a seedy New York hotel to the oppressive atmosphere of an Army newspaper office in Algiers, his stories are firmly anchored in time and place, and his narrative expertise redeems even an occasional farfetched or oversimplified situation.

Albert Maltz, born in 1908, is best remembered as one of the Hollywood scriptwriters who defied the House UnAmerican Activities Committee and was sent to prison because he refused to testify before that committee. Jack Salzman in *Contemporary Novelists* (1972) called Maltz "one of the finest writers of social protest the United States has ever produced." Quite a different opinion was expressed by the *New Republic* reviewer in 1938: "As far back as 1930 Ezra Pound was saying that the proletarian short story was ripe for burlesque. . . . And Maltz, whose talent has little that is actually original, is close to parody: one step more and—horselaugh." Although primarily a scriptwriter (Maltz's credits include *This Gun for Hire*, 1943, and *Naked City*, 1948) and novelist, Maltz concentrated on short fiction for a few years in the 1930's. *The Way Things Are* was published in 1938; it is highlighted by "Man on the Road," which is said to have produced a congressional investigation into the hazards of silicosis, and was reprinted in more trade union journals than any other American story. "The Happiest Man on Earth," a moving story of a depression-harried man's happiness at getting the hazardous job of driving a truck filled with nitroglycerin, subsequently won the O. Henry Award's first prize for 1938. "Afternoon in the Jungle" and "Incident on a Street Corner" are equally memorable depictions of the brutalizing effects of poverty on man.

The four bitter novellas of Richard Wright (1908-1960) comprising *Uncle Tom's Children* were published in 1940; *Eight Men* consists of stories originally published between 1937 and 1957, but not collected until 1961. Together these pieces, concerning long-suffering blacks at the mercy of white indifference or brutality, are a landmark in the new black fiction that was to become so significant in the 1960's and 1970's. Out of burning hatred and indignation, Wright created stories highlighted by vivid scenes and memorable characters exploited, misused, and brutalized by what their author considered the white enemy. For all their power, however, most of Wright's stories seem destined to become more important as social history than as creative literature.

The same is true of the violently aggressive and hate-filled stories of Chester Himes, born in 1909, who began writing during his imprisonment in the Missouri State Penitentiary in Jefferson City. Hatred and indignation characterize his work; his villains are not only the white police establishment but also "ordinary" members of the white community. Best-known for the successful film *Cotton Comes to Harlem* (1940), Himes wrote his stories during a forty-year period; *Black on Black* (1973) is a representative selection of his essays.

Collectively, the work of Hughes, Wright, and Himes is a sad and moving testimonial to racial injustice and its corrosive effect on both victims and their exploiters, permanent landmarks in the literature of the period and seminal influences upon the younger generation of writers who followed them.

The Neon Wilderness, the work of Nelson Algren, born in 1907, was not published until 1947; his Chicago stories, although occasionally lightened by macabre humor and grotesque characters, are close in spirit to the socially conscious prewar fiction. Like Farrell's, Algren's Chicago is a world of first and second generations, spiritually, economically, or emotionally maimed or dying in the jungles of Chicago's West Side; pieces such as "A Bottle of Milk for Mother" and "How the Devil Came Down Division Street" are among the best of the pre-1950 socially conscious stories. (Algren's later collection, *The Last Carousel*, 1973, is considerably less important than its predecessor; unlike many of the extremely prolific authors already discussed, Algren is essentially a two-book man, his reputation resting securely on *The Neon Wilderness* and *The Man with the Golden Arm*, 1949.)

Perhaps the most conspicuous defect of much of the political, sociological, or Marxist-oriented short fiction during the drab years of the American Depression is its overseriousness. In this context, it is not accidental, coincidental, or paradoxical that the prewar years produced a generation of humorists who are too often ignored by literary historians. Outstanding among them is P. G. Wodehouse, whose Bertie Wooster and his man Jeeves have their own secure niche in contemporary literature and film. The United States produced a generation of humorists, many of them associated with *The New Yorker*, headed by James Thurber (who, like Wodehouse, is in a class by himself), along with Dorothy Parker, S. J. Perelman, Robert Benchley, E. B. White, and Leonard Q. Ross (Leo Rosten). In addition to their relatively traditional narrative forms, these writers created their own genre, a kind of hybrid between the essay and the short story. This hybrid form is as much a part of the literary scene as the work of their more "serious" contemporaries, and future social historians should find it as valuable an indication of the temper and tone of the period as the films of Charles Chaplin, Buster Keaton, Harold Lloyd, and Ben Turpin, or the musical comedies of Fred Astaire and Ginger Rogers.

It is also no coincidence that the period saw the emergence of the new science fiction genre, with the founding of *Amazing Stories* in 1926, and *Weird Tales* and *Astounding Stories* a few years later. The movement, however, was short-lived, and by the end of the 1930's, the genre was dying; the real renascence was to come after the war (Ray Bradbury, for example, the most important of the new science fiction writers in the United States, published his first collection, *Dark Carnival*, in 1947; since his major work came out after 1950, no discussion is included here). While the short story has struggled for survival since the 1950's, particularly in England, science fiction and fantasy have flourished.

In England, meanwhile, W. Somerset Maugham continued to produce his extremely popular stories along with several major new writers who would dominate the field during what seems destined to be the last great period of the English short story: H. E. Bates, V. S. Pritchett, Graham Greene, Sylvia Townsend Warner, and William Sansom.

The Two Sisters, the first novel of H. E. Bates (1900-1974), was published in 1926, shortly before his twenty-first birthday; his first collection of short stories, *Day's End and Other Stories*, came out two years later. During his prodigious career, he published some fifty books, including twenty more collections of short stories and five or six volumes of novellas. Although Bates was influenced by Anton Chekhov, Stephen Crane, Sherwood Anderson, and Ernest Hemingway, the most important single influence on his short fiction was A. E. Coppard, and particularly that author's previously mentioned comments on the relationship between the movies and the short story. His visual quality achieved by actualizing Coppard's comments, his rejection of formularized and conventionally plotted stories, and his continuing concern for character, mood, and the evocation of a sense of place were Bates's hallmarks from the beginning; they would remain so throughout his career.

The best of the *Day's End* pieces are set in the "serene pastures" of the Nene Valley in Northamptonshire where Bates was born and reared. Simplicity is the keynote: the best stories are highly concentrated glimpses into the lives of his characters—fragments or single-episode sketches of lonely and unfulfilled individuals presented in moments of crisis, decision, or indecision. Almost without exception, the pictorial and lyrical quality of Bates's language is remarkable; another distinguished short-story writer would say of him a quarter of a century later, "In lucid, effortless prose, Bates can write for the fiftieth time of a field in summer as though he had never seen a field before."

Throughout his long career, Bates would explore other fields, utilize more traditional techniques and methods, and find more exotic settings and more dramatic subjects. "The Child," for example, from his second collection, *Seven Tales and Alexander* (1929), is almost surrealistic, an enigmatic prose poem concerning the effect a naked child creates in her confrontation with a group of panic-striken middle-aged bathers. "Purchases's Living Wonders" from *Something Short and Sweet* (1937), the sixth and darkest of Bates's early collections, is as much allegory as conventional realism, a fablelike account of a midget who becomes a striptease performer in a traveling midget show. "The Palace" and "Breeze Anstey," also from *Something Short and Sweet*, present successively a study of loneliness, frustration, and isolation with almost surrealistic overtones set in a London landmark converted into an internment camp for Austrian and German prisoners during World War I, and a brilliant characterization of a short-lived lesbian relationship that suffers unjustly from the almost inevitable comparison with Lawrence's "The Fox."

At the same time, Bates would return to the Northamptonshire of his earlier stories, both with individual pieces and with *My Uncle Silas* (1939), a collection of brisk and good-natured humorous tales, narrative sketches, and reminiscences centered around a ninety-three-year-old rascal and based on the author's recollections of his own great-uncle.

In the summer of 1941, Bates received a commission as a writer in the Royal Air Force, the results of which were two small collections which climax the remarkable decade and a half begun with *Day's End*. *The Greatest People in the World* (1942) and *How Sleep the Brave* (1943), as much reportage as fiction and published under the soon-recognized pseudonym of Flying Officer X, are concerned with British bomber missions over Europe and the Far East; highly praised and enormously popular, they climax the pre-1950 phase of Bates's career. For various reasons, both financial and otherwise, Bates virtually abandoned the short story for several years; when he returned to short fiction, after becoming internationally famous and for the first time in his career financially rewarded with novels such as *Fair Stood the Wind for France* (1944) and *The Purple Plain* (1947), he was like a man refreshed and exhilarated after a long exile. He produced a dozen collections of stories and novellas, from *Colonel Julian and Other Stories* (1951) to the posthumous *The Yellow Meads of Asphodel* (1976).

There is a temptation to think that any writer as prolific as H. E. Bates "really can't be too good." In his case, the temptation is misleading and the conclusion erroneous. Inevitably, there are misses and near-misses among some two hundred and fifty of his collected stories, but in spite of his productivity, Bates from his early career almost until his death remained a superior storyteller, dedicated craftsman, and keen observer of the human situation.

V. S. Pritchett, born in 1900, began writing seriously in Spain, where he was a correspondent for the *Christian Science Monitor*. *The Spanish Virgin and Other Stories* was published in 1930, followed by *You Make Your Own Life* (1938) and *It May Never Happen* (1945); his most recent work, *On the Edge of the Cliff*, came out in 1979, rounding out a half century of extraordinary achievement. (Like Bates, Pritchett worked with great success in various fields, but he preferred the short story to all other literary forms.)

Whether he is writing a psychological "thriller" such as "The White Rabbit," depicting a few minutes in the lives of a blaspheming young man who desecrates the memory of a youth killed in battle ("The Corsican Inn"), or producing his masterly later stories such as "The Saint," "Sense of Humour," "The Sailor," "Handsome Is as Handsome Does," and "Many Are Disappointed," Pritchett's continuing preoccupation is with the revelation of character.

Pritchett has created a world authentically and convincingly his own: that of the English lower-middle to middle class. It is a world he knew "like the palm of [his] hand," a world of individuals whose small defeats, stalemates, or victories he depicts with calm but interested detachment. It is a world viewed for the most part with a tempered skepticism and enlivened by the author's presentation of the strange or unusual, of the grotesque that exists in the ordinary and the ordinary that is usually inherent in the unusual. It is not, for the most part, a happy world, although at times it is alive with gaiety and humor that can range from the very funny to the macabre. It is a world that has frequently been likened to that of Dickens (a concept Pritchett vigorously rejects) but which seems more Thackerayan than Dickensian; Pritchett's "Vanity Fair," like Thackeray's, is "not a moral place, certainly; nor a merry one, though very noisy" and one usually "more melancholy than mirthful."

Despite his early stated indebtedness to Hemingway and others, almost from the very beginning Pritchett was his own man, finding his own way, his own materials, and his own narrative forms; he could say, simply and honestly: "I do not write for the reader, for people, for society. I write for myself, for my own self-regarding pleasure, trying to excel and always failing [to achieve] the excellence I desire." Perhaps equally worth recalling is Pritchett's love for the short story, the practice of which, he said, "has been the delightful and compensating art and the only kind of writing that has given me much pleasure."

Graham Greene, born in 1904, like Bates and Pritchett, was prolific and versatile, a skilled professional in the best sense of the word; along with them, Maugham, and Coppard, he is regarded by some critics as the most important English short-story writer between the wars. Greene assessed his own contribution more modestly:

> I am only too conscious of the defects of these stories, written at long intervals between 1929 and 1941. The short story is an exacting form which I have never properly practised: I present these tales merely as the by-products of a novelist's career.

The comment is admirable in its sincerity and modesty, and is to a degree justifiable. At his best, as in "The Basement Room," Greene merits a distinguished critic's labeling of him as a "superb storyteller, perhaps the best alive, in the simple and fundamental sense that he immediately captures the reader's appetite for excitement and sustains it by his manipulation of suspense and his unceasing invention." The visual, painter-like quality of even his lesser stories is superb (like Coppard and Bates, Greene learned a great deal from film, and for years he was a distinguished film critic), and even in lesser stories such as "A Little Place off the Edgeware Road," "The Case for the Defense," and "A Day Saved," Greene is never dull. His faculty for effective exaggeration and foreshortening is remarkable, and he at all times possesses the skilled journalist's eye for both the dramatic and significant detail. As in "The Basement Room," he is frequently at his best in depicting frightened or bewildered children in an adult world that to them is often incomprehensible and sometimes terrifying.

Christopher Isherwood, like Greene, was born in 1904, and, like him, did his best work in the novel. Also like Greene, he is a superb journalist whose *Mr. Norris Changes Trains* (1935) and *Goodbye to Berlin* (1939) lie somewhere between reportage and short fiction. Both set in Germany, the first has been called "a series of episodes and Firbankian in-jokes"; each, recording the deterioration of German life under the Nazis, is more akin to "superb journalism" than to fiction.

Sylvia Townsend Warner (1893-1979) was a versatile artist whose work has never received due recognition in the United States. Novelist, poet, and biographer as well as short-story writer, the best-known of her four pre-1950 collections, *The Museum of Cheats*, was published in 1947. The variety of her stories is remarkable; some are disarmingly simple, centering around such an unspectacular incident as a schoolboy's return from holiday; others are complex, meticulously structured, and as predetermined as a Hardy novel. She is equally effective in the realistic tradition of a D. H. Lawrence or the fantasy tradition of a Coppard. Whatever the mood or subject, her stories, with their blending or juxtaposition of somber subject matter and comic spirit, recall Ellen Glasgow's fondness for tragedy that runs, like Friedrich Nietzsche's "divine things," on "light feet." Of her, Thomas Love Peacock's comment that prefaces her most recent collection of short fiction is relevant: "I like the immaterial world. I like to live among thoughts and images of the past and the possible, and even of the impossible, now and then."

James Stern—poet, translator, nonfiction writer, editor, short-story writer, and citizen of the world (Stern was born in Ireland, educated at Eton and Sandhurst in England, was a resident of Africa, France, Germany, and at one time a citizen of the United States before his return to England)—published his best single collection of stories, *The Man Who Was Loved*, in 1952; it was preceded by *The Heartless Land* (1932) and *Something Wrong* (1938). An intelligent observer of mankind, Stern is mainly concerned with a widely varied group of individuals under emotional, psychological, or physical stress. His characters, stimulated by such crises, react violently; their reason is overwhelmed by fears, passion, brutality. Characteristic is the protagonist of "Two Men" ("I must kill, and kill quick"), who is swept away on a torrent of meaningless destruction, or the small boy of "Under the Beech Tree," who, after watching with horror the death struggle of a swan, hangs the body on a tree decorated with the other corpses he has collected. If cruelty tends to motivate many of Stern's best stories, however, it never dominates his artistic integrity; it is never employed for its own sake. His strength lies in his ability to counterbalance cruelty with compassion, abnormality with normality, the grotesque with the commonplace. His stories have beauty and occasional laughter, but the overall impression they leave is one of macabre melancholy; the laughter is that of a dying man in a deserted house, the beauty not far removed from corruption and decay.

World War II all but ended the greatest period in the history of the short story in English. An occasional good story appeared in periodicals from 1940 to 1946, but for the most part the hundreds of so-called "war stories" were shoddy, formularized pieces written to satisfy a well-fed civilian populace's appetite for short fiction about characters and events "over there." Among the best collections of World War II stories, H. E. Bates's Flying Officer X stories have already been mentioned; among the Americans' work, the best single volume is *The Gallery* (1947), by John Burns (1916-1953); it is a series of what the author called "promenades" and "portraits" of American military personnel whose lives cross those of Italians in or around the Galleria Umberto in Naples during the late summer of 1944. Burns was a real talent, and his untimely death was a sad loss. *The Gallery* is an important book, big in concept and achievement and as uncompromisingly realistic as a death certificate.

After *The Gallery*, *The Wolf That Fed Us* (1949), by Robert Lowry, born in 1919, is perhaps the best of the American collections published prior to 1950. Ranging in time from before the United States entered the war to its aftermath, and in settings from New York City and El Paso to Occupied Rome, Lowry's stories capture the essence of his people; he is a first-rate reporter as well as an imaginative writer.

Serenade to the Big Bird, by Bert Stiles (1920-1944), was posthumously published in 1952; it is a series of terse and moving sketches of the narrator's experiences in the United States Air Corps, along with his recollections of the past and his plans for the future, plans never realized as this talented and likable young man was killed while flying escort on a bombing mission in the autumn of 1944. Somewhat reminiscent of William March's *Company K*, *Serenade to the Big Bird* is a moving and powerful book. Major works by other authors, not published until some years after the war, include two novellas, William Styron's superb *The Long March* (1956) and James Jones's *The Pistol* (1958).

Among the individual short stories in one way or another concerned with the war, perhaps the most notable is William Sansom's "The Wall," the first published story of a writer who would become a major figure and one of the most individualistic authors of the post-1950 decades. Other memorable stories range from "Ward 'O' 3(b)" by Alun Lewis and "The Search" by Rollo Wooley—two young English writers each of whom, like Bert Stiles, was killed during the war—to Laurence Critchell's "Flesh and Blood" and J. D. Salinger's "For Esmé—with Love and Squalor." Many of the major English and American short stories and novellas concerned with the war, however, were either not written or not collected until after midcentury (Charles A. Fenton's *The Best Short Stories of World War II*, 1957, is an excellent collection with a knowledgeable prefatory essay).

The first collection of William Sansom (1912-1976), *Fireman Flower and Other Stories*, was published in 1944. Although his first published story, "The Wall," grew out of an incident in which he had participated with the London fire brigade during his wartime service and was sufficiently realistic to be called a "description of actual fire-fighting experience," Sansom is at his best a magician, a magus who transmutes essentially believable characters and situations into myth, fantasy, and the surreal. (One must always keep in mind, however, Sansom's statement that he writes to show "the magic or poetry in ordinary things. That often I seem to write about the extraordinary may seem to deny this. But to me it proves the opposite. I have simply made ordinary things sound extraordinary: in fact conveyed the magic in them.") At the same time, during his long and productive career, he wrote realistic stories, novels, children's books, travel books, and essays with equal effectiveness.

Following *Fireman Flower and Other Stories*, Sansom traveled extensively and wrote copiously. *Three*, a collection of two novellas and a long story, was published in 1946. *Something Terrible, Something Lovely* (1948) is one of his best, a collection ranging from relatively conventional stories of character and incident to tales and sketches, grotesque farces and melodramas, and strange excursions into a world of warped personalities and surreal landscapes and inscapes. Almost without exception, the collection is characterized by adroit storytelling and marvelous evocation of place. "The Equilibriad," (a strange narrative monodrama, the piece concerns the love-hate relationship between an apprehensive myasthenic and his cousin), later collected in *Among the Dahlias* (1957), was also published in 1948, as was *South*, another of the author's most memorable collections.

With *The Passionate North* (1950), Sansom climaxed the first phase of his extraordinary career. It comprises ten stories as varied in form, mood, and substance as their predecessors, ranging from a simple, effective character study of a brief coming-together of a Londoner and a young Scotswoman in a hotel in the moorlands of Scotland ("Time and Place") to "A Waning Moon," which moves from straightforward narrative to an almost surrealistic climax in a desolate slate quarry in the Scottish moors that would not be out of place in Dante's inferno.

Regardless of subject and mood, the best of Sansom's pre-1950 stories tend to share the fact that they concern characters depicted in moments of crisis (sometimes physical, external, tangible, at other times metaphysical, emotional, or spiritual) that cause them to view reality in a new light. Their angle of vision is altered; they see, like their creator, the delight, the terror, the wonder of life. Sansom's continuing sense of wonderment is contagious since his stories are alive with a magic seldom found in contemporary literature.

Originally published in England in two volumes, *Asylum Piece*, by Anna Kavan (1904-1968), is a disturbing and brilliant series of vignettes which depicts the gray world between sanity and insanity. The work was published in the United States in 1946, and was reissued in England and the United States in 1970, twelve years following Kavan's death of an overdose of heroin. Kavan's chronicle of a mental crackup and her slow withdrawal from the real world into a limbo of undefinable terrors was until recently one of the neglected classics of twentieth century literature. It is a painful book to read, wrenching in its depiction of occasional moments of peace and security all too quickly shattered, and Kavan's prose is powerful in its simplicity.

Among the other postwar English writers whose first collections of short stories were published prior to 1950, Angus Wilson, born in 1913, is perhaps the most important. The *Wrong Set* (1949) and *Such Darling Dodos* (1950) are the works of a gifted and versatile satirist whose world (at times reminiscent of that depicted in Aldous Huxley's *Antic Hay*, 1923, and *Chrome Yellow*, 1921) is that of the less wholesome members of the new English middle class—a world of deadbeats, academic harpies, intellectual cripples or crippled intellectuals, and homosexuals. Wilson is a craftsman who never loses control of his subject matter and who seldom indulges in the dubious luxury of creating monsters (as he does in "A Little Companion" or "Mummy to the Rescue") rather than human beings. He creates individuals, not puppets, and his marvelous sense of place and his disciplined prose make even his least palatable scenes a pleasure to read. More important, beneath the frequently malodorous surface of his stories, Wilson's work is alive with a hatred of individual and societal stupidity, indifference, and cruelty that links him to the classic English satirists from Jonathan Swift to Evelyn Waugh, Aldous Huxley, and all the rest.

By midcentury, most of the major figures—Hemingway, Faulkner, and Welty; Coppard, de la Mare, and Bowen—had made their major contributions to what would become the permanent literature of the short story in English. Earlier masters, such as Joyce and Anderson, Lawrence and Mansfield, were dead. Of the major pre-1950 writers, only H. E. Bates and V. S. Pritchett still had much of their best work still ahead of them. The two authors who would be among the most important, perhaps *the* most important, of the next three decades had already published their first collections: John Cheever in 1943 with *The Way Some People Live* and William Sansom with *Fireman Flower and Other Stories* a year later.

The period ended as auspiciously as it had begun, with Faulkner's *Collected Short Stories of William Faulkner* and a large number of new or younger writers with at least one collection of stories in print: Louis Auchincloss (*The Injustice Collectors*, 1950); A. L. Barker (*Novelette: With Other Stories*, 1952); Paul Bowles (*The Delicate Prey*, 1950); Hortense Calisher (*In the Absence of Angels*, 1951); Truman Capote (*A Tree of Night*, 1949); Janet Frame (*The Lagoon*, 1951); Nadine Gordimer (*The Soft Voice of the Serpent*, 1952); William Goyen (*Ghost and Flesh*, 1952); Charles Jackson (*The Sunnier Side: Twelve Arcadian Tales*, 1950); Shirley Jackson (*The Lottery, or the Adventures of James Harris*, 1949); Doris Lessing (*This Was the Old Chief's Country*, 1952); Carson McCullers (*The Ballad of the Sad Café*, 1951); Michael Mc-Laverty (*The Game Cock*, 1947); Brian MacMahon (*The Lion Tamer*, 1949); Vladimir Nabokov (*Nine Stories*, 1947); J. F. Powers (*Prince of Darkness*, 1947); J. D. Salinger (*Nine Stories*, 1953); Mark Schorer (*The State of Mind*, 1947); Delmore Schwartz (*The World Is a Wedding*, 1948); Allan Seager (*The Old Man of the Mountain*, 1950); Jean Stafford (*Children Are Bored on Sunday*, 1953); Wallace Stegner (*The Women on the Wall*, 1949); Peter Taylor (*A Long Fourth and Other Stories*, 1948); Mark Van Doren (*The Witch of Ramoth*, 1950, and *Short Stories of Mark Van Doren*, 1950); Jerome Weidman (*The Captain's Tiger*, 1947); Jessamyn West (*The Friendly Persuasion*, 1945); Christine Weston (*There and Then: Stories of India*, 1947); Tennessee Williams (*One Arm*, 1948); and Edmund Wilson (*Memoirs of Hecate County*, 1947).

William Peden

SHORT FICTION SINCE 1950

Generally speaking, the short story has most often been treated and studied (insofar as it has been studied or treated at all) as if it were a thing apart from the mainstream of conventional literary history and, indeed, somehow separate from a large part of the life of its own times. This isolation of the story, at least for the sake of study and criticism, has not been wholly arbitrary or unreasonable, for throughout its history the short story has, in fact, been something of a special case. Some of the intense pressures on the form, and thus, also, on the authors of short fiction, during the period with which we are here primarily concerned, have been unusual enough to be perceived as being unique. That is to say, oftentimes the makers of short stories, even when they have also been engaged in other kinds of literary creation, have felt themselves to be singularly isolated from literary trends and fashions, even from the main course of literary history. They have, regularly and often, considered themselves to be much more threatened, more endangered than the practitioners of other literary forms—less likely to achieve any recognition than even the poets.

Similarly, the *form* has seemed less likely to endure than even the essay, which has somehow managed to prosper and to thrive, lately under new journalistic management, in a variety of costumes and slight disguises and under a number of other names. There are and have often been times during this period when most story writers must have felt they were engaged in the practice of a literary art form with about as much future possibility as, say, the Elizabethan Pastoral. Certainly most book publishers have viewed the prospect of publishing collections of stories with strictly minimal enthusiasm. Yet this same period—a period of doubt, or at least skepticism, on the part of the artists, or of cynical indifference, on the part of publishers—has seen an extraordinary flowering of the form and the arrival and growth to mature artistry of some of the finest, most gifted writers of short fiction in the whole history of the form. It has been perceived as a period of adversity for the short story and its makers; in an undeniable sense it has been a period marked by great difficulties. At one and the same time, however, we are in the midst, and still far from the tag end, of a period of wonders and riches in which not a few but many of the finest makers of short fiction, judged by broader and deeper standards than those of any one period, have created superb works of art.

It is this kind of paradox with which we must deal—a sense of poverty and adversity on the one hand and a sense of almost inexhaustible energy and achievement on the other. To do so, to understand both these simultaneous aspects of our immediate history and environment, we must consider the short story within the larger context of the modern and "post-modern" literary scene, in all *its* paradoxical, often simply contradictory complexity. In order to do that we must also, and first of all, seek to consider the literary situation as a part of—not antithetical, but, rather, inextricably involved with, ineradicably reflective of—the general movement of history in our times. Thus, although the arts, and preeminently among them literature, may be, even consciously, sternly critical of and at odds with the culture and society of our times; and though most literary artists may very likely consider themselves to be outsiders, perhaps even revolutionaries against the status quo, still, in yet another of the irreducible paradoxes which seem to be so characteristic of our age, both the arts and the artists who practice them, in attitudes and assumptions as well as form and substance, are part and parcel of, almost *inevitable products of*, the very social order and situation from which they feel themselves to be so alienated. In that sense the artists' viewpoint may be said to be "programmed" by the society, and the sense of alienation may be understood as being more conferred than acquired.

Writers of short fiction may not *write for* their editors or magazines or publishers, but their works can reach us only through the cumbersome institutional systems served by editors and magazines and book publishers. Magazine publishing and book publishing are part of the larger business world of getting and spending; and that world in turn succeeds or fails, inflates or depresses together with the economy of the society as a whole. This point is not quite as simpleminded as it may seem. The motion picture industry, for example, is equally wedded to the national—in fact, the *world*—economy. Yet it has been shown in any number of studies that the movie industry thrives and prospers most in situations of recession and that boom times represent a certain decline in movie business. Believe it or not, like it or not, then, one cannot easily conceive of the business of publishing as in any fundamental way separate from the larger society.

Totalitarian societies, which, during precisely our period of interest, have come to define the large majority of the world's political and social systems, do not so much recognize the place and value of the arts *within the system* as they fully understand the need to make use of all of the forms and fashions of art, controlling their creation and coordinating their efforts. It may be (indeed, it has been argued) that totalitarian societies at least do the arts the honor of taking them seriously, while open societies—leaving the arts free to sink or swim, as if art were only a business among businesses—are spared from having to make any judgment about the relationship of the arts and society, of art and life. It has been cogently argued, by Alexander Solzhenitsyn at his Harvard Commencement Address of 1978, that a free, open society can and does have its own forms of censorship which, while less overt and efficient than the familiar official censorship of totalitarian societies, are nevertheless effective at inhibiting the dissemination of new ideas and notions and the awareness of views. That is, a "free" society seems to tend, as if by some natural law, freely to inhibit and limit itself.

The most troublesome manifestation of this tendency is that it serves to confirm and strengthen the prevailing and conventional "mind set" and to interrupt, where it does not actively interdict, the free flow and exchange and the challenge of new ideas. Describing this situation in his Harvard speech, Solzhenitsyn indicated the dangers of accepting, following, and indeed *believing in* "generally accepted patterns of judgment":

> Without any censorship, in the West, fashionable trends of thought are carefully separated from those that are not fashionable. Nothing is forbidden, but what is not fashionable will hardly ever find its way into periodicals or books or be heard in colleges. There is no open violence such as in the East; however, a selection dictated by fashion and the need to match mass standards frequently prevents independent-minded people from giving their contribution to public life. There is a dangerous tendency to form a herd, shutting off successful development.

On the one hand, during this period, the writers of short stories, like the creators of serious literature generally, justly perceived themselves (for a variety of complex reasons) as outsiders, as certainly "independent-minded people" who are and have been greatly restricted, by powerful social and economic forces, in their ability to make any real contribution to public life by and through the means of their art. On the other hand, it does not seem to have been recognized that this very stance, in relation to the rest of society, is traditional enough, conventional enough to be identified as stereotypical.

Our period might fairly be described as a time during which we have seen the apparent triumph of the stereotype, of the "image" over reality, of conventions hardening into clichés, of tradition degenerating into fashion, and of language being polluted and becoming at best a sequence of simplistic gestures. Thus intellection, independent thinking, becomes greatly discouraged by, if not actually replaced by, instantaneous flash cards of feelings.

Serious literature, charged with the preservation, revision, and invention of the language, has been greatly influenced by these trends even as it has fought against them. The paradox, then, is that the same time that has seen serious literature become increasingly irrelevant, evidently insignificant when measured by the standards of the society, has also imposed upon literature a burden of great importance. If the language is to be saved, if images are to be questioned, if clichés are to be tested, and if fashions and habits of thought and feeling are to be recognized for what they are, then it is the function of serious literature to do so by example. This condition makes poets of all writers and thus makes great demands, far beyond the purely aesthetic, on the tellers of tales.

Are these paradoxes really relevant? I think so. I believe that it is from the confusion and conflict of these values among others that our contemporary art forms—and specifically our short fiction—are composed.

I believe it is strongly likely that the times and the experience of World War II—the time just before the war, the time during it, and the immediate postwar years—will be understood as a historical moment of great changes, a huge demarcation forever separating the modern past from the present and future, clearly delineating major and perhaps immutable changes in the art and life of this century. It will be understood not merely as a time of transition or of modest transformation, but, rather, as a time of complex, radical changes of the kind that do not happen, have not happened to any culture or society while that culture or society continued to exist. Only complete and completely mysterious disappearances (the Etruscans, the Trojans, the Empire of the Inca), complete and total defeats (Babylon, Carthage, Byzantium), or total revolutions involving much more than an exchange of the ways of power and the means of production (perhaps China in the twentieth century is the most clear-cut example), offer such a dazzling variety of changes to consider.

At the moment of victory, Great Britain moved to change its form by rapidly dispensing with the images and realities of Empire and world leadership in favor of a place among its own Commonwealth of Nations and a national culture of actively accepted (almost *embraced*) limitations. In America, however, all things were turned upside down. Far from withdrawing, from vanishing, the Americans, and many real and symbolic elements of American life, were suddenly and inexorably a worldwide presence. Soon enough it was a cliché that tubes of American toothpaste were being sold in the bazaars of Timbuctoo and Marakesh, and that "The Pause That Refreshes" was being enjoyed in Bangkok and at the remote and exotic altitudes of Katmandu.

Far from the catastrophe of defeat, the war ended in victory for the Allies and unquestionably for the United States, which, alone among the major nations, had fought and won without being fought over. Far from any kind of social and political change which might be called genuinely revolutionary, the United States seemed to have been able to preserve the health and vitality of its basic institutions intact, partly by constant and flexible adaptation to all kinds of pressures for change, from both within and without, and partly by searching for a clearer, more explicitly defined awareness of the original goals and intentions of the founders of the Republic.

Thus, for example, major changes in the status of American minorities have taken place over the past quarter of a century through the gradual, sometimes simultaneous, but rarely coordinated actions taken by all three primary branches of the Federal government. For this change to occur there had to be genuine pressure and a desire to change, together with a willingness to adapt to changes, coming as much from the majority as from the minorities themselves. Second, and no less significant, there had to be a new and quite different understanding of the complex relationship between the central Federal government and the governments of the separate states before the former could legitimately consider acting on behalf of the interests of the minorities. Technically, prior to World War II, and due to the gradual enlargement of Federal powers during the New Deal years by and through the Supreme Court's reinterpretation of the implications of the Fourteenth Amendment, the relationship between the Federal government and the states had been steadily changing. Now, however, it seems significant that the major changes— as, for example, the Supreme Court's unanimous 1954 decision on the issue of segregation in the public schools—did not happen, were not really considered possible, and indeed were not even seriously envisioned prior to World War II. It is equally pertinent that, although there has been a good deal of unrest and confusion associated with the implementation of that particular Court decision and with subsequent decisions, there has been nothing which even remotely resembles serious revolutionary action, insofar as a revolution by definition necessarily begins with the overthrow of existing institutions of government and power and their replacement by other, different institutions. An often-remarked characteristic of the "revolutionaries" (of various and sundry kinds) in the 1960's was the fact that at no point did they seem to be prepared to offer the prospect of either programs or institutions of their own making.

Many elements of our day-to-day life, most now so familiar that it is difficult to imagine (or, in many cases, to *remember*) how life was without them, were introduced into the culture after World War II. Not only television, whose direct influence on all the other forms of storytelling was immediate and enormous, but also such things as the long-playing record, extensive photojournalism, synthetic fabrics, the supermarket, the shopping center, and the motel are postwar phenomena. Prior to the war, most domestic travel was accomplished on passenger trains. The entire highway and freeway culture, and the mobility which goes with it, is a postwar innovation. Even our national eating habits, for better and for worse, have changed drastically since the Depression years before the war. Frozen foods were a new idea; fast foods were limited to a few items in a few places in a few large cities. Our cooking, at home as well as in restaurants, became adventurously international rather than blandly parochial. Garlic, the green salad, a glass of wine—all these were new to the national table. Much in earlier American cuisine that was regional was soon lost and forgotten and has had to be rediscovered through cook books, in recent years.

These things are, of course, only a very few examples from among very many of how the period from World War II to the present has been a time of radical changes. Because all the changes of the times have been effected within the framework of previously existing systems and institutions, however, the radical nature of all these changes, in sum, in the fabric of our political, social, and cultural life has not been fully perceived or assimilated by those who were and are actually involved. Those who were born into the postwar period have nothing except the memories of their elders with which to measure and define what may be new or old.

The American literary scene has changed so much and in so many ways that the years before World War II might as well be separated from us by centuries. It seems important to discuss, and to seek to understand, some of the changes which have occurred.

Perhaps the greatest single change, and certainly the most lasting, began, modestly enough, during the war. This was the acceptance and then the rapid development of the paperback book, soon becoming another mass-produced product, more or less expendable and designed for mass consumption. Going all the way back to the 1920's, there had been serious efforts, such as that of the Little Blue Book Series of Haldeman-Julius Company, to produce profitable lists of inexpensive paperback books which might actually, it was hoped, compete with the lists of trade books in hardcover produced and sold by the major commercial publishers. There was also the example of prosperous commercial publishing in France, and other European countries, where almost all the trade books were published in paperback and bound, if at all, by the buyer. In the United States, however, the many problems of the sales and distribution of paperback books were seemingly insoluble at the time and in the terms of the times. The situation for any paperback publisher was not made simpler by the concerted efforts of the major hardcover publishers to preserve and maintain the status quo. Moreover, again prior to World War II, the costs of book publishing had remained fairly constant, meaning that a durable hardcover book was not (yet) so expensive as to be prohibitive in comparison and competition with the disposable paperback book. During the war, however, and as a part of "the war effort," the major commercial publishers produced great numbers of paperback books as Armed Forces Editions. This experience awakened many people in publishing to the future potential of paperback publication, and, at the same time, it acquainted millions of readers (many of whom were nonreaders before the war) with the habit of reading paperback books.

Immediately following the war, the G. I. Bill filled the dormant American colleges and universities to capacity. This movement was part, also, of a demographic expansion which did not slacken until the middle 1970's. Paperback books, mostly in reprint but including some original titles as well, offered a quick, efficient, and relatively inexpensive way to furnish textbooks for the new hordes of students. The ready availability of relatively inexpensive titles also served to encourage change and expansion in the curriculum, as did the G. I. Bill itself by attracting older students whose lives and careers had been interrupted by years in the Armed Forces. These students were eager for the opportunities of higher education, but they were also impatient with the old ways of doing things. Some of the implications of the changes in the liberal arts curriculum, particularly as they have had a distinct influence on contemporary literature and on the short story, will be dealt with later. Here it simply should be noted that as a part of the general emphasis on the practical and the pertinent, to satisfy the needs and demands of the veterans studying on the G. I. Bill, the first modern, twentieth century literature (and soon after, contemporary literature) began to be accepted as a respectable area of conventional academic study.

The results of this inclusiveness have by now proved to be a complex, already mixed blessing; but from the first there has been a rapid growth, so that the number of academic courses (including other liberal disciplines such as history, politics, religion, philosophy, and social studies, as well as literature and languages) built around the study of modern and contemporary literature is staggering. It is now possible to be an English major in many, if not most, institutions of higher learning in America and to specialize so thoroughly in twentieth century literature as to have only the most rudimentary acquaintance with the great figures of the past or the periods in which they lived and wrote.

There is another level of irony beginning to be discerned as deriving from the greatly expanded emphasis upon twentieth century literature in academic study. With the real dimensions of the historical past now foreshortened, the recent past becomes the only official history we have. Thus, living writers, whose works have become the staple of academic courses of study, find themselves criticized and even rejected as hopelessly out of date by independent, innovative, and rebellious students. They might as well be Miltons.

Parallel to and roughly simultaneous with the new respectability of twentieth century literature in the academic curriculum, writers themselves began to be hired by the colleges and universities to teach. Prior to World War II, the association between academe and poets and writers had been minimal. A very few poets occasionally gave public readings at the colleges, but only a very few, very distinguished literary figures—Robert Frost, John Crowe Ransom, and Allen Tate being the most notable examples—had official, professional relations with institutions. Soon after the war, however, as a part of the great expansion, the colleges and universities began to hire poets and fiction writers for their faculties. At first they generally taught literature and not creative writing, for there were not more than a handful of creative writing courses in all the United States at that time. Inevitably and soon, however, courses in creative writing began to be offered by poets and fiction writers; and soon they were being offered at graduate as well as undergraduate levels. By now there is practically no institution of higher learning, no cow college or community college, which does not have its poet(s) and fiction writer(s). Hundreds of poets and fiction writers (perhaps by now a thousand or two) are employed as teachers.

Courses in creative writing are (as of this writing) at a peak of popularity throughout the country and appear to be limited in enrollment only by the number of teaching staff available and such mundane considerations as class-room space and scheduling. To furnish the teaching-writing staffs, of the present as well as the future, specialized graduate programs came into being and are now firmly entrenched in academe, solidly established in such organizations as the Associated Writing Programs.

Again, it is clear that this has been a mixed blessing for all concerned; but the postwar development of bringing writers into the colleges and universities could not have come along at a more convenient time for the writers, especially for the fiction writers. In the 1920's and particularly in the 1930's, it had proved possible for a good many of those writers who are now acknowledged and recognized to be our modern masters, our finest serious writers—for example, William Faulkner, Ernest Hemingway, F. Scott Fitzgerald, Katherine Anne Porter, Sherwood Anderson, Eudora Welty, John O'Hara—to earn at least part of their keep through the publication of short stories in the magazines, including the big, mass-market, general "slick magazines," which regularly published a good deal of fiction (in those days more fiction than nonfiction appeared in each issue) and paid well for it. Literary work of high quality was still the exception, however, and there are good reasons to question the perception of the times even though it has been held by many of the writers themselves. In *Writing in General and the Short Story in Particular*, Rust Hills, a prominent fiction editor of the postwar years, expresses doubts that our serious fiction writers really gained much writing for these commercial magazines. There is no doubt now of what happened to the "commercial" short story. "Slick fiction is now not much written, at least in short story form," Hills writes. "Commercial magazines that once emphasized slick fiction expired; new magazines rarely publish fiction at all; magazines that once published a dozen stories an issue, now publish one." The other major source of income for those of our writers who were not fortunate enough to be independently wealthy was the movie industry, which, producing several hundred films a year for a worldwide market, paid well for the rights to stories and novels and also hired many good writers to write screenplays. Among other things, however, the arrival of television in the postwar years resulted in a significant restructuring of the movie industry, away from the concept of the large companies and studios as creative centers. Ever since the war, the movie business has had its ups and downs, but never again have as many pictures been produced; also, the use of writers from outside the industry has been greatly reduced and is now usually irregular and for strictly limited periods.

Academic employment, although essentially a corporate and institutional job and also somewhat less than lucrative, offered the serious writer the security of a regular salary and a good deal of freedom and more time off for writing than most other jobs. Basically the writer (like the musician, the painter, the sculptor, the actor, and so on, all of whom began to find a place for themselves and their work in the universities at about the same time) sold part of his or her time in return for a certain measure of freedom and security. By and large writers proved to be good teachers of literature and of writing; and, like their colleagues the critics and scholars, they had the potential of bringing attention and sometimes distinction to the institutions they served.

The writer, as much as his colleagues, fell under the shadow of the "publish-or-perish" law, which in turn has greatly influenced literary creativity over the past twenty-five years. For one thing, to oversimplify rudely, the writer needed a place to publish his wares. The issue was, in effect, still money; but it was indirect payment. Promotion and increase in salary within the academy was likely to depend on regular published appearances by the writer. (Public readings and lectures, particularly for the poets, began to be a factor also. The precedent of Robert Frost and Vachel Lindsay and the blazing example of Dylan Thomas in the 1950's made this, in a sense, a new form of publication as well as a certain kind of literary show business.) The size of the direct payment from any given magazine, while it might be encouraging or helpful, was secondary in importance to the fact of being published. Thus the period has seen a fantastic growth in the number and kinds of quarterlies, literary magazines, and little magazines. They come and go, flourish and fade quickly, but the actual number of them is still increasing—more than six hundred are listed in the latest edition of the *Directory of Little Magazines and Small Presses*. In any case, the "publish-or-perish" philosophy has clearly set many fiction writers to the regular writing of short stories and to the task of finding (sometimes creating) places to publish them.

The literary magazines have even had an influence, it can be argued, on the general form and structure of the American short story. Because of ever-increasing expenses in all aspects of magazine publication, all but a very few literary magazines must be severely economical. It is easier and cheaper to print more poems than stories; thus, there are usually more poets than fiction writers. The editors of literary magazines are forced to look for short stories that are *quite* short, giving rise to a prose aesthetic of brevity rather than amplitude. Moreover, with enormous competition for a very little space, quality must be clearly recognizable. Even the experimental must be, in a way, consensual. That is, the elements which mark a literary work as "experimental" or avant-garde must be easily identifiable as such—a situation which, at the very least, is not conducive to genuine innovation or originality. All of these conditions can lead us back to the words of Solzhenitsyn and perilously close to the kinds of rigidity and "mind-set" which, he argued, make censorship unnecessary in our society.

It is within the very nature of the system, then, that the literary and little magazines can be (and often are) as inflexible and essentially conservative, no matter how evidently liberal or radical their format may be, as any commercial magazine or film studio. And there is yet another way in which the need for a literary work to be immediately, demonstrably and recognizably of high literary quality can (and does) serve to inhibit creativity. For the writer of some established reputation, this means that there is considerable pressure and temptation to produce work which is demonstrably, recognizably his or her very own: that is, to produce *more of the same*. The result of this pressure and temptation appears to be a possessive staking out of claims to certain specific subjects and themes and an almost obsessive specialization in limited style and tone of voice. At best this produces a certain kind of electric intensity which can, in the hands of an artist, triumph over monotonous sameness, as, for example, in the best work of John Cheever or of Bernard Malamud. It also helps to explain how the mild, relatively modest eclecticism of a successful story writer such as John Updike appears, against that uniform background, to be almost daring and courageous.

In so many ways, some of them still shadowy and uncertain, the experience of World War II had a shattering impact on the American psyche. For the British it was a longer and much more devastating war, and it may be seen and said, by some social historians, to have, in the end, sapped the energies and weakened the will of that great nation and great people. Nevertheless, it cannot be described as an especially *disillusioning* experience for the British; after the sustained honors and carnage of World War I, they had a fair idea of what to expect. For Americans the experience was somewhat different. Although the United States had shared in the final victory in World War I, indeed playing a decisive part in achieving it, the vast majority of the American army was never fully trained and overseas. Casualties among our forces, in the context of trench warfare, were heavy and serious; but, in fact, the great influenza epidemic of 1918 killed more people, civilians as well as soldiers, than did combat. In the end there were combat-experienced veterans to come home, including some who would enjoy literary careers of distinction, such as John Crowe Ransom and J. P. Marquand. Curiously, however, most of the war novels and war stories written by Americans did not come from these veterans, but rather from writers such as Hemingway and John Dos Passos and E. E. Cummings who witnessed combat and suffered from it (Hemingway was seriously wounded) but who were actually peripheral to it as volunteer ambulance drivers who could at any time (like the hero of *A Farewell to Arms*, 1929, only with more ease and convenience) quit and go home. In a sense, although faced with very real dangers from time to time, they could be considered more as reporters of the war than as participants in it. The most celebrated and influential war literature came from these people or from those such as William Faulkner who served in the military but not overseas and not in combat.

What I am trying to suggest is that, in a general way, World War I happened for Americans in such a way as to permit many illusions to persist, to allow a certain general innocence to continue, unfractured. Of course, there is a great mystery attending this historical process of experience and disillusionment. With the Civil War it was America that suffered and experienced the most savage war of the nineteenth century (with the notable exception of the Taiping Rebellion in China about which we have only guesses, not statistics) and, in a real sense, the first modern war. In terms of casualties, in a literal sense, the Civil War is second only to World War II in the numbers of Americans killed and disabled. In a relative sense, based upon the actual population of the United States at that time, it was not only the worst war in American history, but the worst war in all of modern history, its effects surpassing those hideous losses of France and Britain in World War I or Russia in World War II. Interpreting the statistics in the final volume of *The Civil War: A Narrative*, novelist Shelby Foote makes it simple enough to comprehend—"Approximately one out of ten able-bodied Northerners was dead or incapacitated, while for the South it was one out of four, including her noncombatant Negroes." It is less easy to understand how the imaginative truth of this terrible experience was somehow not communicated to the next generations of Americans.

Foote, who, as a combat veteran of World War II, well understands the complexities of feeling, cites the inevitable cynicism of the Civil War veterans and their fears of the future in a world that had changed greatly, and for them strangely, while they were away from it. He also notes a more subtle and ineffable feeling: a deep sense of loss, a sense that, for all its horrors, the war had been the most profound experience of their lives—as he puts it, an awareness that "something momentous was passing from them, something that could never be recaptured." Foote makes the point that in many ways this was the real "lost generation" of the American experience. By and large, they were not involved much in the boom, the expansion, and the triumphs of industrialization which came along in the last three decades of the nineteenth century. "North and South, the veterans were part of this," Foote writes, "but mainly as observers rather than participants, and least of all as profiteers."

Something of the deep-rooted feelings of that generation was expressed by the veteran Oliver Wendell Holmes in his speech at a regimental reunion in Keene, New Hampshire, in 1884:

> The generation that carried on the war has been set aside by its experience. Through our great good fortune, in our youth our hearts were touched with fire. It was given to us to learn at the outset that life is a profound and passionate thing. While we are permitted to scorn nothing but indifference, and do not pretend to undervalue the worldly rewards of ambition, we have seen with our own eyes, beyond and above the gold fields, the snowy heights of honor, and it is for us to bear the report to those who come after us.

The report did not reach through time to the participants in World War II.

Our military unpreparedness was matched by our ignorance and psychological innocence when we were plunged into the war in December of 1941. This time the war was on a huge scale: ten million American men were in the service and located all over the globe. This war lasted a bitterly long time and then ended abruptly, almost absurdly with the introduction of the new, secret, and almost ultimate weapon—the atomic bomb.

Of course—and this, too, is part of the sense of absurdity and part of the reason that the effects of the war are still with us, still being discovered and revealed—the official end of the war was not truly the end of anything. There has not been one day since then that weapons have not been fired and men, women, and children killed in the struggles of issues, and non-issues, that were involved in World War II. The United States has also been involved in two major wars (Korea and Vietnam), not to mention many minor skirmishes.

From that war, then, the veterans returned, bringing with them a confused and confusing weight of raw experience and a frustrating desire to make some sense out of it. They were wounded, inwardly and outwardly, cynical and shocked, and yet at the same time glad to be alive, lucky to be so, and eager to live. They were torn between contradictions, arguably the greatest of which was that the great, professed American value placed on the single individual— a value with strong legal and political as well as an idealistic basis—was expendable and next to meaningless in the midst of the huge impersonal forces which, often by pure and simple accident, took personal fate and, in a sense, personal responsibility almost completely out of the hands of the individual. Who lived or died, suffered or rejoiced, won or lost, was more a matter of blind, implacable chance than of anything the individual might have done or left undone.

This awareness gave, and continues to give, rise to one of the principal concerns of contemporary literature in all its forms: the attempt to find and define the limits of personal freedom and responsibility within the confines of deterministic forces as impeccably indifferent to justice and injustice, to good and evil, as the abstract terms of a mathematical equation. As it had been in Britain during and after World War I, this knotty and profound concern was soonest manifest, in literary terms, in the work of poets such as John Ciardi and Karl Shapiro and William Meredith; and in certain emblematic poems which seemed to become a familiar part of the American literary consciousness, such as Randall Jarrell's "The Death of the Ball Turret Gunner" and Richard Eberhart's "The Fury of Aerial Bombardment." The problem is beautifully incapsulated and expressed, in its stunning ineffability, *as a question*, by Richard Wilbur in "Tywater," a much-anthologized poem about a dead comrade:

> When he was hit, his body turned
> To clumsy dirt before it fell

And what to say of him. God knows.
Such violence. And such repose.

The problem and the essentially insoluble question remain fresh, recent, and painful in the minds and spirits of veterans of those years to this day. In *The Great War and Modern Memory* (1975), his prize-winning study of the literary implications of World War I to Britain and to the world, Paul Fussell, himself a combat veteran of World War II, refers to a comment by the late British novelist, H. M. Tomlinson ("The parapet, the wire, and the mud are permanent features of human existence") and glosses it as follows: "Which is to say that anxiety without end, without purpose, without reward, is woven into the fabric of contemporary life." Psychiatrist Bruno Bettelheim, who suffered something worse than war, namely the horror of the concentration camps, is at this late date (in *Surviving and Other Essays*, 1979) still at honorable pains to try to find moral distinctions and to make reasonable judgments on the basis of that experience. In criticism of what he argues is the unreality at the heart of Lina Wertmuller's film, *Seven Beauties*, he writes:

> Our experience did not teach us that life is meaningless, that the world of the living is but a whorehouse, that one ought to live by the body's crude claims, disregarding the compulsions of culture. It taught us that, miserable though the world in which we live may be, the difference between it and the world of the concentration camps is as great as that between night and day, hell and salvation, death and life. It taught us that there is meaning to life, difficult though that meaning may be to fathom—a much deeper meaning than we had thought possible before we became survivors.

Perhaps it is the knowledge that they are better defined as survivors than veterans that singles out the American writers emerging from the experience of World War II from most of those who came before them.

If the poets reacted first, the story writers were not far behind. There were some outstanding collections in the early postwar years which dealt directly with World War II, books such as James Michener's *Tales of the South Pacific* (1947), *The Gallery* (1947) by John Horne Burns, *The Wolf That Fed Us* (1949) by Robert Lowry, and some extraordinary stories by Irwin Shaw which were collected in *Mixed Company* (1950) and *Tip on a Dead Jockey* (1957). Perhaps the most exemplary and influential, however, especially in terms of tone and attitude, are to be found among the stories of *Nine Stories* (1953) by J. D. Salinger. Only one of these now-classic stories, "For Esmé—with Love and Squalor," is directly concerned with World War II. It is basically built around two scenes (both remembered later in the present time by a first-person narrator), one in England in April, 1944, before D-Day, when the narrator was still training for combat, and the other in Gaufurt, Bavaria, "several weeks after V-E Day," by which time the narrator has come to think of himself in the third person and to see himself as "a young man who had not come through the war with all his faculties intact. . . ." Between those two scenes is, inferentially, by implication, a whole huge war novel—which can simply be imagined by the reader. It is a great *tour de force* and a profoundly moving story, unusual in that it ends strongly on a note of joyous survival. Sadder and more depressing is a story of the aftermath of the war, "Uncle Wiggly in Connecticut," in which two bitter, brittle, wounded young women, drinking through the afternoon together, are the veterans, the walking wounded survivors of World War II marriages to soldiers. Eloise was married to one of Salinger's mythical Glass family—Walt, who survived combat only to be blown up and burned to death by the freak explosion of a Japanese stove. This is a story that ends in cruelty and sorrow and self-pity. These wounded people will not recover easily, if at all.

Salinger's *Nine Stories*, still in print in paperback almost thirty years later, was to prove one of the most influential books of stories of the entire period, and it remains one of the most successful during a time when (as we shall see) books of stories have been almost uniformly unsuccessful in any commercial sense. Clearly, both the author and his work can be taken to stand for the writer-veterans of World War II who have been living with the experience, and trying to make sense and order of it, ever since.

Among many things that happened when the veterans returned from the war and went to college on the G. I. Bill, and when the literature of the modern period began to be offered as a legitimate topic for formal, academic study, was a genuine literary revolution. In a real sense it involved the overthrow of one establishment and its replacement by another. Elements of this change, or changeover, had been at least discernible in the last years of the 1930's and, to an extent, during the war years. In poetry there was a turning away from the "proletarian," often folksy, sociopolitical (and generally leftist in political orientation) verse of the Depression years. A trinity of major figures—T. S. Eliot, Ezra Pound, and William Butler Yeats—emerged from the war years as the recognized modern masters; although, ironically, Yeats was dead, Pound was incarcerated for his professional support of the Axis cause, and Eliot, long since a British citizen, had by and large finished writing his nondramatic poetry and was chiefly engaged in writing plays. (It needs to be noted that this prominence has been subsequently modified, in the last decade or so, by the addition of other "masters" to the pantheon of modern poetry, including especially William Carlos Williams, Wallace Stevens, and the "serious" Robert Frost as distinguished from the more popular image of that poet and his work.) This is not the place to discuss the formal and aesthetic implications of the rise of this triumvirate to its greatest power, prominence, and influence, but there are a number of general aspects which are more directly relevant to the entire literary scene and to the other simultaneous and related things which were happening.

For one thing, acceptance and acknowledgment of the preeminence of Eliot, Yeats, and Pound required an intense study of and revision of the past. All three, each differently, made extensive and eclectic use of the literary past (plundered it, their critics and detractors would say) and of past literary traditions. All three were international, worldwide in orientation. All three were deeply concerned with the great myths and with the mythological roots of modern literature. All three, each in his own way, were strongly set against many aspects of nineteenth century poetry in English, skeptical and critical of the Romantic and the Victorian sensibilities. All three were, to one degree or another, politically and socially conservative. T. S. Eliot was writing extremely influential criticism, helping to revise our appreciation and understanding of the literary tradition, bringing into prominence and modern repute such previously slighted, if not ignored, subjects as the poetry of the Metaphysicals, the poetry and drama of the later and lesser-known Elizabethan and Jacobean dramatists, and the theory and practices of the French symbolists. Remarkably, these interests and enthusiasms of his, together with more general views of literary history and some very specific views of the vocation of the poet in our time, came to dominate; they came to be the establishment views of the English-speaking critical and scholarly world for a solid twenty years after World War II.

It is not Eliot's particular views that it is to our purpose to consider here, however, but, rather, the fact that he could and did manage to impose them on the literary sensibility of a generation—so much so that later writers, poets, and fiction writers also felt compelled to rebel against them, in one way or another, to find their own voices and to create their own work. In other words, what happened to Eliot, Pound, and Yeats (and the other masters of that period who were subsequently recognized and incorporated) *could happen.* It was seen that, just as these three managed to overturn the familiar, accepted, conventional views of the literary tradition of the past, so any views of the past, *including theirs,* could be overturned and replaced by others. Thus the past, including the recent, modern past, became subject to revision, and even to exploitation for present purposes. If this revolution had more or less accidentally happened, it was now understood as a real possibility. *The next revolution might be made to happen.*

Something of this awareness that one could perhaps more fruitfully invent and invest in a coherent program rather than simply wait upon perceived historical process to work itself out is evident in the emergence and solid establishment of the New Criticism in this same postwar period. The terms of the New Criticism had been evolving in the critical work of the Fugitives/ Agrarians (Ransom, Allen Tate, Carolyn Gordon, Cleanth Brooks, Donald Davidson, and so on) for some time. Then, the end of the war found them placed in top-ranking jobs in prominent colleges and universities and often— with, for example, *The Kenyon Review, The Sewanee Review,* the *Southern*

Review, *The Georgia Review*, and, to an extent, *The Virginia Quarterly Review*—in close amiable contact with, where not actually in full control of, prestigious quarterlies and literary magazines. They were in a position to be influential, to have their ideas heard and even acted upon. As critics, they reviewed the new books; as editors and consultants they had a great deal to do with which materials were selected for publication, and which were rejected, by these magazines and others. As teachers they soon had some of the most talented younger writers working under them, people such as Robert Lowell, Peter Taylor, Randall Jarrell, and John Berryman.

Finally, in their own work in both poetry and prose fiction, the New Critics were extremely influential. Oversimplifying (of course), it can be said that the salient feature of the New Criticism was its stringent emphasis on approaching the literary work of art as an aesthetic object in and of itself and, insofar as possible, without any or much concern for such traditional, if secondary, characteristics as its biographical or literary-historical qualities. This approach meant considering and talking about the poem or story in its own terms, and it demanded a new sort of vocabulary and certainly a new awareness of the technical dimensions and qualities of literary art. This meant, then, a new sort of taxonomy, in effect a completely new system of classifying (and finally judging) literary art. Although the New Criticism cannot be said to have had any great influence on the form and shape of the American novel—possibly because, in truth, only shorter and more explicitly unified works can be treated at once so intensively and abstractly—it is generally conceded that the New Criticism has been, and in many ways remains, a powerful and positive influence on the making of poetry and the writing of short stories throughout the English-speaking literary world.

The changes resulting from the triumph of the New Critics were huge ones. There was a complete revision of the literary past, including all the scholarship and criticism devoted to it. Indeed (a surprising and paradoxical result arising from the work of critics who were themselves learned, scholarly, conservative, and deeply interested in history), if followed to its conclusion, there can be said to have been a shattering of the past as classifiable, comprehensible units into disparate parts consisting of isolated, individual literary works whose life is in the present only and is, therefore, a factor of the accident of survival. There was also an enormous influence in the present, the power to influence what can be studied and allowed to survive from the past, what can be made and published in the present, and, thus, an overwhelming influence on the future, in the sense that the future would not now be left to itself to happen, to arrive, but could and would be shaped here and now.

It did not go unnoticed by others that whatever else they may have done or proved, the New Critics showed just how much a few people of close affiliation and like minds could accomplish through concentrated, if not wholly coordinated, activity. In the past, it seemed, literary schools and movements (except in France, where they have always been more like teams than congenial groups of artists) were more or less accidental and spontaneous, so loosely and casually organized as to preclude all but the most rudimentary self-awareness until later, when someone else appears to name and to define the literary movement and to write its history. It may be that the New Critics were the last of these accidental, just-growed-like-Topsy literary movements, or the first of those who have come afterward—schools and movements which have been created by design, arriving, for example, like the Beats of the 1950's, with their future history prepackaged and prewritten.

From the model and the success of the New Critics it was learned, by some alert observers, that given access to even limited means of power and influence, a dedicated group (even if that group is chiefly dedicated to its own advancement) can not only revise the history of the past (like the Soviets), but also shape and write the history of the present, even as it is happening, in such a way as to control the future as well. In any case, the example of the New Critics brought the idea of the *collective* enterprise, of group thought and group activity, into American literary art for the first time—for better or for worse.

Meantime, however, the most startling and revolutionary changes took place in the world of prose fiction, where a number of great but greatly ignored artists were suddenly lifted from relative obscurity to a permanent prominence in our literary history. In 1946, nothing written by William Faulkner or by F. Scott Fitzgerald was in print. With the single exceptions of Fitzgerald's *This Side of Paradise* (1920) and Faulkner's *Sanctuary* (1931), no book by either writer had ever sold more than five thousand copies, and the average sales had been less by far. Fitzgerald was dead, and Faulkner was nearly broke, battling for survival through the rigors of screenwriting. Ernest Hemingway was better known to the public as a colorful figure, but was not really much more widely read. He, too, at that point had produced only one novel, *For Whom the Bell Tolls* (1940), which had enjoyed significant sales. In his case the war, in which he worked as a war correspondent, had seriously interrupted his writing career. Then, in an almost incredible historical irony, before the decade of the 1940's had passed, all three authors abruptly became prominent (and, in a relative sense, highly successful) figures in the American literary scene. By the early 1950's, all three were acknowledged as among the unquestionable modern masters. Faulkner and Hemingway were receiving the medals and prizes from around the world, which they had no doubt deserved, but which had been deferred until their reputations accounted for their practiced artistry. It was too late to give to Fitzgerald the kinds of recognition he had craved, but he was awarded all possible posthumous honor in terms of new editions of all of his work and of extensive and serious scholarly, critical, and biographical studies. He even became the subject of fiction and, lately, has been the subject of drama, in film, on television, and on the stage. He is now a popular symbol of the American literary artist.

How all this came to pass is curious, complex, and probably, even now, largely unfathomable. Many things happened to help the change take place; but at least two things, two parts of the larger picture, are clear and can be considered. First, among the inevitable effects of the introduction of modern literature into the academic curriculum was the immediate need to find representative masters worthy of close study and appreciation, able to be taught and interesting to teach and sufficiently challenging to read—as well as sufficiently different from one another. There *is* a sense in which if Fitzgerald, Faulkner, and Hemingway had not existed in the late 1940's and early 1950's, somebody would have had to invent them. Certainly the professors in the field of modern letters were looking for appropriate masterpieces by appropriate masters to teach. Moreover, they were at one and the same time looking for appropriate subjects to study, to write about, and to publish. They needed figures who could be said, in one way and another, to be worthy peers of James Joyce and (also recently rediscovered) D. H. Lawrence and Marcel Proust and Thomas Mann. The great American artists who had been much neglected and only just recently rediscovered offered the most obviously promising material.

So began the veritable industry of critical and scholarly exploitation of the works of modern (and now postmodern) masters which has persisted and thrives to this day. Indeed the very terms requisite for rediscovery and exploitation were established at the outset. For the young and ambitious critic or scholar of the 1980's, especially the one who wishes to do some original or innovative work, it is now, as it was then, necessary to find a subject which has been in some way neglected by his own predecessors and peers. Chiefly this can be accomplished by dealing with living, still-working writers or by viewing the modern past from the acute angles of some strictly specialized perspective, as in the literature of women writers or of ethnic writers of various colors and religions and national backgrounds. Otherwise the modern literary past now seems relatively fixed and as permanent as any history can be in our time. That is, although the precise rankings and ratings of Eliot, Pound, and Yeats or of Faulkner, Fitzgerald, and Hemingway may change slightly from time to time, go up or go down in response to trends, fashions, tastes, and schemes, still none of these figures seems likely to vanish from the front rank. Too much industry has been expended on establishing that position. Too many critical and scholarly reputations are deeply involved.

One of the profound ironies of the situation (and one which must amuse the ghosts of these great writers of ours) is that in order to redress the injustices of literary history it was necessary to revise and rewrite the past. Although injustice and critical and public neglect were the occasions of and for rediscovery, these authors had to be established retroactively. The result is that it is, at this date, almost impossible to find a history of the first half of the century in which it is not implied, if not fully stated and claimed, that (still for instance) Faulkner, Fitzgerald, and Hemingway were not at the center of the times, not only as masters, but also as *acknowledged* masters. Thus, paradoxically, the truth of the unjust situation which postwar critics and scholars of modern literature set out to redress is undermined by a false perspective. The blame, if any, falls upon an apathetic "reading public" and on a little bad luck. In any case the whole thing has been straightened out.

Simultaneously with the beginnings of academic study of the literature of the modern period came new editions of these great artists and others. Probably none of these was so immediately significant or influential in the late 1940's as The Viking Portable Library editions of Hemingway, Faulkner, and Fitzgerald. Relatively inexpensive, these compact, squat little hardcover editions were, and still are, designed, in the words of the standard book jacket statement, "to offer representative one-volume editions of favorite and classic authors, and the best anthologies on special subjects, in uniform volumes thoughtfully designed for compactness and for ease in reading." Durably bound in cloth, the volumes average about seven hundred pages, containing two to four times as much text as most standard-size books—competition, therefore, to Random House's Modern Library. Editor and critic Malcolm Cowley was one of those at Viking who put together this series of more than fifty volumes. Cowley edited both the *Portable Hemingway* and the *Portable Faulkner* and is to be credited, in the latter assemblage, with reviving Faulkner's career and reputation and directly causing the return of some of Faulkner's earlier work to print. In the cases of both Hemingway and Faulkner, precisely because of the nature and limitations of the anthology format, the short stories of both authors were emphasized, and in both cases sections from novels, which were more or less as self-sufficient as stories, were used—which, in turn, served to add some stature and luster to the short-story form.

It does not undercut either Cowley's critical prescience or his achievement to point out that at least some of his motives, and those of Viking Press, were much the same as those of the academicians and, insofar as it was hoped that the Portable Library books would find a place in the new academe, were closely related to them. The institution, Viking, and the editor, Cowley, were in a profitmaking business. For the modern period, they had to find and publish worthy writers whose work would not be prohibitively expensive. The best bet was writers who were just on the edge of being rediscovered, about to enjoy a rising reputation. Ideally, the Portable editions could, as they did for William Faulkner, actively participate in the author's rediscovery and reevaluation and at the same time could bring a handsome profit to the publisher and distinction to the editor. For once and for all everything worked.

This last part of the literary revolution with which the postwar period commenced probably has had more direct influence on serious writing than anything else. It could be seen, and has been so seen by a generation and a half (already) of writers who have come along since then, more as an almost providential working out of justice than as a fortuitous sequence of events so riddled with variables as to be, by definition, almost unique. In this sense the examples of these masters of the prewar period have been directly in- spirational to the postwar writers. Statistically the odds facing the serious writer in all of the postwar years have been, if anything, much more un- favorable than those faced by the earlier generation. Having lived through one almost complete literary revolution and having seen injustices apparently redressed, however, today's writer cannot be faulted for persisting in the hope, if not the belief, that what has happened once before can happen again. For better or worse, many writers who might, reasonably and practically, have given up the hard habits of the practice of their art for the sake of something more rewarding, have continued to create. This fact has given us the benefit of a rich, varied, and productive period which is perhaps unequaled in excitement, except, possibly, for the last decade or so of the reign of Queen Elizabeth I.

For this state of affairs we can be grateful, even as we must recognize that at least some of the artists' brave assumptions may be hopelessly faulty, or based on inadequate information and a faulty interpretation of history and events. Any belief that there is the faintest possibility of yet another literary revolution in our time is predicated on the faith that there is a real and firm continuity between our own time and the rest of the century; that, except superficially, we are living in the same world, or at least the same kind of a world, as was the earlier generation. It is just as reasonable, and far more plausible, to argue that our resemblances to the prewar world are only su- perficial and that our differences are deeper than we realize—in which case the examples of the modern masters can only be very general in the way, and at almost the same distance, that the lives and art of John Milton or Geoffrey Chaucer or Vergil can sustain a contemporary artist.

Finally, there is a very serious question as to whether, all other things being equal, anything true or just can come to pass in the context of an era that defines itself more by its images than by any reality, an era in which facts and events, as well as people, are conceived of as things to be manipulated, things that *can be* manipulated to serve short- or long-term purposes or interests.

All these are problems with which contemporary writers must learn to live. Such problems cloud our period with uncertainties. Of one thing we can be certain: that at the end of World War II, a literary revolution occurred and turned the creative world upside down.

There are one or two other results of the rise to power and prominence of the New Criticism which ought to be at least cited, if not explored in depth. One result was that, as early as the beginnings of the 1950's, the critic had already become a sort of hero, a "star" within the literary world. Perhaps the importance of Eliot and his critical contributions made this an inevitable probability; in any event, critics—and not only the new critics—assumed important roles in the literary scene. It was the age of R. P. Blackmur, Yvor Winters, Stanley Edgar Hyman, I. A. Richards, Francis Ferguson, Eric Bentley, Leslie Fiedler, F. R. Leavis, Lionel Trilling, and many others. Younger writers such as Randall Jarrell and, later, James Dickey followed behind them, certain that criticism, including active and argumentative book reviewing, was in no way in conflict with their art and, indeed, would prove helpful to the development of artistic reputation. Most of the important critics were poets or fiction writers, or both; although, among the older generation, the creative aspect was generally secondary to the critical act. Lionel Trilling went so far as to argue that, for our own age, it was appropriate to subordinate the creative act. Such a view held that criticism was, at its best, an art form and perhaps a higher (and certainly a more sophisticated and refined) art form than simply fiction-writing or poetry. It thus followed that our finest critics were in fact our finest literary artists.

One result of this heroization of the critic and his act of criticism was that some of the writers, especially those fiction writers who were beginning to rebel against the strictures of "realistic" fiction, added a dimension of literary criticism to their own creative work, as well as emphasized the *sensibility* of the author/narrator/speaker as central and essential to a story. There is a serious, if often implicit, way in which the short stories of some of our writers, who came of age during this period of the rise of influential critics (writers such as John Barth, John Hawkes, Robert Coover, Jonathan Baumbach, Donald Barthelme, William Gass, and various other practitioners and professors of postmodernist fiction, or "metafiction"), contain a strong element of the critical act within the context of the fiction, a sort of self-criticism; or, in another sense, a sort of prepackaged, anticipatory criticism. The elements of literary parody and satire, the deliberate uses of conventions and clichés, the exploration of the narrative *as it is in process*, as if it were a tentative synopsis—all these things depend upon a climate and context of literary criticism and, in one way, predicate the literary critic as the ideal audience for this kind of fiction. Part of this attitude is ironic; but if the irony is to work, there must be a truth in the stature attributed to the literary critic.

Other influences and examples have been at work, leading to the importance of "surrealism" in contemporary poetry and to the postmodernist short story; but one that should not be overlooked is the prestige and power acquired by literary critics in the postwar years. These writers surely felt that they had to come to terms with the tradition of literary criticism as much as with the traditions of poetry and fiction.

Finally, the New Criticism, like any genuine revolutionary force, created its own opposition and backlash. One form that opposition, or counter-revolution, took was in the reassertion on the part of some of the more brilliant and learned scholars of the importance of learning and scholarly discipline in shaping the critical act. Thus, scholars of the various periods of English literature, in reaction to the New Critics, were able to show that the New Critics' ideal of the text as object treated objectively was not only impossible to achieve, but also inherently faulty in its own limited terms.

One seminal, scholarly-critical study, Wayne C. Booth's *The Rhetoric of Fiction* (1961), was at once devastating and liberating. Booth, by depth of argument and by an articulated familiarity with the whole span and spectrum of fiction, was able to persuade that the development of the art of fiction was less evolutionary, less a matter of progress from primitive to sophisticated than had been generally and casually assumed. Moreover, he was able to demonstrate conclusively that some of the leading figures of the modern period—Gustave Flaubert, Henry James, and James Joyce, for example— had not been nearly so "dramatic" or abstracted from their fictional creations as they had professed to be; that, in various ways, the modern authors were as intrusively engaged as had been the eighteenth century masters such as Henry Fielding and Sanuel Richardson.

This argument struck at the heart of some of the tenets of the New Criticism, and also served to give scholarly and critical support to the new writers of postmodern fiction. It is at once amusing (ironic) and perfectly appropriate that when Booth's *The Rhetoric of Fiction* appeared in hardcover from the University of Chicago Press in 1961, it did so with the undeniable benefit of a long book-jacket blurb by the dean of the New Critics, John Crowe Ransom. The way in which Ransom gracefully acknowledges that the New Criticism will have to adjust to and accommodate Booth's scholarship and argument is clearly evident in this sentence from that blurb: "It is like a one-volume encyclopedia in which any practicing critic will find the sort of argument which he himself has been using, but adapted to the whole immense range of effects, many of them quite different from his own." Note that there is, already, an assumed audience for whom this book will, Ransom asserts, be of great practical value: an audience of practicing critics.

It is important to remember that there had to be a very successful revolution before there could be a reaction to it that was meaningful. In this sense it can be argued that even by creating their own opponents, the New Critics have remained the most persuasive influence in English-language literary criticism.

Another quite different result, perhaps largely unintentional, of the rapid deployment and strategical and tactical victories of the New Criticism was the encouragement of the development of contemporary regional literature, beginning with (but hardly confined to) the South from which the New Critics came.

The combination of the national and the international, discovery of the art of William Faulkner with the separate successes of the New Critics in both art and criticism tended again to focus attention on the South as a literary region and unquestionably aroused and inspired a host of Southern writers of all kinds. This condition resulted in a period of great productivity which has continued unabated and undiminished ever since. Further, that example has stirred up similar regional reactions throughout the nation, these being not only geographical in orientation (contemporary literature of the Middle West, Southwest, Northwest, upper New England, the urban centers, and so on), but also grouped together according to other specifically unifying criteria. Thus we have had poetry and fiction identified primarily by religion (Jewish or Catholic); nationality (Irish-American, Latin-American, Native American and so forth); race (black literature); or sex (women's literature).

There are a few central contradictions or paradoxes at work here. First, it was clearly the aim and goal of the New Critics to establish objective standards, both general and specific, which could be applied across the board to most modern and contemporary literature; and in large part they succeeded. Thus, on the one hand, this movement was essentially a centralizing force and therefore parallel to (or part of) the same profound forces at work in the postwar world which were leading politically to an ever-increasing federalism of government and socially to the apparent rapid end of rural and small-town America and its replacement by metropolitan, urban, and suburban centers. So the centralization of criticism was paralleled by the centralization of the American commercial publishing industry, which, with minor exceptions in Boston and Philadelphia, found itself soon after World War II almost exclusively integrated into New York City. Similarly, the communications industry, led by the explosive and rapid development of television, became at once centralized and standardized. Marshal MacLuhan's "global village" came to be the apparent figure for the future. It was believed by some that these forces were so great as to spell the end of distinctive regions and cultures.

As in some other matters, however, the energies of reaction or counter-revolution were already flowing. Seeds of the possible breakdown and disintegration of centralism were already planted and rooted and growing. Thus—as has already been noted by such prominent thinkers as Rene Dubos—by the 1970's all large units and structures and groups, from nation-states to conglomerate institutions to literary schools, seemed threatened by a powerful movement toward smaller and more manageable units. Politically and socially regional (Sunbelt, Snowbelt) and special-interest groups (senior citizens, women, blacks, farmers) were suddenly so important as to be conceived, by some, as radically changing our form of government and the way we live.

In publishing, as the large commercial publishers became larger and more commercial to survive at the expense of serious literature, and especially at the expense of the short story, so the far-flung university presses and small presses began to fill the gap and to perform the functions now neglected by the large-scale, national, commercial publishers. All of this is reflected in, if not wholly contained by, the brief history of the rise of the New Criticism; indeed the same paradox is at the heart of that theory. If they were, at first, centralists in literature, they had also been from the outset Agrarians socially and politically, vigorously resisting the trends in those areas.

There is a fundamental and almost purely literary paradox at the heart of the New Criticism as well. All things considered, it was an exclusive, aristocratic movement. In the beginning of that movement a large number of their own fellow Southerners, including William Faulkner, were declared to be outside the pale, too vulgar or plebian or unrefined in a critical sense to be encouraged to make any contributions to literary art. In the early days, for example, the New Critics regularly disposed of Faulkner as an inspired genius, but essentially as unlettered as Caedmon and badly in need of critical restraint. Certainly he was not viewed as a positive example for literary artists. All this has, of course, changed; but both the success of the New Criticism and the various predictable reactions to it ended by directing contemporary American writing (and thus world writing) into even greater pluralism and individualism. What began as a sort of highly exclusive club has ended in an almost completely inclusive, worldwide democracy of the arts.

Actually related to the literary and critical revolution discussed above, but also separate from it, part of an even larger and more complex process of transformation, the translation of modern and contemporary literature became and has remained a major factor in shaping post-World War II literature. In addition to the influence of British writing, an influence which was at its peak in the years before the war and which (for many reasons) has steadily declined ever since, American writers, and readers, were aware of at least some of the work of the more prominent European artists. With the end of the war, however, and the arrival of America as a superpower, translations of the work of modern literary artists from all over the world became an important part of the English-language literary scene and made an important contribution to it. Suddenly the American reader had at his fingertips the choice of many kinds and forms of fiction; and our writers had, for inspiration and example, far more normative models than any previous generation had possessed.

More dependent upon translation than readers and writers of many other nations, where the fluent use of several languages is a necessity, Americans were paradoxically freed by ignorance to enjoy a far wider eclecticism than others. Gradually, therefore, the literature of modern Europe and of Latin America became a direct influence upon American culture. The modern masters of European and Latin American fiction—figures such as Thomas Mann and Marcel Proust and André Gide; Italo Svevo and Alberto Moravia; Franz Kafka, Robert Musil, and Par Lagerquist; Jorge Luis Borges and Gabriel García Márquez; and so many others—in short order became, however much distorted and changed by the process of translation, as much a part of our cultural climate as our own writers, past and present. And because, small as it may be, the American audience for serious fiction remains larger than that of any other nation (except, perhaps, the Soviet Union), the living literary masters of foreign countries, the older writers such as Borges and Moravia and Max Frisch, or the somewhat younger ones such as Carlos Fuentes or Robbe-Grillet or Heinrich Böll, have come to consider the American audience as much more than secondary. To an extent they must write with an awareness of this audience and, as well, an awareness that their work will in all likelihood reach its largest audience in translation. Acknowledging this fact, Carlos Fuentes, for example, has brought his American translator into the actual creative process, not waiting upon a finished or final manuscript. So has the greatly influential Borges.

If there has been a great influence of foreign literature in translation during our period, however, the reverse flow has been even more powerful and emphatic, making for a much more complex international situation. Immediately following the war, American books began to be widely translated into all the European languages and, in fact, into most of the world's literary languages. This was a new development, but it has continued with unceasing vitality, except for the variable exigencies of the economy and the markets. American fiction in translation has proved to be of great influence elsewhere, and, as in the case of Edgar Allan Poe in the nineteenth century, it has doubled back upon ourselves. That is, foreign writers, influenced by one or another of the American masters, have come to us in translation and, in turn, worked an influence upon our writers. Perhaps the most notable example of this cycle is Gabriel García Márquez, whose *One Hundred Years of Solitude* (1970) was, he asserts, profoundly influenced by the work of William Faulkner in translation. Now García Márquez's work, translated into English, influences and inspires young American writers.

It should also be noted that the complex interchange of translations of modern literature has, at times, had a significant critical influence. Probably the most celebrated example of this influence is in the critical reception of the work of William Faulkner, which, in the superb translations of Maurice Coindreau, reached the French intellectual community. This influence was so great that in 1946, when Malcolm Cowley was trying to put together and publish the *Portable Faulkner*, Jean-Paul Sartre, visiting New York, could tell Cowley (somewhat to Cowley's surprise, even as it delighted and reassured him) that Faulkner was already like a god to the young people of France— *"Pour les jeunes en France, Faulkner c'est un dieu."* Translation and foreign appreciation were factors, then, in the discovery of Faulkner and in the amazing turn for the better his literary reputation took.

For just that reason, as well as for others, most serious writers in America are eager to see their works translated into other languages.

To return to the subject of paperback publishing, the success and the importance of this phenomenon, although it began in close relationship to the academic boom of the immediate postwar years, was very soon of much wider importance than the textbook business. From the first, the publication of serious as well as more popular modern and contemporary writers in paperback editions worked great changes on the nature of the publishing business. Initially, there was no clear distinction, like the one that has become quite definite now, between trade and mass-market paperbacks. As late as the late 1950's drugstores, bus stations, airports—all those places where paperback books were being sold in racks and stacks like magazines—there was an anarchistic array of all kinds of books jumbled together. One found Signet editions of the *Iliad* and of Aristotle in cheek-by-jowl association with the likes of Mickey Spillane and Erskine Caldwell. A surprisingly large percentage of the new titles published in hardcover made their way into paperback without great difficulty and with a modest advance against royalties to be shared equally by the author and the publisher. "I'll wait and buy it in paperback," was a familiar watchword of that time. The significance of this development was that it was almost a very reasonable expectation in those days that one could buy almost any title in an inexpensive paperback edition within a year or so of the hardcover publication.

Meanwhile, although the expenses of book production, promotion, distribution, and so on were gradually being seized and swept along by irresistible inflationary forces (so much so that even in the best heydays of the early 1950's the book production and design departments of hardcover publishers were having to dedicate their efforts to the chore of holding down costs by finding more and more cheap ways of making books) and although the basic sales of serious literature in hardcover editions, poetry and novels and collections of short stories, had not significantly improved since the 1920's (more books in general, more *titles* were being published and sold, but the average sale of individual titles remained roughly the same as it had been a full generation earlier), still the hardcover publisher could at least aim to compensate for both problems by a lucrative paperback sale. In a very short time, however, this secondary factor became an essential consideration. What had been called (and are still so called) subsidiary rights became an essential part of the economic success or failure of a given book. Without a paperback sale, usually in advance of publication, a serious book (almost without exception), indeed almost any book, would automatically fail—it would lose money for the publisher. By the early 1960's, costs of publishing, measured against limited potential for profit even under ideal circumstances, had reached the point where the prompt success or failure of any given title became a more pressing and vital consideration than it had been before.

In the earlier years of this century, however, publishing both here and abroad had often been an adventurous affair, a gambling business, because the risks were small and bearable. For example, with the single exception of his first book, *This Side of Paradise*, no book by F. Scott Fitzgerald published in his lifetime sold as well as *The Great Gatsby* (1925), which apparently sold close to five thousand copies. Since the "break-even point" in those days was roughly fifteen hundred copies, none of those books lost Scribner's much money, if any; and *The Great Gatsby* was actually profitable. Moreover, in the case of Fitzgerald the risk and any losses incurred were more than justified in the long run by the enormous backlist value of the various works of Fitzgerald in the years since his rediscovery and posthumous restoration. Now, however, as a result of inflationary costs and the whimsical vagaries of the capital market (for publishers must borrow most of the money with which to operate), and also of the contemporary methods of strict, cost-accounting bookkeeping, the break-even point for any given title in hardcover is most often estimated at being at least ten thousand copies. This means, among many other things, that nothing published in the entire lifetime of Fitzgerald except *This Side of Paradise*, and nothing published by Faulkner between 1925 and the end of World War II except *Sanctuary*, and nothing of prewar Hemingway except *For Whom the Bell Tolls* could in our times and our terms be classified as anything but a serious financial failure. The implications of this fact are many, but obviously a pertinent implication is that careers similar to those of Faulkner, Hemingway, Fitzgerald, and so many others of that generation are extremely unlikely to happen any more. The days when an author could produce work regularly and in a variety of forms while slowly and cumulatively building up a reputation and a small and dedicated readership until such time as a "breakthrough" could be achieved, are basically gone.

There are some serious "prestige" writers who have been nurtured and brought along by one publisher or another in the old-fashioned way—for example, John Updike at Knopf or Bernard Malamud at Farrar, Strauss, and Giroux, both of whom have been able to publish distinguished collections of stories in a hardcover, commercial format. There is a fundamental difference, however, between these contemporary writers and the earlier masters. In the case of the latter and many of their peers, judgment on their work was deferred and delayed; the feeling was that time would tell, and there was plenty of time. Today there is neither time nor money to wait upon long-term judgments or a change of critical climate. Both almost certainly will come to pass, but not soon enough to matter. Therefore the publisher must *guess* at quality at the outset and then invest in it. That is, an Updike, a Malamud, or a John Gardner is chosen by his publisher more as an act of faith than a matter, at the beginning, of good works. It is a process, on a very small scale, analogous to Calvin's scheme of election and damnation. The publisher/supporter cannot guarantee success on a popular scale, of course; but the publisher can control the situation and the competition to a limited extent. Thus we have another example of that familiar contemporary event: the self-ful-filling prophecy.

It was thought and hoped that the proliferation of mass-market paperback publishing would have any number of wonderfully beneficial effects, among them an increased literacy and a greater sophistication among the existing "reading public." It was envisioned that among the many who bought, and presumably read, paperback books, there would be at least some, perhaps one day even a meaningful percentage, who, becoming accustomed to and at ease with the habit of reading and perhaps becoming attached to certain writers and their subjects, would begin to buy and to read hardcover books also. It was dreamed by a few that the success of the paperback book would serve to increase the still-untapped mass audience for hardcover trade books.

This dream has not yet come true. In fact, so far all available evidence seems to indicate that the two audiences—the paperback readers and the readers of hardcover books—are completely separate and basically different, that there may well be some real transferable sales value in the hardcover best seller which is later published in paperback, but that a paperback success is likely to add almost nothing to an author's subsequent hardcover successes. Movies and television, with all their intricate relationships with both hardcover and paperback publishing, have added more complexity. Again, however, making allowance for the few exceptions—rare examples such as *Love Story* (1970) and *The Godfather* (1969)—these forms of subsidiary rights do not seem to have a significant impact on hardcover sales.

There is one more development in paperback publishing which has had, and is having, a great effect on the fate of serious literature. For some time now the paperback publishers, few in number now and all part of complex conglomerate structures, have been marketing their products differently. Outside the world of college bookstores (no longer a significant part of the business), they have found that the best and most efficient way to sell is to limit strictly the number of titles available for sale and also to limit the lifetime of a given book in the marketplace. Now they sell "blockbusters" only, be-lieving that the public taste is less important than was once imagined. The public, they believe, will buy what is available. By severely limiting the avail-able choices, they can, with a good deal of accuracy, control the sales.

Outside the very limited world of the "trade paperback," available in college bookstores and the like, there is no longer any intent or even interest in trying to "improve" the public taste. It is no longer even a question of "pandering to the public taste," or of "giving the public what it wants." What the public may want or not want is an irrelevant factor in contemporary paperback marketing. Fraud and pollution and the creation of junk have become as common and significant in book publishing as in any other enterprise.

Needless to say, none of this bodes well for the practice or the publication of the short story. With the exception of a very few selected prestigious masters of the form, commercial publishers are not interested in publishing books of stories by anyone. It may be another self-fulfilling prophecy, but commercial publishers are convinced that they simply cannot sell collections of short stories. Books of poetry, they claim, do as well or better; and books of poetry, usually thinner and smaller, cost a little less to produce. If they *have to* throw money away for the sake of literary status and prestige (that is, for a kind of high-class, expensive advertising), it is more sensible to publish poetry than short stories. So they do that—not *much* poetry, mind you, but more than short stories.

The situation would seem very bleak were it not for the fact that this same period has seen fantastic growth in the number and variety of first-rate American short-story writers. In the "Appendix" to *The American Short Story*, William Peden lists "One Hundred-Plus Notable or Representative American Short Story Writers 1940-1975." That list, which is highly selective, is only of *writers*; the *titles* by those authors number in the hundreds. Since many of these living writers are teachers, they have students who, in turn, are writing and publishing short stories. The obstacles against them are great, but the pressure against those obstacles is also enormous.

What has happened since the 1960's is that, in the face of the failure of commercial publishers to do anything much about the short story, new ways and means have been developed. It is now commonplace for university presses and, more and more, small presses to publish collections of stories. Despite the indifference of commercial publishers, the numbers of titles listed in the chronicle reviews in the quarterlies is simply astounding. This is not to deny, however, that there are far more excellent story writers than can be published in book form. Indeed, there are so many that no anthology can even begin to represent them and the variety of their interests; nor can any critical and scholarly studies begin to "cover" the subject.

If commercial paperback publishing did almost nothing to advance literature in our time, it may yet come to pass that the modest paperback printings offered by university presses and small presses will manage to put our gifted writers in touch with an audience. Driven from the marketplace, the short story nevertheless remains a vital and important art form and shows no signs of declining.

A word or two about corruption seems appropriate at this point. Manifest, and evidently shocking to many people, in the whole affair of discovery and deception called "Watergate," it certainly did not begin there. What is relevant to our historical time period and subject is not when corruption in public life, and thus, also, in private life, began; surely the story of Adam and Eve, among other things, establishes the beginning of corruption. What is relevant, rather, is the point at which corruption in public and private life began to be accepted and expected. It is characteristic of the perception of prewar America, a perception more or less shared by foreigners as well as Americans, that the most obvious and conventional forms of mundane corruption—bribery, kickbacks, and all varieties of fraud—were deemed to be widely disapproved of, if not wholly absent from the American scene. War changed that. At the highest levels it was necessary to lie, to steal, to cheat, and to *kill* in order to win that war. Or, to put it another way, there was in World War II, as both Axis and Allies perceived the situation, no real middle ground, no possible compromise. The war was total; surrender would have to be unconditional. Thus everything, all complexity, could be reduced to the question of survival. In the name of survival (victory), all governments, including that of the United States, allowed themselves a dispensation as far as corruption was concerned—unless, as in Nazi Germany or the Soviet Union, no such dispensation was necessary even before the war. For the sake of not merely desirable but absolutely necessary ends, virtually all means imaginable were taken to be allowable.

When such an attitude, necessary or not, becomes national policy at the highest levels, inevitably more than the body politic is infected. Never mind the encouraging example of ruthless and cynical authority—that would be force enough. One must also remember that in such conditions when the individual accurately perceives himself to be utterly expendable, without rhyme or reason except the achievement of the general goal, by and for others, this individual learns that what is at once the extent and limit of his freedom is to be found in wheeling and dealing while he is able, in desperately looking after Number One, insofar as any opportunities to act on his own behalf arise. This is, essentially, the ethic (and the message) of some of our greatest war novels—*Catch-22* (1961), *Slaughterhouse-Five* (1969), *The Naked and the Dead* (1948), the novels of James Jones, and so on. This sad truth seems to be inherent in the short stories of J. D. Salinger.

It was assumed by those who may have been troubled about it that corruption could be reformed when the war was over, that some sort of reform of ethics and manners, style and substance, could and would take place. Clearly it has not, perhaps because, as many thinkers have maintained, the world is still at war. The larger war of which World War II was a phase and a part has not ended. In any case, during World War II corruption began to be expected and accepted within certain limits, those limits chiefly being the ability not to be caught and exposed as a perpetrator of illegal and/or unethical acts. The limits became, in other words, whatever the traffic would bear. Corruption thus entered our lives as a habit and has been sustained as such. The definitions of survival have been extended and expanded. Corporate executives, for example, "fight for survival" to keep their jobs and privileges and perquisites, to maintain a certain standard of living. So do poets and professors of philosophy. What was once, not long ago, easily within the defined framework of corrupt, unprincipled action, is now simply pragmatic.

What are the results of corruption in contemporary life and art as they may affect our literature? For one thing, it has given our poets and fiction writers a powerful subject to deal with. It has increased the elements of satire in post-World War II literature, leading, in America, to the rediscovery of talented prewar satirists such as Nathanael West. Also, because a consequence of corruption is most commonly hypocrisy, literature has turned inward some-what more, for in order for hypocrisy to be revealed and dramatized, it is necessary to depict both inner and outer life, both the world of appearance and the reality. Thus literature has, often as a consequence of trying to deal with the inward and spiritual as well as the outward and visible, become multifaceted. For example, the short stories of Barth, Barthelme, Coover, and other contemporary writers tend (as does all their fiction) to be funny and sad, grotesque and lyrical, parodic and self-parodic, cynical and naïve.

It should not be forgotten that our literary artists live in the same world as everyone else. It is my pragmatic belief, based only on a half century's experience and with no statistical support whatsoever, that corruption seeks and finds its own level, like water. Therefore, there are roughly as many corrupt and hypocritical priests, say, as politicians. Editors of conglomerate publishers are as likely to be corrupt as, for instance, the executives of multi-national corporations. Likewise, the percentage of poets and story writers who are dishonest is roughly the same as the percentage of teamsters or traffic cops, for example. In a major piece of criticism in *The New Yorker* (June 23, 1980), "Why Are Movies So Bad? or, The Numbers," Pauline Kael discusses much the same thing—the rising levels of greed and corruption among the latest generation of movie moguls—and contrasts this generation with the *first* (prewar) generation in the movie business, a generation she names "the vulgarians." Speaking of them, she writes:

> They were part of a different America. They were, more often than not, men who only paid lip service to high ideals while gouging everyone for profits. The big change in the country is reflected in the fact that people in the movie business no longer feel it is necessary to talk about principles at all.

All of the signs and portents, hints and clues, all the forms of evidence indicate that literary artists in their difficult struggle for "survival"—battling for advances and royalties, for grants, awards, prizes, for jobs, for blurbs and book reviews and critical appreciation—are as ruthless, cynical, desperate, and duplicitous as anyone else. It follows that many, if not most, of them will do anything, or at least anything they can get away with, to gain their desired goals. It follows that, in a uniformly corrupt society, they feel they must do so. Because artists are at least inclined to be sensitive and self-aware, it also follows that, at least for a time, at least until they are mercifully able to suppress the pain of self-awareness and self-examination, they are aware that their hypocrisy is double that of the ordinary level. It follows that their rage, being rooted in self-contempt, is extremely intense, which may help to explain the singular anger of so much contemporary literature and its increasing emphasis on caricature at the expense of characterization. This is to suggest, for example, that some of the broad, cartoonlike, comic-strip qualities of much serious short fiction of the last twenty years or so may derive less from an interest in form or from a lack of interest in "realism" than from the simple fact that, for many an artist of our times, reality is very hard and very painful to bear. Of course, once something becomes a literary fashion, it is no longer possible to determine which artists have been moved by genuine pain and self-contempt and which by simple careerism.

Finally, the level of corruption in society taken together with all the possibilities for self-aggrandizement—the academic job, the large number of grants, awards, fellowships, and prizes, most of which did not exist prior to World War II, and, for more than a decade now, the government's direct involvement in the arts by and through such institutions as the National Endowment for the Arts—mean that the postwar writer must spend much more time and energy on such things than did any of his predecessors. In the face of widespread competition for limited rewards, the artist must be either extraordinarily lucky or possessed of extraordinary guile, political savvy, charm, and duplicity.

I am suggesting, then, that a *different sort of person* is likely to be a writer in the post-World War II period than before it. It is, statistically and practically, harder for a serious writer to earn a living and to survive through his art now than it was then. There are enough peripheral and indirect subsidies, however, to make it a worthwhile enterprise for a few—worthwhile by any standards, that is, except those of top management or inherited wealth. We have many contemporary writers, some of them genuinely distinguished, whose sole source of support, albeit both comfortable and adequate, is such living as they can earn by indirect means: that is, such rewards as they can acquire by and through recognition. Thus, for these people (and their number is many), recognition is a matter of survival.

It is safe to say that those who are able, in the face of all temptation, to resist corruption and to maintain their principles are also not likely to inhibit themselves or limit their chances by taking the risks required to do something in thought, word, deed, or all three, that might be called genuinely original. Here, therefore, is yet another force coming out of the war to become part of the texture of quotidian contemporary life, the main thrust of which is substantially conservative. This is one more thing which separates our writers from the prewar modern masters. All things seemed to combine to encourage them to experiment, to seek for adventure, to look for risks. The contemporary writer would be ill-advised to try to follow their example, although he would be equally ill-advised not to honor it with eager lip service.

There is another aspect of the difference between the prewar and postwar generations that ought to be acknowledged—a social difference. It is difficult to think of many writers among the generation of masters in American literature between the wars who were not, at the very least, solidly middle-class in background. They may or may not have gone hungry sometimes, like both Hemingway and Faulkner; they may have been, in fact, poor. Almost all of them, however, came from families with some resources and with both a stake and a position in middle-class America. By assuming the vocation of creating serious literature, they gained nothing either socially or economically, at least at the outset of their careers. Rather they were, in the jargon of sociology, "downwardly mobile," and they risked the disapproval of family and of more conventional friends.

Those who succeeded in the art, however (and, as indicated, their success came during the postwar period), added not only dignity but also an element of promise to the vocation of the serious writer. The artist, as such, acquired a certain social respectability. This, together with other social changes in our culture, has led to the arrival on the scene of a good many writers whose backgrounds are not so traditionally American and middle-class. Beginning in the late 1950's, we witnessed more and more poets and fiction writers who came from groups which previously had had only limited representation on the literary scene: racial and religious and ethnic minorities and writers whose families had been, by any of the usual standards of definition, members of the lower classes, even of what has come to be called the under class. For many of these the vocation of the artist, together with such rewards, direct and indirect, as it may offer, is unquestionably an example of "upward mobility." When even their literacy in the English language, never mind their dedication to literature, separates them from the experience and interests of their families and their class, they are alienated in a new and different way from the way artists of the earlier generation were. In a social sense the earlier generation took its greatest risk, quite aside from success or failure, in chancing a vocation in the arts.

The greatest risk of the postwar generations, however, is in failure. There is therefore a greater emphasis now upon success (that is, recognition) in the art and upon earlier success. The younger generations have more to lose. They have more reason to accept, without serious question or occasion for rebellion, not only the given and currently accepted characteristics of the art form, in details and customs, style and substance (even if the custom calls for recognizable signs of apparent originality), but also the "mind-set" of the larger intellectual community to whom they are beholden for recognition and rewards. So, as serious writers they need not, by definition and by established custom, seek to reflect the thoughts and feelings of the larger society which is, in fact and as a result of the dichotomy within the arts, reflected and represented by the more popular literary artists and forms. Indeed, it is the habit that the serious artist should instead reflect the attitudes of the smaller intellectual community which is his audience. Because this is so, there is much less variety and freedom of expression evident in the work of the younger, postwar generations.

What I am arguing is that a critical cliché concerning the modern and postmodern periods—namely that the first half of the century, the modern period, was the great period of innovation and experiment and that the post-modern period is a time of consolidation of gains—is true enough, but for different reasons from those usually advanced. It is not at all that the modern masters exhausted the possibilities of the novel, the short story, and the poem, but rather that it is simply and practically disadvantageous for the postwar writers to seek to do the same thing. Apparent individuality is not the same thing as originality or innovation.

I am also suggesting that insofar as corruption exists in the literary arts, it extends beyond acts of omission or commission done in the name of reputation and reward, of comfort and security. I am arguing that, unfortunately, in our period there is an extent (as yet unmeasured and perhaps immeasurable) *in which the art itself is also at least vulnerable to corruption*, and that this is one of the most serious literary dangers of our age. When both the making and the judging of an art are possible to corrupt, if they are not already corrupted, what use and value does that art have?

Aside from the competition of television, the ups and downs of the movie business, the new illiteracy, and the affluence that sent people out boating, hiking, swimming, and playing tennis instead of reading books as a leisure activity or pastime, there were other literary changes which have affected fiction. Probably the most important among these has been the growing dominance of nonfiction in the literary marketplace. Before the war there were five short stories in the magazines for every nonfiction article; after the war the situation was permanently reversed. At least partially, this situation derives directly from the war itself, when information was urgent and crucial and when, it was equally apparent, the conventions of modern fiction did not seem adequate or capable of doing justice to the complexities of the subject. This inadequacy, taken together with the frequently fantastic and absurd events of contemporary life, made many writers of fiction distrust the tried and true ways and means of "realistic" fiction. This distrust, although it may well have encouraged the creation of new and interesting kinds of fiction, further alienated what general audience fiction might have had.

In abdicating, fiction writers left the facts and surfaces and manners of contemporary life almost exclusively to the journalists. Nonfiction then began to use and incorporate many of the devices and strategies of fiction, so that the personal essay, in the hands of writers such as John McPhee, Annie Dillard, Edward Abbey, Joan Didion, and Gay Talese, became a sort of first-person short story as well. The interview or article, done in the manner that Tom Wolfe dubbed "the new journalism," soon became almost indistinguishable from the short story. And when, as is sometimes the case, the article deals with a *composite* figure, model, or personality rather than an actual, identifiable character, the difference between an article or essay and a short story is likely to be so fine and so subtle as to be entirely irrelevant.

Meanwhile, ever since the outrage and uproar of the 1960's, the situation has become ever more complex and ambiguous. We have the "nonfiction novel," as Truman Capote styles *In Cold Blood* (1966). We have the work of fiction which uses real characters among and in direct relationship to the fictional ones, as in E. L. Doctorow's *Ragtime* (1975). On the other hand, we have—or *had*, until the Supreme Court decision concerning the libel laws— a plethora of works of popular fiction, such as the works of Jacqueline Suzann or "Henry Sutton," novels which are promoted and sold as telling the real, undisguised, uncensored, unexpurgated facts of the lives of prominent (or notorious) real people, disguised behind fictional names and a few transparent veils of fabrication. In Norman Mailer's *The Executioner's Song* (1979), we have a work that began as reportage, was announced and published as non-fiction, and then was abruptly declared to be a novel by the author (and so accepted by his supportive critics and reviewers), when it became evident that its best chance to rise on the best-seller lists was as a work of fiction. (Here it should be noted that, in terms of sales of trade books on the best-seller lists, nonfiction books have to sell two or three times as many copies to earn a place on the lists.) Among the very few pre-World War II examples of this kind and sort of ambiguity between hard fact and fancy are Hemingway's *Green Hills of Africa* (1935) and *Death in the Afternoon* (1932). In both cases (although this, itself, may have been a fiction), the author insisted that the works were clearly, purely, and simply nonfiction.

It is not at all clear or certain where this may yet lead, if anywhere. What is clear is that the distinctions between fiction and nonfiction have become blurred and vague. It may be, indeed it seems so, that this is something of an advantage to both forms; and it certainly makes the task of those many writers, who do, in fact, practice both forms, much easier.

Another complicating element for all concerned that must at least be mentioned is the changed attitude of journalists toward fact and information. In the war (and so, to an extent, ever since) some facts were, of necessity, withheld or suppressed. Sometimes, for a multitude of purposes, information proved to be misinformation. The necessity of selecting the salient facts, the habit of juggling them when need be, joined with a serious philosophical skepticism that any such thing as "objective" reporting exists; and, beginning in the 1960's with the unembarrassed acceptance of "advocacy reporting" as an honorable form of journalism, all these things led directly to the "media event," to the staged happening, and to the primary importance of the contrived and controlled image at the expense of raw and untidy information. Thus, to a certain extent even pure journalism has become a rhetoric not deeply dissimilar from the rhetoric of fiction.

There is one explicit effect of all this on all fiction, including the short story, of course, insofar as that fiction professes to deal with daily life and the realm of the possible. Fiction writers are required to give evidence of close and accurate observation, which becomes as much a part of their own validation as witnesses as does the reporter's accuracy of quotation. Thus, for example, Ann Beattie is praised for the accurate and authentic and timely (in other words, *correct*) use of the materials of pop culture in her stories and novels.

The ambiguous balance of fact and fiction is elegantly expressed by one of its masters, John Updike, in *The New Yorker* review of the work of Anne Tyler (June 23, 1980), in which he finds reason to praise her fiction for its qualities of reportage ("The brand names, the fads, the bastardized vistas of our great homogeneized nation glint out at us from her fiction with a cheerful authority"). He celebrates her continuing ability "to look close, and to fabricate, out of the cardboard and Magic Markers available to the festive imagination, images of the illusory lives we lead."

Here a few words about *The New Yorker* seem to be in order. In praise of that magazine, it must be said that, week in and week out, it has continued to publish more distinguished short fiction than any other magazine in the country. Since the demise of all the big "slick magazines," it has been the honored custodian of the short story—not merely of and for America, but also for the world. Without *The New Yorker*, we should know even less than we do about the British and Irish story writers; and, over the years, *The New Yorker* has also published a good deal of foreign fiction in translation. Moreover, *The New Yorker*, through a system of contracts and bonuses, pays handsomely for its short fiction, making it at least possible for its regular authors to live off their writing alone. This system supports and encourages such outstanding story writers as J. D. Salinger, John Cheever, Peter Taylor, John Updike, Nancy Hale, Anne Beattie, and Donald Barthelme. Also, *The New Yorker*, despite changes in its editorial staff, has been continuous in its concern for and support of the short story from the beginning. Its record is uninterrupted by World War II; excellent writers graced its pages then, as now. If they never saw fit to publish anything by Faulkner or Hemingway, they did publish such writers as Irwin Shaw and Kay Boyle, for which no one can fault them.

For a while it looked as if *Playboy* might model itself somewhat upon the example of *The New Yorker*; and when Robie Macauley, editor of the prestigious *Kenyon Review*, joined *Playboy* as fiction editor, there was some stirring in the literary world. Not much came of this possibility, however, and most of the best stories published in *Playboy* were by *New Yorker* writers.

The influence of *The New Yorker* on the state of short fiction in America (and the world) has been great, and not only directly on the lives and careers of its own stable of writers but also upon the wishes, hopes, and dreams (and thus upon the subjects, themes, and techniques) of eager, aspiring story writers. In fairness and praise, however, it should be said that the standards of literary taste and intelligence set by the published *New Yorker* stories have had a very salutary effect on the stories of many other writers. Add to this the fact that, as far as commercial publishers are concerned in their outlook toward short fiction, there are all kinds of magazines around, and then there is *The New Yorker*. Collections of stories which have appeared in *The New Yorker* stand at least a chance of being published by major publishers in book form, and with good reason: they have been well-edited and tested in advance, so that the "product" is of known value and quality. Also, the publication of *New Yorker* stories in book form brings a certain local prestige to a commercial publisher whether or not it results in any significant sales. *The New Yorker* is, then, the chief supplier of short stories to the commercial publishers. In that world it sets the tone, the standards, and the style.

Most major American writing is, has been, and will be done elsewhere, these days in the quarterlies and little magazines and sometimes in the special interest and single-issue magazine. If nothing else, however, *The New Yorker* remains important as a surviving general publication devoted to the conservation and maintenance of establishment standards and dedicated to good taste and the celebration of the status quo.

A letter to the editor of *The New York Times Book Review* (July 13, 1980) from Anne Mollegan Smith, managing editor of *Redbook*, served to remind the *Times* and its reviewers and readers of the important part played by *Redbook* (especially during the past decade) in the publication of short fiction. Smith reminds them all that, with an annual total of roughly forty published short stories, *Redbook* stands second only to *The New Yorker* in space allotted to short fiction. She also indicates some of the recent "discoveries" first found, nationally, in *Redbook*'s pages—among them Tim O'Brien, Mary Gordon, John Irving, Lynne Sharon, and Scott Spencer. Smith adds: "*Redbook*'s fiction editors 'discover' these talented writers by doing the hard work of reading the roughly 35,000 unsolicited manuscripts that come to our offices every year. And each year *Redbook* buys at least a dozen—and sometimes as many as 20—stories from this rich resource."

There are a number of things to note in her statement of fact. First, she takes some pride in the fact that her fiction editors apparently do their job, that they actually read all those manuscripts. She is referring, of course, to the *unsolicited* manuscripts; and, in fairness, it must be said that most magazines, and book publishers as well, have long since given up dealing with the unsolicited manuscripts, "the slush pile." One must ask, however, what is the relative state of things when a managing editor finds cause for pride in asserting that her subordinates do what they are presumably paid to do in reading the work submitted by unsung and unknown authors? Surely this indicates—even as the mind boggles at the magnitude of the reading chore— that, by and large, discovery of new talent is not the usual function of magazine editors anymore. The figures she takes pride in, a dozen or maybe twenty out of thirty-five thousand, further emphasize this point. In any case, it should be noted that Smith is surprisingly honest about the process: "With odds of 35,000 to 12 (or at most, 20), an unsolicited fiction submission to *Redbook* does not have an easy time getting accepted." She also makes no claims that the stories selected for publication are, *de facto*, the "best" of the batch. What is really indicated here is, in plain numbers, the extent to which the system has broken down, that it seems no longer possible, in conventional ways, for even the most serious and dedicated publishers of short fiction to begin to perform their proper task; that the system is such that it cannot any longer lay claim to offering a representation of contemporary fiction.

A more positive view might take as its point of departure the incredible number of short stories being created and submitted, against all those odds, in the hope of possible publication. Surely those figures indicate that creativity is, as yet, undiminished and undaunted, no matter how sadly dwindled are the prospects of publication.

Finally, the fact that such a letter, written in the context of a reply to a book review which failed to mention *Redbook* while citing and listing some of "the few remaining magazines" that publish short stories, was deemed necessary indicates the great gap of ignorance and indifference with which everyone—writer, editor, publisher, reader—must contend. If the professional book reviewer, and, as well, the large and well-paid staff of *The New York Times Book Review*, is unaware of the facts about *Redbook*, a national magazine created and published right there in New York City, then how can the rest of us hope or pretend to keep up? And how can *they*, the journalists of our literature, profess to be doing their job and earning the power and prestige and privileges accorded them if they are unable to keep up with the literary activities in their immediate neighborhood, let alone claiming to oversee the activities of the nation at large?

Clearly the situation is that the "national" magazines cannot do their job and that *The New York Times Book Review* is unable or unwilling to do its job. I can think of no more emphatic and easy proof that New York is no longer, if indeed it ever was, a *national* literary center and that it no longer has, except by custom and tradition, much power or influence. For where there is small power to do good work or to reward good work, where there is only the power to do harm or to ignore good work, then that power, being almost purely negative, is in its final stages. If, for a good part of this century, the rest of the nation has been dominated in a literary sense by New York,

that almost classically colonial situation is changing fast. If this were really
an empire we are thinking of, all the available information seems to lead
straight toward the conclusion that the days of this empire are numbered.

In late 1979, Bantam Books published *A Geography of Poets: An Anthology
of the New Poetry*, edited by Edward Field. This work offers, in its own terms,
a better sense than most anthologies (or, for that matter, critical studies) of
the sudden largeness, complexity, and diversity of the American literary scene.
It offers, by analogy at least, a model not otherwise available of the plurality
and excitement of the contemporary short story and of the incapacity of the
contemporary systems of publication and recognition not only to contain and
represent the facts, but also even to describe in outline what is happening.
There is some value, then, in briefly looking at *A Geography of Poets*. In size
and scope it is the most ambitious and extensive anthology in many years,
presenting roughly six hundred poems by 228 poets. Fields has written a useful
and revealing introduction, which combines a more or less "official" general
history of the movements and directions in American poetry since World
War II with some of his personal history and his own reactions to things as
a poet. When, at the age of thirty-eight, and after being rejected by twenty-
two publishers, he won the Lamont Award for his first book of poems in
1963, he was able to go across this big country on poetry reading tours. It
was then that he "began to discover a lot of good poets everywhere I had
never heard of before." He decided to put together an anthology which gave
some sense of the real geography of poetry in America here and now—"By
presenting the poets of each area I might reveal a whole world of poetry still
undiscovered or ignored by the New York publishers." The results are the
most interesting and inclusive gathering of recent American writing (of any
kind) that I know of, with interesting effects and side effects.

For example, there are inevitably many "stars," or "names," included; but
with so many poets from so many places to be represented it is to be observed
that none of these well-known poets stand out in context as obviously and
inherently superior, distinctly better than any of the others. With all poets
offering best-foot-forward, there are as many good feet as the shiny boots of
a marching band. An intelligent observer coming to American literature in
general and contemporary American poetry in particular for the first time,
might have real difficulty singling out the more prominent and successful poets
(in terms of grants, prizes, awards, laurels, reviews, recognition) from among
this gathering. The "major" figures are, in fact, not distinguished from or
different from the others. I believe that much the same condition applies to
the contemporary short story, that the conditions required for the application
of the labels "major" and "minor" are no longer meaningful and that, therefore, the terms themselves are not so much without meaning (for they continue
to be used by critics as if they had some meaning) as without factual reference
in reality. That is to say, simply, the terms are no longer *true*. I would argue

(as indeed I have been) that except for the work of certain undisputed masters of the prewar period, there have been no genuine "major" figures in American fiction since World War II. This is not to say that the work created by writers during our period has been "minor," but only to argue that, despite all the assertions of official and unofficial critical histories, there have been no artists who can honestly be described as standing head and shoulders above the herd.

At a writers' conference at the University of Rhode Island in July of 1980, Kurt Vonnegut, Jr., announced to the students that though the novel itself may not be dead yet, it seems clear to him that Norman Mailer, Joseph Heller, and himself are "the last major novelists" in America. He might, more accurately and honestly, have said that he and they are probably among the last (for a time) who can be called "major" novelists.

The second important point proved by Field's anthology—and one which again applies well to the situation of the short story—is that the anthology, in its very success demonstrably proving the necessity of its method as the only way to create a model that represents the truth and the facts of the present situation, is also self-destructive, proving at one and the same time that *no* anthology can do justice to the contemporary scene. For one is fully aware that, using exactly the same sort of organization and criteria that Field did, one could create an anthology of identical size, with a similar number of poets and poems, and one with work of the same high level of literary quality, and could do all this without repeating one poet or one poem. Precisely the same thing is true of the short story. This means, frankly, that most of the anthologies of poetry and of the short story of the 1950's, 1960's and 1970's do not even begin to reflect honestly or to suggest or to attempt to describe and deal with the many and various things that have been happening in the literature of our time.

There are precious few scholarly-critical studies of the short story during the period we are concerned with; perhaps this is because of the plethora of anthologies, most of which offer at least some brief chronological history, together with notes and checklists. There is, however, (in my opinion and best judgment) one really first-rate study of the contemporary short story, both generally and specifically, although it is almost exclusively limited to the American short story—William Peden's *The American Short Story: Continuity and Change 1940-1975*. (This is a revised and enlarged version of an earlier study by Peden, *The American Short Story: Front Line in the National Defense of Literature*.) Peden's study is thorough, wide-ranging, and seminal in the best sense, in that it at once leads the way toward and makes possible future studies of the short story.

There are, as already indicated, a great many anthologies of all kinds dealing with the short story and offering many examples and at least some critical and historical judgment. Many of these are quite good and useful, although many more seem to be merely mechanical and imitative of one another or, at best, urgently gimmicky and innovative. The best of all the anthologies published so far (in my judgment) is *The Norton Anthology of Short Fiction*, carefully assembled and edited by R. V. Cassill, who, in addition to creating outstanding fiction of his own, both short stories and novels, for more than thirty years, has also earned an enviable reputation as one of our most vital and influential teachers of the critical appreciation and the writing of short fiction.

There are a number of ways to keep up with the short story on a yearly basis. First of all, there are the competitive annual anthologies—*Prize Stories: The O. Henry Awards*, edited by William Abrahams and published by Doubleday, and *The Best American Short Stories*, published by Houghton Mifflin and, since the death of longtime editor Martha Foley, put together by a different editor each year. Neither of these volumes, their titles to the contrary, is limited to American stories, but to stories published over a given year in North American (including Canada) publications. Over the years, *The Best American Short Stories* has proved to be more eclectic and adventurous while, by and large, the taste of William Abrahams has been safely conservative. Both these anthologies have been put on notice by a relatively new arrival in the field—*The Pushcart Prize: Best of the Small Presses*, which, although it also publishes poetry, ranges farther and wider in its search for quality than either of the commercial anthologies. Finally, for a sense of new and future directions in the short story, there is the *Intro* series of the Associated Writing Programs, which annually offers representative and outstanding work by beginning writers.

We have reached the point where the reference book is the essential starting place for study and understanding. Things are happening so quickly and thoroughly that almost any reference book will be somewhat out of date, behind the action of the times, by the time it appears in print. Even so, there is no other way to consider the contemporary scene without grotesque distortions.

In his most recent book *The Tale Bearers: Literary Essays* (1980), V. S. Pritchett, himself the author of some ten collections of short stories, deals specifically with the short story in only one of his twenty-three essays about fiction writers. That essay, "Satan Comes to Georgia," is about the art of Flannery O'Connor and is, in particular, concerned with her collection of stories *Everything That Rises Must Converge* (1965). In this essay he notes that, in the modern time frame, "English writers were slow starters in the art of the short story." He cites with approving understanding the notion of the great modern Irish story writer, Frank O'Connor, "that anarchic societies are the most propitious for an art so fundamentally drawn to startling dramatic insights and the inner riot that may possess the lonely man or woman at some unwary moment in the hours of the day."

There may well be something to the Frank O'Connor-V. S. Pritchett theory, for it is certainly true that the British short story has been less important and influential in the postwar period than one might have expected. Those two terms—"important" and "influential"—help to define the circumstances and the problem. In the late 1940's and early 1950's, Britain, although war-torn and war-weary, was still a vital center for serious literature in the shared native language. One important factor at the time was that publishing costs were so much lower in Great Britain that, as in the United States before the war, it was possible to break even with smaller sales. One result of that fact was that from the late 1940's until the early 1960's there was a great deal of *exchange* of serious titles between Britain and the United States. Although this exchange somewhat favored the American writers in terms of quantity and, as well, favored the younger and newer American writers (for the British seemed to want to keep up with the latest trends and developments in America, whereas the American publishers have been mainly interested in the work of known and well-established British authors), at least for a time there was a considerable activity of exchange. Very often this included the publication of collections of short stories by American writers. With the exception of a few old-time regulars at *The New Yorker* (V. S. Pritchett, for example), and an occasional collection by a very prominent British author such as Graham Greene or Joyce Cary, there have not been a great many British collections published in America.

There have been collections which appeared in association with other, somewhat peripheral circumstances. For example, Alan Sillitoe's *The Loneliness of the Long-Distance Runner*, consisting of the title piece (a long story or short novel) and eight short stories, was published by Knopf in 1960, following the considerable success of Sillitoe's novel *Saturday Night and Sunday Morning* (1959) in both Britain and the United States. Both the novel and the stories are in the process of being turned into films. More recently, in the same vein, stories of prewar British writers such as A. E. Coppard and H. E. Bates, after achieving some recognition when seen by large audiences as television series dramas made by BBC and shown in America through the auspices of public television have been published in trade paperback editions; as, also, have the stories comprising *The Glittering Prizes* by Frederick Raphael. Occasionally a British writer has achieved sufficient success and repute here to merit publication in hardcover of short stories. A recent example is *Stories* by Doris Lessing (1978), which is, in fact, a collection of all her short fiction published from 1958 to the present, except for her stories set in Africa. Not many British collections have been published in America, however, and practically none of the experimental work produced by younger British writers has been published here or, indeed, is even known here. Such a significant collection as *Statement Against Corpses* (1964), containing stories by B. S.

Johnson and Zulkiar Ghose, never found an American publisher.

In presenting this experimental gathering of examples of "a literary form which is undeservedly neglected," something of the sense of what the authors perceived themselves to be struggling against can be seen in the opening sentence of a brief prefatory note at the outset of the book: "These short stories have been written in the knowledge that the form is in decline, but in the belief that this is due to no fault inherent in the form." It is hard to imagine a more defensive posture of apologia than that; but there were reasons enough. By that time, early in the 1960's, Britain's economy was deeply troubled. Publishing costs matched those in America, and the core of the serious reading public in Britain (once deemed solid as the Rock of Gibraltar) was shrinking. This, then, fairly well marked the end of the easy exchange between the serious writers of Britain and America; except for very prominent writers and for the best-sellers, the exchange in the future would be severely limited.

By the end of the 1970's, the situation had worsened in one respect. Publishing costs in Britain had so inflated that the average British hardcover book cost twice as much as its American counterpart. This, in turn, served to limit the extent of cultural exchange. Battling for survival, some British commercial firms began to open American branches in order to publish some books directly in the United States, and also to market their own books more aggressively and competitively. These, however, were to be books aimed at the potential mass markets; there was no place for the British short story on their lists.

Meanwhile, neither American university presses nor the small presses have been eagerly seeking out and publishing British collections, although we know from the magazines that there are still solid and interesting stories being written there. There are, as yet, no British equivalents to kinds and numbers of small, independent presses to be found in America. For more than a decade, then, there has been very little to encourage the contemporary British story writer. It would be a bleak picture if it were not for the examples set by Greene and Pritchett and Lessing, for example, of prominent fiction writers known chiefly as novelists (or, in Pritchett's case, as critic and essayist) spending time and energy on the difficult form of the short story against discouraging odds. Only a handful of the most prominent American fiction writers of recent years—one thinks of Updike and Cheever and Bernard Malamud and Joyce Carol Oates—have been regularly productive in the short story form. The others either cannot afford the time to work on stories or might have too much difficulty getting a collection published. The result is a surprising number of important fiction writers who have settled (so far) for one distinguished collection of stories: for example, Wright Morris, Robert Penn Warren, Kurt Vonnegut, Jr., and Saul Bellow. Even the prolific John Gardner has produced only one collection of stories.

Seen against this background, the production and the publication of several volumes of short stories by Graham Greene and V. S. Pritchett and Doris Lessing is an impressive achievement and an exemplary contribution to the welfare of the short-story form. These distinguished writers, like most of the British writers of stories in our time, create solidly crafted, well-made, basically old-fashioned stories. They have never shared the American interest and excitement in technique for its own sake. What shines through the best British short stories is a mastery of the given form, not an exploration of or search for new frontiers. B. S. Johnson was an exception, an extraordinarily gifted writer of experimental fiction, but he died young.

In summary, then, the years since World War II seem not to have been especially prosperous or productive ones for British short fiction. Certainly in vitality and influence they in no way match the years leading up to World War II. Yet at the same time, we owe a debt to writers of great distinction, such as Graham Greene, who clearly love the short story and who have worked hard, making a sacrifice, to keep the classic short story alive and well when many of our own most prominent serious writers, perhaps unwilling to waste time on a small audience and on very small rewards, have turned away from the form. At this writing the fate and future of the short story in Great Britain is seriously in doubt, and the influence of the British story in the literary world at large is minimal.

The creative writing programs, graduate and undergraduate, throughout the United States have led to an increased (and arbitrary) specialization, a separation between poetry and prose fiction. Very few students are encouraged to study both. Indeed, a certain competition between the two "fields" has developed in many institutions. Thus the ideal of the man of letters, still a prominent goal in the prewar years, has largely been laid to rest. At least among the younger writers, poetry and prose seem to have less immediate influence on each other. It is also already noticeable that certain highly structured institutions have developed easily identifiable styles, so that many of the recent graduates, especially in poetry, tend to write in and around certain predictable stances and tropes. There remains, however, enough competition and variety among institutions that, in prose fiction at least, the possibility of an imposed national style seems remote. Meanwhile, whatever else, the writing programs have unquestionably increased the basic standards of reading and writing at a time when those standards, among students nationwide, are greatly imperiled.

It has been the thesis of this essay that a series of complex changes and developments have served to make the literary world, in almost all its aspects—creation, publication, criticism, and so on—fundamentally different from the literary world in the first half of this century, the years leading up to World War II. I have argued that there have been many fundamental changes in American life, of which these changes in things literary were a part. I have attempted to demonstrate that most of the people involved, writers, publishers, critics, and reviewers, have not fully assimilated the changes or the new facts of life in the second half of our century—that most of these people, deeply involved in the literary life of our times, have modeled their careers and actions on the inapplicable examples of the past. Another point of this essay has been that, of all the serious literary forms of our times, the short story has probably suffered most from the complex of forces which have radically changed the situation of serious literature.

Out of some sort of grand historical irony, however, the period with which we are dealing, during which the short story has been most troubled and threatened, has witnessed an unprecedented flowering and flourishing of the form. There are so many fine writers of excellent stories around that to attempt to list them would be foolishly arrogant; it would require an encyclopedia. It is, therefore, the implicit and explicit argument of this essay that, in the face of such worthy energy (and richness, diversity, and abundance of gifts), negative forces are destined to be either overwhelmed or outwitted. If the system cannot accommodate such a surge of genuine creativity and energy, then it is the system which will change and be changed.

What all this must mean, then, is that we are in the midst of an exciting period of swift and thorough transition, moving through a confused and confusing present time into a future which is at least partly cloudy with as-yet-unimagined possibilities. It seems clear that the unstifled and uninhibited human impulse to create fiction will be a part of that future. Meanwhile, here in the present, the concision, the evocative range, and the variety of form of the short story have become singularly apt as a medium for the times. It is here and now that the novel and even the journalism of our times have borrowed from the ways and means of the short story to their own advantage. Thus, it might be argued that even in the face of indifference and adversity, the short story has become, triumphantly, the appropriate fictional art of the age.

George Garrett

LANGUAGE AND NARRATIVE IN THE BIBLE

Throughout antiquity, there was a common belief in the value and efficacy of language. For ancient peoples, words were alive and vital; they had an independent existence of their own and did not depend upon those who uttered them. Words, it was commonly agreed, possessed a unique force and power, almost a character. When released in speech, they could have an indelible effect. Thus, when used in magic formulae, words had the potency to do things; they could cast spells and remove spells. The very word *spell*, as in *spellbound*, testifies to the galvanizing power of words and language and story.

Among Native Americans there is a clear understanding of the power of language to do things, to effect change. A Chippewa song to assist the dying testifies to the power of language to transform life from physical to spiritual, from this world to the next, and it suggests also an amazement at the power of the song:

> You are a spirit,
> I am making you a spirit,
> In the place where I sit
> I am making you a spirit.

In most primitive song, the words are part of a complex unit. The words are often sung, and the singing is usually accompanied by some kind of action such as clapping, stamping the feet, or dancing. Words and music and movement together constitute a single entity. Thus the power inherent in the words, which is never separate from action, is made clear. As early as 2850 B. C. an Egyptian myth told of creation by the power of the word, and, as recently as the twentieth century, a six-and-a-half-year-old child told Jean Piaget, "If there weren't any words, it would be very bad; you couldn't make anything." Words are treated with such great respect because they give a measure of mastery over a part of the world. They order the chaos and so create things. Surrounding what we thus express there is space, silence, mystery.

The ancient Hebrews reflect this nearly universal sense of the power of language. The Hebrew *dabar* ("word") is from a root which means "to get behind," "to push," and suggests therefore the projection forward of what lies behind, the translation into action of what is at first in the thought. In the Hebrew understanding, the word is effective: it accomplishes what it is spoken to do. A compelling example is the story of Isaac and his twin sons, Jacob and Esau (Genesis 27). The aged Isaac, now blind, asks his elder and favorite son Esau to bring venison, prepare a favorite dish, and then receive his father's blessing. The mother, however, conspires with her favorite son Jacob to steal the blessing. She dresses the delicate and effeminate Jacob in animal skins to imitate the feel and the smell of his rough and animallike brother. Thus clad, he brings the favorite dish to his father, whose suspicions of the quick success in the hunt are allayed by Jacob, who lies, "God helped me." Isaac then calls his son close to him so that he can be sure it is in fact Esau. His suspicion is aroused again. He asks pointedly whether it is in fact Esau, and Jacob assures him that it is. The father, although not entirely sure ("the voice is Jacob's voice, but the hands are the hands of Esau," he says), gives Jacob the blessing reserved for the firstborn. The blessing is no sooner spoken than Esau dramatically enters with the game. When it is apparent what has happened, Isaac and Esau are both shaken and helpless in the face of what cannot be altered: the words of blessing, now spoken, are already at work effecting what Isaac spoke them to achieve. Even though the blessing is obtained by deception and even though that deception is found out only seconds after the blessing was mistakenly given, it cannot be changed. The two pitiful figures, Isaac and Esau, to whom the reader's heart goes out, never suggest that the blessing can be canceled, abrogated, or altered. It was spoken and it stands, for words have power to accomplish things, and that power, when released, is independent of human control. Esau can only plead, "Have you nothing left for me?" and the father does the best he can with what additional blessing remains in him.

All words are effective, but most of all God's words accomplish what they are spoken to do.

> For as the rain cometh down,
> and the snow from heaven,
> and returneth not thither,
> but watereth the earth,
> and maketh it bring forth and bud,
> that it may give seed to the sower,
> and bread to the eater:
> So shall my word be that goeth forth from my mouth:
> it shall not return unto me void,
> but it shall accomplish that which I please,
> and it shall prosper in the thing whereto I sent it. (Isaiah 55:10-11)

The divine word always works, without fail. *Ruach* in Hebrew can mean "wind" or "breath" or "spirit." The words of God are not only formed by the expulsion of his breath but are charged with the live-giving vigor of His spirit. So it is no surprise to find in the Hebrew Bible that God created the universe by His word.

> By the word of the Lord were the heavens made;
> and all the host of them by the breath of his mouth.
>
> For he spake, and it was done;
> he commanded, and it stood fast. (Psalm 33:6,9)

The classic statement of God's creative word is the account of creation given in Genesis 1:

> And God said, Let there be light: and there was light. . . . (1)
> Let there be a firmament in the midst of the waters, and let it divide the waters from the waters . . . and it was so. (6-7)
> Let the waters under the heaven be gathered together unto one place, and let the dry land appear: and it was so. (9)
> Let there be lights in the firmament of the heaven . . . and it was so. (14-15)
> Let the waters bring forth abundantly the moving creature that hath life . . . And God created . . . every living creature that moveth. . . . (20-21)
> Let the earth bring forth the living creature after his kind . . . and it was so. (24)
> Let us make man in our image . . . so God created man. . . . (26-27)

The response to each command "and it was so" is not to be read as a surprise. Rather, creation follows naturally from the divine utterance. God said the word, and it happened. Moreover, in that simple, resounding *fiat lux* is heard the expression of the sovereign, unchallengeable will of the absolute and transcendent Lord to whom all nature, all creation is totally subservient.

Creation came from the word of the Lord, but it is not finished, for the creative and life-giving word of God is, in the thought of the Bible, a continuing experience.

> Then they cry unto the Lord in their trouble,
> and he saveth them out of their distresses.
> He sent his word and healed them,
> and delivered them from their destructions. (Psalm 107:19-20)

> He sendeth forth his commandment upon earth:
> his word runneth very swiftly.
> He giveth snow like wool:
> he scattereth the hoar frost like ashes.
> He casteth forth his ice like morsels:
> who can stand before his cold?
> He sendeth out his word and melteth them:

God's words above all are effective; and the test of a true prophet (that is, a speaker of God's words to His people) is whether or not what the prophet says takes place.

> The prophet, which shall presume to speak a word in my name, which I have not commanded him to speak . . . that prophet shall die.
> And if thou say in thine heart, How shall we know the word which the Lord hath not spoken? when a prophet speaketh in the name of the Lord, if the thing follow not, nor come to pass, that is the thing which the Lord hath not spoken, but the prophet hath spoken it presumptuously: thou shalt not be afraid of him. (Deuteronomy 18:20-22)

As these words from Deuteronomy imply, the speech of God can also be destructive:

> The voice of the Lord is powerful;
> The voice of the Lord is full of majesty.
> The voice of the Lord breaketh the cedars:
> Yea, the Lord breaketh the cedars of Lebanon. (Psalm 29:4-5)

> The heathen raged, the kingdoms were moved:
> he uttered his voice, the earth melted. (Psalm 46:6)

Jeremiah understood the word of God to be both destructive and creative.

> And the Lord said unto me, Behold, I have put my words in thy mouth.
> See, I have this day set thee over the nations and over the kingdoms, to root out, and to pull down, and to destroy, and to throw down, to build, and to plant. (Jeremiah 1:9-10)

In the prophets, the objective, dynamic character of the word of God is clear. The prophet is seized by a mysterious power which sometimes crushes and torments him ("But his word was in my heart as a burning fire shut up in my bones, and I was weary with forbearing, and I could not," says Jeremiah 20:9) and which sometimes fills him with joy. ("Thy words were found, and I did eat them; and thy word was unto me the joy and rejoicing of mine heart," says Jeremiah 15:16.) Thus the word is always greater than the prophet who speaks it. He receives the word only to transmit it; his function is to be a messenger who delivers the message of another: "Thus saith the Lord." In the process of transmission, however, the spoken word becomes a living person; the prophets are consumed with their message. Isaiah's lips must be cleansed so that they can give forth the divine communication (Isaiah 6:1-10). God's communication with Jeremiah is more direct and more intimate (Jeremiah 1:4-10). With Ezekiel, God is more dramatic as God invades completely and takes over Ezekiel's private life (Ezekiel 2:8-3:3; 24:15-18). Prophet and message become one, and the message is both word and event. Christians claim that this identification of person with word is seen and heard most clearly in Jesus Christ:

"And the word was made flesh, and dwelt among us, (and we beheld his glory, the glory as of the only begotten of the Father,) full of grace and truth" (John 1:14).

Historical Consciousness

A second feature of Hebrew religion, besides its understanding of the power of words and language, is its historical consciousness. The locus of God's speaking to His people is in their historical experience: He reveals Himself to them in their history. Others have believed that gods have directed their destiny, but the special characteristic of biblical faith is that it believes that God binds Himself to historical events to make them the vehicle of the revelation of His purpose. His people do more than listen or know intuitively; they experience Him and His power to rescue and set free. The knowledge of God is associated with events that occurred in human life which are interpreted in such a way as to reveal the nature of God and humanity. It is this rooting in history that differentiates biblical religion from that of other people of those times, whose literature exhibits no such interest in history.

History in the biblical understanding is not a succession of cycles or swings of a pendulum; it is a meaningful progress toward a goal. It is a story en route to a destination: the future in which the full purpose of God will be made clear. In this view, nature is not independent but is instead the servant of history. Even when images and metaphors are drawn from nature or borrowed from other places such as the Canaanite storm god Baal, they are always set within a historical context.

Given the understanding that God is known in history, which is moving toward a destination, storytelling is important, even essential, in preserving and setting forth this history. The language about God in the Bible is the language of narrative filled with pictures drawn from human experience and human society. The knowledge of God is the knowledge of His claim upon His creation, and this is not the private possession of the knower. According to biblical religion, knowing God is not holding certain ideas about God, but rather an event in the interaction between two personalities. This relationship is not a timeless or static one existing in the realm of ideas; rather, it is something which happens, and the characteristic word form in the language of the Bible is not the substantive but the word of action, the verb. God steps into the world He has made and acts. The knowledge of God was not something to be known but something to be done. Knowledge and truth involve things to be done: "If we say that we have fellowship with him, and walk in darkness, we lie, and do not the truth" (1 John 1:6). Living is seen pictorially as walking, and truth is something one is to do.

In the Bible, knowing is an event in the intercourse between two personalities ("To know" is a remarkably profound Hebrew euphemism for sexual intercourse). Thus the Bible is not a book of speculative theology. It says nothing about God as He is in himself nor of humanity as it is in itself. The Bible speaks only of God, who is from the first related to humanity and of humanity, which is from the first related to God. This two-sided relationship is not developed as a doctrine but is set forth as happening in a story. The relationship is such that it cannot be adequately expressed in abstract formulations, for it is not a static or timeless relationship. Rather, it changes and develops and progresses, not always in a smooth way or a clear direction.

Biblical theology, therefore, is essentially a theology of recital in which the biblical faith is confessed by narrating the formative events of Hebrew history as the redemptive work of God. (See G. Ernest Wright's *God Who Acts: Biblical Theology as Recital*.) The distinctiveness of the Bible consists in its close attention to the facts of history and tradition because these facts are taken to be the facts of God. Biblical theology is fundamentally an interpretation of history, a confessional narration of historical events as the acts of God, events which led backward to the beginning of history and forward to its goal.

The Old Testament presents five chief revelatory events in which the faith centers: the patriarchs who were called by God and who received certain promises from Him; the deliverance from slavery in Egypt in fulfillment of God's promises; the testing in the wilderness and the reception of the Law which was the formation of the nation; the conquest of Canaan, the land of promise, as a gift from God; and the establishment of the monarchy principally under David. Of these, the call and promises to the fathers, the deliverance from Egypt, and the gift of the land are central.

The New Testament continues this understanding. In it, Jesus Christ is a new event, yet He can be understood only in relation to the former events which depict what God was doing for His people. Of the experience of Jesus Christ, His life and teaching, His suffering and death, and His resurrection and gift of the Spirit are central. C. H. Dodd in *The Apostolic Preaching* (1939) has identified six elements in the core proclamation of the early Church as revealed in the book of the Acts of the Apostles: the new age, the time of fulfillment has come; the new age has come through the ministry, death, and resurrection of Jesus in accordance with the Scriptures; God has therefore exalted Christ as Lord; the existence of the Church is proof of God's gift of the Spirit; the Messianic age will soon be consummated in the return of Christ; and everyone must therefore repent. This proclamation is interpretative, yet it too takes the form of recital, based on an interpretation of the narrative of the Old Testament Scripture. A story is told and its meaning is expounded.

This biblical preference for narrative is in part a defense against the temptation of idolatry, which is understood as an attempt to confine God and His nature to human creations and formulations. The faith is greater than human attempts to express it, and the suggestive nature of narrative helps keep this fact clear. There is, however, more to this "salvation history" than the mighty divine acts of deliverance and rescue which establish security and hope. Biblical history is also filled with suffering, tragedy, defeat, war, destruction, disillusionment, and death. It is also the biblical confession that God can be active in each of these experiences: the whole of history can be revelatory.

Narrative rests upon the immensely rich mystery of time, or better, of temporality, for it is not merely a linear reaching; and narrative is the only adequate vehicle in which to carry the multivalent diversity of human experience. It is capable of yielding infinitely new meaning. In telling the biblical story, therefore, the narrators do not begin with universal laws or principles. God's action goes instead from the particular to the general. Universal history is made by the selection of a tiny and insignificant nation to be the light of the nations. In the telling of the story, moreover, God's presence is not always unambiguously revealed. The events of history are not confused with God's presence itself. God's presence (perhaps better His "coming," which is more dynamic) in history is that of the hidden God whose intentions always remain full of mystery to human sight. (See Isaiah 45:15; 55:8.) Yet the hidden God is also the one who comes at certain moments in time to demonstrate through certain events His being and His intention to set free. The events of history are not only a revelation by which God showed Himself to the world; they are also a redemption by which He saved the world.

The distinctive style of this narration of God's acts in history is simplicity. Erich Auerbach in *Mimesis* (1968) observes that in classical literary criticism the sublime style was always to be kept distinct from the low style. It was the distinctive greatness of Holy Scripture, however, that "it had created an entirely new kind of sublimity, in which the everyday and the low were included, not excluded, so that, in style as in content, it directly connected the lowest with the highest." Boileau described the opening speech of Genesis, "God said, Let there be light," as truly "sublime," with even something of the divine in it, because of the grandeur and immensity of the conception expressed in utter simplicity.

Even when the Bible speaks of secrets and riddles which are revealed to very few men, it does so in unpretentious language so that all who are filled with faith can understand. St. Augustine described the proper spirit of those who approach Scripture: "They should strive toward what is incomprehensible not as if they were going to comprehend but as if they were about to participate." Only the intellectually arrogant are excluded from such a view; the humble and simple are at no disadvantage.

The Design of Biblical History

The grand scheme of history that is recorded in the Bible is radically different from classical histories. It has an overall imaginative structure, from a retrospective view of the beginnings of the universe to a prophetic view of the consummation at the end. M. H. Abrams in *Natural Supernaturalism* (1971) identifies five characteristics of biblical history which distinguish it from Graeco-Roman views: It is finite, not cyclic, so that its events occur only once; it has a sharply defined plot with a beginning, a middle, and an end; there is God the "hidden author," who has planned it and who directs it all; the key events are abrupt, cataclysmic, and mark a drastic, even an absolute difference; and the biblical pattern is symmetrical, beginning with the creation of heaven and earth and ending with the creation of a new heaven and a new earth.

The story begins in a garden (Genesis), but it ends (Revelation) in a city. The setting progresses from rank, untamed nature into which the man was put to control and tend, to the city, the ultimate expression of humanizing civilization which includes the garden of paradise within it. Northrop Frye, in the *Anatomy of Criticism* (1971), has suggested that there are three principal organizing metaphors in the Bible: the garden, the sheepfold, and the city; and the last vision includes them all. In the new Jerusalem a river of pure water flows from the throne of the Lamb through the center of the city in a garden or park with trees on both sides. Human work on the natural, vegetable world produces the garden; human work on the animal world yields the domestication of sheep and the sheepfold; human work on the mineral world shapes the stones of the solidly built city of God.

Throughout the story runs the experience of the presence of God in the midst of His people. The presence is ever real, ever elusive. This elusive presence (see Samuel Terrien, *The Elusive Presence*, 1978) can best be captured in a narrative describing the experience of the continuity and change of a God whose story changes in a wonderful way. The stupendous saga as described by St. Paul begins with Adam and Eve, since whose time the whole of creation has been awaiting the coming of Christ, Who will end all travail. It is a story the conception of which is so grand that St. Paul felt that we but see "in a glass darkly."

Varieties of Narrative in the Bible

While the Bible can be read as a grand and coherent history, most biblical scholars, especially for the last two centuries, have identified not only books in various genres but various strands of material underlying the existing forms of the individual books. The Hebrew Bible is divided into the Law, the early and the later Prophets, and the Writings. The Law books also tell the history. The Writings include Ruth (sometimes described as a short story), Jonah (a droll tale), and Esther (a grim patriotic record). The other Writings—poetry, proverbs, wisdom writings—are not of concern here, nor are the specific books of Laws nor much of the writings of the Prophets. The New Testament begins with the Gospels according to Matthew, Mark, Luke, and John and continues with the Acts of the Apostles. Letters by St. Paul and others follow. For Christians, the Bible concludes with the Apocalypse or the Revelation of St. John the Divine. Of the New Testament books, the Gospels and specifically Jesus' parables are of interest here.

The narratives of Genesis as we now have them are masterfully handled. They generate interest, as do all stories, by arousing tension and then releasing it. They are not "historical" in the modern sense of the term; that is, they do not make critical assessment of their sources. Rather, traditional material is worked together to form a coherent and compelling pattern. For example, Genesis 1-11 gives a universal setting for the more particular stories of one people, Israel, which follow.

Genesis 1 and 2 present, it is often observed, what appear to be two rather separate and distinct accounts of creation, the first chapter (thought to be the more recent) giving a lofty conception emphasizing the power given to men and women over all creation; the second chapter (thought to be the older) provides a smaller conception emphasizing human weakness and affinity to the soil. The first chapter tells the familiar story of the week of creation culminating in the Sabbath; the second chapter gives no notice of time. The first chapter begins with a watery chaos, like Babylonian stories of creation; the second chapter begins with a waterless wasteland, like the Canaanite stories. In the first chapter male and female are created together on the "sixth day." In the second chapter, God makes the man, then wonders where to put him; so He makes a garden. Seeing that the man is unhappy alone, He makes the animals; and when none of them serves as a proper companion, He finally creates the woman. Thus creation is bracketed by the two human beings.

Yet the two disparate traditions are so joined that many readers are not aware of any discrepancy. Chapter 1 is an ideal beginning for the grand story which follows. Its description of creation marks the dawn of history, just as the story itself in Genesis 1 may have been partially shaped by the observation of the dawning of the day, from the twilight slowly revealing the outlines of the earth to the emergence of the sun, the vegetation, and the creatures of earth, chief among which, we believe, is humanity.

The narrative continues with the fall of humanity into a state of sin, disobeying the command of God. (Every paradise has one thing which must not be done, G. K. Chesterton observes in *Orthodoxy*, a "doctrine of conditional joy.") Upon discovery of the sin, God questions first the man, forcing an admission of guilt from him, and then questions the woman, forcing an admission of guilt from her as well. The serpent is not questioned (God does not converse with creatures other than human) but is rather cursed to crawl on its belly. Later, in talking to the man God curses the ground too, but He does not curse the two people; He only punishes them. Before, the account suggests to many readers, the man and the woman were equal. Now, after the fall, a hierarchy is set up: male dominates the female. All relationships have been distorted by the disobedience: between humans and animals, between mothers and children, between husbands and wives, between male and female, between man and the soil, between man and his work. In an expression of concern, God clothes the couple and sends them, thus protected, from the garden.

Wickedness persists, and the world declines into the chaos out of which it was formed. Order had so degenerated that "the sons of the gods" had intercourse with human women and created a race of giants, the Nephilim. This bit of uncharacteristic and undisguised mythology is included in the biblical account to indicate the depth of the world's descent into evil. The great flood comes to destroy and to cleanse for a new beginning. Noah and his family alone are preserved; everything else dies. The account of the flood is a carefully organized chiastic plan:

1 Order disintegrates	6 God remembers and storm stops
2 God's address	7 Birds sent from the ark
3 Command to build the ark	8 Command to leave the ark
4 Entrance into the ark	9 God's address
5 Storm rises and rages	10 Restoration of order
and swells to its climax	

This crisis passed, God commands the new family, as at the beginning, to be fruitful and increase. The survivors, however, are no longer required to be vegetarian; meat-eating is allowed, apparently as a concession to the less-than-perfect condition of the race. Finally, the rainbow is set in the sky as a sign of the divine promise never again to destroy all creatures in such a flood.

As the story of the primeval history began with the creative power of speech, so the primeval portion concludes with the story of the interruption of the building of the tower of Babel (Genesis 11:1-9). On the surface it is a childish explanation of the diversity of human speech, but on a deeper level it illustrates the potentialities of language and imagination which are corrupted by human pride. The people in Shinar (Babylon) said to each other, "Let us make brick . . . let us build us a city and a tower, whose top may reach unto heaven; and let us make a name [for ourselves]." The Lord Who "came down to see the city and the tower" said, "Behold, the people is one, and they have all one language; and this they begin to do: and now nothing will be restrained from them, which they have imagined to do." So he confused their language and scattered them (this theme is not uncommon in world mythology; see Theodore Gaster, *Myth, Legend, and Custom in the Old Testament*, 1969).

Next, the story of a particular people is told against this large background of universal primeval history. Abraham is summoned to uproot his family, leave his ancestral land, and travel to a place which God will show him (Genesis 12). It is the archetype of an epic journey in search of spiritual truth. In Genesis 15 there is a deeply disturbing account of the covenant which God makes with His chosen patriarch. In a stunned trance, the chosen man dimly perceives the terror of the choice. God promises the aged Abraham that he will make him into a great nation. The suspense mounts: how will this promise be fulfilled? Perhaps it will be through a slave born in Abraham's house? No, says God; it will be a child of Abraham's own. A substitute then, begotten with an Egyptian slave girl, Hagar? No, says God at length; a child of Abraham and Sarah. The aged husband and wife laugh.

The promised son, Isaac, is born, but the anguish of being chosen by God is still to increase. In the profoundest personal experience in the entire history of the patriarchs, Abraham is commanded by God to sacrifice his long-awaited son (Genesis 22). The object of the ordeal seems to be to test Abraham's faith in God's ultimate purpose. It was one thing to start for an unknown promised land; it is another to maintain confidence when all seems lost. It is a powerful and compelling story, told with a minimum of modifiers. As is usually true of oral tales, there is no report of internal emotion, yet the emotion is there, just below the surface, revealed in small physical details and fragments of conversation.

In what Søren Kierkegaard called "the teleological suspension of the ethical," God tells Abraham to "take your son Isaac, your only son, whom you love" (each phrase builds the impact of what is shortly to follow). In Moriah, Abraham is to offer Isaac as a sacrifice "on one of the mountains which I will tell thee of." The vagueness of the place recalls the vagueness of the location of the Promised Land earlier. Abraham obeys, and, although there is no report of his feelings, the reader sees his stunned reaction in the brief phrases which describe his actions. Nearly in silence, we imagine, he "rose up early in the morning" (before anyone could ask what he was doing or where he was going), "saddled his ass, and took two of his young men with him, and Isaac his son" (how long he had waited to use that phrase, "his son"), "and clave the wood for a burnt offering, and rose up and went. . . ."

Three days later they reach the appointed place, and Abraham speaks at last. He tells the two men to wait with the animal. "I and the lad" (no name now—Abraham is distancing himself from the act) "will go yonder and worship and come again to you." It is a deliberate lie to allay any suspicion, yet it is in fact the truth. Abraham then lays the wood upon "Isaac his son," treating the child like a beast of burden or a sacrificial animal—distancing himself still further from the dreadful act. He takes, the text says leanly and grimly, "the fire in his hand and a knife," and they both go together. There is a shared humanity and paternal relationship nevertheless. The boy, aware that something is not right, asks in innocence and in fear, "Where is the lamb?" The father in a subtle evasion says, "God will provide himself a lamb," meaning Isaac, yet, unknown to him at this point, foreshadowing what in fact will happen.

At the nameless place, Abraham builds an altar, lays out the wood, dreading all the while, we may imagine, what must inevitably follow. Unable to delay the act any longer, he binds his son and "laid him on the altar upon the wood." Then comes the terrifying sentence, "And Abraham stretched forth his hand, and took the knife to slay his son." The name of the child is not given here, but the relationship is stressed. Such is the terror of the act for father and for son. The resolution is quickly told. At the last moment a voice calls out Abraham's name twice (so there will be no mistaking the urgency of the command). Already the language softens. He is not to lay his hand upon the boy nor do anything to him, for Abraham's faith is proved. He looks up and finds a ram caught in a thicket and offers that instead of his son.

Finally, the praiseworthy story of Joseph (Genesis 37-50) provides a re-markably suitable conclusion to the book of Genesis. The story reflects a high degree of narrative skill and describes a world in which God is remote. The human plane is the primary focus of the story. Earlier in Genesis, God con-versed directly with people; dreams and visions were clear and understand-able. Now, God is further off and does not speak directly; dreams require an interpreter. A gifted man becomes the intermediary and replaces the angelic messenger. Although God is no longer visibly active in human affairs, His function is nevertheless crucial: to remember, to keep in mind, and so to keep alive the events of human history. A principal theme of the story of Joseph is knowledge versus ignorance (or forgetfulness)—particularly God's knowl-edge, which is His providence, in the face of human (and apparently also divine) forgetfulness (Genesis 40:23).

The two planes of the story are held together by an effectively dramatic device whereby the reader is cast in a role analogous to that of God: The reader remembers while others forget. The reader keeps Joseph in mind and recalls promises previously made to him. The reader knows God's plan before Joseph does, and the reader, moreover, knows how the story will turn out, for the descendants of Joseph still live, and in them he is alive. The reader thus sees the overarching purpose not by hearing about it but by participating in it; he is thereby convinced of the certainty of the patriarchal traditions. From the beginning, however, the reader's attitude toward Joseph is complex, since he can sympathize both with the point of view of the brothers, who think Joseph an unsufferably proud tattletale, and with that of the father, who loves him because "he was the son of his old age."

Joseph dreams twice, and the dreams are told not only to Joseph's family but also to the reader, who, like Jacob, remembers and waits to see what will happen. Reuben saves Joseph from death by putting him into a pit, intending to rescue him when no one is looking. In the absence of Reuben and at the urging of Judah (the identities of the less cruel brothers are given), Joseph is sold. Reuben returns to the pit and finds Joseph gone; the reader sympa-thizes with Reuben, but knows what has happened and is confident that Joseph lives.

In Egypt, Joseph is betrayed by Potiphar's wife, but the reader knows he is innocent. In prison he grows into a responsible leader, and when he is at last released, he becomes thoroughly Egyptian. Meanwhile, his father remains alive and grieves for his son whom he thinks dead. When the brothers come to Egypt seeking grain, the reader watches Joseph, knowing, unlike the broth-ers, his true identity. When Judah accurately reports the conversation with his father, the brothers' new honesty is sure, and the reconciliation takes place. The reader sees the story from God's point of view, not from that of any one character, knowing what is happening in Egypt and in Canaan, remembering the events of the story, responding to the devices of paradox and symmetry, and seeing the pattern as it emerges from the events. Yet the reader is more than a close listener to a skillfully told narrative; he is also a participant in the theological point which the story makes: that there is a pattern and a masterful creative hand constantly at work in men's affairs.

Finally, however, there is surprise, for the reader is not, after all, omniscient. We do not know what happened to Potiphar's wife nor why Judah's sons displeased God. Most of all we are not fully prepared for the new information about the sale of Joseph that the brothers impart to him and to us in Joseph's presence:

> We are verily guilty concerning our brother, in that we saw the anguish of his soul, when he besought us, and we would not hear; therefore is this distress come upon us. (Genesis 42:21)

We did not know this before, and the depth of the agony of the parting was more cruel than we had suspected. Thus the reader is above the events of the story but beneath the realm of God. The reader is, after all, not quite like God, and there can still be surprises.

The narrative portions of the New Testament are the four Gospels and the Book of the Acts of the Apostles. The Gospels are more interesting for students of literature because they represent a peculiar Christian genre, the Gospel. Contrary to earlier opinion, the Gospels now seem related to the literature of the time and are perhaps Christianity's adaptation of the Graeco-Roman genre of didactic biography.

Of the four canonical gospels, that according to Mark was probably written first, about A.D. 65-70; Matthew and Luke were written about 80-90; John about 90-100. The first three—the "synoptic" gospels (Greek: "one view")—share a common chronology and viewpoint. The Fourth Gospel has its own chronology and point of view which are impossible to reconcile completely with the synoptic accounts.

The synoptics, beginning with Mark, edited and arranged already-existing material from narrative and discourse traditions so that the climax of Jesus' life—his death and resurrection—are shown to be the climax of the gospel account. The gospels are therefore not biographies in the modern sense of the term, for they omit most information about Jesus' childhood and about early influences on him and concentrate instead on his death and resurrection. Half of Mark's gospel, for example, is given to the telling of the last seven days of Jesus' life.

In the synoptics there is a basic agreement as to the order of events and the kind of teaching which Jesus engaged in: sayings interspersed with parables. There is considerable duplication and overlapping between the three, but there are also some noteworthy differences. The infancy narratives in

Matthew and Luke are quite different; Mark has none. Mark omits nearly all of the sayings of Jesus. The relationship between the three synoptic gospels is a continuing subject of scholarship and conjecture.

The synoptics suggest that Jesus' ministry lasted one year (only one Passover is mentioned); the Fourth Gospel suggests that his ministry lasted three years (three Passovers are mentioned). Furthermore, the exact order of events during his ministry is not the same. In the synoptics, for example, the incident of Jesus driving the moneychangers from the temple occurs at the beginning of the last week of his life as a prelude to the Passion, while in the Fourth Gospel, the incident takes place at the beginning of Jesus' ministry as a prelude to his whole work. In the synoptics, the Last Supper is a Passover meal; in the Fourth Gospel it occurs earlier, and Jesus dies as the Passover lambs are being killed. In the synoptics Jesus teaches by short sayings and parables; in the Fourth Gospel he is given to long discourses in the pattern of miraculous sign followed by a long discourse of explanation and explication.

The approach of the gospel writers, then, was to take the material about Jesus' life available to them and to arrange it freely and creatively into a coherent, forceful narrative which set forth their understanding of what that life meant. That the four accounts do not entirely agree in style, spirit, and approach is a testimony to the creativity and imagination of their authors. Chronological consistency and factual authenticity are less important than the authors' interpretation of the meaning of Jesus Christ.

Bibliography

Auerbach, Erich. *Mimesis: The Representation of Reality in Western Literature.*

Frei, Hans. *The Eclipse of Biblical Narrative.*

Gros-Louis, K. R. R., J. S. Ackerman and T. S. Warshaw, eds. *Literary Interpretations of Biblical Narratives.*

McDonald, D. B. *The Hebrew Literary Genius.*

Moulton, R. G. *The Literary Study of the Bible.*

Petersen, Norman R. *Literary Criticism for New Testament Critics.*

Price, Reynolds. *A Palpable God: Thirty Stories Translated from the Bible with an Essay on the Origins and Life of Narrative.*

Robertson, David. *The Old Testament and the Literary Critic.*

Speiser, E. A. *Genesis.*

Talbert, Charles H. *What Is a Gospel? The Genre of the Canonical Gospels.*

Terrien, Samuel. *The Elusive Presence: Toward a New Biblical Theology.*

Wright, G. Ernest. *God Who Acts: Biblical Theology as Recital.*

Philip H. Pfatteicher

NARRATIVE ELEMENTS IN SIX BOOKS OF THE OLD TESTAMENT

Genesis, Exodus, Judges, Job, the Song of Solomon, and Ezekiel represent the major literary types found in the Old Testament. The first three are narratives, each very different in structure and historical scope; Job, both prose and poetry, represents Hebrew wisdom literature; the Song of Solomon, the Bible's most sensuous book, is a collection of lyrics; Ezekiel is prophecy: visionary, vivid, oratorical. To study narrative elements in these six books is to confront many forms of narrative and many purposes for their use.

When attempting to understand the Bible as literature we must keep in mind that we are not dealing with texts of which the history of composition is known with any certainty. We do not know, for example, through how many centuries of oral transmission the stories of Genesis passed before they were committed to writing. Nor do we know precisely how the many stories in this book came to be collected into the Hebrew text now established. Scholars, adapting linguistic evidence, have devised somewhat differing theories of authorship and editorial revision for each book of the Old Testament, but these theories are subject to change as new evidence from archaeology or text analysis is presented. Thus, when we speak of the "structure" of one of these books, or of any piece of narrative therein, we are addressing the arrangement of words in the particular text we are using (if we are interpreting one of the many English translations, then what we conclude is modified even further. When we speak of structure, we are not in any valid way stating authorial intent. In the present analysis, structure refers to perceived patterns of thought, imagery, and the like that convey kinds of meaning familiar to modern readers and considered reasonable by Biblical scholars.

The following analyses of narrative are based largely on the texts of the Authorized (King James) Version (English, 1611), the English Bible in longest continuous use and of greatest impact on English-speaking writers. However, significant conflicts between the Authorized Version and more recent scholarly opinions will be noted, where pertinent.

Genesis

Encompassing in less than forty thousand words the history of the world from Creation to the settling of the descendants of Jacob in Egypt, this narrative conveys both the sweep of time and the distinct personalities of the Hebrew patriarchs; both the incomprehensible power of Yahweh and the very human moods of the Lord, manifested in discourse with human beings. Genesis is a narrative of powerful, litanylike repetitions such as the catalog of the days of Creation (Chapter 1), the listing of the generations from Adam to Noah and from Noah to Abraham (5:10-11); it is also a narrative of sudden halts in the chronological flow, oases where we focus for a moment on individuals, including Nimrod, "a mighty hunter before the Lord" (10:9), and Lamech, who cried out, ". . . I have slain a man to my wounding, and a young man to my hurt" (4:23).

For most of its fifty brief chapters, Genesis retells key incidents in the lives of a few people, particularly Adam, Noah, Abraham, and Jacob, important in Jewish history not so much for their deeds as for the specific words of command or promise they received from Yahweh—words of power to mold the future. The structural unity of Genesis derives primarily from the fulfilled expectations engendered by these words. The statement "And God said, Let there be light: and there was light" (1:3) establishes the pattern of effective divine speech which continues through the book, the Lord speaking to man not always the expected message at the expected time (for example, the Lord's sentence of alienation, not death, to Cain, or the Lord's declaring that ninety-year-old Sarai [later Sarah] would give birth), but always the resonant message at the necessary time. Besides structural unity, the use of speech to reveal divinity characterizes Yahweh as empathetic, reflective on and concerned for creatures. The use of speech not only makes Yahweh appear accessible to humankind, but also enables the narrator to present a few bits of interior monologue which open to us, very slightly, the mind of God. The first of these occurs just before Yahweh expels Adam and Eve from Eden:

> And the Lord God said, Behold, the man is become as one of us, to know good and evil: and now, lest he put forth his hand, and take also of the tree of life, and eat, and live for ever . . . (3:22),

a statement which, however we interpret Yahweh's motives, reveals the divine action to be performed out of design rather than in hasty wrath or vengeance.

Accompanying the emphasis on speech, intimate dialogue in particular, is the notable lack of visual or tactile description. The flow of events and critical speeches does not stop so that a person or place may be evoked in colors and textures. Adjectives and adverbs are few. The only noteworthy description in Genesis is of Noah's ark, the dimensions and materials of which are specified in Yahweh's command to Noah. Setting, however, is very important, although within any story very few objects, persons, and conditions will be mentioned. The sense of place is characteristically evoked by naming familiar locales (the plains of Mamre, the city of Nahor, and so forth), a tactic more meaningful to the people of the region than to us, or landmarks (such as water wells and stone pillars). Because they are so few, almost all noted objects take on symbolic importance, especially if they are used in more than one story (for example, the wells by which both Rebekah and Rachel were found). The very naming of objects from Genesis conjures up remembrance of the stories which contain them: the serpent, the olive leaf, the ram in the thicket, the mess of pottage, the coat of many colors.

The one type of description about which Genesis is precise is ritual or quasiritual description. The building of the ark falls into this category, as does Abram's sacrifice (15:9-11), which precedes his covenant with Yahweh, and the instructions by which wives are obtained for Isaac and Jacob in Padan-Aram. Perhaps the ritual atmosphere is also responsible for the preoccupation with specific number prevalent throughout Genesis: the exact dimensions of the ark, the exact ages of all the generations of Adam, the number of animals for sacrifice, the exact number of armed men in Abram's household, the length of journeys, and so on. Even more impressive than the numbers is the profusion of personal names, a device perhaps even more effective than the naming of places for instilling in the reader, ages after the events, a feeling of identification with figures whose names, fathers' names, and children's names are all that have been recorded of their lives. To the modern English reader the names mean almost nothing, of course, except in the power of their sheer number to impress us with how fully was fulfilled Yahweh's commands to be fruitful and multiply, and Yahweh's promise to Abraham that his seed would "multiply . . . as the stars of the heaven, and as the sand which is upon the sea shore" (22:17).

Major Divisions of Genesis
Creation (I) (1). Thought by many scholars to have been written as late as 500 B. C. (from oral sources far more ancient), this chapter introduces us to God as speaker and seer. The advancing creation on each of the six days is set in motion by the words "And God said. . . ." After each creative burst the narrator comments, ". . . and God saw that it was good," thus introducing the reflective characteristic of God that eventuates in the drastic reconsideration of his Creation in the flood story. This chapter culminates in the creation of humankind: "male and female created he them" (1:27).

Creation (II) and Eden (2-3). Written as much as four hundred years earlier than Chapter 1, this section contains the familiar story of the creation of Eve from Adam, the Fall, and Yahweh's curses on man, woman, and serpent. This is the first of the typically intimate scenes set in named places with named characters conversing with Yahweh and using important objects.

Cain; the generations of Adam (4-5).

Noah (6-9). This section is marked by the ritual specificity of the building of the ark, the precise chronology of the endurance of the flood, and, perhaps most important, Yahweh's decision to "destroy man whom I have created from the face of the earth" (6:7), an act followed after the flood by Yahweh's rainbow-marked covenant to protect and nurture Noah's line.

The generations of Noah (10-11). This section includes, besides the precise chronology of the "begats," the cataclysm of the tower of Babel, by which, states Yahweh, man learns the limits of his power to effect his imaginings (11:6).

Abram (12-15). Here we read of the movement of Abram and his nephew Lot from Ur, of the Chaldees to Canaan, and their struggle to wrest a home from the people of the area. This section culminates in Abram's detailed sacrifice, after which Yahweh makes his first promise of greatness to Abram.

Yahweh's promise to Hagar (16).

Abraham and Sarah (17-18). Yahweh's covenant with Abram, now Abraham, and Sarai, now Sarah, including the command that male children be circumcised; this section includes the marvelous dialogue between Yahweh and Abraham in which the patriarch "haggles" to save the people of Sodom.

Lot and the destruction of Sodom (19).

Interpolated, anachronistic story of Abraham, Sarah, and Abimelech (20).

Birth of Isaac and Abraham's pact with Abimelech (21).

The sacrifice of Isaac and the ram in the thicket (22). This most suspenseful scene in Genesis reinforces the theme of Yahweh's closeness to man by dramatizing Yahweh's seeming abandonment of Abraham; one of several tests of faith in Genesis, this is the only one in which a man is asked to perform a socially abhorrent act to affirm his worthiness. The story, in its climax, demonstrates Yahweh's difference from pagan gods which indeed demanded human sacrifice.

The death of Sarah and Abraham's bargaining for burial ground (23).

Isaac and Rebekah (24). This chapter recounts the ritualistic fulfillment of Yahweh's command that a wife for Isaac be sought among the people of Abraham's home country, not among the peoples of Canaan. The focus of the narrative is on the precision with which the command is carried out.

The death of Abraham and the birth of the twins, Esau and Jacob (25).

Isaac and Abimelech (26); See Chapter 21. This reiteration of the pact with Abimelech shows the use of narrative repetition to emphasize a principle, here the ethnic purity of Abraham's descendants.

The blessing of Isaac (27). This story of Jacob's trickery of Esau establishes

Jacob's opportunistic personality and the enmity of the brothers; symbolically, the writers forecast the struggle between Israel and the Edomites, supposed descendants of Esau.

Jacob, Rachel, and Laban (28-29). This narrative repeats in the succeeding generation the ritual search for a wife among the peoples of Abraham's native land; the twist in this story is Jacob's enterprising sojourn among these people, during which he uses his subservience to Laban to accumulate wealth and power.

Jacob's children (30). In Rachel is exemplified again the barren woman eventually blessed with powerful offspring, and the younger sibling who achieves dominion over the elder, in this case Leah.

Jacob's besting of Laban and his return to Canaan (31). This story, by including the theft of Laban's household gods among Jacob's triumphs over his master, implies the superiority of Yahweh over the despised gods of Israel's neighbors; the story concludes with the ritual pact of friendship between these peoples.

Jacob's fear of Esau and his wrestling with the "man" (32). In one brief chapter the wealthy Jacob returns to contend with his fear of the tricked Esau, wrestles—symbolically and literally—with Yahweh, and emerges with a clear awareness of his task as Israel, father of his people. Incredibly resonant, this chapter blends the narrative devices of symbolic naming, divine speech, and ritual action.

The reunion of Jacob and Esau (33).

The rape of Dinah (34). This chapter powerfully reiterates the principle of nonmiscegenation and the consequences of violation for the neighbors of Israel.

The death of Rachel in childbirth and the death of Isaac (35).

The generations of Esau (36).

Joseph and his brothers (37).

Judah and Tamar (38). In this story the line of Jacob breaks the proscription against miscegenation, with disastrous results; importantly, however, the chapter closes with miscegenation established, because no longer do the descendants of Abraham seek marriages among the people of Padan-Aram. This point is enacted by the narrative, not specified.

Joseph and Potiphar's wife (39). This narrative is juxtaposed with the Judah story to demonstrate Joseph's greater self-control, and, therefore, his fitness to rule; as always, the point is made by implication rather than explicitly.

Joseph, interpreter of dreams (40).

Pharaoh's dream (41). The first confrontation between Israel and Egypt is dramatized here; not only is Joseph's indispensability to Pharaoh shown, but also his absolute piety in announcing the Lord as the source of his power.

The reconciliation of Joseph and his brothers (42-45). This story reemphasizes Joseph's strength to overcome both vengeance and loneliness. It also presents the desolation of old Jacob and implies, by contrast with his remarkable youth, the inevitability of misfortune.

The journey of Israel to Egypt (46-47).

Jacob's blessing on Ephraim and Manasseh (48). The poignant recapitulation of Jacob's life and his deliberate preference of the younger over the elder, thus reiterating this theme of Genesis.

Jacob's prophecies for his sons and his death (49).

Joseph's leadership and his death (50). Here are reaffirmed Joseph's reverence for his ancestors, his importance in Egypt, and his humility as leader. Genesis concludes with his prophecy of Israel's return to Canaan.

Exodus

Exodus differs from Genesis as narrative primarily in its narrower scope and in its focus on one principal character, Moses. Exodus spans the life of Moses from birth to mature manhood. Thirty-eight of its forty chapters span the little more than a year between Yahweh's call to Moses to return to Egypt to confront Pharaoh and the completion of the ark and tabernacle described to Moses by Yahweh at the foot of Mount Sinai. The first chapter rapidly accounts for the several generations between Joseph and Moses, with emphasis on the enslavement of the prolific Israelites by a new Pharaoh "which knew not Joseph" (1:8). Chapter 1 introduces the canny Israelite midwives, who thwart the dull-witted Pharaoh's order to murder male Hebrew infants. Chapter 2 tells another story of a clever Israelite outwitting the slower Egyptians: Moses' mother and sister contrive not only to save the infant, but to have him brought up in the Pharaoh's household (the Joseph theme repeated). The chapter then covers in a few verses Moses' growth to manhood and his escape from Egypt for killing an Egyptian. This chapter follows the model of Genesis in that the passage of many years is indicated by the telling of a few incidents from crucial stages of a character's life, the character's actions, rather than explicit statements by the narrator, revealing his personality.

The Exodus narrative, by opening with the acts of people rather than of Yahweh, gives the reader a different perspective on events from that held by the reader of Genesis. In the earlier book, the reader looks with Yahweh— the only ever-present character—on the actions of humankind, which to a great extent merely fulfill Yahweh's express commands and promises. The reader of Exodus works and travels with Moses and his people, who spend much of the book in doubt of and sometimes resistant to Yahweh's nature and commands. In the opening chapters, Yahweh appears briefly to watch over and bless the Israelites, but only in the third person; Moses, until his call late in life, does not even know that he is Hebrew and has no knowledge of Yahweh or of the Israelite tradition. Throughout Exodus the Israelites display little understanding of their God, while Abraham, Isaac, and Jacob remain little more than well-known names to them; the narrative places the people frequently at odds with Moses, their mediator, and emphasizes spatially the distance between Yahweh and the Israelites by locating the Lord's appearances on mountainsides and in other spots prohibited to all but Moses and his protégé Joshua. As readers we look up toward Yahweh rather than down upon his people.

The more earthly orientation of Exodus is reinforced by a style far more physically descriptive than that of Genesis. Where, for example, Genesis had been virtually barren of color words, Exodus abounds with them, particularly in the lengthy and repeated descriptions of the building materials of the ark and tabernacle:

> Moreover thou shalt make the tabernacle with ten curtains of fine twined linen, and blue, and purple, and scarlet. . . . (26:1)
> And thou shalt make fifty taches of gold. . . . (26:6)
> And thou shalt make curtains of goats' hair to be a covering upon the tabernacle. . . . (26:7)

Even more pronounced, as this passage shows, is the scrupulous specificity of the building instructions, their importance shown by the narrator's having Moses repeat them to the people, and to us, after Yahweh has given them to Moses, and the reader. The same specificity marks all the ritual instructions in the book, including the passover ritual given Moses by Yahweh (12:1-13) and the divine pronouncements of the law code to guide the wandering nation (primarily 20-23).

The entire book can be described as moving from a focus on the Hebrew people as enslaved, remote from their God, and in need of a leader, to an explicit affirmation of the law and care of Yahweh, as understood and maintained by the newly founded class of priests—whom Moses represents and idealizes. The scenes in which this charismatic holy man participates are chosen to demonstrate the different talents and virtues which the priest/leader must possess; these scenes also demonstrate the need for a special group of men trained to exercise these abilities. In his lengthy negotiations with Pharaoh (5-12), he shows the righteous persistence of the child of Yahweh; in his dealings with his "stiff-necked" people, he shows infinite patience mingled with just wrath (primarily 32); and most important, in his dialogues with Yahweh, he never relents in his obedience to the Lord nor in his care for his people. Again, Chapter 32 provides the best instance; after the Hebrews' building of the golden calf drives Moses to destroy the sacred tablets and Yahweh to thoughts of genocide, Moses' anger cools to allow him to negotiate for his people's reprieve:

> Wherefore should the Egyptian speak, and say, For mischief did he bring them out, to slay them in the mountains, and to consume them from the face of the earth? Turn from thy fierce wrath, and repent of the evil against thy people.
> Remember Abraham, Isaac, and Israel, thy servants, to whom thou swarest by thine own self, and saidst unto them, I will multiply your seed as the stars of heaven, and all this land that I have spoken of will I give unto your seed, and they shall inherit it for ever.
> And the Lord repented of the evil which he thought to do unto his people. (32:12-14)

Significantly, after this incident, the virtual climax of the story, the people display no further recalcitrance (in Exodus, at least) and the narrative moves surely toward the building of the ark and tabernacle in perfect accord with Yahweh's directions. The closing verse captures this mood of faith restored:

> For the cloud of the Lord was upon the tabernacle by day, and fire was on it by night, in the sight of all the house of Israel, throughout all their journeys. (40:38)

Judges

Much more so than either Genesis or Exodus, Judges evinces the explicit opinions of one or two editors collecting and interpreting the ancient stories. Attempting to account for the religiopolitical history of the many generations of Israel between the death of Joshua and the rise of Samuel, a first group of editors (c. 600 B. C.) juxtaposed well-known stories of military leaders, prophets, and assassins from different tribes of Israel within an interpretive framework which sees the defeats and victories of Israelite forces as God's punishment for idolatry or his reward for repentance and fidelity. Although none of these remarkable leaders is a judge in the strict sense (for example, Jephthah is a general, Deborah a prophet, Ehud a clever assassin), each "judges" Israel and its enemies by violently enacting the will of the Lord. These judges are made to seem to follow one another chronologically, usually after lengthy periods in which Hebrew idolatry has led to political subjection. The overall effect is of a roller coaster of Israelite fortunes. For example, the victory of Deborah and Barak over Sisera (4-5) is followed by the comment, "And the land had rest forty years" (5:31), only to be followed immediately by "And the children of Israel did evil in the sight of the Lord: and the Lord delivered them into the hand of Midian seven years" (6:1). Soon, however, Israel's "cries unto the Lord" (6:7) are rewarded by deliverance through Gideon (6-8).

The final chapters of Judges (17-21) establish a new theme, embodied in the refrain "In those days there was no king in Israel; but every man did that which was right in his own eyes" (17:6), noted several times in this section and in the very last verse. The direct intervention of Yahweh in this section is limited to a brief first-person response to a prayer the gathered tribes offer before taking the field against the erring tribe of Benjamin. The ideal of strict adherence to Yahweh, which had moved the first seventeen chapters, is replaced by the political ideal of monarchy as a cure for instability. The latter section in a sense contradicts the former, which includes the story of ambitious Abimelech (9-10), made king in Israel despite the wise counsel of Jotham, who argues against kingship as an unnatural order (9:7-20). These conflicting points of view have led scholars to speculate that Chapters 17-21 were added by later editors (c. 500 B. C.) of writings from monarchic Israel before its fall in 722.

Despite the editorial framework and the emphatic points of view, the individual stories of the heroes retain their distinctive narrative forms and the "judges" themselves their frequently unideal characteristics. The tales stand out from the chronological, didactic frame by their paratactic internal structure, their fairy-tale-like use of hyperbole, and their sharp focus on vivid dramatic events. Parataxis is striking in Jephthah's story (11-12:7), for example, in which two related events, Jephthah's rash oath (11:30-36) and the Ephraimites' fatal mispronunciation of "Shibboleth" (12:5-6), are juxtaposed without transitional comment; in the Samson story (13-16) the three examples of Samson's lust for pagan women are paralleled without the narrator's explicit pointing of the message. Hyperbole is best shown in the Samson story, also, in such memorable anecdotes as the hero's slaying of a thousand men with the jawbone of an ass, his pulling up the gates of Gaza, and his firing the crops of the Philistines. Another fairy-tale technique, the riddle, is also important in the Samson story; a third, the test of quality—here, the test of divinity—is central to the story of Gideon (6:20-40).

Dramatic intensity, particularly in the confrontations between men and women, is perhaps more responsible than any other factor for the power of these stories. Deborah and Barak, Jael and Sisera, Jephthah and his daughter, Samson and the woman of Timnath, Samson and Delilah: these stories are marked by spare, soul-revealing dialogue and such memorable acts as Jael's driving the nail into Sisera's temple, Jephthah's despair as his daughter dances to meet him, and Delilah's cutting of Samson's seven locks. In these stories it becomes clear—no narrator tells us—that Yahweh has judged his wayward people through men and women little more virtuous or clear-headed than we are, but capable of astonishing passion and decisive action at pivotal moments in tribal and national history.

The judges of Israel: Othniel (3:9-11), Ehud (3:15-30), Shamgar (3:31), Deborah (4-5), Gideon (6-8), Abimelech (self-proclaimed king, 9), Tola (10:1-2), Jair (10:3-5), Jephthah (11-12:7), Ibzan (12:8-10), Elon (12:11-12), Abdon (12:13-15), Samson (13-16).

Job

Job as a story is much like Plato's *Symposium* as a story: little happens, an extraordinary amount is said on a single topic, and the main character is unforgettable. However, where the Platonic debate takes place in a spirit of leisure and has a clear winner, the Biblical debate emerges out of a man's near-despair and ends in a silence which mocks the exchange of opinions. The words of Job, his three erstwhile comforters, and Elihu, the young self-appointed wise man, are swallowed up in the whirlwind out of which God speaks directly to Job.

Formally, Job consists of the lengthy debates in verse surrounded by two brief prose narratives, which to many scholars are later, unnecessary additions of material from a folk version of the story, but which others see as giving the reader needed detachment from the arguments of Job and his friends. The first prose piece presents us Job, the man of vast wealth, one "perfect and upright, and one that feared God, and eschewed evil" (1:1). From Job in his affluence we turn to God in his majesty, confronted by Satan, who declares that no human, even Job, can remain God's servant under great suffering. God tells Satan to do his will on Job to test the man's faith. When Job responds to the death of his children and the loss of all his property by worshiping God, the Lord allows Satan to test Job further by smiting him "with sore boils from the sole of his foot unto his crown" (2:7). Still Job praises God, even though his wife urges him to "curse God, and die" (2:9). At this point, Job's three friends, Eliphaz, Bildad, and Zophar, arrive to mourn with him. The prose narrative ends and the verse orations begin. At their conclusion, forty chapters later, prose again begins. We are shown Job, now at peace with himself and God, restored through the Lord's blessing to an affluence and prestige "more than [at] his beginning" (42:12).

The initial prose piece, presented without the narrator's explicit approval or explanation of God's action, gives the reader knowledge which neither Job nor his friends possess; thus, throughout the book we remain unconvinced by the friends' hammered argument that Job's misfortunes are God's punishments for his sins. Our knowledge also keeps us from fully identifying with Job's escalating resentment at God's plaguing of him (for example 7), his sense of remoteness from God (9), and his emerging self-righteousness in the face of God's injustice (31). The irony of the book's structure, however, is that Job's arguments are so eloquently stated that we do identify with his despondency. Not only is his quest for ultimate justice close to that of each person, but also his drive to know God and to be justified before him is perfectly embodied in the pounding rhythms and vivid reiterations of Hebrew verse:

> Did not I weep for him that was in trouble?
> Was not my soul grieved for the poor?
> When I looked for good, then evil came unto me
> and when I waited for light, there came darkness.
> My bowels boiled and rested not:
> the days of affliction prevented me.
> I went mourning without the sun:
> I stood up, and I cried in the congregation,
> I am a brother to dragons,
> and a companion to owls. (30:25-29)

The deeper irony of the book's structure, however, is that the very power of Job's language reveals that his confidence in his righteousness is actually pride in his ability to argue. He eventually silences his opponents in the debate—without converting them—and thereby sets himself up for a demonstration of divine power which forces him to admit the arrogance of his plea for what he had ignorantly called justice. Fittingly, God's demonstration is rendered in the form of a voice speaking "out of the whirlwind" (38:1). This poetry exceeds even Job's in eloquence:

> Hast thou entered into the springs of the sea?
> Or hast thou walked in the search of the depth?
> Have the gates of death been opened unto thee?
> Or hast thou seen the doors of the shadow of death?
> Hast thou perceived the breadth of the earth?
> Declare, if thou knowest it all. (38:16-18)

After Job realizes his fault and repents "in dust and ashes" (42:6), the concluding prose passage adds the final irony. Although the reader might well reason—as the three friends would—that Job's earlier rebukes have earned for him further afflictions, God instead admonishes the three and commands them to sacrifice on Job's behalf:

for him will I accept . . . ye have not spoken of me the thing which is right, like my servant Job. (42:8)

The reader is left to ponder Job's righteousness: does it consist only of his repentance, or is it embodied, ironically, in his violent refusal to see God as the simple rewarder/punisher which the three friends had pictured? The concluding prose leaves to the reader the task of justifying God's ways; we are merely told of Job's great blessings during the rest of his one hundred forty years.

Song of Solomon

Interpreters still dispute the structural coherence of this exquisite collection of lyrics, just as they debate whether the ancient writers and compilers intended it as religious allegory as well as a celebration of sexual love. Many see in the Song of Solomon fragments of a drama: dialogues between a pair of lovers, the woman's yearning for her beloved, and further dialogues between the woman and her skeptical fellow townspeople. Others see the Song of Solomon as the run-together elements of a fertility-cult ritual which somehow became integrated into Yahwism. Perhaps most now judge the Song of Solomon to be semi-independent love lyrics, held together by repeated passages, reiterated imagery, and a common theme: the desire for marriage between man and woman.

The repeated passages, recurring unexpectedly but in appropriate contexts, serve as *leitmotiven* for the entire Song of Solomon:

> His left hand is under my head,
> And his right hand doth embrace me.
> I charge you, O ye daughters of Jerusalem,
> by the roes, and by the hinds of the field,
> that ye stir not up, nor awake my love,
> till he please. (2:6-7; 3:5; and again 8:3-4)

The Song of Solomon ends, in fact, with a verse first heard in the woman's initial call to her lover:

> Make haste, my beloved,
> and be thou like a roe or to a young hart
> upon the mountains of spices. (2:17 and 8:14)

Providing even more coherence to the Song of Solomon than the repetition of whole passages are the reiterated images, which, drawn from nature and from man's handiwork, vividly convey the Song of Solomon's sensuality:

> I am come into my garden, my sister, my spouse:
> I have gathered my myrrh with my spice;
> I have eaten my honeycomb with my honey;
> I have drunk my wine with my milk:
>
> Eat, O friends; drink,
> yea, drink abundantly, O beloved. (5:1)

... his hands are as gold rings set with the beryl:
his belly is as bright ivory overlaid with sapphires. (5:14)

The Song of Solomon cannot be said to possess narrative unity, but it does set forth brief symbolic scenes which reinforce the drive for union so eloquently expressed by the lovers' images and their repeated praises and pleas:

I rose up to open to my beloved;
and my hands dropped with myrrh,
and my fingers with sweet smelling myrrh,
upon the handles of the lock.
I opened to my beloved; but my beloved had withdrawn himself,
and was gone:
my soul failed when he spake:
I sought him but I could not find him;
I called him, but he gave me no answer.
The watchmen that went about the city found me,
they smote me, the wounded me;
the keepers of the walls took away my veil from me. (5:5-7)

Come, my beloved, let us go forth into the field;
let us lodge in the villages.
Let us get up early to the vineyards;
let us see if the vine flourish,
whether the tender grape appear,
and the pomegranates bud forth;
there will I give thee my loves. (7:11-12)

Ezekiel

The uses of narrative within a work of prophecy—intended less as story than as exhortation—are amply demonstrated in Ezekiel. This most graphic and visionary of the Old Testament prophetic books employs four major narrative types: recollections of visions, instructions for rituals, allegories, and prophesied events. Empowering all four types are the words of Yahweh voiced by the prophet: words meticulously descriptive, threatening, and compassionate.

Although scholars now judge the book to be the work of later editors (as late as 250 B. C.) besides that of the real Ezekiel and his disciples, the book displays remarkable coherence of voice and tone.

Chronologically, the book is strictly linear in structure, Ezekiel taking us from the "fifth year of King Jehoiachin's captivity" (593 B. C.) to the twenty-fifth, with the recounted events being his dramatic calls from Yahweh and the visions, duties, and prophecies which follow each movement of the spirit. The early calls proclaim Ezekiel's role as prophet of the destruction of Judah (especially 3) and Yahweh's justifications and descriptions of that fall (to 33:21). After the fall occurs, the catastrophic visions are succeeded by pictures of restoration. The most eloquent of these envisions Israel as a tender flock cared for by the shepherd Yahweh (34); the most detailed (40-48) instructs the Israelites how to build the new temple in the new Jerusalem.

Ezekiel's visions of Yahweh are unmatched in the Old Testament for vividness and variety:

> And I saw as the colour of amber, as the appearance of fire round about within it, from the appearance of his loins even upward, and from the appearance of his loins even downward, I saw it as it were the appearance of fire, and it had brightness round about. . . .
> And when I saw it, I fell upon my face, and I heard a voice of one that spake. (1:27-28)

While the visions that precede the fall of Judah inspire terror, those that follow engender hope:

> And he said unto me, Son of man, can these bones live? And I answered, O Lord God, thou knowest. (37:3)
> Thus saith the Lord God unto these bones; Behold, I will cause breath to enter into you, and ye shall live. (37:5)

While Ezekiel fulfills part of his prophetic task by retelling to us his visions, he also reports Yahweh's command that he perform rigorous rituals to inflame others with repentance (as in 5). He must also undergo ordeals: dumbness, lack of movement for more than a year, and the sudden death of his wife:

> Also the word of the Lord came unto me saying,
> Son of man, behold, I take away from thee the desire of thine eyes with a stroke: yet neither shalt thou mourn nor weep, neither shall thy tears run down. (24:15-16)
> So I spake unto the people in the morning: and at even my wife died; and I did in the morning as I was commanded. (24:18)

Perhaps the character of the prophet is shown best in the contrast between the many verses which he uses to narrate his visions of the divine and the brief accounts of his own suffering.

Ezekiel is most effusive in speaking forth Yahweh's prophecies and the justifications for his acts. While God's plans are often stated directly, as in Chapter 20 wherein Yahweh recalls his bringing forth the Israelites from Egypt, at other, more memorable times extended allegories carry the doom. In Chapter 16, for example, Yahweh speaks of Israel as the maiden he has saved and cared for, only to see her turn harlot for the idols of all nations:

> Thou hast also taken thy fair jewels of my gold and of my silver, which I had given thee, and madest to thyself images of men, and didst commit whoredom with them. (16:17)

For this evil, proclaims the prophet,

. . . I will judge thee, as women that break wedlock and shed blood are judged; and I will give thee blood in fury and jealousy. (16:38)

In fury and in reflection, in pain and in hope, Ezekiel as narrative presents a history of prophecy and pivotal events during twenty years of Israel's captivity. Since Ezekiel is the prophet's own words, in structure if not fully in fact, the book also presents us with the character of a remarkable narrator: seer, sufferer, poet.

Bibliography
Bowra, C. M. *Primitive Song.*
Chase, Mary Ellen. *The Bible and the Common Reader.*
Good, Edwin M. "Job and the Literary Task," in *Soundings.*
Henn, Thomas R. *The Bible as Literature.*
Laymon, Charles M., ed. *The Interpreter's One-Volume Commentary on the Bible.*
Lord, Albert B. *The Singer of Tales.*
Olrick, Axel. "Epic Laws of Folk Narrative," in Alan Dundes' *The Study of Folklore.*
Thompson, Leonard. *Introducing Biblical Literature: A More Fantastic Country.*

Christopher J. Thaiss

RUTH, ESHTER, AND JONAH

Ruth

The book of Ruth is set in the time of the Judges (twelfth century B. C.). It is likely, although by no means agreed, that it was written much later, perhaps in the fifth century. The author is unknown.

The book falls rather naturally into six scenes which progress with dramatic complications and with increasing precision and focus: from the land of Moab, to the town of Bethlehem, to the harvest fields of Boaz, to the threshing floor, to the gate of judgment, to the marriage bed. Each of these scenes is punctuated by a blessing which is associated with that particular location and event. The first scene takes place in Moab. There Naomi, bereft of her husband and two sons, blesses her two daughters-in-law:

> . . . Go, return each to her mother's house: the Lord deal kindly with you, as ye have dealt with the dead, and with me.
> The Lord grant that ye may find rest, each of you in the house of her husband. (1:8-9)

The central verb in the blessing, "deal kindly" or "keep faith" or "recompense," is a key theme of this short book which emphasizes God's ultimate dependability and kindness. Each of the daughters-in-law does find a home, although each in a different way: Orpah apparently in the household of her late husband and Ruth in the household of her new husband, Boaz.

The second scene of the book is the only scene of the six which has no blessing of God or by God. The absence of a blessing emphasizes Naomi's grief and desolation; she can say no kind words because of what she has gone through: she has experienced God's perverse ways and assumes that she has been cursed. In place of a blessing, she says, ". . . the Lord hath testified against me, and the Almighty hath afflicted me." Whatever happens—good or bad—is God's doing, and He has chosen for her affliction and calamity. We smile at Naomi's wallowing in her grief, denying her name, responding to the women's greeting by a lugubrious emphasis on her bitter experience so that they will know and so that she will not forget even amid the joy of homecoming, "I went out full, and the Lord hath brought me home again empty." Actually, left to herself, she was fortunate enough, according to her own view of success and failure as directly related to reproduction, since she had a husband and bore two sons. God intervened, however, and brought her home empty, as if He did not want her to be happy. This nadir of the narrative is reached, paradoxically, in Naomi's home country.

The desolation, however, is only preparation for the abundant blessing which follows. God's affliction of Naomi and the absence of a blessing is replaced in scene three with not one but three blessings. In the harvest fields the reapers and Boaz greet one another with gracious words of mutual blessing—this farm is a courteous and reverent place. "The Lord be with you. And they answered him, The Lord bless thee" (2:4). Additionally, Boaz in his conversation with Ruth blesses her in what is a central verse of the book: "The Lord recompense thy work, and a full reward be given thee of the Lord God of Israel, under whose wings thou art come to trust" (2:12). Boaz thus acts to incorporate Ruth into the harmony of his farm.

Later, Naomi, learning of the man's generosity, blesses him in what is the third blessing of this scene, "blessed be he that did take knowledge of thee" (2:19), and, learning his identity, she says, "Blessed be he of the Lord, who hath not left off his kindness to the living and to the dead" (2:20). As she had exaggerated her grief earlier, now she swings to the other extreme and is suddenly—too suddenly?—confident of God's care, not only of the living but of the dead as well. She will not, however, let herself forget that she has experienced the death of her husband and her sons. Nevertheless, the scene abounds in good will and generosity, both human and divine. It is a harvest of blessing, signifying the harvest to come, both in the fields and in the lives of the principal characters of the story.

The fourth scene takes place at the threshing floor. When Boaz discovers Ruth in his bed, he says, "Blessed be thou of the Lord, my daughter. . ." (3:10). He is grateful most of all because the young foreigner was attracted not to the young farmhands but to Boaz himself: "thou hast showed more kindness in the latter end than at the beginning, inasmuch as thou followedst not young men, whether poor or rich," he says in almost disbelieving gratitude and astonished joy.

At the threshing floor not only is the grain being sorted out, but also the responsibility for Ruth and her line must be settled. The complication of the nearer kinsman is mentioned, and Boaz and Ruth sleep as the suspense builds. But there is promise here of a rich harvest—at night as Ruth asks Boaz to spread his skirt over her in adoption and in the morning as Ruth spreads her skirt to receive the grain that Boaz gives her. The sexual and the reproductive implications of these parallel gestures are obvious.

At the gate of judgment in the fifth scene, the suspense increases as the nameless nearer kinsman agrees to buy the field which belonged to Elimelech and all seems lost to Boaz. The kinsman balks, however, at also taking the girl who goes with the field, and the responsibility to provide descendants for Ruth and Elimelech belongs finally to Boaz. The kinsman proves to be no more of a lasting problem than the famine that drove Naomi and her husband from Judah. Boaz says in triumph,

. . . I have bought all that was Elimelech's, and all that was Chilion's and Mahlon's, of the hand of Naomi.
Moreover Ruth the Moabitess, the wife of Mahlon, have I purchased to be my wife, to raise up the name of the dead upon his inheritance, that the name of the dead be not cut

off from among his brethren, and from the gate of his place: ye are witnesses this day.
                                                                    (4:9-10)

This triumphant renewal takes place at the very "gate of his place," Bethlehem. In reply, the elders give a threefold marriage blessing:

> The Lord make the woman that is come into thine house like Rachel and like Leah, which two did build the house of Israel: and do thou worthily in Ephratah, and be famous in Bethlehem: and let thy house be like the house of Pharez, whom Tamar bare unto Judah, of the seed which the Lord shall give thee of this young woman. (4:11-12)

By this marriage the past and the present and the future are joined.

Finally, in the last scene at the marriage bed and the bed of birth, the women say to Naomi when Ruth has borne a son,

> Blessed be the Lord which hath not left thee this day without a kinsman, that his name may be famous in Israel.
> And he shall be unto thee a restorer of thy life, and a nourisher of thine old age: for thy daughter-in-law, which loveth thee, which is better to thee than seven sons, hath born him. (4:14-15)

Naomi and the dead son and the child and the daughter-in-law are all included in this blessing. Naomi takes the child as if it were her own (legally it would be considered Elimelech's) and nurses him. The neighbors, whom Naomi told to change her name from Pleasant to Bitter, give the child his name Obed and say, "There is a son born to Naomi." Ruth is all but forgotten in the joy of the birth.

A blessing, then, is central to each of the six scenes of this book. Ruth the foreigner blesses no one but is part of each blessing, either as recipient or cause. Moreover, the blessings are progressive. In the first scene, Naomi blesses her two daughters-in-law; in the second there is no blessing; in the third, things change and Boaz blesses Ruth and Naomi blesses Boaz; in the fourth Boaz blesses Ruth; in the fifth God is asked to bless Ruth and Boaz and their descendants; and in the sixth the women bless God for his goodness. Thus, throughout the story there is a clear progression, although it occurs not without complication and suspense. What appears to be simply good fortune is revealed to be the providence of God.

The story is built on contrast: famine and harvest, loss and possession, death and life. Yet in a deeper sense the story can be seen to have its foundation not in contrast but in the identity of humanity and nature, the wholeness of the cosmos, and the sympathetic actions of nature and people. The land is laid waste by famine, and Naomi's marriage is devastated by death. Both the land and Naomi are rendered infertile, and reproduction seems impossible. The land is revived by God's visitation, and Naomi is at last given a child again, although through her daughter-in-law. As the people celebrate the harvest, Naomi rejoices in the birth of a son.

The situation is a balance between the famine with which the narrative begins and the harvest with which it concludes. The famine has to do with agriculture and with human relationships, bringing death to the fields and to Naomi's husband and sons. The harvest has to do with agriculture and with human relationships, bringing life to the fields and to the now childless Naomi. Grief leads to joy, death to life, hopelessness to the abundant fulfillment of hope. The progression is from loss to desolation to good fortune to hope to redemption to possession.

There are careful balances in the narrative, and throughout the book the locations and the characters and the conversation and the events are set in pairs. The six scenes form three sets of interlocking frames: scenes one and six deal with marriage, its end and its beginning; scenes two and five deal with the town of Bethlehem; scenes three and four have to do with the harvest, both agricultural and human. There are two basic locations: Moab and Bethlehem. The conversation progresses by twos, often in question-and-answer form. This careful balancing of scenes, characters, events, and conversation suggests a basically stable—if not exactly static—picture. Such is the essence of the idyll. Moreover, this stability enforces the theme of the steadfastness of God, who works quietly and unobtrusively, but steadily.

The characters reflect the stability of God. Ruth and Boaz, like God, are steadfast and unchanging, gracious even toward foreigners—Ruth to Naomi and Boaz to Ruth. They reflect on an earthly level the dependability and the resolution of God. The number two, then, seems to be the organizing principle, and pairs seem to be the pattern of the narrative. Yet careful examination indicates that the pattern is more complex than simply balancing, and groups of not two but three are also of increasing importance throughout the narrative.

At the beginning, there are three pairs: Naomi and Elimelech, Mahlon and Chilion, Orpah and Ruth. Eventually three of those six people start out for Judah. On the way, Naomi three times tells her daughters-in-law to go back to their homes, but after the third command Ruth silences her with forceful oratory in three pairs of promises:

> . . . whither thou goest, I will go; and where thou lodgest, I will lodge: thy people shall be my people, and thy God my God: where thou diest will I die, and there shall I be buried. . . . (1:16-17)

After that speech, we imagine, Ruth and Naomi go on together in silence. Chapter two progresses with pairs of statements, but the chapter ends with a three-part conversation between Naomi and Ruth which prepares readers for the richness of the harvest which is soon to follow. The fourth scene repeats the pattern of the third. The conversation progresses in pairs until the last exchange between Naomi and Ruth.

In the last chapter of the book, scenes five and six, the number three becomes prominent. The scene at the gate begins with three pairs of lines. Boaz makes his threefold exclamation of victory, and the elders give the threefold marriage blessing. In scene six, at the birth of the child, the women give a threefold blessing of God, and the little family is expanded to three members: Boaz and Ruth and Obed.

The numbers in the narrative have contracted and expanded as the surprising work of God unfolds. Three had left Judah for Moab, and three had begun to return from there. Soon, however, Orpah went back and two returned to Bethlehem. The women there recognize only one—Naomi wallowing in her grief—but soon to the two, Naomi and Ruth, comes a third, Boaz; and by the time the story is finished, there are four: Boaz and Ruth and Obed and Naomi.

In this story it may be Naomi who is most like God. Throughout, she is the controlling character, even while she herself is being imperceptibly controlled by the ultimately gracious hand of God. In an essentially stable setting, she is the one character who changes. She moves from exaggerated sorrow to unexpected hope to triumphant joy, even as the story moves from famine to harvest, from death to life, from grief to promise.

Esther

The book of Esther is not a religious book; the name of God is not mentioned. Its spirit is a narrow fanaticism which is in marked contrast to the spirit of Jonah and Ruth. The meaning of the book of Esther is uncertain—whether to explain the popular folk festival of Purim; to tell a mythological tale of Elamite divinities; or to teach the virtue of fortitude. The one praiseworthy thing about the book is its plot.

Ahasuerus, when rebuffed by his queen, chooses Esther, a Jew, in her place. Esther's cousin Mordecai gives her information about a plot against the king, and the plotters are hanged. Haman, an overbearing anti-Semite, when Mordecai does not do obeisance to him, has the king execute a decree that all Jews in the kingdom will be killed on the thirteenth of Adar. Esther, after Mordecai's warning that she will not escape the extermination, plots against Haman by inviting him to a royal banquet. The king, who cannot sleep, has the book of history read to him as a soporific, but by chance the portion read reminds him of Mordecai's role in foiling the earlier plot against him. The king, seeing Haman, who is always hanging around, even at night, asks, "What shall be done unto the man whom the king delighteth to honor?" Haman, thinking that the man is himself, suggests royal apparel, the king's horse, and a crown. He is told to deliver these to Mordecai.

At the banquet Esther asks the king that the life of her people be spared and accuses Haman of being responsible for the plot against him. The king leaves the room; Haman beseeching Esther for mercy falls on her couch; the king returns, thinks Haman is about to ravish the queen, and has Haman hanged on the gallows that Haman had prepared for Mordecai. An edict is sent to the empire revoking the earlier condemnation, and on the thirteenth of Adar the Jews, instead of being slaughtered, do to their enemies what their enemies had planned against them. After the slaughter, at Esther's request, Haman's ten sons are hanged and what was to have been a day of desolation for the Jews becomes instead a day of feasting and gladness.

The plot is skillfully crafted. The rise of the Jews occasioned by the selection of Esther leads to Esther's replacing Vashti as the favorite. The revenge plotted by Haman as a result leads to his promotion over Mordecai. The revenge by the Jews occasioned largely by a series of chance happenings at night and at the banquet leads to Haman's replacing Mordecai on the gallows and Mordecai replacing Haman in the hierarchy of the empire.

Like the book of Jonah, Esther abounds in fantastic exaggeration. Ahasuerus gives a banquet to display his wealth, and the feast lasts 180 days. The candidates for Vashti's place are each prepared for a full year—six months with oil of myrrh and six months with "sweet odors and with other things for the purifying of women"—before they can spend a night with the king. Haman erects a gallows seventy-five feet high. When the reversal of fortune comes, the Jews kill five hundred in Shushan and then seventy-five thousand.

The book also abounds in letters and writing and repetitious legal-sounding language. It is a government and a society which delights in written records. Letters are sent to each royal province saying "that every man should bear rule in his own house" after Vashti's refusal to obey her husband. A writ is issued to the king's satraps and officers authorizing the murder of Jews on the thirteenth of Adar. The king has the chronicle of daily events read to him. The earlier writ is recalled and in its place are sent letters giving the Jews permission to kill anyone who might attack them. After the killing, Mordecai sends letters to all the Jews establishing the fourteenth and fifteenth of Adar as a time of feasting and celebration. Finally Esther has letters sent wishing peace and security to the Jews.

Most interesting of all perhaps is the characterization. The king is weak and dull and cannot think for himself; he must always be told what to do. He first appears presiding over an elaborate display of his wealth, and when "merry with wine" he orders the seven eunuchs to bring Vashti before him wearing the royal crown. She refuses to appear. The king is enraged and consults with his wise men, who tell him that Vashti's refusal to obey her husband's request will establish a dangerous precedent for every woman to disobey. (The insecurity of the male population could not be more apparent.) The king does what he is told. Later, it is suggested to him that he have beautiful young virgins brought to him so that he may choose one to replace Vashti. Again he does as he is advised. Haman suggests the royal decree

allowing the murder of all Jews, and it is done. The king comes to the banquet
to which Esther invites him and attends the following night also when invited.
He is not master in his own house, but is obedient to his wife. He wants to
honor the man who saved him from the traitors and asks Haman what to do.
At the second banquet he says to Esther all he ever says to her (he is not
much of a conversationalist), "What is thy petition . . . it shall be granted
thee . . . even to the half of the kingdom." When she says that her people
are to be slain, the king in his ignorance of what is happening in the kingdom
asks, "Who is he and where is he that durst presume in his heart to do so?"
He finds Haman flung across Esther's couch and misses the point of what is
happening. He is a sensualist who cannot think of anything other than physical
pleasure—banquets, drink, sex. It is suggested to Ahasuerus by one of the
eunuchs that Haman be hanged on the gallows he erected for Mordecai.
Ahasuerus then allows Esther to issue a writ in his name "in whatever terms
you think fit." Finally, therefore, it is a woman who rules in the kingdom.

Haman is a whining bully who seeks to insinuate himself into royal preferment; Mordecai is a faithful and good man. It is the women, however, who
have all the important ideas in the story. Esther is the heroine, but even she
needs to be urged by Mordecai not to think selfishly that she will be able to
escape if her people are killed. It is Vashti who is the one thoroughly honorable
character who refuses to be used by the king as a possession when he decides
to display his wealth.

Jonah

One of the most amusing stories in the Bible is the droll book of Jonah.
Unlike the other prophetic books, Jonah is not a collection of prophetic
utterances but is, rather, a narrative about an otherwise obscure eighth century
prophet (2 Kings 14:25). The author writes of him in the third person in a
satirical tone. Significant details are lacking, such as the name of the land
where the fish left Jonah and the name of the king to whom Jonah preached.
The language, which includes Aramaisms and a number of words not found
elsewhere in the Old Testament but which are found in later Hebrew literature, is not the language of the eighth century. The outlook is more like that
of the fifth century B. C.

The book is entirely narrative. There are no prophecies; even Jonah's
preaching to Nineveh is not recorded. Fantastic elements abound. There is
a series of divine miracles: the storm, the appearance of the big fish, the
miraculous growth of the gourd and of the worm that destroys it. The historic
city of Nineveh was never a "city of three days' journey" across, and no
Assyrian king was ever called "King of Nineveh." The title is as absurd as
"King of London." The entire city of Nineveh—both humans and animals—
is converted instantly once Jonah preaches there. The book is therefore perhaps best understood as a short story with a moral. The historical prophet

is used as the ridiculous representative of a narrow nationalism.

The narrative is one of symbolic action. Like Ruth, the book is an imaginative creation set in the remote past (or in a timeless setting) to teach God's mercy, power, and universality. It is a story primarily to instruct. Except for Jonah himself, all the characters in the story are likable—even the animals. The sailors in whose ship Jonah attempts to flee from God's command to go to Nineveh are devout; they pray when their ship is in danger and urge Jonah to pray also. When by lot they conclude that it is Jonah who has caused the storm, they row hard to bring the ship to land. When at last to save their lives and their ship they throw Jonah overboard (as he had begged them to do), they pray to God for forgiveness. When the storm ceases, they fear God, offer a sacrifice, and make vows.

The nameless "King of Nineveh," hearing but the sentence "Yet forty days and Nineveh shall be overthrown," immediately repents and causes all his city, even the animals, to do the same.

Jonah is a more complex and less likable character, an egotistical braggart, who is indiscreet in his boasting. God tells him to go overland to the east, so he gets on a ship going west. While the storm which he has caused rises, Jonah sleeps. The ship's master awakens him to his duty to pray. When the lot falls on Jonah, he brashly boasts, "I am a Hebrew; and I fear the Lord, the God of heaven, which hath made the sea and the dry land." This cant does not impress the sailors whom he had told earlier that he has fled from God's presence, apparently thinking that God is God only on a part of the dry land.

"What shall we do?" they ask. "Cast me forth into the sea; so shall the sea be calm unto you: for I know that for my sake this great tempest is upon you," he replies. The speech may appear generous, but we know that it is not; it is, rather, an attempt to implicate them in his death and so avoid God's call permanently, since he will appear to be submitting to God's control while making it impossible for him to obey the command. It is a marvelously diabolical plan.

After his imprisonment inside the fish, Jonah is left on dry land somewhere, and again God repeats his call, for Jonah has not gotten away. This time Jonah obeys. With one phrase from him, the city converts. Jonah is angry at his remarkable success and says to God in effect, "See, I told you this would happen. I know your character better than you do." Yet again he offers to have his life taken so that he will not have to face what he does not wish to see. Jonah, who had gone west toward the end of the Mediterranean (Tarshish is perhaps Cadiz in Spain) to avoid preaching to Nineveh, now in exaggerated obedience goes to the extreme east side of the city and sits down to sulk. A gourd grows miraculously to shade him from the heat of the sun, but the next day God prepares a worm to destroy it and sends an east wind to buffet Jonah.

The short book ends with a question: we are not told whether Jonah is convinced, and the question is left for each reader to answer. The mariners change their mind and throw Jonah into the sea. Jonah changes his mind and goes to Nineveh after all. The king changes his mind and repents. Even God changes his mind and "repented of the evil that he had said he would do unto them; and he did it not." The readers are left to change their minds as they will when they are thus confronted with the foolishness of nationalistic exclusivism.

Bibliography
Campbell, Edward F., Jr. *Ruth*.
Hals, Ronald M. *The Theology of the Book of Ruth*.
Moore, Carey A. *Ruth*.

Philip H. Pfatteicher

PARABLES OF JESUS OF NAZARETH

The relationship between Jesus and other storytellers of His time is only now beginning to be examined; but it does appear that the influence of others upon His stories was not significant. Although there are a few references to Jesus and Christianity in Pliny the Younger, Tacitus, Suetonius, Josephus, and the Talmud, knowledge of His biography is confined to the New Testament. He was probably born in Bethlehem of Judea (although some say Nazareth) *circa* 4 B. C.; Herod, who was king when Jesus was born, according to Matthew's Gospel, died in 4 B. C. In approximately A. D. 27-29 ("In the fifteenth year of the emperor Tiberius," Luke's Gospel dates it, but how those years are counted is uncertain), Jesus began a public ministry after being baptized by John the Baptist at about the age of thirty (Luke 3:23), although John 8:57 may suggest a later age. After an itinerant ministry of one to three years, preached principally throughout Galilee but finally within Jerusalem, He was executed by order of the Roman governor of Judea, Pontius Pilate, who was governor, A. D. 26-36. His followers first scattered, then gathered again, claiming to have encountered Him alive after His crucifixion. They collected and edited recollections about Him, His deeds, and His words, and thus began the Christian movement.

Jesus Himself wrote nothing. Information about His words and works come from His immediate followers and their disciples as recorded in the four canonical Gospels—according to Matthew, Mark, Luke, and John—of the New Testament. Although other apocryphal Gospel accounts also exist, their reliability is uncertain. Jesus, especially as the first three Gospels portray Him, was a master storyteller, teaching almost exclusively by means of parables; some were very brief (a sentence or two), others more extended. A parable is a species of figurative language which has at its heart a comparison; that is, a parable is a metaphor with a double and paradoxical purpose: it is meant both to conceal and to illustrate. It thus has a kinship to riddle and to allegory.

At the end of the nineteenth century, Adolf Juelicher advanced the view that Jesus' parables were not allegories with a series of connected references, but, rather, stories with one main point dealing with some general religious truth. Recent studies suggest that the line cannot be demarcated so sharply and neatly between allegory and parable, since they are related genres in which many intermediate states occur.

In both parable and allegory, one starts with an idea and looks for an image to represent it. In allegory, two stories are told simultaneously; when the allegory is successful, the elements in the story not only represent their referents but are also identical with them. A parable is less full in its correspondences; it is a self-contained story with internal coherence of its many elements, and the pattern of these events implies a connection with the world of ideas outside the parable. Parables, like certain metaphors, articulate a referent so new, so alien to consciousness, that the referent can be grasped only within the metaphor itself. To make this articulation, parables draw upon the familiar world and tell remarkably ordinary, human stories. Unlike myth, a parable tells a story which is absolutely possible in everyday experience. At the same time, however, parables surprise, for the familiar is used in a new way. Old ways of thinking are challenged, and resistance to change may impede one's understanding.

The meaning of the parable, therefore, is often at least partially hidden. Jesus told His disciples, "Unto you it is given to know the mystery of the kingdom of God: but unto them that are without, all these things are done in parables:/that seeing they may see, and not perceive; and hearing they may not hear, and not understand. . . ." (Mark 4:11-12). When a metaphor or parable contains a radically new vision, it yields absolutely no information until after the hearer has entered into it and experienced it from the inside. Metaphors and parables, therefore, are not only ways of communicating; they are also ways of knowing. There is no way around the parable; it cannot be done away with once one has perceived "the point" since the point of the parable is its story, the structure of the little drama, the plot. Parables are useful precisely because they do not tie down ideas and confine them; rather, parables release ideas and allow them to expand and grow.

The parable, then, cannot be reduced to one "meaning." Rather, it generates ever new meanings, arresting the hearer; and, by leaving the hearer in enough doubt about the precise application, teases him into thought that issues in action. The shortest, most condensed of all Jesus' parables is this:

> Again, the kingdom of heaven is like unto treasure hid in a field; the which when a man hath found, he hideth, and for joy thereof goeth and selleth all that he hath, and buyeth that field. (Matthew 13:44)

Three is a key number in storytelling; both secular and religious stories abound in threes, and this short parable is the first of a group of three (see also Matthew 13:45-46, 47-49). In this condensed parable, moreover, three critical moments emerge: finding the treasure, selling everything else, and buying the field.

In this example, the reader is impressed with the good fortune of the man who found the treasure (albeit wondering whose it had been and why it got hidden away and whether the discoverer had a right to it), on his joy in selling all that he had, and on his triumph, for no one else got to the treasure first. Beyond that, the reader is expected to see more. The parable tells of the encounters which form our experience; they are the chance encounters which revolutionize all which we are and will be. Discovery leads to a reversal in one's thinking and being, a conversion, a shift in direction, outlook, and vision which fires the imagination and the life. Discovery leads to renewal, and the renewal issues in decision; having been changed by an encounter, one acts accordingly.

Another story of reversal which challenges accepted ideas is the familiar parable of the Good Samaritan. Classified by some as an example rather than a parable, illustrating what one should do or avoid, it is a full and compelling story. It focuses on the reactions of three people to one in need. A man on the dangerous road from Jerusalem to Jericho is beaten, robbed, and left for dead. Two clerics (a priest and a Levite, a member of the priestly tribe) see him and pass by, avoiding him. According to the Law, their avoidance of one who seemed dead is correct: contact with a corpse would defile them and render them unable to perform their religious duties until they were ritually purified. An outsider, however, a Samaritan who is ostracized by the Jews of the time, goes to the injured man, tends to his wounds, and puts him on his own animal while he, who had been riding, now walks. The Samaritan takes the injured man to an inn and cares for him through the night. When he leaves in the morning, apparently assured of the man's recovery and also wishing to ensure his own anonymity, he pays for the man's stay and promises the innkeeper that when he returns he will pay whatever further charges there may be.

This story is told in answer to the question "Who is my neighbor?" Jesus tells the story and then turns the question on the questioner: "Which now of these three, thinkest thou, was neighbor unto him that fell among thieves?" The lawyer whose question prompted the story replies, "He that showed mercy on him," and Jesus concludes, "Go, and do thou likewise." The question is not "Who is my neighbor," but "Whose neighbor can I be?" The clerics in the story, traditionally good, become bad, and the Samaritan, traditionally bad, becomes good. The world, like the original question, is turned upside down. The story reopens closed options and overturns set judgments and established conclusions.

So, too, is the most extended and complex parable, that of the Prodigal Son, a story of reversal. It is perhaps better called the Parable of the Two Sons. The younger son of a man asks for his inheritance, journeys to a far country, and wastes his money on "riotous living." A famine occurs just when the son has spent the last of his money, so he hires himself out as a servant of a man who sends him to feed his pigs (an unclean and abhorrent animal to Jewish Law); he would have eaten the pigs' food, but "no one gave unto him." At last, he recalls that his father's hired servants had more than enough to eat, while the son, far from home, is famished. He prepares a speech to give to his father and sets out for home. When he is still a distance away, his father, who apparently has been watching for him, sees him and runs to him in a torrent of emotion and compassion. The son begins his speech, but before he can get to his request—"make me as one of your hired servants"—the father interrupts, telling the servants,

> Bring forth the best robe, and put it on him; and put a ring on his hand, and shoes on his feet:
> and bring hither the fatted calf, and kill it; and let us eat, and be merry: for this my son was dead, and is alive again; he was lost, and is found. (Luke 15:22-23)

The second son enters; this blocking character, coming in from the field (he too has been away from home, but not far), hears the celebration, and learning the cause is angry and will not go in. The father therefore comes out to him and, in an action paralleling his going out to the younger son, asks him to come in. In his jealousy, the elder brother professes his constant faithfulness to his father, but complains, "thou never gavest me a kid, that I might make merry with my friends:/but as soon as this thy son [not 'my brother'] was come, which hath devoured thy living [not exactly; the inheritance had been given to him] with harlots [perhaps the elder brother's invention, a clue as to what he would do if he had the courage to take his inheritance and leave; the earlier report mentions only 'riotous living' and says nothing about harlots], thou hast killed for him the fatted calf" (Luke 15:29-30). The father patiently corrects him: "It was meet that we should make merry, and be glad: for this thy brother [not merely 'my son'] was dead, and is alive again; and was lost, and is found" (Luke 15:32). No further comment is necessary. This parable of the Lost Son with its three characters is itself part of a group of three parables in Luke's Gospel: the Lost Sheep (15:3-7), the Lost Coin (15:8-10), and the Lost Son (15:11-32).

Not all the parables, however, move from sadness to joy; some are tragic and stress exclusion rather than inclusion. In the parable of the talents (Matthew 25:14-30), a man who is to travel to a far country entrusts his goods to his servants, giving to one five talents, to another three, to another one, "to every man according to his several ability." The man with five talents trades with them and makes five more; the man with two talents does the same and doubles his holdings; but the man with one hides it in the ground. At length the master returns. The man with ten talents presents them to the master and hears, "Well done, thou good and faithful servant: thou hast been faithful over a few things, I will make thee ruler over many things: enter thou into the joy of thy lord." The man who now has four talents presents them and hears the same words. Finally the man with one talent brings it to the master, saying to him, "I knew thee that thou art an hard man, reaping where thou hast not sown, and gathering where thou hast not strewed:/and I was afraid, and went and hid thy talent in the earth: lo, there thou hast what is thine." The master replies harshly:

> Thou wicked and slothful servant, thou knewest that I reap where I sowed not . . .
> thou oughtest therefore to have put my money to the exchangers, and then at my coming

I should have received mine own with usury.
Take therefore the talent from him, and give it unto him which hath ten talents. . . .
And cast ye the unprofitable servant into outer darkness: there shall be weeping and
gnashing of teeth.

This parable, which progresses slowly with dialogue and repetition, building
suspense, offers insight into self-recognition. It moves from the man's refusal
to take a risk, through the repressed guilt which he projects onto someone
else, to the loss of all opportunity for a meaningful existence. It is a grim and
powerful story which beclouds the hearer and conceals as much as it reveals.

Another parable of exclusion is the Parable of the Wedding Guest (Matthew
22:11-14). Concentrated and dramatic, the parable is attached to another
which tells of a king who, since the invited guests will not come to his son's
wedding banquet, gathers all he can find "both bad and good." When the
king enters the hall, he sees a man who is not wearing a wedding garment.
He asks politely, "Friend, how camest thou in hither not having a wedding
garment?" The man is speechless. Therefore, because he is speechless, the
king has him bound hand and foot, taken away, and cast "into outer darkness;
there shall be weeping and gnashing of teeth." The man's speechlessness is
at the heart of the parable. He has no defense, no reply; he simply stands
there stupidly before the king. Speech is central to human existence, the
parable implies, and being human involves the capacity to hear words and
to answer. Since conversation with this man is impossible, he is excluded from
all human (and divine) society.

Some parables are oddly comic. The parable of the Unjust Steward (Luke
16:1-9) is an example. A rich man learns that his steward has apparently been
wasting his master's goods and calls the man to account, "for thou mayest no
longer be steward." The man wonders what to do. "I cannot dig; to beg I am
ashamed." Proud and not adept at physical labor, he devises a scheme: he
calls each of his master's debtors and has each one reduce the bill he owes.
We hear him say in hushed and urgent tones, "Take thy bill, and sit down
quickly, and write fifty." The master commends the unjust steward because
he has done wisely, "for the children of this world are in their generation
wiser than the children of light." The steward cleverly takes care of himself.
Jesus concludes the parable, "And I say unto you, Make to yourselves friends
of the mammon of unrighteousness; that, when ye fail, they may receive you
into everlasting habitations." A crooked manager who knows enough to look
out for himself and his future welfare becomes a rebuke to Jesus' disciples
who do not care.

Bibliography
Crossan, John Dominic. *In Parables*.
Jeremias, Joachim. *The Parables of Jesus*.
Jones, G. V. *The Art and Truth of the Parables*.

Perrin, Norman. *Jesus and the Language of the Kingdom.*

Ricoeur, Paul. "Listening to the Parables: Once More Astonished," in *Christianity and Crisis.* 34:23 (January 6, 1975), pp. 304-308.

TeSelle, Sallie McFague. *Speaking in Parables.*

Via, Da O., Jr. *The Parables:. Their Literary and Existential Dimension.*

Philip H. Pfatteicher

THE ADAPTATION OF BIBLICAL STORY BY WRITERS OF SHORT FICTION

Archetypes, Allusions, and Adaptations

The use of the Bible in works by writers of short fiction is so extensive that no single study, even of great length, could begin to account for all of it, much less explore it. The biblical heritage is so deeply ingrained in Western culture that it might be said that no writer has been uninfluenced by it, although perhaps not every writer is aware of the biblical influence on his work. Therefore, to observe that a particular writing has "used" biblical material is to say almost nothing; even to show at length how certain Bible stories or storytelling methods have been employed by a writer in a given tale may tell us nothing about the author's conscious process. So-called Christ and Adam figures abound in the literary landscape, if one is inclined to name them so.

A more concrete form of biblical influence shows itself in explicit allusions to biblical names and stories and in paraphrase or direct quotation of Bible passages. Scholars have delighted in probing the relevance of allusions toward understanding respected works. Book-length studies of biblical allusions by William Shakespeare, John Milton, James Joyce, and others have been written. Again, however, what has been said with the assertion that an author has alluded to the Bible by, for example, naming a character Peter or by writing that "all is vanity"? One may be saying merely that the author has used a traditional name or a proverbial expression that happens to appear in the Bible. Even when the biblical derivation of a name or passage is beyond dispute, as in Herman Melville's explicit citing of Ishmael as an outcast, one can merely speculate the author's reasons for the allusion. Is he saying that, like the Ishmael of Genesis, the Ishmael of the novel is only an outcast from men, not an outcast from God? Or is he perhaps being ironic, since his Ishmael is the only one saved, while the rest of the crew is destroyed? Furthermore, does any biblical allusion carry with it the author's intent as to how much of the biblical source may be relevant toward understanding his work? In other words, how much of the Bible is being alluded to in an allusion? When the walking stick of Goodman Brown's companion turns into a serpent, is Nathaniel Hawthorne alluding to Yahweh's transformation of Moses' sheep-hook or to the magic trick of the Egyptian priests, or to both? When, in *The Bear* (1942), William Faulkner states that Ike becomes a carpenter because Christ had so chosen, how fully is the writer asking us to parallel their lives?

There is a third kind of inquiry that allusion provokes but does not help the reader to carry out: when a writer alludes to a biblical personage or passage, is he implying a commentary on the source? Sometimes the writer may thus intend, but much more often the writer depends on the allusion to provoke connotations of which presumably the reader will automatically think.

Deliberate use of the Bible in order to comment on a figure or event is clearly seen only in the extensive adaptations of biblical episodes by writers. Authors in every genre have produced and continue to produce such works. Biblical "epics" on film first appeared in 1915, and in recent years television audiences have seen new biblical films each Christmas and Easter. Since 1970, several Broadway musicals, including *Jesus Christ Superstar* and *Joseph and the Amazing Technicolor Dreamcoat*, have adapted biblical themes. Archibald MacLeish's *J. B.* (1958), based on Job, is the best-known of modern Bible-inspired plays. William Faulkner's novel *A Fable* (1954), Gian-Carlo Menotti's opera *Amahl and the Night Visitors*, and T. S. Eliot's poem "The Journey of the Magi" exemplify modern biblical adaptations in other genres.

Writers of short fiction and novellas have frequently adapted biblical episodes, although certainly not with the great frequency with which they have employed biblical names and symbols for allusive purposes. The motives behind allusion differ greatly from those which inspire adaptation. By being allusive the writer merely pushes the reader toward associating one set of ideas with another. The nature of the relationship is not clear. For example, although Frank O'Connor titles a story "Judas," readers cannot tell how O'Connor means the source story to shape their perspective on O'Connor's own tale, which concerns a lad who feels guilty about leaving his mother alone one evening so that he might spend time with a young woman. O'Connor makes the allusion because he wants the reader to see the story in the context of betrayal and guilt; no one could reasonably suggest that O'Connor's purpose is to have us understand the Bible story in modern terms.

The writer who adapts biblical material to modern contexts wants the reader to reconsider the contemporary relevance of the source story. Not only does the writer feel that the reader will learn more about the present by reexperiencing the story, but he also feels it essential to reshape the text so that the reader will relate to it in specific ways. The adapter inhabits a place somewhere between the literal translator and the overt exegete: the former strives to make the text, "as it is," available to new readers, whereas the latter experiences the story for the reader, so to speak, and presents an abstract. Those who may legitimately be called biblical adapters seem, at one extreme, to be translating almost exclusively, with little invention; at the other, their work contains little narrative and much direct commentary. What sets the adapters apart from either the translators or the commentators, however, is their reliance on storytellers' techniques to move their readers. Thus, although Reynolds Price's collection *A Palpable God* (1978) contains his word-for-word translations of thirty stories from both Testaments, he decides where, at beginning and end, to break each tale from its context in the Bible; moreover, he arranges his tales so that Old and New Testament stories alternate, the individual juxtapositions determined by thematic relationships rather than by chronology or by the order of the books in the established versions. Daniel

Berrigan's *A Book of Parables* (1977), in which commentary predominates, derives its power from Berrigan's experiments with point of view, personal narrative, and speaker characterization.

With exceptions such as Price's book and some of Berrigan's narrative essays, the short stories and novellas of the biblical adapters fall into three rough categories: (1) the Bible story as explicit theme for the modern story; (2) the modern parallel-plot story; (3) the Bible story itself retold from a different point of view. These categories conveniently differentiate important ways of using biblical sources, and each story tends to employ one method more than the others, although the modes often overlap within stories. Each of the following sections will consider a few of the stories that make up the categories.

The Bible Story as Theme

This category contains such stories as Hawthorne's "Rappaccini's Daughter," Mary Wilkins Freeman's "On the Walpole Road," Arthur C. Clarke's "The Star," and Roger Zelazny's "A Rose for Ecclesiastes." Each differs from the other in the way the author uses biblical material as theme and in the extent to which it is used.

The Hawthorne story, set in Renaissance Padua, presents a magnificent garden, unlike any other in the world, created, as it were, by the brilliant Dr. Rappaccini, who is unexcelled in his knowledge of poisonous plants. Rappaccini's garden exudes perfumes deadly to all creatures except his daughter, Beatrice, who indeed can live only in the fatal air of the plants. Viewing this scene, young Giovanni Guasconti, a student who has taken lodgings over the garden, speculates that this place may be "the Eden of the present world" and Rappaccini himself its "Adam."

The idea of Eden establishes a polarity in the story between fallenness and purity, with the garden an ironically fallen Eden and the old world outside comparatively healthful and unspoiled. For young Guasconti, the garden—especially its "Eve"—has powers of attraction that throw him into internal battle between desire for Beatrice and fear of destruction. His desire triumphs; he becomes more and more a creature of the garden, exuding the same perfume as Beatrice and the flowers. He wittingly becomes Rappaccini's "experiment," although he loathes his susceptibility and Beatrice's allure.

What makes the story a genuine exploration of the theme of Eden and the Fall is that Hawthorne is not satisfied with the simple inversion of the fallen paradise; he goes on to double the irony: the deadly Beatrice herself dies after drinking Giovanni's "gift" of "blessed herbs . . . almost divine in [their] efficacy." Her last words attribute her death not to the herbs but to Giovanni's selfish hatred of her nature. "Oh, was there not," she asks, "from the first, more poison in thy nature than mine?" The polarity vanishes. The narrator calls Beatrice the "poor victim of man's ingenuity and of thwarted nature, and of the fatality that attends all such efforts of perverted wisdom." Rappaccini's garden, seemingly so alien to the world, is merely one more of fallen man's attempts to transcend his nature. As commentary on Genesis, the story reasserts the irrecoverability of Eden; it shows that paradise is not a place, as Rappaccini and Giovanni would see it, but a state of mind and heart which recedes further and further the more effort people exert to recover it.

Though "Rappaccini's Daughter" introduces the Fall as an idea, it explores it through narrative, not argument, and so its commentary is indirect. The same may be said even more emphatically about Freeman's "On the Walpole Road," which comments on Revelation without mentioning the book, but merely by alluding to the New Jerusalem and including a brief opening discussion of life after death.

In this light-hearted, anecdotal tale, two New England farmwives, Almiry and Mis' Green, chat about the weather, neighbors, and relatives as they ride home from the Walpole market on a dusty afternoon. Old Mis' Green speculates that there will not be "anything very frightful 'bout Gabriel's trumpet. I think it's goin' to come kinder like the robins an' the flowers do in spring, kinder meltin' right into everything else, sweet an' nateral like." When Almiry warns that "that ain't accordin' to Scripture," Mis' Green asserts, paraphrasing Corinthians, that "It's me a-seein' the Scripturs, an' it's you a-seein' the Scripturs . . . an' we'll never reely know how much is straight till we see to read it by the light of the New Jerusalem."

This first and last mention of the theme is followed by talk about a brewing thunderstorm and then, associatively, by Mis' Green's story about a memorable thunderstorm on the day of her Uncle Enos' funeral twenty years earlier. Although the "Scripturs" do not reappear explicitly in the tale, the opening discussion of how they are to be read puts the ensuing anecdote about the funeral into a universal context. It focuses the reader's attention on two topics: differences in individual perspective and reward and punishment after death. Since the anecdote is Mis' Green's, all its violent elements, including the storm and the lightning-caused fire which burns Uncle Enos' barn and hay crop, are subsumed within her serene outlook. She draws no connection between the story destruction and what she tells of Uncle Enos' remarkable selfishness, although the reader might imagine that Almiry, if Freeman had given her the chance, might have taken a more apocalyptic view of the events of Enos' burial day. Mis' Green does speculate about the punishment due Uncle Enos, but she speaks of it in terms of what people will say about him after death, not in terms of divine retribution.

As commentary on the Bible, Freeman's work seems to recommend 1 Corinthians 13 ("now we see through a glass darkly") as a check to the too-easy drawing of analogies between the visions of Revelation and "explanations" of natural events. If this is Freeman's argument, however, she makes it implicitly through juxtaposing the discussion of the Bible and Mis' Green's anecdote.

More explicit as commentary is Roger Zelazny's "A Rose for Ecclesiastes," one of many science fiction stories to explore biblical ideas in the context of humankind's encounters with alien cultures. In the story, Gallinger, the narrator, finds a striking similarity of tone between Ecclesiastes and the sacred texts he is given permission to examine by the high priestess of a doomed race of Martians. He becomes convinced that the race can be saved by their discarding what he considers the nihilism imposed by their religion. He becomes determined to revoke their despair when his Martian lover becomes pregnant with his child—an event which refutes the Martians' conviction of their infertility. He invades their most secret ritual to plead that, as does Ecclesiastes, their own existing texts may represent only a tiny fraction of their religious thought, and that they need not resign themselves to brief lives stunted by an "all is vanity" philosophy. To his amazement, the priestesses greet his words with joy: they proclaim him the "prophet" predicted in their most sacred texts—texts that he has not read. Gallinger, who throughout the action projects a self-confidence and sense of superiority that alienate him from other humans, is humbled by this revelation that he is merely playing a role determined millenia before.

The climax of this story implies—it does not state—a different view of Ecclesiastes from that on which Gallinger had acted. Whereas he had interpreted the Preacher's message as desperate, the work of a dying subculture, the climax sustains the Preacher's warning against ambition and naïve optimism as attitudes which destroy people of a thriving culture such as Gallinger's.

Unlike "Rappaccini's Daughter," "On the Walpole Road," or "A Rose for Ecclesiastes," Arthur C. Clarke's "The Star" takes as its main matter the narrator's attempt to understand a piece of Scripture. The story opens with his telling the reader that his Christian faith (he is a Jesuit priest) has been all but shattered by his recent voyage to the Phoenix Nebula, three thousand light years from Earth. Not until the very end of the story does the reader learn that the nebula, which had become a supernova—the brightest of exploding stars—about six thousand years earlier, must have been, according to calculations, the star of Bethlehem. What shatters the narrator's faith is the voyagers' discovery of a vault built by the inhabitants of the doomed star's planets not long before the explosion. This vault contains records in all forms of a beautiful culture in some ways superior to man's. "Oh, God," wonders the priest, "there were so many stars you could have used. What was the need to give these people to the fire . . . ?" This question, which concludes the story, is asked after the narrator has already speculated at length about the existence of God. This discovery, he asserts, does not deny God: "God has no need to justify His actions to man. He who built the universe can destroy it when He chooses." Nevertheless, these thoughts do not mend the narrator's spirit, even if he remains intellectually unbroken. The story ends, leaving the narrator, like Job before the whirlwind, proclaiming God, but wondering who he is proclaiming and why.

The Parallel-Plot Story

Simple plot parallels need not imply commentary on the stories paralleled or even the use of one story as a source for the other. Not every story of a charismatic leader who frees his people and builds a nation helps anyone understand Exodus or is meant to. True biblical adaptations in this category take as their explicit subject the correlation between a modern event and a biblical event, or they present a parallel plot with such clear allusions to the biblical story that the reader can hardly avoid making the correlation himself.

Among the stories which expressly aim at a clearer understanding of the biblical text are Daniel Berrigan's "Eve and the Bible Salesman" and "The Patience of Job in Detroit," both from his collection, *A Book of Parables.* In "Eve and the Bible Salesman" Berrigan proposes understanding how in Eden "there were no rules." To do this, he focuses on Eve, whose mind "seemed to have the exact, monochromatic character of the story itself." He places her in a modern context: "in a house in a clearing where the trees brushed the windows on windy nights. . . ." To understand, he imagines her beneath the fruit-bearing tree, putting out her hand—"no one told her to do it"—and catching the loosened fruit:

> The ruddy mirror cleared. Something happened to her at that moment, I think. Everything that came to be known later, in cruder times (after much tragedy and gross miscalculation as well as the spoilage of vast numbers of children, rotting like fruit in rancid barrels) the word was "education."

He imagines her making love to "the man" and then reflecting on her dreams; but he corrects himself: "she never said such things. The sentence is too reflective, it arches back on itself."

Of the Fall itself he is almost loath to speculate. He calls himself "the gigantic child who kneels clumsily at the front window of the doll house. His very breath can cloud the proceedings within, he can work havoc by inadvertence." He finally attempts Satan: a Bible salesman with a smooth line. "What did he know that she didn't know? Simply, everything we know, consequences. Not a threat or a curse or a sentence to be passed, but our world." Berrigan's narrator concludes the story by admitting failure. "We cannot imagine that world, let alone desire it. We can only despise it, and secretly mourn."

"The Patience of Job in Detroit" unfolds in the narrator's greater certainty of events and in his even greater wonder in their presence. Here the relationship between the Bible story and the modern instance is symbiotic: the narrator seeks to understand Job so that he might comprehend old Demos, his cancer-ridden landlord; he tells Demos' story so that he might understand Job. The plot of Demos' story is really parallel to that of Job only because the narrator points up the analogies. He sees the Adversary of Job not only in Demos' cancer but also in the black tenant who steals Demos' keys and then periodically raids his house. Himself he casts into the role of Job's would-be friends, although his sin is not, like theirs, to condemn Job, but to try to escape Demos' incessant need to talk (he says that this need explains the talkiness of Job). When he finally learns to accept his role as Demos' listener, he is able to find in the dying old man a source of faith and hope. His ultimate picture of the old man coincides with his image of Job: "He knows who is there, he draws his ragged breath like a mandarin, his head tosses bulkily, sick and starved, all but transparent, a grave heavy with Easter seeds. . . ."

A third modern parallel plot also adapts Job; but Zelazny's "For a Breath I Tarry" introduces the parallel only through direct quotations from the Bible story before embarking on an un-Joblike narrative of the superrobot Frost's quest first to understand Man and then to become human. Were it not that Zelazny precedes Frost's quest with a debate between "Solcom" and "Divcom, the Alternate" regarding Solcom's supremacy, and were it not that Zelazny had written of Divcom's robots "going to and fro in the Earth and up and down in it," the reader would hardly recognize Zelazny's story as a commentary on Job. Once the parallel is proposed, however, the reader is inclined to read Frost's story as it relates to Job's.

So read, "For a Breath I Tarry" attempts to make the reader imagine a new perspective on Job's quest to comprehend God. As one views Frost's machine-bound efforts to comprehend Humanity fail time after time, one is led to a new appreciation of the unfathomable distance between Machineness and Humanness; those who know human life but cannot describe it see their creature, their tool, stumble toward understanding aided only by the crude instruments of analysis they have given it. By analogy, Zelazny leads readers to a new appreciation of Job's crying need and feeble ability to understand divinity. While viewing the even feebler, but more definite, attempts by other robots to "explain" humanity to Frost, one sees the arguments of Job's friends for the conventional babble they are.

The infinite superiority of Frost to his supposed advisers is demonstrated by Frost's successful translation into a man at the climax of the story. Although this event takes Zelazny's story far from the simple parallel to Job and closer to Genesis 1, it does suggest the radical turning point at Job 38 when suddenly Job begins to comprehend the Lord's voice out of the whirlwind.

The Bible Story Retold from a Different Point of View

More common as a literary kind than either the Bible story as explicit theme or the parallel-plot story is the Bible story itself retold from a different point of view. This kind of story does not radically shift the setting of the biblical original, but in shifting point of view from the limited third person most characteristic of Bible narrative the author changes plot and characterization to varying degrees. As with the two other modes of biblical adaptation, this mode depends for its effectiveness on the reader's knowledge of the biblical original from which it differs and upon which it comments. Characteristically, these stories never deny any of the details found in Bible stories, although particular characters may deny them or be confused about their perceptions. Almost always these stories explore avenues of thought or action merely opened by the Bible narratives.

Mark Twain's satiric *Extracts from Adam's Diary* (1904) and *Eve's Diary* (1906) shift points of view so far from that of Genesis that the inhabitants of Eden sound like two of Twain's canny Missourians. In Twain's Eden, fallenness is a fact of character even before the Fall. Although Adam notes that with Eve's eating of the apple (literally) death entered the garden, no change in Adam's attitudes, or in Eve's, occurs after it—except that each begins to become clothes-conscious.

Twain's interest is in stereotyping male and female behavior, with Adam the "superintendent" who keeps accounts and maintains the status quo. He deplores Eve's talkativeness, her passion for change, and her insatiable curiosity. When Twain gives the reader Eve's diary, however, one sees these so-called flaws revealed as virtues, though the virtues of the fallen world: creativity, the quest to know (science), and the appreciation of beauty. Twain thus gives one a conventional male stereotype of woman, then negates it by providing the woman's perspective in prose far more poetic and thoughtful than Adam's.

While the first two-thirds of the story (excerpts from each diary alternate) show Adam and Eve at odds, the final third expresses Eve's magnificent devotion to Adam and Adam's much slower realization of his need for her. By the close, some forty years after the Fall, the satiric mood has given way entirely. Adam's final comment, at Eve's grave, shows his own transformation: "Wheresoever she was, *there* was Eden."

Equally humorous, but intended as serious commentary on the nature of biblical prophecy, is Berrigan's "The Whale's Tale," the Jonah story from the leviathan's point of view. Berrigan's purpose is twofold: to stress Providence in the whale's swallowing of Jonah and to stress the necessary humility of the prophet, whom the whale claims to be by nature impatient, arrogant, and self-righteous. The author describes Jonah in the belly of the whale; the whale then speculates on Jonah's future career. Although Berrigan's emphasis on the whale as savior does not deny the events of the Bible story, it does considerably differ from it in tone. From the whale's point of view, Jonah's adventure in the sea is not God's physical and mental torture of the chosen man who has violated his trust, but an absolutely essential step in the preparation of the prophet.

Although the book exceeds the short story in length, no survey, however brief, of modern biblical adaptation in short fiction should overlook Pär Lagerkvist's novella *Barabbas* (1949). Unequalled in intensity as a fictional quest to understand Christ's sacrifice, the story shows how Barabbas, "the acquitted," proceeds over many years from suffering to suffering—often in the name of Jesus—but never achieves Christian faith. The classic story of one who *would* believe, *Barabbas* takes its title character from Golgotha, where he witnesses the Crucifixion, to the Cyprian copper mines where he befriends a Christian zealot later martyred, to Rome, where he dies, beside but apart in spirit from Peter and the other Christians crucified by Nero. Abandoned as an infant and nurtured to steal, deceive, and murder, Barabbas stands in awe of Christ's dictum, "Love one another," but never acts on those words, or even comprehends them. From Golgotha forward, Barabbas witnesses for Christ, lies for Christ, destroys for Christ, kills for Christ, and even dies for Christ; but love is beyond his power.

In contrast to Barabbas are the believers, who follow Christ or his legend for many reasons, most of them superficial, at least to Barabbas, who suffers their hatred for his having the public's pardon. Nevertheless, this brutally honest book refuses to judge those who scorn Barabbas; by never venturing into the minds of others, Lagerkvist forces the reader to judge the characters' motives; he intimidates the reader's condemning spirits by depicting Barabbas himself vividly as a man given less to judging than to wonder at the power which enables these flawed people to perform acts of charity and courage.

Ultimately, the book does not judge even Barabbas. On his own cross, this follower of Jesus—to all Roman eyes a Christian, but in his heart one who doubts—cries out, "To thee I deliver up my soul." To whom does he now speak: to Christ or, as the narrator wonders, to death, "that which he had always been so afraid of"? The book only makes the simple narrative statement: "And then he gave up the ghost." It well may be that Lagerkvist has presented a drama of the true martyr rather than of the man without faith. The reader must decide.

Close in some respects to *Barabbas* is Leonid Andreyev's "Lazarus," one of several biblical retellings by this author. Andreyev's portrait of Lazarus as "grave and silent . . . horribly changed and strange" corresponds with Lagerkvist's brief description of the same figure in *Barabbas*. Where Lagerkvist enhances the somber mood of his tale with spare, muted descriptions, however, Andreyev contrasts Lazarus' hollow eyes and chilling aspect with the gaiety, richness, and color of all that surrounds him. Moreover, where Lagerkvist limits the reader to Barabbas' perspective, Andreyev at times shifts his focus from Lazarus in order to probe the minds of others, including the Emperor Augustus. Indeed, the sharpest contrast is drawn between the vigorous reasoning of those who encounter Lazarus and the deathly opaqueness of Lazarus' character. Rather than having a personality, Lazarus projects the annihilation of personality from his eyes. All who look into those eyes turn mad or desperate; to them "there was no more a sense of time; the beginning of all things and their end merged into one. . . . A man was just born, and funeral candles were already at his head, and then were extinguished. . . ."

Not a death's head, Lazarus, in returning from death, becomes the illusion of life beyond death. He shatters minds because his eyes refute the hope of an afterlife. Unlike Barabbas, who in Lagerkvist's treatment emerges as a memorable personality who became a symbol by accident, Andreyev's Lazarus is ultimately shown to be no more than the symbol of human illusion. What Andreyev indirectly demonstrates is that, without that illusion, man creates nothing and quickly perishes.

Bibliography
Ackerman, James, and Thayer Warshaw. *The Bible as/in Literature*.
Baker, Carlos. "The Place of the Bible in American Fiction," in *Religious Perspectives in American Culture*.
Lewis, C. S. *The Literary Impact of the Authorized Version*.
Mann, Thomas. *The Tables of the Law*.
Maus, Cynthia P. *The Old Testament and the Fine Arts*.
_____ . *The New Testament and the Fine Arts*.
Moseley, Virginia. *Joyce and the Bible*.
Schneidau, Herbert N. *Sacred Discontent: The Bible and Western Tradition*.

Christopher J. Thaiss

THE FABLE TRADITION

Although it is impossible to trace the genre of the fable to a single source or a first writer, it is known that the fable tradition has its roots far back in ancient history; in fact, the fable is perhaps one of the earliest forms of the short story. Although readers have most often come to associate the fable with Aesop, even to the extent of attributing to Aesop fables written at a much later time, the fable tradition actually flourished in many cultures other than that of ancient Greece, as proven by the existence of fables in diverse ancient writings.

From the time of its very inception, the fable seems to have entailed the notion of allegory. According to the definition of the ancient Greeks, whose fables are most familiar to the Western world, the fable is a story, a tale, a narrative; the Greeks made clear the fable's fictional nature by terming it μυθos (from which comes the word "myth") and thus distinguishing this sort of tale from the historical tale, which was termed λογos, or ιοτοριx. Nevertheless, although the tale was fictive, its intent was to portray allegorically a reality of some kind, and this basic assumption concerning the fable's nature has characterized the fable throughout centuries of varied treatment.

As it most commonly appears, the fable personifies animals, or occasionally plants, or sometimes even the elements of nature, so as to reveal some truth; ordinarily that truth concerns a particular aspect of human behavior, although some fables which are aetiological (such as how the turtle got its shell) have come to be attached to the genre. The use of animals to represent human truth may have come about in part because people are familiar with animals, often living in close association with them. Moreover, certain animals have been perceived as displaying various attributes or patterns of behavior which have come to be associated with them, such as the wiliness of the fox and the rapaciousness of the wolf. Although it is difficult now to determine whether the animals actually possess such traits or whether the fable has taught the reader to perceive the animals as possessing such traits, the fact is that certain animals have come to embody an identifiable symbolic meaning. Human familiarity with both the animals themselves and with their distinguishing characteristics makes them particularly well-suited to metaphorical or allegorical uses.

Even though the early fables occasionally included gnomic lines, the fables were not written with specific morals attached but relied instead on implication and inference. The practice of adding epimythia, statements which overtly present the fable's moral purpose, became very popular in the Middle Ages when the fables were used for moral instruction. Since these medieval fables are the ones that are known best, the fable has come to be identified with moral didacticism; in its genesis, however, the fable's purpose seems to have been merely to contain wisdom.

The most famous writer of fables is, of course, Aesop. By the time of the Middle Ages his fables existed in many variant forms—in verse and in prose, and in many languages such as French, German, Latin, and English. Although Aesop was not the only source of medieval fables, many of the most popular are traceable ultimately to Aesop, by means of such redactors as Demetrius Phalereus, Phaedrus, Babrius, Avianus, and Gualterus Anglicus. Since Aesop probably did not write his fables down, the reader is obliged to rely on the testimony of these later writers who claim that their collections are based on Aesop's work. The extent to which Aesop is responsible for all the fables attributed to him cannot be finally determined, but it is known that he is associated with the beginning of the genre as it developed in Greece.

There were earlier users of the fable than Aesop, but their work, for the most part, has been lost. Archilochus, a Greek poet believed to have lived on the island of Paros in the seventh century B. C., composed a number of fables concerning the fox and the monkey, the fox and the eagle, and the fox and the hedgehog, but unfortunately his work survives only in fragments. Another early fable is that of Hesiod, a Greek poet who lived in Boeotia and who wrote around 700 B. C. His fable of the hawk and the nightingale, contained in the poem "Works and Days," is one of the oldest known of the Greek fables:

> A hawk catches a nightingale and carries her in his claws high up to the clouds. In response to her pitiful wailing the hawk asks why she screams, since her master has her and she will therefore go wherever he wishes to take her; if he wishes to eat her he will, or if he wishes to let her go, he may do so. The hawk points out that one who tries to match strength with someone stronger will not only lose the battle but will be hurt as well by shame.

Hesiod claims that this fable is for the barons, who will understand it.

Even older is the fable in Judges 9:8-15, concerning the trees who seek a king:

> The olive tree, when asked to reign over the other trees, responded by inquiring if it should leave its rich oil, which honors gods and men, so as to sway over the trees. The fig tree, also asked, similarly inquired if it should leave its good fruit in order to reign. In like manner the vine inquired if it should leave its good wine, which cheers gods and men. The bramble, when asked, responded that if the trees were in good faith anointing it as king they should take shelter in its shade, but if they were not, that fire should come out of the bramble and burn up the cedars of Lebanon.

Despite such earlier fables as these, however, it is with Aesop, who is believed to have lived in the sixth century B. C., that the fable has come to be most closely associated. Much of Aesop's life remains a mystery, although tradition has it that he was a Phrygian slave who was owned by Iadmon of the island of Samos, that he was ugly and deformed, and that he was killed by the people of Delphi. How much of this legendry is true one cannot know. From the testimony of Herodotus, Aristophanes, Xenophon, Plato, and Aristotle, scholars today have concluded that Aesop did exist and that he was known as a fabulist who concerned himself with moral and satirical lessons; Plato, for example, tells of Socrates amusing himself during the last days of his life with Aesop's tales. Beyond this, however, there is no real way of verifying "facts" about Aesop's life.

Similarly there is a lack of absolute information about Aesop's canon. The first collector of Aesop's fables of whom there is knowledge is Demetrius Phalerus, who was reported to have assembled Aesop's fables in prose in the fourth century B. C. This collection is not now available, although it was, apparently, the source used by the later fabulists Phaedrus and Babrius. Phaedrus, a Roman who lived in Greece in the first century A. D., wrote a collection of fables in Latin verse which included Aesopic tales as well as new fables which Phaedrus himself wrote concerning contemporary social and political events. While Phaedrus states in his Prologue that he is merely putting into verse stories which Aesop invented, he does in some instances attribute a particular fable to Aesop, such as the tale of the dog and the meat:

> A dog carrying a piece of meat in his mouth while crossing a river sees his reflection in the water; believing that he sees another dog also carrying meat, he snatches for the reflection, letting fall the meat he held in his mouth. In addition to failing to get that which he coveted, he also loses that which he already had.

In its simplicity, its brevity, and its implied meaning, this fable is typical of the early Aesopic tradition.

Babrius, like Phaedrus, was a Roman who is believed also to have lived in the second half of the first century; like Phaedrus, Babrius added to the Aesopic fables tales of his own composition, in the collection he wrote in Greek verse. Again like Phaedrus, Babrius refers to Aesop in his Prologue, explaining that his intent is to soften and sweeten Aesop's sometimes hard or stinging iambic lines. One of the best known of the Aesopic fables is that of the fox and the grapes, which is included in the Babrius collection:

> A fox, seeing several bunches of grapes hanging from a vine, leaped in vain to pick the fruit, which was ripe and purple. Being unable to reach the grapes he went away, remarking as he went that the grapes were sour, and not ripe at all as he had thought.

To these two sources, Phaedrus and Babrius, and through them to Aesop, are traceable most of the fables which were popularized in the Middle Ages and which have become part of our fable lore.

Along with Phaedrus and Babrius, another writer of the first century A. D. to whom readers are indebted for a particular popular fable, is Horace, a Roman poet who included in his *Satires* (35, 30 B. C.) the fable of the town mouse and the country mouse. Horace explains that this fable's purpose is to illustrate the care that accompanies wealth:

> When the country mouse entertains his city friend, the city mouse scorns the meal of peas, oats, and bacon rinds. Since life is so short, the city mouse explains, one should seek pleasure, which can be found in the city. Once there, the country mouse finds that indeed luxuries abound and delicious food is available, but when the watchdogs are let loose, frightening the country mouse half to death, he decides that his quiet home and simple food are quite sufficient for him.

This fable was used repeatedly by later writers to demonstrate the virtue of the simple life and the wisdom of keeping one's proper place in the social hierarchy.

Both the Phaedrus and the Babrius collection were used extensively by later writers. The Babrius collection was put into Latin verse, perhaps around A. D. 400, by Avianus, a Roman writer of whom little is known. The Avianus fables, because of their simplicity, were popular in medieval schools as exercises in grammar and composition; fables had been recommended for this purpose as early as the first century A. D. by Quintilianus, a rhetorician who prized the Aesopic fables as aids in memorizing, reciting, and composing. The Avianus fables were also used by Alexander Neckham for his *Novus Avianus* of the late twelfth century, on which a number of later French versions rely. The Phaedrus translation of the fables was the basis for the tenth century *Romulus* collection in Latin prose, which circulated widely in manuscripts of varying contents. This collection, which was said to be directly derived from Aesop, was extremely popular. In the twelfth century, Gualterus Anglicus (Walter the Englishman) translated this *Romulus* collection into Latin verse; it is also from Walter's translation, known in the Middle Ages as *Esopus*, *Ysopet*, or *Isopet* (or the *Anonymous Neveleti*, since the collection was published anonymously by Nevelet in 1610), that many later French and Italian versions are derived.

Also writing fables in the twelfth century was Marie de France, who drew on both the *Romulus* collection and the *Roman de Renart* (c. 1175-1205), the tales of Reynard the fox, for her fables, many of which referred to contemporary society. Another French writer, whose fables were influenced by the work of Marie, by the *Romulus* collection, and by Hebrew lore, was Rabbi Berechiah ben Natronai ha-Nakdan, who, toward the end of the twelfth century, wrote his *Fox Fables*. In spite of the title, however, not all the fables concern the fox, as, for example, the fable of the mouse who overeats:

> A mouse who was black and thin went through a hole into a granary where he ate until he was immensely fat. When he was ready to leave he discovered he could not fit through the hole. A cat informed him that unless he vomitted up what he had eaten and grew thin, he would never be able to leave and would never see his father again. This story is for one who covets the wealth of others but who eventually loses what he gains.

Like other writers and collectors of fables in the Middle Ages, Berechiah attached an epimythia, a brief concluding passage which made explicit the fable's moral application.

This custom of using fables specifically for didactic purposes became in the Middle Ages part of the fable tradition. Fables were used by medieval preachers as exempla, to illustrate Scriptural or doctrinal points and to portray moral and immoral behavior. Such churchmen as Jacques de Vitry, who included fables in his collection of exempla, and Odo of Cheriton, who collected fables specifically to be used in sermons, helped to popularize the moralization of fables. As a consequence, the fables possessed today almost uniformly have a moral attached.

In addition to being used by medieval preachers as exempla and by medieval teachers as exercises in language and composition, fables were used by medieval poets for both didactic and aesthetic ends. Geoffrey Chaucer, writing in the last half of the fourteenth century, immortalized in "The Nun's Priest's Tale" the fable of Chauntecleer, the proud cock who lets himself be tricked and captured by the fox, but who then in turn tricks the fox into permitting him to escape. This same fable was also used by Robert Henryson, a Scots poet working approximately a century later, who reworked a number of well-known tales for his volume of *Morall Fables of Esope* (1621). In Henryson's hands the fable was a vehicle not only to point a moral but also to convey social and political commentary. Typical of Henryson's treatment of the genre is his fable of the sheep and the dog:

> A dog who is poor falsely claims before the ecclesiastical court that a sheep owes him a loaf of bread. The court, composed of the sheep's natural enemies, is presided over by a wolf as judge. Although the sheep makes a noble defense, pointing out the prejudicial atmosphere and the unfairness of the court, he loses the case and must sell his wool to pay the dog.

The *Moralitas* which follows explains the fable's allegorical significance: the poor shivering sheep is like simple folk who are oppressed on all sides but who suffer particularly from the corruption in the civil and ecclesiastical courts. The sheep plaintively asks God why He sleeps so long and permits such evil to go unchecked in the world. The large part which the *Moralitas* plays in Henryson's fables is evident in such poems as this, wherein Henryson devotes sixteen stanzas to the fable itself and nine stanzas to the explanation of the moral. Henryson's collection of thirteen fables, to which are appended such extended *Moralitates*, perhaps develops to its poetic extreme the convention of the epimythia.

Working at approximately the same time as Henryson in the fifteenth century was Heinrich Steinhöwel, who, using the prose *Romulus* collection, published a reworking of the Aesopic fables around 1480. Steinhöwel added to the fables promythia, statements at the beginning of the fables concerning their moral purposes. It is believed that Steinhöwel's *Äsop*, or a French translation of Steinhöwel by Machaut, or both, were used by William Caxton when he began, in 1483, to print his *Aesop*, which was one of the first of the fable collections printed in English.

The Middle Ages was clearly one of the great periods of growth and popularity for the fable, a time during which the form was widely and successfully used for such diverse purposes as instruction and entertainment. The fable experienced similar major revivals of interest in the late seventeenth century and in the eighteenth century, when it was taken very seriously as a literary genre.

The seventeenth century revival of interest in the fable was due in large part to the work of the Frenchman Jean de La Fontaine, who published twelve books of fables between 1668 and 1694. He is perhaps more responsible than anyone else for moving the fable into the realm of poetry. Although he claimed to be unoriginal, to be merely translating and adapting from Aesop and Phaedrus, his originality was made manifest in the lyrical and dramatic verse with which he transformed his material. Followers of La Fontaine included such writers as John Gay and Robert Dodsley, the Spanish writer Tomás de Iriarte, the German writer C. F. Gellert, and Ivan Krylov, a Russian writer of the late eighteenth and early nineteenth centuries.

La Fontaine's innovative treatment of the genre did, however, provoke a counter movement. In response to what he perceived as La Fontaine's revolutionary and inappropriate poeticizing of the form, Gotthold Lessing, writing in Germany in the eighteenth century, initiated an opposing trend for fabulists. His intent, as indicated in his 1759 collection, *Fabeln*, was to return to the original conventions of the Aesopic fable, to make the fable not poetic but philosophical. His fables, accordingly, were short, simple, and pithy. An interesting example is that of the nightingale and the lark:

> What can be said to poets who go on flights above their readers' understanding? As the nightingale inquired of the lark, does one soar so high deliberately, so as not to be heard?

The controversy in the eighteenth century over the nature of the fable was of great interest to writers and critics; in contrast to scholars of other times who dismissed the form as suitable primarily for the purposes of teaching and preaching, eighteenth century scholars considered the fable to possess genuine literary respectability. After this great flowering of interest, however, the fable fell into disuse as a literary form.

Nevertheless, in the twentieth century the genre may be experiencing a revival, or perhaps a rebirth in a new form; the work of such writers as Donald Barthelme, John Barth, Kurt Vonnegut, Jr., Jorge Luis Borges, and Gabriel García Márquez has been said to be, in various ways, akin to the fable. These writers may, however, be redefining the genre as they explore, through it, the notion of story. For the most part, fabulists prior to the twentieth century used the fable as a vehicle for transmitting a specific message and kept its form discrete. In contrast, some twentieth century writers of short fiction employ the fable not because of the form's didactic abilities but because of the form's magical essence—its enchantment as an older form of story. Such contemporary writers frequently blend the fable form directly into a narrative and do not, in consequence, make a clear definition between the two genres. In such works there often results a mix of the fantastic and the realistic; fabulous narrative elements which abrogate scientific laws are blended with firmly realistic narrative elements. Other contemporary writers, however, keeping the form of the fable discrete, include fable segments within a larger narrative framework; John Barth, for example, in a self-conscious use of the form, uses wisdom figures within a narrative to tell tales within tales, and García Márquez uses fablelike short-story elements within his narrative form.

While many contemporary writers of short fiction do not use the fable form didactically—Kurt Vonnegut, Jr., for example, seems to indicate that the moral is that there is no moral—other conscious fabulists such as James Thurber have deliberately sought a didactic end. Part of the appeal of Thurber's satire is that the form serves as a commentary upon the content; part of his fables' humor and irony depends upon his use of what many see as a childish form to convey sophisticated ideas. Consequently, in contrast to those contemporary writers of short fiction who use the fable to convey a nebulous world view and who move into the fable's magical world as a retreat from the realistic world, Thurber is more in the tradition of Aesop in using the fable form purposefully to convey a sharply satiric commentary upon human behavior.

The tradition of the fable, then, persists in the twentieth century world, albeit in a seemingly changing form. Originally a "short story" which usually depended upon elements of narrative, drama, and dialogue, the form in its infancy used fantasy, usually in the shape of personified animals, to convey human reality. The form's roots were thus firmly located in the psychological desire to remove human truths to a simpler realm, specifically the world of animals. This desire to simplify and simultaneously mythify human experience is surely basic to much imaginative writing. At the same time, the early form of the fable was concise and pithy, readily engaging the mind and achieving the immediate effect of an understanding on one plane—that is, on the plane of the supernatural or the extraordinary—which could be transferred to and which would inform another plane—the plane of reality and human experience. The form's ability to achieve this immediate understanding made it perfectly suited to didactic ends.

In the twentieth century, however, except when used by such consciously traditional fabulists as Thurber, the fable seems to be changing in two important ways: one rarely sees a direct one-to-one correspondence wherein the fabulous world and the real world are juxtaposed, wherein a fictive creature reveals truth about real human beings; and similarly one rarely finds a direct moralization. Whereas the fable developed as an apologue, a fiction created to edify, in contemporary usage the fable has become primarily a device of fantasy, a fictional technique used to evoke a magical world. The contemporary fabulist, then, in refocusing the genre upon fantasy, uses the form for the effect of creating enchantment, thereby preserving and continuing one of the earlilest purposes of the story.

Evelyn Newlyn

THE SAGA AND THÁTTR

The term "saga" (pl. "sögur") is Old Norse in origin and means "a saw" or "saying." After written language supplemented oral language in the North, the word "saga" was extended to include any kind of legend, story, tale, or history written in prose. As a literary term, "saga" refers more specifically to prose narratives written in medieval Iceland. The sagas are traditionally classified according to their subject matter. The main types of sagas are *Konungasögur* (Kings' Sagas), *Íslendingasögur* (Sagas of the Icelanders or Family Sagas), *Sturlunga saga* (Saga of the Sturlungs), *Byskupasögur* (Bishops' Sagas), *Fornaldarsögur* (Sagas of Past Times), *Riddarasögur* (Sagas of Chivalry), and *Lygisögur* (Lying Sagas). In general, Family Sagas and Kings' Sagas are of highest literary merit. Their excellence ranks them among the finest work of the European Middle Ages.

Closely associated with the saga in medieval Icelandic literature was the tháttr (pl. thættir), a shorter prose form which is related to the saga in roughly the same fashion as a short story is to a novel: the most evident difference between the two is length. Tháttr literally means "a single strand," as of rope. The Icelanders early extended this meaning metaphorically to refer to parts of written works. Episodes of narratives, chapters of histories, or sections of law were thus known as thættir. Icelandic short stories came to be called thættir because many of them are preserved as anecdotes or strands in sagas, particularly in the Kings' Sagas.

While the term "saga" has made its way into popular modern nomenclature as a label for an epiclike narrative, the word "tháttr" has no cognate descendant in English, and has but recently been accorded attention as a genre with its own governing rules. The common habit of embedding short stories in the sagas suggests why the Icelandic thættir have either been overlooked or absorbed into a general discussion of saga literature. Enough versions of single stories exist both as separate manuscripts and as episodes in the sagas to indicate that the stories had a recognizable identity of their own, more or less independent of the host texts. Genre distinctions in medieval Icelandic writing were not particularly definitive. Terms such as "frásaga" (story, narrative), "æfentyri" (adventurous exploits), and "hlut" (part) mingle with "saga" and "tháttr" as reference terms in the literature. On occasion a narrative referred to in one place as a tháttr is called a saga in another. Although more sophisticated and telling differences between saga and tháttr were established through practice of the arts, the boundary between stories and sagas remained fluid.

Evidence of the strong ties and shifting boundaries between the saga and tháttr forms has provoked ongoing speculation about the original relationship between the two. The once-held belief that tháttr were oral tales recorded by scribes and then linked into sagas has been discarded. Sagas and thættir represent a sophisticated confluence of numerous sources both written and oral, and are dependent as well on the genius of their individual authors. While the origin of saga and tháttr writing is a matter of speculation, it can be said that the two are related emanations of the deeply rooted storytelling traditions of Northern Europe.

Storytelling, poetry recitation, and their descendant written forms have historically been the most favored of all arts in Scandinavia and particularly in Iceland. This affection for and mastery of the literary arts in Iceland has been attributed to strong urges of an emigrant culture to preserve knowledge of its European ancestral history. Medieval Icelandic manuscripts are the single preserve of certain heroic Germanic myths and tales which were part of a shared tradition of the Northern peoples. The old literature was lost in Germany and England, where Christianity arrived early. In Scandinavia, where Teutonic mythology and religion held sway for centuries longer (Sweden did not have a Christian bishop until the twelfth century), some of the old myths and stories were preserved, mainly in two Icelandic texts known as the *Eddas*. The *Poetic Edda* (ninth to twelfth century) contains heroic, didactic, and mythological poems which allude to events, legends, and beliefs of the Teutonic tribes. The *Prose Edda* (c. 1220) relates mythological and heroic stories of the pre-Christian North and provides an elaborate poetics for the poetry associated with the legends.

Medieval Icelanders had material as well as patriotic motives for their literary efforts. Those who note the preponderance of writing and the relative absence of other artistic endeavors in Iceland point out the lack of native materials necessary for practicing other arts.

Those who engaged themselves in such vigorous literary activity on a remote and rural island several hundred miles from the European mainland were by majority Norwegian emigrants who came to Iceland during the reign of Harald Fairhair. Harald's ambitious rise to power during the later decades of the ninth century clashed with the Norwegian landed gentry whose livelihoods and properties were threatened by the young monarch's expansion. Rather than suffer servitude or death many chose emigration westward. Various other causes, including hope for a better life and need to escape the law, brought more settlers.

From all accounts, the Icelanders were industrious and enterprising farmers, exceptionally literate and particularly skilled in self-government and law. Those who could argue the law and bring cases to just settlement were highly regarded. The Icelandic pioneers organized assemblies called "Things" which ruled the country by democratic process. They elected to their head not a monarch, but a lawspeaker, part of whose job it was to recite the entire body of law each three years. The first law of the land was a customary one, added to and refined at the annual assembly and passed by memory between generations. An old law formula recited in *Grettir's Saga* gives evidence that alliterative techniques aided in memorization and so rendered law into a poetry of sorts. This law system, suggested by district assemblies in Scandinavia, was unlike any other the world had known. Democratic assemblies ruled the entire country of Iceland for more than eight hundred years before such an idea began to infect Western history on a larger scale. Although the system was far from utopic in practice, it commanded the respect and loyalty of the people. Words were the recognized bond of the body democratic; they were to replace force as the *modus operandi* of government. Against this vision of rational and peaceable government struggled old revenge codes from the heroic tradition. Conflicts between law and violence and the law's frequent incapacity to stop violence became major themes in the Family Saga literature.

Christianity was adopted by assembly vote in the year 1000. One of the most important legacies of the new faith was the access its missionaries provided to written language. Icelanders quickly learned the Latin the churchmen brought and became familiar with its texts. They also put the new alphabet to most vigorous use in the practice of vernacular and sometimes secular literatures. Young Icelanders furthered their educations in Europe or at home. By the early twelfth century there were two bishoprics in Iceland, at Skalaholt and Holar. Both sees supported schools where chieftains sent their sons. At Holar, Icelandic farmboys learned Gregorian chant and Latin versification from a French clergyman. Class distinctions were few, thus allowing the new learning to spread rapidly.

Christianity, with its attendant teachings and written language, initiated Iceland into European traditions. Biblical lore and Christian ethics were added to the Icelanders' stock of old Germanic stories and myths without replacing the older literature. Confident of the value of their own history, Icelanders gave over their enlarged knowledge to the service of the stories of their own peoples. Possibilities for preservation became virtually unlimited. Stories, law, and history had found their harbor on vellum. Before the era closed, Iceland produced a prodigious amount of hagiography, historiography, homiletics, astronomy, grammars, laws, romances, and story, much of it in Icelandic.

The oldest manuscripts which are preserved in Iceland are from the twelfth century; the earliest text is thought to have been a legal code. Ari Thorgilsson (c. 1067-1148) is regarded as the father of Icelandic vernacular history. His *Libellus Islandorum*, commonly called *Íslendingabók (c. 1120, Book of the Icelanders)*, comments on the settlement of Iceland, on exploration voyages to Greenland and Vinland (America), and on other important political data associated with the founding of the island republic. *Book of the Icelanders* well reflects the respect for historical data and interest in biography which continued to be evident in the later Kings' Sagas and Family Sagas; it is written in a style free from embellishment; it is sober and thorough but not without touches of human interest.

Of more central importance to the evolution of the distinctly literary sagas and thættir is *Landnámabók (Book of Settlements)*, which was also first written in Ari Thorgilsson's time and is sometimes attributed to him. *Book of Settlements* is a rich depository of historical and legendary anecdotes about four hundred of Iceland's first settlers. The work documents land claims, describes farmsteads, and gives accounts of feuds, law cases, and marriages. It lavishes special care on genealogy, naming the pioneers' descendants and ancestors as fully as the author's knowledge allows. The author weaves dramatic incident and brief character sketches in with the more sober demographic and historical data. About Ingolf, who was Iceland's first settler, *Book of Settlements* reports that as soon as he saw Iceland he threw his high-seat pillars into the sea and made settlement where they landed. Details of ordinary life, both comic and domestic, interlace the carefully prepared documentary. One section describes a dale named for a cow, and another tells about a man who lost his life in battle when his belt broke and his britches fell. In the *Thórdarbók* version of *Book of Settlements*, the author justifies his compilation, noting that civilized peoples are always eager "to know about the origins of their own society and the beginnings of their own race." Historians continued to expand and revise *Book of Settlements*, issuing it in various editions during the thirteenth and fourteenth centuries.

The first document to which the name "saga" is attached is the fragmentary *Oldest Olafs saga helga (St. Olaf's Saga)* from the late twelfth century. Although primarily a hagiographic account of King Olaf Haraldsson (St. Olaf, c. 995-1030), the saga does contain several thættir made lively by verbal exchanges. *St. Olaf's Saga* was likely composed at the Benedictine monastery in northern Iceland. Such monasteries carried on a wide range of literary activities, not all of them religious in nature. Translations of European histories were undertaken and biographies of kings were written with an eye to more than the kings' saintly virtues. Most of these early works are lost.

The popularity of sagas about kings is evidenced by the compilation of the *Morkinskinna (Rotten Skin)* in c. 1220. *Rotten Skin* is a collection of biographies of eleventh and twelfth century Norwegian kings which incorporates thirty thættir, among them *Halldor Snorrason*, *Ivar's Story*, and the most famous tháttr, *Audun and the Bear*, one of the most beautiful pilgrimage stories in world literature.

When the Icelandic biographers of kings set to documenting the lives of long dead Norwegian monarchs, they turned to the skaldic verse which celebrated their subjects. The fixity of the verse patterns and the conventionality of the kennings (elaborate metaphors) made the poetry a more reliable medium for accurate preservation of the kings' lives than oral tales.

Skaldic verse had its origins in Norway, but Icelanders became its greatest practitioners. Several of Iceland's pioneers were skalds, including the most famous of all skaldic poets, Egil Skallagrimsson, whose two beautiful poems,

Head Ransom and *Lament for My Sons*, are centerpieces in *Egil's Saga*. Many Kings' Sagas are liberally interspersed with skaldic poems, but it would be a mistake in most cases to think of Kings' Sagas as merely prose expansion of the tighter verse forms. The numerous histories which grew out of the skaldic tradition seem to have directed attention to the art of biography for its own sake. These Kings' Sagas, especially those found in the *Rotten Skin* and *Flateyjarbók* manuscripts, are also host to dozens of thættir which feature as their subject a meeting between an Icelander and a Norwegian or Danish king. These short stories probably gave rise to techniques, characters, and themes more purely fictional than the histories which embody them. The subject matter of the thættir is not often traceable to skaldic verse.

Practitioners of skaldic poetry became favorite subjects for both saga and tháttr writers. A number of heroes of the great Family Sagas—Egil, Gisli, Grettir, and Gunnlaug among them—are also famous poets. The Kings' Sagas contain many stories which feature a Norwegian king and his skald. Even heroes who are not poets can grace a scene with a skaldic verse when the occasion warrants.

Side by side with the newer written forms, stories continued to be recited; such performances also provided subject matter for the writer of sagas and thættir. In *Rotten Skin* is recorded the story of a young Icelander visiting a European court. It is Yuletide and the boy makes the court company merry each night with his stories. As Christmas draws near the boy's spirits fall, for his stock of stories is nearly spent. He tells King Harald he has but one final story, the story of Harald's own adventures abroad. The king is delighted by this unexpected attention and arranges it so the story lasts for the twelve nights of the festival.

Medieval Icelanders told stories about stories and stories about poems. They recorded poems about past events which were made into stories with poems embedded in them; they celebrated those who recited and wrote verse and tale. Clearly the literary arts and its practitioners were accorded a position of honor, and what the bards praised in their ancestors they put into practice themselves.

The medieval Icelander who has most clearly come to embody the Icelandic desire to preserve antiquarian literature is Snorri Sturluson (1179-1241), a historian and poet who simultaneously practiced the more pragmatic arts of law and diplomacy. Snorri's work is impressively diverse. He is the author of the so-called *Prose Edda*, which is a compendium of Germanic mythology, a catalogue of kennings and a poem of more than one hundred stanzas authored by Snorri. The poem is accompanied by a commentary on the stanzaic and metric forms of each verse. Other works attributed to Snorri include the masterful collection of Kings' Sagas known as *Heimskringla* (c. 1230-1235), one part of which is the distinguished *St. Olaf's Saga*. Snorri has been called the author of *Egil's Saga*, although that is a matter of conjecture.

During the thirteenth century, the powerful Sturluson family dominated Icelandic political affairs. Snorri undertook diplomatic missions to Norway and was powerful in Icelandic politics, serving twelve years as Lawspeaker. His talents as historian, literary critic, antiquarian, sagaman, and poet rank him as the most prominent literary figure of his age. He was also an influential and wily chieftain who was deeply involved in the internecine struggles of the day and who was neglectful of family obligations. It was his own estranged son-in-law who, leading sixty men, murdered Snorri from ambush in response to an order from the Norwegian king.

This incident serves to point up the state of general lawlessness which plagued the Icelandic Republic in the thirteenth century. (The Saga of the Sturlungs gives lurid account of these days.) While the old democratic system of assembly rule had never matched in practice what it held in theory, legend at least had it that for several generations the country was, for the most part, at peace. The prestigious assemblies had continued to function, and respect for the law had kept violent family feuds from turning into general lawlessness. By the first decades of the thirteenth century, however, Iceland's political and social life had become a welter of competing factions. The Norwegian crown, the assemblies, and the church bishops vied to impose a gaggle of rules and counterrules. The lines of authority were so indistinct that no group hesitated to use force to advance its position.

It was during these last chaotic days of the Icelandic Republic (Norway assumed jurisdiction over the country in 1262) that the most sophisticated of all the sagas, the Family Sagas, were written. These Sagas of Icelanders owe important debts to the centuries of interest in law, history, and kings' lives which preceded them. Yet the blend of national history, genealogy, local legend, and character anecdote gathered into stories with structures and aesthetic values of their own is quite unlike earlier sagas or Continental literature of the same period.

Nowhere else in Europe (excluding the British Isles) had prose been adopted for such clearly literary purposes: the medium of the Continent's literature was still verse, and the subject matter was heroic and traditional when it did not take up prevailing Christian motifs. In Europe, the thirteenth century was the age of scholasticism, and its literature was written mainly under the inspiration of the Christian faith. Dante's *Divine Comedy* (c. 1320) stands as the age's crowning achievement.

The Icelanders knew the heroic tradition well. This hoard of common experience, which found voice in works as diverse as *Beowulf* (c. 1000), the *Poetic Edda*, and *The Nibelungenlied* (c. 1200), was kept alive mainly by Icelanders. Nor were the Icelanders unaffected by the Christian literature or courtly romance. Thomas of Brittany's *Tristan* (c. 1160) was translated into Old Norse as *Tristrams saga ok Ísöndar* in 1226, and numerous other translations followed.

Such material engaged the imaginations of the Family Saga writers and supplied them with a storehouse of conventional stories, cosmological schemes, and codes of heroic behavior, but the subject matter and the ethos of the Family Sagas spring from a native source. Sagamen took their ancestors' history and their own knowledge of the Icelandic landscape and transformed the Icelandic experience into narratives and stories which, in retrospect, read remarkably like novels and short stories. The high literary merit of the Family Sagas has made them widely known outside of Iceland and linked the name "saga" with their particular subject matter. The more than one hundred and twenty sagas and thættir thought to have been written during the thirteenth century provide a remarkable fictional portrait of the tenth and the first third of the eleventh centuries. The sagamen rendered their histories in human terms. They were interested in individual men and women and the drama their lives provoked. By aesthetically arranging these incidents, which often range over a century and involve scores of characters, the sagamen aroused interest in the moral dimensions of his ancestors' acts and the larger questions which they raised about human destiny in general.

The saga writer's techniques are those which are often associated with modern realistic fiction. Verisimilitude is of primary importance. Characters are not drawn as types but are faithful portraits of individuals. Characters speak as people do to one another and are revealed through action. Description is minimal and lyrical effusion is absent. The imagery is spare, homely, and solid, free of affectation and exaggeration.

Presumably the authors of the Family Sagas did not have in mind a literary experiment when they wrote their stories. More likely they sought to reduplicate the actual features of life as they thought it had existed for their ancestors and as they had come to know it. For a long time it was thought that the sagas provided reasonably accurate histories of the Icelandic pioneers and their descendants. Research conducted in the past thirty years, however, has shown that the sagas are not reliable as histories nor as indices to local geography, although they take historical events and lives of historical persons as their subject. It is far more accurate to describe the sagas as well-composed fiction. The manner of presentation is the historian's but the effect is literary. Pertinent genealogies are recorded, local customs explained, and place names accounted for as the stories unfold. Use of the authorial "I" is almost totally absent, and point of view is established by selection of detail and juxtaposition of scenes rather than by interpretive commentary.

Saga language also suggests the historian's objective tone. Concrete nouns are its hallmark. Verbs tend to be generalized and clauses strung loosely by means of parataxis. Interpretive adverbs and adjectives are avoided, and, when employed, they are determining rather than descriptive. Descriptions of landscapes or of persons are consequential. If a river is filled with floating chunks of ice, someone will surely jump from one to another or swim between them. When fantastic elements or dreams break into a realistic account, verisimilitude is not lost. For example, the same language is employed in *Grettir's Saga* when the monster Glam attacks Grettir as when the opponent is human or the scene less dramatic.

Language spoken in the Family Saga is terse and laconic. It is never rhetorical or stylized. Dialogue typically occurs at dramatic moments and so increases tension and reveals character. Forceful and felicitous language is accorded the highest respect: lawspeaker, poet, and wit have the day. To die with a quip on one's lips is a measure of heroic stature. Vesteinn dies complimenting his assailant on his effective blow and Attli falls noting that "broad spears are becoming fashionable nowadays."

Family Sagas tend to be episodic. Individual scenes begin and end in rest. They are related to one another by movement through time as well as by cause and effect patterns generated by the action. Characteristically a saga closes decades or even centuries after it begins, and this remorseless passage of time is often associated with fate. The saga's episodic structure attains its unity through juxtaposition and symmetry among its lesser parts. Reliance on techniques of short fiction is apparent: the scene is the basic unit of the Family Saga, and the larger effects of the narrative rely on the successful realization of each scene and the arrangement of those scenes.

Although bound into a close family by the commonality of the Icelandic historical milieu and shared method of construction, the Family Sagas support a range of character types and thematic interests broader than other medieval literatures. *Laxdaela Saga* has as a main theme the decline of the generous habits which prevailed during the pioneer generations. Unn the Deep Minded, who gave wise counsel until the day of her death, is mother of the Laxdaela clan and emblem of pioneer largesse. *Laxdaela Saga*'s central story is of the imperious Gudrun who forces her third husband to kill Kjartan, her former lover and her husband's cousin. Kjartan is a hero in the old tradition and also one of the first to practice Christianity in Iceland. His death ushers in a more violent era; Gudrun takes control and sets off revenge killings which disrupt the entire district. Peace is finally won, but in an atmosphere less luminous and expectant than that of the pioneer age. *Eyrbggja Saga* also has a district's history as its subject and shares some characters with *Gisli's Saga*. The powerful Snorri godi, known for his strength and wiliness in a number of sagas, figures in many scenes, and his attempts to advance his career by means of shrewd planning and outright trickery provide focus in the otherwise diffuse history of the Snaefelsness region. *Eyrbggja Saga*'s author had a strong antiquarian interest. Hauntings and old religious rites figure prominently in the saga. Strict adherence to the heathen viewpoint does not admit the romantic and heraldic details which decorate the latter half of *Laxdaela Saga*.

Several of the finest sagas are biographies. *Egil's Saga* preludes the story of the famous warrior-poet with a long and well-wrought section about Egil's father, grandfather, and uncle and their conflicts and alliances with Harald Fairhair. Egil himself is portrayed as a Viking with a lusty appetite for brawling and ransacking. He has a series of confrontations with European royalty, managing in the most extreme situation to save himself from Eirik Bloodaxe's wrath by composing and reciting a poem in praise of the king. In his mature years, Egil settles in Iceland and is one of the few saga heroes to die of old age. In his last years Egil becomes old and blind and is mocked by servants, but his contrariness exerts itself to the last. He takes his treasure and buries it without a trace.

Gisli's Saga and *Grettir's Saga* are biographies of Iceland's two great outlaws. Both heroes are poets. Gisli is a man obsessed by the desire to protect family honor; he kills his sister's husband to avenge the killing of his wife's brother. He is found out and outlawed, and his enemies pursue him and drive him to take up undignified poses and disguises to save his life. He is also terrorized by bloody, prophetic dreams which appear in the saga as verses given him by dream women, one bright and one dark. Gisli makes brave defense and is portrayed as a far greater man than those with whom he does battle. *Gisli's Saga* distinguishes itself by its intensely concentrated telling. A foreboding and tragic tone sounds throughout.

Grettir's outlawry is longer and less ominous than Gisli's. Like Egil, Grettir is a precocious and taciturn child. After a brilliant youthful career as a land-cleanser, Grettir's great strength is arrested by a curse placed on him by the monster Glam. The battle scene between Grettir and Glam is one of the finest in saga literature. The reckless young hero hears how Glam has ravaged the Vatnsdale district and is anxious to test his strength against such an opponent. He is warned from such opportunism but he pays no heed. Grettir defeats Glam but is cursed by the dying monster to a life of fear and solitude. Grettir's outlawry, which follows this battle, is the result of a false charge. He is eventually forced into the interior of the island where he lives as a solitary, fending off those who come to kill him for bounty. Despite his perilous situation, Grettir becomes a gentler and more dignified man during his nineteen years of outlawry. He dies a tragic death, but the saga ends with the lucky adventures of Grettir's half-brother, which are presented in the "Spés tháttr."

Njal's Saga is called the greatest of all the Family Sagas. It encompasses the two biographies of Gunnar of Hlidarendi and Njal, which are followed by the story of Kari's vengeance. This intricately designed triptych is woven into a whole by the author's imaginative grasp of every feature of his narrative. Gunnar lives his life within the framework of the old heroic code, but he is not a lucky man. He arouses the envy of lesser men and has a wife who steals. He is unable to stop a chain of events which leads him to kill three members of the same family, a situation which Njal has predicted will lead to his death. Gunnar is hunted down and murdered in his own house, a victim of lesser men. His wife, Hallgerd, a sinister force in the saga, betrays him. Gunnar's friend and mentor, Njal, is a lawyer and a prophet of sorts who devotes his life to an attempt to replace the old revenge codes with justice and law. His attempts are insightful and trusting but finally fruitless. His own sons kill Njal's foster son, and after other violent developments, Njal and his family are burned in their house by Flosi. Njal's son-in-law Kari takes revenge. Reconciliation is finally achieved after Kari and Flosi are both absolved in Rome. The reconciliation is confirmed when Kari marries Flosi's niece, the young woman who instigated the burning of Njal. On a larger plane this saga takes as its subject the upheaval and redefinition of values associated with the coming of Christianity to Iceland. Njal himself has certain characteristics of the Christian martyr. *Laxdaela Saga* and *Grettir's Saga* contemplate this same theme from different points of view.

The great age of Family Saga writing seems to have ended about 1300, a time just postdating the passing of the Icelandic Republic into Norwegian control. Of the major Family Sagas only *Grettir's Saga* is thought to have been written later. Authors of the later era turned their attention to mythic and heroic themes drawn from the Germanic heritage. They wrote what are known as Sagas of Past Times, which have as their subjects fantastic, heroic, and supernatural events of the remote past.

The most notable of the Sagas of Past Times is the *Völsunga Saga*, which opens by recounting the earliest days of the tribe of the Völsungs. The flower of the clan is Sigurd, the most popular of all Northern heroes. Sigurd kills the dragon Fafnir and comes into possession of the Nibelungen wealth. Later he is betrothed to the Valkyrie Brynhild, but the affair comes to tragedy when Sigurd, under a witch's spell, forgets Brynhild and marries another woman. Brynhild is married into the same family and eventually urges her husband to kill Sigurd. When the deed has been accomplished, Brynhild throws herself on Sigurd's funeral pyre. The remainder of the saga follows the life of Sigurd's widow, Gudrun, and the revenge killings her children carry out. Stories and characters of the *Völsunga Saga* are common to all Germanic peoples; *The Nibelungenlied* is based on the same tales which also form the basis for Wagner's Ring cycle.

The author of the *Völsunga Saga* relied heavily on the eddic poems which include all the elements of his story. The prose in *Völsunga Saga* is notably passionless and lacks the verisimilitude which the solid presence of the Icelandic landscape and historical personages gave to the Family Sagas. The Sagas of Past Times in general do not retain the high literary standards of their predecessors, although sagas such as *Ragnar Lodbrook's Saga*, *Orvar Odd's Saga*, and *Hrolf Kraki's Saga* are popular as swashbuckling adventure stories. Icelandic romances of chivalry (*Riddarasögur*) and the fairy tale or Lying Sagas (*Lygisögur*), which were based on foreign models, captured the interest of fourteenth and fifteenth century writers. These outlandish adventures are written in an ornate and verbose style. The day of the Family Saga had passed; although Family Sagas were collected and copied during the fourteenth and fifteenth centuries, and were doubtlessly read, they were no longer written.

Away from the European mainstream, Icelandic writers created a literature of psychological realism worthy of compare to nineteenth and twentieth century fiction. At the same time, the Family Sagas found a unique place within the humanistic tradition of the Middle Ages. Sagamen were, of course, Christian. The importance of an individual life, the emphasis on selflessness, forbearance, and conciliation as well as other Christian values exert quiet force when they appear as qualities of fine men and women, whether they are pagan or Christian. The pagan heroic code, with its stringent and violent demands, comes to clash with these gentler ideas. Such conflicts may be within an individual, between family members, or argued in the courts. Whatever the dramatic forum, the importance of the immediate conflict is never sacrificed to point up an abstract principle. Family Sagas are primarily good stories well told. The best of them retain allegiance to district history and genealogy without allowing antiquarian interests or Christian creed to obscure their aesthetic designs.

The Family Sagas number around thirty-five and are anonymous. They vary in length from a few pages to more than four hundred. *Njal's Saga* is the longest, and both *Egil's Saga* and *Grettir's Saga* are more than three hundred pages long. Most of the longer sagas deal with heroes and families in the Northern and Western regions of Iceland. *Njal's Saga* is set in the South. The sagas which are set in Eastern Iceland are fewer in number and they are shorter. Among them are two fine sagas, *The Vapnfjord Men* and *Hrafnkel's Saga*. *The Vapnfjord Men* is the story of a friendship between two brothers-in-law which disintegrates when they are alienated by a Norwegian merchant and quarrel over a box of silver. After one friend casts off his sick wife, who is the other friend's sister, a feud opens and continues into a second generation. Reconciliation is achieved only after a young man kills his best-loved uncle in answer to an earlier killing. Half-hearted battles between the inheritors of the quarrel convince them that it is more honorable to end the fighting.

Hrafnkel's Saga is a masterpiece of short fiction. It relates the story of the precocious son of an Icelandic pioneer who rises quickly to district prominence. Hrafnkel kills his shepherd for riding his horse and is brought to trial by the shepherd's family. Judgment is passed against Hrafnkel, and he loses his wealth and is tortured at the confiscation trial. Later, after abandoning his heathen practices, Hrafnkel rises again to district renown. He takes revenge on his opponents by killing an innocent man, and this time there is no retort. Hrafnkel remains in control and enjoys great prestige. The saga makes exceptionally fine use of landscape features to forward its plot, and the dialogues spoken at the National Assembly are among the best in Family Saga literature. Characters in this tightly woven saga are finely and individually drawn.

Short sagas stand midway between the saga and the tháttr genres. *Hrafnkel's Saga*, for example, is a saga although in the main it tells a single strand story. In English collections it is often placed among Icelandic stories. At thirty-five pages, it is longer than a tháttr and a good deal shorter than the generational sagas. Such commonality of subject matter and similarity of technique do bind saga and tháttr and might well indicate that they are shorter or longer redactions of the same prose form. As noted earlier, boundaries between saga and tháttr are not explicit. Despite the wide common ground, however, certain provinces belonging only to the tháttr reveal its closer affinities to the modern short story.

One hundred short stories are usually named as thættir. Approximately forty-five of these fall into a group which features an Icelander as protagonist, and among this group are the most distinguished of the stories. Tháttr length runs from a single page to about twenty-five pages, the average being between ten and twelve standard printed pages.

While the Family Sagas typically take as heroes famous men or families, the thættir usually choose a common man. Thættir about Icelandic farmers cluster around the lives of saints, historic heroes, folklore heroes, or kings. By far the most popular subject matter is the Icelander who travels to the court of a European king; these thættir outnumber all others by approximately five to one. Such a predominance of one sort of short story may be an accident of preservation, but it is more likely that the Kings' Sagas, which host them, provided a kind of yeast for the development of such short stories. One suspects they are fictional and imaginative, even fanciful outgrowths associated with the serious business of relating kings' biographies.

A tháttr tends to focus on a single character. At first the hero may appear to be a fool, who later proves himself to be inventive and insightful. Many tháttr heroes are poets, and some are simple, anonymous travelers. These protagonists are usually young men strayed away from home, equipped with a native wit or goodness which is hidden under an offhanded ingenuousness. In a typical tháttr of the King and Icelander type, the Icelander speaks with one or more monarchs, often alienates himself in the initial meeting, and leaves court intent on proving his true worth to the king. The moments of recognition and reconciliation tend to be complimentary to both king and Icelander; a spirit of equality unites the common man from the North with the powerful monarch. The effect is clearly patriotic, revealing the pride the Icelanders took in the most ordinary among their ancestors.

Hreidar the Fool is one such story. Hreidar is the younger of two brothers and said to be barely able to care for himself, but it is apparent almost immediately that he is a very canny fool. Hreidar traps his brother into taking him abroad with him, where he manages to meet King Magnus. Magnus is charmed by his eccentricity and invites Hreidar and his brother to stay at court. The king predicts that Hreidar will lose his even temper and learn to be clever with his hands.

When he is rudely teased by some of King Harald's men, Hreidar does lose his temper and kills a man. He seeks asylum with an upland farmer, and while in hiding, tries his hand at metalsmithing. When Harald and his men arrive to capture Hreidar, he is well enough hidden to escape detection. He is willing to risk his life for a joke, however, and bursts into Harald's presence handing him a gilded silver pig he has made. Before Harald realizes the pig is an insult, Hreidar races away and returns to King Magnus, for whom he recites a poem and is rewarded with an island. Hreidar gives the island back at Magnus' suggestion and returns to Iceland where, as the text says, he put aside his foolishness and became a successful farmer.

In brief, the lowly Icelander has his way with everyone. His foolish cleverness reveals Harald to be a harsh and tempestuous man and Magnus to be a good ruler and counselor. For his own part, Hreidar has an entertaining series of adventures and returns home a wise and more mature man.

The tone in such a story is noticably lighter than in the Family Sagas. Thættir are infused with the optimistic outlook of the Christian Middle Ages, in contrast to the Family Sagas, whose scope tends to be epic and serious. While there are many comic moments in the Family Sagas, the burden of bringing alive the ethos of an age imposes epic obligations on an author. The tháttr writer is free from such weighty obligations. While a character like Hreidar shares nobility of spirit with a saga hero like Hrafnkel, the tháttr author is not burdened with the long-term consequences of his hero's deeds except in the most general way. The tháttr writer, for example, need not confront his hero's death. The tháttr form may well have encouraged writing stories which were more fictional than historical. The interchange between Icelander and king typically has far more moral and psychological consequence than historical importance. Ivar in *Ivar's Story* is an Icelandic poet residing at the court of King Eystein. Ivar asks his brother to tell Oddney back in Iceland that he wishes to marry her. Ivar's brother does not deliver the message; instead he marries Oddney himself. Ivar hears the news and becomes downcast. The King cannot understand his sorrow and calls Ivar to him and offers him land, gifts, and other women, but Ivar is not solaced. The King can think of nothing else to offer except his companionship. Ivar accepts Eystein's offer of friendship. Each day before the tables are cleared, Ivar joins the King and speaks of Oddney to his heart's content. Soon the poet's happiness returns and he remains with King Eystein.

The tháttr writer seems to have enjoyed a greater imaginative freedom because he was not bound to make aesthetic sense of a vast amount of time. Since he wrote about a moment often unmarked in history and about an Icelander whose life was not particularly noteworthy, he could turn his attention to the creation of a fictional environment. The thættir are not analyses of historical deeds whose consequences are national in scope; they are tributes to the characters of kings. The stories also celebrate the characters of common Icelanders who call forth the true natures of the kings they visit. Likely the Icelandic writers knew little about life in Norway or about its landscape, so focus tended to remain on character and dialogue, which were explored and exploited to the exclusion of other features. The thættir characters found themselves in realistic dilemmas and extricated themselves through dint of their imaginations, or, as in the famous case of Audun, by innocence and goodness. The story is called *Audun and the Bear*.

Audun is a Westfjord man of very modest means who gives all his money for a Greenland bear which he wishes to present to King Svein of Denmark. When Audun lands in Norway, King Harald, having heard about the precious bear, invites Audun to court, hoping to buy it or have it given to him. In a graceful show of honesty and naïveté, Audun tells Harald he wishes to deliver the bear to Svein. Harald is so startled by the man's innocence that he sends him on his way even though Norway and Denmark are at war. Audun finally makes his way to Svein, but not without begging for food and selling half of the bear to do so. Svein is pleased and supplies Audun with silver for a pilgrimage to Rome. When Audun returns to Svein's court after his journey south, he is reduced to a beggar and the kings' men mock him. Svein recognizes Audun and richly rewards him, praising him as a man who knows how to care for his soul. Audun refuses a position in Svein's court in order to return to Iceland to care for his mother. On his way home, he visits once more with Harald and at the Norwegian monarch's request tells him about the gifts Svein has given him. Among those gifts is an arm ring which Svein has instructed Audun to keep unless he can give it to a great man to whom he was obligated. Audun gives the ring to Harald, because, as he says, Harald could have had his bear and his life but took neither. Audun sails back to Iceland and is considered a man of great luck. In the few scenes of this story, the tháttr author gathers peace, goodwill, generosity, and integrity around this modest Icelander, who, without consciousness, becomes a model of the medieval pilgrim.

The thættir as a group, although they are restricted in subject matter, tend to take the shape of modern short stories; they develop character swiftly and pointedly through action. They are dramatic rather than narrative. Genealogy is curtailed if it is used at all. The ominousness of fate and the burden of history are usually dispensed with. Language is terse and witty, often with a lightness appropriate to its subject.

During the fourteenth century, the themes of the Sagas of Past Times were also taken up by tháttr writers. These stories tend to lack the tension, the energy, and the comic juxtaposition of earlier thættir. The old patterns are visible but without the solidity that the stories of Icelanders in the kings' courts have. The setting shifts to prehistoric Europe and the plots often read as bawdy folk tales. In the story *Gridr's Fosterling, Illugi*, for example, the young prince's playmate, Illugi, wins royal favor by killing a revenant and is allowed to accompany the prince on an ocean voyage. When Illugi swims to shore for fire to save the ship's crew from freezing, he wanders into the cave of an ogress who tests his courage before allowing him her daughter's favors. The monster is a queen under an evil spell. Illugi destroys the spell and marries the daughter. The queen marries the prince and all live happily ever after.

When this sort of subject matter replaced the realistic action and individual characters of the earlier thættir, the stories became less distinguishable as a genre and certainly less akin to modern fiction.

This shift in subject matter indicates a stronger bonding with the European literatures. The popularity of the adventure and the fantastic tale were prompted by the Continental interest in romance. Certain of the later thættir are strong and resemble the best *fabliaux*. The strongest stories of this group are usually reliant on historical matter and the learned tradition, as their predecessors were, rather than on folktale. "Spes Tháttr" which concludes *Grettir's Saga*, is an example. Because of their optimistic character, thættir do have natural affinities to *fabliaux*, but the tháttr's strengths are particularly its own. The use of realistic characters, few and vividly dramatized scenes, vigorous dialogue, and definitive imagery give the medieval Icelandic short story a distinct place in the history of European short fiction.

Bibliography

Andersson, Theodore M. *The Icelandic Family Saga.*
——————. *The Problem of Icelandic Saga Origins.*
Einarsson, Stefan. *A History of Icelandic Literature.*
Gordon, E. V. *An Introduction to Old Norse.*
Harris, Joseph C. *The King and the Icelander: A Study in the Short Narrative Forms of Old Icelandic Prose.*
Jones, Gwyn. *A History of the Vikings.*
Ker, W. P. *Epic and Romance.*
Nordal, Sigurd. *Sagalitteraturen.*
Schier, Kurt. *Sagaliteratur.*
Turville-Petre, G. *Origins of Icelandic Literature.*

Helen Menke

BALLAD NARRATIVE

This essay describes the distinctive narrative style found in the traditional folk ballads first of Britain and later of the United States. These ballads share many elements with narrative folk songs of the rest of Europe as well as with oral-poetic forms throughout the world, such as their quasiformulaic vocabulary of set phrasings. They also show distinctive characteristics, especially their "incremental repetition" with its spectrum of dramatic effects: haunting, ironic, emphatic, grimly comic. The ballads form an inheritance for modern readers and writers, capturing the voice of ancient and still highly effective storytelling and bearing the credentials of definitive popularity in their various forms. These traditional works represent exactly what their original audience—a broad audience that endured for centuries—most wanted to hear. They are also important for their influence on literary creation during the last two centuries.

The ballads are stanzaic narrative songs, sung to a tune repeated for each stanza; they were generally not merely chanted or recited. Most are cast into quatrain verse, and the most common form of stanza is an alternating tetrameter and trimeter, 4/3/4/3, with the second and fourth lines rhyming. Some have very long histories as recognizable, individual entities, telling a given story to a given tune or assortment of tunes. As oral-traditional song, however, such a ballad may have been recovered from various singers in widely varying verbal forms, in which, for example, the names of principal characters may differ, portions of the story may be amplified or omitted, and length may vary by more than the entire length of a short version. Yet these variations do not constitute the identity of the story in the way that a literary artist's distinctive details produce a unique story which is closely modeled on a story type. The identity of the ballad story consists of what it shares with other versions rather than how it differs from them. The story does not belong to its singer, even if he or she has modified or embellished it, or inadvertently garbled some of it, or changed the names. The story remains the familiar possession of the people for whom he or she is the present singer, one of a long line.

The ballads of England and Scotland are not traceable to known authors. Anonymity of author does not in itself, of course, suppress the personal voice of that author—consider *Sir Gawain and the Green Knight* (c. 1370). The ballad style, however, effaces all that would be individual in its writer. There is no personal commentary and no individual manner of expression. The question of who these ballad authors may have been has been vigorously disputed for more than a century and is not settled now. Essentially, the two parties in the long dispute have been those who argued (sometimes romantically) for communal authorship, and those who argued (sometimes snobbishly) for individual poets set apart from ordinary folk by profession, by class, or merely by genius. What is now fully appreciated is that the laconic, forceful, highly objective manner of the ballads, like many of their specific formal features, is at least in part the effect of their having been *transmitted* through generations of traditional singing, whatever the ultimate origins of the songs may have been. In this they resemble folktales, except that the link to music in folk song is a strongly conservative influence; the tune or tunes of a ballad, which have been shown to remain attached to the same story (although our records of tunes used long ago are sketchy) over many generations, hold together the essence and many of the details, the plot and much of the language, of the ballad. It is significant to note here that the singing style, especially among the Scots and the American mountaineers, expresses this impersonality: the ballads are sung in a high, stylized, nasal delivery with minimum effect, regardless of what type of story is being sung.

We know that the earliest ballads, essentially similar to those still sung in the twentieth century from unbroken tradition, already existed in the thirteenth century. The oldest ballad known is "Judas," recorded in a manuscript in the thirteenth century; other ballads record specific historical occurrences of the fifteenth and sixteenth centuries, and it has been argued that some features of the ballads evolved in the eighteenth century. Thus, there is an extended history through which old ballads were cherished and new ones brought into being. Throughout this long history, many ballads undoubtedly arose and then disappeared without leaving a trace. What remains to us today of the British tradition, except for a very few later retrievals, is contained in the great collection published between 1882 and 1896 by Francis James Child, so that ballads are commonly referred to by their reference numbers in that collection—for example, "Barbara Allen" is known as Child No. 84.

While individual authors left no legible stamp on the ballads, the men, women, and children who sang these ballads over the generations established in them a distinctive and powerfully effective narrative style. There is great variety in the ballads, whether they be short or long, comic or tragic, historical or supernatural or domestic; yet they all share the essential elements of ballad style. Some of these elements may be briefly illustrated.

The ballads tell their stories with a strict economy that is an example and a challenge to the discipline of writers of other narrative forms. In remarkably few words, the ballad encapsulates its whole dramatically effective story; and it does this without a traditional beginning. A ballad often begins abruptly with the crucial action already under way. This is the device known in epic narratives as beginning *in medias res*, and it has been adapted to various forms of fiction; but in ballad the beginning is particularly abrupt, in proportion to the brevity of the mode:

> Rise up rise up now Lord Douglas she says
> And put on your armor so bright
> Let it never be said that a daughter of thine
> Was married to a lord under night. (Child 7B)

In cases in which the opening lines (usually the first half quatrain) are devoted to a conventional and even languid time-marking, the transition to the story itself is still equally abrupt:

> It fell on a day, and a bonny summer day
>   When corn grew green and yellow
> That there fell out a great dispute
>   Between Argyll and Airly. (Child 199A)
>
>   * * *
>
> It fell and about the Lammas time
>   When husbandmen do win their hay
> Earl Douglass is to the English woods
>   And a' with him to fetch a prey. (Child 161B)

The conventional opening lines in these last two examples illustrate a paradox in the style of ballads. The stories begin abruptly and move swiftly, and yet many of their techniques seem to retard movement. The oral tradition uses stock expressions, as in these two beginnings, which establish setting and describe characters and what they do. Such tags may do little more for the story than refrain lines, which sometimes have no reference to the story at all:

> A knicht had two sons o sma fame
>   Hey nien nanny
> Isaac-a-Bell and Hugh the Graeme
>   And the norlan flowers spring bonny. (Child 18B)

These refrain lines, which may descend from connections between the singing of ballads and community ring dances, slow the narrative; at the same time, they remind us that the ballad narratives were sung in an unhurried way (early observers called the folk singing style "drawling"). The stock expressions, which sometimes seem to be inserted quite casually and unnecessarily, also make the narrative seem leisurely. Yet there is an urgency and immediacy to the stories, with their swift beginnings, transitions, and endings.

This paradox of simultaneous urgency and leisure runs through all ballad narrative. It is visible in the repetitive patterns which F. B. Gummere called "incremental repetition," by which advance comes through slight change within nearly identical recurrences of lines or whole stanzas:

> And aye she served the lang tables
>   With white bread and with wine
> And aye she drank the wan water
>   To had her colour fine.
>
> And aye she served the lang tables
>   With white bread and with brown

> And ay she turned her round about,
> Sae fast the tears fall down. (Child 62A)

Such patterns of repetition place great dramatic emphasis on the change introduced and mark time until that change appears—the slowing effect is even more pronounced when the lines are heard measured out to their music. Yet to balance this savoring of crucial detail, the ballads generally leave out almost all other detail and pass swiftly from one crux to another. This overall narrative method in the ballads has been described by Gummere as "leaping and lingering." The narrative moves swiftly, almost without connectives, from one scene to another, then pauses with repetition and, in particular, with dialogue. This characteristic movement has been interestingly compared by M. J. C. Hodgart to the effect of cinema: the pace is an alternation of speaking scenes, on the one hand, and gaps on the other. Attention cuts quickly from one sharply focused incident or speech to another, without intervening transitions.

The scenes upon which the ballads are built are composed largely of dialogue. A speech by any character usually occupies a minimum of one line, and more generally one half or whole stanza. It is often paired with a reply from another character of similar length and phrasing; their talk makes up the entirety of many scenes.

> Will ye gang to your men again
> Or will ye gang wi me?
> Will ye gang to the high heavens,
> Wi my dear son and me?
>
> I winna gang to my men again,
> For they would be feared at me;
> But I would gang to the high heavens,
> Wi thy dear son and thee.
>
> It's for nae honour ye did to me, Brown Robyn,
> It's for nae guid ye did to mee;
> But a' is for your fair confession
> You've made upon the sea. (Child 57)

Such stanzas as these are usually printed with quotation marks separating the speeches from narrative and from one another, but it is important to remember that all ballad texts are only transcriptions of sung versions, and that punctuation marks cannot be sung. These stanzas are printed without quotation marks to make clear that who speaks, and how, must be inferred from what is said. A listener to the rest of the story has, of course, an advantage over the reader who sees only these stanzas. All words of all speakers, however, are sung by the same singing voice; ballad singers do not do dramatic, interpretive singing performances. The words in the speeches themselves must

cue our sense of who is the speaker. When the speeches are similar—a proposition and a retort, a question and an answer—the crucial variation may be
small, and we may have to wait for it to appear in the middle or latter part
of the speech. These considerations do not suggest that the ballads are highly
suspenseful: an important difference between them and the work of modern
writers is that they are for the most part stories already familiar to their
audience. Most hearings of them are rehearings; all singings are resingings.
Rather, the point is that the narrative method is itself highly dramatic, presenting what happens in the words of the characters, which become the words
of the singer. They are highly immediate, no matter how familiar.

The effect of these shifts of scene and speaker; the dramatic foreground
focus and the omission of most background; and the abrupt and then lingering
pacing found in the ballads can be seen in a short complete text of one of the
most famous ballads, "Sir Patrick Spens."

> The king sits in Dumferling toune,
>   Drinking the blude-reid wine:
> O whar will I get guid sailor,
>   To sail this schip of mine?
>
> Up and spak an eldern knicht,
>   Sat at the kings richt kne:
> Sir Patrick Spens is the best sailor
>   That sails upon the se.
>
> The king has written a braid letter,
>   And signd it wi his hand,
> And sent it to Sir Patrick Spens,
>   Was walking on the sand.
>
> The first line that Sir Patrick red,
>   A loud lauch lauched he;
> The next line that Sir Patrick red,
>   The teir blinded his ee.
>
> O wha is this has don this deid,
>   This ill deid don to me,
> To send me out this time o' the yeir,
>   To sail upon the se!
>
> Mak hast, mak haste, my mirry men all,
>   Our guid schip sails the morne:
> O say ne sae, my master deir,
>   For I feir a deadlie storme.
>
> Late late yestreen I saw the new moone,
>   Wi the auld moone in hir arme,
> And I feir, I feir, my deir master,
>   That we will cum to harme.
>
> O our Scots nobles wer richt laith
>   To weet their cork-heild schoone;

Bot lang owre a' the play wer playd,
Thair hats they swam aboone.

O lang, lang may their ladies sit,
Wi thair fans into their hand,
Or eir they se Sir Patrick Spens
Cum sailing to the land.

O lang, lang may the ladies stand,
Wi thair gold kems in their hair,
Waiting for thair ain deir lords,
For they'll se thame na mair.

Haf owre, haf owre to Aberdour,
It's fiftie fadom deip,
And thair lies guid Sir Patrick Spens,
Wi the Scots lords at his feit.

The much admired dramatic force of this work derives most, perhaps, from the complete omission of the actual climactic event of the story, to say nothing of the suppression of background fact. Such reduction or suppression is also valued in modern short fiction, and a ballad such as "Sir Patrick Spens" testifies how far this economy can be taken to gain dramatic effect. We are not told what the sailing expedition was for; we are not sure whether treachery has drawn this assignment for Spens; and we are never told directly about the shipwreck. Other ballads may situate their narrative or dialogue immediately after their implied awful event, or before it; by subtlety and indirection, which are admirable models for the writer of effective narrative prose today, they convey what seems too overwhelming to be directly reported.

It is likewise significant that we do learn a good deal that the ballad does not state directly about the arrogance and practical ignorance of the lords and courtiers, and about the loyalty and courage shared by Spens and his canny sailors. It is important that the impersonality of the dramatic presentation does not keep the ballad from expressing strong views and values—views hostile to the distant king, much more hostile to the idle and elegant nobles, and perhaps a bit less hostile to the ladies of those nobles (these distinctions are subtly and incisively made, with no direct statement of disvalue), and, conversely, views favorable to the mariners and their beloved captain. These are not personal values, not the vision of a single creative artist, but rather the views and values of the original ballad's audience.

The folk ballads have had wide influence among literary writers, the makers of artful written narratives, since they began to be appreciated by the literate during the eighteenth century. Their most conspicuous impact was on the romantic poets, notably Samuel Taylor Coleridge and John Keats. (The "Lyrical Ballads," 1798, of William Wordsworth owe more to the broadside street literature of the London printing shops than to the oral ballads of the countryside.) Their remarkably forceful narratives have, however, been appreciated by a wide variety of writers since the age when Samuel Johnson remarked with some annoyance that "It is in the power of any man to rush abruptly upon his subject, that has read the ballad of *Johnny Armstrong*." (The history of ballad influence is traced in A. B. Friedman's *Ballad Revival* (1961) through the nineteenth century and into the narrative verse of twentieth century poets.)

More recently, folk ballads have had a significant influence on popular culture, as seen in the popularity of folksingers in the 1960's. During the 1970's, some entertainers continued to reproduce certain short traditional ballads, others adapted folk narrative material to rock accompaniment, and still others imitated ballad style in their own new songs. This return in popular culture to the manner and some of the materials of oral folk song, both lyrical and narrative, testifies to the continuing power of ballad stories and styles.

Bibliography

Bronson, Bertrand. *Ballad As Song*.
Buchan, David. *Ballad and the Folk*.
Fowler, David. *Literary History of the Popular Ballad*.
Friedman, A. B. *Ballad Revival*.
Gerould, G. H. *Ballad of Tradition*.
Hodgart, M. J. C. *Ballads*.
Lomax, Alan, ed. *Folk Songs of North America in the English Language*.
Sargent, Helen Child and George Lyman Kittredge, eds. *English and Scottish Popular Ballads*.
Wells, E. K. *Ballad Tree*.

Mark W. Booth